GLOBAL CITY-REGIONS

Trends, Theory, Policy

Global City-Regions

Trends, Theory, Policy

Edited by

ALLEN J. SCOTT

OXFORD
UNIVERSITY PRESS

OXFORD
UNIVERSITY PRESS

Great Clarendon Street, Oxford OX2 6DP

Oxford University Press is a department of the University of Oxford.
It furthers the University's objective of excellence in research, scholarship,
and education by publishing worldwide in

Oxford New York

Auckland Cape Town Dar es Salaam Hong Kong Karachi
Kuala Lumpur Madrid Melbourne Mexico City Nairobi
New Delhi Shanghai Taipei Toronto

With offices in

Argentina Austria Brazil Chile Czech Republic France Greece
Guatemala Hungary Italy Japan South Korea Poland Portugal
Singapore Switzerland Thailand Turkey Ukraine Vietnam

Oxford is a registered trade mark of Oxford University Press
in the UK and in certain other countries

Published in the United States
by Oxford University Press Inc., New York

First published 2001
Published new as paperback 2002

British Library Cataloguing in Publication Data

Data available

Library of Congress Cataloging in Publication Data

Data available

ISBN 0–19–829799–8 (hbk.)
ISBN 0–19–925230–0 (pbk.)

5 7 9 10 8 6 4

Typeset by Graphicraft Limited, Hong Kong
Printed in Great Britain
on acid-free paper by
Biddles Ltd.
King's Lynn, Norfolk

Contents

List of Figures

List of Tables

List of Abbreviations

ABICALÇADOS	Association of Shoe Manufacturers
ADB	Asian Development Bank
APEC	Asia-Pacific Economic Cooperation
ASEAN	Association of Southeast Asian Nations
ASSINTECAL	Association of Synthetic Component Manufacturers
BAP	best available policy
BAT	best available technology
BOD	biological oxygen demand
BOT	Board of Trade
BSR	Bohai Sea Rim
CARICOM	Caribbean Community and Common Market
CBD	central business district
CBO	community-based organization
CDS	city development strategies
CERIS	Center for Settlement and Immigration
COMDEX	Computer Dealers Expo
DTB	Deutsch Terminbörse
EDUCO	Educación con Participación de la Communidad
ESCJ	Economic Strategy Council of Japan
EU	European Union
FDI	foreign direct investment
FTA	free trade agreement
GATT	General Agreement on Tariffs and Trade
GaWC	Globalization and World Cities
GDP	gross domestic product
GEMS	Global Environmental Monitoring System
GNP	gross national product
GOL	government on line
GST	goods and services tax
GTA	Greater Toronto Area
GTSB	Greater Toronto Services Board
ICAM	Instituto de Capacitación de Manizales
IMD	International Institute for Management and Development
IMF	International Monetary Fund
IPO	initial public offering
IPPUC	Instituto de Pesquisa e Planejamento de Curitiba
IQ	intelligence quotient
JETRO	Japan External Trade Promotion Organization
KANU	Kenyan African National Union
KLAFIR	Korea Local Authorities Foundation for International Relations
KNCFH	Korean NGOs and CBOs Forum for Habitat II

KRIHS	Korea Research Institute for Human Settlements
LQ	location quotient
M&As	mergers and alliances
MATIF	Marché à Terme International de France
MENPROSIF	Mendoza Provincial Program on Basic Infrastructure
MERCOSUR	Argentina, Brazil, Paraguay, and Uruguay Common Market
MNC	multinational corporation
MOCT	Ministry of Construction and Transportation
MOFE	Ministry of Finance and Economy
MOIR	Ministry of Industry and Resources
NAFTA	North American Free Trade Agreement
NASDAQ	National Association of Securities Dealers Automated Quotation
NATO	North Atlantic Treaty Organization
NGO	nongovernmental organization
NYSE	New York Stock Exchange
OECD	Organization for Economic Cooperation and Development
OJIB	Ontario Jobs and Investment Board
OSDC	Office of State Deputy Comptroller
PAU	Plan de Activación Urbana
PIT	personal income tax
SSHRC	Social Science and Humanities Research Council
TNC	transnational corporation
UCLA	University of California, Los Angeles
UN	United Nations
UNCHS	United Nations Centre for Human Settlements
UNCTAD	United Nations Conference on Trade and Development
UNEP	United Nations Environmental Program
UNESCAP	United Nations Economic and Social Commission for Asia and the Pacific
UNESCO	United Nations Educational, Scientific, and Cultural Organization
WHO	World Health Organization
WTO	World Trade Organization

Preamble

This book comprises an edited selection of the proceedings of an international conference on global city-regions held under the auspices of the School of Public Policy and Social Research at the University of California, Los Angeles, 21 to 23 October 1999. The conference attracted an audience of some three hundred and fifty people, comprising a mix of academics, governmental officials, business people, community leaders, and others, from more than thirty-two countries. An intensive series of addresses, paper presentations, panel discussions, and workshops over the three days of the conference generated a vibrant and many-sided discussion about the emergence of global city-regions and their role in the contemporary world system.

In spite of the extremely wide range of theoretical and political opinion represented at the conference, there seemed to be broad agreement to the effect that a series of distinctive phenomena that we might generally refer to as "city-regions" are indeed making their appearance as major elements of the current world scene, and that their advent is intrinsically related to intensifying levels of globalization. Most conference participants were also apparently willing to approve the notion that the relationship between city-regions and globalization is reflexive in nature. On the one hand, city-regions are arranged in a worldwide mosaic whose basic outlines are a function of globalization processes; on the other hand, globalization itself is in significant degree mediated through the same worldwide mosaic of city-regions. This nexus of global-urban relations offers critical clues about the social, economic, and political dynamics that are currently shaping the texture of human life in much of today's world, in economically developed and developing countries alike. Notwithstanding the broad consensus at the conference about these points of departure, the proceedings were also marked by many disagreements in regard to the detailed logic and dynamics of global city-regions and the policy challenges that they pose. The different claims that were expressed span the entire gamut from wholehearted support for current economic liberalization trends to equally forceful endorsement of strong social agendas, with many varied shades of opinion ranged between these end points. These divergences crop up repeatedly in the chapters that follow and no attempt has been made to reduce the discontinuities that separate them, though the editorial commentary inserted at various stages offers an interpretative overview of the discussion as it unfolds. Thus, if the book does not set forth settled and uncontroversial conclusions—nor could it given the current state of our knowledge—it provides, by the same token, an initiation into a deeply contentious and urgent debate, and puts the question of global city-regions firmly on the analytical and policy agendas.

Many individuals and associations contributed to the success of this enterprise. A very special note of gratitude is due to the Wallis Foundation of Los Angeles and its trustee, Jeffrey Glassman, for generous financial support that made it possible to mount the basic organizational structure of the conference and to bring in many distinguished speakers and guests from all over the world. Other major sponsors were the J. Paul Getty Trust, the John D. and Catherine T. MacArthur Foundation, and the Albert and Elaine Borchard Foundation. The following organizations and agencies also made significant material contributions: The Capital Group Companies, Inc., ARCO, the Government of Quebec, the Australian Consulate General in Los Angeles, the South Coast Air Quality Management District, the Trust Company of the West, the Milken Institute, *La Opinión*, and the Center for the New West. In addition, a number of centers and programs at UCLA provided important support; I wish to acknowledge, in particular, the contributions made by International Studies and Overseas Programs, the Center for International Business Education and Research, the Center for European and Russian Studies, the Latin American Center, the Center for Pacific Rim Studies, and the Lewis Center for Regional Policy Studies.

Special thanks are due to the conference organizing committee, which worked long and diligently to mold the final conference program. Members of the committee were John Agnew, Stephen Commins, Linda Griego, Eugene Grigsby, Robert Rodino, Edward Soja, Michael Storper, Lynne Zucker, and the editor of this book. A number of private and public agencies also participated actively in conference program planning activities. These included: The Organization for Economic Cooperation and Development; the Southern California Industrial Areas Foundation; the South Coast Air Quality Management District; the United Nations Educational, Scientific, and Cultural Organization; and the World Bank. A particular note of gratitude is due to the conference coordinator, Nga Nguyen, and to her assistants, Selene Mak, Jill Shernowitz, and Lee Melreit for their extremely able management of conference planning and organization activities. In addition, Anita Mermel and James Tranquada were responsible for many valuable backup services, and Leslie Evans provided inspired editing of the conference proceedings before their final submission to the publisher. Chase Langford redrafted all graphic materials into the final form in which they appear here.

Neither the conference nor the book would have been possible without the initial prompting of Dr Barbara Nelson, Dean of the School of Public Policy and Social Research at UCLA. Her enthusiastic encouragement and help throughout the extended period of preparation for the conference were critical to its eventual success. On behalf of all of those who participated in what turned out to be something of a watershed event, I wish to thank her and all the other faculty and staff at the School for Public Policy and Social Research for their gracious and generous support throughout this enterprise.

Allen J. Scott
Los Angeles, 1 January 2000

Introduction

ALLEN J. SCOTT

Globalization is both a growing force in our daily lives and a subject of rapidly intensifying debate. Much less evident in prevailing discourse, but surely of equal practical significance, is a new regionalism that appears to be on the rise, and that is rooted in a series of dense nodes of human labor and communal life scattered across the world. The new regionalism stands in opposition to the view of the world as a borderless space of flows that is sometimes set forth in discussions of the future course of international development. It does not represent the antithesis of globalization, however, but is its counterpart in a world from which geography has not yet been—and cannot yet be—abolished.

These nodes constitute distinctive subnational (i.e. *regional*) social formations whose local character and dynamics are undergoing major transformations due to the impacts of globalization. Many of them are foci of significant new experiments in local political mobilization and reorganization as different social groups within them strive to deal with the stresses and strains to which they are increasingly subject as a result of globalization. Many of them, too, are now starting to take on definite identity and force as economic and political actors on the world stage. The new regionalism, then, differs in the first instance from an older regionalism in which the individual regions within any national territory were apt to be much more subservient to the dictates (but also more shielded from outside turbulence by the protective cloak) of the central state. We shall henceforth refer to these regional social formations as *global city-regions*.

An initial, though admittedly inadequate, way of identifying the emerging system of global city-regions is simply to assimilate it into the worldwide network of large metropolitan areas as shown in Figure 0.1. This maneuver offers a rough impression of the kinds of phenomena that are the focus of this book, though not all the metropolitan areas shown are equally caught up in processes of globalization, and, more importantly, not all global city-regions can be simply equated with existing large metropolitan areas. That said, and to the degree that we *can* describe global city-regions in this manner, Figure 0.1 demonstrates that they are emphatically of major importance in today's world. As Figure 0.1 also shows, major city-regions occur in both economically advanced and in developing countries. Furthermore, and contrary to many recent predictions, large cities all over the globe continue to grow in size. In 1950, there were 83 cities in the world with populations of more than one million (two-thirds of them being

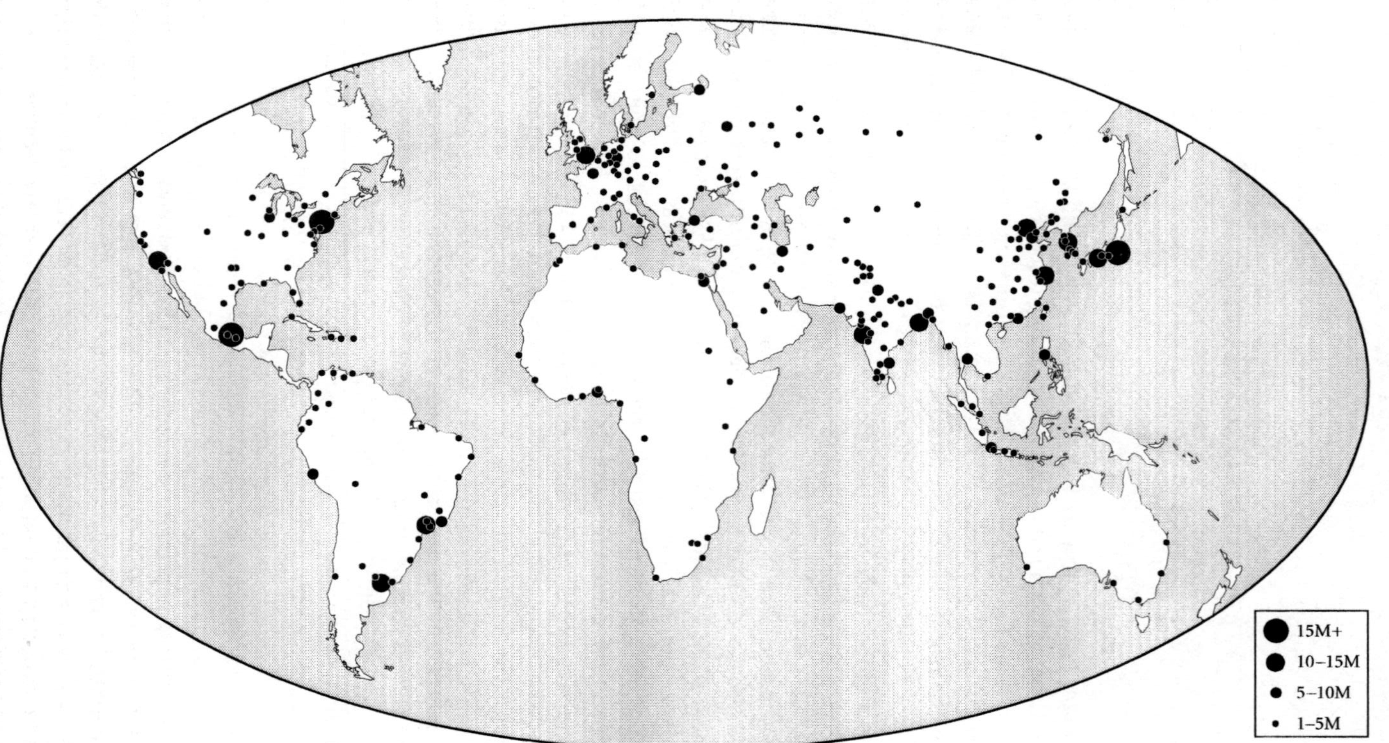

Figure 0.1. *World distribution of metropolitan areas with populations greater than one million*

Source: UN 1995

Table 0.1. *The world's thirty largest urban areas ranked by estimated 2000 population*

	Urban Area	Population (millions)				
		1950	1970	1990	2000	2015
1	Tokyo, Japan	6.9	16.5	25.0	27.9	28.7
2	Bombay, India	2.9	5.8	12.2	18.1	27.4
3	São Paulo, Brazil	2.4	8.1	14.8	17.8	20.8
4	Shanghai, China	5.3	11.2	13.5	17.2	23.4
5	New York, USA	12.3	16.2	16.1	16.6	17.6
6	Mexico City, Mexico	3.1	9.1	15.1	16.4	18.8
7	Beijing, China	3.9	8.1	10.9	14.2	19.4
8	Jakarta, Indonesia	n.a.	3.9	9.3	14.1	21.2
9	Lagos, Nigeria	n.a.	n.a.	7.7	13.5	24.4
10	Los Angeles, USA	4.0	8.4	11.5	13.1	14.3
11	Calcutta, India	4.4	6.9	10.7	12.7	17.6
12	Tianjin, China	2.4	5.2	9.3	12.4	17.0
13	Seoul, South Korea	n.a.	5.3	10.6	12.3	13.1
14	Karachi, Pakistan	n.a.	n.a.	8.0	12.1	20.6
15	Delhi, India	n.a.	3.5	8.2	11.7	17.6
16	Buenos Aires, Argentina	5.0	8.4	10.6	11.4	12.4
17	Metro Manila, Philippines	n.a.	3.5	8.0	10.8	14.7
18	Cairo, Egypt	2.4	5.3	8.6	10.7	14.5
19	Osaka, Japan	4.1	9.4	10.5	10.6	10.6
20	Rio de Janeiro, Brazil	2.9	7.0	9.5	10.2	11.6
21	Dhaka, Bangladesh	n.a.	n.a.	5.9	10.2	19.0
22	Paris, France	5.4	8.5	9.3	9.6	9.6
23	Istanbul, Turkey	n.a.	n.a.	6.5	9.3	12.3
24	Moscow, Russia	5.4	7.1	9.0	9.3	n.a.
25	Lima, Peru	n.a.	n.a.	6.5	8.4	10.5
26	Teheran, Iran	n.a.	n.a.	6.4	7.3	10.2
27	London, U.K.	8.7	8.6	7.3	7.3	n.a.
28	Bangkok, Thailand	n.a.	n.a.	5.9	7.3	10.6
29	Chicago, USA	4.9	6.7	6.8	7.0	n.a.
30	Hyderabad, India	n.a.	n.a.	n.a.	6.7	10.7

Note: n.a. = data not available.

Source: United Nations 1995.

located in the economically advanced countries); in 1970 there were 165 such cities; and in 1990 there were 272 (two-thirds of them now being in the economically developing countries). The United Nations' assessment of future population trends in the world's thirty largest metropolitan areas (see Table 0.1), indicates that this growth can be expected to continue over at least the next few decades.

If global city-regions bear a marked affinity to metropolitan areas as they are commonly defined, what also typifies them—and what Figure 0.1 and Table 0.1

fail fully to capture—is that their form and substantive makeup are also much influenced by processes of territorial and political amalgamation at the local scale. These processes have only begun to operate in a systematic manner in recent years, and they are not always evident in any given instance. Where they are observable, they usually entail some sort of effort to construct interterritorial bases of collective action and identity, especially in circumstances where adjacent territorial units possess some degree of functional interdependence, but have hitherto been administratively or politically separate. The basic objective in these cases is almost always to build regional political competence, and to bring together fragmented territorial units, formally or informally, in pursuit of mutual aid and advantage in the face of the mounting challenges that globalization is now bringing to the fore at the local level.

City-region development is arguably most common where at least some of these territorial units are already strongly urbanized and where there is some tendency to spatial polarization within any given set. Thus, one particularly recurrent form is exemplified by the basic figure of a central metropolitan area with a hinterland of variable extent comprising less densely developed ancillary territory. Another frequent form is represented by spatially overlapping or convergent urban areas—i.e. conurbations—again with a surrounding hinterland area. Yet another consists of alliances of geographically distinct but proximate urban centers working together in order to harvest the benefits of mutual cooperation, such as the new groupings or "synergy networks" of medium-sized cities that are springing into being in the new Europe of the regions. Some of these putative city-regions may sometimes even spill over beyond conventional national boundaries, as in the cases of Copenhagen-Malmö, San Diego-Tijuana, or Singapore-Johor-Batam. In official European Union circles the recent geographical appearance of these different sorts of new urban-regional entities is widely referred to in terms of a so-called infranational revolution.

Across the world, such entities are becoming the focal points of what Brenner (1998) has identified as a new global city-centric capitalism. They function as territorial platforms for much of the post-Fordist economy that constitutes the dominant leading edge of contemporary capitalist development, and as important staging posts for the operations of multinational corporations. Above all, they are important centers for flexible-manufacturing sectors, as exemplified by high-technology or neoartisanal industry, and for service sectors, as exemplified by new media or business and financial activities. As Chapter 1 of this book argues in some detail, sectors like these have a special locational affinity for global city-regions because they thrive on the productivity- and innovation-enhancing effects of dense and multifaceted urban milieux that are simultaneously embedded in worldwide distribution networks. Moreover, the geographic structure of these networks tends more and more to override purely political boundaries so that they are increasingly free from regulatory supervision on the part of national states. In these senses, then, and as the chapters that follow reiterate, city-regions are coming to function as the basic motors of the global economy (Scott 1996), a proposition that points as a corollary to the further important notion that globalization and city-region development are but two facets of a single integrated reality. This notion leads again to the remark that global city-regions today are facing enormous and unfamiliar pressures, so that they are increasingly being induced to search by trial and error for appropriate models of political response. Above all, and in view of the upsurge of global markets, city-regions far and wide have strong incentives to deal in one way or another with those aspects of regional collective order that help to sustain or enhance their competitive economic advantages.

In developing countries, these pressures are especially severe, and even more so in an era when national import-substitution policies are virtually everywhere in retreat before more export-oriented approaches to national economic development. In some countries, these approaches have also gone hand-in-hand with a distinct loss of enthusiasm for the polarization-reversal policies that prevailed at an earlier period. In any case, export-oriented producers in developing countries have a high (though by no means universal) propensity to congregate together in large cities, thus putting further heavy burdens on them. These are the bases from which the tasks of securing and cultivating appropriate niches on world markets are oftentimes most successfully carried out, for it is here that the infrastructures, skills, and auxiliary services needed to sustain production at global standards are for the most part concentrated. Hence, and notwithstanding a complementary process of multinational branch-plant development in various hinterland areas in developing countries, a few large city-regions tend to be the essential and privileged channels through which these countries interact with the global economy.

On the social front, as well, city-regions in all parts of the world are experiencing tremendous internal breakdowns, both directly and indirectly, as a result of globalization, and, again, these are most severe in economically developing countries (see Chapters 11–14 below). Cities, of course, have always been foci of social problems, many of them related to the pervasive phenomena of social segmentation and heterogeneity that predictably occur in dense population centers. In the new global order, these problems are reasserting themselves in often sharply dysfunctional form. In the first place, large global city-regions today are marked by unusually high levels of income inequality. Members of the upper tiers of urban society (managers, professionals, technicians, and so on) have seen their incomes rise dramatically in the recent past, in part as a result of the expanding high-level economic opportunities created by globalization. By contrast, members of the lower tiers are frequently faced with stagnant or (in ascending economic cycles) with slowly rising incomes. Despite some upward mobility of individuals who start out in these lower tiers, a chronic condition of depressed wage levels at the bottom end of contemporary urban society is maintained by the existence of a large underbelly of sweatshops and low-wage service activities in almost all major global city-regions, whose voracious demands for cheap labor constantly stimulate new inflows of immigrants. In the second place, large-scale immigration has turned city-regions—as complex as most of them already were in terms of their social makeup—into vortexes of hitherto unprecedented cultural, ethnic, and racial variation. This feature, which is in and of itself a potentially positive development, leads to deepening problems and predicaments given the virtually universal absence of effective economic, institutional, and political arrangements for integrating the newcomers into urban society except as low-wage and predominantly casual labor reserves. In the context of the income inequalities that already abound in global city-regions, the net result invariably is an exacerbation of the overall climate of social tension.

Thus, in addition to the issues of economic policy alluded to above, global city-regions are also confronted with the latently explosive social conditions that are being generated within them as they develop, grow, and become more enmeshed in ties to other parts of the world. Any attempt to deal with these conditions is likely to meet with formidable obstacles. In particular, no matter how well-meaning any program of reform may be, it is unlikely to be successful if it consists solely of top-down mandates. Equally important is the bottom-up imperative of reconstituting the public interest to elicit the consent and social reintegration of all elements of urban society. Effective action, whether from the top or the bottom, must in part, of course, be consolidated at the national level (a significant dimension being the income-redistributing activities of central states), and one can be rightly skeptical about the possibilities of definitive solutions being found solely at the local level. Yet the local *can* be an important arena of social reconstruction in its own right, as well as being a conduit through which diverse national policies are mediated. The local is all the more important given the psychic and political distance of the central state from many of the constituencies that make up modern global city-regions, as compared with the immediacy and relevance of the local community. It is in this light that we can begin to understand something of the numerous new kinds of social movements and civil organizations that are now springing forth in large city-regions as spontaneous responses to problems of social exclusion and marginalization. The local level, too, has become a renewed focus of persistent calls for more radical practices of democratic participation and representation, as ever-widening circles of urban society demand a greater voice in public decision-making. Many of these demands go so far as to envisage the possibility of extending the full entitlements and obligations of citizenship to recent immigrants and other socially marginal groups. Concomitantly, the nature of citizenship itself is currently being subject to much fresh scrutiny, and in some parts of the world (Amsterdam being a prime example), practical attempts are actually under way to extend the franchise not just to those who are nationals of the central state, but also to those who, whatever their nationality by birthright, have made a long-term commitment to life in the local community.

To many commentators today, globalization as an economic phenomenon is synonymous with neoliberalism as a political ideology, the two often being thought of as virtually inseparable forces in modern capitalism. But globalization and neoliberalism are not the same thing, despite their current historical conjunction. Other versions of globalization are entirely possible and workable in practice. If the arguments made *passim* in this book have any validity, neoliberalism as a political correlate of current economic trends is actually rapidly approaching exhaustion, if only in the sense that it is oblivious to the fact that the markets upon which it pins its faith are themselves, and of necessity, grounded in institutional, legal, and political frameworks that call for constant extramarket superintendence. There can accordingly be no universal market society, but only historically specific kinds of markets. Among the viable alternatives to neoliberalism waiting in the wings is some form of social democratic or social market system of regulation. This is likely in the end not only to be more viable as a means of economic governance at every level, from the global to the local, but also more socially fair, and hence more politically legitimate over the long run. As argued in Chapter 1, what social democracy offers is a clear commitment to promoting those institutional arrangements necessary for long-run success in the modern post-Fordist economy, together with a practical concern for reducing the many injustices that fester in the absence of adequate social protection, while acknowledging that markets have efficiency-seeking properties that are extremely desirable, all else being equal.

The future course of globalization is still largely open to negotiation, and the political debates that will be waged in the coming decades over its principal directions of change will in all likelihood be highly charged. These debates will almost certainly revolve in part around the question of city-regions and their deepening role as points at which globalization processes crystallize out on the geographic landscape and as active agents in shaping globalization itself. The chapters that follow expand greatly on these debates. They do so by means of theoretical analysis and empirical description together with critical explorations of many of the different policy choices that seem to lie ahead. The authors of these chapters deal in detail with such matters as the internal economic functions and external linkages of global city-regions, their social constitution and dynamics, the governance problems that they pose, their incidence and attributes in developing countries, and, again, the multiple policy challenges that flow from their peculiar association with globalization. Editorial commentaries directed specifically to these chapters are collected in the brief introductory essays that introduce each main part of the book.

This volume, it is hoped, will help to lay the foundations for more informed discussions of the urgent and perplexing political choices that we will assuredly face as the worldwide mosaic of city-regions identified here takes on sharper and more complex outlines in the decades ahead.

REFERENCES

Brenner, N. (1998). "Global cities, global states: global city formation and state territorial restructuring in contemporary Europe." *Review of International Political Economy*, 5: 1–37.

Scott, A. J. (1996). "Regional motors of the global economy." *Futures*, 28: 391–411.

United Nations (1995). *World Urbanization Prospects.* New York: United Nations Department of Economic and Social Information and Policy Analysis, Population Division.

PART I

OPENING ARGUMENTS

Chapter 1 provides an overall conceptual map of the questions, debates, and empirical particulars raised by an investigation of global city-regions. The chapter ranges widely over many pertinent issues from the economic foundations of global city-regions to their emerging political relations, and if it strives to articulate definite points of view on these matters, it is in no sense designed to bring closure to this still emerging field of inquiry. As the expositions in the rest of the book unfold, numerous additional analytical and descriptive details are elaborated, and at the same time, significant divergences of theoretical and political conviction become apparent. Chapter 1 offers a framework for accommodating these details and a backdrop against which the arguments and disagreements that run through the book as a whole can be evaluated. An integrated overview is thus provided, but without sacrificing the rich palette of varied opinion that exists about the social dynamics and meaning of these new geographical phenomena designated here *global city-regions*.

1

Global City-Regions

ALLEN J. SCOTT, JOHN AGNEW,
EDWARD W. SOJA, AND MICHAEL STORPER

There are now more than three hundred city-regions around the world with populations greater than one million. At least twenty city-regions have populations in excess of ten million. They range from familiar metropolitan agglomerations dominated by a strongly developed core such as the London region or Mexico City, to more polycentric geographic units as in the cases of the urban networks of the Randstad or Emilia-Romagna. Everywhere, these city-regions are expanding vigorously, and they present many deep challenges to researchers and policymakers as we enter the twenty-first century. The processes of worldwide economic integration and accelerated urban growth make traditional planning and policy strategies in these regions increasingly problematical while more fitting approaches remain in a largely experimental stage. New ways of thinking about these processes and new ways of acting to harness their benefits and to control their negative effects are urgently needed.

The concept of *global city-regions* can be traced back to the "world cities" idea of Hall (1966) and Friedmann and Wolff (1982), and to the "global cities" idea of Sassen (1991). We build here on these pioneering efforts, but in a way that tries to extend the meaning of the concept in economic, political, and territorial terms, and above all by an effort to show how city-regions increasingly function as essential spatial nodes of the global economy and as distinctive political actors on the world stage. In fact, rather than being dissolved away as social and geographic objects by processes of globalization, city-regions are becoming increasingly central to modern life, and all the more so because globalization (in combination with various technological shifts) has reactivated their significance as bases of all forms of productive activity, no matter whether in manufacturing or services, in high-technology or low-technology sectors. As these changes have begun to run their course, it has become increasingly apparent that the city in the narrow sense is less an appropriate or viable unit of local social organization than city-regions or regional networks of cities. One tangible expression of this idea can be observed in the forms of consolidation that are beginning to occur as adjacent units of local political organization (provinces, *Länder*, counties, metropolitan areas, municipalities, *départements*, and so on) search for regionwide coalitions as a means of dealing with the threats and the opportunities of globalization. In this process, we argue, global city-regions have emerged of late years as a new and critically important kind of geographic and institutional phenomenon on the world stage.

In what follows, we attempt to bring these remarks into closer conceptual focus. Our discussion is driven by five main questions:

1. Why are global city-regions growing rapidly precisely at a moment in history when some analysts are claiming that the end of geography is in sight, and that the world is turning into a placeless space of flows?
2. How have forms of economic and social organization in city-regions responded to globalization, and what new problems have been created as a consequence?
3. What main governance tasks do global city-regions face as they seek to preserve and enhance their wealth and well-being?
4. Is it possible for the less economically advanced parts of the world to harness the potential benefits of global city-region development to their own advantage, and what are the main drawbacks of such development for them?
5. How can we define the public interest in culturally heterogeneous global city-regions? In particular, how are traditional notions of democracy and citizenship being challenged by the emergence of global city-regions and in what ways can they be made more effective in this new context?

Cutting across all of these questions are the competing claims of the two main political ideologies that seem most clearly poised to assume prominent roles in modern capitalist societies in the decades immediately ahead, namely, a currently dominant neoliberalism, and—most evident today in certain parts of the European Union—a new social democratic (or social market) perspective. These two ideologies offer in theory and practice quite contrasting visions of the future of global city-regions.

THE NEW REGIONALISM IN GLOBAL CONTEXT

In the immediate postwar decades almost all of the major capitalist countries were characterized by strong central governments and tightly bordered national economies. These countries formed a political bloc within the framework of a Pax Americana, itself underpinned by a network of international arrangements (the Bretton Woods system, the World Bank, the IMF, GATT) through which they sought to regulate their economic relations. Although international trade and investment flows expanded rapidly in the postwar period, they scarcely disrupted the ability of nation-states to implement domestic economic policies. One consequence of this situation was that each country had its own peculiar national institutional structure that in greater or lesser degree shaped social and demographic processes and sustained a distinctive national urban system.

Today, globalization has brought about significant transformations of this older order of things. There are many institutional experiments now under way that are leading in the direction of a new social and political organization of space.

This new organization consists above all of a hierarchy of interpenetrating territorial scales of economic activity and governance relations, ranging from the global to the local, and in which the emerging system of global city-regions figures prominently. Four main points need to be made about this hierarchy.

1. Huge and ever-increasing amounts of economic activity (input–output chains, labor migrations, trade, foreign direct investment, international business operations, monetary flows, and so on) now occur in extensive cross-national networks. As globalization moves forward, it creates conflicts and predicaments that in turn activate a variety of political responses and institution-building efforts in regard to these networks. Examples include the major international financial and business arrangements that are already in place, such as the G7/G8 group, the OECD, the World Bank, the IMF, and a newly streamlined GATT, now known as the World Trade Organization. While these particular political responses to the pressures of globalization remain limited in scope and real authority, they are liable to expansion and consolidation as capitalism continues to globalize.

2. In part as a corollary of these same pressures, there has been a proliferation over the last few decades of multination blocs such the EU, NAFTA, MERCOSUR, ASEAN, APEC, CARICOM, and many others. These blocs, too, represent institutional responses to the stresses created by the steady spilling over of national capitalisms beyond their traditional political boundaries. They remain in various stages of development at the present time, with the EU being obviously in the vanguard. However, because they involve only small numbers of participants, they are clearly more manageable as political units (i.e. internal transactions costs problems are relatively restrained and consensus is easier to attain) in comparison with actual or putative global organizations.

3. Sovereign states and national economies remain dominant elements of the contemporary political and economic landscape, though they are clearly undergoing deep transformation. Individual states no longer enjoy the same degree of sovereign political autonomy that they once possessed, and under conditions of intensifying globalization they find themselves less and less able or willing to protect all the regional and sectional interests within their jurisdictions. Numerous economic sectors have been subject to massive debordering over the last few decades so that it is increasingly difficult, if not impossible, to say precisely where, for example, the American economy ends and the German or Japanese economies begin. As a result, some of the regulatory activities that were formerly carried out under the aegis of the central state are being assimilated into institutions at supranational levels of definition; at the same time, other functions have been drifting down to institutions whose range of operation is more local or regional.

4. Accordingly, and most importantly for the purposes of the present chapter, there has been a resurgence of region-based forms of economic and political organization, with the clearest expression of this tendency being found in certain large

global city-regions. That said, the economic and political trajectories of these city-regions cannot be fully understood except in relationship to the complex hierarchy of interpenetrating territorial scales referred to above.

The notion of a resurgence of region-based economic and political organizations requires further elaboration. The propensity for certain types of economic activity—manufacturing and service sectors alike—to gather together in dense locational clusters appears to have been intensifying in recent decades. This quest for mutual proximity on the part of all manner of economic agents at the present time is in significant degree a strategic response to heightened economic competition which—in many segments of the economy—has intensified uncertainty and placed a premium on learning and innovation. Clustering enables firms to respond to these challenges by allowing them greater levels of operational flexibility and by enhancing their innovative capacities. Globalization has accentuated this process, though it is by no means the exclusive cause of it, so that with the internationalization of markets, the economies of global city-regions have grown accordingly. Large city-regions are thus coming to function as territorial platforms from which concentrated groups or networks of firms contest global markets. At the same time, many regions are now subject to intensified cross-border competitive pressures. They are thus faced with the choice of either submitting to these pressures passively, or engaging actively in institution-building and policymaking in an effort to turn globalization as far as possible to their benefit. The choice is an especially critical one for city-regions because central governments nowadays are finding it increasingly difficult to deal with the varied demands of all the different localities that they oversee, especially as the latter are often marked by quite idiosyncratic problems. To complicate this state of affairs, many city-regions are also finding themselves faced with important new tasks of local political integration and representation. These tasks are of special urgency at a time when global city-regions function more and more as poles of attraction for low-wage labor migrants from all over the world, so that almost everywhere their populations are becoming increasingly polyglot and interspersed with marginalized social groups. As a consequence of this, many city-regions today are being confronted with pressing issues related to political participation and the local reconstruction of political identity and citizenship.

The new map of the world that is coming into being as these trends take their course can in large degree be represented in terms of the four intersecting territorial scales of economic and political relations described above, together with a series of cross-cutting relational forms ranging from international civil bodies to the far-flung operations of multinational corporations. At the geographic base of the whole system lies a mosaic or archipelago of large city-regions constituting one of the principal structural networks of the new global economy (Veltz 1996). It is to the economic functions of these localized economic systems that we now turn our attention.

CITY-REGIONS AS THE MOTORS OF THE GLOBAL ECONOMY

It has long been predicted that improvements in transportation and communications technologies, in terms of both cost and quality, will eventually undermine any need for urban concentration. With each round of technological change in this area, scholars and journalists keep telling us that large-scale urbanization is a thing of the past. But with each such round of development cities not only do not disappear, they become larger and more important. This is because although advances in modern transportation and communications technologies enable many forms of economic and social interaction to occur over ever-greater distances, in other cases they actually heighten the need for proximity. The key to understanding why this is true lies in the ways that different economic activities are interconnected in terms of what we might call their transactional or network relationships to each other and to the rest of the world.

In very schematic terms, two different kinds of productive activity are typically to be found in any advanced economic system, each of them corresponding to a fundamentally different type of network structure. On the one hand, certain kinds of production are highly routinized: they rely on forms of knowledge that are relatively well codified and on machines and work processes where repetition is the dominant pattern of action. In economic terms, this means that it is possible to plan this sort of activity with some degree of confidence and to carry it out at very large scales. The necessary materials and inputs used in production can thus often be acquired according to a given schedule, and they can be purchased in large volumes. This means, too, that these materials and inputs can be brought in cheaply over large distances, for the ability to plan and to purchase in large volumes means that their unit costs can be kept low. Under these circumstances, the linkages between functionally related firms are likely to have a rather limited impact on locational decisions, and firms will be relatively free to seek out locations quite distant from one another. In practice, and because production is routinized in this type of system, the chosen locations will often coincide with pools of cheap, unskilled labor, sometimes far from any major urban center.

On the other hand, we find economic sectors where quite different kinds of conditions hold. Vast areas of the contemporary economy involve activities where enormous uncertainty prevails, and where there are strong limits on producers' abilities to routinize or simplify their operations, especially in regard to their mutual interactions. In high-technology industry, for example, producers are frequently faced not only with rapid shifts in basic technologies themselves, but also with demands for their products that vary greatly from one customer to another and from one moment to the next. In high-level business and financial services, the changing project-oriented and client-oriented product means that firms must be organized so as to vary the mix of skills and resources that they bring to each particular job; further, the skills and resources themselves (especially human intellectual assets) are not widely available because they are quite specialized. In industries faced with markets that fluctuate because of constant design changes or fashion effects (more broadly, product differentiation processes), firms must be prepared to change and recombine equipment and labor and to monitor shifts in the market, often on a day-to-day basis.

In the latter circumstances, firms find it difficult to routinize their operations and to plan their relations with other firms, or even with their own workers over extended time frames. They come to depend on networks that facilitate change and recombination, in contrast to the more rigid kinds of networks that typically underpin the first group of firms. Change and recombination are potentially very costly, however, because they depend on high levels of access to a wide variety of information and resources. Firms need to know what different kinds of suppliers and (shifting) market opportunities are available to them. Workers need to know about alternative job opportunities, especially where labor markets are characterized by high levels of flexibility. Often, and in spite of the informatics revolution, the knowledge underlying these processes is quite tacit. Acquiring this economically useful knowledge in a timely fashion depends on human relationships and on being able to interpret the information in meaningful ways. Simultaneously, where economic specialization and flexibility are strongly present, rapid shifts in underlying networks of transactions occur as firms negotiate new contracts or restructure their buying and selling relationships, and as workers shift from one job to another. These are networks, in short, that are characterized by high levels of uncertainty, instability, and complexity. In these circumstances, the costs of transacting rise greatly as distance increases, and with the geographical scattering of producers, inefficiencies rapidly set in.

At the same time, producers in these industries gain significant competitive advantages from their copresence in the dense transactional networks that come into being as they buy and sell from each other, hire workers from the local labor pool, participate in both formal and informal business associations, and so on. These networks underpin an atmosphere rich in constantly shifting bodies of information (much of it quite informal) about technologies, markets, and product designs. As such, they help to foster economic creativity and innovation in many different types of sectors, including, in particular, some of the most dynamic leading edges of the contemporary economy such as high-technology industry, services, and cultural products industries.

In the postwar years, and up until about the early 1970s, most of the major capitalist economies seemed to be moving steadily toward greater routinization of production, especially in manufacturing. However, for a variety of complex reasons, beginning with the economic crises of the early and mid-1970s, economic environments tended to become much less stable than they had been, forcing firms in many sectors to adopt more flexible technologies and organizational patterns. In addition, new digital technologies were now encouraging destandardization of production processes, just as rising incomes and proliferating market niches were stimulating a search for wider product variety. For all of these reasons, the second type of production described above has come to be pervasive, if not now dominant, in the advanced capitalist societies, so that increasingly important shares of output and employment are now accounted for by flexibly networked production systems or value chains.

These arguments lead to the essential question of the relationships between these flexibly networked systems and large cities, and this question hinges fundamentally on the issue of economic productivity, performance, and innovation. For one thing, the different firms and actors that participate in these networks all receive a tremendous boost to their efficiency by being part of tightly linked and spatially concentrated clusters, not only because clustering greatly mitigates transactions costs, but also because of the flexibility and information effects referred to above. For another, creativity and innovation within the production system are much enhanced, in part because of the great variety of different skills, sensibilities, and experiences embodied in the labor force, and in part because the agglomeration of interdependent producers in one place increases the probability of encounters in which novel insights and/or economically useful knowledge are engendered. In addition, firms have greater access to a more varied group of suppliers and business opportunities than they would have if they were all at widely separated locations. The local availability of a wide range of specialized suppliers and workers permits firms to be more flexible, and frees them from investment in the excess inventories that would otherwise be necessary where the risks of breakdowns in supply chains or market outlets are high. Overhead costs can be kept to a relatively low level because equipment and inventories are stored, as it were, in the networked collectivity of producers. Workers, too, are able to tap into richer bodies of local labor market information as well as to increase their access to potential job opportunities, thus enhancing their ability to change jobs, or to find new jobs when they are unemployed. Of course, the contemporary economy is also marked by well-developed long-distance supplier relationships and recruiting activities. But oftentimes, as we shall see, these relationships also feed into highly localized production networks.

Productivity and performance are thus raised by urban concentration in two ways. First, concentration secures overall efficiency of the economic system. Second, it intensifies creativity, learning, and innovation both by the increased flexibility of producers that it makes possible and by the enormous flows of ideas and knowledge that occur alongside the transactional links within localized industrial networks. Such networks are typically to be found at the economic cores of the world's major city-regions today, and in many cases, they are the basis of significant new rounds of urban expansion. Moreover, the economies of these city-regions are to an increasing degree tied in to world markets, thus stimulating yet further growth, which in turn encourages more specialized producers to appear in any given network. The films of Hollywood, the semiconductors of Silicon Valley, the banking and financial services of New York and London, and the fashions of Paris all represent the outputs of clustered flexible production networks whose fortunes are strongly tied to world-market demand. Other examples include mechanical engineering in Baden-Württemburg and Bavaria, the small-firm craft-based industries of northern Italy, the jewelry industry in Bangkok, or furniture production in Guadalajara, Mexico. In this manner, global city-regions come to function increasingly as the regional motors of the global economy, that is, as dynamic local networks of economic relationships caught up in more extended worldwide webs of interregional competition and exchange.

To be sure, this description is only a starting point for a fuller analysis of the economic structure of global city-regions. But the essential key to understanding why, in an era of generally declining transportation and communication costs, we still have a world that is organized around large urban regions (rather than around a more diffuse pattern of location), lies in the ways in which the economies of these regions have become so closely tied in with clustered flexible networks of firms that compete on increasingly extended markets.

THE SOCIAL GEOGRAPHY OF GLOBAL CITY-REGIONS

The forces shaping the emergence of global city-regions have had marked impacts on their internal social geography—patterns of social stratification, intrametropolitan income distribution and demographics, and ways of daily life. Three striking outcomes dominate these localized effects of globalization and economic restructuring.

The first is the increased cultural and demographic heterogeneity induced primarily by large-scale migration into global city-regions. Migration has been oriented most insistently to the largest city-regions, creating some of the most culturally diverse urban agglomerations in history. As with so much that has been happening in this age of intensified globalization, this increased cultural heterogeneity is associated with both explosive dangers and creative new opportunities for social mobility and social justice.

The second main outcome is a pronounced change in the spatial morphology of global city-regions. Whereas most metropolitan regions in the past were focused mainly on one or perhaps two clearly defined central cities, the city-regions of today are becoming increasingly polycentric or multiclustered agglomerations. Two extreme examples of such multiclustered agglomerations are represented by Shanghai and the Pearl River Delta, global city-regions that each contain more than thirty million inhabitants. Moreover, in virtually all global city-regions there has been a rapid growth of outer cities and edge cities, as formerly peripheral or rural areas far from old downtown cores have developed into urban centers in their own right. The blurring of once rigid and clearly defined boundaries has been an integral part of the globalization process and the new information age, and this is now reflected in the increasingly ambiguous meaning of what is urban, suburban, exurban, or indeed rural or not urban at all. Thus, what has been happening can be described as a simultaneous and complex process of decentralization and recentralization of the city-region. Many older established central agglomerations have been experiencing an outflow of certain population groups and employment activities, but the spaces they have vacated have also typically been reoccupied by new immigrant communities and economic functions. At the same time, new poles of urban growth are being created in the periphery, stretching and pinning down the urban fabric in a recentered regional constellation of cities. Here again there arise both positive and negative consequences for political and economic health and well-being.

The third major effect of globalization and economic restructuring on the social geography of city-regions is closely related to the previous two, but is even more challenging in its direct political and policy implications. It is becoming apparent that globalization and its associated forms of economic change tend to widen the gap between the wealthy and the poor in economic, social, and spatial terms. Globalization intensifies these trends by stimulating the growth of high-wage occupations in large cities while promoting (especially in a context of large-scale immigration from low-wage countries) the proliferation of marginal, low-skill jobs. For example, in the early 1990s it was reported that the disparity between wealth and poverty had grown in all the developed industrial countries, in both big and small cities. This gap tends to peak in the largest global city-regions, particularly because a high proportion of the rich tends to live in these places. In many such places, too, there is rapid growth of the welfare-dependent urban underclass as well as of the working poor, as represented, for example, by households with multiple jobholders who are nonetheless unable to live comfortably above the poverty line.

Any attempt to explain the detailed causes of increasing segmentation and socioeconomic inequalities in global city-regions is inevitably highly controversial, and there are many analysts across the political spectrum who argue that the observable disparities in these regions are a result of rapid economic growth rather than of globalization as such. Whatever the final verdict on this question may be, there is good reason to place the issue of rising levels of social and spatial segmentation high on the policy agenda in any discussion of the problems facing the development of global city-regions in the new millennium. At the level of national policy, for example, there seems to be a perplexing trade-off between social protection and job generation. In comparison to most of Western Europe, the United States has been very successful with regard to job generation but much less so in dealing with rising socioeconomic inequalities. Even in the European Union, however, there are cases where both objectives have been met simultaneously, as in Denmark or the Netherlands. Hence, there are several different policy contexts where mutual learning might be highly productive and where some progressive middle ground or third way (Giddens 1998) might be profitably explored between free-wheeling neoliberalism and traditional welfare statism.

At the scale of the city-region, there are further pressing social policy challenges. High on the list of these challenges is how best to accommodate expanding immigrant populations, for there can be little doubt that immigration, especially into the larger global city-regions, will continue well into the twenty-first century. There is much evidence to suggest that immigrant populations play a vital role in regional economic development, both as cheap labor and as innovative entrepreneurs, especially in sectors marked by many small firms and flexible production arrangements such as clothing, electronics, and a wide variety of services. However, without appropriate measures for social integration, housing, and education, it is likely to prove difficult to maintain or enlarge the productive role of immigrant workers in global city-regions and avoid political clashes with the domestic workforce.

The rising levels of social segmentation observable in most global city-regions have stimulated some innovative local responses. In the United States, for example, in the absence of adequate local government attention to their interests and problems, many low-income groups are now forming into a wide diversity of self-help and community-based organizations, and this trend is no doubt likely to intensify in the future. New coalitions of this type with their focus on such basic needs as shelter, water, health, decent jobs, and living wages will almost certainly play a growing role in the reorganized civil society of global city-regions in the future. Yet the merits of this kind of substitution of civil for governmental action are debatable, for there is no guarantee that it will generate those equitable forms of social protection that are among the cornerstones of democratic practice in many societies. A very different kind of situation exists at the opposite end of the economic spectrum in global city-regions. Those at the top of the income ladder seem increasingly to be withdrawing from civil society and civic responsibility into fortressed households and gated communities, creating their own kind of private residential governance structures or "privatopias" (Mackenzie 1994). As we shall see below, this fundamentally undemocratic approach to the organization of urban space is even more marked in a number of developing countries. In the new geography of the global city-region social distance as well as economic distance between the haves and have-nots is steadily on the rise.

The sociospatial reorganization of global city-regions has had other negative consequences as well. As these cities have grown and extended outward, and as their populations have become more and more diverse, a complex set of spatial mismatches in the location of jobs, housing, and transit facilities has been created, giving rise to severely adverse effects on the quality of life as well as (indirectly) to many negative environmental impacts. At one extreme, this state of affairs has compounded the problems of the inner city poor, for as good jobs disappear to the outer cities, the existing housing stock becomes excessively run down and overcrowded, and homelessness rises. At another extreme, rapid outward expansion of the urban fringe often creates isolated peripheral areas where families attracted by cheap housing find themselves stranded so far from their jobs that they must travel for extended periods of time each way to work.

The culturally heterogeneous, polycentric, socially and spatially segmented global city-region is thus a highly fragmented chess-board of uneven development sprawling ever outward. The expanded city-region functions as a vital platform of competitive advantage and generative growth in the global economy, but at the same time this regional world of production often rests upon institutional structures of governance and planning that are inadequate to maintain effective social order, not to mention continued economic health (Storper 1997). The creation of new and responsive frameworks of regional governance capable of sustaining economic development, instigating a sense of cooperative regional identity, and promoting innovative ways of achieving regional democracy and economic fair play is the great challenge for the future.

NEW GOVERNANCE ISSUES IN GLOBAL CITY-REGIONS

Until recently, regions as political entities were mainly thought of as administrative units nested within the territory of the nation-state. Regions were thus coterminous with the local level of government, or constituted subterritories within a national territory, mere lower levels in a hierarchy of administrative-cum-political arrangements from more to the less general and significant. To be sure, federal states have always engaged in relatively more power sharing between different levels of government than have unitary states, but in the postwar period, even federal governments have tended to exert more and more influence over lower levels through increased fiscal transfers designed to realize ambitious national goals. In both cases, regions were for the most part seen as units for efficient administration of public goods and services that for technical reasons were best delivered at this geographical level. Beginning in the 1970s, however, a new regionalism began to emerge and steadily to superimpose itself on this older devolutive regionalism. The new regionalism is not so much an effect of initiatives flowing out from central government as it is a direct local response to stresses and strains set in motion by the emergence of the city-region as an important actor in the world economy.

The term *governance* is now widely employed to describe the multifaceted types of social and economic coordination at issue here. Concretely, many processes of governance today involve not just agencies of government but also non-governmental organizations, civil associations, private-public partnerships, and so on. The term can apply equally well to coordination of the complex economic and social environment of the global city-region as a whole as it can to collective action in regard to specific segments of urban life (such as particular sectors of production or individual neighborhoods). One important domain of governance can be identified in relation to possible and actual responses of city-regions to the new global competition. The global market and new transportation and communications technologies have encouraged a restructuring of economic competition such that city-regions now increasingly emerge as privileged sites of generalized competitive advantage (Keating 1997). In this context, the specific character of different regions is of critical importance: local policies are increasingly being formulated to intensify competitive advantages, encourage new firm formation, improve the economic environment for local firms, and make the local business climate more attractive to mobile capital. These activist local economic development policies differ markedly from previous (top-down) approaches to regional development that tended to focus on questions of equity between regions within a given national territory. Indeed, since the incentives to creative intervention are greatest for those wealthy metropolitan areas with the most at stake in global competition, local competitive policies frequently work against equity between regions.

Here, a number of dilemmas haunt local economic development policies. One of these is connected to the widespread practice of seeking to promote development by attracting inward investment. This usually involves competitive bidding wars between different places, i.e. locational tournaments, especially directed at attracting the branch plants of transnational firms. In the USA, this practice is generally favored by central-city business elites who are most likely to benefit from it, while various neighborhood groups see themselves as being excluded from any benefits that may accrue. Moreover, much research from both the United States and Western Europe suggests that policies devoted to assisting and retaining existing firms are more effective in stimulating local economic growth than are policies committed to capturing inward investment. Competitive tournaments with other city-regions in the effort to attract mobile capital probably offer a much lower (perhaps even negative) rate of return per dollar expended to the local community. Yet even if we accept that coordination of the diverse synergies in global city-regions is likely to be the most effective way to proceed, how best to promote these synergies and how to design institutional frameworks for this purpose is by no means clear.

In recent times, the term governance has acquired two broadly opposing connotations with respect to the role of the public sector. One of these signifies the merging of the public and private in loose partnerships, where the idea of government as a set of political relations (involving struggles and debates over both objectives and policies) is replaced with the idea of the public sphere as a relatively limited set of arrangements for harmonizing various private interests under conditions of strict market failure. From this essentially neoliberal viewpoint, city-region governance would involve the replacement of confrontation or competition between private and public interests with a technocratic approach to the solution of local problems. This line of attack tends to put a premium on the creation of a positive "business climate," so that the locality becomes more attractive to new investors and firms can more effectively organize for successful interplace competition. In other words, what is good for local firms is seen as being good for the entire city-region. A second sense of the term sees governance as involving a set of complex institutional reactions to the broader problems of economic and social adjustment in the emerging global-local system. From this more institutionalist point of view, the governance of city-regions is part of a larger problem of contemporary global coordination. There is no single geographical scale at which political regulation of the world economy or of its component parts can be secured. The critical issue here is coordination across geographical scales, between the policies pursued at supranational, national, and regional levels, involving both formal and informal coordination, and the possibilities of popular input into their formation and implementation at all levels (Hewitt de Alcántara 1998, Scott 1998).

As city-regions emerge into prominence as durable elements of the global system, they face many daunting tasks. One of these is concerned with achieving the right mix of cooperation and competition between firms. Balancing the return to short-term competitive behavior by firms with the need for long-term cooperation among them to ensure steady local economic growth via resource pooling and mutual learning is a major challenge. Another concerns the ability of the national and supranational political units within which global city-regions are embedded to coordinate their interactions. A further task concerns the codification of local practices, either in terms of fixed rules of government or flexible rules of interorganizational and interindividual negotiation, the former maintaining formal safeguards over representation but at the expense of responsiveness to rapid socioeconomic change. Finally, there is the delicate problem of efficient and streamlined public action in the face of rapidly shifting external conditions versus public accountability. Without a high degree of accountability local social inequities (in the form of income and wealth disparities, differential access to local foci of power, disparities in public goods and service provision between different areas within the city-region, etc.) created by the drive to efficiency are apt to lead to social conflict and instability (Jessop 1998).

GLOBAL CITY-REGIONS IN DEVELOPING COUNTRIES

The processes of urban and regional development we are describing here are not limited to the wealthiest countries. They are global in extent; indeed, many of the largest global city-regions are located outside of the developed world. Some of the most prominent examples include Bangkok, Buenos Aires, Cairo, Jakarta, Lagos, Mexico City, Rio de Janeiro, São Paulo, Shanghai, or Teheran.

In many cases, such city-regions developed as the principal concentrations of advanced economic activity in their national economies. In some countries, rapid industrialization is dependent on the spatial concentration of infrastructure and productive activity. The modern productive sector requires access to a wide range of suppliers and services, which initially can be made available at reasonable cost in only a small number of places in these countries, due to their limited overall level of development. Particularly when there is a national push for rapid industrial development, it tends to result in superagglomerations. These large urban centers also become the privileged basing points for the biggest national and transnational companies. The location of such companies in these cities reinforces local growth and sustains a complex tertiary sector in the national economy.

Such development often acts as an attraction for the rural poor in these countries, who go to the city in search of higher incomes. This pull factor, coupled with the extensive modernization of agricultural activity and policies that push people off the land, frequently generates extremely high rates of local population growth, and results in a situation where a small number of cities in these countries comes to account for a high proportion of the national population. This further helps to explain the phenomenon of megalocephalic urban development in developing countries.

It should be emphasized that the extreme urban concentration found in many developing countries results from the combination of two essential dynamics: one of these concerns forces similar to those found in developed countries and that lead to the appearance of large productive clusters; the other involves the particular circumstances of developing countries, consisting of an initial state of relatively low levels of urbanization, restricted modern sectors, and unevenly developed infrastructure. When these countries are confronted with national policies favoring rapid industrial development, the result is the appearance of one or a small number of hyperlarge urban regions.

The social and environmental problems engendered by this process of urbanization are often more pronounced than in the developed countries, all the while sharing certain of their basic features. Even with spatial concentration of infrastructure as a strategy to generate modern industrial development, infrastructural conditions in these city-regions are frequently far from adequate. Transportation, sanitation, housing, and water systems are generally unevenly distributed in metropolitan space, and severe shortages are common. Indeed, there are often such great discrepancies between social need and economically feasible supply that one can speak of veritable crisis conditions in many such cities. To this must be added an understanding of social and economic power in many developing nations. Poor, disenfranchised rural populations are often pushed off the land by unjust economic policies, by physical violence, or by the monopolization of land resources by the rich. They end up in cities, where again they are subject to the economic and social turmoil involved in becoming part of the urban subproletariat.

In developing countries it is even more difficult to resolve the problems and predicaments of global city-regions than in developing countries. In the first place, even though these regions are often far richer than the rest of the national territories in which they are located, they also invariably contain populations marked by huge economic disparities. In the absence of progressive income redistribution policies, it becomes effectively impossible to finance needed improvements in infrastructure and services. In the second place, precisely because there is a limited number of city-regions that can function as basing-points for the most modern parts of the economy, and as points of contact with the global economy, there is usually a diminished tendency to spatial dispersion of population and economic activity so that relaxation of the pressures on these centers is unlikely to occur. For example, even though the São Paulo metropolitan area accounts for a smaller share of national economic output in Brazil today than in 1970 (45 percent as opposed to 65 percent), it continues to grow and spread in absolute terms at a rate that makes it quite difficult for infrastructure supply to catch up to demand. This experience contrasts with that of many developed countries, where smaller city-regions often absorb enough of national growth at a certain point to flatten the urban hierarchy (in relative terms), and to reduce pressures on the biggest city-regions. Most developing countries, therefore, remain trapped within a cycle of megacity growth.

Because of the nature of development processes based on rapid industrialization and high levels of internal population migration, the populations of global city-regions in developing economies are almost always highly segmented in terms of social class, income, and, sometimes, racial, terms. These city-regions then assume spatial forms that express this social segmentation, as reflected above all in the segregation of rich and poor. At one extreme, one finds massive poor communities living in shantytowns, *favelas*, and *bidonvilles*, and at the other the more spacious and well-equipped communities of the middle classes and the rich. In many such global city-regions, there are complex social frictions having to do with the combination of segregation, inequality, and proximity. Violence, or the fear of it, becomes a central preoccupation of the upper classes, pushing them toward forms of fortress settlements, gated high-rise communities surrounded by walls and guarded entries. This architecture of fear only exacerbates the fragmented character of urban space, and generates additional problems for infrastructure provision, as the rich attempt to secede socially and politically from the space of the urban community as a whole.

Recently, the global city-regions of many developing countries have been affected by a double economic trend. First, there are certain tendencies for the movement of economic activities outward from their metropolitan cores and into exurban fringe areas; second, there is a limited tendency in some countries for the migration of routine productive activities to smaller towns, i.e. activities that have become less dependent on the advanced services and inputs only found in the largest urban areas. But, as already noted, these tendencies are far from being strong enough to stem the growth of large cities in the national economy or to reduce the enormous pressure on infrastructure and services in the major city-regions.

Continuing economic globalization has greatly reinforced the attractiveness of global city-regions in developing countries for major national and transnational firms. In many countries, firms that used to produce primarily for the national market are finding themselves faced with the effects of trade liberalization and the dismantling of national policies that provided protection and incentives. The concomitant requirement that they sell more of their output on global markets, and compete against imports, makes many of them more dependent on the advanced production conditions available only in global city-regions. Hence, globalization, liberalization, and—in some cases—privatization of formerly nationalized industries, may reinforce the economic attractiveness of the main city-regions and exacerbate the developmental problems referred to above. In addition, many countries are now abandoning regional policies that aimed at encouraging decentralization within the national territory, and they are doing so either for budgetary reasons or because they are redefining the goals of economic policy away from the protection of national markets and toward promoting an export-orientation for their industrial and service sectors. In some cases, this has unleashed interregional bidding wars for new investments, so that even though advanced activities go increasingly to the main city-regions, other regions now pay dearly—often to multinational corporations—for such investment as they can attract, further weakening national and local fiscal capacities to provide public goods, which are sorely needed to compete more effectively in the new, globally competitive economy.

Many of the current attempts in developing countries to deal with the problems of their city-regions are based on policy frameworks that are likely to be inadequate, or that are imported from developed countries into contexts so fundamentally different that their outcomes are often perverse. For example, experiments in privatizing urban services have been suggested or attempted in a number of places. But privatization in a context where basic universal service and infrastructure provision have not yet been attained is likely to aggravate classical market failures, while leading to improved services only for those who already have them. Tradable rights in certain services (e.g. rights to resell water) are likely to have some short-term efficiency improving effects, but will do little to ensure the extension of infrastructure to the population that does not yet have it. Decentralization of taxing and infrastructure- and service-building authority is likely to enable the richer regions to devote more of their resources to their own problems, assuming that they have effective management systems for doing so, but it could result in even greater interregional disparities within the national territory. Political decentralization, involving the participation of NGOs and community associations, may be helpful in achieving somewhat greater democratic voice and in mobilizing certain kinds of disenfranchised populations, but it is difficult to imagine it resolving the extreme gaps between rich and poor and supplanting the role of transparent, universal democratic processes in articulating needs and rights in urban governance. Fundamentally, many such reforms appear most useful in societies that have already attained a relatively advanced level of economic and social development, where certain public goods, levels of education and health, skills, literacy, and participation have already been achieved, and where the question is now how to make governance of complex systems work better.

Global city-regions in developing countries represent the best and the worst of the development process. They are places where highly productive and innovative economies are often in evidence, but they are also places where the multifaceted market failures, historical imbalances, and brutal power relations of the development process are painfully in evidence. Large cities in developing countries thus constitute a particularly problematical variant of the phenomenon of global city-regions in general. That said, and despite the desperate social conditions that are commonly found in the large cities of these countries, economic development in one way or another is probably more likely to be achieved in combination with large-scale urbanization than in its absence.

DEMOCRACY, CITIZENSHIP, AND GLOBAL CITY-REGIONS

Modern thinking about democracy developed alongside the expansion of the territorial state in Europe from the sixteenth century on. Actual practice, of course, had older roots in some of the cities of ancient Greece and in the late-medieval resurgence of civic republicanism in the Italian city-states. But by the nineteenth century in Europe and elsewhere the fate of democracy was increasingly tied to that of the territorial state. Indeed, the right to national self-determination has become one of the primary measures of democratic practice, enshrined in the Charter of the United Nations. States, of course, have traditionally been the key referent of the political; a whole range of ideals and the practices built up around them—citizenship, obligation, general authority, rights, political representation, and so on—have been tightly associated with the achievement of statehood. Key debates in political theory and jurisprudence reflect the close ties of these ideals and practices to the history of states and the political struggles that have occurred in order to establish and control distinctive, bordered territories. For example, the roles of obligation and dissent are defined almost entirely in terms of loyalty to specific states and their institutions; debates about the optimum size of community for democracy are always conducted in terms of various territorial entities; and social groups conceived of as capable of self-rule are typically defined in terms of geographical contiguity or adjacency (Agnew 1995).

The authority of even the most powerful territorial states today, however, is being redefined in relation to a world economy that is no longer a sum of distinct national economies in highly controlled interaction, but is rather based on economic, social, cultural, and informational flows that straddle the boundary-making and territory-protecting activities of states. In this context, it is increasingly difficult to think about essential political concepts such as democracy and citizenship as being exclusively attached to the unified territorial unit of the nation-state. The emerging world of global city-regions poses two particular problems given conventional understandings of democracy and citizenship. The first is that city-regions do not always fit neatly within existing state boundaries. In contemporary Europe, for example, urban spheres of influence frequently and increasingly flow across international boundaries. The second is that the city or region itself potentially becomes the object of primary loyalty and membership rather than the state in which it is located, a transformation that would already seem to be incipiently under way in such countries as Canada, Germany, or Italy. With economic life and social existence increasingly tied to the fate of the city and its region rather than to the state, some aspects of citizenship may begin to become associated once more, as they were in earlier historical periods, with city-regions and not with states.

The latter point has a number of important implications. One is that residence in a city-region and not just official state citizenship now becomes a significant basis for political activity. For example, in many cities with substantial immigrant populations, there are now serious proposals on foot to allow immigrants to vote in local elections, and this has extensive reformist possibilities. Another is that with increases in the exchange of people, goods, and capital between city-regions all over the world, these multiple flows will not be effectively regulated at the local level. Thus, at the very time when city-regions are facing ever greater burdens of economic, social, and fiscal responsibility, they are also being faced with forces they cannot hope to control. Consequently, effective governance in the new world system would also entail the creation of supranational and global levels of interregional regulation, and for this, new forms of political organization will be needed. In the absence of complementary structures of regulation at higher levels of political authority, then, the current devolution of power from states to city-regions can in some ways only aggravate the democratic deficit in the current world of territorial states attempting to control increasingly diffuse networks of economic power (Held 1991).

The achievement of multilevel democratic governance faces two crucial barriers. The first is the continuing conflation of citizenship with nationality. The second is that powerful states have been the main advocates of globalization. The U.S. government, for example, through its sponsorship of the World Trade Organization and financial liberalization has been the most important enabling agent of economic globalization. It can thus scarcely be expected to endorse political reforms that essentially undermine its power, unless the course of globalization deepens so much that a reassertion of state power becomes next to impossible. Today, we are still quite far from that possibility.

IDEOLOGICAL AND POLITICAL CHALLENGES IN THE NEW WORLD SYSTEM

The world system appears to be moving into an economic and political configuration quite different from the old center-periphery model of international development, where whole states were on one or the other side of the great development divide. The profound changes that have been occurring on the economic front are increasingly giving rise to diverse institutional and political responses and experiments in coordination at different geographic levels from the global to the local. The political and institutional shifts going on at each territorial scale are poorly understood, but the scale that is represented by the emerging global mosaic of city-regions is certainly one of the most puzzling. Precisely because these city-regions constitute the basic motors of a rapidly globalizing economy, much is at stake as they steadily sharpen their political identities and institutional presence.

As the complex trends alluded to in these pages become more and more apparent, a further question arises as to what macropolitical or ideological formations are best suited to define institution building and policymaking efforts in the coming decades. Giddens (1998) has forcefully argued that two main sets of political principles appear to be moving toward a major contest for ascendancy. One of these is a currently dominant neoliberal view—a view that prescribes minimal government interference in and maximum market organization of economic relations (and that is sometimes but erroneously taken to be a virtually inescapable counterpart of globalization). In view of what we have written above, neoliberalism, certainly in the version that crudely advocates laissez-faire as a universal panacea for economic problems, would seem to offer a seriously deficient political vision, notwithstanding the current vigorous expansion (in some quarters at least) of the global casino economy. The other is a new social democratic or social market perspective, which, especially in Western Europe, has enjoyed notable electoral success of late. On the economic front, social democratic approaches are prepared to acknowledge and to work with the efficiency-seeking properties of markets where these are consistent with standards of social fairness and long-term economic well-being, but to advocate selective intervention where they are not. As such, a social democratic politics would seem to be well armed to face up to the tasks of building the political infrastructures and enabling conditions (at every territorial scale) that are each day becoming more critical to sustained high levels of economic performance and social stability as the new world system comes increasingly into focus. At the city-region scale, in particular, and to repeat, these tasks can be centrally identified with the compelling need to promote those local levels of efficiency, productivity, competitiveness, and social fairness that markets alone can never fully secure. At the same time, the question of local democratic practice—how to define the substantive content of citizenship and how to establish appropriate forums of popular participation—is inescapably joined to the more technocratic issues raised by the challenges of economic coordination in global city-regions (Ascher 1998).

Globalization has potentially both a dark, regressive side and a more hopeful, progressive side. If the analysis presented here turns out to be broadly correct, then those views that have been expressed of late by some commentators to the effect that any deepening trend to globalization must constitute a retrograde step for the masses of humanity can be taken as a salutary warning about a possible future world, but by no means as a representation of *all* possible future worlds. Globalization under the aegis of a triumphant neoliberalism would no doubt lead to greatly increased social inequalities and tensions within city-regions and exacerbate the discrepancies in growth rates and developmental potentials between them. Alternative and realistic possibilities can be plausibly advanced, however, as indicated above, and some form of reconstructed social democratic politics would seem to offer a viable, fair, and persuasive way of facing up to these questions.

REFERENCES

Agnew, J. (1995). "Democracy and Human Rights after the Cold War," in P. J. Taylor, R. J. Johnston, and M. J. Watts (eds.), *Geographies of Global Change: Remapping the World in the Late Twentieth Century*. Oxford: Blackwell.

Ascher, F. (1998). *La république contre la ville*. Paris: Odile Jacob.

Friedmann, J., and Wolff, G. (1982). "World City Formation: An Agenda for Research and Action." *International Journal of Urban and Regional Research*, 6: 309–44.

Giddens, A. (1998). *The Third Way: The Renewal of Social Democracy*. Cambridge: Polity.

Hall, P. G. (1966). *The World Cities*. London: Weidenfeld and Nicolson.

Held, D. (1991). "Democracy, the Nation-State, and the Global System," in D. Held (ed.), *Political Theory Today*. Stanford: Stanford University Press.

Hewitt de Alcántara, C. (1998). "Uses and Abuses of the Concept of Governance." *International Social Science Journal*, 155: 105–13.

Jessop, B. (1998). "The Rise of Governance and the Risk of Failure: The Case of Economic Development." *International Social Science Journal*, 155: 29–44.

Keating, M. (1997). "The Invention of Regions: Political Restructuring and Territorial Government in Western Europe." *Environment and Planning C*, 15: 383–98.

Mackenzie, E. (1994). *Privatopia: Homeowner Associations and the Rise of Residential Private Government*. New Haven: Yale University Press.

Sassen, S. (1991). *The Global City: New York, London, Tokyo*. Princeton: Princeton University Press.

Scott, A. J. (1998). *Regions and the World Economy: The Coming Shape of Global Production, Competition, and Political Order*. Oxford: Oxford University Press.

Storper, M. (1997). *The Regional World: Territorial Development in a Global Economy*. New York: Guilford Press.

Veltz, P. (1996). *Mondialisation, Villes, et Territoire: l'Economie de l'Archipel*. Paris: Presses Universitaires de France.

PART II

ON PRACTICAL QUESTIONS OF GLOBALIZATION AND CITY-REGION DEVELOPMENT: THREE PLENARY ADDRESSES

This segment of the book comprises edited transcripts of three plenary addresses to the Conference on Global City-Regions given by Kenichi Ohmae, world-renowned business consultant and author, James D. Wolfensohn, president of the World Bank, and Lucien Bouchard, premier of the Province of Quebec, Canada. These three individuals are leading figures in the world of practical politics and/or business, and the work of each of them is deeply intertwined in one way or another with the fate and fortunes of global city-regions.

The three chapters that follow attest powerfully to some of the varied challenges and opportunities brought to the fore by the phenomena of globalization and city-region development. They also highlight the perplexities that those in significant decision-making and advisory positions in the modern world must face up to as these phenomena become ever more deeply entrenched. No matter whether the central issues are concerned with how particular localities can best harvest their competitive advantages in an era of globalization (as discussed by Ohmae), or how stubborn problems of poverty can be resolved (Wolfensohn), or how a distinctive regional culture like that of Quebec can survive and prosper in the new world order (Bouchard), these chapters dramatically illustrate the complexity as well as the contentiousness of the policy issues that are at stake.

Ohmae argues that city-regions with high levels of human capital development and an ability to contest global markets through their strategic command of the tools of the cybereconomy will emerge as the most prosperous foci of prosperity in the world of the twenty-first century. He sees multinational corporations as being important participants in this process, and he avers that the most successful global city-regions in the future will be those that offer such corporations the most advantageous sites for their operations. Ohmae's argument combines a strong conviction about the efficacy of open markets with an optimistic vision of the potentialities of the virtual economy, and while contrasting perspectives are expressed in other parts of this book (see, for example, Chapters 1 and 19), his point of view represents an extremely important tendency in the current debate on globalization, and his statement makes the case with clarity and vigor.

Wolfensohn's remarks focus on problems of poverty in the less developed parts of the world today. Wolfensohn ascribes an important role to business in building the foundations for an attack on the multiple dilemmas that such regions face, but he emphasizes that civil society and government must also be deeply involved in the search for practical solutions. The World Bank has always been resolutely committed to this search, but as Wolfensohn tells us, the Bank is also now less and less inclined to channel its development programs through national states, and instead is adopting a new strategy of attempting to deal with the problems at their roots by working directly with local agencies and officials. Here again the renewed significance of the region as both agent and medium of social change is evident.

Bouchard's view of the new Quebec combines laissez-faire elements on the economic side with a more social democratic approach on the social side. The particular interest and urgency of Bouchard's statement, of course, resides in the circumstance that Quebec is not only a well-developed urban-economic region but also a distinctive cultural formation struggling to maintain its identity in the Canadian confederation. Just as many culturally distinctive European regions have found that their survival appears to be best assured within the supranational continental bloc represented by the European Union, Quebec too is increasingly inclined to calculate that its future can be most effectively secured by consolidation of its regional status within the NAFTA area.

A common thread running through each of these three chapters is their insistence on the intense significance of global city-regions as elements of the new world order. Indeed, there would seem to be a growing consensus these days across a wide spectrum of opinion (globalist and antiglobalist, neoliberal and social democrat, etc.) that some dramatically new regionalist model of development is making its historical and geographical appearance in relation to international trends and pressures. This theme also provides a unifying link across all of the chapters in the book, for in spite of their many points of disagreement, they are all concerned with the task of understanding how this regionalist model is emerging into concrete reality and how the policy problems that it raises can be most effectively dealt with.

2

How to Invite Prosperity from the Global Economy Into a Region

KENICHI OHMAE

The world, economically and in management terms, has become a network of prosperous regions, prosperous city-regions. It is particularly interesting to note that in today's world, countries or regions the size of cities are prospering, while at the same time there are cities the size of countries having problems. I summarize the critical economic success factors in this new globalized world (which dates from about 1985) into the "Four Cs": Communication/information, Capital/investment, Corporation/industry, and Consumers/individuals.

The "Four Cs" are working very well in some of the smaller countries, regions, and city-states. They have capital and communications infrastructure and they have attracted corporations and citizens to create a nuclei for prosperity. In contrast, cities the size of countries are suffering from "Three Ps": Population explosion, Poverty, and Pollution.

Why is this happening? To me it is clear that these gigacities are not prospering partly because of governance issues and partly because of disparities created in the host country by accommodating one megacity within its infrastructure. Most countries are not really prepared for having one primadonna across the nation. The issue to address therefore is that of megacities out-growing the infrastructure of what was known as a "country"—to become part of the global economy in their own right.

THE FOUR DIMENSIONS OF THE GLOBAL ECONOMY

If you look closely at the prosperous regions of the world, they do in fact, look like city-states. In size, they typically range from three to five million people. I refer to this size as the "optimal business unit"—a manageable unit able to prosper in the global marketplace. That is at least my observation of what is happening. Let us analyze this further and discuss *why* this is happening. I will conclude, ahead of my own discussion, that this trend is going to accelerate further as we move into the next century.

This concept is better understood by imagining four dimensions to the economy—or alternatively four parallel economies: the first is the *real economy*, which is the economy created by industrialization in a country. Simultaneously we are moving into a second economy, a *borderless economy*, in which the entire world is becoming the marketplace as well as a networked production place. The third economy has rapidly taken shape: the *cybereconomy*, which tends to be characterized by countries or regions with IQ-intensive industries. The next millennium will see very IQ-intensive *borderless* interaction among people, companies, and regions. The fourth economic dimension emerging on the horizon is what I refer to as the *equation-based* or *multiples economy.* These are the economies that seek out options, hedges, or other multiplier effects that can rapidly increase wealth. This economy manifests itself in the stock market and in other types of direct banking. These sorts of multipliers are not the cybereconomy per se. Cyberspace helps to create a multiples economy, but unless you have a way of multiplying your wealth—five times, ten times, twenty times, or sometimes even more—you will not be a successful participant in the global market. Money is attracted to regions with individuals and organizations with prospects for high multiples. By necessity, capital flows across national borders to find these multiples—and cyberspace is an important vehicle to support that flow.

My point is that we are moving very quickly from the real world, the real economy, into the borderless economy, the cybereconomy, and into the multiples-based economy. This is occurring so fast that very few people, very few companies, have come to grips with the full implications of this "C" change. I have just finished writing a book entitled *The New Invisible Continent*, due to be released by Harper. It took me a long time to develop this book—almost four years—primarily because it deals with very complex issues. What I present in the following discussion are some of the conclusions drawn from that book.

MAKING THE SHORT LIST

As a corporate adviser, my role is to advise companies where to invest. The CEOs of major companies are so busy that unless you are on the short list of investment opportunities, you will not even be considered as a possibility. There are dozens of regions and cities that would like to attract the capital and corporate presence of some of my clients, but unless you have made it to the short list, you will be bypassed. To make it to the short list, you must offer real value and, ultimately, capture the investor's imagination.

Sometimes I work on the other side, the receiving end. I have worked with a number of countries and regions to help them attract investments and corporate migration. This, too, is a marketing challenge. It is imperative to demonstrate the real value you have to offer and then make absolutely sure that you are among the top three choices in the minds of the decision-makers. If you are not in the top three, you are out of the game. It becomes essential, therefore, to segment and objectively assess the potential competition. To make sure that for a particular purpose, *your* city, *your* region, *your* country is the best—it all comes back to marketing. This is a major reason why management consultants have become involved in public policy issues over the last two decades.

DECLINE OF THE NATION-STATE AND THE RISE OF CYBERCITIES

In the past we attempted to establish prosperity from within; the nation-state mentality where wealth was produced from *within* the nation. I do not think that this kind of wealth is enough today unless you are blessed with oil deposits, gold deposits, or a network of colonies that produce wealth for you. We have graduated from the economy that relies on wealth created only by the people within its own borders. That is clearly not enough anymore. The key now is to bring the global economy in to work for you—and then have them stay and even breed within. You become a base for prosperity, not only for people from immediately within the region but also from the outside, as Singapore has done in spilling over to neighboring nations. Hong Kong has done the same. These prosperous regions tend to have positive spillover effects, supporting larger numbers of people to achieve better living standards and higher per capita income.

As a consultant, I carefully observe the flows of money, information, corporations, and consumers. The notion of a "flow of consumers" may seem peculiar to you. Today, however, consumers cross their national borders to shop—physically and through cyberspace. For a country like Japan, with the idiosyncrasies of high market prices, seventeen million Japanese people travel abroad each year to places like Europe to do low-cost shopping. Now, the airfares are so low that a shopping spree to Europe pays off! That is why we have so many Japanese youngsters traveling to Italy to go brand shopping.

So how do we invite prosperity from the global economy into a region? One of the reasons this has become a key question is because of the Information Revolution—the shift from an industry-based economy to an IQ-based economy. Indeed, Alvin Toffler declared twenty years ago that the world would be IQ-based—it is clear that we have already made this shift. This structural shift means that the value propositions of regions change. This simultaneously necessitates a change in the method of marketing prosperity to that region.

In the old paradigm, national sovereignty was very important. There were solid lines of national borders. Organizations were pyramid-shaped—both corporate and government organizations. Wealth was found or created in minerals and the soil, and arguably also through military force. Land mass was important. Land of your own, or perhaps the land of a colony. Jobs were primarily in manufacturing.

The situation today, however, is very different. Today, the United States has 75 percent of its workforce in services; Japan is now at 67 percent; the majority of the working population is no longer in manufacturing. The effects of this change have seen governments turn to protect weak domestic industries. Japan champions this. If you are weak in Japan you are automatically protected. If you are strong, you are automatically unpopular.

So, stable local jobs tend to be in services, while manufacturing industries shift to low-cost production locations. At this point, inviting and attracting a strong global corporation base to your region is critical. Ireland has, for example, been able to attract some of the strongest, globally competitive, IQ-based industries to its shores. That is why the country is doing quite well. It also helps to explain why nation-states, operating by their traditional definition, are on the decline. The notion of wealth creation from within has become very difficult to maintain because to achieve it, the government either has to exploit their own people or exploit somebody else's—unless of course you are blessed with oil and minerals from the soil.

Key industries have become fundamentally borderless, and by key industries, I refer essentially to three: transportation, financial institutions, and telecommunications. Inherently these industries are borderless anyway. I mean, transportation crosses borders, capital from financial institutions criss-crosses borders, and telecommunications by definition is a global industry.

These three key industries shape the borderless economy. Despite this, most political systems are biased toward special interests, and these special interests tend to be weak industries—traditional establishments. The unfortunate result is a bunch of politicians serving the interests of the nineteenth century while the consumers, corporations, and the economy itself move into the twenty-first century. The gap between the two is a century wide. No wonder we have gigantic problems at hand.

As the new economy takes shape, the optimal size of the "global business unit" emerges. In the international management arena, we use the term "global business unit." Essentially we ask, what is the best business unit size to combat the competition on behalf of the customers? You may be surprised to learn that the optimal size shrinks rather than expands. I estimate that the optimal size of a global business unit has shifted to something like three million people. Let us discuss why this shift has taken place.

The concept of an optimal global business unit size intersects with the evolution of existing nation-states, which at one time were central to the operation of global business. First, then, let us discuss the definition of "nation-state." The United Nations is the principal institution to define "nation-states." Personally, however, I do not think the UN is capable of defining what they mean by "nation-state." They are, at best, ambiguous and extremely confusing. One new member of the United Nations is the Republic of Nauru, with a population of ten thousand people—smaller than the daytime population of some office buildings. Nauru consists of twenty-one square kilometers with one phosphate deposit—a sole wealth-creating device that will be depleted in a few years' time. They do not even have their own currency. (They use Australian currency because the mining company happens to be Australian.) Still, their GDP per capita is quite attractive; by definition it is a prosperous country. But is this really a country? If Nauru is a country, you have to explain to me why Taiwan is not a country. Taiwan has its own currency, its own constitution, its own military, and a sizable population of twenty-one million.

So back to the United Nations: What do they mean by "a country"? Their definition is very simple. If they vote for something to be a country, it is a country. There are exceptions, however. The five permanent members of the UN Security Council can veto a vote by the member states. If they veto the vote, it is not a country. Would you mind asking the Security Council, "What do you mean by country?" Well, even the General Assembly doesn't have the courage to ask that. That is why we do not really know what we mean by "a country." Despite the absence of this fundamental building block, we have formed the IMF, the OECD, and UNESCO to carry on operations with nation-states—with the UN as the assembly of representatives of the nation-states. It clearly remains a nineteenth century game.

Fortunately, we do not need to waste time redefining the term "nation-state" on behalf of the UN. The real economy is moving ahead, with a new reality of "city-regions" and "city-states." Therefore, while the term "nation-states" has potential to cause inconvenience, we are not inconvenienced. This is a blessing, and perhaps offers a potential solution, as "country" is no longer a unit of prosperity. Look at the globe and all of the different countries. Then identify all of the separate prosperous regions within these countries. Catalonia, with Barcelona as its epicenter, is a prosperous part of Spain. It is even more true to say that Catalonia is a prosperous independent part of the European Union (EU). In the context of the EU, Catalonia's ties with the rest of Spain become less of a political problem. Another example is Lombardia. In terms of size, Lombardia is the fourth largest region in Italy although it is unquestionably the most densely populated. It is not necessary to form a political group to declare independence from Italy, because Italy is less meaningful today, with Rome merely used as a recycling device.

Let us now turn to one of the poorest countries on earth: India, three hundred dollars per capita GNP—excuse me, it has now improved to six hundred. Go straight to Bangalore and you will see a cybercity with a future. Bangalore has more IQ-based, mathematically competent people, in absolute numbers, than anywhere else on earth. Hyderabad in Andhra Pradesh is close behind, and Chandrababu Naidu, the chief minister of Andhra Pradesh, was reelected, thank goodness, in this month's election (October 1999—Ed.). Pune, in Maharashtra, is third in the cybereconomies of India. So although you may be born in one of the poorest nations on earth there is opportunity to be quite prosperous—by linking through satellite communications to the cybereconomy of the rest of the world.

One of the companies in Bangalore, Infosys Technologies, has just listed their stock on NASDAQ. First they achieved a $2.5 billion market capitalization. More than one hundred out of three thousand of their employees became instant millionaires. A common financial goal in India is for a family, in their lifetime, to save $35,000. Eight hundred people surpassed this lifetime achievement on that day. Now the stock is selling at three times the IPO price. This means Infosys has created over two hundred millionaires and its founder, Narayan Murthy, has become the richest Indian. This defies and disables the traditional caste system. Nowadays, therefore, if you are competent, you can work for GE or Bell Atlantic using satellite communications. You may also continue to live in Bangalore and enjoy a cost of living one-fiftieth of the cost of living in Japan. You will live like royalty. That is the tremendous impact of the network and it is a true story.

Another company called Satyam of Hyderabad has plans to list very shortly on NASDAQ. DCM DataSystems may also follow; and there are some 120 companies I know of in India that would eventually qualify. If fly-by-night dot.com companies can be sold on NASDAQ, I can recommend 120 Indian software companies that could do equally as well, if not better, on the NASDAQ—and that is at American prices. Once they are listed on NASDAQ, they are priced by the global standard. Israeli companies are doing exactly the same.

Do you see what I am trying to say? "Countries" are no longer units of prosperity. China is another outstanding example. China as a country has huge problems—and in all likelihood will continue to have problems. But China is not a basket case. China's key technological cities will do well as long as Beijing doesn't interfere. Another example is Scottsdale, Arizona. Scottsdale-Phoenix has a population today of 2.8 million people. It is a wonderful cyber-based economy and is very prosperous. Las Vegas is almost a miracle story, with a population of 1.2 million and an industry that now accommodates a series of conventions. COMDEX, for instance, is a major convention held in Las Vegas in mid-November. People from all over the world travel to participate in these conventions. For a city that previously survived on prostitution, divorce, and gambling, Las Vegas now boasts high-technology conventions, tourism, family resorts, and retirement homes—two entirely different worlds. I can now use the words "Las Vegas" at the dinner table with my children—where previously I abstained from talking of those business meetings.

REGIONAL TRADE BLOCS AND NONALLIANCE

In parallel with the emergence of these supercities or regions, economic blocs such as NAFTA, EU, MERCOSUR, and ASEAN are forming. It starts to become very clear that we are witnessing the dilemma of nonalliance. Nonalliance works with charismatic leaders because these leaders have the unique ability to make two different things look similar. In the old days, it was the United States versus the Soviet Union, and nonalliance had some meaning. To resist an alliance with either of the two brought all kinds of benefits from both sides. Yugoslavia, Indonesia, India, and Egypt were four champions of nonalliance.

However, all of these countries are now in trouble—except for Egypt, which continues to have strong charismatic leadership under Mubarak. Nonalliance is the culprit. You can try to define your own country using other countries, but unless you can define your own role within the global map, you will not prosper. How will the rest of the world view you? You may say, "I am not the United States, or I am not such and such," but that is not good enough. This is at the root and at the heart of the Canadian problem. If you ask the Canadians today, "What are you?" Most will say, "Well, we are not Americans. We are a member of North America, but we are not Americans." So, what are you?

This is also Quebec's problem, and it is a serious one. Unless Quebec citizens put themselves on the global map they will not prosper. It is not good enough simply to position themselves on the Canadian map. It is a phase of the old economy and it is imperative to their prosperity that they create their own place on the map of North America and on the map of the world. That is why the Quebec issue is greater than an internal issue of a country known as Canada.

Switzerland also has a soul-searching problem. Switzerland is permanently neutral. Neutral to *what*? Being neutral to hide some wealthy people's money is fine, because you have sovereignty, banks have sovereignty, but neutral to *what*? Switzerland is not a member of the EU; they do not use the Euro, the European currency. All we can do is wish this country good luck. Neutrality today means less than it did historically because the world is not so bipolarized. Everyone is seeking the good life; everyone is looking for prosperity. In that sense, the Russians, the Chinese, the Indonesians, the Indians, and the Americans are the same. We are not neutral to wealth, right?

I have already introduced what I see as the four dimensions of the twenty-first century economy. Let us revise these and then think about the issues we have just raised in terms of the dimensions:

- *Real-world economy*. This is the economy we know. Production of chemicals and machinery, etc.
- *Borderless economy*. Fifteen years ago I wrote a book entitled *The Borderless World*; now it is here and real. I also wrote a book, in 1985, called *Triad Power: The Coming Shape of Global Competition*. In it I said that a corporate alliance across Japan, Europe, and America was a must to survive, to serve the customers. Today, we read every day in the papers of the formation of some new kind of triadian alliance—it is a daily event. In the days of writing my book there were not many examples, but I could see forces at work shaping the economy in this direction.
- *Cybereconomy*. I do not have to explain this one at length. It is a large part of our economy. We can do shopping on the web and have it delivered by FedEx. I can also buy airline tickets in cyberspace and have them delivered by FedEx or UPS, and it is cheaper than any agency in Japan.
- *Multiples-based economy*. A principal example of this is to acquire stock in companies with prospects to increase your investment market value by fifty times. This is what Cisco Systems does. And with seventy times multiples, they could acquire any company they want on earth. In the old days, if you wanted to acquire a company for $100 million, you went to the bank and borrowed $100 million. Nowadays you use the strength and buying power of your company's stock at seventy times multiples and acquire the company very cheaply. This is possible because the stockholders of the acquired company believe that under your company, their multiples will continue to improve. In the traditional bank-based economy, it was 1:1. Now we use 5:1, 20:1, 70:1, and long-term capital management use 250:1! That is a little too risky for me, but the optimal size

of the multiples may be around thirty to forty times, as long as you are in the right industry and the right place at the right time.

Winners in the twenty-first century will be those able to take advantage of all four dimensions of the new economy—including the old one, the real economy. You cannot live in cyberspace alone. Let us face it, this is a tremendous challenge as 99 percent of the managers I know today are good at one thing—managing in the real economy. They have only just begun trying to understand the cybereconomy. After about ten to fifteen years of experience, they may have some grasp of the borderless economy—but in all likelihood they will feel uncomfortable and unfamiliar with it. Some managers have no understanding of the multiples' economy at all. They still deal with banks without considering transacting in the multiples' dimension.

I believe the turning point for all of this was about fifteen years ago: The year 1985, to me, is like the transition from BC to AD. It was a critical time. When historians look back at this century from, say, 2050, they will say 1985 was the epoch shift. Pre-1985 will be referred to as "BG" and post-1985 will be referred to as "AG." BG represents the "Birth year of the American Godzilla companies": Oracle, established 1977; Sun Microsystems, 1982; Dell, 1984; Cisco Systems, 1984; Quantum Fund, 1984; Gateway, 2000, CNN, 1985. . . . And then there was Windows Version 1, 1985. In the fourteen years since 1985, Bill Gates has become the richest man on earth and Microsoft's market capitalization just passed the GNP of South Korea. Hence, BG and AG: before Gates, and after Gates. This was a paradigm shift in the economy—due primarily to the emergence of the cybereconomy and the Internet.

New key factors for success have emerged since the founding of the Internet. The tools used by these Godzilla companies include extensive use of cyberspace, leverage, multiples, arbitrage, and simultaneous globalization. Take Cisco Systems. They do not require physical presence to sell their products because 75 percent of their sales are web-based. Companies such as FedEx and UPS then facilitate global distribution. You do not have to be in 180 countries to be selling in 180 countries. It is simultaneous globalization—I call it the sprinkler model. It is not like a cascade that slowly gathers momentum; it is "bang!"—and the sprinkler releases to the entire the world. These new companies are not timid newcomers to the market either—they are voracious and aggressive eaters. You probably do not want to hold a product Microsoft is interested in. Before you know it they will devour your entire company. Do not become too attractive to Cisco Systems either, because with their command of multiples, they will buy any company they like for the technology. It saves time. They do not have to spend time and energy developing attractive products themselves.

It is crystal clear to me that something changed around 1985. If you assess corporate growth rates, you have to use totally different curves to show post-1985 rates. These Godzilla companies grow ten times faster than anything we have known in the past—ten times. I have to believe that the chromosomes of corporations have changed; it is a mutation problem. I cannot otherwise explain why companies can grow from zero to $20 billion in such a short time. In the physical world, it is impossible. In the multiples economy, however, you go to the stock market and trade at a price-earnings ratio of 60 to 100 times. With a multiple of that strength, you are in a position to buy, in totality, companies of critical importance to your distribution, or your technology. Then while you grow, you outsource the difficult things such as administration, compensation, and executive training. The sophistication of the market appreciates and accepts this.

A word of warning: If you are still using old management textbooks, throw them away, because they are no good. You will need them for historical reasons, but otherwise they are basically useless. They will not help you to reach the new benchmark. We live in a totally different world and it is important to share this view quickly as the majority of people are still trudging along old management paths. It is the Dells, Sun Microsystems, Cisco Systems, Oracles, and Microsofts of this world that have grown their sales, on average, ten times faster than anything we have previously known. That is why I refer to them as Godzillas. Actually, Godzilla is a Japanese invention. But although we have a couple of them in Japan, like Softbank, most Godzillas are American.

There are certainly ways to jumpstart this new type of corporation. As a management consultant, I know there are ways to do it. The first step is awareness of the new forces at work changing the business and economic environment.

COUNTRIES: HOW TO HARNESS THE FOUR Cs AND ESCAPE THE THREE Ps

Let us revisit our discussion of countries, because countries have no idea what is happening in the corporate world. As mentioned, it is essential to harness the four fundamental forces at work. This has been my lifetime theme. I have been saying this for twenty years: Communication, Capital, Corporations, and Consumers—the "Four Cs." The prosperous regions tend to work smoothly with these "Four Cs." Not-so-prosperous megaregions tend to be characterized by the "Three Ps": Poverty, Population, and Pollution.

I believe that the formation of large economic blocs will accelerate regional autonomy. Regions that successfully promote the Four Cs and offer opportunities for other cities and regions that were previously unsuccessful will prosper. For example, because of the formation of the EU, I think people in the UK are more relaxed about debating whether or not Scotland or Wales should have their own parliaments; and after three hundred years, Scotland recently held its first assembly, with Queen Elizabeth present. Wales is headed in the same direction. Northern Ireland will also become less of a problem, because if you view the situation in the context of the entire EU, the issues are not as antagonistic. Catalonia and Lombardia are good examples of this. Their problems are not as difficult as they were ten years ago.

NAFTA is also making subtle "psychological" differences to countries or regions such as Puerto Rico (two times voted down to join the United States);

Costa Rica; and Trinidad-Tobago—a very prosperous one-million-person region-state. Quebec also, when analyzed in this context, will find a solution. If they cannot find a solution in the context of NAFTA or the global economy, there is no hope for them anyway. ASEAN has provided the Chinese city-regions with a better probability of success. Indonesian "rebels" also need not worry as much as they used to about Jakarta in this new greater economic bloc.

The formation of greater economic blocs like the EU pose a very interesting challenge to the traditional nation-state, however. After all, what is a nation-state without full control of the military? In the EU, NATO manages military forces; the currency in two years' time will be the Euro; and in regards to legislative power, a significant portion of national law-making bodies will have to coordinate with Brussels. What about the power to grant permits and licenses? These are now mutually recognized no matter who issues them. What does it then mean to set national standards for a doctor's license or teacher's license, when all other EU members' standards must be certified as also acceptable?

As such, "countries" are now only left with "champagne diplomacy." (Diplomats usually toast each other with expensive champagne when they agree to misinform or deceive others. Champagne toasting is also a prelude to trade negotiations.) But what is diplomacy without military and currency tools? "Champagne diplomacy" will therefore also become obsolete, as military, currency, and trade issues are managed by superregional institutions like NATO and the EU.

This is a large-scale experiment in Europe. It suggests that the two or three remaining centrally controlled supernations will also have to come to grips with the realities of the borderless world. I predicted in *The Borderless World* that we would see the end of the Soviet Union as such. I did not predict it would happen so soon, however. Indonesia is a concern. It will have to reconsider its strong, separate, nonaligned state to enable any opportunity to participate in the new world economy. China, too, will discover that strong central control will eventually destroy them. Why? Because to participate in the global, cyber- and multiples-based economies require highly educated people. The key factor for success is IQ. It means allowing people to learn freely everything they need to know to participate effectively in the high technology world economy. This would mean outright defiance of directions and orders from Beijing. It poses a serious dilemma for China's government. It will prove to be more than they can control other than by military force. China in its current form cannot prosper.

The same is true for Japan. Instead of the military, the Japanese government uses money to impose control. We sprinkle money "from the sky" to poor regions and we squander $2 trillion to stimulate the economy to attempt to recover from the banking crisis. All to no avail. Where China uses military, we use money. But alas, we have no money today. We borrow from our children and now from our grandchildren and each year our generation is stealing about US$4,000 on average from our grandchildren whom we haven't even met yet! Japan steals from the next generation to try to solve last year's problem.

I continue to propose reform for Japan. I proposed a structure of governance that creates a Doshu Federation of Autonomous Regions—a Doshu republic. I proposed this ten years ago and people hated it. "Japan divided?!" It was very negatively received. This structure is not so unpopular today, however. Today, three of the four major political parties have adopted the idea as part of their public policy and marketing. They all claim to have invented the concept.

To summarize, in the old view, the optimal size of the economy was large; a hundred million and more was better. Now, we are talking about very different, globally networked, regions where the market is the world. You do not have to have the market residing within your borders, because *the whole world is the market.* Intelligent, highly trained citizens are essential for this type of wealth to be created and sustained. The optimum population of an economic unit is half a million to 3 million: small enough to be flexible in regard to laws and infrastructure and to establish a coherent interface with the global economy. These are the primary reasons why I say that the optimal size of prosperity has shifted.

I have many other examples I could share with you, but these are the most fundamental points incorporated into my new book, entitled *The New Invisible Continent.*

3

The World Bank and Global City-Regions: Reaching the Poor

JAMES D. WOLFENSOHN

In my capacity as president of the World Bank, I spend a good deal of my time dealing with issues of city-regions in the developing world. Let me talk for a few minutes about the problems I see in terms of the expansion of our planet, and about the development of global city-regions in that part of the world where I work.

I should tell you I had these problems brought home to me very strongly after my last visit to Los Angeles. I came at the invitation of the Cardinal to take a look at the South-Central area of the city. I visited the St Francis Cabrini Community Center, which deals with immigrants, and the problems of poverty. Shortly after that I went to Honduras, where I visited a center—if that is what it could be called—a sort of dilapidated house that was available to street kids. The kids came in every day, because they had nowhere to live; they left their drugs and their weapons at the door; and there was Father Albert who looked after them. There was also a very tough-looking guy who was there to try to guide and assist them. And he spoke English. So I asked him, "Where did you learn English?" He said, "In South-Central." I said, "Do you know St Francis Cabrini Community Center?" He said, "Yes, but I didn't make use of it, so they arrested me and threw me out of the country." There he was, reformed, telling the kids that if they went down his path the chances were that they would end up in jail. He was telling them that they should not end up in South-Central Los Angeles to make trouble.

This curious nexus between my visit to Los Angeles and a visit to an environment in Honduras that catered to street kids brought home to me that geographic boundaries are no longer relevant. Indeed, as one looks at Los Angeles, one thinks in terms of emigration from the very countries that I go to. One is so conscious of this as one goes to South-Central Los Angeles and hears Spanish and where everyone has come from. There is a direct and immediate link that is forged between developing countries and global city-regions like Los Angeles.

I mention this because I deal with the issues that affect the five billion people who live in developing and transitional economies. Quite recently our world welcomed its six billionth inhabitant. Of that six billion people, three billion live on less than $2 a day, and 1.2 billion live on less than $1 a day. In fact, people on welfare in the United States have larger incomes than 70 percent of the people in the world. So we have a somewhat different picture of development in our country compared to what we see elsewhere.

As one thinks of the next twenty-five years, just as this conference looks forward to the twenty-first century, we see an increase from six billion to eight billion people. Ninety-eight percent of that increase will be in developing countries. Only 2 percent will be in developed countries. And virtually the entire increase of two billion people in developing countries will be in major city-regions and other urban areas. This is a dramatic demographic shift and as a result we can surely expect a large increase in urban poverty, particularly in parts of Sub-Saharan Africa and East and South Asia.

CHALLENGES IN THE MANAGEMENT OF GLOBAL CITY-REGIONS

This poses an absolutely fantastic challenge to the management of global city-regions. It poses a challenge to the governments of the countries in which these city-regions are growing. It poses a huge challenge to those of us in the international community who want to try and assist in the fight against poverty, in the establishment of a sustainable environment, and in the development of a more just world. This issue of poverty is not just a moral and a social issue. It *is* surely a moral and a social issue, but it is more than that. It is the issue, really, of whether our children are going to live in a world that is peaceful; whether they are going to live in a world where there is equity; and whether they will live in a world that will impact the developed countries by means of economics, of trade, of health, of crime, of drugs, of wars, because we are now clearly one huge global community.

Imagine my friend in Honduras—just one example out of many these last few months. Everything links us together. While rural poverty remains an enormous challenge, the issue of poverty is now to a very large extent focused on city-regions. That is why this conference is so important. It is important because the dimensions of management of global city-regions have become central to the issue of poverty reduction or eradication, and, in fact, central to the issue of peace.

But you cannot look at global city-regions without thinking about the environment in which they operate. I was fascinated by what Mayor Richard Riordan told us about the issues that face him in Los Angeles—safety, health, nutrition, clean neighborhoods, streets without potholes, empowering neighborhoods, education, and so on. But what he did not have to address was the need in his city for a comprehensive legal system, a need here for the protection of property rights, a need here for honest judges, for financial supervision and control. He did not have to address issues of corruption or of an absence of trained leaders. He did not have to refer to a lack of people with the capacity to enter government, or to work in civil society. But all these issues are of major significance in the developing and transitional economies.

At the World Bank we have just completed a remarkable study in which we interviewed 60,000 people in sixty countries, all of them living on under a dollar a day. I quote just one of them: "I don't know whom to trust, the police or the criminals. We work and hide indoors, our public safety is ourselves." Of the 60,000 people we interviewed, when they described what it is like to be poor, they talked about the issue of lacking any voice whatsoever. They talked about a total distrust of government. They talked about enmity toward the police. Women talked about the fear they feel in their daily lives. The views of poor people in developing and transitional economies are quite different from what they are in Los Angeles or in any other developed country. And the challenges are greater, because in the developed world, the population in the next twenty-five years will grow by 2 percent. Cities in developing countries will double in size. They do not have the infrastructure. Streets without potholes are not an issue when you do not have streets. These are issues at the core of the five billion—soon to be six billion—people in the developing and transitional economies. And that is part of our world. That is not an optional extra. It is something that we need to deal with now.

EMPOWERING THE PEOPLE OF THE SLUMS

As you know, I have had the opportunity in my time to lead a very privileged existence, in terms of my interests in the arts and culture and so on. I also took a great interest in the environment and in issues of poverty. It is only when you go and visit these countries and you go into the slums and the villages, which I have had the privilege of doing, that you get a real sense of the people and the issues they face. The first and most important thing that you learn is that the very best people you meet are in the slums and villages. These are people who are basic in their ideas. They have a very clear idea of what they want. They are entrepreneurial. They do not want charity, they want a chance. They want an opportunity to transform their lives. Empowerment is the key, but without help they cannot do it themselves, because the infrastructures do not exist. Given no governance, or in many cases limited governance, given no legal system, an ineffective or oppressive police system, dishonest judges, the cancer of corruption—which is the thing that all 60,000 people mentioned because corruption affects the poor more than it does rich people or the middle class—given all of these issues, the poor need the chance and resources to manage and determine their world. These are the frontal issues that we need to attack in that world of which I speak.

One of the ways that they can be tackled is by better governance and assisting the management of city-regions. We are moving now in the work that we do at the Bank from nation-state lending, to provincial and state lending, to urban lending. It is a function of size, and it is a function of practicality. If you are trying to design programs to reach people, it is just impossible to do it at the top only. This is a practical matter. Support and encouragement for appropriate management of city-regions is crucial to the whole issue of national development.

If you are trying to encourage investment and the potential investors come into a city and get a picture of it as a place where you cannot walk outside because someone will knock you on the head, or the place looks dreadful, or you are shaken down as you come into the city itself, this gives an impression that is hard to remove when you are talking about encouraging new investment. But the issue is more than just one of image. City-regions can be and are the engines of growth. They are the places for opportunity. Thus, it becomes absolutely central for the Bank to try and work with governments to support their efforts in terms of city-region development.

I had the pleasure of visiting Johannesburg last week, where I saw my friend the city-manager Ketso Gordhan, who is here with us tonight. In Johannesburg, he and his colleagues have decided that what they need to do is to have a comprehensive approach to the development of the city. They are looking not just at handouts, not just at the issue of having to provide services to people in poverty. They recognize that the only way you can deal with issues of urban development is on a comprehensive basis. Their plans are quite remarkable, and they are drawing on experience from the outside. They are looking at these townships and the issues of poverty in a way that is optimistic. They are seeking to enfranchise the people. The issue there is not looking at the poor with pity but as part of the solution.

CITIES ALLIANCE, A GLOBAL COALITION OF CITIES AND THEIR DEVELOPMENT PARTNERS

This sort of local leadership is truly inspiring and it was examples like this that drove the World Bank and the United Nations to join forces to assist developing city-regions meet their main challenges. So it was fitting that last May, Ketso Gordhan helped the Bank and the United Nations Center for Human Settlements launch the Cities Alliance, a global coalition of cities and their development partners. This Alliance aims to do two main things: to support the process through which city dwellers themselves can participate in defining their vision for their city, and to commit to nationwide and citywide programs of slum regeneration that will help the urban poor get their share of the economic promise of cities. The challenge for the Alliance is enormous but the urban poor must be the business of every one of us if we are to achieve successful, sustainable city-regions.

What we have to do in all our efforts is to transform our thinking about poverty, about slums and misery, to think of the people who live in city-regions not as the objects of development, but rather as agents of change. We need to help empower them and make them part of the solution. It is abundantly clear on the evidence of all the work that we have done at the Bank, and that other institutions have done, that empowerment, accountability, and responsibility within poverty areas is the way we can make the lives of the people better. I can give you dozens of examples. In fact, I and Professor Akin Mabogunje, who is with us here tonight, recently had the opportunity of visiting the slum areas of Lagos where we helped put in some drainage in the market district. It is a place that is unlike anything in Los Angeles, but it is vibrant. It is thriving. We got rid of the excess water, and you have a humming marketplace, run by women—traders, savers, entrepreneurs. It gives you faith in the ability of people to lift themselves out of poverty if they can get a bit of help and guidance, for example, on the legal procedures that can give them access to property rights. So what we need to be thinking about for those cities is a coalition for change. A coalition of private sector, civil society, and international institutions, accountable to local governments and representatives, can come together to support those cities in an orderly and organized way, in much the way that Johannesburg is doing.

SUCCESS STORIES IN SLUM REGENERATION

There are many examples of success stories in slum regeneration, whether it is in Rio, or in Jakarta, or in Kampala. We in the Bank have had the privilege of helping to lift five million people in urban slums out of poverty in Indonesia. We have worked with millions of people in Brazil. I have been to these areas, and their stories make you want to weep. I remember in 1997 when I was in the favelas of Rio. We had put in a program of water provision and sewage disposal, and I went in to meet the women. As often happens, if you have been in these places, they want to show you the toilet. So they take you to it and they flush it, because that is something that allows them to live a more civilized life. The water and sewage disposal facilities are put in privately. They are self-supporting. And it saves the women from walking down the hill for two hours a day with these yoke-like poles over their shoulders with water buckets on the ends, and then walking back up the hill. All this I saw, and thought, how remarkable it is. Then I went for a drink with all the women. One of them came up to me and shook a piece of paper in my face, which was her water bill. She showed me that she had paid five reals, or whatever the amount was, for that month. Then others came up. And then the mayor of Rio told me, "Jim, they're not showing you this to show you that they've paid. This is the first time in their lives that they have had a piece of paper with their name on it. They are now recognized, they're now part of society." By bringing in infrastructure, by giving them a chance, and by giving them recognition, you unleash a force of people who are now transforming their city and their environment.

I say this to you because the process is not magic, it entails trusting people. It is trying to come together with government, civil society, and the private sector to put in infrastructure and to try and come up with programs that provide the poor with infrastructure and financial facilities and opportunities for jobs and legal systems, and protection from corruption. If you can do that, the challenge of the next two billion people becomes manageable.

Our responsibility at this conference, whether we are from developed or developing countries, is to forge alliances that will allow us to work together to give opportunities to people in poverty. We should do it for moral reasons; we should do it for reasons of equity and justice; we should also do it for reasons of self-interest, because otherwise we cannot withstand the tide over the next twenty-five years of an increase of two billion people, who will flood into global city-regions, increasing the numbers of people living on $2 a day from three billion to four billion.

The front lines are in the city-regions. These are the places where we have to fight the poverty issues because that fight also has an impact on rural areas. It has an impact on the security of countries, and on peace. And it has an impact on South-Central Los Angeles in terms of the number of people who are coming here from less economically developed areas.

I am grateful to have had the opportunity to address you tonight. Because I believe the challenge in developing and transitional economies is not just an issue for people who work in the World Bank and other similar institutions. The fight against poverty in global city-regions is a fight for everyone. It is truly a fight for peace and stability on our planet, and it is this fight that I hope you can address in the meetings you have over the next few days.

4

Quebec in an Era of Global City-Regions

LUCIEN BOUCHARD

Let us, first of all, define the subject. Global city-regions are metropolitan areas where local economic activity and political issues are closely related to the world system. The theme you have chosen for your conference is a clear indication that the challenges posed by the globalization of the economy and the emergence of planetary cultural references involve each and every one of us. These challenges range from adjusting to countless changes in our daily lives to having to contemplate the prospect of world government. This conference is a major step in the understanding of the issues and challenges raised by the emergence of a global world.

QUEBEC AND GLOBALIZATION

With a population of only seven million people, differentiated by its language, culture, and strong democratic institutions, some of which go back more than two hundred years, Quebec is directly concerned by globalization. After all, one of the main characteristics of this global movement is the powerful forces of homogenization that accompany it. Moreover, our economy had to evolve from the extraction of natural resources to one that is increasingly based on high-technology exports. This could not be done by looking inward but, rather, by meeting the challenges that globalization brought to our doorstep.

We chose to meet world competition head-on rather than seek protection from it. As a matter of fact, we have been the greatest promoters of free trade with the United States and we are eagerly anticipating its extension to the three Americas. U.S. Commerce Secretary William Daley said in Montreal that NAFTA "would have never been completed without the tireless efforts and vocal free trade advocacy of the people and government of Quebec."

A feature of global city-regions is the emergence of economic environments somewhat akin to industrial clusters, which are believed by many to be the best approach to stimulate competitiveness. The government of Quebec adopted such an approach twenty years ago, in order to galvanize its most vibrant and promising economic sectors, such as biotechnology, aerospace, information technologies, and transportation. We felt that this was the best way to tap into the knowledge of our world-class universities and to get the most out of a well-trained, productive, and stable workforce.

It is also said that industrial clusters foster creativity and innovation. This is certainly true of our recent experience with the world of multimedia, which is booming in Montreal. In just a few years, Montreal has become a leading multimedia center. We have gone from virtually no jobs in that field, five years ago, to more than two thousand now. Within five more years, through our *Cité du multimédia*, as many as ten thousand more jobs will be added, according to our most conservative projections.

To face the challenges of globalization, we have also sought to make our schools and other learning institutions focal points to face the new world created by the technological changes brought on by the information age.

AN ECONOMY INTEGRATED TO THE CONTINENT

I need not demonstrate how fully Quebec's economy is integrated with that of the continent. The nature and direction of trade flows speak for themselves. Quebec firms sell their goods and services mainly to the United States and also to the rest of the world. As a matter of fact, 58 percent of our overall production is shipped to customers outside our borders. Last year, we exported $47 billion worth of goods to the United States, which represented 84 percent of our international exports. Moreover, Quebec's GDP is the sixth largest in the Americas. You might also be surprised to learn that Quebec is the USA's eighth largest trading partner, behind Canada, Japan, and Mexico, the top three, but well ahead of countries such as France, Italy, and Korea.

At the institutional level, Quebec is the only international member of the Council of State Governments, to which the fifty American states belong. Also, Quebec is either a full or associate member of three regional groupings involving the New England and Great Lakes states. These groupings are concerned with issues ranging from energy and the environment to trade and tourism. The links we are creating through them are becoming more and more important in shaping our public policy agenda.

MONTREAL AS A GLOBAL CITY-REGION

Greater Montreal is a global city-region. It boasts 40 percent of Quebec's population and accounts for 50 percent of its industrial output. There is no doubt that Montreal is the regional motor driving Quebec's place in the global economy. A recent study of fifty-two North American and European cities shows that Montreal is truly a global city and a highly competitive one. Montreal is fifteenth among major North American cities in terms of population. But it now ranks ninth for the number of high-technology companies; seventh for the number of jobs in information technology; sixth in the pharmaceutical and biotechnology sectors; fifth in aerospace; and it stands at the very top for the proportion of the population working in high technology.

Montreal is also Quebec's main cultural window, from which Quebec shines and through which the world calls on us. Montreal is a place where Quebec's new identity, as a francophone yet pluralistic society, is being shaped.

Global city-regions often are culturally mixed, and as such are faced with problems of political participation and the reconstruction of local political identity and citizenship. This reality applies to Montreal, which is a truly cosmopolitan metropolis. Sixty percent of the workforce—and 80 percent of our engineers—are bilingual, and 6 percent of the population speak three languages or more, the highest rate in Canada. Under a program we have just announced, called "The Decade of the Americas," we will double the number of trilingual persons within the next ten years. Thus, the teaching of Spanish and other languages will be encouraged.

When describing global city-regions, academics underline that one of their main challenges is to integrate large immigrant populations. In Quebec, we have made French our official and common language, while fully respecting minority language rights. We have sought to build a citizenship based on modern civic values. We believe that these policies have largely contributed to our current linguistic and social equilibrium.

It is appropriate for cities and regions to play an international role, especially for the purpose of economic promotion, but also for cultural reasons. For instance, Montreal and Quebec City have extensive international relations. As a matter of fact, the Quebec government has nurtured these efforts. We have also been very supportive of Montreal International, an agency that is the Montreal area's chief economic promoter. Its creation is the result of a concerted approach by several local and regional governments and organizations, as well as the private sector. We have given consistent support to the activities of Montreal on the international stage whereby our metropolis has created links with numerous large cities all over the world.

The same is true for Quebec City, which has built comprehensive networks with the French-speaking world and with other cities in different countries. One of Quebec City's windows to the world is due to its membership in the exclusive club of cities designated as World Heritage Sites under UNESCO.

EFFECTS OF GLOBALIZATION

The challenges that come with globalization are fascinating. One of these is the need to take advantage of the international solidarity created by the outstanding capacity of the worldwide communications system to address earnestly North-South issues. Another challenge has to do with the redesign of the powers of the states through multilateral treaties. This implies a reassessment of the role of the state. In Quebec, one of the issues that concerns us directly is that of cultural diversity. My government took a clear position on the need to preserve such diversity and is committed to play a direct and active role in this area.

It has become a truism to say that national boundaries are increasingly blurred. The gradual lowering of economic barriers and increasingly dominant cultural parameters have created a world where one has to be the best, not just to thrive, but merely to survive. This is true whether we are talking of technology, manufactured goods, or cultural products. The fact that national boundaries are being whittled away by freer trade and cultural influences does not mean that states are becoming irrelevant. In every national capital, decisions are made that concern both local and international issues. Every day, as well, national life is extended through bilateral and multilateral treaties whereby member states have reshaped the architecture of their interventions.

There is another reason why states must remain active. Whether we are talking about economic or cultural issues, we cannot leave unbridled market forces to dictate what the world of tomorrow will be like. This may not seem important to culturally secure or economically dominant groups, but it is essential to the survival of the cultural identity of smaller nations. The notion of cultural diversity then becomes a basic tenet of both national and foreign policy.

A few years ago, the former secretary general of the United Nations, Mr Boutros Boutros-Ghali, described his vision of the world. Mr Boutros-Ghali said, "a healthy globalization of modern life presupposes sound identities. For globalization that is excessive or poorly understood could also crush cultures, meld them into a uniform culture from which the world has nothing to gain. . . . An orderly world is a world made up of independent nations, open to one another and respectful of their similarities and differences."

As globalization becomes more and more a reality in the fields of trade, finance, travel, information, and, to some degree, culture, much of the interaction flowing from it is virtual. Meanwhile, in the real world, urban areas are forever expanding, generating social, cultural, and economic problems that are very concrete. This is especially true in less developed countries. Solving these problems will dictate, to a large extent, public policy agendas for the foreseeable future.

Globalization seems to overtake every field of activity, creating much insecurity along the way and leaving individuals with a pervasive feeling of powerlessness. Yet, neither the individual nor the state is totally powerless. There is room left for government action aimed at mitigating the unavoidable consequences of globalization. There are several ways of coping with these. One is obvious and accessible to everyone. By raising awareness of global issues among individuals, we contribute to making each person a potential global participant. Remember that, not long ago, as we became more aware of living in a global village, where environmental issues are everyone's concern, the most potent slogan was "Think globally, act locally." Today, the age of information puts at everybody's fingertips the power to inform, influence, and act. Through the Internet, and related information technologies linking persons, organizations, and governments, people now have the power to think locally and act globally.

COPING WITH GLOBALIZATION AT THE INSTITUTIONAL LEVEL

Professor Scott and his colleagues, in the theme paper prepared for this conference (Chapter 1), raised a most relevant question. They asked, namely, "what alternative institutional arrangements need to be developed to deal with . . . region-wide policy issues to ensure effective governance of . . . the emerging new world order?" We would do well to look at Europe as a model for the integration of city-regions to the political and institutional landscape. Europeans have recognized the role of regions and city-regions in a number of ways. These attest to their deep understanding of regional issues as factors shaping local responses to the economic challenges of globalization.

Together with the economic and political integration they have initiated, European Union members have established a Council of European Regions. Their treaty provides for mandatory consultation of cities and regions on various issues such as railways, roads, waterways, public health, education, youth, culture, and what Europeans call economic and social cohesion—which we would call here social balance or the social contract. This approach is perfectly consistent with the movement toward greater economic integration and harmonization of social, cultural, and foreign policies.

Finally, under the Maastricht Treaty, more than 170 regions are officially recognized and can assert their positions directly before the European Commission and Parliament.

CONCLUSION: KEEPING CITIES, REGIONS, AND INDIVIDUALS FROM BEING MARGINALIZED

We must find more ways, in North America, for our cities, regions, and states to cooperate to deal with the outside world. Too often, we perceive each other as competitors, instead of potential allies. The authors of this conference's theme paper wrote that the great challenge of the future will be "the creation of new and responsive frameworks of regional governance capable of sustaining economic development." They add that these new frameworks will have to integrate "a sense of cooperative regional identity, and promote innovative ways of achieving regional democracy and economic fair play."

The challenges that global city-regions face are in many ways the same that beset Quebec. We have to integrate growing immigrant populations and make them welcome. We also have to create an environment that is conducive to economic growth, while meeting global competition head-on. Finally, we must ensure that all have a voice in shaping the world they share. Whether at home or around the world, we must not let social and economic distance grow between the haves and the have-nots. This is something to which my government is particularly sensitive. I had the opportunity to discuss these matters recently in Moncton during the Francophone Summit. Many policies we adopted in Quebec in recent years have been directed to this goal.

Whatever model we devise to govern ourselves in the future, it must be flexible enough to recognize nations and the original contribution they can all make to a changing world.

PART III

THE GLOBAL CITY-REGION: A NEW GEOGRAPHIC PHENOMENON?

The phenomenon of large-scale urbanization has been a persistent topic of debate throughout the twentieth century. As the debate has evolved, various labels have been employed to designate the principal object of inquiry: the million city, the primate city, the metropolis, the conurbation, megalopolis, world city, global city, and so on, with each new phase of the debate bringing increasingly higher levels of theoretical and empirical complexity into view. The idea of the "global city-region" represents a new phase of development of this conceptual lineage, though its close relationship to all that has gone before must also be clearly recognized. As Hall writes in Chapter 6, the global city-region represents "a new scale of urban organization," both in terms of its polynucleated but integrated internal structure (sometimes extending over a radius of scores or even hundreds of miles from its center of gravity), and in terms of its privileged position within far-flung global networks of commercial, social, and cultural transactions. Indeed, much of what is most important about the urbanization process today can arguably best be understood not so much in terms of national urban systems, but, as suggested in Chapter 1, in terms of a worldwide mosaic of interrelated city-regions. The rise of city-regions as major articulations of world geography is further underpinned by the formation of new regional institutional infrastructures in response to the many local social and economic breakdowns that result from the increasing global interconnectedness of large agglomerations.

The four chapters that make up this part of the book provide an extended elucidation of these remarks. These chapters all deal with the dual character of city-regions as nodes in global networks and as complex places with powerful internal logics and meanings. Hall proposes a series of specific empirical criteria (in terms of the attributes and external linkages of city-regions) by which the degree of their insertion into the modern world system can be evaluated. By his reckoning there are only some ten cities in the world today that can unambiguously be deemed as being global in status. Nevertheless, there are large numbers of other cities that are at least in some degree caught up in globalization processes, and, more importantly, that are experiencing rapid intensification of their cross-national relationships. Sassen offers a distinction between *global cities* and *global city-regions*, on the grounds that the former represent a more limited set of phenomena and are bound by a narrower spatial circumference. As such, the essential features of the global city, according to Sassen, are its functions as a center of information-intensive business and financial activities, and its role as a dense locus of power and inequality. In contrast to the more ambitious claims about the nature of global city-regions as laid out in Chapter 1, Sassen prefers to define these phenomena as global cities plus additional tracts of surrounding territory, giving them a more complex but also less sharply focused social identity. Camagni and Friedmann advance the discussion by providing synoptic accounts of the multiple synergies that run through global city-regions and that constitute their competitive advantages. Camagni makes the important point (*contra* Paul Krugman) that economic competition can occur between territories just as much as it can between firms, in the sense that city-regions (not to mention other kinds of spatial ensembles) represent composites or collectivities of externalities and complementary public goods, and these constitute important foundations of regional competitive advantage. As such, they deeply affect the attractiveness of any given region to mobile capital investments and they represent a critical element of individual firms' abilities to contest wider markets. This theme is picked up again in more detail by Porter in Chapter 9.

5

Global City-Regions in the Twenty-first Century

SIR PETER HALL

There are two questions, separate but interrelated. First, what do we mean by a "global city"? This is an old question, much discussed, but not satisfactorily answered. We need to resolve it before we can proceed to the second and novel question, which is the subject of this symposium: what do we mean by a "global city-region"?

DEFINING THE GLOBAL CITY

A major review of the global-cities literature has come recently from the Globalization and World Cities Study Group and Network at the University of Loughborough, led by Peter Taylor and John Beaverstock. We can echo their conclusion that "Positioning world cities in a global urban hierarchy has become a preoccupation for the many scholars of international urban studies" (Beaverstock, Smith, and Taylor 1999: 2). Table 5.1, from their paper, compares some of the attempts over the last thirty years, beginning with the present author. They comment:

> From the seminal work of Peter Hall (1966) to the comprehensive analyses of London, New York, Tokyo, and Paris in the mid-1990s (Llewelyn-Davies 1997), or international financial centers towards the end of the millennium (*The Economist* 1998), the central facet of the world city literature has been to *rank* cities according to their disproportionate geoeconomic power in the world-system. (Beaverstock, Smith, and Taylor 1999*a*: 446.)

Looking back over these thirty years of work, they identify four major approaches that have led to "standardized" rankings of major cities. The first phase sought to identify the strategic domination of certain world cities in the world-system by analyzing and ranking the locational preferences and roles of multinational corporation (MNC) headquarters in the "developed" world (Hall 1966, Hymer 1972, Heenan 1977). Then, building upon Hall (1966) and especially Hymer (1972), a second approach centered upon the decision-making corporate activities and power of MNCs, in the context of the new (spatial) international division of labor discovered in the late 1970s (Fröbel, Heinrichs, and Kreye 1980). This approach, which includes such key works as Cohen (1981),

Table 5.1. *Cited major cities*

Authors	Major cities identified[a]
Budd (1995)[b]	Tokyo, London, New York, Paris, Frankfurt
Cohen (1981)	Tokyo, London, Osaka, Paris, Rhine-Ruhr
Drennan (1996)[b]	London, New York, Tokyo
The Economist (1992)[b]	New York, Tokyo, London
The Economist (1998)[b]	London, New York, Tokyo
Feagin and Smith (1987)	New York, London, Tokyo
Friedmann (1986)	London, Paris, New York, Chicago, Los Angeles
Friedmann (1995)	London, New York, Tokyo
Friedmann and Wolff (1982)	Tokyo, Los Angeles, San Francisco, Miami, New York
Glickman (1986)	New York, Tokyo, London, Paris
Hall (1966)	London, Paris, Randstad, Rhine-Ruhr, Moscow, New York, Tokyo
Heenan (1977)	Coral Gables (Miami), Paris, Honolulu
Hymer (1972)	New York, London, Paris, Bonn, Tokyo
Knox (1995*a*, *b*)	London, New York, Tokyo
Lee and Schmidt-Marwede (1993)[b]	London, New York, Tokyo
Llewelyn-Davies (1997)	London, Paris, New York, Tokyo
Martin (1994)[b]	London, New York, Tokyo, Osaka, Chicago
Meyer (1986)[b]	New York, London, Paris, Zurich, Tokyo
Muller (1997)	London, New York, Tokyo
O'Brien (1992)[b]	London, Frankfurt, Paris, Hong Kong, Singapore
Reed (1981)[b]	London
Reed (1989)[b]	New York, London
Sassen (1991)	New York, London, Tokyo
Sassen (1994*a*, *b*[b])	New York, London, Tokyo, Paris, Frankfurt
Short *et al.* (1996)	Tokyo, London, New York, Paris, Frankfurt
Thrift (1989)	New York, London, Tokyo
Warf (1989)[b]	New York, London, Tokyo

Notes:

[a] Limited to the top five cities identified in the global urban hierarchy.

[b] Specific studies identifying International Financial Centers.

Source: Beaverstock, Taylor, and Smith 1999*a*, Table 1.

Friedmann and Wolff (1982), Friedmann (1986), Glickman (1987), Feagin and Smith (1987), and to some degree Knox (1995*a*, *b*) and Thrift (1989), has enriched the "theoretical" approach taken to world-city studies, but has also acted as a major catalyst for work in the 1990s. A third approach has firmly associated the cities within the urban hierarchy with their propensity to engage with the internationalization, concentration, and intensity of producer services in the world economy. The key work here is undoubtedly that of Saskia Sassen, in *The Global City* (1991) and *Cities in a World Economy* (1994). Finally, a fourth approach identifies major cities and their relative positions through rankings of international financial centers. The pioneering work here has come from Howard Reed (1981). These four approaches, it could be suggested, are perhaps not quite as distinct as they may seem: thus Sassen's producer services include Reed's financial services.

A key argument of the Loughborough group is that many of the approaches—even the classics, such as Friedmann (1986, 1995) and Sassen (1991, 1994)—concentrate simply on measuring data on global city *attributes*, while ignoring the critical importance of understanding the mutual *relationships* between individual members of a system of cities (Taylor 1997: 324–25). Perhaps the best recent example of the attribute approach comes from John Short and colleagues at the University of Syracuse, who present comparative data in order to try to disprove much of what they say is the conventional wisdom about so-called global cities—in particular, the primacy of London and New York. Their data (ranked in Table 5.2) show that in 1995, in terms of the head office location of the largest banks ranked by assets, the score was Tokyo 16, Paris 11, Frankfurt 6, New York 5, and London 5; in terms of headquarters of the world's largest industrial corporations in 1993, the scores were Tokyo 17, New York 6, London 5, and Chicago, Seoul, and Osaka 4 each; in terms of Stock Exchange market valuation, the order in 1992 was New York $3,888 bn., Tokyo $2,321 bn., London $933 bn., Paris $328 bn., and Frankfurt $321 bn.; in terms of headquarters of the top 50 foreign banks in the USA (in terms of assets in 1994), the score was Tokyo 14, Paris 6, Osaka 4, Toronto 3, and London 3. Finally, in terms of international air passengers (in 1992) the numbers were London 59,003,000, Paris 32,369,000, Frankfurt 23,711,000, Hong Kong 22,061,000, New York 19,609,000, and Tokyo 19,022,000 (Short *et al.* 1996, 703–08).

These data are very suggestive, but—as the Loughborough group argue—they tell us nothing about the mutual relationships among the members of this system of cities; we have to infer, for instance, that, because of a concentration of high-level service activities such as international banks, a city is exceptionally well connected. To some degree, as Beaverstock and Taylor point out, this emphasis is simply due to the abundance of data on attributes and the relative paucity of data on relationships. There are some exceptions: for instance, air traffic data and telecommunications traffic data. But they suffer from lack of differentiation: air traffic figures for Miami, for instance, are distorted by the huge tourist traffic into and out of Florida—and similarly, though perhaps to a lesser degree, with the figures for London as compared with other major cities, presented in Figures 5.1 and 5.2.

However, this raises yet another complication. High-level global cities can be distinguished by a high degree of concentration of four particular clusters of advanced services: command and control functions (government, international agencies, headquarters of major private corporations); financial and business services (ranging from commercial services such as accountancy, law, and advertising to public relations, management consultancy, and the design professions

Table 5.2. *World-city data*[a]

City	Rank						
	Economic command functions						
	Banks[b]	Stocks[c]	HQs[d]	Air traffic[e]	Population[f]	Olympic games[g]	Rolling Stones[h]
Tokyo	1	2	1	6	1	1	1
London	5	3	3	1			2
New York	4	1	2	5	5		
Paris	2	4	7	2		2	3
Frankfurt	3	5	13	3			
Amsterdam	12	9		7		2	
Seoul	12	5		13	4	1	
Brussels	7		17			2	3[i]
Munich	9		9	20		1	
Zurich	14	7		9			
Toronto	11	6		16		2	
Osaka	6		6		6		
Los Angeles			15	11	13	1	
Mexico City					2	1	2
Singapore		14	8				
Beijing	8					1	
Hong Kong		8		4			
Madrid			12	18		2	
Milan	10	11					
Rome	13		10	12			
Montreal	15					1	
Buenos Aires					10		2
Moscow					11	1	
Sydney		10				1[j]	

Notes:

[a] Includes cities ranked among the top fifteen cities in any two or more categories.

[b] Hundred largest banks' head offices, 1995 (see Table 5.2).

[c] Major stock exchanges in the world, 1992 (see Table 5.3).

[d] Headquarters of the world's largest industrial corporations, 1993 (see Table 5.4).

[e] Airports having world's highest international passenger traffic volume, 1992.

[f] Largest population centers, 1991 *(United Nations Demographic Yearbook)*.

[g] Cities that have hosted (1) or applied for hosting (2) the Summer Olympic Games since 1964.

[h] Concerts of the Rolling Stones World Tour, 1995.

[i] Three concerts in Wechter, Belgium.

[j] Host City, 2000.

Source: Short *et al.* 1996: Table 9.

of architecture, civil engineering, fashion, and interior design); tourism of both the leisure and business varieties; and cultural and creative industries, including the live performing arts, museums and galleries, and the print and electronic media (newspapers, magazines, books, film, television, radio). These activities prove to be highly symbiotic: thus business services attract business travelers who may also use cultural facilities; urban tourism and culture are mutually supportive.

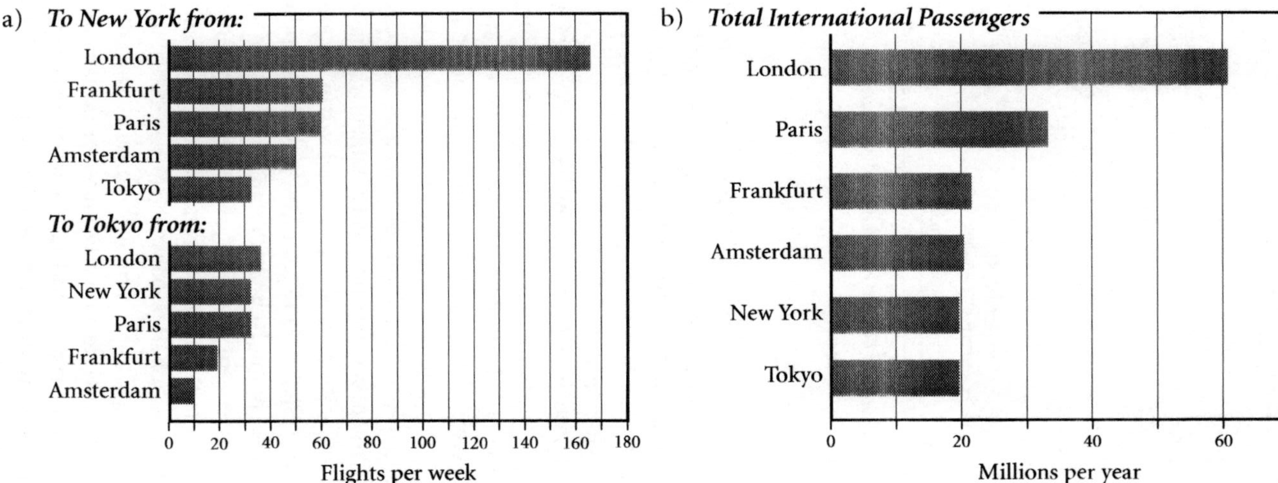

Figure 5.1. *Indices of international air traffic: (a) weekly frequency of direct flights to New York and Tokyo, and (b) total international passengers*

Source: London First Centre 1995

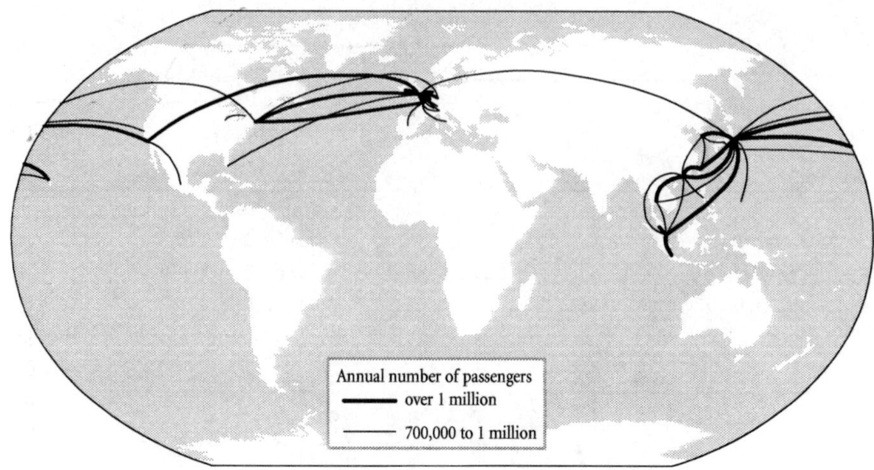

Figure 5.2. *The world's busiest international air routes, 1991–92*
Source: London First Centre 1995

The fact that London is the first international airport system in traffic terms reflects the fact that it is simultaneously a major business center, and a major cultural center, and a major tourist center, and all these are synergistic; likewise with competitor cities like Paris, Amsterdam, or Rome (Llewelyn Davies 1997; Association of London Government 1997).

There is an additional problem here, created by the existence of national boundaries. Despite major advances in European integration in the last decade—the Single European market, Economic and Monetary Union, the Schengen agreement for the effective abolition of borders—Europe is still a system of separate nation-states, with separate languages and cultures, in a way that the United States, Canada, and Australia (and other continental-scale nations, such as China, Brazil, and Argentina) are not. Very evidently, this combination of state power, language, and culture creates protected urban systems in a way that more open and uniform systems do not. In Europe, small capital cities such as Brussels, Copenhagen, Stockholm, Helsinki, Vienna, and Lisbon have a command over their national territories—in terms of governmental systems, legal systems, and the mass media—that is quite disproportionate to their size. And this combines in some cases with traditional specialisms (such as Zürich in banking, Milan in fashion, or Paris in art) that create a nonhierarchical urban pattern (Hall 1995). Some cities in other continents also display niche specialisms (e.g. Boston and San Francisco for financial services, and Los Angeles for media), but because no other continent has so many small nation-states with long cultural histories, no other presents quite this degree of nonhierarchical richness. And, of course, international boundaries completely distort comparisons of international air traffic: it is no accident that European airports figure so prominently in Figure 5.1.

Table 5.3. *Percentage change in city citations,* Financial Times, *1990–95*

Cities	1990 (Rank)	1995 (Rank)	Change
London	27 (1)	28 (1)	+1
Other UK	15	23	+8
Other European—not UK	26	18	−8
Brussels	5 (=3)	5 (=3)	0
EUROPE	68	69	+1
New York	11 (2)	7 (2)	−4
Other North American	11	14	+3
NORTH AMERICA	22	21	−1
Tokyo	5 (=3)	5 (=3)	0
Other East Asian	2	2	0
EAST ASIA	7	7	0
REST OF THE WORLD	3	3	0

Source: Beaverstock *et al.* 1999, from the *Financial Times* (various, 1990 and 1995).

This poses a basic question: as Beaverstock *et al.* (1999: 2) comment, on most indicators London is the most important city in Europe, but how in relational terms is it connected to other European cities? And does that place it at the apex of a hierarchy, or is the relationship more complex and nonhierarchical? Attribute data alone will not supply the answer to these questions. Nor even, perhaps, will relational data: Figure 5.2 is very suggestive, with its particularly strong linkages between London, New York, and Tokyo; but there are a wide range of regional or continental linkages between each of these cities and other cities in the same part of the world. How far these relationships are symmetrical, suggesting equality between the centers, or how far asymmetrical, suggesting a hierarchy, cannot be read from the map.

In order to overcome this basic problem, the Loughborough group has used three different ways of measuring relationships between cities: first, content analysis of leading business newspapers; second, tracing out personnel migration; and third, detailed analysis of producer services, in particular the structure of branch offices of large producer services such as accountancy or law (Beaverstock *et al.* 1999, 2000*a*).

The first approach is illustrated by Tables 5.3 and 5.4, from their work in progress, which show news references to other cities from the *Financial Times*, published in London, and the *Wall Street Journal*, published in New York. Both show a bias towards Europe; both show London, New York, and Tokyo as the most prominent places. (And, to a considerable degree, the rankings reflect the place of publication; doubtless Paris would be prominent in a French business paper, or Frankfurt in a German one). Other cities' rankings, however, show a great deal of volatility: in the *Wall Street Journal* Bonn slides from fourth place to fifteenth between 1990 and 1995. This analysis, though suggestive, suffers of course from the problem that it is not a direct measure of relationships and is influenced by

Table 5.4. *Percentage change in city citations,* Wall Street Journal, *1990–95*

Cities	1990 (Rank)	1995 (Rank)	Change
London	7 (=2)	11 (1)	+4
Other UK	0	4	+4
Other European—not UK	23	25	+2
Bonn	6 (=4)	2 (15)	−4
Frankfurt	3 (=9)	5 (=4)	+2
EUROPE	30	37	+7
New York	5 (7)	9 (3)	+4
Other North American	11	14	+3
Washington D.C.	6 (=4)	5 (=4)	−1
NORTH AMERICA	22	21	−1
Tokyo	12 (1)	20 (2)	+8
Other East Asian	2	2	0
Beijing	7 (=2)	4 (6)	−3
Shanghai	6 (6)	1 (20)	−5
EAST ASIA	7	7	0
REST OF THE WORLD	3	3	0

Source: Beaverstock *et al.* 1999, from *Wall Street Journal* (various, 1990 and 1995).

what happens to be newsworthy at any particular time. The apparent decline of Bonn, for instance, must reflect that it was much in the news in 1990, just after the fall of the Berlin Wall and the effective reunification of Germany. It also lost most government functions, but only in 1999, after the period of this comparison.

A second and more direct measure is international migration of highly skilled and specialized professional and managerial workers. Table 5.5 reports a study by the Loughborough group, based on interviews and questionnaires, showing personnel movements from London-based investment and merchant banks. It demonstrates an overwhelming concentration of flows to New York at both dates, and a very sharp diminution as we move down the urban hierarchy: London, it appears, has strong relations with a few European and East Asian cities, but with very few other cities anywhere. This of course reflects the strong degree of concentration in the international financial system (Beaverstock *et al.* 1999: 6). The Loughborough team conclude that this method has value in illustrating the relative magnetism of different centers for high-level mobile personnel, but that it is very time-consuming and labor-intensive.

The third suggested approach is through the geographical organization of branches of large producer services firms. Though it does not record actual transactions, of course, it does lay bare firms' spatial strategies. The overseas branches constitute a city's outward relations, allowing us to infer the geographical relationship between any given pair of cities. Table 5.6 shows some results.

Tables 5.7 and 5.8 show the results of an extension of this work by the Loughborough group, based on an analysis of 69 firms in advertising, banking

Table 5.5. *Skilled international migration from City of London-based investment and merchant banks to international office networks, 1988 and 1993*

City of London migrants 1988[a]		City of London migrants 1993[b]	
New York	136	New York	63
Hong Kong	46	Tokyo	23
Sydney	21	Hong Kong	20
Tokyo	16	Paris	16
Paris	10	Sydney	11
Singapore	5	Madrid	11
Others	15	Others	49
Total	249	Total	193

Notes:
[a] Complete data derived from sixteen banks: Barclays de Zoete Wedd, Barings & Co., Brown Shipleys, Citicorp, County NatWest Bank, Goldman Sachs, Guinness Macon, Hambros, Hill Samuel, Kleinwort Benson, Lazards, Nomura International, Robert Flemings, Rothschilds, Schroders, and S. G. Warburg.
[b] Incomplete data derived from nine banks: Hambros, HSBC Investment Bank, Kleinwort Benson, NatWest Markets Bank, Nomura International, Paribas, Rothschilds, S. G. Warburg, Standard Chartered.

Source: Beaverstock *et al.* 1999.

Table 5.6. *World-city coverage of the ten largest London and New York law firms beyond their "home" (EU and USA) regions*

London		New York		
City	Presences	City	Presences	Lawyers
Hong Kong	9	London	9	209
Singapore	8	Hong Kong	8	109
New York	7	Paris	7	139
Moscow	6	Tokyo	6	42
Tokyo	6	Frankfurt	4	22
Bangkok	3	Singapore	4	36
Beijing	3	Brussels	3	19
Ho Chi Minh	3	Budapest	3	18
Prague	3			
Shanghai	3			
8 other cities	11	25 other cities	30	
Total	62	Total	74	

Source: Beaverstock *et al.* 1999, based on ESRC-funded research, 1997–98 (cf. Beaverstock, Taylor, and Smith 1999*b*).

Table 5.7. *Percentage levels of linkage to London*

City	Producer Service				
	ACC	ADV	B&F	LAW	AVG
Amsterdam	73	62	26	6	42
Atlanta	80	10	3	0	23
Bangkok	47	48	37	11	36
Barcelona	40	52	29	8	32
Beijing	40	43	26	15	31
Berlin	67	10	11	6	24
Boston	67	24	16	8	29
Brussels	80	76	26	54	59
Budapest	40	38	24	17	30
Buenos Aires	47	38	39	5	32
Caracas	47	43	26	6	31
Chicago	87	29	32	20	42
Copenhagen	67	62	3	0	33
Dallas	73	24	11	14	31
Düsseldorf	93	57	16	5	43
Frankfurt	80	48	66	23	54
Geneva	47	14	37	3	25
Hamburg	73	38	14	0	31
Hong Kong	73	52	76	54	64
Houston	53	5	26	14	25
Istanbul	33	62	21	3	30
Jakarta	60	43	42	6	38
Johannesburg	73	38	32	0	36
Kuala Lumpur	53	38	39	0	33
Los Angeles	73	67	42	34	54
Madrid	67	76	53	11	52
Manila	40	43	34	5	31
Melbourne	67	57	32	6	41
Mexico City	67	48	47	8	43
Miami	47	38	26	12	31
Milan	87	71	50	11	55
Minneapolis	47	14	0	0	15
Montreal	73	48	21	0	36
Moscow	53	38	39	28	40
Munich	67	5	14	2	22
New York	93	90	95	68	87
Osaka	67	0	16	0	21
Paris	93	71	61	48	68
Prague	33	57	32	14	34
Rome	60	14	18	8	25
San Francisco	80	43	39	18	45
São Paulo	60	57	45	9	43
Santiago	60	43	32	5	35

Table 5.7. *(cont'd)*

Seoul	67	43	47	0	39
Singapore	53	67	79	31	58
Shanghai	40	33	32	5	28
Stockholm	67	67	8	8	38
Sydney	87	76	55	8	57
Taipei	53	43	50	5	38
Tokyo	93	43	76	32	61
Toronto	93	76	39	6	54
Warsaw	40	43	26	18	32
Washington, D.C.	87	5	14	60	42
Zürich	67	57	61	5	48

Source: Taylor, Walker, and Beaverstock 1999.

Table 5.8. *Average percentage linkage to London by regions*

Region	No. of cities	Average linkage
Western Europe	16	41
Pacific Asia	12	40
USA	11	39
Eastern Europe	5	33
Latin America	5	37
Old Commonwealth	5	45

Source: Taylor, Walker, and Beaverstock 1999; cf. Beaerstock *et al.* 2000*b*, Table 3.

and finance, accountancy and advertising services, and legal services, across 262 cities for 1997–98, showing their linkages with London. The tables show the percentage probability, on entering a London office, of that firm having a branch in another city. Brussels dominates in law, other European cities in advertising. New York emerges as London's main partner; in banking and finance New York stands well ahead of Tokyo, Hong Kong, and Singapore in the three top positions; in advertising New York is again dominant; in law, New York and Washington are above Brussels; in accountancy, New York, Paris, Tokyo, and Toronto share top place.

The extreme right-hand column in Table 5.7 shows the average scores across all four producer services. The Loughborough group uses this to define an index of London External Relations. The London-New York link is clearly in a category of its own, scoring 87; it is designated a "prime link." The next, Paris-London (68) and Hong Kong-London (64) connect London to other world regions and are designated as "major links." What emerges is the worldwide scope of London's linkages, as shown in Table 5.8. The 54 cities fall into five groups: 16 in Western

Europe, 12 from Pacific Asia, 11 from the United States; there are 5 each from Eastern Europe, Latin America, and the Old Commonwealth (Australia, Canada, and South Africa).

The Loughborough group relies heavily on these four categories of producer services: taking their cue from Sassen (1991: 126), they treat world cities as particular "postindustrial production sites" where innovations in corporate services and finance have been integral to the recent restructuring of the world economy, or globalization. Although services, both directly for consumers and for firms producing other goods for consumers, are common to all cities, what distinguishes global cities are advanced producer services or corporate services, which tend to be highly concentrated in a limited number of leading cities with "a specific role in the current phase of the world economy" (Sassen 1991: 126).

The basic unit of analysis in the Loughborough group assessment, therefore, is the producer service firm. The firms they consider all have multicity, multistate locations. Ideally, such a study should deal with all global corporate service firms in all advanced producer service sectors, but lack of data precludes this. Their resulting "GaWC Inventory of World Cities" is produced by aggregating the information from the four listings of all centers for each of the four services (accountancy, advertising, banking, and law). Their analysis involves three stages. First, they find the global competence of service firms in terms of their presence in cities. Second, aggregating for each city, they find the global service centers for a given service sector. And third, by aggregating service center results by city, they identify world cities of different degrees of corporate service provision.

They consider 122 cities in all. For each, a score of three indicates a prime center, two a major center, and one a minor center. Given four sectors, the result is a series of estimates of world city-ness ranging from 1 to 12. Cities and their scores are shown in Table 5.9.

The division of cities into different classes has been carried out using simple logical criteria. Any city scoring 10 or above must be a global service center in all four sectors. Where it is a minor center for a particular service, this must be compensated for by the other three being prime. In addition it must be prime in at least two sectors, and the other two must be major designations.

Ten cities qualify as Alpha world cities. As might be expected, there are no surprises here: 3 of the 10 cities are from the United States, 4 from Western Europe, and 3 from Pacific Asia. Any city scoring 7 to 9 must be a global service center for at least three of the four sectors and must be a major or prime center in at least two sectors.

Ten cities also qualify as Beta world cities. The same three world regions are represented as for prime world cities, but with "outer" cities appearing: Sydney, Toronto, Mexico City, and Moscow. In addition, a third world region appears: São Paulo in South America.

It is at the bottom end of the scale where uncertainty emerges. The Loughborough group comment:

Table 5.9. *The Loughborough Group "GaWC" inventory of world cities (Cities are ordered in terms of world city-ness values ranging from 1 to 12)*

A. *Alpha world cities*
- 12: London, Paris, New York, Tokyo
- 10: Chicago, Frankfurt, Hong Kong, Los Angeles, Milan, Singapore

B. *Beta world cities*
- 9: San Francisco, Sydney, Toronto, Zürich
- 8: Brussels, Madrid, Mexico City, São Paulo
- 7: Moscow, Seoul

C. *Gamma world cities*
- 6: Amsterdam, Boston, Caracas, Dallas, Düsseldorf, Geneva, Houston, Jakarta, Johannesburg, Melbourne, Osaka, Prague, Santiago, Taipei, Washington
- 5: Bangkok, Beijing, Rome, Stockholm, Warsaw
- 4: Atlanta, Barcelona, Berlin, Buenos Aires, Budapest, Copenhagen, Hamburg, Istanbul, Kuala Lumpur, Manila, Miami, Minneapolis, Montreal, Munich, Shanghai

D. *Evidence of world-city formation*

D(i) Relatively strong evidence
- 3: Auckland, Dublin, Helsinki, Luxembourg, Lyon, Mumbai, New Delhi, Philadelphia, Rio de Janeiro, Tel Aviv, Vienna

D(ii) Some evidence
- 2: Abu Dhabi, Almaty, Athens, Birmingham, Bogota, Bratislava, Brisbane, Bucharest, Cairo, Cleveland, Cologne, Detroit, Dubai, Ho Chi Minh City, Kiev, Lima, Lisbon, Manchester, Montevideo, Oslo, Rotterdam, Riyadh, Seattle, Stuttgart, The Hague, Vancouver

D(iii) Minimal evidence
- 1: Adelaide, Antwerp, Århus, Athens, Baltimore, Bangalore, Bologna, Brasilia, Calgary, Cape Town, Colombo, Columbus, Dresden, Edinburgh, Genoa, Glasgow, Gothenburg, Guangzhou, Hanoi, Kansas City, Leeds, Lille, Marseille, Richmond, St Petersburg, Tashkent, Tehran, Tijuana, Turin, Utrecht, Wellington

Definitions: World city-ness values produced by scoring 3 for prime center status, 2 for major center status, and 1 for minor center status.

Source: Beaverstock, Taylor, and Smith 1999*a*, Table 6 and Table 7.

the most interesting feature of our final inventory of world cities will be the identification of cities below the top levels. This is a grey zone where it is unclear whether or not we are dealing with world cities or some "sub-level" of city. Our purpose in devising an inventory of world cities is not to simply replace the grey zone by a strict boundary. Rather, we will keep a "fuzzy" lower "frontier" to our list of cities by recording the global presence in cities below our chosen world city threshold. The need is not to eliminate the grey area but to investigate it and that is the spirit in which we have approached this classification exercise. (Beaverstock, Smith, and Taylor 1999: 5.)

They define cities scoring 4 to 6 as Gamma world cities. All these cities must be global service centers for at least two sectors, and in at least one of those it must be a major center. This definition captures thirty-five further cities, again distributed largely across the three main regions, but with another three representatives from South America. In addition, Africa has its first city in the list, Johannesburg, but there are still no world cities in South Asia or the Middle East (if we count Istanbul as European).

The remaining sixty-eight cities are designated as having evidence of world-city formation processes, although the evidence is not strong enough to label them world cities. The most interesting among them are 12 which score 3; here is found one Middle East city, Tel Aviv, and two South Asian cities, Mumbai and New Delhi. Perhaps these signify the early stages in filling the voids on the global world-city map.

The resulting list of ten "Alpha" world cities, ten "Beta" world cities, and thirty-five "Gamma" world cities contains no major surprises: the cities that appear in Table 5.2 tend to be Alpha world cities in Table 5.9, with only one or two exceptions. The main interest of the Loughborough inventory lies in the lower levels of world city-ness, in the "fuzzy zone" below the Alpha and Beta centers. The regional concentration is quite remarkable: this is a concrete expression of what has been called "uneven globalization," which Peter Taylor instances as an example of the tendency to monopolization in the capitalist economy (Taylor 1999: 9).

The work of the Loughborough group is undoubtedly the most rigorous attempt yet made to define systematically the relationships that are central to the concept of a global city. But it still opens up as many questions as it answers. In particular, the tail of the distribution confirms what has long been suspected: that, below the relatively small number of cities that have generally been awarded global city status, there is a relatively large number of cities with a marginal claim to inclusion, which, however, lack several key attributes. That might lead to their dismissal out of hand. But that would be a mistake. It is precisely at this level that one best comes to understand the force of the ties that link global cities, and that may allow the isolation of a quite large category of specialized or niche-economy cities. And this category may be crucially important in policy terms, because it allows a city to make its own bid for occupation of some crucial niche market, as when Glasgow became European City of Culture in 1990 or City of Architecture in 1999, or when Bilbao suddenly launched itself on to the world's consciousness with the Guggenheim museum, or when a city like Seoul or Sydney attracts the Olympic Games. There is more than one route to global city status, and cities are discovering that fact for themselves.

DEFINING THE GLOBAL CITY-REGION

If global cities are defined in terms of their *external* information exchanges, logic suggests that global city-regions should be defined in terms of corresponding *internal* linkages. Information moves in two ways: electronically, and inside people's heads for face-to-face exchange (Hall 1991). The latter movements may occur daily on a regular basis (commuting) or less frequently and/or more irregularly (business meetings). We have very few data on these movements, with the exception of commuting; but this is a very indirect measure, since we have no direct indication of what information the commuters exchange when they reach their destination. Attempts have been made in a few cities to record all information exchanges through diaries (Goddard 1973; Carlstein, Parkes, and Thrift 1979), and these indicated clearly that electronic exchanges were invariably more routine in character (using "programmed" information) and served as a prelude to face-to-face meetings where "unprogrammed" information was exchanged. These studies were made in an era before the personal computer or e-mail, and before the spread of the globalized economy, yet the same point has been underlined by more recent studies (Mitchell 1995, 1999). Because of this basic fact, the dense cores of traditional cities still offer major agglomeration economies, as argued three quarters of a century ago (Haig 1926).

However, it is also clear that increasingly sophisticated systems of electronic exchange permit flexible mixtures of the two kinds of exchange. Specialist consultants can operate effectively from home bases up to two hours' travel time from metropolitan cores, since in this way they can travel when needed to offices in these cores or, through air and rail connections, to offices in other metropolitan centers. High-quality fast transportation networks, in the form of highways or high-speed rail links, are crucial here. Further, their key meeting places may no longer be located in traditional downtown areas. Increasingly, professional and managerial workers function in a variety of geographical spaces: they may process electronic information in home offices in suburbs or the remote countryside, in airplanes and trains and hotels and airport lounges; they may meet face-to-face in all these places as well as in convention centers (which may be purpose-built, or in adapted hotels, or in converted country houses), or in new-style offices such as IBM's UK headquarters at Bedfont Lakes outside London Heathrow airport, which features a central cafeteria-type atrium surrounded by hot-desk cubicles.

What does this mean for the internal geography of global city-regions? It implies huge complexity and sophistication. The high-level intelligence and control functions of the global cities are increasingly dispersed across a wide geographical area, limited only by certain geographical constraints of time-distance. Though traditional face-to-face locations retain their power, they are increasingly supplemented by new kinds of node for face-to-face activity. The resultant geographical structure is quintessentially polycentric:

1. *The traditional downtown center*, based on walking distances and served by a radial public transportation center. This serves the oldest informational services (banking, insurance, government) and is found in the cores of old cities: the City of London, Châtelet-Les Halles, Downtown Manhattan, Maronouchi/Otemachi.
2. *A newer business center*, often developing in an old prestige residential quarter, and serving as the location of newer services that have expanded in the twentieth century, such as corporate headquarters, the media, new business

services (advertising, public relations, design): London's West End, the 16e arrondissment, Midtown Manhattan, Akasaki/Roppongi.

3. *An "internal edge city,"* resulting from pressure of space in traditional centers and speculative development in old industrial or transport land, now redundant, near to them: London Docklands, La Défense, World Financial Center, Shinjuku.
4. *An "external" edge city*, often located on the axis of the main airport, more rarely a high-speed train station: London Heathrow, Paris Charles de Gaulle, Amsterdam Schiphol, Stockholm Arlanda, Washington Reagan/Dulles corridor.
5. *"Outermost" edge city complexes* for back offices and R&D, typically at major train stations twenty to forty miles distant from the main core: Reading, St Quentin-en-Yvelines, Greenwich (Connecticut), Omiya, Shin-Yokohama.
6. *Specialized subcenters*, usually for education, entertainment and sporting complexes, exhibition and convention centers: Royal Docks (London), Milton Keynes (Open University), Tokyo Waterfront. These take a great variety of forms and locations: some are on reclaimed or recycled land close to the traditional core, some are older centers, formerly separate and independent, that have become progressively embedded in the wider metropolitan area (Oxford, Cambridge, Uppsala, New Haven). Some of these may take on new functions: witness the emergence of the Cambridge region as a major high-technology center ("Silicon Fen") since 1970.

Within this increasingly polycentric structure, there is increasing specialization: many functions—back offices, logistical management, new-style headquarters complexes, media centers, and large-scale entertainment and sport—relocate over time to decentralized locations, albeit at different speeds and with different effects. In the extreme case, the Asian megacity (best represented by the Pearl River Delta region of China), this is mediated by state planning, but in a highly flexible way: core command-and-control functions are concentrated in Hong Kong, other service functions in Guangzhou, while other routine manufacturing and service functions are scattered across the cities of the delta. But the entire region is by definition highly centralized on a global scale (Xu and Li 1990, Yeung 1996, Sit and Yang 1997, Hall 1999). The form bears some similarities to Gottmann's megalopolis, first identified by him on the Northeastern urban seaboard of the United States (Gottmann 1961); but it is infinitely more complex, because more highly interconnected. Here, as around Shanghai, around Jakarta, and around Singapore, we see the beginnings of a new urban form that in some cases even transcends national boundaries: a city-region on a vast scale, networked externally on a global scale and internally over thousands of square kilometers: the precursor of a new scale of urban organization.

REFERENCES

Association of London Government. (1997). *The London Study: A Socio-Economic Assessment of London*. London: ALG.

Beaverstock, J. G., Lorimer, H., Smith, R. G., Taylor, P. J., and Walker, D. R. F. (1999). *Globalization and World Cities: Measurement Methodologies. GaWC Research Bulletin 2.* Loughborough: University of Loughborough, Department of Geography. Posted on the Web: http://www.lboro.ac.uk/departments/gy/research/gawc/rb/rb2.html.

——, Smith, R. G., and Taylor, P. J. (1999). *A Roster of World Cities. GaWC Research Bulletin 5.* Loughborough: University of Loughborough, Department of Geography. Posted on the Web: http://www.lboro.ac.uk/departments/gy/research/gawc/rb/rb5.html.

——, Smith, R. G., Taylor, P. J., Walker, D. R. F., Lorimer, H. (2000*a*). "Globalization and World Cities: Some Measurement Methodologies." *Applied Geography*, 20: 43–63.

——, Smith, R. G., Taylor, P. J., (2000*b*). "World-City Network: a New Metageography?" *Annals of the Association of American Geographers*, 90: 123–34.

——, Taylor, P., Smith, R. G. (1999*a*). "A Roster of World Cities." *Cities*, 16: 445–58.

——, Taylor, P., Smith, R. G. (1999*b*). "The Long Arm of the Law: London's Law Firms in a Globalising World Economy." *Environment and Planning, A*, 31: 1857–76.

Budd, L. (1995). "Globalization, Territory, and Strategic Alliances in Different Financial Centers." *Urban Studies*, 32: 345–60.

Carlstein, T., Parkes, D., Thrift, N. (1978). *Human Activity and Time Geography.* (*Timing Space and Spacing Time*, vol. 2.) London: Edward Arnold.

Cohen, R. B. (1981). "The New International Division of Labor, Multinational Corporations, and Urban Hierarchy," in M. Dear and A. J. Scott (eds.), *Urbanization and Urban Planning in a Capitalist Society.* London: Methuen, 287–315.

Drennan, M. P. (1996). "The Dominance of International Finance by London, New York, and Tokyo," in P. W. Daniels and W. F. Lever (eds.), *The Global Economy in Transition.* Harlow: Addison Wesley, 352–71.

The Economist (1992). "Financial Centers: Rise and Fall." 27 June, 3–26.

—— (1998). "A Survey of International Financial Centers—Capitals of Capitals." 9 May.

Feagin, J. R., and Smith, M. P. (1987). "Cities and the New International Division of Labor," in M. P. Smith and J. R. Feign (eds.), *The Capitalist City.* Oxford: Blackwell, 3–36.

Friedmann, J. (1986). "The World City Hypothesis." *Development and Change*, 17: 69–83.

—— (1995). "Where We Stand: A Decade of World City Research," in P. L. Knox and P. J. Taylor (eds.), *World Cities in a World System.* Cambridge: Cambridge University Press, 21–47.

——, and Wolff, G. (1982) "World City Formation: An Agenda for Research and Action." *International Journal of Urban and Regional Research*, 6: 309–44.

Fröbel, F., Heinrichs, J., and Kreye, D. (1980). *The New International Division of Labour.* Cambridge: Cambridge University Press.

Glickman, N. J. (1987). "Cities and the International Division of Labor," in M. P. Smith and J. R. Feagin (eds.), *The Capitalist City.* Oxford: Blackwell, 66–86.

Goddard, J. B. (1973). "Office Linkages and Location." *Progress in Planning*, 1, part 2.

Gottmann, J. (1961). *Megalopolis: The Urbanized Northeastern Seaboard of the United States.* New York: Twentieth Century Fund.

Haig, R. M. (1926). "Toward an Understanding of the Metropolis." *Quarterly Journal of Economics*, 40: 179–208, 402–34.

Hall, P. (1966). *The World Cities.* London: Weidenfeld and Nicolson.

—— (1991). "Moving Information: A Tale of Four Technologies," in J. Brotchie, M. Batty, P. Hall, and P. Newton (eds.), *Cities of the 21st Century: New Technologies and Spatial Systems.* Melbourne: Longman Cheshire, 1–21.

—— (1995). "Towards a General Urban Theory," in J. Brotchie, M. Batty, E. Blakely, P. Hall, and P. Newton (eds.), *Cities in Competition: Productive and Sustainable Cities for the 21st Century*, Melbourne: Longman Australia, 3–31.

—— (1999). "Planning for the Mega-City: A New Eastern Asian Urban Form?" in J. Brotchie, P. Newton, P. Hall, and J. Dickey (eds.), *East West Perspectives on 21st Century Urban Development: Sustainable Eastern and Western Cities in the New Millennium.* Aldershot: Ashgate, 3–36.

Heenan, D. A. (1977). "Global Cities of Tomorrow." *Harvard Business Review*, 55 (May–June): 79–92.

Hymer, S. (1972). "The Multinational Corporation and the Law of Uneven Development," in J. Bhagwati (ed.) *Economics and World Order from the 1970s to the 1990s.* New York: Collier-Macmillan, 113–40.

Knox, P. L. (1995*a*). "World Cities and the Organization of Global Space," in R. J. Johnston, P. J. Taylor, and M. J. Watts (eds.), *Geographies of Global Change.* Oxford: Blackwell, 232–48.

—— (1995*b*). "World Cities in a World System," in P. L. Knox and P. J. Taylor (eds.), *World Cities in a World-System.* Cambridge: Cambridge University Press, 3–20.

Lee, R., and Schmidt-Marwede, U. (1993). "Interurban Competition? Financial Centers and the Geography of Financial Production." *International Journal of Urban and Regional Research,* 17: 492–515.

Llewelyn-Davies Planning (1997). *Four World Cities.* London: Comedia.

London First Center (1995). *London Business Briefing: International Business Travel.* London: London First Center.

Martin, R. (1994). "Stateless Monies, Global Financial Integration, and National Economic Autonomy: The End of Geography?" in S. Corbridge, R. Martin, and N. Thrift (eds.), *Money, Power, and Space.* Oxford: Blackwell, 253–78.

Meyer, D. R. (1986). "The World System of Cities: Relations Between International Financial Metropolises and South American Cities." *Social Forces,* 64: 553–81.

Mitchell, W. J. (1995). *City of Bits: Space, Place, and the Infobahn.* Cambridge, Mass.: MIT Press.

—— (1999). *e-topia: "Urban Life, Jim—But Not as We Know It."* Cambridge, Mass.: MIT Press.

Muller, P. O. (1997). "The Suburban Transformation of the Globalizing American City." *Annals of the American Academy of Political and Social Science,* 551: 44–58.

O'Brien, R. (1992). "Global Financial Integration: The End of Geography." New York: RIIA.

Reed, H. C. (1981). *The Preeminence of International Financial Centers.* New York: Praeger.

—— (1989). "Financial Center Hegemony, Interest Rates, and the Global Political Economy," in S. Y. Park and M. Essayard (eds.), *International Banking and Financial Centers.* London: Kluvier Academic Press, 247–68.

Sassen, S. (1991). *The Global City: New York, London, Tokyo.* Princeton: Princeton University Press.

—— (1994*a*). *Cities in a World Economy.* London: Pine Forge Press.

—— (1994*b*). "The Urban Complex." *International Social Science Journal,* 139: 43–62.

Short, J. R., Kim, Y., Kuus, M., Wells, H. (1996). "The Dirty Little Secret of World Cities Research—Data Problems in Comparative Analysis." *International Journal of Urban and Regional Research*, 20: 697–719.

Sit, V. F. S., and Yang, C. (1997). "Foreign-Investment-Induced Exo-Urbanisation in the Pearl River Delta, China." *Urban Studies*, 34: 647–77.

Taylor, P. J. (1997). "Hierarchical Tendencies amongst World Cities: A Global Research Proposal." *Cities* 14: 323–32.

——, Walker, D. R. F., and Beaverstock, J. V. (1999). *Introducing GaWC: Researching World City Network Formation.* GaWC Research Bulletin 6. Loughborough: University of Loughborough, Department of Geography. Posted on the Web: http://www.lboro.ac.uk/departments/gy/research/gawc/rb/rb2.html.

Thrift, N. J. (1989). "The Geography of International Economic Disorder," in R. Johnston and P. J. Taylor (eds.), *A World in Crisis? Geographical Perspectives.* Oxford: Blackwell, 16–78.

Warf, B. (1989). "Telecommunications and the Globalisation of Financial Services." *Professional Geographer*, 41: 257–71.

Xu, X.-Q., and Li, S.-M. (1990). "China Open Door Policy and Urbanization in the Pearl River Delta Region." *International Journal of Urban and Regional Research*, 14: 49–69.

Yeung, Y. M. (1996). "An Asian Perspective on the Global City." *International Social Science Journal*, 147: 25–31.

6

Global Cities and Global City-Regions: A Comparison

SASKIA SASSEN

Each phase in the long history of the world economy raises specific questions about the particular conditions that make it possible. One of the key properties of the current phase is the ascendance of information technologies and the associated increase in the mobility and liquidity of capital. There have long been cross-border economic processes—flows of capital, labor, goods, raw materials, tourists. But in the twentieth century these took place largely within the interstate system, where the key articulators were national states. The international economic system was ensconced largely in this interstate system. This has changed rather dramatically over the last decade as a result of privatization, deregulation, the opening up of national economies to foreign firms, and the growing participation of national economic actors in global markets.

It is in this context that we see a rescaling of what are the strategic territories that articulate the new system. With the partial unbundling or at least weakening of the national as a spatial unit due to privatization and deregulation and its associated strengthening of globalization, come conditions for the ascendance of other spatial units or scales. Among these are the subnational, notably cities and regions; cross-border regions encompassing two or more subnational entities; and supranational entities, i.e. global digitized markets and free trade blocs. The dynamics and processes that get territorialized at these diverse scales can in principle be regional, national, or global.

I locate the emergence of global cities in this context and against this range of instantiations of strategic scales and spatial units (Sassen 2000*a*, *b*, *c*). In the case of global cities, the dynamics and processes that get territorialized are global. Thus the formulation of global city-regions (Scott *et al.* 2000; see also Scott 1998; Storper 1997) represents the elaboration of yet another strategic scale. Clearly, as a territorial scale and as an analytic construct in many ways it overlaps the global city, in that the latter is likely to be contained by the region. Yet they may well be quite diverse both as a territorial scale and as an analytic construct.

In this chapter I examine first some of the differences entailed by each of these constructs—global cities and global city-regions. This is a first attempt at this comparison, stimulated by the chapter of Scott, Agnew, Soja, and Storper. Their focus on the region has allowed me to specify with greater clarity what is specific to the global city focus, and what a focus on the region adds to our understanding of the broader process of globalization and its spatializations. There follows a more in-depth discussion of the features that specify the global city construct, this being the one I am better equipped to discuss given my role in developing it. This discussion should be read in juxtaposition with the chapter by Scott *et al.*, which examines the global city-region concept in depth. If there are two features that mark the global city they are, first, a particular interaction of centrality and networks, and second, not unrelated to the first, a particular dynamic of power and inequality. I explore certain aspects of these two features in the final two sections.

ELEMENTS IN A NEW CONCEPTUAL ARCHITECTURE

The globalization of economic activity entails a new type of organizational structure. To capture this theoretically and empirically requires, correspondingly, a new type of conceptual architecture. Constructs such as the global city and the global city-region are, in my reading, important elements in this new conceptual architecture. The activity of naming these elements is part of the conceptual work. There are other, closely linked terms which could conceivably have been used: world cities,[1] "supervilles" (Braudel 1984), informational city (Castells 1989). Thus choosing how to name a configuration has its own substantive rationality.

When I first chose to use global city (1984) I did so knowingly—it was an attempt to name a difference: the specificity of the global as it gets structured in the contemporary period. I did not choose the obvious alternative, world city, because it had precisely the opposite attribute: it referred to a type of city which we have seen over the centuries (e.g. Braudel 1984; Hall 1966; King 1990), and most probably also in much earlier periods in Asia than in the West (Abu-Lughod 1989; King 1990). In this regard it could be said that most of today's major global cities are also world cities, but that there may well be some global cities today that are not world cities in the full, rich sense of that term. This is partly an empirical question for me; further, as the global economy expands and incorporates additional cities into the various networks, it is quite possible that the answer to that particular question will vary. For instance, the fact that Miami has developed global city functions beginning in the late 1980s does not make it a world city in that older sense of the term. (See also Abu-Lughod 1999, Short and Kim 1999, Shachar 1990.)

Thus I would argue that the choice of the term global city-region also comes with that same specificity—incorporating the particular features of the current phase of economic globalization. We would have to hypothesize as to whether future phases will have global cities and global city-regions as core elements of the organizational structure of a global economy.[2] But while these two concepts factor in the specificity of the current phase, they have distinctive theoretical and empirical dimensions.

Regional vs. City Scale

A first difference concerns the question of scale. The territorial scale of the region is far more likely to include a cross-section of a country's economic activities than the scale of the city. It is likely, for instance, to include as key variables manufacturing and basic infrastructure. This, in turn, brings with it a more benign focus on globalization. The concept of the global city introduces a far stronger emphasis on strategic components of the global economy, and hence on questions of power. Secondly, the concept of the global city will tend to have a stronger emphasis on the networked economy because of the nature of the industries that tend to be located there: finance and specialized services. And, thirdly, it will tend to have more of an emphasis on economic and spatial polarization because of the disproportionate concentration of very high- and very low-income jobs in the city compared with what would be the case for the region.

Overall, I would say, the concept of the global city is more attuned to questions of power and inequality. The concept of the global city-region is more attuned to questions about the nature and specifics of broad urbanization patterns, a more encompassing economic base, more middle sectors of both households and firms, and hence to the possibility of having a more even distribution of economic benefits under globalization. In this regard, it could be said that the concept of the global city-region allows us to see the possibilities for a more distributed kind of growth, a wider spread of the benefits associated with the growth dynamics of globalization.

Both concepts have a problem with boundaries of at least two sorts, the boundary of the territorial scale as such and the boundary of the spread of globalization in the organizational structure of industries, institutional orders, places, and so on. In the case of the global city I have opted for an analytic strategy that emphasizes core dynamics rather than the unit of the city as a container—the latter being one that requires territorial boundary specification. Emphasizing core dynamics and their spatialization (in both actual and digital space) does not completely solve the boundary problem, but it does allow for a fairly clear trade-off between emphasizing the core or center of these dynamics and their spread institutionally and spatially. In my work I have sought to deal with both sides of this trade-off: by emphasizing, on the one side of the trade-off, the most advanced and globalized industries, such as finance, and, on the other side, how the informal economy in major global cities is articulated with some of the leading industries. In the case of the global city-region, it is not clear to me how Scott *et al.* specify the boundary question both in its territorial sense and in terms of its organization and spread.

Competitiveness for Cities and for Regions

A second difference is the emphasis on competition and competitiveness, much stronger in the global city-region construct. In my reading, the nature itself of the leading industries in global cities strengthens the importance of cross-border networks and specialized division of functions among cities in different countries and/or regions rather than international competition per se. In the case of global finance and the leading specialized services catering to global firms and markets—law, accounting, credit rating, telecommunications—it is clear that we are dealing with a cross-border system, one that is embedded in a series of cities, each possibly part of a different country. It is a de facto global system.

The industries that are likely to dominate global city-regions, on the other hand, are less likely to be networked in this way. For instance, in the case of large manufacturing complexes, the identification with the national is stronger and the often stronger orientation to consumer markets brings to the fore the question of quality, prices, and the possibility of substitution. Hence competition and competitiveness are likely to be far more prominent. Further, even when there is significant off-shoring of production—as in the auto industry, for instance—this type of internationalization tends to be within the chain of production of a given firm. Insofar as most firms still have their central headquarters associated with a specific region and country, the competition question is likely to be prominent and, very importantly, sited—i.e. it is the United States versus the Japanese auto manufacturers.

Finally, the question of the competitiveness of a region is deeply centered in its infrastructure. To some extent this is also a crucial variable in the case of global cities, but it is, probably, a far more specialized type of infrastructure. The regional scale brings to the fore questions of public transport, highway construction, and kindred aspects, in a way that the focus on global cities does not. Again, it reveals to what extent a focus on the region allows for a more benevolent appreciation of competitiveness in a global economy, because a focus on the regional infrastructure is far more likely to include strong consideration of middle-class needs in this regard. In contrast, a focus on the global city will tend to bring to the fore the growing inequalities between highly provisioned and profoundly disadvantaged sectors and spaces of the city, and hence questions of power and inequality.

Cross-border Transactions, for Global Cities and for City-Regions

A third difference, connected to the preceding one, is that a focus on networked cross-border dynamics among global cities also allows us to capture more readily the growing intensity of such transactions in other domains—political, cultural, social, criminal. We now have evidence of greater cross-border transactions among immigrant communities and communities of origin and a greater intensity in the use of these networks once they become established, including for economic activities that had been unlikely until now. We also have evidence of greater cross-border networks for cultural purposes, as in the growth of international markets for art and a transnational class of curators; and for nonformal political purposes, as in the growth of transnational networks of activists around environmental causes, human rights, and so on. These are largely city-to-city cross-border networks, or, at least, it appears at this time to be simpler to capture the existence and modalities of these networks at the city level. The same can be said for the new cross-border criminal networks. Dealing with the regional scale does not necessarily facilitate recognizing the existence of such networks from one region to the other. It is far more likely to be from one specific community in a region to another specific community in another region, thereby neutralizing the meaning of the region as such.

THE GLOBAL CITY MODEL: ORGANIZING HYPOTHESES

This section continues the effort to specify the differences and overlaps between the two constructs, but does so by focusing on the basic hypotheses that organize the model of the global city. In this regard, it should be read alongside the chapter by Scott, Agnew, Soja, and Storper on global city-regions.

There are six hypotheses through which I organized the data and the theorization in *The Global City*. I will discuss each of these briefly as a way of producing a more precise representation that should facilitate comparison with the construct of the global city-region.

First, the geographic dispersal of economic activities that marks globalization, along with the simultaneous integration of such geographically dispersed activities, is a key factor feeding the growth and importance of central corporate functions. The more dispersed a firm's operations across different countries, the more complex and strategic its central functions—that is, the work of managing, coordinating, servicing, and financing a firm's network of operations.

Second, these central functions become so complex that increasingly the headquarters of large global firms outsource them: they buy a share of their central functions from highly specialized service firms: accounting, legal, public relations, programming, telecommunications, and other such services. Thus while even ten years ago the key site for the production of these central headquarters functions was the headquarters of a firm, today there is a second key site: the specialized service firms contracted by headquarters to produce some of these central functions or components of them. This is especially the case with firms involved in global markets and nonroutine operations. But increasingly the headquarters of all large firms are buying more of such inputs rather than producing them in-house.

Third, those specialized service firms engaged in the most complex and globalized markets are subject to agglomeration economies. The complexity of the services they need to produce, the uncertainty of the markets they are involved with, either directly or through the headquarters for which they are producing the services, and the growing importance of speed in all these transactions, is a mix of conditions that constitutes a new agglomeration dynamic. The combination of firms, talents, and expertise from a broad range of specialized fields makes a certain type of urban environment function as an information center. Being in a city becomes synonymous with being in an extremely intense and dense information loop. This is a type of information loop that as of now still cannot be replicated fully in electronic space, and has as one of its value-added features the fact of unforeseen and unplanned mixes of information, expertise, and talent, which can produce a higher order of information. This does not hold for routinized activities that are not as subject to uncertainty and to nonstandardized forms of complexity. Global cities are, in this regard, production sites for the leading information industries of our time.

A fourth hypothesis, derived from the preceding one, is that the more headquarters outsource their most complex, unstandardized functions, particularly those subject to uncertain and changing markets and to requirements of speed, the freer they are to opt for any location because the more the work actually done in the headquarters is not subject to agglomeration economies. This further underlines that the key sector specifying the distinctive production advantages of global cities is the highly specialized and networked services sector. In developing this hypothesis I was responding to a very common notion that the number of headquarters is what specifies a global city. Empirically it may still be the case in many countries that the leading business center is also the leading concentration of headquarters, but this may well be because there is an absence of alternative locational options. But in countries with a well-developed infrastructure outside the leading business center, there are likely to be multiple locational options for such headquarters.

Fifth, these specialized service firms need to provide a global service, which has meant a global network of affiliates or some other form of partnership, and as a result we have seen a strengthening of cross-border city-to-city transactions and networks. At the limit this may well be the beginning of the formation of transnational urban systems. The growth of global markets for finance and specialized services, the need for transnational servicing networks due to sharp increases in international investment, the reduced role of the government in the regulation of international economic activity and the corresponding ascendance of other institutional arenas, notably global markets and corporate headquarters —all these point to the existence of a series of transnational networks of cities. We can see here the formation, at least incipient, of transnational urban systems. To a large extent it seems to me that the major business centers in the world today draw their importance from these transnational networks. There is no such thing as a single global city—and in this sense there is a sharp contrast with the erstwhile capitals of empires.

A sixth hypothesis, is that the growing numbers of high-level professionals and high-profit-making specialized service firms have the effect of raising the degree of spatial and socioeconomic inequality evident in these cities. The strategic role of these specialized services as inputs raises the number and value of top-level professionals. Further, because talent can have an enormous effect on the quality of results, proven talent is at a premium. The necessity for speed also favors selecting proven talent. The likely effect is rapidly to bid upward the structure of rewards. Types of activities and of workers lacking these attributes, whether in manufacturing or industrial services, are likely to get caught in an opposite cycle.

In the first four hypotheses, my effort was to qualify the emerging dominant discourse on globalization, technology, and cities, which was predicting the end of cities as important economic units or scales. I saw a tendency in that viewpoint to see the global economic system as only a function of the power of transnational corporations and global communications. My counterargument was, and remains, that the capabilities for global operation, coordination, and control contained in the new information technologies and in the power of transnational corporations need to be produced. By focusing on the production of these capabilities we add a neglected dimension to the familiar issue of the power of large corporations and the capacity of the new technologies to neutralize distance and place. A focus on the production of these capabilities shifts the emphasis to the *practices* that constitute what we call economic globalization and global control.

A focus on practices draws the categories of place and work process into the analysis of economic globalization. These are two categories easily overlooked in accounts centered on the hypermobility of capital and the power of transnationals. Developing categories such as place and work process does not negate the centrality of hypermobility and power. Rather, it brings to the fore the fact that many of the resources necessary for global economic activities are not hypermobile and are, indeed, deeply embedded in place, notably places such as global cities, global city-regions, and export processing zones.

This entails a whole infrastructure of activities, firms, and jobs, that is necessary to run the advanced corporate economy. These industries are typically conceptualized in terms of the hypermobility of their outputs and the high levels of expertise of their professionals rather than in terms of the production or work process involved and the requisite infrastructure of facilities and nonexpert jobs that are also part of these industries. Emphasizing place, infrastructure, and nonexpert jobs matters precisely because so much of the focus has been on the neutralization of geography and place made possible by the new technologies.

Recapturing the geography of places involved in globalization allows us to recapture people, workers, communities, and more specifically, the many different work cultures, besides the corporate culture, involved in the work of globalization. It also brings with it an enormous research agenda, one that goes beyond the by now familiar focus on cross-border flows of goods, capital, and information.[3]

Finally, my detailed examination of three particular cities in that early work brought to the fore the extent to which these cities collaborate through their very specific advantages rather than simply competing with each other. In focusing on global finance it became clear that the growth of the major centers was partly derived from the growing network of financial centers. In looking at the broader network it also became clear to what extent it was and remains characterized by a pronounced hierarchy among this growing number of centers that constitute it.

In my reading of the Scott *et al.* chapter, I see some of these same hypotheses operating, even though not specifically formulated. But there are clearly also differences and unclear overlaps. In the two final sections I want to develop two particular issues that illustrate in a specific fashion some of the overlaps and differences in the two constructs.

NEW FORMS OF CENTRALITY

Several of the organizing hypotheses in the global-city model concern the conditions for the continuity of centrality in advanced economic systems in the face of major new organizational forms and technologies that maximize the possibility for geographic dispersal. Historically centrality has largely been embedded in the central city. Have the new technologies and organizational forms altered the spatial correlates of centrality?

My argument is that today there is no longer a simple straightforward relation between centrality and such geographic entities as the downtown, or the central business district. In the past, and up to quite recently in fact, the center was synonymous with the downtown or the CBD. The spatial correlate of the center can assume several geographic forms. It can be the CBD, as it still is largely in New York City, or it can extend into a metropolitan area in the form of a grid of nodes of intense business activity, as we see in Frankfurt and Zurich (Hitz *et al.* 1995). The center has been profoundly altered by telecommunications and the growth of a global economy, both inextricably linked; they have contributed to a new geography of centrality (and marginality). Simplifying, I identify four forms assumed by centrality today (Sassen 2000*b*: chapter 4).

First, while centrality can assume multiple spatial correlates, the CBD in major international business centers remains a strategic site for the leading industries. But it is one profoundly reconfigured by technological and economic change (Graham and Marvin 1996, Burgel and Burgel 1996, Péraldi and Perrin 1996). Further, there are often sharp differences in the patterns assumed by this reconfiguring of the central city in different parts of the world, notably the United States and Western Europe (Veltz 1996, Kunzmann 1994, Sassen 2000*b*, Hitz *et al.* 1995).[4]

Second, the center can extend into a metropolitan area in the form of a grid of nodes of intense business activity. One might ask whether a spatial organization characterized by dense strategic nodes spread over a broader region does in fact constitute a new form of organizing the territory of the "center," rather than, as in the more conventional view, an instance of suburbanization or geographic dispersal. Insofar as these various nodes are articulated through digital networks, they represent a new geographic correlate of the most advanced type of "center." This is a partly deterritorialized space of centrality. Indeed much of the actual geographic territory within which these nodes exist is part of an older social geography—the suburb or the metropolitan region—which is not part of the new grid of digital networks, and is in that sense partly peripheralized.[5]

This regional grid of nodes represents, in my analysis, a reconstitution of the concept of region. Far from neutralizing geography, the regional grid is likely to be embedded in conventional forms of communication infrastructure, notably rapid rail and highways connecting to airports. Ironically perhaps, conventional infrastructure is likely to maximize the economic benefits derived from telematics. I think this is an important issue that has been lost somewhat in discussions about the neutralization of geography through telematics.

It is this second form of centrality which intersects most clearly with the global city-region. In my reading, this space of centrality is distinct from the more encompassing construct of the global city-region, which is a fundamentally territorial space.

Third, we are seeing the formation of a transterritorial "center" constituted, partly in digital space, via intense economic transactions in the network of global cities. These networks of major international business centers constitute new geographies of centrality. The most powerful of these new geographies of centrality at the global level bind the major international financial and business centers: New York, London, Tokyo, Paris, Frankfurt, Zurich, Amsterdam, Los Angeles, Sydney, Hong Kong, among others. But this geography now also includes cities such as Bangkok, Seoul, Taipei, São Paulo, Mexico City. The intensity of transactions among these cities, particularly through the financial markets, trade in services, and investment, has increased sharply, and by orders of magnitude. At the same time, there has been a sharpening inequality in the concentration of strategic resources and activities among these cities compared to others in their same countries, a condition that further underlines the extent to which this is a cross-border space of centrality.[6]

In the case of a complex landscape such as Europe's we see in fact several geographies of centrality, one global, others continental and regional. A central urban hierarchy connects major cities—Paris, London, Frankfurt, Amsterdam, Zurich—many of which in turn play central roles in the wider global system of cities. These cities are also part of a wider network of European financial/cultural/service capitals, some with only one, others with several, of these functions, which articulate the European region and are somewhat less oriented to the global economy than Paris, Frankfurt, or London. And then there are several geographies of marginality: the East–West divide and the North–South divide across Europe, as well as newer divisions. In Eastern Europe, certain cities and regions, notably Budapest, are rather attractive for purposes of investment, both European and non-European, while others will increasingly fall behind, notably in Rumania, Yugoslavia, and Albania. We see a similar differentiation in the south of Europe: Madrid, Barcelona, and Milan are gaining in the new European hierarchy; Naples, Rome, and Marseilles are not.

Fourth, new forms of centrality are being constituted in electronically generated spaces. For instance, strategic components of the financial industry operate in such spaces. The relation between digital and actual space is complex and varies among different types of economic sectors. But it is increasingly becoming evident that the highly complex configurations for economic activity located in digital space contain points of coordination and centralization. I return to some of these issues in the next and final section of the chapter.

IN THE DIGITAL ERA: MORE CONCENTRATION THAN DISPERSAL?

What really stands out in the evidence on the spatial organization of the global financial industry is the extent to which there is a sharp concentration of the shares of many financial markets in a few financial centers.[7] London, New York, and Tokyo (notwithstanding a national economic recession) regularly appear at the top *and* represent a large share of global transactions. London, followed by Tokyo, New York, Hong Kong, and Frankfurt account for a major share of all international banking. London, Frankfurt, and New York account for an enormous world share in the export of financial services. London, New York, and Tokyo account for over one third of global institutional equity holdings—this as of the end of 1998 after sharp declines in Tokyo's value compared to 1996. At the end of 1998, twenty-five cities accounted for 83 percent of the world's equities under institutional management. These twenty-five cities also accounted for roughly 48 percent of the total market capitalization of the world, which stood at US$20.9 trillion in early 1999. London, New York, and Tokyo account for 58 percent of the foreign exchange market, one of the few truly global markets; together with Singapore, Hong Kong, Zurich, Geneva, Frankfurt and Paris, they account for 85 percent in this, the most global of markets.

This trend towards consolidation in a few centers also is evident within countries. In the United States, for instance, all the leading investment banks are concentrated in New York, with only one other major international financial center in this enormous country, Chicago. Sydney and Toronto have equally gained power in their continental-sized countries and have taken over functions and market share from what were once the major commercial centers, Melbourne and Montreal respectively. Similarly with São Paulo and Bombay, which have gained share and functions respectively from Rio de Janeiro in Brazil and New Delhi and Calcutta in India. These are all enormous countries and one might have thought that they could sustain multiple major financial centers. In France, Paris today concentrates larger shares of most financial sectors than it did ten years ago and once important stock markets such as Lyon have become "provincial," even though Lyon is today the hub of a thriving economic region. Milan privatized its exchange in September 1997 and electronically merged Italy's ten regional markets. Frankfurt now concentrates a larger share of the financial market in Germany than it did in the early 1980s, and so does Zurich for Switzerland, which once had Basel and Geneva as very significant competitors of sorts. This story can be repeated for many countries. What stands out is that this pattern towards the consolidation of one leading financial center is a function of rapid growth in the sector, not of decay in the losing cities.

We are seeing, then, both consolidation in fewer major centers across and within countries *and* a sharp growth in the numbers of centers that become part of the global network as countries deregulate their economies. São Paulo and Bombay, for instance, joined the global financial network so to speak after Brazil and India deregulated their financial systems, at least partly. This mode of incorporation into the global network is often at the cost of losing functions that they had when they were largely national centers, functions now superseded by the entry into their urban landscape of leading, typically foreign, financial, accounting, and legal services firms to handle the new cross-border operations. The incorporation typically happens without a gain in the share of the global market that they can command even though they add to the total volume in the global market and even though capitalization in their national market can rise sharply.

Why is it that at a time of rapid growth in the network of financial centers, in overall volumes, and in electronic networks, we have such high concentration of market shares in the leading centers? Both globalization and electronic trading are about expansion and dispersal beyond what had been the confined realm of national economies and floor trading, so to speak. Indeed, given globalization and electronic trading one might well ask why financial centers matter at all.

The continuing weight of major centers is, in a way, countersensical. The rapid development of electronic exchanges, the growing digitalization of much financial activity, the fact that finance has become one of the leading sectors in a growing number of countries, and that it is a sector that produces a dematerialized, hypermobile product, all suggest that location should not matter. In fact geographic dispersal would seem to be a good option given the high cost of operating in major financial centers. Further, the last ten years have seen an increased geographic mobility of financial experts and financial services firms.

There has been, indeed, geographic decentralization of certain types of financial activities, aimed at securing business in the growing number of countries becoming integrated into the global economy. Many of the leading investment banks have operations in more countries than they had twenty years ago. The same can be said for the leading accounting and legal services and other specialized corporate services. This is true also for some markets: for example, in the 1980s all basic wholesale foreign exchange operations were in London. Today these are distributed among London and several other centers (even though their number is far smaller than the number of countries whose currency is being traded). But these trends do not undermine the patterns of ongoing concentration described above.

There are, in my view, at least three reasons that explain the trend towards consolidation in a few centers rather than massive dispersal.

The Importance of Social Connectivity and Central Functions

First, while the new telecommunications technologies do indeed facilitate geographic dispersal of economic activities without losing system integration, they have also had the effect of strengthening the importance of central coordination and control functions for firms and for markets.[8] Major centers have massive concentrations of state of the art resources that allow them to maximize the benefits of telecommunications and to govern the new conditions for operating globally. Even electronic markets such as NASDAQ and E*Trade rely on traders and banks that are located somewhere, typically in a major financial center.

To maximize the benefits of the new information technologies you need not only the infrastructure but a complex mix of other resources. Most of the value added that these technologies can produce for advanced service firms lies in the externalities. And this means the material and human resources—state of the art office buildings, top talent, and the social networking infrastructure that maximizes connectivity.

Social connectivity has a dimension in the production of "information" as well. There are two types of information that matter to these operations. One is the datum, which may be complex but comes in the form of standardized information easily available to these firms: e.g. the details of a privatization in a particular country. The second type of information is far more difficult to obtain because it is not standardized. It requires interpretation/evaluation/judgment. It entails negotiating a series of datums and a series of interpretations of a mix of datums in the hope of producing a higher order type of information. Access to the first kind of information is now global and immediate thanks to the digital revolution. But it is the second type of information that requires a complicated mixture of elements, not only technical but also social—what we could think of as the social infrastructure for global connectivity. It is this type of social infrastructure that gives major financial centers a strategic role.

In principle, the technical infrastructure for connectivity can be reproduced anywhere. Singapore, for example, has technical connectivity matching Hong Kong's. But does it have Hong Kong's social connectivity? We could probably pose the same rhetorical question for Frankfurt and London. When the more complex forms of information needed to execute major international deals cannot be gotten from existing databases, no matter what one can pay, then one needs the social information loop and the associated de facto interpretations and inferences that come with exchanging and analyzing information among talented, informed people.[9] The process of making inferences/interpretations into "information" takes quite a mix of talents and resources.[10]

In brief, financial centers provide the expertise and the social connectivity that allows a firm or market to maximize the benefits of its technological connectivity.

Cross-border Networks

Second, the global financial system has reached levels of complexity that require the existence of a cross-border network of financial centers to service the operations of global capital. But this network of financial centers will increasingly differ from earlier versions of the "international financial system." In a world of largely closed national financial systems, each country duplicated most of the necessary functions for its economy; collaborations among different national financial markets were often no more than the execution of a given set of operations in each of the countries involved, as in clearing and settlement. With few exceptions, such as the off-shore markets and some of the large banks, the international system consisted of a string of closed domestic systems. The global integration of markets pushes towards the elimination of various redundant systems and makes collaboration a far more complex matter, one that has the perhaps ironic effect of raising the importance of leading financial centers.

This has brought with it a new kind of "merger," one that connects financial markets across borders. The two most important forms are the consolidation of electronic networks that connect a very select number of markets and the formation of strategic alliances among financial markets. The Chicago BOT is loosely linked to Frankfurt's futures exchange, DTB; and the Chicago Mercantile Exchange to Paris MATIF. The NYSE is considering linking up with exchanges in Canada and Latin America and has opened talks with the Paris Bourse. The National Association of Securities Dealers acquired the American Stock Exchange in June 1998. This has set off other combinations. NASDAQ's parent is having similar talks with Frankfurt and London. Perhaps most spectacular was the linkup between the London Stock Exchange and Frankfurt's Deutsche Borse in the summer of 1998, with the goal of attracting the top three hundred shares from all over Europe—a blue-chip European exchange. Paris reacted by proposing that some of the other major European exchanges should create an alternative alliance. This alliance has recently been instituted among Paris, Amsterdam, and Brussels.

The implication of these cross-border networks is that these various centers do not just compete with each other: there is collaboration and division of labor. In the international system of the postwar decades, each country's financial center, in principle, covered the universe of necessary functions to service its national companies and markets. The world of finance was, of course, much simpler than it is today. In the initial stages of deregulation in the 1980s there was a strong tendency to see the relation among the major centers as one of straight competition among New York, London, and Tokyo, the heavyweights in the system. But in my research on these three centers I found clear evidence of a division of labor already in the late 1980s (Sassen 2000*a*). What we are seeing now is yet a new pattern, where this cooperation or division of functions is somewhat institutionalized: strategic alliances not only between firms across borders but also between markets. There is competition, strategic collaboration, and hierarchy.

Denationalized Elites and Agendas

Third, national attachments and identities are becoming weaker for these global players and their customers. Thus the major U.S. and European investment banks have set up specialized offices in London to handle various aspects of their global business. Even French banks have set up some of their global specialized operations in London, inconceivable even a few years ago and still not avowed in national rhetoric.

Deregulation and privatization have weakened the need for large financial centers to remain purely national. The nationality question simply plays differently in these sectors than it did even a decade ago. Global financial products are accessible in national markets and national investors can operate in global markets. It is interesting to see that investment banks used to split up their analysts team by country to cover a national market; now they are more likely to do it by industrial sector (see, for example *Latin American Finance*, various issues).

In my *Losing Control?* I described this process as the incipient denationalization of certain institutional arenas. I think such denationalization is a necessary condition for economic globalization as we know it today. The sophistication of this system lies in the fact that it only needs to involve strategic institutional areas—most national systems can be left basically unaltered. Japanese firms operating overseas adopted international accounting standards long before Japan's government considered requiring them. In this regard the wholesale side of globalization is quite different from the global consumer markets, in which success necessitates altering national tastes at a mass level.

Major international business centers produce what we could think of as a new subculture. The long-standing resistance in Europe to M&As, especially hostile takeovers, or to foreign ownership and control in East Asia, signal national business cultures that are somewhat incompatible with the new global economic ethos. I would posit that major cities contribute to denationalizing corporate elites. Whether this is good or bad is a separate issue; but it is, I believe, one of the conditions for setting in place the systems and subcultures necessary for a global economic system.

CONCLUSION

Globalization has brought with it a change in the scales at which strategic economic and political processes territorialize. Global cities and global city-regions have emerged as major new scales in this dynamic of territorialization. As categories, they share key propositions about economic globalization but overlap only partly in the features they each capture. This chapter began the task of elaborating a comparison.

Economic globalization and telecommunications have contributed to produce new spatialities for the urban that pivot on cross-border networks and territorial locations with massive concentrations of resources. In the case of cities, this is not a completely new feature. Over the centuries cities have been at the crossroads of major, often worldwide, processes. What is different today is the intensity, complexity, and global span of these networks, the extent to which significant portions of economies are now dematerialized and digitized and hence the extent to which they can travel at great speeds through some of these networks, and the numbers of cities that are part of cross-border networks operating at vast geographic scales.

The new urban spatiality thus produced is partial in a double sense: it accounts for only part of what happens in cities and what cities are about, and it inhabits only part of what we might think of as the space of the city, whether this be understood in terms as diverse as those of a city's administrative boundaries or in the sense of a city's public imaginary. Even though partial, this new urban spatiality is today strategic.

NOTES

1. Originally attributed to Goethe, the term was relaunched in the work of Sir Peter Hall (1966) and more recently respecified by John Friedmann (Friedmann and Wolff 1982). See also Stren (1996) and Friedmann (1995).
2. Here Arrighi's analysis is of interest in that it posits the recurrence of certain organizational patterns in different phases of the capitalist world economy, but at higher orders of complexity and expanded scope, and timed to follow or precede particular configurations of the world economy. (Arrighi and Silver 1999).
3. Further, by emphasizing the fact that global processes are at least partly embedded in national territories, such a focus (e.g. Taylor 2000, Brenner 1998, Sassen 1996) introduces new variables in current conceptions about economic globalization and the shrinking regulatory role of the state (see generally Olds *et al.* 1999). That is to say, the space economy for major new transnational economic processes diverges in significant ways from the duality global/national presupposed in much analysis of the global economy. The duality national versus global suggests two mutually exclusive spaces—where one begins the other ends. One of the outcomes of a global-city analysis is that it makes evident that the global materializes by necessity in specific places and institutional arrangements, a good number of which, if not most, are located in national territories and ensconced in national legal frameworks.
4. In the United States, major cities such as New York and Chicago have large centers that have been rebuilt many times, given the brutal neglect suffered by much urban infrastructure and the imposed obsolescence so characteristic of U.S. cities. This neglect and accelerated obsolescence produce vast spaces for rebuilding the center according to the requirements of whatever regime of urban accumulation or pattern of spatial organization of the urban economy prevails at a given time. In Europe, urban centers are far more protected and they rarely contain significant stretches of abandoned space; the expansion of workplaces and the need for intelligent buildings necessarily will have to take place partly outside the old centers. One of the most extreme cases is the complex of La Defense, the massive state of the art office complex developed right outside Paris to avoid harming the built environment inside the city. This is an explicit instance of government policy and planning aimed at addressing the growing demand for central office space of prime quality. Yet another variant of this expansion of the "center" onto hitherto peripheral land can be seen in London's Docklands. Similar projects for recentralizing peripheral areas were launched in several major cities in Europe, North America, and Japan during the 1980s.
5. Pierre Veltz's (1996) work is an important contribution to this analysis. See also Mozère, Péraldi, and Rey (1999) and Castells (1996).
6. The pronounced orientation to the world markets evident in such cities raises questions about their articulation with their nation-states, their regions, and the larger economic and social structure (see, e.g. Brotchie *et al.* 1995). Cities have typically been deeply embedded in the economies of their region, indeed often reflecting the

characteristics of the latter; which is still true. But cities that are strategic sites in the global economy tend, in part, to disconnect from their region. This conflicts with a key proposition in traditional scholarship about urban systems, namely, that these systems promote the territorial integration of regional and national economies.

7. See Sassen 2000*b*: chapter 3 for a more detailed presentation of data and sources on the subject covered in this section. Among the main sources are the International Bank for Settlements (Basle); IMF national accounts data; specialized trade publications such as the *Wall Street Journal*'s *WorldScope*, MorganStanley *Capital International; The Banker*; data listings in the *Financial Times* and in *The Economist*; and, expecially for a focus on cities, the data produced by Technimetrics, Inc.
8. A growing number of financial markets have "owners" now and are run by something akin to firms, and hence are also subject to central management functions.
9. It is the importance of this input that has given a whole new importance to credit rating agencies, for instance. Part of the rating has to do with interpreting and inferring. When this interpreting becomes "authoritative" it becomes "information" available to all.
10. Risk management, for example, which has become increasingly important with globalization due to the growing complexity and uncertainty that comes with operating in multiple countries and markets, requires enormous fine tuning of central operations. We now know that many, if not most, major trading losses over the last decade have involved human error or fraud. The quality of risk management will depend heavily on the top people in a firm rather than simply on technical conditions, such as electronic surveillance. Consolidating risk management operations in one site, usually a central one for the firm, is now seen generally as more effective. This has been the decision made by several major banks: Chase and Morgan Stanley Dean Witter in the United States, Deutsche Bank and Credit Suisse in Europe.

REFERENCES

Abu-Lughod, J. L. (1989). *Before European Hegemony: The World System A.D. 1250–1350.* Oxford: Oxford University Press.

—— (1999). *New York, Los Angeles, Chicago: America's Global Cities.* Minn.: University of Minnesota Press.

Arrighi, G. and B. Silver. (1999). "Part IV. Scholarly Controversy: Chaos and Governance," in D. E. Davis (ed.), *Political Power and Social Theory*, vol. 13. Stamford, CT: JAI Press, 239–315.

Braudel, F. (1984). *The Perspective of the World*, vol. 3. London: Collins.

Brenner, N. (1998). "Global Cities, Glocal States: Global City Formation and State Territorial Restructuring in Contemporary Europe." *Review of International Political Economy*, 5: 1–37.

Brotchie, J., Barry, M., Blakely, E., Hall, P., and Newton, P. (eds.). (1995). *Cities in Competition: Productive and Sustainable Cities for the 21st Century.* Melbourne: Longman Australia.

Burgel, G., and Burgel, G. (1996). "Global Trends and City Politics: Friends or Foes of Urban Development?" in M. A. Cohen, B. A. Ruble, J. S. Tulchin, and A. M. Garland (eds.), *Preparing for the Urban Future: Global Pressures and Local Forces.* Washington, DC: Woodrow Wilson Center Press, 301–35.

Castells, M. (1989). *The Informational City.* London: Blackwell.

—— (1996). *The Networked Society.* Oxford: Blackwell.

Friedmann, J. (1995). "Where We Stand: A Decade of World City Research," in P. L. Knox and P. J. Taylor (eds.), *World Cities in a World System.* Cambridge: Cambridge University Press, 21–47.

——, and Wolff, G. (1982). "World City Formation: An Agenda for Research and Action." *International Journal of Urban and Regional Research*, 6: 309–44.

Graham, S., and Marvin, S. (1996). *Telecommunications and the City: Electronic Spaces, Urban Places.* London: Routledge.

Hall, Sir P. (1966). *The World Cities.* New York: McGraw Hill.

Hitz, Keil, Lehrer, Ronneberger, Schmid, Wolff (eds.). (1995). *Capitales Fatales.* Zurich: Rotpunkt Verlag. (Note: The editors are listed in this work without first names or initials.)

King, A. D. (1990). *Urbanism, Colonialism, and the World Economy: Culture and Spatial Foundations of the World Urban System.* The International Library of Sociology. London and New York: Routledge.

Kunzmann, K. R. (1994). "Berlin im Zentrum europäischer Stadtnetze," in W. Süss (ed.), *Hauptstadt Berlin. Band 1: Nationale Hauptstadt Europäische Metropole.* Berlin: Berlin Verlag, 233–46.

Mozère, L., Péraldi, M., and Rey, H. (eds.). (1999). *Intelligence des Banlieues.* La Tour d'Aigues: Editiones de l'Aube.

Olds, K., Dicken, P., Kelly, P. F., Kong, L., and Yeung, H. W.-C. (eds.). (1999). *Globalization and the Asian Pacific: Contested Territories.* London: Routledge.

Péraldi, M., and Perrin, E. (eds.). (1996). *Réseaux Productifs et Territoires Urbains.* Toulouse: Presses Universitaires du Mirail.

Sassen, S. (1996). *Losing Control? Sovereignty in an Age of Globalization.* The 1995 Columbia University Leonard Hastings Schoff Memorial Lectures. New York: Columbia University Press.

—— (2000*a*). *The Global City: New York, London, Tokyo.* Princeton: Princeton University Press. (Revised edition; originally published 1991.)

—— (2000*b*). *Cities in a World Economy.* Thousand Oaks, California: Pine Forge/Sage Press. (Revised edition; originally published 1994.)

—— (2000*c*). *Cities and their Cross-Border Networks.* Tokyo: United Nations University Press.

Scott, A. J. (1998). *Regions and the World Economy: The Coming Shape of Global Production, Competition, and Political Order.* Oxford: Oxford University Press.

——, Agnew, J., Soja, E. W., and Storper, M. (2000). "Global City-Regions." Chapter 1, this volume.

Shachar, A. (1990). "The Global Economy and World Cities," in A. Shachar and S. Oberg (eds.), *The World Economy and the Spatial Organization of Power.* Aldershot: Avebury, 149–60.

Short, J. R., and Kim, Y. (1999). *Globalization and the City.* Essex: Longman.

Storper, M. (1997). *The Regional World: Territorial Development in a Global Economy.* New York: Guilford Press.

Stren, R. (1996). "The Studies of Cities: Popular Perceptions, Academic Disciplines, and Emerging Agendas." in M. A. Cohen, B. A. Ruble, J. S. Tulchin, and A. M. Garland (eds.), *Preparing for the Urban Future: Global Pressures and Local Forces.* Washington, DC: Woodrow Wilson Center Press, 392–420.

Taylor, P. J. (2000). "World Cities and Territorial States under Conditions of Contemporary Globalization." The 1999 Annual Political Geography Lecture. *Political Geography*, 19: 5–32.

Veltz, P. (1996). *Mondialisation Villes et Territoires: L'Economie d'Archipel.* Paris: Presses Universitaires de France.

7

The Economic Role and Spatial Contradictions of Global City-Regions: The Functional, Cognitive, and Evolutionary Context

ROBERTO CAMAGNI

This chapter is concerned with the nature and the role of global city-regions seen in a theoretical perspective, and with the contradictions of their current evolutionary trends relating to their spatial layout. In our investigation of the role of global cities, we have also dealt with the cognitive dimension. This is a dimension not normally included in the geographical approach (which is mainly of a functional character), but being increasingly emphasized in nonconventional economic approaches. It allows us to link the economic role of spaces to the new logic governing decision-making processes under conditions of dynamic uncertainty. It also makes it possible to take fully into account the strong multiplier effects at work in large global cities, led by the new international information-intensive functions, considering not only the traditional agglomeration advantages and increasing returns, but also the place/node interaction and the symbolic roles of such cities.

These processes, however, are giving rise to contradictions in the physical form of global cities, whose settlement patterns, largely unconstrained by planning regulations (which are particularly weak at the city-region scale for institutional and political reasons), tend to evolve in response to a series of short-term and fragmented decisions made by uncoordinated agents. Powerful forces of "urban overload" and "crowding-out" caused by increases in land rent push residential and economic activities outside the boundaries of the densely populated city core, generating long-term negative feedback effects on mobility patterns and the environment of the whole city-region.

In order to cope with these contradictions, it is necessary for a new alliance to be forged between market forces and planning (and between their respective supporters in the research sphere), in order to counteract the worrying trend towards divergence which has emerged in recent international debate. This chapter is organized in three sections, each of which explores a specific context:

1. *The functional context.* Examining some evidence regarding globalization and its effects on large cities, it is claimed that such cities do in fact find themselves in direct competition with each other;
2. *The cognitive context.* Looking at global cities as functional and symbolic entities, a classification of the economic role of big cities is presented, based on both a spatial and a cognitive logic;
3. *The evolutionary context.* Considering the metropolitan settlement pattern, an attempt is made to identify the social costs of a sprawling metropolis, taking the Milan metropolitan area as a case study in order to investigate the mobility costs associated with different typologies of urban expansion (infilling, extension, linear development, sprawl, and large concentrated projects).

THE FUNCTIONAL CONTEXT: GLOBALIZATION AND THE COMPETITION BETWEEN CITIES

Globalization, understood as the growing planetary interdependence of societies and territories, is a process that has been taking place for many decades. It is therefore not surprising that some, taking a structural perspective, claim that it is nothing new, while at the other extreme others say that it represents a clear-cut revolution in our conceptual and operational framework.

However, if we consider that common representations and symbolic codes do not evolve in a parallel, incremental fashion, but tend to emerge abruptly, and that these representations are powerful determinants of the behavior of numerous economic agents interlinked by mutually dependent decision-making, imitation, and cumulative reactions, then we are obliged to take globalization seriously as a new point of reference for the interpretation of economic and urban phenomena.

Globalization is increasing the competitive pressure on firms, and hence on cities and regions, through many different channels: international trade (and we refer here to the "internationalization" process), foreign direct investment ("multinationalization"), financial integration, and the "globalization" of information, knowhow, and technologies (Gordon 1994). In this connection, I will limit myself to just three statistics as an illustration:

1. international trade has grown over the last thirty years at a rate that is the double the world's GDP (Figure 7.1);
2. international foreign direct investments over the past twenty-five years have grown at four times the rate of world GDP (OECD 1992, UNCTAD 1998) (see Tables 7.1 and 7.2);
3. foreign direct investment (FDI) increasingly involves the tertiary sector, which has a strong urban and metropolitan bias. These sectors currently represent more than 60 percent of the stock of outward FDI in countries such as Japan, Germany, and Italy, and more than 50 percent in countries like the United States and France (OECD 1999) (Table 7.3).

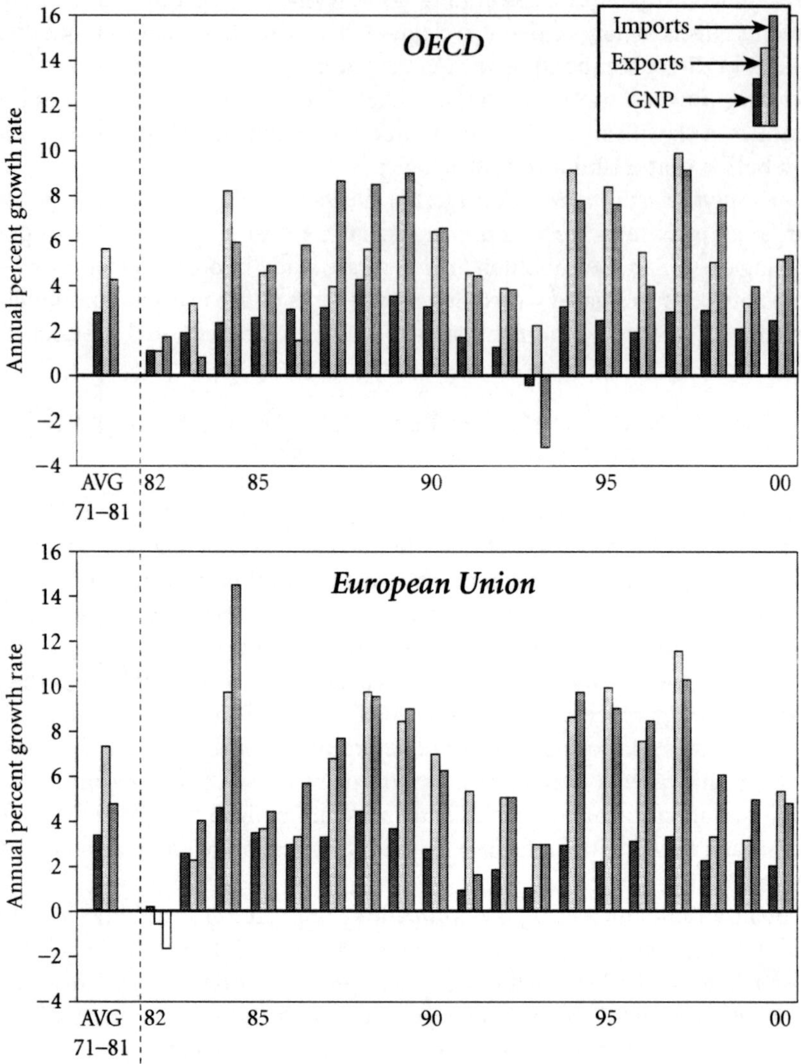

Figure 7.1. *Growth rates of GNP, exports and imports*
Source: OECD 1999

It is easy, therefore, to imagine that cities, and large cities in particular, compete with each other to attract these huge flows of resources. This conclusion was recently challenged by an authoritative economist, Paul Krugman, on two, logically different, grounds. First, it was argued that only companies but not territories compete with each other; secondly, that whenever local authorities try to intervene in affecting the competitive advantage of their territories, they end up with

Table 7.1. *Inward foreign direct investments by country*

	1985–90[a]	1991	1992	1993	1994	1995	1996	1997[b]
Millions of dollars								
World	159,331	158,936	175,841	217,559	242,999	331,189	337,550	400,486
Developed countries	129,583	114,792	120,294	138,887	141,503	211,465	195,393	233,115
of which, EU countries	63,186	78,777	83,793	80,935	71,580	116,792	92,398	108,172
Developing countries	29,090	41,696	51,108	72,528	95,582	105,511	129,813	148,944
Share on world's FDI inflows (%)								
World	100	100	100	100	100	100	100	100
Developed countries	81	72	68	64	58	64	58	58
of which, EU countries	40	50	48	37	29	35	27	27
Developing countries	18	26	29	33	39	32	38	37
Annual growth rate (%)								
World			11	24	12	36	2	19
Developed countries			5	15	2	49	−8	19
of which, EU countries			6	−3	−12	63	−21	17
Developing countries			23	42	32	10	23	15
Inward FDI stock as a percentage of GDP								
	1980	1985	1990	1995	1996			
World	4.6	6.4	8.3	10.1	10.6			
Developed countries	4.8	6	8.3	9.1	7.6			
of which, EU countries	5.5	8.2	10.8	13.2	13			
Developing countries	4.3	8.1	8.7	15.4	15.6			

Notes:
[a] annual average
[b] estimates

Source: UNCTAD 1998.

Table 7.2. *Outward foreign direct investments by country*

	1985–90[a]	1991	1992	1993	1994	1995	1996	1997[b]
Millions of dollars								
World	180,510	198,143	200,800	240,900	284,261	352,514	333,629	423,666
Developed countries	169,155	189,782	179,984	205,810	241,481	306,465	283,476	359,236
of which, EU countries	93,652	106,362	109,157	97,410	120,595	159,234	150,927	179,801
Developing countries	11,331	8,324	20,714	34,929	42,512	45,642	49,161	61,138
Share on world's FDI outflows (%)								
World	100	100	100	100	100	100	100	100
Developed countries	94	96	90	85	85	87	85	85
of which, EU countries	52	54	54	40	42	45	45	42
Developing countries	6	4	10	14	15	13	15	14
Annual growth rate (%)								
World			1	20	18	24	–5	27
Developed countries			–5	14	17	27	–8	27
of which, EU countries			3	–11	24	32	–5	19
Developing countries			149	69	22	7	8	24
Outward FDI stock as a percentage of GDP								
	1980	1985	1990	1995	1996			
World	4.9	5.9	8.1	9.9	10.8			
Developed countries	6.5	7.5	9.8	11.5	10.1			
of which, EU countries	6.3	10.4	11.8	14.6	16.8			
Developing countries	0.5	1	1.8	4.5	4.9			

Notes:
[a] annual average
[b] estimates

Source: UNCTAD 1998.

Table 7.3. *Stock of foreign direct investments: shares by sector 1986–96*

Country	Sector	Inward		Outward	
		1986	1996	1986	1996
USA	Manufacturing	0.33	0.41	0.40	0.35
	Services	0.51	0.50	0.35	0.54
UK	Manufacturing	0.35	0.32	0.36	0.44
	Services	0.32	0.54	0.40	0.47
France	Manufacturing	0.38[a]	0.38	0.50[b]	0.36
	Services	0.55[a]	0.58	0.46[b]	0.57
Germany	Manufacturing	0.48	0.20	0.61	0.30
	Services	0.52	0.79	0.31	0.68
Italy	Manufacturing	0.61	0.48	0.29	0.30
	Services	0.36	0.77	0.58	0.64
Japan	Manufacturing	0.70	0.55[c]	0.26	0.28[c]
	Services	0.30	0.45[c]	0.55	0.66[c]

Notes:
[a] Data referred to 1989.
[b] Data referred to 1987.
[c] Data referred to 1994.
Source: OECD 1999.

a sort of neomercantilism, detrimental to the fair allocation of resources which should be based on objective elements, neutrally evaluated by the market (Krugman 1996).

I can see four arguments that contradict this vision:

1. Firms use locations as competitive tools, and increasingly use global mobility to optimize production and distribution costs. Location territories, on the other hand, are not just the passive objects of location decisions by firms, but communities made up of economic subjects who act in their own interest by trying to keep or attract firms. Workers, subcontracting firms, suppliers of intermediate inputs, services, and factors, are all agents that can achieve their goal not just by competing on prices and wages with other communities (sites), but also by upgrading the quality of their service through direct or indirect tools which involve the community and the local public administration. Locations are in a sense bought and sold on a global market, where demand and supply confront each other.

2. Firms more and more rely on externalities, in the form of public goods, supplied by the local public administration. The endowment of human capital and social overhead capital, which are usually cited in international economics textbooks as sources of the comparative advantage of nations and regions, refer precisely to the action of these territories and their governments (though in a short-term formalized model they may be treated as exogenously given).

3. More and more local firms require selected external assets and "specific resources" that cannot be easily obtained via spontaneous market developments. Therefore firms are increasingly engaged in a cooperative process with other local firms, (collective) actors, and the public administration for the conception and provision of these resources. A good way of depicting this process is through the concept of local "milieus," based on the interactions or "untraded interdependencies" (using Michael Storper's expression) that occur within the local territory and enhance its competitiveness and innovative capability. These effects are in part spontaneously generated, representing an important basis for the increasing of local returns often advocated by Krugman, and in part dependent upon specific and explicit cooperation among local actors, requiring some form of local governance. In both cases, the competitive weapons reside more outside the single firms than inside them, i.e. more in the local milieu than in a specific firm located in its geographical space.

4. Local territories and milieus compete and cooperate with each other, building their own comparative or competitive advantages. This is good for the entire economy if we hold the view of a "generative" development process taking place from below, rather than a process quantitatively defined at the macroeconomic level and then attributed in a "competitive" way to each territory (only in this last case would the efforts developed by the single territories result in a zero-sum game in relation to the competitive distribution of a predefined payoff). Cities, given their nature of clusters of public goods and externalities, enhancers of interaction and local synergy, and given also the political accountability and representation of their elected administration, may be considered competing actors on the global scene.

Territories have therefore become important economic operators, performing the crucial tasks of enhancing the static and dynamic efficiency of local firms, as will be shown in greater depth in the following section.

THE COGNITIVE CONTEXT: GLOBAL CITIES AS FUNCTIONAL AND SYMBOLIC ENTITIES

The main aim of this chapter is to examine the relationship between the economic function, size, and spatial form of global city-regions. A wider and deeper interpretation of their role may in fact help to understand the links between absolute size, cumulative or multiplier effects that go far beyond those usually encountered in regional economics, and the urgency of taking into consideration the potential negative effects on their internal efficiency deriving from their size and spatial form.

A new understanding of the role of global city-regions may be reached integrating two logical dimensions (Figure 7.2):

1. A *spatial logic*, distinguishing two theoretical approaches: the *territorial approach*, interpreting the city as a "place" in a two dimensional space, and

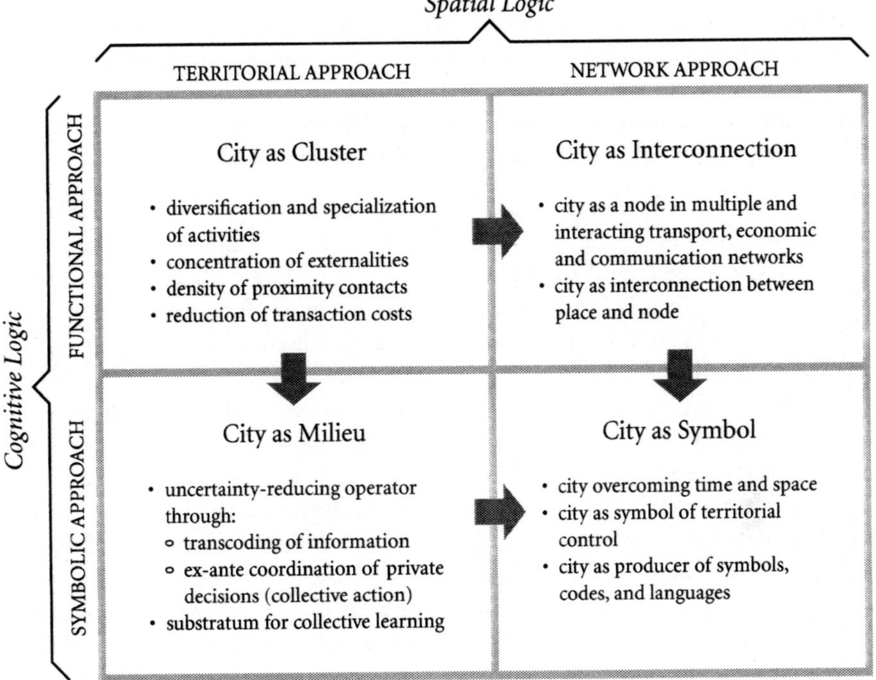

Figure 7.2. *The roles of global cities: a theoretical taxonomy*

the *network approach*, interpreting the city as a node in a global network of transterritorial relationships.

2. A *cognitive logic*, referring to the various forms of rationality involved in the behavior of economic agents (following Herbert Simon's well-known distinction [Simon 1972]): a "substantive" rationality, implying a *functional approach*, involving optimization among perfectly known alternatives; and a "procedural" rationality, implying a *symbolic approach*, typical of a condition of imperfect information and widespread uncertainty about alternatives, about the moves of other actors, and the possible outcomes of present decisions. In this latter condition, decisions are tied to established routines, imitation processes, interchange of opinions and "feelings," ex-ante coordination among actors, as well as shared representations, codes, and symbols.

Combining the two dimensions, we end up with a double-entry picture, encompassing a meaningful taxonomy of roles of the global city.

A. According to the first typology, which derives from a functional/territorial logic, cities are *clusters* of activities generating a host of synergetic effects (called agglomeration or urbanization economies) which cumulatively enlarge the overall size of the agglomeration. The main increasing returns stem from a number of different effects:

- the wide diversification of urban activities, and the specialization of single economic units;
- the concentration of public goods and social overhead capital, which create a huge concentration of positive externalities;
- the density of contacts, thanks to geographical proximity;
- the reduction in transaction costs, also due to proximity.

All these effects are well known and have long been recognized in the literature on urban development and innovation diffusion. In a dynamic setting, they imply and generate strong local multiplier effects, à la Keynes or Leontief, stemming from input–output relationships or interactions between export-oriented and residential activities, and from cumulative processes à la Myrdal, Kaldor, Krugman, via the increasing efficiency of an expanding local economy.

B. The second typology, emerging from the functional/network logic, considers the city as a *node* and *interconnection* in long-distance networks. Strong synergetic processes originate whenever the city acts as a node in multiple planetary networks, including transport and communication networks, but also the nonmaterial networks centered around specialized activities, professional relationships, power relationships, and headquarters functions. Even more important, multiplier effects and increasing returns stem from the interdependence between the size of the city and its nodal role; this is due to critical mass effects in generating *demand* for external connectivity and to the effects of *supply* of external connectivity on the competitiveness of local activities.

C. But, as shown in the lower part of Figure 7.2, there are also other aspects of the city—connected with the role of symbolic logic—which are frequently overlooked by territorial theorization. This view represents the city as a *milieu* that, according to the theory developed by GREMI[1] (Camagni 1991, 1999), performs the crucial function of reducing dynamic uncertainty, to the benefit of local economic actors. In a turbulent environment characterized by difficulty in information collection, processing, and assessment, strong interdependence between the decisions of different actors, and great complexity in the external environment, economic actors find in the local milieu the necessary support for coping with uncertainty. In fact this milieu—consisting of shared values, common representations, and codes; a sense of belonging or even patriotism; trust, common professional background, and economic specialization—helps by facilitating two crucial tasks:

- The *transcoding* of external information and its evaluation, allowing more accurate interpretation and faster utilization in decision-making and in developing new business ideas. This occurs in many ways, including informal contacts, imitation, mutual assessment of "rumors," and so on, which in innovation theory are considered to fulfill a crucial function;[2] in a word, it occurs through a "socialized" or "collective" process (Camagni 1991).
- The *ex-ante coordination* of private decisions in order to permit collective action, both in business behavior and in the provision of public or collective goods.

> Some of the main obstacles to collective action are considered, by economic theory, to be the cost of information collection and the risk of opportunistic and free-riding behavior. In both cases, the existence of a local milieu limits these costs, thanks to geographical and organizational proximity and the establishment of common codes for cooperation through trust and for the punishment of improper behavior. When these costs reveal themselves to be excessive, the public sector may be called on to enforce some of the rules or contribute directly to the development and implementation of local schemes; its visibility, accessibility, and accountability with respect to the local community reinforces the synergetic effect.

The uncertainty-reducing function of large city-regions represents a valuable advantage also for households, as far as job search and professional careers are concerned; the diversification and breadth of the metropolitan labor market in a sense represent an insurance against the risk of unemployment or underemployment.[3]

But the local milieu performs a second task, always in a functional/procedural logic: it supplies the permanent substratum for collective learning processes.

Numerous theoretical and empirical studies have indicated that learning processes are essential to innovation, and require a host of tacit, immaterial, and informal exchanges, which happen mainly *inside* large firms. An interesting parallel to this process, occurring within small-firm-intensive local environments, has been pointed out recently: in this case the learning processes develop mainly *outside* the individual firm (which is small and generally short-lived), but *inside* the local labor market, through the chains of professional upgrading and mobility of skilled labor. The local milieu—which can be either an industrial district or a city[4]—becomes the substratum in which long-term "collective" learning processes are embedded to the advantage of the local economy (Camagni 1995). The creation of this milieu, centered around the productive "vocation" or competitive advantage of the local area, generates a cumulative process that reinforces the competitive advantage itself.

D. The last typology (emerging from the symbolic/network logic) concerns the city as a *symbolic entity*. Economists, though acknowledging its relevance, are not at their ease in dealing with this subject. I therefore limit myself to listing the main symbols that can be (or have been) associated with the city, and in particular large cities:

- the city as both "place" and "node," represented by the ancient Egyptian hieroglyphic for the city which consists of a cross (the external networks) inside a circle (the place); this synthesizes the coexistence of two territorial roles: the development of a local, territorial society or civilization and good accessibility to other global nodes;[5]
- the city as a device that allows us to overcome both space and time: distance being overcome through the participation in global networks and time through both the "memory" of the past, preserved in its monuments, museums, and archives, and the anticipation of the future in its propensity continuously to create the new;[6]

- the city as a symbol (and a concrete actor) of territorial control: "the place from which a territorial control is established" (Roncayolo 1990: 29). This is a theme already present in the reflections of nineteenth century thinkers, who spoke about the "contradiction," or antithesis, between city and countryside (Friedman 1979, Camagni 1996: Introduction). Roncayolo also points out the apparent paradox between "the geographical reality of the city, on the one hand, which dilutes itself in processes of generalized urbanization [and], on the other, the city as a symbolic actor, driving force of communication systems, which gathers new strength. Cities fight each other using images and representations, as well as fiscal incentives" (Roncayolo 1990: 241, our translation);
- the city as a creator of symbols: the place where social codes, languages, rules, conventions, and representations are established and passed on to the rest of the world. It is interesting to note that one of the latest symbols to be produced, the Internet, has created a new style and market which is mainly urban. In the production and exchange of information via the Internet, usually associated in common wisdom with remote "electronic cottages," the top fifteen metropolitan core regions in the United States, representing 4.3 percent of total population, account for around 20 percent of Internet hosts and are the driving forces in the growth of the network (Graham 1999).

Symbols and representations guide important decision-making processes involving strategic choices.[7] An interesting example is the rush for metropolitan locations of headquarters and commercial facilities in European countries by global players (mainly large financial institutions and multinational companies) which followed, not the implementation, but simply the announcement of, the European Single Market in Delor's White Paper in 1985. Large capital cities in all EU countries faced a booming demand for central locations, which determined a parallel boom in land rents and prices, for a period lasting up to 1992—ironically, the formal starting year of the Single Market! (see Figure 7.3).

How does a "global city" status relate to the preceding typology of roles of the big city? The linkages are very tight, as:

- agglomeration and size provide critical mass and top-level quality to urban factors and activities, a first crucial precondition for globalization;
- networking and interaction over long distances provide the second precondition for globalization, in terms of planetary visibility and accessibility;
- the development of an urban milieu provides the psychological and synergetic context for the establishment of long-term learning processes and the conditions for the selection and reproduction of global decision elites in democratic societies;
- the "global city" status amounts to both the outcome of a symbolic representation process that builds upon actual economic functions and a rhetoric addressed to the cumulative strengthening of such functions and the related economic and political leadership they secure to the city.

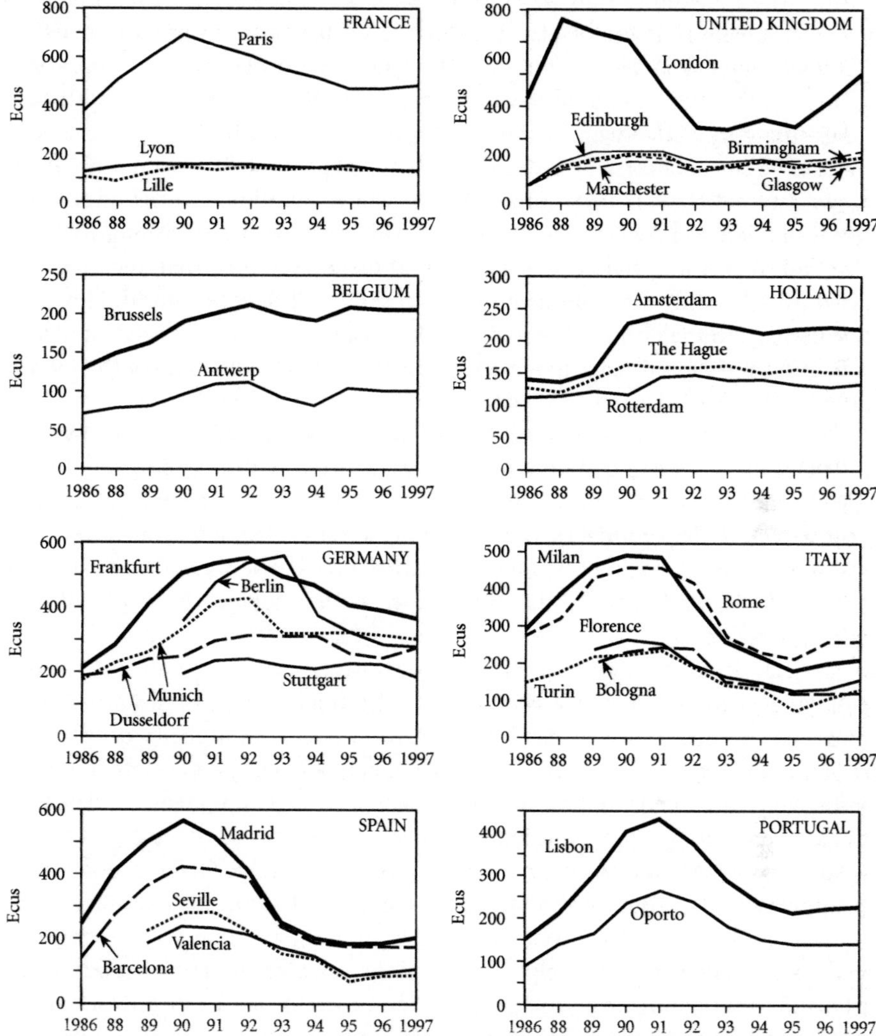

Figure 7.3. *Rental values of office space (ecus per square meter, 1986–97) in European cities*

Source: Gabetti Holding data

THE EVOLUTIONARY CONTEXT: SPATIAL CONTRADICTIONS AND METROPOLITAN FORM

The above discussion about the different roles assigned to global cities according to different types of cognitive logic shows just how much the traditional approach to optimal urban location and optimal city size—comparing costs and benefits in the functional sphere—needs to be widened if it is to encompass expectations and symbolic representations of the city, the evaluation of risks in turbulent environments, and the search for strategies to reduce uncertainty. This means that the balance between overall benefits and costs shifts to a higher level, implying the acceptance of lower levels of collective welfare and urban sustainability (Camagni and Gibelli 1996; Camagni 1998; Camagni, Capello, and Nijkamp 1999).

What is more, the different roles assigned to the global city interact with each other in a cumulative way, pushing the overall size of urban systems ever upwards. The city appears to be losing control over its physical dimension, since it has grown beyond the territorial limits within which traditional forms of political representation and governance have effect. The problem of establishing accountable and responsible planning institutions at the level of the urban region is one faced by urban administrations and communities all over the world. However, due perhaps to the political costs of this process, i.e. the need for intermunicipal solidarity, and the still unclear benefits of proper physical planning of the metropolis, only a few attempts have achieved even partial success.[8]

The general answer to the challenge of urban sustainability, pursued by both the planning system and spontaneous market forces, is the structuring of large urban regions in a polycentric form, organized around dense interconnected transport networks. This model theoretically has two advantages: it avoids overloading each individual center, thereby safeguarding the efficiency and sustainability of the "places," and provides the overall critical mass apparently necessary for a "global-city" status.

Deriving from this, however, are two contrasting settlement patterns, representing the extreme spatial archetypes for the microterritorial scale of settlement: a "compact polycentrism," organized around a multiplicity of relatively compact and diversified centers, and a "sprawling polycentrism," where the single settlements are made up of mainly monofunctional, low-density urbanizations. There is now intense international debate about the pros and cons of these abstract patterns—the choice resting on a complex multicriteria evaluation. It is important that future evolution as well as present conditions are taken into consideration (due to the problem of irreversibility), and that both micro- and macro-level efficiency are weighed up (at the scale of the neighborhood, the city, and the urban region) along with at least three other major issues, namely car dependency, urban quality (how to preserve an "urban effect"), and social conditions (equity and segregation).

In the following section I shall concentrate on the mobility issue, summarizing the present state of the debate and presenting the main conclusions of a quantitative analysis of the metropolitan area of Milan, which addressed the issue of the social costs of alternative settlement typologies.

Settlement Patterns and Urban Form: The Mobility Issue

The huge problems relating to mobility in large metropolitan areas and urban regions derive from the recognized failure of the market system of decentralized and fragmented decisions, in presence of externalities. Mobility patterns depend on the supply of transport infrastructure, which is facing increasing difficulty in meeting the enormous growth in mobility demand (itself increasingly complex and unsystematic), which in turn depends on the unconstrained location decisions of firms, developers, and households. In the absence of appropriate planning guidance and consensus, the decisions of single actors tend mainly towards suburbanization, generating an increasing burden on other actors, the territory, and the community, producing a vicious cycle of road construction and further suburbanization. On the other hand, strict regulatory measures have often proved ineffective and counterproductive, due to the lack of flexibility and ability in managing the complex nature of modern mobility demand.

A growing literature exists and much research has been undertaken on this subject, contributing to a lively international debate animated also by international institutions such as the European Union and the OECD, on the advantages of compact versus sprawling city forms. This debate, in which important and deep reflections are intermixed with more ideological viewpoints, can be summarized as follows.

Suburbanization, which used to be a typically North American phenomenon, is increasingly affecting European cities too, as a consequence of a vast array of factors including changes in lifestyle, the attraction of more natural nonurban environments, the rapidly decreasing quality of life in many city centers, and, not least, as a reaction to innercity congestion. This location strategy by individuals and firms has apparently proved effective according to a private logic, as the resulting mobility pattern—accompanied by heavy public infrastructure investment in suburban roads—has led to an increase in average trip speed (empirically tested for North American cities by Gordon and Richardson (1995) and for some European cities with an efficient transport system like Paris by Massot (1998)).

Unfortunately, the higher average speed has not resulted in shorter commuting times, but in increasing distance traveled; commuting times show a remarkable stability through time in all territorial systems, leading many scholars to think about an anthropologic constant in the form of a fixed time-budget constraint, averaging one hour, for daily trips in all societies.

Average journey-to-work distances (one way) in a sample of large international cities recently analyzed by Newman and Kenworthy (1999) show the following increases between 1980 and 1990 (see Table 7.4).

Table 7.4. *Average journey-to-work lengths in a sample of large international cities (km)*

	1980	1990
North America	13.0	15.0
Australia	12.0	12.6
Metropolitan Toronto	10.5	11.2
Europe	8.1	10.0

Source: Newman and Kenworthy 1999.

In all metropolitan areas of the United States, average commuting distances rose from 13.6 km. in 1983 to 18.6 in 1995 (Cervero 1998: 32). Increasing average distance means exponentially growing vehicle-kilometers traveled overall in the expanding metropolises and cumulatively increasing suburbanization.

Decentralization of jobs following decentralization of population, even if at lower rates, has not provided a better match between residential and working locations, as witnessed by the increasing distances traveled. It has determined, or codetermined, a dramatic fall in transit ridership, as the physical layout of public transit systems is generally oriented in a radial pattern around the city center, not serving scattered suburban locations efficiently. The same effect derives increasingly from the dispersal of residential locations in low-density settlements, leading to the almost complete car dependency of American cities.

Increasing commuter travel results in higher fuel consumption, as the growth in travel easily exceeds the higher fuel efficiency increase brought about by the car technology; this was even registered in the United States where fuel efficiency almost doubled between 1973 and 1988, and oil consumption increased by 20 percent.

The price systems and fiscal policy of most advanced countries were proactive with respect to the emergence of highly transportation-intensive lifestyles and residential location patterns. Increasing fuel efficiency of cars and long-term fall in the real price of oil (not just in the United States, but also in most European countries) helped the substitution of mass transit trips by private car use: in the United States the real price per kilometer traveled decreased by 47 percent between 1973 and 1988, while the average transit price increased in real terms by 47 percent. Furthermore, unlike Europeans, American motorists pay only 60 percent of the cost of road construction, maintenance, and administration, through taxes and user charges (Cervero 1998: 35). The general unpaid hidden costs of road traffic are estimated by the OECD and U.S. Natural Resources Defense Council at about 5 percent of GNP of advanced countries, made up of congestion costs (2 percent), and the costs of pollution, accidents, social disruption, and global climate change.

In the case of the United States, the upper estimate of these costs, related to a passenger-kilometer unit base, equal the hidden subsidies to transit riders for capital and operating costs. These figures are often utilized by proroad advocates to underline the intrinsic cost and economic disadvantage of mass transit, but unit figures should not be used in a situation where transit commuters represent 3.5 percent of total commute trips in the country. What emerges is evidence of an entire socioeconomic system locked into a car-dependent settlement and mobility pattern.

The relationship between settlement structure and transport modal choice emerges as a cumulative and long-term one, where the key factor is the relative competitiveness of the two modes, private and public. When the initial competitiveness of the transit system is jeopardized by increasingly dispersed locations, its relative appeal to consumers decreases sharply and the cost of new

Table 7.5. *Activity intensity: population and job density per hectare*

	1960	1970	1980	1990
American cities	26	25	22	23
Australian cities	27	22	19	18
Canadian cities: Toronto	52	60	59	65
European cities	113	102	87	82
Asian cities	—	260	232	251

Source: Newman and Kenworthy 1999.

infrastructure investment and operation improvement correspondingly skyrockets. The average relative speeds of the two modes, defined on the entire existing network, can give a misleading image of their relative performance, as the actual speed of the transit system may be relatively high on some arcs, but low and close to zero on others and for most metropolitan origins and destinations, due to lack of public service or time-consuming interconnections with other modes.[9]

Therefore, the element under scrutiny is the form of the metropolis, and in particular the relationship between its spatial layout and transportation network, with the relative compactness of the settlement structure and consequent overall urban density adopted as critical indicators. In fact, average density appears to be closely associated with per capita gasoline consumption, as shown by the well-known hyperbolic relationship estimated by Newman and Kenworthy. This relationship per se does not reveal a direct, causal relationship between the two variables, but the existence of at least three different settlement models: the European, the Asian, and the American—characterized by very different average urban densities, associated with equally different levels of car use and energy consumption through a complex set of long-term evolutionary processes involving the architecture of transportation networks and lifestyles. But this same relationship was proven to hold also in the case of single metropolitan areas with reference to the density of their neighborhoods or municipalities (New York, Melbourne, Milan, Paris, etc.); this leads us to suggest that the density and compactness of settlements could be used as planning policy targets and tools to achieve lower levels of car dependency.

Unfortunately, while both American and Australian cities have recently stopped or even reversed the historical trend towards decreasing metropolitan densities, the same does not hold for European cities, which are apparently following, some decades later, the same suburbanization trend of the former (this is particularly clear in the case of Brussels, Frankfurt, and London). The figures are clear in this respect (see Table 7.5).

Density, of course, should not be the sole policy variable, just as car dependency reduction is not the sole goal, although it has significant economic, environmental, social, and aesthetic drawbacks for the city. The policy response should be to provide alternative settlement patterns for the long term, by building a new collective vision of the modern sustainable city, through integrated land-use/transportation/pricing policies.

Settlement Typologies and Collective Cost: The Case of the Milan Metropolitan Area

The metropolitan area of Milan, in its strictest sense, coincides with the Milan province and encompasses 4.4 million people. In a wider sense, it also encompasses many areas outside the administrative province (including Como, Varese, Pavia, Cremona) and even outside the Lombardy region (towards Novara, in neighboring Piedmont, and Piacenza in Emilia-Romagna), including some 7–8 million people.

In a recent research work (Camagni, Gibelli, and Rigamonti 1998), the effects of different typologies of urban expansion (expansion by infilling, extension, linear development, sprawl, and concentration on large projects) on mobility patterns and land consumption were measured, considering the single municipalities (186) within the Milan province. Each municipality was allocated to a single (or double) typology by inspection of air cartography of the area at two points in time, 1981 and 1991.

Regarding land consumption, a first interesting element emerged (Figure 7.4). Sprawling urbanization and linear expansion along the main axes are the most land-consuming typologies, while expansion through large and compact projects and infilling are the least land-consuming typologies. However, the entire territorial system is slowly adjusting to the new condition of land scarcity with a lower rate of land consumption per residential unit built in the last decade with respect to the past.

Furthermore, an *index of collective impact of mobility* was constructed using the weighted sum of commuter trips (weighting differently each trip according to mode and length) divided by actual trips. Simple regression analysis showed a strong positive influence of absolute population size and density on the share of the public mode. The indicator of collective impact of mobility, on the other hand, is strongly affected by the age of the housing stock (new building development showing a higher impact) and by demographic growth rates (rapidly growing municipalities have higher indicator levels) (see Figure 7.5 and Table 7.6). Multiple regression analysis confirmed the previous results, both with respect to the index of mobility impact (see Table 7.7) and to the share of the public mode. Population density was found to be significant as a determinant of the share of public transport, but also a statistically significant variable determining the level of the impact index (with the right, negative, sign). An important variable in determining the share of public transport (see Table 7.8) is given by its relative performance in terms of the average commuting trip time: this performance, on its turn, as already explained and empirically confirmed, depends on the relative compactness of the settlement patterns—the size and density of population in each municipality[10] (see Table 7.9).

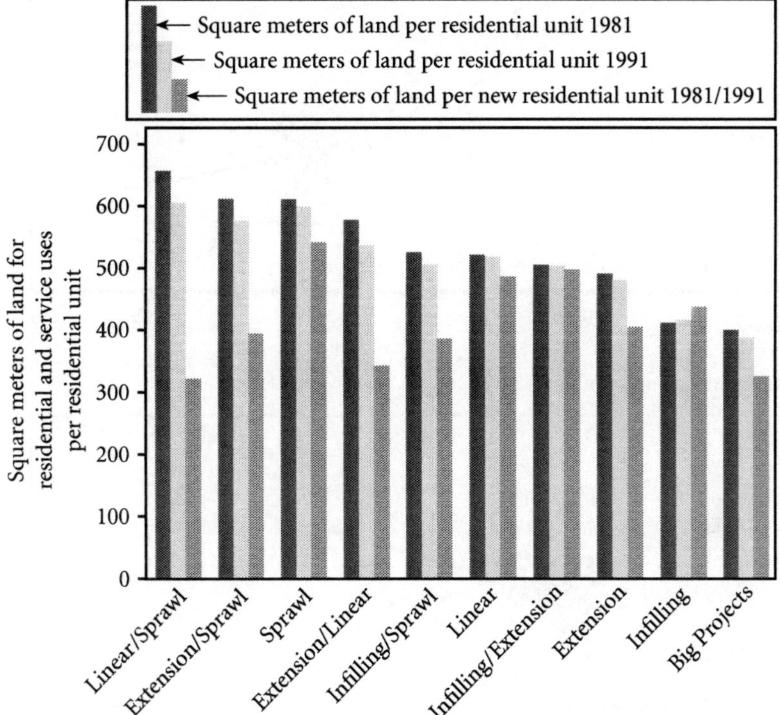

Figure 7.4. *Land consumption by types of urban expansion, municipalities of Milan province*
Source: Camagni, Gibelli, and Rigamonti 1998

This empirical analysis confirms some of the statements made above: the relationships between settlement patterns and collective costs are complex and affected by cumulative and circular effects. New visions for sustainable cities should be developed and implemented using differentiated tools, ranging from settlement patterns to private mobility costs, from urban density to public mode supply, its attractiveness, and performance.

CONCLUSIONS

The aim of this chapter is threefold. First, it shows how globalization increases competition between cities and territories, pushing local communities to upgrade the quality of local territories. Second, it underlines the multiple roles performed by global city-regions—the investigation includes functional as well as symbolic roles, touching on the systems of symbolic representation and the need for reduced uncertainty. Third, it attempts to show how significant multiplier and synergetic effects linking these different roles end up by increasing urban size, making it necessary to consider the sustainability of the ever-expanding physical footprint of the city.

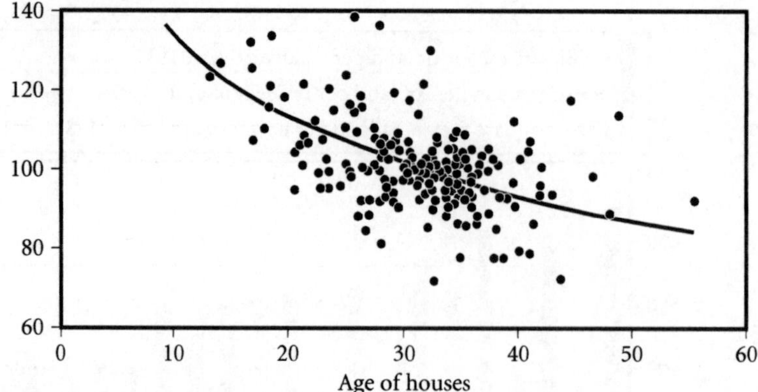

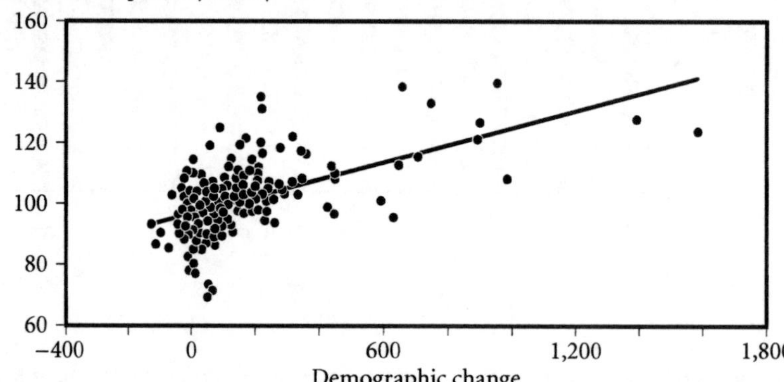

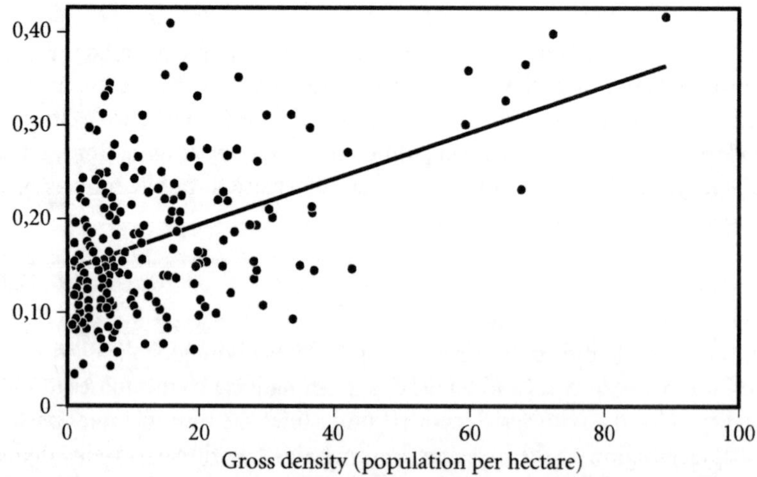

Figure 7.5. *Forms of settlements and mobility patterns in the metropolitan area of Milan*
(a) relationship between index of journey impact and demographic change,
(b) relationship between index of mobility impact and age of houses,
(c) relationship between collective mode share and gross population density.

Source: Camagni, Gibelli, and Rigamonti 1998

Table 7.6. *The results of the simple regression analyses*

				R^2	St.T
Impact index	= 96.99	+26.84	Demographic growth rate	0.33	8.49
Impact index	= 200.63	−28.99	ln(age of housing stock)	0.32	−9.39
Share of public transport =	−0.06	+0.027	ln(population)	0.118	4.96
Share of public transport =	0.14	+0.000002	Population density per sq.k.	0.189	6.54

Table 7.7. *The results of the multiple regression analysis: Dependent variable: impact index*

Independent variables	Coefficient	Student's *T*
Constant	1.386	34,175
Age of the housing stock	−1.202E-02	−10,47
Population change (%) 1981–91	7.540E-04	5,466
Density: Inhabitants/sq.m.	−1.660E-05	−3,313
R^2	0.588	

Table 7.8. *The results of the multiple regression analysis: Dependent variable: share of public transport*

Independent variables	Coefficient	Student's *T*
Constant	0.351	9.347
Trip time public/private transport	−1.018E-03	−8.024
Growth rate of population 1981–91	−1.482E-04	−1.939
Net density: inhabitants/urbanized land	1.708E-05	5.502
R^2	0.508	

Table 7.9. *The results of the multiple regression analysis: Dependent variable: trip times on public transport*

Independent variables	Coefficient	Student's *T*
Constant	55.303	58.656
Net density: inhab/urbanized land	−1.514E-03	−5.592
Population 1991	−6.211E-05	−2.207
R^2	0.310	

Sprawling settlement patterns represent only a short term and partial answer to the growing congestion of the central areas, as they impose an increasing burden on the territory in terms of irreversible car dependency and the extension of commuting catchment areas. Polycentric networks of compact centers can represent a viable alternative spatial pattern for avoiding a dramatic fall in the quality of metropolitan territories.

NOTES

1. The GREMI (*Groupe de Recherche Européen sur les Milieux Innovateurs*), chaired by the present author, is an international group of scholars located at the Sorbonne University, Paris, for the purpose of studying innovative environments. The "innovative milieu" is defined as the set of relations uniting a local production system, a set of actors and their representations, and an industrial culture, which together generate a localized dynamic process of collective learning. Some of the basic constituent elements of the local milieu are: mobility of specialized labor within the local labor market, innovation imitation, interfirm cooperation and linkages, common codes and conventions, and a sense of belonging.
2. At the Global City-Regions Conference, Saskia Sassen came close to this concept speaking about the relevance of "information interpretation" in the globalizing economy, and localizing this crucial function in the global city.
3. The role of "*assurance tout risque*" played by the large city was also underlined by Veltz (1996).
4. The theoretical parallel between the milieu and the city has been traced by the author in a recent work, the common element being the presence of relational capital (Camagni 1999).
5. Along similar lines, the great Jewish theologian Franz Rosenzweig speaks about the city as "wandering root," a synthesis of nomadism and territoriality. Born in history as antithesis to nomadism, a response to the need of stability and safety, a way of building and transmitting to subsequent generations a culture and identity, the city is still crossed by multiple flows—modern forms of nomadism—from daily trips for work, leisure, and social relations purposes, defining the local (metropolitan) life-basins ("*bassins de vie*"), to long-distance transport and communication flows, defining the support space, the control space, and the cooperation space of the city, increasingly globalized.
6. The French philosopher Dagognet writes: "*Nous définissons la Cité comme ce qui permet de vaincre ensemble le temps et l'éspace, donc tout ce qui nous limite, rien moins donc d'une réussite philosophique prométhéenne. On conçoit alors qu'elle inquiète le Ciel, qui est défié.*" (Dagognet 1984: 221, quoted from Ansay and Schoonbrodt 1989). Anthony Giddens (1993) speaks about the reshaping of time and distance with reference to social life as an effect of globalization.
7. Kenichi Ohmae, at the Global City-Regions Conference, spoke about the necessity of "touching the imagination" of managers, in their decisions about locations.
8. Metropolitan governance represents a prime concern of the Urban Affairs Department of the Territorial Development Service of the OECD, as witnessed by many recent initiatives.
9. Newman and Kenworthy's sample of 46 large international cities show that the average speed of metro trains is higher than that of cars not only in Asian cities (38 km/h vs. 25), but also in European ones (41 vs. 36). There is only a small negative difference for cities in Canada (33 vs. 40), Australia (35 vs. 45) and the United States (37 vs. 51). These differences could not explain why commuters rely increasingly and so heavily on private cars. But if one compares the average trip time for the two modes by neighborhoods of origin, the times for suburban neighborhoods are substantially lower for the private car, even in European cities.

10. Improved econometric analyses of the Milan cases are presented in Camagni, Gibelli, and Rigamonti (2000).

REFERENCES

Ansay, P., and Schoonbrodt, R. (1989). *Penser la ville: choix de textes philosophiques.* Bruxelles: AAM Editions.

Camagni, R. (1991). "Technological Change, Uncertainty, and Innovation Networks: Towards a Dynamic Theory of Economic Space," in R. Camagni (ed.), *Innovation Networks: Spatial Perspectives.* London: Belhaven-Pinter, 121–44.

—— (1995). "Global Network and Local Milieu: Towards a Theory of Economic Space," in S. Conti, E. Malecki, and P. Oinas (eds.), *The Industrial Enterprise and Its Environment: Spatial Perspectives.* Aldershot: Avebury, 195–214.

—— (1996). *Principes et modèles de l'économie urbaine.* Paris: Economica.

—— (1998). "Sustainable Urban Development: Definition and Reasons for a Research Programme." *International Journal of Environment and Pollution,* 1: 6–26.

—— (1999). "La ville comme *Milieu*: de l'application de l'approche GREMI à l'évolution urbaine." *Revue d'Economie Régionale et Urbaine,* 3: 591–606.

——, and Gibelli, M. C. (1996). "Cities in Europe: Globalisation, Sustainability, and Cohesion," in Presidenza del Consiglio dei Ministri—Dipartimento Politiche Comunitarie, *European Spatial Planning.* Rome: Poligrafico dello Stato, 91–179.

——, Capello, R., and Nijkamp, P. (1999). "New Governance Principles for Sustainable Urban Transport," in M. Beuthe and P. Nijkamp (eds.), *New Contributions to Transportation Analysis in Europe.* Aldershot: Ashgate, 213–50.

——, Gibelli, M. C., and Rigamonti, P. (2000). "Urban Mobility and Urban Form: The Social and Environmental Costs of Different Patterns of Urban Expansion." Paper presented to the Fortieth Congress of the European Regional Science Association, Barcelona, August.

Cervero, R. (1998). *The Transit Metropolis.* Washington, DC: Island Press.

Dagognet, F. (1984). *Le nombre et le lieu.* Paris: Librerie Philosophique Vrin.

Friedmann, J. (1979). "On the Contradiction between City and Countryside," in H. Folmer and J. Oosterhaven (eds.), *Spatial Inequalities and Regional Development.* Den Haag: Martinus Nijhoff, 23–46.

Giddens, A. (1993). *Sociology.* Cambridge: Polity Press.

Gordon, P., and Richardson, H. (1995). "Sustainable Congestion," in J. Brotchie, M. Batty, E. Blakely, P. Hall, and P. Newton (eds.), *Cities in Competition.* Melbourne: Longman Autralia, 348–58.

Gordon, R. (1994). *Internationalization, Multinationalization, Globalization: Contradictory World Economies and New Spatial Division of Labor.* Santa Cruz, CA: Center for the Study of Global Transformations, University of California, Santa Cruz, Working Paper no. 94/10, August.

Graham, S. (1999). "Global Grids of Glass: On Global Cities, Telecommunications, and Planetary Urban Networks." *Urban Studies,* 36 (5–6): 929–49.

Krugman, P. (1996). "Making Sense of the Competitiveness Debate." *Oxford Review of Economic Policy,* 12: 17–25.

Massot, M. H. (1998). "Les échelles territoriales de la mobilité domicile-travail et de la mobilité locale," in N. May, P. Veltz, J. Landrieu, and T. Spector (eds.), *La ville éclatée.* Paris: Editions de l'Aube, 92–108.

Newman, P., and Kenworthy, J. (1999). *Sustainability and Cities: Overcoming Automobile Dependence.* Washington, DC: Island Press.

OECD. (1992). *Technology and the Economy.* Paris.

—— (1998). *International Direct Investment Statistics Yearbook.* Paris.

—— (1999). *Economic Outlook.* Paris, July.

Roncayolo, M. (1990). *La ville et ses territoires.* Paris: Gallimard.

Simon, H. (1972). "From Sustantive to Procedural Rationality," in C. B. McGuire and R. Radner (eds.), *Decision and Organization.* Amsterdam: North Holland.

UNCTAD. (1998). *World Investment Report.*

Veltz, P. (1996). *Mondialisation, villes, et territoires. L'économie d'archipel.* Paris: PUF.

8

Intercity Networks in a Globalizing Era

JOHN FRIEDMANN

Although terms like "global" and "globalization" have become part of everyday speech, they are rarely used with precision. There are two schools which look at very different facets of globality. The first, represented most recently by George Soros in his popular *The Crisis of Global Capitalism* (1998), emphasizes financial markets that transfer trillions of dollars each day from one part of the globe to another in search of short-term gains in money markets, stocks, and hedge funds. Soros calls it the amoral world of market relations and seeks to separate it, categorically, from human society, where, he argues, moral relations prevail. Like a modern-day Robin Hood, Soros makes his billions in the aggressive, speculative world of finance and gives away much of this amorally gotten wealth in the world of moral relations where he assumes the mantle of philanthropic citizen. Seemingly unable to reconcile this contradiction between amoral markets and moral society, he defends himself against critics by saying that each world is governed by a different set of rules: it would be financially ruinous, he says, to play the game in the first with the rules of the second.

The second school working within the framework of globality can be identified with a group of Los Angeles regional geographers and planners, particularly Allen Scott (1996) and Michael Storper (1997). The geographers tend to privilege the "real" economy with its traditional factors of production: land, labor, capital, and information over the fictive economy of speculative finance capital. They emphasize technology, innovations, entrepreneurship, as they occur in specific regional clusters of economic activity. Each of these clusters has a specific physical setting, historical trajectory, and set of external economies, chief among which is the face-to-face talk of people in an industry that allows them to make sense of information, learn about innovations, strike up alliances, raise capital, and make informed business decisions (Storper 1997). The real economy of regions and interregional relations depends on regional resources, and its time horizon is the *longue durée* of sustainable development. As someone who has taught at UCLA for twenty-seven years, I share the geographers' love for the world of the "real" economy, and this is the approach that I shall take in this chapter.

It remains to clarify what I mean by "globalizing" in my title. I understand globalization as an ongoing process that ties local/regional economies into global networks of information and markets. Although national borders remain more or less in place, they have become increasingly porous. In the "real" economy, and contrary to the hopes of "market fundamentalists," we are never in a "borderless world." But we are in a world where there is a growing interconnectedness of events on a globe-spanning scale. This web of connections may or may not remain intact, and as even George Soros admits, it will require—indeed, it already requires—new regulative institutions at the world level. Whatever these might turn out to be, an increasingly interconnected world involves individuals as well as collective actors, including cities and regions, in new sorts of relationships among themselves. My chapter is about some new relationships that are beginning to emerge, and that are centered on large city-regions. I will address six interrelated propositions. Some of them are already fairly well understood while others are still the object of ongoing debates. The six are these:

1. a limited number of city-regions are the major nodes and focal points of a globalizing economy;
2. finding an appropriate form of governance continues to be a critical concern for these regions;
3. in today's world, city-regions are increasingly responsible for managing their own development;
4. the sustainable development of city-regions requires giving greater attention to the creation and conservation of regional wealth in its multiple forms;
5. city-regions have much to gain (and nothing to lose) by associating with other regions in networks, especially, if not exclusively, across national borders, in the continuing quest for sustainable development;
6. city-regions situated in geographical proximity to each other, but embedded in national economies of different levels of economic achievement and sharing cultural affinities, can collectively strengthen their competitive position by collaborating with each other in the creation of a sustainable common wealth.

CITY-REGIONS AS FOCAL POINTS IN A GLOBALIZING ECONOMY

Open any publication of the World Bank, and you are immediately confronted with an array of statistics collected for each nation-state in the world, beginning with so-called national accounts. This pattern has been with us for so long—more than half a century—that we assume it to be the only reasonable way to conceive of territorial economies. In the past, there have been alternative constructs that would take the region as their basic unit for analysis (Perloff and Leven 1964). Interesting as these attempts were to focus on smaller units than national economies, they failed to take root in what was already then a globalizing system of nation-states.

A new beginning was made with a series of publications that attempted to link the growth of city-regions with the global system (Friedmann and Wolff

1982; Friedmann 1986, 1995, 1998*b*; Sassen 1991, 1994; Knox and Taylor 1995). And more recently, Michael Storper's monumental work on metropolitan regional economies has furnished a solid theoretical basis for new thinking about territorial development (Storper and Salais 1997; Storper 1997). Adopting a Schumpeterian framework of entrepreneurial capitalism, Storper stresses the strategic importance of face-to-face interaction, learning, and innovation in the rise of leading metropolitan economies. Each region, he argues, has certain "conventions" or unwritten codes of doing business. It is these conventions, together with its leading industries, that trace the distinctive profile of regional economies.

Following Storper's logic, it would make a great deal of sense to think, for example, of the American economy as a set of interactive regions based on key cities such as Los Angeles, Seattle, Denver, Dallas, Chicago, New York, Miami, and so forth (Pierce 1993). The same could be said also for other large, continent-sized countries such as China, India, Indonesia, Russia, and Brazil, countries that are far less internally articulated than North America. Australia is a good example. This country of a continent-sized national economy, with its 18 million people, is largely clustered around five metropolitan areas that themselves are only weakly linked to each other. Each of these cities has its own hinterland funneling resources to the center, and it is this center that links the regional into the global economy. Nearly a hundred years ago, the separate colonies of Victoria, Tasmania, South Australia, New South Wales, Queensland, and Western Australia decided to reconceive themselves as the political Commonwealth of Australia, which ultimately came to be symbolized in the new nation's planned capital city of Canberra. But the old pattern of quasi-city-states remains to this day.

If we look further, we will discover a large number of city-states and quasi-city-states where nation and city-region coalesce. Leaving aside Singapore and Kuwait, both well-known examples of bona fide city-states, one thinks of the ministates of Central America (each dominated by its capital city), Slovakia, the Czech Republic, and Slovenia in central Europe, the three Baltic states of Estonia, Latvia, and Lithuania, and even the much larger Thailand, whose vital core is the metropolitan region of Bangkok. Uruguay, Ireland, Barcelona/Catalunya, and Montreal/Quebec are among many others that come to mind.

But if indeed the economies of the twenty-first century are perhaps best understood as conglomerates of city-regions, why has this not been reflected in official thinking? It is of course true that the world of national economies is deeply ingrained in the institutional structure of global governance, beginning with the United Nations. Undoubtedly, this is a major obstacle. But the principal reason, in my view, is the difficulty authoritatively to define the boundaries of an alternative construct, not to replace the nation-state but to add yet another level of complexity. Or to put it otherwise, the difficulty has been to define a level of city-regional governance that can speak authoritatively for the region as a whole. I will return to this question in the next section.

Things are beginning to change, however. National boundaries are becoming increasingly permeable to flows of information, commodities, people, ideas, and images. This is part of what we mean when we say that the world is globalizing (Amin 1994). States have responded to this challenge by yielding some of their sovereignty to suprastate organizations, a process most clearly visible in Europe, but true on a world scale as well, as all sorts of new alliances are being struck (Held 1995, Sassen 1996, Linklater 1998). At the same time, states have begun to devolve important powers to local governments, most significantly to city and provincial levels. And as we move into the new century, I expect that we shall see a strengthening of both these supra- and subnational governance arrangements.

The picture that is emerging is one of localized production and trade in a complex web of public, private, and mixed institutional relations, ranging from planetary to local. At present, the system is dominated by some thirty or forty "world cities," but, with continuing urbanization, long-term economic growth, and greater interconnectedness among city-regions, the number of these global "hubs" will perhaps double over the coming decades. Still, the nation-state is not about to disappear. Realistically speaking, we can probably expect more states to declare themselves at least nominally sovereign, as this or that ethnic group succeeds in asserting its territorial claims (e.g. East Timor). But in a world of struggling interdependencies, any sort of territorial sovereignty, in the strong sense of supremacy, must be judged an illusion. Nation-states may set the institutional framework for regional development, and perhaps provide some policy parameters and financial resources for local development. But the world's major city-regions will themselves become significant actors, planning, promoting, and guiding their own development within a dynamic and continuously evolving global economy. To do this effectively, however, they will first have to face up to the primordial requirement of constituting a viable institutional arrangement of regional governance.[1]

REGIONAL GOVERNANCE A CRITICAL CONCERN

In some ways, our language is much too blunt to capture the elusive, multifaceted dynamics of urbanization. The statistical concept of urban is of only limited use: the concentration of a population above a certain threshold size and living at densities that are relatively higher than settlements in the surrounding (rural) areas. There are other, equally deficient, definitions based on, for example, administrative criteria. And to specify the "urban" still further, economic criteria may be added, such as the requirement that the population in question engage in predominantly nonagricultural activities.

All this is straightforward enough in a context where urban are contrasted with rural areas. But the latter designation is, of course, an equally imprecise and, for the most part, empty category, not least in societies where the great bulk of the population is no longer engaged in farming, where farming itself has become a transnational business, and where free-standing small towns and villages are an endangered species. Some European planners have proposed a new category of *neorural* to capture the new phenomena, where land-based production systems, ecological protection, and quality of life coalesce in new combinations (Gulinck and Dortmans 1997). But these phenomena could as easily be treated as neourban.

I will not attempt here to disentangle the various meanings of these terms that are, after all, in everyday use even when their scientific definition remains contested. Instead, I want to turn to the concept of city-region in the sense that I am using this term here, as a functionally integrated area consisting of both a core or central city (or cities) which usually lends its name to the area in question and, contiguous with it, a region that serves the multiple collective needs of this city and provides a space for its future expansion. The needs of a large city are many—and some city-regions are very large, indeed.[2] They include urban satellites (such as New Towns and so-called Edge Cities), reservoirs, water and sewage treatment plants, solid waste disposal facilities, oil and chemical complexes, electric power plants, open recreational spaces and amusement parks, wetlands, intensive agriculture, horticulture, and small livestock production, airports and harbors, industrial and warehousing districts, wholesale markets, tourist attractions, historical landmarks, and more. All these elements can usually be found within a radius of forty to sixty miles from the central city. Within this complex of seemingly incompatible land uses, the traditional distinction between urban and rural ceases to be useful, as even remaining farms and allotment gardens are now routinely referred to as *urban* (Losada *et al.* 1998). Accepting this terminology, we may in fact view the whole of the city-region as a new form of urban landscape.[3]

City-regions of this magnitude typically overlap with multiple jurisdictional boundaries of governmental and administrative units that, more often than not, act at cross-purposes with each other, rendering any sort of concerted action problematical. And yet, as I shall argue, the inability of most city-regions to work towards a vision of the common good is a major failing that renders much of the talk about *sustainable* development little more than ideological cant.

The awareness that city-regions require some arrangement of common governance is, of course, nothing new (Sivaramakrishna 1996). Many cities in Western Europe (Berg, Braun, and Meer 1993; Lefèvre 1998), North America, and Asia (Laquian 1995) have wrestled with this problem since at least the 1950s, none too successfully. With very few exceptions, U.S. cities, representing one end of the spectrum, exhibit extreme fragmentation, single-purpose regional districts (transportation, air quality management, etc.), and for the most part very small general-purpose governments that jealously guard their prerogatives, competing fiercely against each other for potential jobs and tax dollars. To call this a system of checks and balances is to give it more credit than is due. In practice, it is a system incapable of timely and concerted action. Another extreme is given by the governance structures of major Australian cities (Murphy and Wu 1999). Following British practice, Australian municipalities are called Local Councils and exist entirely at the sufferance of their respective state governments. It is the state government that is responsible for planning and other important urban functions. The elected government of Victoria, for example, presides over a state of four-and-a-half million people of whom more than 70 percent reside in the officially designated metropolitan area of Melbourne. Victoria is thus a quasi-city-state. The Commonwealth government has very little say about what happens in Victoria's cities throughout the country other than as a byproduct of national policies that are not specifically urban, such as those on immigration. It is the federated states that hold the real power in their respective city-regions.

Australian city-regional governance is a top-down system. Enshrined in the constitution, it came into being at the time of federation. But in Western Europe and Canada, the approaches to metropolitan governance (as it is called there) have been more experimental, especially over the last decade or two. Christian Lefèvre (1998) describes recent European experiences with forming metropolitan authorities in the following words:

> Metropolitan governance highlights values of negotiation, partnership, voluntary participation and flexibility in the constitution of new structures. In doing so, it presents us with a radically different idea of the institution [of metropolitan governance]. It is no longer presented at the start, created in advance, ready-to-use, but appears as the result of a constitutive process. It is the process which radically transforms yesterday's metropolitan model. Metropolitan governance does not consider the institution to be pre-established—on the contrary. The objective to be achieved (roughly speaking the form and content of the metropolitan authority) is not fixed in advance but becomes the product of the system of actors as the process unfolds. Thus, the process has its own dynamic, fed by the actors themselves. But this feeding is not left to chance; it is done through specific forms and negotiated procedures which frame and punctuate the process. Unlike the classic metropolitan model where the process of constitution was generally short but where implementation proved . . . defective, the process here is long, and may stop or slow down at any time, but the result seems less uncertain because the legitimacy of the institution is produced by all the actors during the process of constituting the metropolitan government. (p. 18.)

Lefèvre's formulation captures the idiosyncratic processes of today's experiments with metropolitan (or city-regional governance). But the actual processes, and how they should be assessed, are a great deal more complicated than even Lefèvre suggests. To begin with, I would question whether the objective of such a process is simply the formation of a "metropolitan authority" as the paragraph quoted above declares. Metropolitan governance is not a good in itself, nor is it merely a question of efficient service provision, which may or may not be subject to economies of scale. Rather, I would argue, behind the exercise of regional governance is a vision (frequently contested, to be sure) of a good city (Friedmann 1998*a*). But whose vision? This surely is a matter of inclusiveness in the representation of Lefèvre's actors. To bring together local officials and business interests into a "partnership" is one thing, but the further inclusion of organized "civil society," especially of the least vocal among them, is altogether something different, and may give rise to a radically different vision of the good city. And although the constitution of a system of metropolitan governance is important, the powers retained by the smaller territorial units that form an integral part of the region are equally important. This question of the "territorial division of powers" is discussed in the European Union under the so-called *principle of subsidiarity* which refers to the delegation of powers to the lowest level of governance compatible with effective and efficient performance. Finally, there are the matters of transparency and democratic accountability in governance without which any system will inevitably get stuck in a quagmire of corruption. Evidently, then, "metropolitanization" ends up being a political process that has different outcomes for different cities.

SUSTAINABLE DEVELOPMENT AND THE CREATION OF REGIONAL WEALTH

The idea that exports are the basis of a region's economy, propelling it to ever greater heights, has become part of the accepted folk wisdom among politicians and academics alike. Its first theoretical formulation was by the American historian Douglass C. North in 1955. Eighteen years later, Paauw and Fei (1973) reformulated this doctrine in terms of national economies, with particular application to Southeast Asia, where it soon became known as the strategy of export-led growth, paving the way to the market fundamentalism recently decried by George Soros (1998). The strategy privileges export production over production for domestic markets and posits a virtuous circle of balanced interregional trade in the context of a spatial division of labor. What the theory does not tell us is why exports should beget exports over the long term, why all regions are bound to gain from unrestricted trade, how commodity exports are to be produced and by whom, and what happens if deficits show up in place of the expected balance. Without answers to these questions, the theory of export-led development remains incomplete, and development strategies based on it are likely to have unwanted consequences.

Let me begin with the question of what happens when a region's growth is stunted at very low levels, and its trade with other regions runs a long-term deficit, with imports outpacing exports by a large margin. In this case, the region becomes a natural candidate for transfer payments from elsewhere (the national treasury, Brussels, bilateral aid, the World Bank) and will also begin to draw down its initial fund of wealth-creating resources by a process of *systematic neglect or disinvestment*. Six interrelated resource complexes are required to sustain a region's ability to export; "mining" them undermines and ultimately destroys its capacity to produce future wealth. The six include:

1. *human capital*, which includes those things that nurture our ability to become healthy productive human beings: good nutrition, housing, health care, and education;

2. *social capital*, which is a robust, self-organizing civil society and its institutions, deeply engaged with the everyday life of local communities;
3. *natural resources*, both renewable and not, and having economic value, such as ground water, productive land, attractive landscapes, forests, fisheries, and minerals;
4. *environmental resources*, which include the quality of the air we breathe, the water we drink, and the capacity of land to sustain life;
5. *economic and social infrastructure*, such as for transportation, electric energy, water supply, sewage treatment, solid waste disposal, as well as hospitals and schools which are directly related to human capital formation; and
6. *directly productive plant and equipment*, from office buildings to factories.

Together, these resource complexes constitute the productive assets of a region. But what happens if a city-region should fail to invest in them or worse, allow them to run down because of persisting trade deficits, or because increased exports—and this is the other possibility—put excessive pressures on regional assets, which are allowed to degrade despite the apparent flourishing of production for export? Disinvestment can assume many forms: heavily polluted, unhealthy environments; speculative property investments; aging "rust-belt" industries; the steady depletion and contamination of ground water resources; persistent shortages of water and power; the massive spread of underserviced shantytowns and slums; poorly maintained, inadequate, and obsolete infrastructure; the degradation of formerly attractive landscapes into. . . . It is an unhappy list that has become a familiar sight in many parts.

Even so, the relationship between asset degradation and regional fortunes is not always clearly understood. My argument is that the two circuits of regional development—regional wealth-creation and intercity trade—must be kept in a rough balance. *Sustainable development is never bestowed from the outside but must be generated from within the regional economy itself.*[4] The frenzied competitive search for external capital that seems to motivate so many city-regions has just the opposite effect. It drains the region's most precious assets rather than adding to them. The two circuits are not automatically self-balancing; unless appropriate measures are taken and the necessary long-term investments made, sustainable development will be jeopardized.

Poor city-regions with low or negative trade balances may think that they can afford to neglect the circuit of wealth creation while they offer financially attractive deals to foreign capital. But this philosophy of "grow now, correct imbalances later" is deceptively seductive. The deterioration of wealth-creating assets and the failure adequately to invest in them has long-term hidden costs that must be counted whenever local governments, in a celebratory mood, tote up the foreign direct investment (FDI) dollars committed by multinational firms. Although it is true that some disinvestment can be rectified later, there is no assurance that the circuit of intercity trade will continue to flourish without constantly attending to the condition of regional assets as well.

THE FORMATION OF INTERCITY NETWORKS

Broad considerations of this sort have recently led important European cities to form a series of loose alliances among themselves. In the early 1990s, the European Commission reported the existence of thirty-seven collaborative intercity networks (Kunzmann 1995). One of the first of these, and in some ways the most interesting, is EUROCITIES, which got its start in 1986 with an explicit political agenda: to press for a Europeanwide urban policy and thus for the formal recognition by Brussels of cities as significant centers of subnational governance. In addition, the founding cities hoped to increase the transfer of knowledge, experiences, and best practices among themselves and to facilitate the implementation of practical projects. Last but not least, they wanted to assist cities from outside the Union to integrate themselves into the EU and support their "continuing progress towards democratic government and a market economy." Membership is open to democratically elected city governments, as well as to their "economic and scientific partners" (Chambers of Commerce and universities) in cities having a regional importance, with a minimum population of 250,000 and "an international dimension." By mid-1997, EUROCITIES had grown to include sixty full-member cities, sixteen associate-member cities (from beyond the EU), and eleven economic and scientific partners.

The EUROCITIES document, *A Charter of the European Cities* (1996), reveals a good deal about this oldest of intercity networks. The Charter was specifically addressed to the European Commission in an attempt to amend the basic Treaty of the Union. Its preamble is a remarkable statement of a political tradition that reaches nearly a millennium into the past.

> Cities are one of the characteristic features of European civilization. Their ancient history, their tradition of autonomy and pluralism and their ability to blend diverse cultures into a real local community have given rise to several developments of significance in the world: from the period of free communes and cities through the principle of self-government to the very idea of citizenship. The variety of political, cultural, and social experience of European cities has given them an exceptionally rich and diverse quality of life. (EUROCITIES 1996: 6.)

Here, in a few sentences, we have an heroic appeal to history, municipal autonomy, cultural diversity, the communal tradition, democratic governance, and citizenship. A number of more substantive statements elaborate on this revealing declaration which lays claim to no less than European civilization (paraphrased from EUROCITIES 1996: 6–9):

- *Cities as the basis of European integration.* Cities root citizens in their institutions and traditions. They are also the first and essential political and institutional point of contact for those who choose to move, whether EU citizens or not, in a Europe where immigration and cultural and ethnic pluralism are increasingly widespread. Local authorities in cities can play a vital role in developing the dialogue between society and the system of democratic representation, in leading the fight against racism, xenophobia, and intolerance, and ensuring that the benefits of city life are available to everyone.

- *The principle of local self-government.* Despite having evolved far beyond its intergovernmental origins, the European Union has not yet come to terms with its responsibilities as a truly supranational organization, necessitating intense cooperation with local and regional authorities as well as with member states. To do this, regional and local authorities must be recognized as essential levels of government, and the principle of local self-government must be considered as a basic right.
- *The principle of subsidiarity, or proximity.* The Treaty of Maastricht was the first clearly to state the principle of subsidiarity and to address the institutional dimension of intrastate powers. Perhaps better described as the principle of proximity, it states that decisions should be taken at higher levels of government only when there are manifest reasons for doing so. This principle has still not been recognized as applying *below* the level of member states. Cities' aim is not the suppression or reduction of policies at European or national levels, but their coordination with those of local government and the activities of civil society.
- *Cities as partners in European policies.* European cities wish to become partners with the national governments and Community institutions in defining and implementing regional and urban policies. Cities have a vital interest in seeing concrete policies put in place on a number of issues (a) including the development of trans-European networks linking cities to each other; (b) combining the development of these networks with the demand to spread the benefit of economic growth and maintain the environmental balance necessary to ensure their sustainability; and (c) incorporating the long-term aims of social cohesion and employment creation in all relevant EU policies.
- *European citizenship.* Cities have an important role to play in the realization of European citizenship, specifically in developing local democracy, in guaranteeing the balance between the rights and responsibilities of all those who live in their communities, in promoting the equality of the sexes, and in enabling the active participation of citizens in the processes of government.
- *The challenge of social exclusion.* The Treaty must reflect the major preoccupation of urban governments with the problems of unemployment, poverty, and social exclusion. Cities want to see a greater emphasis on the Union's duty to promote social cohesion and a more active commitment to combating disparities *within* communities as well as *between* regions and, above all, to ensure equal opportunities for all the citizens of Europe.

This is a powerful agenda; it is also a plea for the vital importance of the metropolis as an organized political community and critical actor in development, mediating between the suprastate of the EU and the local citizenry. Remarkably, it encapsulates an ideology to which the nearly eighty cities of this European network subscribe, a statement of what unites them beyond their frequently divisive economic interests.

Above all, the Charter contains a multitiered vision of European governance that declares cities (and civil society) as partners in the conception and implementation of urban and regional policies, along with provincial, regional, national, and supranational authorities. EUROCITIES, headquartered in Brussels, also engages in more practical activities, some of them funded by the European Commission, including projects in the fields of intercultural education, economic development, urban renewal, transportation, telematics, and the environment.

I want to turn briefly to European city networks, because the idea of strategic networking appears to have caught the imagination of the new Europe *sans frontières économiques*. But as the Union looms ever larger in the economic sphere, historical forces begin to reassert themselves, and an older Europe of cities and regions—especially of ethnic regions, from Scotland and Wales to Euskadi and Wallonia—begins to reassert itself. Many forces are at work here, but I would argue that intercity networks, at least in the case of EUROCITIES, are partly a strategic move to place an explicitly urban agenda on the table of the European Commission. For many years, Brussels has attempted to placate traditional regions bypassed by globalization, channeling substantial "compensatory" funds in their direction. Realizing that this policy is likely to be continued, EUROCITIES have urged a Europe not only of regions but of "of cities *and* regions" to ensure that their own increasingly pressing needs are not forgotten in the annual fiscal dispensation.

More economically inspired networking has generally been on a much smaller scale, as in the case of cross-border relations between southeastern England and northwestern France (Church and Reid 1996), the twin cities along the U.S.–Mexican border (Herzog 1990, Sklair 1993), or the Hong Kong Special Administrative Region and Guangdong Province in China (Chu and Ho 1997, Lin 1997). In Asia, these cross-border zones are often referred to as "growth triangles" (Douglass 1995, 1998; Chen 1995), an essentially arbitrary geometry. Finally, a very different but interesting example of a specific cross-border collaboration is the planning framework that has been developed for the Benelux countries, involving no less than five planning authorities, each having very different cultural assumptions: the Brussels Capital Region, Wallonia, Flanders, the Netherlands, and Luxembourg (Zonneveld and Faludi 1997).

In the next section, I would like to examine a much larger-scale but still regionally focused example of what may become one of the most important urban-industrial regions in the world. Here, as I see it, cities and provinces from within the same cultural complex but with very different actually realized economic potentials—northeastern China, the two Koreas, and southern Japan—face a unique challenge to develop a vast urban-industrial complex through intercity/regional networking.

INTERCITY COLLABORATION: THE CASE OF THE YELLOW SEA REGIONAL COOPERATION ZONE

The heart of what I shall call the Yellow Sea Regional Cooperation Zone is the Chinese Bohai Sea Rim (BSR). This region, according to Liu and his colleagues, "is the leading political and cultural center in China as well as the main economic focus of the northern part of the country. As defined [here], it covers an area of 514,000 km^2 embracing Beijing and Tianjin Municipalities and Hebei, Liaoning, and Shandong Provinces" (Liu, Zhang, and Linge 1997: 123). The concept of combining two municipalities (with provincial status) and three provinces into an economic macroregion arose in 1984 as part of China's newly adopted "open door" policy. As stated in one document, the Bohai region was to be " 'an aggregation of thirteen cities of different sizes,' organized to promote mutual assistance 'as well as developing regional specialization and labor division in economic structure based on comparative advantages' in order to 'integrate the economic activities of different cities and counties, to explore natural resources jointly with pooled technology and labor, and to share capital, urban and regional infrastructure, and harbor facilities for export-oriented industrial production' " (Chang *et al.* 1992: 61, cited in Liu, Zhang, and Linge 1997: 123). Furthermore, the Ninth (current) Five-Year Plan suggests that a Bohai Sphere Zone should be one of seven proposed economic regions in the country that would gradually take shape in accordance with their geographic position and internal development.

The idea that the Bohai Sea Rim (which is essentially a Chinese conception) should, with international participation, gradually evolve into a larger Yellow Sea Regional Cooperation Zone was first launched by Korean scholar Won Bae Kim in the early 1990s (Kim 1990, 1991, 1998; Douglass 1998). It is this enlarged, international dimension that I should like to explore further. The region includes some of the world's largest cities. If we set a compass in the center of the Yellow Sea and draw a circle with a radius of 1,000 km—about one hour's flying distance—we encompass not only the whole of the Chinese Bohai Sea Rim (and even Shanghai, the "dragon head" of the Yangtse River Basin) but also the two Koreas and the southern-most portions of Japan, from Osaka to Hiroshima and Fukuoka (see Figure 8.1). By way of comparison, the same circle set in the heart of Europe would enclose all major urban centers of the EU, from London to Athens. Looking at the Chinese BSR alone, its 1990 population of 203 million is expected to grow to 243 million within twenty years (equivalent to the entire population of the United States in 1990), with better than half of it classified as living in cities (Linge 1997: 140). When we add to this the two Koreas and southern Japan, we arrive at a total projected population base for the year 2010 of roughly 350 million.

The Yellow Sea Regional Cooperation Zone is thus a potential power house capable of rivaling the European Union. Within a relatively tight space, it arrays Japan and the Republic of Korea, two of the world's leading national economies, alongside that of China which has been growing at catch-up rates of more than

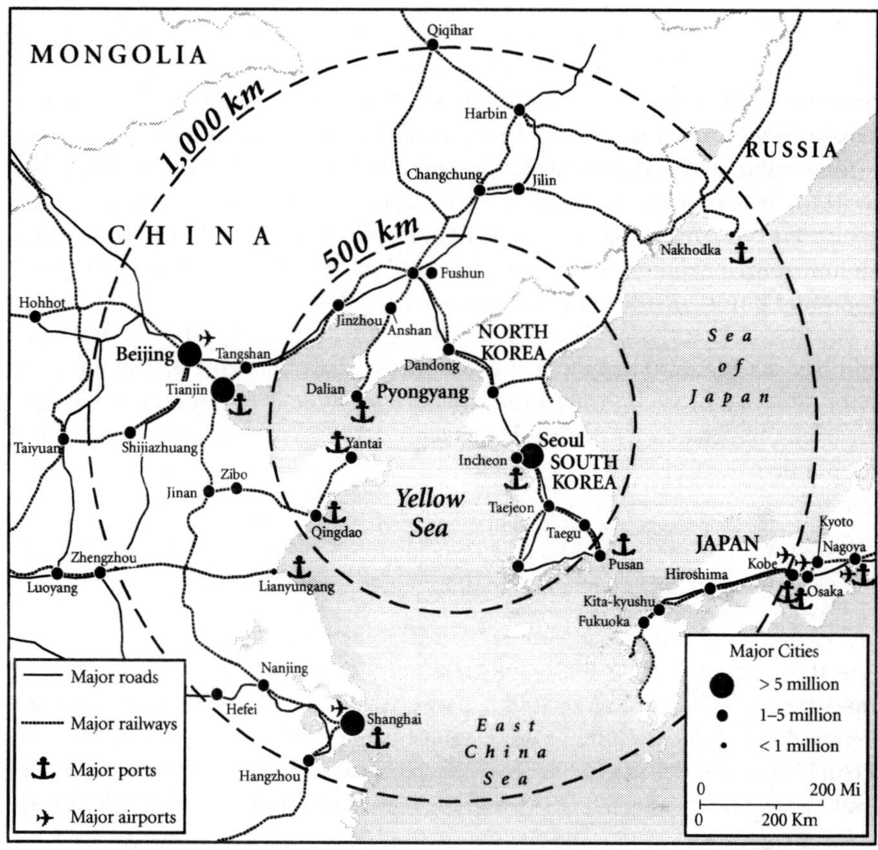

Figure 8.1. *Yellow Sea rim region*

8 percent for the last fifteen years and is likely to keep on growing at hyperrapid speed for at least an equivalent period. Moreover, and this is an important consideration for collaborative development, China, Korea, and Japan share a common cultural tradition centered in China, even though, in political terms, they are now far apart.

Despite its economic might, the Yellow Sea macroregion faces enormous challenges. Some of China's poorest peasants eke out a living in its mountain regions, and their future can only improve if a robust, diversified economy is strengthened, and agricultural productivity is raised through the application of advanced dry-farming techniques (Linge 1997: 136). More important even than poverty eradication (which is also a very serious problem in North Korea) is the fact that much of the heavy industry in the Chinese and North Korean portions of the Yellow Sea Rim threatens to turn into a gigantic "rust belt" unless major structural reforms occur. Heavy industries in both countries are state-owned, and although the Chinese government is currently attempting to make their own state industries more competitive and financially accountable, partly through privatization or in partnership with Western multinationals, hundreds of thousands, if not millions, of workers are losing their jobs along with housing, social services, and retirement benefits, all of which are firm-specific. At the moment, most of these industries would be incapable of surviving in a global business environment, and a sudden switch to an open market would savage them, just as it did in the former Soviet economies. Other major problems include severe water shortages, dwindling ground water reserves, heavily polluted rivers and sea shores, some of the worst air pollution in Asia, and a permanently congested transport infrastructure (Linge 1997).

The one competitive advantage relative to South Korea and Japan that the region still has is a plentiful supply of low-cost labor. This opportunity has not gone unnoticed by Korean industrialists who have begun to invest heavily in the BSR, especially the Shandong peninsula (Fukagawa 1997). As Liu, Zhang, and Linge (1997) point out:

> investors are recognizing that the BSR has the potential to become part of a wider regional cooperation zone that would benefit participating countries because of their geographical proximity, cultural and ethnic affinities, complementary and diversified economies, and large markets. (p. 134.)

A start has thus been made on international collaboration in the Yellow Sea macroregion. Diplomatic relations between the Republic of Korea and the People's Republic of China were established in 1992, and opportunities for expanding collaboration are now widely recognized to exist. An Association of East Asian Cities has been formed, and the mayors of nine Chinese, South Korean, and Japanese cities are meeting annually to discuss common issues (W. B. Kim, personal communication). Add to this the eagerness of China's national planners to integrate the region with the globalizing world economy and to maintain the economic growth momentum that has been built up, and it is evident that a strengthened institutional framework should be given serious consideration. It is true that the conditions for an institutionalized intercity network such as EUROCITIES do not exist at present. Cities in northeast Asia are neither autonomous nor do they have the civic and democratic traditions that fire the imagination of West Europeans. Despite initiatives at decentralization, the heavy hand of central administrations is still very much in evidence throughout the macroregion, even in the governance of local affairs. Finally, there is no equivalent to the European Union Treaty and no Brussels.

Despite these differences, an institutional framework can be created that would encourage not only trade but collaborative relations across a wide range of issues touching on the future of city-regions in the Yellow Sea Rim. The following is a mere sketch, concrete in intention but without the detail that would breathe life into the concept. I would like to propose the establishment of an *Intergovernmental Council for the Integrated Development of the Yellow Sea Regional Cooperation Zone.* Council members from China, the two Koreas, and

Japan would be appointed by their respective national governments and include, among others, provincial governors and big-city mayors.

The broad purpose of this Council would be to promote and facilitate the integrated and sustainable development of the macroregion. Its activities would be funded with contributions from its institutional membership as well as from multilateral and bilateral sources. The Council would be served by a small technical secretariat and planning unit on the model, perhaps, of the spatial structures plan initiative of the Benelux countries that I mentioned earlier (Zonneveld and Faludi 1997). Intercity and interregional networking would be encouraged by the Council, with special committees set up to consider priority areas for common action, such as tourism, trade and business relations, transportation infrastructure, urban technologies, and cultural exchanges. Finally, the Council could initiate and monitor projects of its own. One concrete idea for such a project would be a *Yellow Sea International Research and Technology Center* (established with the backing of the scientific academies of member countries) to come up with concrete solutions to practical problems such as the use of seawater in industrial production, water recycling, industrial and municipal waste treatment, regenerating industrial wastelands, and the development of sustainable fisheries.

It seems to me that there are four conditions that must be met if a project of intercity networks in the Yellow Sea Regional Cooperation Zone is to succeed. *First*, it must be based on *complementary* interests, so that all parties stand to gain something from continuing cooperation. *Second*, the project requires a *strategic vision* that, even as it proceeds from simple beginnings, moves towards an increasingly broader range of objectives. *Third*, the project requires an *institutional base* that, in my proposal, would be the Intergovernmental Council for regional cooperation. And *finally*, the project needs *ongoing practical actions* that, step by step, lead to visible and beneficial outcomes for all concerned. This is my reason for suggesting a Yellow Sea International Research and Technology Center that would begin to address some of the region's urgent problems, such as the use of seawater in industrial production, and would facilitate the transfer of technologies from city to city and from region to region with positive-sum outcomes for all. The gradual emergence of the EU over the past forty years has been precisely such a gradual process based on conditions of interest complementarity, strategic vision, institutional development, and technical exchange. When, in the year 2050, we look back on the historical evolution of the Yellow Sea Cooperation Zone, we will see that the progress made was the result of just these first modest steps.

NOTES

1. The great champion of a system of city-regional development is undoubtedly Jane Jacobs, particularly in her excellent, if iconoclastic study, *Cities and the Wealth of Nations* (1984). Ms Jacobs cuts through a lot of professional cant on why some regions grow

while other stagnate or decline. Her trenchant critique is unfortunately marred by an insistence that a "genuine" development of urban economies hinges on their ability to replace imports with their own production. This principle flies straight in the face of the widely accepted theorem of export-orientation in regional growth.

2. UN projections for 2000 are of fifteen cities with more than 12 million people, headed by the Tokyo agglomeration with its 28 million. The number of so-called megacities is expected to increase to thirty-three by 2015 (United Nations 1995).
3. The concept is, in fact, not new at all, but it is only now beginning to be acknowledged as an urban form. See Friedmann and Miller (1965). What *is* new, though, is the emphasis on transnational activities located outside the urban core.
4. This is a key point in Jane Jacobs's (1984) analysis and with which I am in full accord.

REFERENCES

Amin, A. (ed.). (1994). *Post Fordism: A Reader.* Oxford: Blackwell.

Berg, L. van den, Braun, E., and Meer, J. van der. (1993). *Governing Metropolitan Regions.* Aldershot: Avebury.

Chang, S-D., Hu, X.-W., and Sun, J.-J. (1992). "Tianjin: North China's Reviving Metropolis," in Y.-M. Yeung and H. W. Hu (eds.), *China's Coastal Cities: Catalysts for Modernization.* Honolulu: University of Hawaii Press, 41–68.

Chen, X.-M. (1995). "The Evolution of Free Economic Zones and the Recent Development of Cross-national Growth Zones." *International Journal of Urban and Regional Research*, 19 (4): 593–621.

Chu, S. W.-K., and Ho, K. C. (1997). *City-States in the Global Economy: Industrial Restructuring in Hong Kong and Singapore.* Boulder: Westview Press.

Church, A., and Reid, P. (1996). "International Networks and Competition: The Example of Cross-border Cooperation." *Urban Studies*, 33: 1297–318.

Douglass, M. (1995). "Global Interdependence and Urbanization: Planning for the Bangkok Mega-Urban Region," in T. G. McGee and I. M. Robinson (eds.), *The Mega-Urban Regions of Southeast Asia.* Vancouver: University of British Columbia Press, 45–77.

—— (1998). "World City Formation on the Asia Pacific Rim: Poverty, 'Everyday' Forms of Civil Society and Environmental Management," in M. Douglass and J. Friedmann (eds.), *Cities for Citizens: Planning and the Rise of Civil Society in a Global Age.* Chichester, New York: John Wiley & Sons.

EUROCITIES. (1996). *A Charter of the European Cities: Towards a Revision of the Treaty on European Union.* Brussels: EUROCITIES.

Friedmann, J. (1986). "The World City Hypothesis." *Development and Change*, 17: 69–83.

—— (1995). "Where We Stand: A Decade of World City Research," in P. L. Knox and P. J. Taylor (eds.), *World Cities in a World System.* Cambridge: Cambridge University Press, 21–47.

—— (1998*a*). "The Common Good: Assessing the Performance of Cities," in H. Dandekar (ed.), *City, Space, and Globalization: An International Perspective.* Conference Proceedings. Ann Arbor: University of Michigan, College of Architecture and Urban Planning.

—— (1998*b*). "World City Futures: The Role of Urban and Regional Policies in the Asia-Pacific Region," in Y.-M. Yeung (ed.), *Urban Development in Asia: Retrospect and Prospect.* Hong Kong: Hong Kong Institute of Asia-Pacific Studies, The Chinese University of Hong Kong.

——, and Miller, J. (1965). "The Urban Field." *Journal of the American Institute of Planners*, 31: 312–19.

——, and Wolff, G. (1982). "World City Formation: An Agenda for Research and Action." *International Journal of Urban and Regional Research*, 6: 309–44.

Fukugawa, Y. (1997). "The Northeast Asian Economic Zone: Potential for the Latecomer," in E. K.-Y. Chen and C. H. Kwan (eds.), *Asia's Borderless Economy: The Emergence of Subregional Economic Zones.* St. Leonards, NSW (Australia): Allen & Unwin.

Gulinck, H., and Dortmans, C. (1997). "Neo-Rurality: The Benelux as a Workshop for New Ideas about Threatened Rural Areas," in W. Zonnveld and A. Faludi (eds.), *Vanishing Borders: The Second Benelux Structural Outline.* Special issue, *Built Environment*, 23: 37–46.

Held, D. (1995). *Democracy and the Global Order: From the Modern State to Cosmopolitan Governance.* Cambridge: The Polity Press.

Herzog, L. (1990). *Where North Meets South: Cities, Space, and Politics on the U.S.–Mexican Border.* Austin: University of Texas Press.

Jacobs, J. (1984). *Cities and the Wealth of Nations: Principles of Economic Life.* New York: Vintage Books.

Kim, W. B. (1990). "The Future of Coastal Development in the Yellow Sea Rim." *Journal of Northeast Asian Studies* (Winter): 307–19.

—— (1991). "Yellow Sea Economic Zone: Vision or Reality?" *Journal of Northeast Asia Studies* (Spring): 35–55.

—— (1998). "Economic Cooperation between China's Shandong Province and Korea's West Coast Region and Measures to Establish Regional Alliance." *Korean Spatial Planning Review*, 27: 1–18. In Korean; abstract in English.

Knox, P. L., and Taylor, P. J. (eds.). (1995). *World Cities in a World System.* New York: Cambridge University Press.

Kunzmann, K. (1995). "Strategische Städtenetze in Europa: Mode oder Chance," in H. Karl and W. Henrichsmeyer (eds.), *Regionalentwicklung im Prozess der Europäischen Integration.* Bonn: Institut für Europäische Integrationsforschung e.V. Bonner Schriften zur Integration, Europa Verlag.

Laquian, A. (1995). "The Governance of Mega-Urban Regions," in T. G. McGee and I. M. Robinson (eds.), *The Mega-Urban Regions of Southeast Asia.* Vancouver: University of British Columbia Press, 215–41.

Lefèvre, C. (1998). "Metropolitan Government and Governance in Western Countries: A Critical Review." *International Journal of Urban and Regional Research*, 22: 9–25.

Lin, G. C. S. (1997). *Red Capitalism in South China: Growth and Development of the Pearl River Delta.* Vancouver: University of British Columbia Press.

Linge, G. (ed.). (1997). *China's New Spatial Economy: Heading Towards 2020.* Hong Kong: Oxford University Press.

Linklater, A. (1998). *The Transformation of Political Community: Ethical Foundations of the Post-Westphalian Era.* Cambridge: Polity Press.

Liu, Y., Zhang, L., and Linge, G. (1997). "The Bohai Sea Rim: Some Development Issues," in G. Linge (ed.), *China's New Spatial Economy: Heading Towards 2020.* Hong Kong: Oxford University Press.

Losada, H., Martinez, H., Vieyra, J., Pealing, R., Zavala, R., and Cortés, H. (1998). "Urban Agriculture in the Metropolitan Zone of Mexico City: Changes over Time in Urban, Suburban, and Peri-urban Areas." *Environment and Urbanization*, 10: 37–54.

Murphy, P., and Wu, C.-T. (1999). "Governing Global Sydney: From Managerialism to Entrepreneurialism," in J. Friedmann (ed.), *Urban and Regional Governance in the Asia Pacific.* Vancouver: University of British Columbia, Institute of Asian Research.

North, D. C. (1955). "Location Theory and Regional Economic Growth." *Journal of Political Economy*, 63: 243–58.

Paauw, D. S., and Fei, J. C. H. (1973). *The Transition in Open Dualistic Economies: Theory and Southeast Asian Experience.* New Haven: Yale University Press.

Perloff, H. S., and Leven, C. L. (1964). "Towards an Integrated System of Regional Accounts: Stocks, Flows, and the Analysis of the Public Sector," in W. Z. Hirsch (ed.), *Elements of Regional Accounts.* Baltimore: Johns Hopkins.

Pierce, N. R. (1993). *Citistates: How Urban America Can Prosper in a Competitive World.* Washington, DC: Seven Locks Press.

Sassen, S. (1991). *The Global City: New York, London, Tokyo.* Princeton, N J: Princeton University Press.

—— (1994). *Cities in a World Economy.* Thousand Oaks, CA: Pine Forge/Sage.

—— (1996). *Losing Control: Sovereignty in an Age of Globalization.* New York: Columbia University Press.

Scott, A. J. (1996). "Regional Motors of the Global Economy." *Futures*, 28: 391–411.

Sivaramakrishna, K. C. (1996). "Urban Governance: Changing Relations," in M. A. Cohen, B. A. Ruble, J. S. Tulchin, and A. M. Garland (eds.), *Preparing for the Urban Future: Global Pressures and Local Forces.* Washington, DC: Woodrow Wilson Center Press.

Sklair, L. (1993). *Assembling for Development: The Maquila Industry in Mexico and the U.S.* U.S.–Mexico Contemporary Perspectives 5. San Diego: University of California at San Diego, Center for U.S.–Mexican Studies.

Soros, G. (1998). *The Crisis of Global Capitalism.* London: Little, Brown, & Co.

Storper, M. (1997). *The Regional World: Territorial Development in a Global Economy.* New York: Guilford Press.

——, and Salais, R. (1997). *Worlds of Production: The Action Frameworks of the Economy.* Cambridge, MA: Harvard University Press.

United Nations. (1995). *World Urbanization Prospects: The 1994 Revision.* New York.

Zonneveld, W., and Faludi, A. (eds.). (1997). *Vanishing Borders: The Second Benelux Structural Outline.* Special issue of *Built Environment*, 23 (1).

PART IV

THE COMPETITIVE ADVANTAGES OF GLOBAL CITY-REGIONS

Competitiveness, as Porter points out below, is not just a function of the capacity and competence of the individual firm, but resides, too, in the general milieu or locational environment that surrounds it. Porter argues (as do the authors of Chapters 1, 6, and 7) that a particularly rich kind of milieu is represented by the dense clusters of economic activity (together with their attendant local labor markets and other social appendages) that typically constitute the functional bases of global city-regions. These milieux almost always function as fountainheads of positive externalities helping to sustain high levels of economic performance in local firms. In this context, firms are simultaneously transmitters and receivers of benefits or competitive advantages embedded in commercial and noncommercial transactions alike. The locational proximity of the firms in any given cluster, moreover, ensures that these benefits retain high levels of potency at their point of consumption. Among the many positive features of this situation, one of the most important—in view of its role in sustaining dynamic competitiveness—revolves around the innovative impulses continually sparked off in dense interactive industrial systems.

To an increasing degree, then, competitive advantage resides not so much in natural resource endowments as it does in forms of social and political organization. Porter illustrates this point by reference to Houston, Texas, where local reserves of raw petroleum have long since been reduced to minor significance, but where a major business complex based on petroleum-industry services continues to grow and thrive. Precisely because competitive advantages in the modern world are to such a significant degree dependent on organizational rather than natural endowments, they can sometimes be actively built up in particular places by appropriate forms of policy intervention. Even places that have been subject to long-term economic decay are not entirely or necessarily beyond repair. As Porter suggests, the apparently hopeless cases of many American inner cities may yet be susceptible to recovery by cultivating their inherent but long suppressed competitive advantages based on centrality and population density.

The latter remarks point to possibilities for constructing creative new relationships between business and government in upgrading the competitive advantages of global city-regions. Courchene's chapter is in effect an extended exploration of this theme via an investigation of the regional political economy of the province of Ontario and the Toronto metropolitan area within the framework of NAFTA. Courchene shows how provincial policies over the 1990s have tended to steer Toronto away from its traditional role as a focal point of the Canadian economy and toward a new role as the nucleus of an extended global city-region whose functional context encompasses North America and the wider world. This change has been wrought in a series of political maneuvers involving both a decisive turn to neoliberalism by the government of Ontario, and the administrative consolidation of the formerly fragmented Toronto metropolitan area into a single megacity. In the process, Toronto's primary external commercial connections are being reorientated from a predominantly east–west axis to a predominantly north–south axis, and Toronto has emerged as one of North America's largest and most dynamic cities, with a diverse and booming local economy.

The propensity for new forms of business-government collaboration to make their appearance in global city-regions raises many questions about the political meanings and objectives of this collaboration. To a significant degree (as exemplified by the varied opinions set forth in the present book) these questions turn on the relative merits of competitiveness-enhancing policy agendas on the one hand, and more socially oriented programs on the other. Oddly, perhaps, there appears to be a wide domain of agreement to the effect that some form of public or collective action is needed to sustain high levels of competitive performance in global city-regions, though a wide gap separates those who advocate such action in order to promote purely business interests and those who see it as also serving wider social purposes. The disagreements evident here are symptomatic of a wider clash of views about practical issues of development, growth, and competition in general as globalization runs its course. Just as the debate on globalization itself is currently moving into high pitch, so the specific problems of global city-regions are increasingly the object of intense and many-sided disputes, not least about the role that public policy should or should not play in their economic progress, distributive performance, and social well-being.

9

Regions and the New Economics of Competition

MICHAEL E. PORTER

This conference, in which so many interesting people have come together to explore the intersection of geography, competition, the environment, and society, comes at a time in the world economy that is puzzling to many observers. The process of globalization seemingly should make location and regions less important, but it appears to be doing just the opposite. Many government and company leaders are struggling to understand what it all means. Is there a role for national or state governments? What is that role? Should companies worry about where they locate operations and take a proactive role in their communities, or is that obsolete thinking?

There are some very substantial changes underway in the nature of competition, the sources of competitiveness, and the principles of economic policy. These changes have been underway for some time, but only recently are they becoming evident. What is the new agenda they are defining? What roles does it suggest for companies, governments, and other institutions? This chapter aims to describe the outlines of this new economics of competition and the prominent role that regions and cities play in it.

TRANSITIONS IN COMPETITION

The new economics of competition can be summarized around six transitions that are increasingly driving prosperity. I will outline each of them briefly. The balance of this chapter will develop the theoretical foundations and some of the policy implications.

From macroeconomics to microeconomics. Historically, most country economic policy has focused on the macroeconomic issues—e.g. government budgets, inflation, and interest rates. Indeed macroeconomic policy *is* economic policy in many countries. Increasingly, however, macroeconomic policy has become table stakes. A sound macroeconomic policy is essential, but no longer provides enduring prosperity because all countries are pursuing the same aims with similar policies. Moreover, countries that fail to deliver sound macroeconomic policies are punished by global capital markets, which limit the discretion national leaders have about macro policy.

Increasingly, the drivers of prosperity and economic policy are moving to the microeconomic level—to the capabilities and behavior of units below the whole economy such as individuals, firms, industries, and clusters. There are some who believe that with sound macroeconomic policies the improvement in microeconomic conditions takes care of itself. However, in an increasing number of countries with solid macro policies, among them New Zealand, Britain, and Australia, growth in per capita income is disappointing due to microeconomic weaknesses.

From current productivity to innovation. In the last two decades, economic policy in most countries has been focused on what one might call getting the national house in order. This has involved steps to address the inappropriate roles government played in the past: deregulating, privatizing, restructuring, reducing unnecessary business costs, improving poorly performing infrastructure, etc. Yet the progress on current productivity is beginning to reach the point of diminishing returns, especially in advanced economies. The future agenda is increasingly becoming one of enhancing the capacity for innovation—how to create an environment in a country, state, or region that supports the creation and commercialization of new ideas. Gains in productivity from reversing poor policies and emulating best practices from elsewhere produce major benefits, but they are largely one-time benefits. Sustained productivity growth requires the capacity to innovate.

From economywide to clusters. At the microeconomic level, most policy thinking has addressed aspects of the business environment that affect all industries in the economy, or broad sectors such as manufacturing or services. While the economy as a whole remains an important unit of analysis, however, economywide influences are rarely competitive advantages. Much competitive advantage in advanced economies arises from things that are cluster-specific. Clusters are groups of interconnected firms and industries in the same field that arise in particular economic areas. Clusters arise because of local externalities of various sorts including the benefits of proximity for many types of interfirm transactions (especially those involving ideas and technology) as well as access to specialized institutions and inputs. While having good roads, a sensible overall tax policy, and intellectual property protection are all important to a productive economy, then, the defining sources of competitive advantage are often more specialized.

From internal to external sources of company success. There are parallel changes going on in thinking about the competitive advantages of companies. Historically, most work on company strategy has taken an internal or company perspective. Indeed, the assumption implicit in almost all the literature on management is that company success is driven by what a company does and the choices it makes about how to organize and compete. However, there is growing recognition that company success also has much to do with things that are outside the company. Recognition of the importance of supplier relationships and the benefits of partnering were early examples of this perspective. Now, it is becoming more apparent that supplier relationships, partnerships, and many other resources that firms draw upon have much to do with the locations at which company activities are based. Traditional thinking about industrial location concentrates on business costs such as taxes and utility rates. Recent research suggests that locational influences on competitive advantage are far broader. The environment in which a company is based has much to do with the choices it makes and the capabilities it can draw upon efficiently. This amounts to a rather radical change in our perspective on competition. In 1999, for example, there was for the first time an economic geography module in the core strategy course at the Harvard Business School.

From separating to integrating economic and social policy. Historically, economic policy has largely been seen as a subject in and of itself. Economic policy and social policy have been two different disciplines pursued by different groups of players. Today it is becoming increasingly clear that we can no longer separate economic from social. Increasingly, the challenge will be to integrate the two. For example, my work on problems of distressed inner city areas in the United States suggests that alleviating this distress will require the integration of both economic and social approaches. Either alone—relying on a rising tide to lift all boats or on large investments in social spending to redress inequalities—will not be successful. And "Third Way" approaches, which represent a sort of splitting the difference, lack a firm conceptual grounding.

From national/cross-national to regional and local. The nation-state has been the principal geographical unit of economic analysis, and the locus of economic policy has tended to be national. Today, the geographic unit of interest is becoming more varied. On the one hand, many dimensions of economic policy must now be addressed at least in part at the cross-national level. On the other hand, the drivers of prosperity are increasingly subnational, based in cities and regions.

The more that one thinks in terms of microeconomics, innovation, clusters, and integrating economic and social policy, the more the city-region emerges as an important unit. Issues or policies that span nations or are common to many nations will be increasingly neutralized, and no longer sources of competitive advantage.

However, it is not a matter of one unit of geography supplanting another. While the relative emphasis is shifting, all levels remain important. A region in the United States will not prosper if the United States as a nation does not adequately protect intellectual property, or fails to work with other countries on issues that span national borders. The task is to integrate the city-region with other economic units, and adopt a more textured view of the sources of prosperity and economic policy that encompasses multiple levels of geography.

SOURCES OF RISING PROSPERITY

In order to develop these ideas further, we must understand the theoretical foundations of economic prosperity in the modern economy.[1] In global competition, prosperity is no longer based on natural resources, military power, political influence, or the presence of large-scale firms. Instead, the roots of a high and rising standard of living lie in the productivity with which a given economic area can utilize its human, capital, and physical resources. It is rarely what a nation inherits that determines its prosperity in the global economy, but the productivity with which enterprises can operate there. Productivity determines the wages that can be sustained and the returns to capital and natural resources employed. Competitiveness, then, is determined by productivity. While a decade ago there was no accepted definition of competitiveness, there is increasing understanding that the only meaningful definition of competitiveness is productivity.

Treatments of productivity tend to focus on efficiency, or the unit output per man hour or dollar of capital employed. However, the proper conception of productivity encompasses the *value* of the products and services that can be created in a given economic area (e.g. uniqueness, quality, features) as well as the efficiency with which they can be produced. Rising per capita income comes as much or more from driving up the value of products (and the prices they can command) as it does from increasing the efficiency with which generic or standard products are produced.

The central role of productivity in prosperity renders industrial policy thinking obsolete. All industries offer possibilities to raise productivity and, with it, improve prosperity. Sophisticated technology can be applied to the production of virtually any product or service. There are no high-technology and low-technology industries, only companies that apply high-technology or low-technology methods. Prosperity has less to do with what an economic area produces than how it goes about doing so.

Many natural resources are becoming less valuable as globalization expands their supply and technology or creates new substitutes. The most prosperous economic areas do not export natural resources or even physical products per se (which can be produced in many locations) but intellectual capital in various forms. A good example is the oil and gas cluster in Houston. Very little of the world's oil and gas is produced in Texas anymore, and even less of it is produced near Houston. In terms of the creation of intellectual capital, advanced technology, and high wages, however, the world center of oil and gas is in Houston.

The traditional distinction between domestic and foreign companies has also largely been superceded. In terms of its impact on the prosperity of an economic area, the ownership of a company is secondary to what the company chooses to do in that area. The profit flowing to owners is normally small relative to the wages a company pays and the other impacts it has on an economic area; much of the profit itself is typically reinvested. Ownership itself is also becoming more international. If a foreign company chooses to locate highly productive activities in an economic area, this supports rising wages and serves to upgrade other local firms and industries. Conversely, a domestic company that produces using unproductive methods will constrain local wages and may hurt other locally based firms that depend on the company for goods and services. The choice of what a company will do in a location is, in turn, a function of the quality and efficiency of the business environment there—on productivity.

Finally, traditional distinctions between local industries and traded industries are breaking down, a fundamental issue facing Japan (see Porter, Takeuchi, and Sakakibara 2000). Japanese policymakers thought that they could separate the export industries, many of which were highly competitive, from local industries such as distribution, agriculture, transportation, and food processing, many of which are highly uncompetitive. Local industries in Japan have been protected and blocked from restructuring to provide employment opportunities and a sort of retirement system. Yet the inefficient local Japanese industries have driven up the costs of export industries, while the idiosyncratic structure of the local industries has impeded the ability of many companies that depend on them in some way to compete in international markets. National productivity depends on the productivity of *both* local and traded industries.

PRODUCTIVITY AND THE MICROECONOMIC BUSINESS ENVIRONMENT

Productivity in a given economic area is clearly influenced by the quality and stability of the macroeconomic and political environment. Unstable macroeconomic policies and an unreliable political system deter investment and shorten time horizons. While a sound macroeconomic, political, and legal context is a precondition for high levels of productivity, however, it is not sufficient. Wealth is actually created by the microeconomic capabilities of an economy—the capacity of individuals, firms, markets, and associated institutions to produce valuable output using efficient methods. The association between microeconomic environment and GDP per capita is revealed in statistical research (Porter 1998*a*, and 1999*b*). Using survey data from fifty-five countries, a composite index of the microeconomic competitiveness based on common factor analysis explains more than 84 percent of the variation in GDP per capita.

Macroeconomic policy defines a context in which firms have an opportunity to be productive. Microeconomic circumstances determine whether an economy actually is productive. The framework in *The Competitive Advantage of Nations* provides one way of modeling the microeconomic environment of an economic area in terms of four influences:

1. the *quality and specialization of the inputs* available there—e.g. human resources, capital markets, technological base, and physical infrastructure;
2. the *quality of local demand*—the sophistication of the local customer base and the demand-side pressures giving firms special insight into customer needs and pushing them to upgrade;
3. the *context in which rivalry takes place*, a function of the incentives for investment- and technology-intensive forms of competition and the intensity of local rivalry;

4. the *availability and quality of related and supporting industries*, which influences the productivity of accessing components, services, and machinery and the flexibility and speed of innovation.

This complex array of microeconomic factors, inputs, institutions, incentives, and pressures provides the underpinning of productive forms of competition.

The role of local competition in a global economy has been especially controversial. In a recent book (Porter, Takeuchi, and Sakakibara 2000), we have investigated the role of local rivalry in Japan, a country where it is widely believed that lax antitrust policy contributed to competitive success. In a sample of industries, the dominant variable explaining Japan's world export share was the extent of fluctuation in Japanese (home) market share among the leading competitors, a measure of local rivalry. Competitive industries, such as cameras, were ones where local market share fluctuated substantially. Uncompetitive industries, such as polyethylene film, were ones where market share rarely changed. We also collected data on all registered cartels in post-World War II Japan. Industries in which there had ever been a cartel were almost never competitive.

The vitality of rivalry has very strong implications for policy in developing countries where monopolies are prevalent and numerous barriers to competition are present. Without a strong commitment to competition, including a strict antitrust policy, a country is unlikely to progress economically. This result is verified statistically using data from *The Global Competitiveness Report* (Porter 1998*a*, 1999*b*).

CLUSTERS AND THE BUSINESS ENVIRONMENT OF REGIONS

Clusters are geographic concentrations of interconnected companies, specialized suppliers, and service providers; firms in related industries; and associated institutions (for example, universities, standards agencies, and trade associations) in particular fields that compete but also cooperate. There is a long tradition in the literature in economics, regional science, and other disciplines that takes note of the tendency of firms to agglomerate in geographical regions in particular fields. These literatures continue to add to our knowledge of the phenomenon, and the contributions are too numerous to summarize here.[2] My work has sought to integrate the concept of agglomeration with the learning on competition and competitive strategy in a global economy.

A cluster is a series of connected industries producing products and services that are related in a variety of ways. The concept of clusters focuses not so much on the agglomeration of a single industry but on the externalities across industries. Such externalities, in the form of such things as relationships with suppliers and firms in related industries and access to local institutions, take on great importance in modern competition. The Norwegian maritime cluster provides a good example. Norway is a location with high costs of labor and other basic inputs, but controls 10 percent of all the world's sea-borne trade. The cluster includes shipping companies, the traditional core industry, but also ship and other vessel builders, specialized service providers (e.g. lending, insurance, legal), shipboard and cargo-handling equipment, standard-setting and classification organizations, specialized education providers, and an array of other related industries (e.g. offshore oil and gas production). The productivity of Norwegian maritime-related firms supports high local wages and a high standard of living.

Clusters are present in virtually all economies, but are most associated with advanced economies. It appears that cluster formation is fundamental to economic development, because it is necessary to support more sophisticated and productive forms of competition. The relationship between clusters and economic development is supported by the available statistical evidence. Cluster attributes, such as the quantity and quality of local suppliers, prove to have a strong positive association with GDP per capita. It also appears that economic growth is led by clusters. In Norway, for example, recent research has revealed that the clustered industries have grown faster than other industries in the economy between 1988 and 1998 (Norwegian School of Management 1999).

Clusters can be national in scope, arising almost exclusively within the borders of a single nation, such as the case of Norwegian maritime. Clusters also sometimes cross national borders, but more often they are geographically concentrated *within* nations. As firms, suppliers, related industries, and other institutions are concentrated in close proximity, the productivity and innovation advantages of clusters often rise.

A good example is California wine. This cluster encompasses less than the state of California and is contained in a number of counties. Within these counties, there is not only a concentration of wine producers but also independent grape growers, suppliers to wine producers and grape growers (such as winemaking equipment, barrels, bottles, caps, and labels), specialized services providers such as public relations and advertising, information companies such as trade publications (e.g. *The Wine Spectator*), and specialized institutions such as the programs in wine-related education and specialized enology research at the University of California at Davis.

A cluster is much more than simply an economic organization facilitating production efficiency. The essence of a cluster lies in the exchange of insights, knowledge, and technology, and in offering a structure that offers the incentives and flexibility to innovate. A California-based wine company can innovate more easily than an isolated wine producer, for example, because it can readily assemble all the elements needed to do so. Location within a cluster facilitates continuous improvement, encourages strategic differentiation, and creates pressures for innovation (Porter forthcoming).

MAPPING CLUSTERS

Clusters represent a new way of conceptualizing and dividing up economies. Defining clusters precisely, and linking cluster development to performance, has been hampered by limitations in standard industrial classification systems. Economic data has traditionally been collected based on aggregates such as manufacturing and services. Within these categories, industries are grouped based on product similarity rather than the strength of externalities. Our cluster mapping project has begun the process of defining the boundaries of clusters statistically. The essence of a cluster lies in externalities that cross industry boundaries as well as boundaries between categories such as components, machinery, and services. We test for externalities by examining the locational correlation of employment across states or economic areas in pairs or groups of industries. In other words, where there is employment in one industry in an economic area, do we also find employment in another industry? Locational correlation is an indication of cross-industry linkages. Given the size and diversity of the U.S. economy, the distribution of employment across states and economic areas provides a unique opportunity to test for clustering in this way.

The methodology begins by separating industries that are inherently local (e.g. restaurants, local utilities, local services) from industries that trade products and services across economic areas. Local industries are not concentrated geographically; employment in them is widely distributed across all economic areas.[3] Such industries can be isolated using statistical methods. We estimate that local industries represent approximately 64 percent of total U.S. private employment, an important reminder that not all economic activity is global or even national in competitive scope.

The other 36 percent of employment is in industries that compete across economic areas. These industries represent the minority of employment, but they are the drivers of economic development. Traded industries have higher average wages ($35,373 vs. $23,164 in 1996), and directly or indirectly *create the demand for the local industries*. Using locational correlation of employment across states, we identified fifty traded clusters in the economy (see Figure 9.1). Some industries have linkages to more than one cluster. Among traded industries, a small number of industries (less than 1 percent of employment) are geographically concentrated purely because of traditional comparative advantages in terms of the location of natural resources.

Defining cluster boundaries using this approach requires adjustments for spurious correlation. Two industries can exhibit locational correlation if they are part of two different clusters but ones which are both strong in the same one or two states. We eliminated spurious correlation using detailed examination of industry definitions and input-output tables (which reveal one form of interindustry linkage).

Figure 9.2 illustrates the patterns of locational correlation in the information technology cluster. Taking electronic computers as the core industry (1.00), the locational correlation of computer employment with employment in prepackaged software is .726; with magnetic and optical recorders, .778; with electronic components, .860; with telephone and telegraph apparatus, .773; and so on. These correlations reveal the tightness of fit within a cluster.

Upstream	Industrial and Supporting Functions	Final Consumption Goods and Services
• Ceramics and glass • Chemical products • Forest products • Information technology • Materials for construction and building • Metal manufacturing • Oil and gas • Optical goods • Plastics • Rubber	• Aerospace engines • Aerospace vehicles and defense products • Analytical instruments • Automotive • Communications equipment • Education and knowledge creation • Farm machinery and construction equipment • Financial services (except insurance) • Insurance • Heavy construction services • Marine equipment and technology • Motorcycles and bicycles • Motor-driven products • Power generation • Power transmission and distribution • Prefabricated enclosures • Production technology • Publishing and printing • Transportation and logistical services	• Apparel • Building fixtures and equipment • Crops based agriculture • Confectionery and baked goods • Dairy products • Entertainment • Fishing and fish products • Footwear • Furniture • Hospitality and tourism • Jewelry and precious metals • Leather products • Lighting and electrical equipment • Malt beverages • Meat processing • Medical devices and health services • Packaged personal goods • Pharmaceuticals • Textiles • Tobacco • Wine

Figure 9.1. *Clusters of traded industries*

It is important to note that employment patterns in the traded industries include some employment in dispersed sales, service, and distribution facilities of firms that have their primary headquarters in a particular economic area. This means that employment patterns will *understate* the actual degree of clustering in the economy. Nevertheless, locational correlation analysis reveals strong cluster linkages that are consistent with more qualitative assessments of groups of externalities among industries.

Mapping clusters across geography reveals strong concentrations of cluster employment in particular regions and cities. Figures 9.3 and 9.4 show maps, by county, of employment in two representative clusters, the information technology cluster and the automotive cluster. The figures indicate counties in which employment in the cluster has a location quotient (LQ) of greater than one. (The LQ is greater than 1 if the employment in a cluster in a county is greater than that county's average share of employment in the United States.) The findings are striking. There are strong cluster concentrations in particular regions. Moreover, the counties with high LQs are almost invariably *contiguous*, verifying a strong influence of proximity in cluster location.

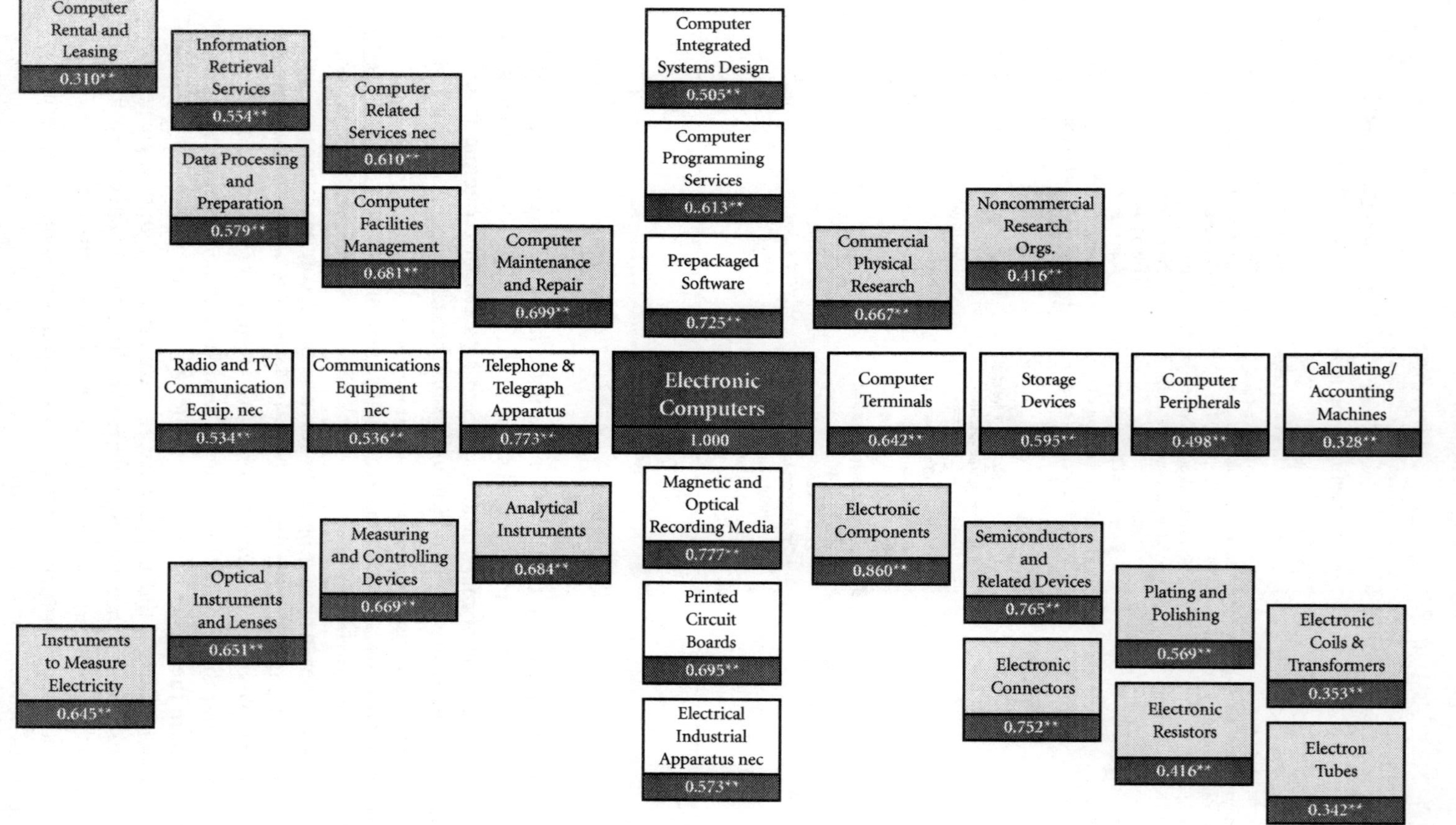

Figure 9.2. *Information technology cluster: locational correlation of employment with core industry in U.S. states (Double asterisk indicates significant at the 95% level)*

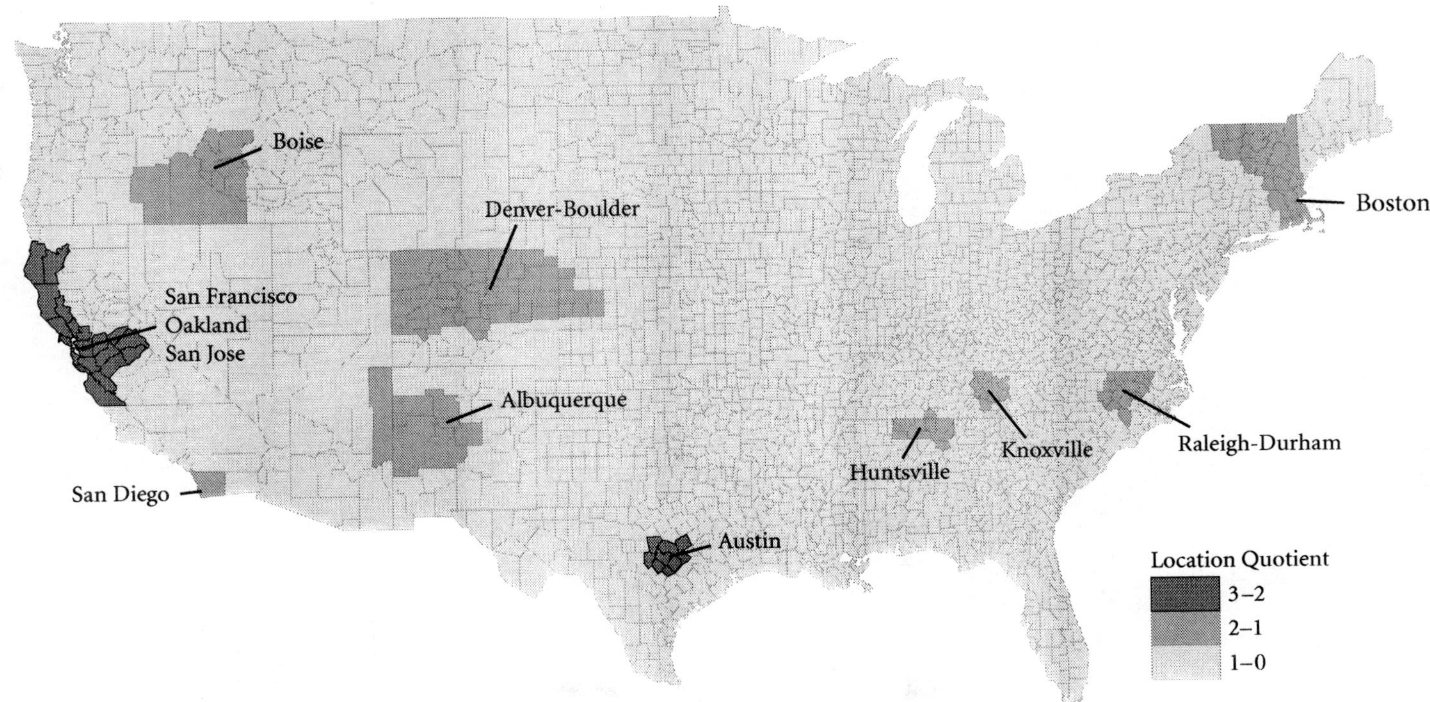

Figure 9.3. *The geography of the information technology cluster in the United States*

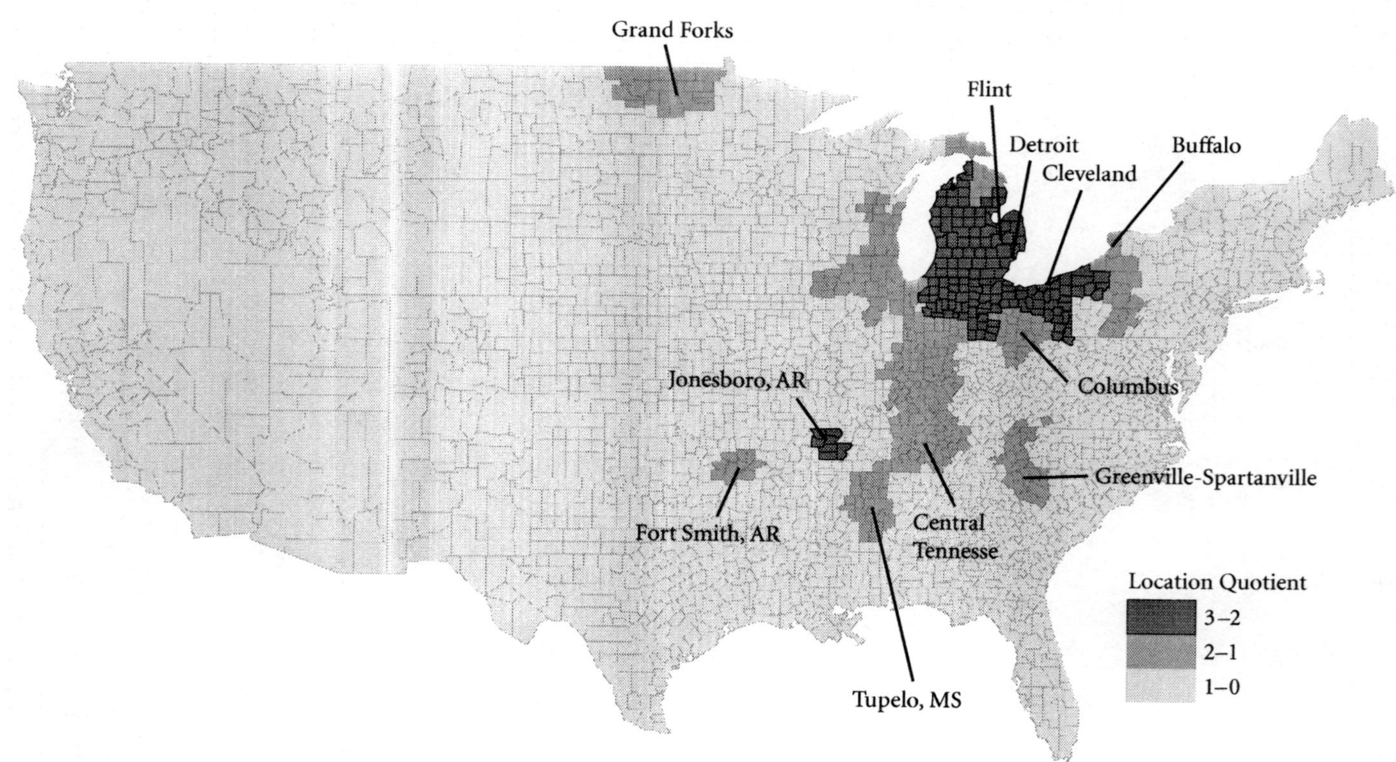

Figure 9.4. *The geography of the automotive cluster in the United States*

The data and methodology are being used to explore the evolution of clusters over time, the overlaps between clusters, the link between clustering and patenting, and the relationship between clustering and economic performance (e.g. employment growth, average wages).

CLUSTERS AND INNOVATION

While improving current productivity is a central challenge for economic policy, future prosperity and sustained economic development will hinge increasingly on innovation. The successful assimilation, development, and commercialization of new products and process underpins long-term productivity growth. Innovative capacity is one step removed from today's prosperity. Innovation drives the rate of long-run productivity growth and hence *future* competitiveness.

Recent research has modeled the sources of innovative capacity in an economic area as falling into three broad categories (Porter, Stern, and Furman 1999). The first is the *common innovation infrastructure*. This refers to the common pool of institutions and resource commitments that support innovation in many fields. These can be seen as the elements of the diamond that are cross-cutting and which influence innovation in many if not all industries (e.g. investment in basic research, investment in education, the extent of the network of universities conducting research and training scientists and engineers) and the policies that broadly affect the incentives for innovation in any industry (e.g. intellectual property laws).

The second element of innovative capacity is *cluster-specific conditions*. While the common innovation infrastructure is important, innovation is also strongly affected by circumstances in particular fields such as specialized inputs, unique demand conditions for particular types of products, and access to specialized suppliers. This is why nations and regions are invariably more innovative in some fields than others.

Innovation tends to be facilitated by the presence of a cluster, particularly where the cluster is concentrated geographically. Innovations in related industries tend to feed on each other. Firms within a cluster are often able to perceive new buyer needs more clearly and rapidly than can isolated competitors. For example, Silicon Valley and Austin-based computer companies plug into customer needs and trends quickly and effectively, with an ease nearly impossible to match elsewhere. Firms within a cluster can also often commercialize innovations more rapidly and efficiently because of their ability to source easily needed components, machinery, and services. Small entrepreneurial firms grow up within clusters to meet newly emerging needs overlooked or too small for established players. Reinforcing these other innovation advantages of clusters is the sheer pressure —competitive pressure, peer pressure, and constant comparison—that arises in geographically concentrated clusters.

The final element of innovative capacity in an economic area is *the quality of linkages*. The strength of the interaction between the common innovation infrastructure and cluster-specific conditions also matters. For example, are there effective institutions in place to migrate basic science into established or nascent clusters? Do the strongest clusters provide sustained support back to the common institutions? While measuring the strength of these interactions is difficult, they represent a key element of the national innovation environment in an economic area.

Statistical analysis in seventeen OECD countries between 1973 and 1993 revealed a strong and consistent relationship between measures of the strength of national innovative capacity and per capita international patenting (Stern, Porter, and Furman 1999; Porter, Stern, and Council on Competitiveness 1999).

An international patent is one that is filed in both the home country as well as abroad. The research used the number of patents that were approved in both the country of the inventor as well as by the U.S. Patent and Trademark Office. Patenting is an imperfect measure of innovation, but is "the only observable manifestation of inventive activity with a well-grounded claim for universality" (Trajtenberg 1990: 183). Obtaining a patent in a foreign country is a costly undertaking, which is only worthwhile where a commercial return is anticipated. Hence, international patenting isolates innovations of commercial significance. Moreover, the fact that all patents were also granted by the U.S. Patent and Trademark Office not only ensures consistency in standards but also controls for "new-to-the-world" technologies.

Overall, the measures of the strength of national innovative capacity explained more than 99 percent of the variation in international patenting, highlighting the strong relationship between measures of innovative capacity and observed innovative output.

While the research just described focused on innovation at the national level, it is clear that the true locus of innovation is regional and local. Many elements of the common innovation infrastructure vary by region. Equally or more important, however, cluster circumstances vary strongly by region. Our cluster mapping project is just beginning to explore the relationship between clustering and patenting activity at the level of states, economic areas, and counties. Preliminary results suggest a strong relationship between innovation and clustering. New learning on innovation will require moving beyond aggregate patterns of innovation and national-level research to investigate the microeconomics of innovation in particular geographic areas. Innovation policy will also increasingly require a state and local dimension. U.S. states, for example, are beginning to play a much more active role in innovation policy, with some states actually allocating public funds for basic and development research.

APPROPRIATE ROLES OF GOVERNMENT

The new economics of competition involves changed roles for government. Government's role is clearly more than providing a stable macroeconomic policy. Government must also work to improve the microeconomic business environment that affects all industries. It must improve the quality of the inputs and infrastructure firms draw upon, such as the basic education system, the logistical infrastructure, and communications infrastructure. Government must also create a system of rules and incentives to encourage more productive modes of competition across the economy, in areas such as antitrust, investment incentives, intellectual property protection, and so forth.

There is growing recognition, however, that there are additional roles for government at the cluster level. In addition to pursuing policies to benefit the economy as a whole, states and regions are beginning to see their economies as a collection of clusters, and looking for ways to enhance productive potential at the cluster level. In the United States and elsewhere, there are numerous cluster initiatives that are creating a new type of working relationship between business and government.

Cluster development is not the same as industrial policy. Industrial policy is based on the premise that some industries are more beneficial to prosperity than others, and that nations or regions should employ subsidies and other policies to distort competition in their favor. Cluster theory, in contrast, posits that *all* clusters can contribute to rising prosperity and that the task is to improve the business environment to allow existing and emerging clusters to be more productive. In traditional conceptions of economic policy, government-business interactions focus on lobbying over tax breaks and efforts to reduce business costs such as unemployment insurance and dealing with regulatory burdens. In cluster development, the aim is to remove obstacles and constraints to upgrading productivity at the cluster level, whether they be specialized skill pools or the need for more innovation-friendly regulatory standards. Reducing business costs remains important, but cluster development recognizes a wider array of relevant business costs as well as going beyond costs to allow firms to be more effective. Government and business must work together to understand what the particular constraints are and relax them.

The medical device cluster in the Minneapolis/St. Paul area illustrates that cluster development involves not just government but also initiatives by the private sector and local universities. In the Twin Cities, policy choices by the state and city governments were prominent in the upgrading of the cluster. For example, the Minnesota government instituted a technology licensing program at the state university. It began marketing the state as a leading center of health technology ("The Great State of Health") which was more effective than a generalized appeal to attract any company in any field to locate there. A full-time "Health Care Industry Specialist" was appointed in the Department of Trade and Economic Development to coordinate the various interfaces between government and the cluster. Although government initiatives were important, however, the private sector also pursued a variety of initiatives by itself, often through trade associations. For example, university and technical college programs were developed in particular specialties where there were skill shortages, and the cluster trade group, the Medical Alley Association, is active in many other areas.

Once the role of clusters in competitiveness is understood, a new and more constructive relationship between business and government is possible.

Regions or cities can begin the process of economic development by understanding where they have areas of strength. In modern global competition, economic areas must specialize and even subspecialize. In Minneapolis/St. Paul, for example, the uniqueness in health technology lies in the cardiovascular area. In Connecticut, there is a bioscience cluster that includes an array of large pharmaceutical company research centers. While Connecticut is unlikely to supplant Boston or the West Coast anytime soon, there are subfields in which Connecticut has uniqueness (Connecticut Department of Economic Community Development 1999, 1998). These should guide the process of cluster development.

Distinctions between high technology and low technology should not lead regions to turn away from fields. Every field can become high technology, from agriculture to logistics. Not all industries will grow, and employment in a cluster may decline as it is upgraded, but every cluster offers the potential to support higher living standards. An example is the oil and gas cluster in Houston. Oil and gas would seem to be a mature, low technology field, and is vulnerable to ups and downs in oil prices. Economic planners in Houston have sometimes sought to reduce dependence on the sector. However, a closer look at the oil and gas cluster reveals an extraordinary level of technology. The axes of technological development are ultra deepwater offshore drilling and advanced reservoir recovery. Deepwater drilling requires dynamically positioned vessels costing $300 million or more, filled with sophisticated equipment, much of which is built in Houston. The oil and gas cluster is one of the largest users of superconductors for modeling seismic data to support exploration and production. Cutting-edge materials used in oilfield equipment to deal with high pressure and harsh conditions can seed new industries. While total employment in the cluster is down from the past peak, the average wage in the cluster has risen markedly. Houston generates the highest value added per worker of any oil and gas cluster in the world.

INTEGRATING ECONOMIC AND SOCIAL POLICY

Economic and social policy have traditionally been seen as separate agendas involving different organizations and programs. In the new economics of competition, however, social and economic policy are integrally interconnected. A productive economy requires well-educated workers with a sense of opportunity, who are healthy, have adequate housing, and who are willing to invest in upgrading their capabilities. Moreover, protecting the environment enhances productivity rather than detracts from it, because corporate pollution is a sign of waste and poor technology. Reducing pollution involves more productive use of resources (Porter and van der Linde 1995).

There is no conflict between a healthy economy and a just and fair society (see Porter 1999*c*). The same things that are good for people are good for the economy, if one sees prosperity in productivity terms. There is no substitute for helping people be successful in the economy rather than attempting to distort economic outcomes via intervention and redistribution, and no substitute for a healthy economy in creating the resources needed to address social needs. "Third Way" thinking, which seeks a middle ground between society and the economy, is flawed because integration of social and economic does not require compromise in either direction. Most of the apparent conflicts between the economy and society have to do with an overly simplified view of competition and bad public policies, which fail to equip citizens to prosper in the economy and create bad incentives through the way social programs are structured.

The particular social challenge where I have devoted the most attention is America's inner cities, where poverty in the United States is concentrated.[4] Inner cities have been seen as primarily a social problem, to be addressed with large amounts of both public and philanthropic spending on social programs. This approach has not succeeded, because it has failed to recognize that poverty in cities is also an economic problem. Without a viable economic base and job creation in or near inner cities, no amount of social spending will redress inequality.

The premise has been that job growth must inevitably occur in the suburbs. Yet for many types of businesses it is more efficient to be located in the urban core. Policy errors and poor city administration drove up business costs in urban cores and drove out companies. Our research also reveals that many companies leave the inner city not because they want to, but because they cannot find a site for expansion. While there is plenty of vacant land in inner cities, political barriers have prevented the assembly and development of usable sites. By looking at the fundamentals of prosperity in new ways, then, it becomes evident that the traditional demarcation between rich areas and poor areas is not inevitable but the outcome of faulty policy choices.

A paradigm shift is needed here, from reducing poverty to creating income, jobs, and wealth that widen prosperity to all of our citizens. Inner cities can build a viable economic base once we stop thinking about them as disadvantaged areas and start thinking about their inherent competitive advantages in a regional economy. We need to focus on market opportunities, not community deficiencies. The existing and potential advantages of the cities most often lie in their strategic location, in an underserved local market demand, in the potential for integration with citywide and regional business clusters, and in available human resources in a worker-constrained economy.

Regions must see inner cities as having an important role in an efficient metropolitan economy. Clusters that benefit from an inner-city location include health care, entertainment and tourism, education, financial services, transportation and logistics, food processing and distribution, logistically sensitive manufacturing, recycling/remanufacturing, commercial support services, and consumer retailing and services.

There is now a substantial body of research highlighting the competitive advantages of urban cores as business locations, documenting the types of growth businesses already located in these areas, and charting the policy approaches required to improve the business environment in areas that have been largely neglected. The disadvantages of inner cities as business locations must be addressed directly, not offset by subsidies. Ironically, success will come not from seeing inner cities as special areas needing special approaches, but from practicing more traditional economic development activities in these areas.

CONCLUSIONS

Prosperity in the modern, global economy is increasingly rooted in the microeconomic capacity of economic areas, both in terms of current productivity and the capacity for innovation. The microeconomic perspective also highlights better ways to connect economic and social policy. Disadvantaged parts of regional economies will only become more prosperous if we apply the same thinking about competitiveness in these areas as we do to the rest of the economy.

The nation-state has been the principal geographical unit of economic analysis, and the locus of economic policy has tended to be national. The more that one thinks in terms of microeconomics, innovation, clusters, and integrating economic and social policy, however, the more the city-region emerges as an important unit. Many of the most important levers for competitiveness arise at the regional level, and reside in clusters that are geographically concentrated.

However, it is not a matter of one unit of geography supplanting another. While the relative emphasis is shifting, nations and cross-national institutions remain important. The task will be to integrate the city-region with other economic units, and adopt a more textured view of the sources of prosperity and economic policy that encompasses multiple levels of geography. This will be an agenda that will occupy policymakers and scholars for years to come.

NOTES

1. These ideas were first developed in *The Competitive Advantage of Nations* (Porter 1990). They have been developed, extended, and tested empirically in other books and articles, including Porter 1995, 1996, 1998*a*, 1998*b*, and Porter (forthcoming).
2. References can be found in Porter (1998*b*) and Porter (forthcoming).
3. The ownership of local industries can span economic areas, as in restaurant chains. In local cases, however, the location of ownership seems to have less economic significance than in traded industries.
4. Porter (1995). For further references, please see http://www.icic.org, the website for the Initiative for a Competitive Inner City.

REFERENCES

Connecticut Department of Economic and Community Development. (1998). *Partnership for Growth: Connecticut's Economic Competitiveness Strategy.* Hartford, CT. (February.)

—— (1999). *Industry Clusters: Progress Report, November*. Hartford, CT.

Norwegian School of Management. (1999). "Value-Creating Norway Project." Seminar materials. Oslo: Norwegian School of Management (December).

Porter, M. E. (1990). *The Competitive Advantage of Nations.* New York: The Free Press.

—— (1995). "The Competitive Advantage of the Inner City." *Harvard Business Review*, 73 (3): 55–71.

—— (1996). "What Is Strategy?" *Harvard Business Review*, 76 (6): 61–78.

—— (1998*a*). "The Microeconomic Foundations of Economic Development," in *The Global Competitiveness Report 1998.* Geneva: World Economic Forum, 38–63.

—— (1998*b*). *On Competition.* Boston: Harvard Business School Press. Particularly the chapter on "Clusters and the New Competitive Agenda for Companies and Governments," 197–287.

—— (1999*a*). *Competitive Strategy: Techniques for Analyzing Industries and Competitors.* New York: The Free Press.

—— (1999*b*). "Microeconomic Competitiveness: Findings from the 1999 Executive Survey," in *The Global Competitiveness Report 1999.* Geneva: World Economic Forum, 30–53.

—— (1999*c*). "Inequality, Capitalism, and the Morality of Competition." Unpublished working paper (revision of 13 December).

—— (Forthcoming). "Location, Clusters, and Company Strategy," in G. Clark (ed.), *Handbook of Economic Geography*. Oxford: Oxford University Press.

——, Stern, S., and Council on Competitiveness. (1999). *The New Challenge to America's Prosperity: Findings from the Innovation Index.* Washington, DC: Council on Competitiveness (March).

——, Takeuchi, H., and Sakakibara, M. (2000). *Can Japan Compete?* Tokyo: Diamond; Basingstoke, UK: Macmillan; New York: Basic Books.

——, and van der Linde, C. (1995). "Toward a New Conception of the Environment-Competitiveness Relationship." *Journal of Economic Perspectives*, 9 (4): 97–118.

Stern, S., Porter, M. E., and Furman, J. L. (1999). *The Determinants of National Innovative Capacity.* Harvard Business School Working Paper no. 00-034 (18 October).

Trajtenberg, M. (1990). *Economic Analysis of Product Innovation: The Case of CT Scanners.* Cambridge: Harvard University Press. Particularly the chapter on "Patents as Indicators of Innovation," 183–224.

10

Ontario as a North American Region-State, Toronto as a Global City-Region: Responding to the NAFTA Challenge

THOMAS J. COURCHENE

The severe economic fallout of the early 1990s recession represented a watershed in the evolution of the Canadian province of Ontario and, within the province, of Toronto and the Greater Toronto Area (GTA). Four years after the onset of the recession, Ontario's employment still languished at roughly 96 percent of its prerecession peak. And employment in the GTA fell by nearly 10 percent from peak to trough. On the fiscal front the economic fallout was nothing short of spectacular: Ontario's then-governing New Democratic Party (Canada's version of a social democratic party) oversaw five consecutive years (1990–95) of deficits in excess of $10 billion, for an overall increase in government debt of nearly $60 billion, surely a record for a subnational government, anywhere, anytime. Thus, by 1995, Canada's most powerful and populous province[1] was verging on "fiscalamity."

With the 1995 election of Mike Harris and his fiscally conservative and market-oriented Progressive Conservative party, the role of Ontario (and Toronto) within Canada and North America changed in a dramatic and irreversible manner. Ontario effectively superceded the erstwhile conception of itself as the economic and focal point for a trans-Canadian east–west economy and turned its attention and its policy arsenal to take advantage of the emerging opportunities ushered in by the Canada–U.S. Free Trade Agreement and by NAFTA. In *From Heartland to North American Region-state* (1998), Colin Telmer and I argue that the powerful message of the recession was that the former pan-Canadian, or east–west, economic perspective was leaving Ontario ill-prepared to address the open borders of NAFTA. Likewise Toronto, long ensconced in the comfortable pew as the natural and national center for the provision of pan-Canadian

The author gratefully acknowledges the generous support he was given in writing this chapter. In particular, I would like to thank several Ontario government officials for providing insight and information on both Ontario and Toronto. Brian O'Riordan of G. P. Murray Research also provided needed input. I relied heavily as well on the recent Evolution of Toronto Forum and, in particular, the papers by Joe Berridge, Meric Gertler, Michael Mendelson, and Enid Slack. Given the interpretive nature of the ensuing analysis, it is with more than the usual caveat that I take full responsibility for what follows.

public goods and services, realized that this was no longer a viable economic future. Hence, Toronto and the GTA also had to make a key transition—from a national economic capital with a significant international reach to a full-blown global city intimately tied to NAFTA's emerging geopolitical reality. I hasten to add that neither Ontario nor Toronto has abandoned its east–west role: rather, the focus is shifting markedly to ensure that they are positioned to become competitive and to excel in a north–south economic environment and, within this, to preserve and promote their east–west hegemony.

The role of this chapter is to describe and assess these transformations in terms of their implications for Toronto, for Ontario, and for the Canadian federation. Even though the presence of a powerful international city is an absolute prerequisite for donning the mantle of a North American region-state, the initial focus in what follows is on the latter, namely the attempt by Ontario to redesign itself politically and economically to become a "heartland" of North America. Within this framework, I then address the challenges and opportunities facing Toronto and the GTA as a global city-region. Admittedly, this may well tilt the analysis too much in the direction of linking Toronto's global city aspirations and performance to the associated and far-reaching changes in the underlying nature of the Canadian federation itself. Nonetheless, as powerful as Toronto is economically, it remains politically very weak: Canadian cities are essentially creatures of their respective provincial governments, with no direct links to the federal government (Ottawa was forced to abandon its short-lived Ministry of Urban Affairs a couple of decades ago). Thus, the obvious economic dynamism of Toronto is necessarily circumscribed by the division-of-powers and policy evolution of the Canadian federation, at least thus far.

The analysis proceeds as follows. In the next section I focus on the emergence of Ontario as a North American region-state, including the pressures arising from globalization and the information revolution, the shift toward a "regional-international interface," and the implementation of policies designed to privilege Ontario and Ontarians in the emerging North American geoeconomic reality. The section concludes with a series of implications for Ontario, for its sister provinces, and for the Canadian federation itself.

Given the dominant position of Toronto and the GTA within Ontario, the evolution of Ontario toward region-state status is, in effect, also the evolution of Toronto toward global city-region status. In "Toronto as a global city-region" I focus in more detail on opportunities and challenges facing Toronto as it competes head-to-head with U.S. global city-regions—its strategic location, the well-balanced nature of its economic base, and its recent and likely future evolution in light of the wide-ranging policy initiatives undertaken by region-state Ontario. A brief conclusion completes the chapter.

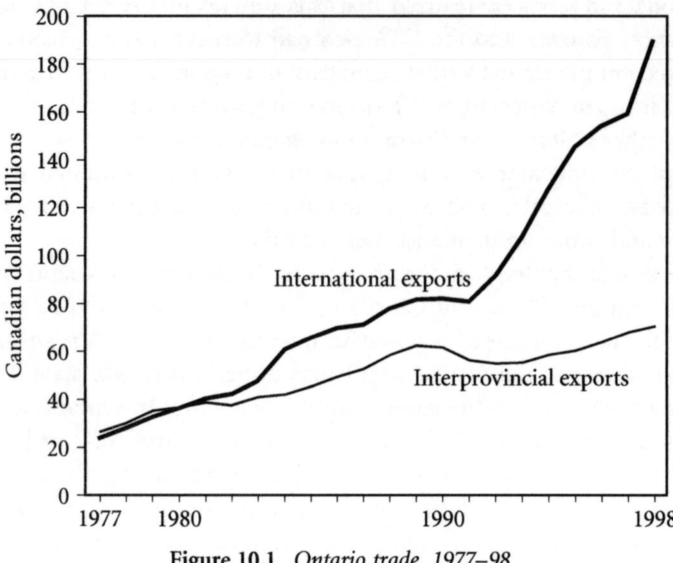

Figure 10.1. *Ontario trade, 1977–98*
Source: Ontario Ministry of Finance

ONTARIO AS A NORTH AMERICAN REGION-STATE

Ontario's Regional-International Interface

The principal dilemma of contemporary economic geography is the resurgence of regional economies and of territorial specialization in an age of increasing ease of transportation and communication. (Storper 1995: 107)

National boundaries have become increasingly irrelevant in the definition of market and production spaces while regions, rather than countries, are emerging as key policy arenas. (United Nations 1990: iii)

On the global economic map, the lines that now matter are those defining what may be called "region-states." (Ohmae 1993: 78)

In *From Heartland to North American Region-State* (Courchene and Telmer 1998) these visions of the emergence and role of region-states inform our analysis of Ontario's transition from Canadian heartland to a powerful North American region-state. By far the most important factor driving this transition is Ontario's rapidly increasing North American trade integration. From Figure 10.1, as recently as 1981 Ontario's international exports and its interprovincial exports (i.e. exports to Canada's other provinces) were roughly equal, in the neighborhood of C$40 billion each. By 1998, however, Ontario's international exports soared to almost $200 billion, nearly three times the value of its 1998 interprovincial exports. As a percentage of Ontario's GDP, international exports increased from just above 30 percent in 1981 to over 50 percent in 1998, while interprovincial exports, also just above 30 percent in 1981, fell to under 20 percent by 1988.[2] While international exports include exports to all countries, roughly 90 percent of these exports are to the United States, so that Ontario's exports to the United States now account for roughly 45 percent of its GDP. This is an astounding degree of cross-border integration. This is even true for the Americans: the two-way Ontario–U.S. trade is second only to their two-way trade with Japan.

To this, one should add two other factors. The first is that all of Canada's provinces are becoming more integrated tradewise with the United States. The second is that Canada's provincial or regional economies are not only quite distinct industrially but have cyclical fluctuations that are not synchronized east–west. This led Telmer and me (1998) to assert that Canada is less and less a single national (east–west) economy and more and more a series of north–south, cross-border economies. In turn this means that a Great Lakes economy like Ontario may well want to integrate its school-to-work and welfare-to-work subsystems, among other policy areas, in a manner that will differ from how a Pacific Rim economy like British Columbia might want to forge those integrations. Hence, this economic diversity across Canada's provincial/regional economies will lead rather naturally to policy diversity or asymmetry.

Finally, the Canadian federal government is contributing to this trend toward decentralization and asymmetry at the provincial level. For example, over the past few years it has transferred responsibility for training to the provinces. This follows the earlier devolution of powers relating to key aspects of forestry, mining, energy, and tourism. Beyond this, Ottawa has agreed to constrain the operations of the federal spending power in areas of exclusive provincial jurisdiction. This adds a "push" factor, as it were, to the earlier factors that are pulling Ontario in the direction of a North American region-state.

However, Ontario's large and increasing regional-international interface on the one hand and its accretion of powers on the other do not translate directly into the province becoming a North American region-state: rather, it might evolve, instead, into a highly decentralized province within the Canadian federation. What region-state status requires and implies is that Queen's Park becomes the focus for preserving, promoting, and enhancing Ontario's economic future in North America. But this is exactly what Ontario is currently all about. In detailing Ontario's key policy initiatives toward this end it is appropriate to frame them within a conceptual framework relating to the modus operandi of region-states.

Region-States as Embodiments of Untraded Interdependencies

It is much more difficult to sort out the analytics relating to region-states than to document their empirical existence. In general, the relevant literature (most of it European) falls into the "evolutionary" economics school rather than the neoclassical school. Specifically, the emphasis is not on equilibria (as it would be if the analysis were neoclassical), but on innovation, on agents of change, and on the role of institutional and structural elements. Indeed, the emphasis on path-dependency, on feedback mechanisms, and on irreversibilities is central to this literature and predates the appearance of these concepts in mainstream economies as reflected, for example, in the recent literature on endogenous growth.

One important strand of this rich regional literature relates to the role of *local milieux* in generating networking which, in turn, can be characterized by organizational principles and linkages that encourage flexibility, the creation and transmission of knowledge, skill formation, mutual trust among partners, and so on (Lecoq 1991: 239). Thus, these "*milieux innovateurs*" are, at the same time, *organizational* (in the sense that they embody a set of institutions, rules, conventions, and practices) and *territorial* (in the sense that they are embedded in the social and economic infrastructure of the region).

Geographer Michael Storper (1994), among others, extends this analysis by postulating that the success of Silicon Valley, Route 128, and other industrial "hot spots" must reside in what he calls *untraded interdependencies.* The "untraded" aspect is critical, since it implies that to access these interdependencies one must be located in the regional economy:

> Thus, regional economies constitute the nexus of untraded interdependencies which emerge and become, themselves, specific but public assets of production communities (assets of coordination, i.e. frameworks of collective action), and which underpin the production and reproduction of other specific assets such as labor and hardware. (1995: 106)

An alternative way to conceive of these untraded interdependencies is to view them as "locational externalities," hopefully *positive* locational externalities but they could obviously be negative as well. One could conceive of a series of these externalities—one set might relate to the interdependencies at the industry/production level, another could involve the forward and backward linkages among education/training, income support and labor and product markets, and a third might involve the set of public goods. Focusing on the third of these, a firm locating anywhere in North America has access to an international public good—NAFTA. If, among Canada, the United States, and Mexico, the firm chooses to locate in Canada, it gains access to Canadian public goods (such as medicare for its workers) but foregoes access to the comparable U.S. and Mexican national public goods and/or infrastructures. And if the firm locates in Ontario, it acquires the Ontario set, not the Alberta or Quebec set, of provincial public goods. Because we have focused our example on public goods, it is fairly easy to see that they are inherently untradeable—one accesses them by location, not by markets (although one could in some cases use markets to attempt to replicate another jurisdiction's public goods, e.g. a firm in the United States could provide medicare for its workers). Indeed, one might extend Storper's conception by suggesting that the process of competitive federalism can be viewed as an attempt among subnational units to compete with each other in the provision of these untraded interdependencies or positive locational externalities. The new twist, drawing from the emerging regional-international interface, is that this competition in Canada is less and less along east–west (interprovincial) lines and more along cross-border (international) lines. For example, Ontario probably takes due notice of tax rates in British Columbia and Nova Scotia. But it is far more concerned about tax rates in Michigan, Ohio, and New York.

The above analysis is admittedly tentative and incomplete. The literature on networking and externalities in light of internationalization and the informatics revolution is literally exploding. Indeed, one could probably come at the concept of a region-state entirely from a networking framework. For example, sociologist Manuel Castells in his sure-to-be classic *The Rise of the Network Society* (1996) offers the following assessment of the implications of globalization and the informatics revolution:

> The global economy emerging from information-based production and competition is characterized by its *interdependence*, its *asymmetry*, its *regionalization*, the *increasing diversification within each region*, its *selective inclusiveness*, its *exclusionary segmentation*, and, as a result of all these features, an extraordinarily *variable geometry* that tends to dissolve historical economic geography. (p. 106, emphasis in original.)

This is fully consistent with my own views of the supplanting of the traditional national-national relationship with the regional-international interface and the emergence of the region-state.

Ontario and Untraded Interdependencies

While the evolution of Ontario toward region-state status began well before the Harris government came on the scene (in 1995), it is nonetheless the case that the policies of neither the Peterson (1985–90) nor Rae (1990–95) governments would qualify Ontario as a region-state in terms of the definition developed above. For example, the Peterson Liberals never did buy into the FTA, at least not officially. Nor did Rae's NDP government buy into the FTA or NAFTA. And neither premier accepted the rationale underpinning the GST (Canada's version of a value-added tax), namely its export/import neutrality and, therefore, its inherent resonance with the concept of a North American region-state. Beyond this, one can probably make a case that in terms of attracting foreign investment, Peterson and especially Rae were engaged in creating *negative* locational externalities—Peterson by embarking on an incredible spending spree that left Ontario among the high-tax, high-transfer provinces in Canada (and especially in North America) and Rae by doubling the province's indebtedness and triggering successive decreases in its credit rating. (Nonetheless, much of the rapid increase in Ontario's international exports (Figure 10.1) occurred prior to the 1995 ascension to power of the Harris Conservatives).

With the Harris government, all of this changed. Ontario bought into the full range of federal policies designed to promote export penetration and competitiveness. Moreover, by setting the province's fiscal house in order, including significant cuts in personal income taxation, the Harris Conservatives have certainly made Ontario a more attractive business location within North

America. Beyond this, I would suggest that the ongoing institutional/municipal revolution ought to be considered as an integral part of creating untraded interdependencies or positive locational externalities.

In more detail, one can divide these sweeping policy initiatives into two separate episodes. The first was the Harris Conservatives' election platform—the *Common Sense Revolution*. The legacy of the province's two previous governments was a dramatic increase in both debt and tax rates. As already noted, the annual deficits over the five-year period 1990–95 never once dipped below $10 billion, with a cumulative debt accumulation in the order of $60 billion. Not surprisingly, therefore, the *Common Sense Revolution* focused on returning the province to fiscal sanity—a balanced-budget over the five-year mandate, a 30 percent reduction in Ontario's personal income tax rate,[3] a near-25 percent reduction in the number of politicians, a 15 percent cut in the provincial bureaucracy, and a promised 750,000 new jobs. All of this was legislated within the first six months of their taking office and, basically, fully implemented during their first mandate. The Harris Conservatives were reelected in 1999, with further tax cuts an integral part of their campaign platform—an additional 20 percent cut in provincial personal income taxes and a 20 percent reduction in the education component of property taxes.

Lest one attribute the strong economic performance of the province of Ontario since 1995 solely to the Harris Conservatives' legislative agenda, one should note that their coming to office coincided with the fiscal turnaround engineered by Canada's federal Finance Minister Paul Martin. Hence, the Ontario Conservatives were fortunate to inherit low interest rates, low inflation, low federal deficits, and, thanks to a sharp depreciation in the exchange rate, a highly competitive Canadian economy (vis-à-vis the United States).

Less than a year into their initial election mandate, the Harris Conservatives launched another revolution, which I refer to as the "institutional-municipal" revolution. This was an unbelievably broad set of reforms, all announced in a single week in January of 1996 and referred to as the "Megaweek" proposals. These included:

- a complete restructuring of the Ontario hospital system, including the closing and consolidation of many hospitals;
- a restructuring/amalgamation of Ontario municipalities, including the creation of the megacity of Toronto (on which, more later);
- a wholesale restructuring of provincial-municipal powers, shifting "hard" services (services relating to property and infrastructure) to the municipalities and moving "soft" services (education, health, and welfare) to the provincial level (although the municipalities will still be responsible for funding 20 percent of welfare costs);
- a new municipal Act accompanying this restructuring that enhanced the scope for municipal maneuverability;
- a major consolidation of school boards in the province;

- a property tax reform shifting to market-value assessment;
- a decrease in provincial transfers to various public-sector institutions such as schools and universities. And, added later:
- the privatization of Ontario Hydro.

Underpinning much of this was an effective declaration of war against public sector unions with the result that citizens have had to suffer through several provincewide strikes, especially in the education sector.

As noted, this was an incredibly ambitious reform agenda. While not downplaying the ideological underpinnings of these two revolutions, the untraded interdependencies framework provides an *analytical* perspective for these dramatic reforms, namely to enhance Ontario's locational advantage within the North American market. In particular, part of being competitive within North America implies an efficient public sector. This is especially important for Ontario (and Canada) since our public sector is much larger than the American counterpart. While it is not as yet clear whether this dramatic institutional revolution will increase public sector productivity, there is no question that this is its intent.

At this juncture, it might appear that we are equating the notion of a region-state and positive locational externalities with the existence of laissez-faire capitalism. This is not necessarily the case. Region-states can be exponents of either communitarian or individualist capitalism and they can be high or low transfer economies. In Ontario's case the confusion arises because the Harris government inherited a fiscal crisis and it had to sort this out as the first priority in terms of privileging Ontario and Ontarians in the North American context.

By way of summary, Table 10.1 presents the defining features of the "old" (heartland) Ontario as well as the salient characteristics of the "new" (region-state) Ontario. Beyond this, it is important to emphasize that Ontario is well positioned to become a North American "economic motor." For example, disposable income within one-day's trucking of Toronto exceeds $2 trillion (US$). This constitutes as large a one-day's market as that for Boston, or New York, or Detroit. Toronto is Canada's financial capital, with the third highest concentration of financial services activity in North America, after New York and San Francisco. Ontario is the home of 41 percent of Canada's aerospace sales; one-half of chemical production; 50 percent of the industrial design industry; 90 percent of Canadian shipments of the metal, die, and mold industry; 91 percent of Canada's foreign banks; 90 percent of Canada's top advertising agencies; 90 percent of public accounting firms; 80 percent of the top law firms; and, more generally, home to more than 1,000 multinational enterprises. (For more detail, see Courchene and Telmer 1998, chapter 9).

Thus, Ontario has the ability and the desire to jettison its erstwhile role as the heartland of Canada and become a North American region-state. With what consequences?

Table 10.1. *Heartland vs. region-state Ontario*

Panel A. Heartland Ontario: selected defining characteristics	Panel B. Region-state Ontario: selected defining characteristics
• Ontario was so prosperous and so diversified economically—and so powerful politically—that Canadian policy had little choice but to be cast in a pro-Ontario light. • Relatedly, the management of the big levers of economic power always kept a close eye on Ontario, e.g. if the minister of finance was not a Toronto MP then at least Toronto would be well represented in the key economic portfolios. • Since Ontario could generally count on the federal government to further the province's interests, heartland Ontario was in favor of a strong central government. For example, Queen's Park did not assume the role of economic policymaker that L'Assemblée nationale did for Quebec. There was no need for this since Rideau Street was essentially an extension of Bay Street, and Ottawa delivered—the auto pact, the NEP, nuclear power for Ontario Hydro. • Not surprisingly, therefore, Ontarians tended to direct their attention and loyalties to Ottawa, more so than other provincial residents. • While Ontario obviously desired sufficient influence to defend its own interests, its preference was to block offending legislation of a sister province rather than by acquiring further provincial powers. For example, it did not take up Ottawa's invitation to opt out of federal programs, as did Quebec. Had it done so, other provinces would surely have followed and this would have served to reduce Ottawa's influence. • With aspects of the National Policy still in play, Ontario's interests were more in the direction of freeing up internal trade than in pursuing freer trade with the United States. This was especially true in the high energy-price era where Ontario	• Ontario is a North American region-state and the province will advance its interests within this larger, and effectively, global environment. Specifically, Ontario will pursue this new (largely) economic role by actively promoting a regional-international interface and, in particular, by attempting to create a favorable set of untraded interdependencies (positive locational externalities) designed to privilege Ontario and Ontarians within North America. • Queen's Park is evolving and will continue to evolve in the direction of assuming powers and influence sufficient to deliver on this new role. • Ontario remains fully committed to the "Canadian dream." But this will not be the former heartland relationship. For example, Ontario will give high marks to Ottawa policy that maintains fiscal integrity, low inflation, and an overall competitive environment. • Ontario will become much more involved in issues relating to interprovincial redistribution. It will remain a strong supporter of equalization, but will insist on equal treatment for its citizens from other federal redistributive programs ("fair shares" federalism). • In protecting its own interests, Ontario may still wish to block offending legislation in a sister province (as under heartland), but it now will have no qualms about acquiring greater powers. This is "provincial rights if necessary but not necessarily provincial rights." • International free trade is "in." Nonetheless, Ontario will also attempt to preserve and promote east–west markets. Part of this will be via the pursuit of an effective economic union. Indeed, Ontario will likely attempt to link its commitment to the social union to the

Table 10.1. *(cont'd)*

Panel A. Heartland Ontario: selected defining characteristics	Panel B. Region-state Ontario: selected defining characteristics
wanted full access to the energy-related megaprojects of the energy provinces in tandem with a "buy Canadian" preference. • Ontario was not a leader in social policy. Some of this related to the economic diversity of the province and some of it to innate conservatism, but there was also an understanding that social policy leadership by Ontario would trigger regional equality concerns from other provinces, with Ontario ultimately playing a large paymaster role. • In general, Ontario was able to wheel, deal, and compromise and to manage its privileged position to ensure that Canada's interests coincided with Ontario's interests.	commitment by other provinces to the economic union. • As a result of increased decentralization and the likelihood of increased asymmetry as different provinces choose alternative approaches to forge their human capital subsystems, intergovernmentalism or codetermination will emerge as new governance instruments. Ontario will play a leading role here. • To be a successful region-state, Ontario will have to become a leader in policies related to the creation of human capital. With human capital at the cutting edge of competitiveness and with skills and education the key to a high-wage economy, an integrated approach to this subsystem must become a defining characteristic of Ontario as a region-state. Ontario is not yet on track here.

Source: Courchene (1999b) and Courchene and Telmer (1998, chaps. 2 and 10).

Region-State Ontario: Implications

Ontario's transition from Canadian heartland to North American region-state carries with it a series of rather profound implications—for Ontario (and Toronto), for internal Ontario governance, for its sister provinces, for the federation, and for the evolution of Canadian industry. I shall limit myself to three resulting implications.

Ontario's Economic Mission Statement

Far and away the most convincing evidence that Ontario has indeed donned the mantle of a North American region-state is the publication of an Ontario "economic mission statement" by the Ontario Jobs and Investment Board (OJIB 1999), the chair of which is Premier Harris. Figure 10.2 presents a summary overview of the mission statement. The emphasis on knowledge and skills, innovation, global outreach, economic development, and generating a favorable investment climate are the chosen strategies to deliver on the overall "vision" (namely, that "Ontario is the best jurisdiction in North America to live, work, invest, and raise a family") and the accompanying "mission" (namely that "Ontario will achieve sustainable economic prosperity with the best performing economy and

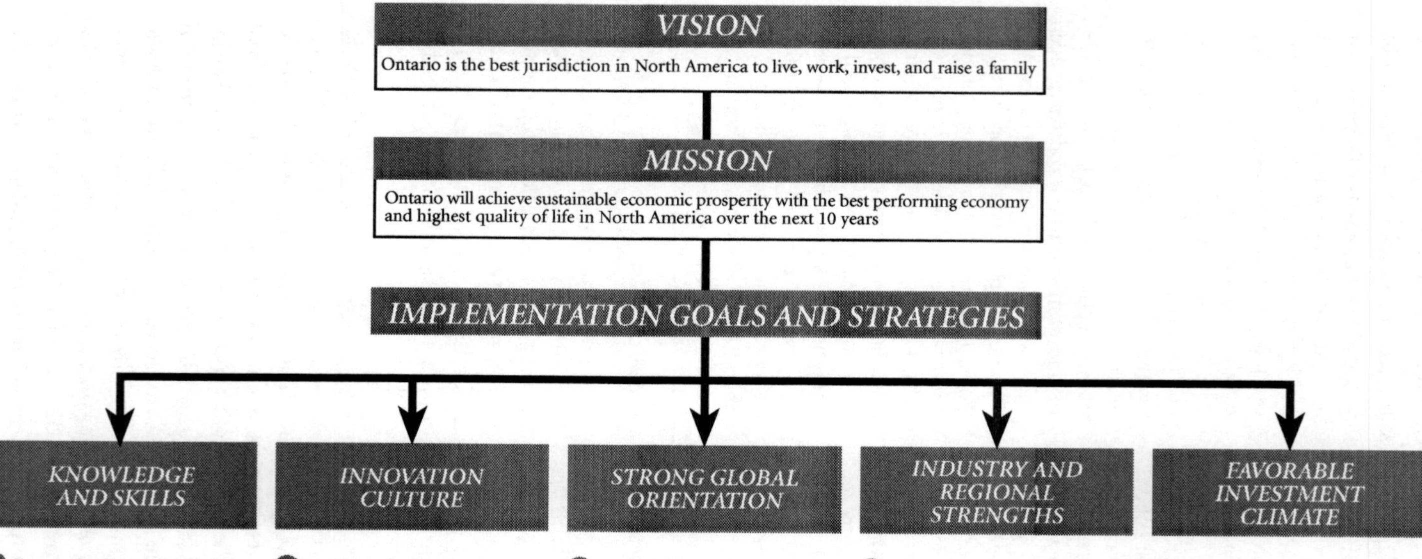

Figure 10.2. *Ontario's economic mission statement*

Source: Ontario Jobs and Investment Board 1999

highest quality of life in North America over the next ten years"). Since OJIB consulted widely in developing this economic mission, it can and should be viewed as a governmental and societal project to privilege Ontario with a set of "untraded interdependencies" that will allow it to excel as a region-state. I would hazard a guess that no other subnational jurisdiction anywhere has developed as focused a mission statement designed to maximize the opportunities presented by globalization and the information revolution. To be sure, these are only words, but the already-announced next step for OJIB is to proceed with "benchmarking," i.e. developing and publishing performance indicators relating to the components of the mission statement.

Of particular importance to the ensuing analysis on Toronto as a global city-region is the focus that the mission statement places on the role of city-regions:

> Around the world, cities are the focal points for creativity, innovation, production and the supporting infrastructure. Ontario's largest urban areas will continue to be central in our economic development strategies. . . . [Hence the mission statement will] give prior attention to the economic challenges and opportunities facing the Greater Toronto Area and Golden Horseshoe—Canada's only global scale city-region.

Thus, the province of Ontario is not only fully committed to advance the prospects of Toronto as a global city-region but recognizes that success in this endeavor is essential if Ontario is to become an effective North American region-state.

Ontario-Triggered Changes in the Federation: The Personal Income Tax

The policies of region-state Ontario are bound to have an impact on overall Canadian policy and governance. Thus far, the most significant such example relates to Canada's shared personal income tax (PIT) system. Canada's approach to PIT sharing is frequently viewed as a model for federal systems. Ottawa sets the definitions for income and the basic rate and bracket structure. The provinces then apply a single tax rate to the federal tax rates. These provincial tax rates vary considerably, but average close to 50 percent, which means that the provinces receive roughly one-third of total PIT revenues. The provinces can also mount various tax credits, low-income tax reductions, and high-income surtaxes. Ottawa charges a small collection fee for these add-ons, but collects the basic provincial tax share free of charge. Thus, the shared PIT is decentralized (in that the provinces are free to vary their single tax rate) and harmonized (there is only one form to fill out). Quebec is not part of Canadian PIT sharing: it has a separate PIT system for provincial revenues. In its 1997 provincial budget, Ontario argued that the existing system was too constraining and indicated that it might follow the Quebec route of establishing its own PIT collection system. Ottawa responded by allowing all provinces, beginning in 2001, to apply their own rate and bracket structures against the commonly determined federal tax base. (In public-finance terminology, this represents a shift from the current "tax on tax" approach to a "tax on base" or "tax-on-income" approach). Alberta has already indicated that it will use this new flexibility to mount a *flat* tax for its PIT share.

Hence, in pursuing region-state status, Ontario will now have an additional degree of freedom—full personal income tax flexibility with respect to both tax rates and tax brackets for its share of the PIT.

Toronto and the Bank Mergers Issue

As a bridge between the focus on Ontario and the focus on Toronto, the recent controversy over bank mergers is especially instructive. Specifically, the Royal Bank and the Bank of Montreal agreed to merge, as did the Canadian Imperial Bank of Commerce and the Toronto-Dominion Bank. In terms of market value, these banks represented the top four of Canada's six "national" banks, all four of which were effectively headquartered in Toronto. These proposed mergers merit further highlight.

An assessment of the environment that led to these proposed mergers might run along the following lines. In the 1970s, many large corporations began to realize that, as capital markets became more developed, they no longer needed their financing through the banks but could go directly to the capital markets. Canadian policy reacted to this by striking down the prohibition on banks owning investment dealers. (Actually, Ontario took the lead here, since regulation of investment dealers is a provincial jurisdiction in Canada. Once Ontario signaled its willingness to remove the former ownership restrictions on investment dealers, Ottawa followed by allowing the banks to own them.) As the banks gobbled up most of the investment dealers, this allowed them to recapture some of the corporate market. But neither time nor markets stand still. In particular, a significant number of corporations are becoming so large that they require syndicates of banks to meet some of their financing needs, and this trend is going to continue. If Canadian banks do not become larger (in a capitalization sense), they will neither have the capacity to finance many of these corporations nor be sufficiently large to participate in the syndications. A niche strategy might save the individual banks as ongoing companies but, in aggregate, their combined strength and presence will fall short of what Canada and, particularly, Ontario need for future economic development; increasingly we will likely have to rely on U.S. and foreign institutions to finance key aspects of our economy, with all that this implies for sovereignty and made-in-Canada economic development.

One does not have to agree to this assessment of the merger issue to recognize that it has profound implications for Ontario's region-state future and in particular for the evolution of Toronto. Better capitalized banks with an enhanced ability to become state of the art in terms of the emerging technology as well as the potential to operate more effectively internationally would surely contribute to Toronto's role as a major financial player in North America. Moreover, associated with being a major financial player comes a whole range of related services—accounting, legal, advertising, securities, and the like. Not surprising, key economic institutions in Toronto were in full support of the mergers, since the resulting enhanced capital base of the new banks would allow them to play a key role in spearheading Toronto's global city aspirations.

However, while Ontario and Toronto had a north–south view of the evolution of finance and banking, Ottawa had an east–west view. This issue can be phrased differently and more generally. Canada's nationwide banking system is also a key Canadian social or socioeconomic institution. In this context, the prospect that the mergers would result in the closing of branches elsewhere in the country was viewed as unacceptable. To be fair, there *is* a social or solidarity aspect of our national banks. But what the merger issue highlighted is the deep societal division between the emerging requisites of north–south competitiveness and the traditional requisite of east–west solidarity. In the event, Canada's finance minister disallowed these mergers: east–west solidarity won this round, but the game is hardly over.

There is a far more pervasive and troubling policy challenge at issue here. Canada, from the 1879 National Policy onward, has fostered an east–west economy and society. But the three key planks of the National Policy (high tariffs, transportation subsidies, and settlement of the west) are no longer in play, so that trade is once again (as in the pre-National Policy era) following the natural north–south geographical dictates. As a result, some of this east–west infrastructure has, in economic terms, now become a "stranded asset." Left to the interplay of markets, economic agents will aggressively pursue the north–south economic and trading potential. Does government policy largely oversee this private sector transition, or does it attempt to counter these trends by viewing banks and other economic activities as an integral part of our east–west *social capital*? This highlights one of the key differences between Toronto as a global city and, say, U.S. cities such as New York, Los Angeles, and Chicago. Unlike the latter, Toronto is home base for a very substantial range of "national" commercial and cultural enterprises. Indeed, its potential economic dynamism in the emerging north–south geoeconomy arises, to a considerable degree, from this role as the dominant pan-Canadian player in the provision of these "national" goods and services. The prospect that Toronto would now convert this east–west dominance to develop a powerful north–south presence may not sit well with many Canadians. The fact that Toronto has no real alternative but aggressively to adopt a north–south perspective does not mean that this inevitable adjustment will come easily on the political front. This is part of the rationale for approaching global-city Toronto from a division-of-powers (i.e. provincial) framework, rather than from the traditional urban studies approach. Nonetheless, both perspectives are essential and both will be the focus for the remainder of the chapter.

TORONTO AS A GLOBAL CITY-REGION

The evolution of Ontario toward region-state status is, for all intents and purposes, about the evolution of Toronto in the direction of becoming a global city-region. Thus, most of the above analysis is, at base, applicable to Toronto and to the GTA. Indeed, the relationship goes both ways: without Toronto as a powerful economic engine with an international reach, there would be no Ontario region-state. With this caveat, I now turn my attention to the Toronto city-region.

With its roughly 4.5 million people the Greater Toronto Area (GTA), defined below, constitutes just over 40 percent of Ontario's population but 50 percent of its GDP. In turn, this means that the GTA accounts for roughly 20 percent of overall Canadian GDP. As already noted, this places the GTA in quite a different environment from that for any U.S. metropolitan area. Specifically, the dominance of Toronto in the Canadian economy and society means not only that all Canadians have a stake in Toronto's future but, as well, are likely to be far from indifferent in terms of how the city evolves. This is one of the rationales for approaching Toronto's future from the perspective of the political evolution of Ontario, and also the evolution of other provinces. Another is that Canadian cities in general, Toronto included, are creatures of their respective provinces and, as such, have few of the key economic and social policy levers at their own discretion.

The Geography of the GTA

The upper panel in Figure 10.3 portrays the geography of the five regions that constitute the GTA—Metro Toronto, Halton, Peel, York, and Durham. Until recently, Metro was comprised of six municipalities—Etobicoke, York, North York, East York, Scarborough, and the city of Toronto. As part of the amalgamation process associated with earlier-noted "Megaweek" initiatives, the province eliminated these six municipalities of the former Metro Toronto and created the megacity of Toronto (henceforth referred to simply as Toronto). The ring of the four regions around Toronto is typically referred to as the "905 area," so-named because it recently acquired a separate area code, leaving Toronto with its original 416 area code. Based on 1996 data from Statistics Canada, Toronto's median income for 1996 was $19,000, with higher median incomes in the 905 area—Durham ($25,300), Halton ($27,500), Peel ($23,300), and York ($23,200). For comparison purposes, Ontario's median income is $21,000.

This is an arbitrary definition of the GTA. As the 1996 GTA Task Force Report noted (1996: 23, henceforth referred to as the Golden Report after its chair, Anne Golden), if one were to adopt Jane Jacobs's "economic energy" dimension of a city-region, this would encompass the "Golden Horseshoe"—the urban area from Oshawa to Niagara, with Toronto at the core. In terms of the lower panel of Figure 10.3, the Golden Horseshoe would swing around the tip of Lake Ontario through to Buffalo. Indeed, the degree of economic interdependency is such that one might also include the corridor to the U.S. Midwest, i.e. the area from Toronto to Kitchener-Waterloo, London, and on to Windsor (and Detroit). When combined with the Golden Horseshoe, this larger area is typically referred to as the "Golden Triangle" (effectively the area encompassed by the Toronto–Buffalo–Detroit triangle). While the other areas of Ontario—Kingston and eastern Ontario, Ottawa and the national capital region, and the vast north and western areas of the province—are also progressively becoming more integrated with Toronto, they are more in the nature of economic hinterlands (except perhaps

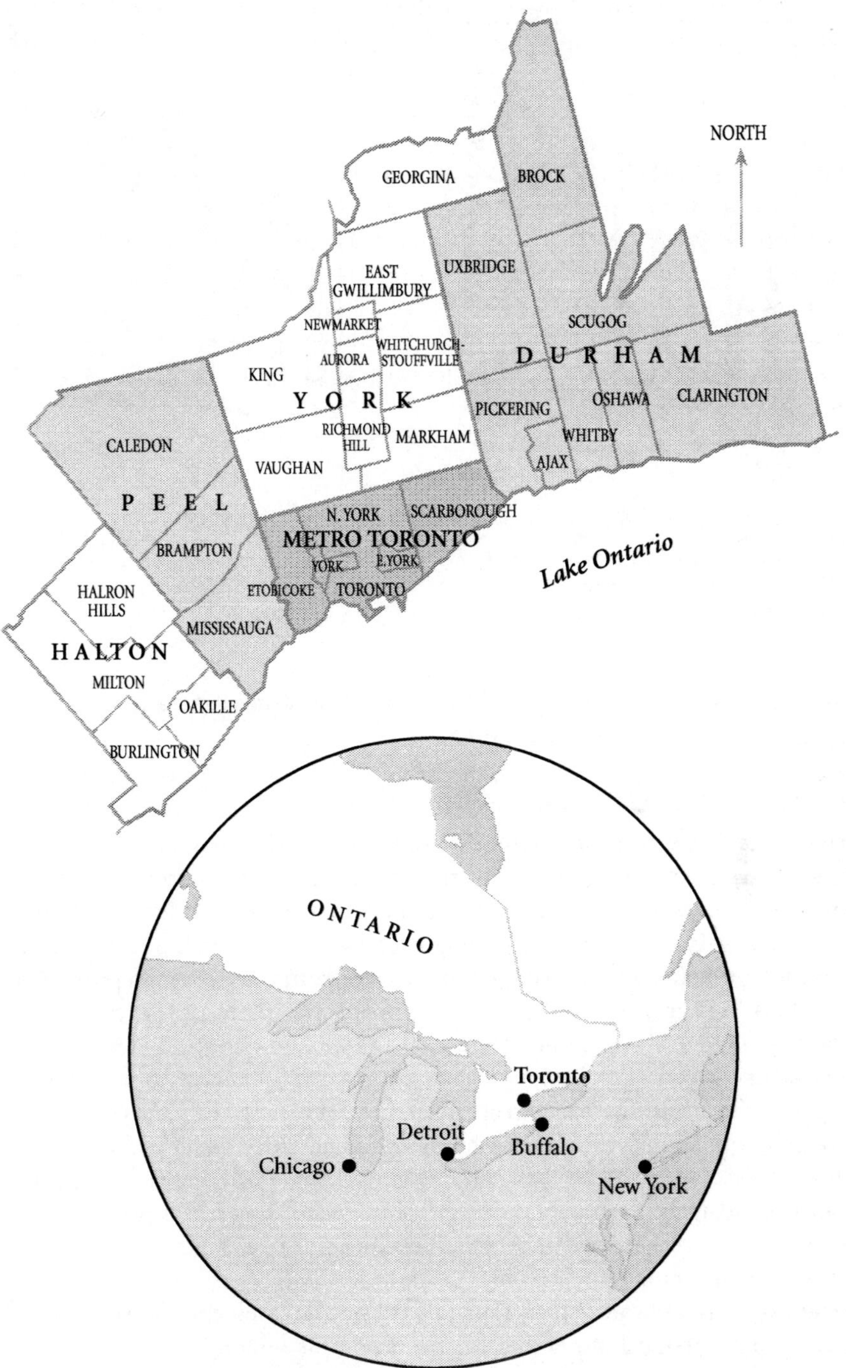

Figure 10.3. *The geography of the Greater Toronto area and its regional context*

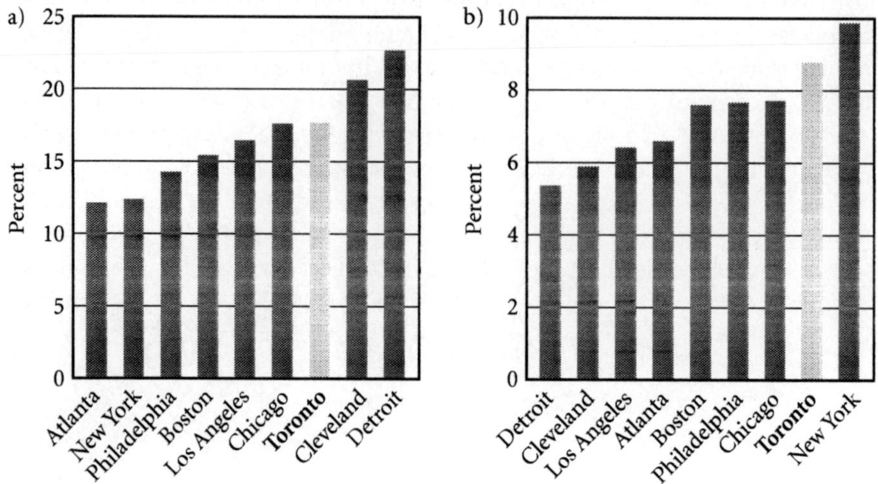

Figure 10.4. *Manufacturing and service employment in North American cities, 1994*

(a) manufacturing as a percentage of total employment, (b) finance, insurance, and real estate as a percentage of total employment

Source: The Boston Consulting Group

for Canada's version of "Silicon Valley" in the Ottawa area) and are typically not viewed as an integral part of the GTA.

Toronto's Economic Base

Beyond the fact that most of Ontario's economic, social, and cultural strengths relate primarily to the role and influence of the GTA, it is instructive to focus in more detail on the various "engines" of growth that are driving Toronto's and the GTA's economic dynamism. Thankfully, Meric Gertler (1999) has provided such an analysis. His first observation, drawn in part from the Golden Report, is that Toronto is "unusually well-balanced" in comparison with major U.S. city-regions. From Figure 10.4, Toronto ranks third after Detroit and Cleveland in terms of the share of manufacturing in total employment and second after New York for employment in finance, insurance, and real estate. As already noted this reflects Toronto's preeminent position in the hierarchy of Canadian cities, i.e. it is far and away the financial, industrial, services, and cultural[4] capital of Canada. The obvious challenge facing Toronto is to capitalize on this enduring legacy and to grow it in the much more competitive North American context, a context where Toronto currently ranks ninth (some say eighth) in terms of the ten Canada–U.S. metropolitan regions with more than four million people (Golden Report 1996: 23).

First and foremost among Gertler's economic pillars or clusters is the automotive sector. Facilitated by the 1965 Canada–U.S. Auto Pact, the GTA is home to assembly plants of the American "majors"—GM, Ford, and DaimlerChrysler—as well as Honda's plants in Alliston. Supporting this continentally integrated auto-assembly superstructure "is a substructure of rapidly growing and increasingly sophisticated producers of automobile parts" (Gertler 1999: 4). Not only is the auto sector key in its own right, but much of the rest of the GTA and Ontario economy is driven off the automobile sector (one in six GTA jobs are auto-related). Moreover, and in part counter to the overall perspective of this chapter, the impact of the Auto Pact was fully to integrate the GTA and Ontario into the North American automobile market far in advance of the FTA or NAFTA agreements and, therefore, far in advance of Ontario's donning its region-state mantle. (This serves as an important reminder to readers that not everyone is enamored with my vision of Ontario as a region-state. And no doubt the ensuing analysis of Toronto as a global city will also find plenty of detractors).

Gertler (1999) also focuses on several other key GTA "pillars":

- *Information and communications technology.* Nortel Networks, IBM Canada, and Celestia.
- *Advanced engineering and aerospace.* Bombardier, Husky Injection Moulding Systems.
- *Finance.* Toronto is the effective headquarters for the big-five Canadian banks, is the dominant center for investment banking activity (nine of Canada's ten largest investment dealers have Toronto home offices), and is Canada's major player in the insurance industry. The Toronto Stock Exchange is the third largest in North America. In addition it is important to recall that while banking, per se, is federally regulated, the province of Ontario regulates the investment dealers (and the Toronto Stock Exchange) as well as most financial services brokers.
- *Business services.* As Canada's services capital, Toronto is home to an impressive array of legal, accounting, advertising, industrial design, and consulting enterprises that now are becoming key "traded" sectors.
- *Health and education.* Toronto is at the center of Canada's premier complex for medical education and research. The University of Toronto is the obvious depository for many of the international centers of excellence that are incorporated in the details of Ontario's mission statement (articulated earlier), since it sits atop the impressive system of the forty Ontario universities and colleges.
- *Cultural industries.* Toronto is now the third largest live theatre center in the English-speaking world, after London and New York (Golden Report 1996: 58) and the second or third largest in North America in terms of film production (Berridge 1999: 1). Relatedly, the GTA's Sheridan College has an international reputation in terms of computer graphics and animation, which provides a drawing card well beyond the cultural sector.

In addition to these and other dynamic clusters and attributes, much of Toronto's innovation comes from the fact that it is the national and natural focal point for attracting the best and the brightest of Canadian talent. However, this may be in the process of changing significantly. Recent data indicate that high-skilled and professional Canadians are increasingly attracted to the United States—the number of temporary FTA/NAFTA visas has risen from 16,000 or so in the early 1990s to nearly 100,000 in 1997. This is becoming a major public issue in Canada, with concern directed toward our high taxes, the falling Canadian dollar, and our productivity shortfall. More to the point of this paper, Ontario's policies and its mission statement are in large measure directed to providing an economic environment designed to ensure that the province, and especially the GTA, can retain our best talent. This is yet another rationale for embedding the future of Toronto within the larger evolution of Ontario.

Beyond this, Toronto is far and away the preferred location for most of Canada's immigrants. Indeed, the city of Toronto is arguably the most multicultural (or multinational) of all Canadian–U.S. metropolitan areas. An astounding 45 percent or so of Toronto's (not the GTA's) residents are foreign born or have parents who are foreign born, suggesting that the global reach of Toronto will transcend the NAFTA economy.

This, then, is the *potential* of Toronto as a global city. To be sure, its current strengths reflect, in part, the thrust of overall Canadian policy. As noted, Toronto and the GTA were the obvious beneficiaries of the National Policy. Not only did Toronto emerge as the privileged hub for the production of national goods and services across an incredibly wide industrial spectrum, but many hundreds of U.S. enterprises established Canadian (largely GTA) subsidiaries to "leapfrog" the tariff. Moreover, the 1965 Auto Pact privileged Ontario with an industrial and manufacturing base that has served to anchor a much more diversified and dynamic industrial and manufacturing infrastructure.

And then came the 1989 Canada–U.S. Free Trade Agreement and the devastating 1990s recession, which effectively brought Toronto and the GTA face-to-face with its economic future. Is Toronto's future that of the economic, financial, and cultural capital of Canada, while maintaining an important north–south linkage? Or does Toronto's economic future lie primarily in aggressively pursuing north–south integration while maintaining a dominant east–west role? From the admittedly subjective perspective of this author, the resolution of this dilemma can be parsed as follows: (1) Toronto has little alternative but to pursue the latter option; (2) the dominance of the homeowner-based politics of Toronto (Berridge 1999) suggests that Torontonians themselves (as distinct from 905 residents) may well have opted for the former; and (3) by donning its North American region-state vision, the province of Ontario is effectively, and appropriately, forcing Toronto into a global city-region framework. Not to put too fine a point on all of this, Ontario's "mind of state" has effectively and permanently altered Toronto's "state of mind" in terms of its economic future.

Backing up a bit, part of Toronto's 1990s economic decline was linked to the fact that the recession was more or less worldwide. Moreover, one can also lay a lot of the blame (in terms of the severity of the recession) on the Bank of Canada's price-stability strategy, which served to appreciate the Canadian dollar from 76 Canadian cents per U.S. dollar in 1986 to 89 cents in 1991, thereby wreaking havoc with Canada's, and particularly Toronto's, manufacturing and services industries.

There was, however, another and more ominous factor at play in terms of Toronto's fortunes—the inevitable integration imperative arising from the FTA and the attendant information revolution. There were, and are, two aspects to this challenge. The first is that the "open borders" policy of the FTA and NAFTA allows for quite dramatic rationalization of cross-border economic activity. Fast off the mark was the rationalization of U.S. subsidiaries operating in Canada since the Canadian market could now be serviced from the United States. Beyond this, Toronto faces a related challenge. One way to express this is to note that for a considerable range of economic activity, Toronto is Buffalo's international city! Buffalo and other proximate U.S. locations are, under an open borders environment, within easy economic striking distance of Toronto and the GTA and they are "armed," as it were, with a legal, institutional, and fiscal regime that is arguably more suited to aggressive competition. All told, this amounts to a clarion call to Toronto and Ontario that their erstwhile privileged position operating as Canada's heartland is now under siege and that Ontarians have no choice but to become aggressive players in the new geoeconomic reality.

The second is that selected aspects of Toronto's dominance in Canada are also coming under challenge. It should hardly come as a surprise that other provinces and cities are also progressively looking north–south and, as such, they will also be focusing on ways in which they can forge cross-border linkages of their own and, in doing so, wean themselves from Toronto's influence. For example, the recent sale of British Columbia-based MacMillan Bloedel to U.S. Weyerhaeuser generated commentary to the effect that at least Weyerhaeuser was a Pacific Region firm, not a Toronto-based firm. This is the emerging north–south reality and mentality in action. Actually, this should eventually play in Toronto's favor. The fact that other regions will begin to pursue north–south opportunities should pave the way for Canadians to allow Toronto and the GTA similar leeway. Note that none of this suggests that Ontario and Toronto will in any way forgo pursuing any east–west economic opportunities, as Ontario's strong support for the recent Agreement on Internal Trade makes clear.

Ontario's economic fortunes over the last half of the 1990s have been nothing short of spectacular. Thanks to the earlier-noted restructuring, to the long-lived U.S. economic boom, and especially to the depreciation of the Canadian dollar (it fell from its 89 cent peak in 1991 to a low of 63 cents in the summer of 1998 and at the time of writing it is in the range of 68 cents), Ontario and the GTA literally took off. Exports more than doubled. Moreover, fully 50 percent of Canada's impressive job growth since 1995 has occurred in Ontario. This period coincides with the coming to power of the Harris government, so that there is much debate in Ontario and Canadian circles in terms of how much of this growth would have occurred naturally and how much is a result of the more competitive environment ushered in by the Harris government's policies. Perhaps the best way to answer this is to note that Premier Harris won reelection in 1999, the first back-to-back majority governments in Ontario since the 1960s.

The Political/Institutional Revolution Revisited

In the run-up to the creation of the megacity, and, more generally, the municipal/institutional revolution, a rich menu of alternative approaches to the evolution of Toronto and the GTA were incorporated in an impressive set of reports and panels. The most important of these has already been referred to—*Greater Toronto*, the report of the Task Force on the Future of the Greater Toronto Area (1996), chaired by Anne Golden. The Task Force was struck in a time frame (Spring 1995) where the city of Toronto was still suffering from the lingering effects of the 1990s recession, even though the level of economic activity in the *rest* of the GTA had already surpassed its prerecession peak. Hence, a significant part of the Task Force's agenda was devoted to addressing the "apparent and potential further decline in economic attractiveness of the core of the GTA" (Golden Report 1996: 17). At the heart of this economic concern was the divergence in property tax rates between then-Metro Toronto and the 905 region. Essentially, Toronto had higher commercial property taxes than the 905 area and relatively lower residential property tax rates. Toronto argued that its higher tax rates were triggered by its higher "needs"—among other things, a larger welfare case load and a much more serious "homelessness" problem than 905. The 905 area responded by arguing that Toronto's services were far too generous. In any event, the Task Force concluded that "the tax system puts Metro business at a serious disadvantage in comparison to businesses in other parts of the [GTA] region, and encourages businesses to migrate from Metro to other GTA municipalities, which exacerbates the problem of [Metro's] eroding tax base" (Ibid.: 11–12). Arguably, there were other factors also at play in this migration of businesses from the core to the 905 area—e.g. space constraints in the core and the attraction of locating enterprises in the 905 area where, increasingly, their valued employees were residing. In any event, the property tax issue along with an application of the principle of subsidiarity dominated the Task Force recommendations for the evolution of the GTA:

Our report is premised on a vision of Greater Toronto as *the place where people and businesses that can choose to be anywhere, choose to be.*

Our recommendations to support this vision include:

- a framework for a Greater Toronto economic strategy that focuses on both physical and human infrastructure;
- a common assessment system for Greater Toronto, based on Actual Value, with a program to cushion the impacts on those adversely affected;
- equalization of property taxes that businesses in the GTA pay for education;
- removal of the barriers to efficient infrastructure investment to allow for a more sustainable urban form;
- removal of overlap and friction between the Province and municipalities through a financially neutral disentanglement of responsibilities;
- improved coordination for services that cross boundaries, without centralizing service delivery;

- replacement of the five existing regional governments with a single, streamlined Greater Toronto Council with a more limited range of functions; and
- giving local municipalities added powers and responsibilities to deliver a wide range of services more efficiently. (1996: 9–10.)

The last two bullets, among others, embrace the principle of subsidiarity. In the words of the Task Force (1996: 174):

> The Task Force agrees that, wherever possible, services should be delivered by local municipalities to ensure maximum efficiency and responsiveness to local needs and preferences. The Greater Toronto Council will have only those responsibilities for services that are key to our competitiveness, require planning and coordination at a region-wide basis, or cannot be provided at the local level. All other services previously delivered at the regional level will be devolved to local municipalities.

Thus, the Task Force's proposals would have effectively eliminated the five regional governments, with a selected set of functions transferred upward to the GTA level and the remainder passed downward to the municipal level.

A second task force was the so-called Who Does What Panel, chaired by former Toronto mayor, David Crombie. Graham and Phillips (1998: 185–6) summarize the recommendations of the WDW panel as follows:

> In total, the WDW Panel made over two hundred recommendations, including proposals for a more permissive municipal act (based on the Alberta model); property-assessment based on current value and use; amalgamation in general and, specifically, some consolidation of the GTA municipalities; and (following the Golden Report) the creation of a Greater Toronto Area Services Board to replace the five regional governments of the GTA. In terms of disentanglement, the panel's recommendations reflected the principle that hard services should be municipally funded and delivered, while human services (social assistance, public health, child care, and homes for the aged) should be the full responsibility of the province.

In general terms, these two reports, in tandem with a myriad of ensuing conferences, have served to provide an important analytical backdrop for the longer term evolution of Ontario's provincial-municipal relations and, in particular, of the GTA. In specific terms, while the Ontario government's restructuring of the GTA did fall back on some of these recommendations, it also departed significantly from some of the key features. For example, it did not embrace the subsidiarity conception of the Task Force Report. Rather, and as already noted, it eliminated the six municipalities of the former Metro Toronto region and created the single megacity of Toronto, leaving five regional governments in place—Toronto, Halton, Peel, Durham, and York (see Figure 10.3). It did, however, create a Greater Toronto Services Board (GTSB) with a vague mandate to focus on infrastructure issues, especially transportation, as they relate to the GTA. Relatedly, the province also mandated GTA-wide sharing of those components of the residential property tax dedicated to financing welfare and other enumerated social services. In terms of the property tax, the province did institute provincewide, market-value assessment replete with much more provincial control in rate setting. And as part of this increased provincial control of the property tax base the province assumed control over the funding of education. The quid pro quo for assuming responsibility of education was to transfer responsibility for some "hard service" functions to the municipalities along with a continuing role in financing some social services (20 percent of welfare and all of social housing, etc.). Graham and Phillips (1998) provide a comprehensive overview of this complicated and controversial restructuring process.

My personal view is that this is a welcome interim equilibrium within a longer term evolution. The core of this interim equilibrium is the shift toward market-value assessment of the property tax base and greater provincial control over rate-setting. For this to be workable, there needs to be some restructuring of boundaries to internalize the externality arising from the fact that there is a divergence in terms of where citizens earn their income and where they consume services. Hence the rationale for municipal amalgamation, not only for the megacity of Toronto but for most other Ontario cities as well. And as an added bonus from the province's vantage point, the creation of the megacity merged the high-business-tax preferences of the former city of Toronto with the more competitive-oriented policies of the other five former municipalities. Arguably, the new megacity is now more attuned to a global city-region mentality and more attuned to the larger vision of Ontario as a North American region-state. Most important of all in terms of future evolution, the embryonic GTSB has, despite its vague mandate and lack of resources, the potential to serve as a launching pad for initiatives in the direction of generating a unity of economic purpose across the entire GTA.

Prior to addressing these pressures for further evolution, it is appropriate to address one of the themes of Chapter 1, namely the social geography of global city-regions:

> It is becoming apparent that globalization and its associated forms of economic change tend to widen the gap between the wealthy and the poor in economic, social, and spatial terms. Globalization intensifies these trends by stimulating the growth of high-wage occupations in large cities while promoting . . . the proliferation of marginal, low-skill jobs. For example, in the early 1990s it was reported that the disparity between wealth and poverty had grown in all the developed industrial countries, in both big and small cities. (Scott *et al.* 2000.)

Available evidence in Canada (e.g. Beach and Slotsve 1996) suggests that while market incomes in Canada are polarizing, overall income inequality (market income plus government transfers) is not as yet showing much evidence of diverging further. In part, this is because Canada has quite dramatically targeted its income support programs toward addressing inequality, e.g. the former universal family allowance has long-since been replaced by income-tested and even refundable tax credits. Nonetheless, there are growing concerns relating to the income-distribution implications of globalization on the one hand and the market-oriented policies of the Harris government on the other. For example, when the Conservatives took office in 1995 they scaled back welfare payments by 21 percent (which put the province somewhere in the middle of the Canadian provinces) and embarked on a program of workfare. It is probably fair to say that, ideologically, Ontario is now far more polarized than at any time in memory. However, even under the old Toronto region, with its six independent municipalities, there was tax-base sharing across the region in terms of policy areas such as welfare and homelessness. Under the new Toronto megacity structure, tax and expenditure sharing is obviously full and complete. Moreover, and as already noted, the new initiatives call for tax-base sharing across the entire GTA for selected social services. To be sure, this will not relieve the core of its social problems (e.g. homelessness), but the financing of these challenges will not be left solely to the revenue-sharing capacity of the core. Beyond this, of course, all megacity and GTA residents have access to Canada's European-style social envelope—"free" hospital and medical insurance, a generous income-tested support system for the elderly, federal employment insurance, and a growing federal presence in terms of addressing child poverty—as well as refundable tax credits under the income-tax system and a new federal child benefit that Ontario has restructured to provide support for working-poor families. Thus, while the "hole in the donut" or, given the GTA's geography as portrayed in Figure 10.3, the "hole in the croissant" (Slack 1999), challenges on the social front of an emerging global region-city are apparent, the financing of these challenges is such that, in principle at least, all similarly situated GTA residents are on a "level paying field." Where there is much more concern is on the cyclical front. Toronto and the GTA are in the midst of a sustained economic boom. What happens if and when growth slows, given the largely transfer-dependent status of all Ontario municipalities, not just the megacity? This is a convenient entrée to some speculation on the likely further evolution of Toronto and the GTA.

The Future of Toronto as a Global City-Region

Bird and Chen (1998) note that provinces are the principal beneficiaries of the devolution of power within the Canadian federation. On the one hand, Ottawa has devolved selected powers to the provinces (training, forestry, mining, etc.). On the other hand, the recent evidence is that powers within provinces have been transferred upwards from municipalities to the provinces. This is certainly true for Ontario, where, for example, Queen's Park has taken effective control over education on the expenditure side and of the property tax base and rates on the revenue side. As also noted, this is best viewed as an "interim equilibrium." Kenichi Ohmae's contribution in this volume argues that global city-regions are progressively the dynamic motors of economic growth and, as such, more powers will eventually accrue to these city-regions. The purpose of this section is to focus on those areas where the global city-region of Toronto is likely to expand its importance and influence.

The Infrastructure Dimension

The Greater Toronto Services Board (GTSB) has the long-term potential for forging an integrated approach to those areas that are critical to enhancing GTA-wide competitiveness and exporting potential. Foremost among these areas is the issue of physical infrastructure (e.g. transportation) and, over the longer term, human capital infrastructure. Admittedly, as currently constituted, the GTSB is in no position to deliver on this: it has "no direct elections, no clear mandate, no taxing powers, no democratic accountability, and no independent powers" (Mendelson 1999: 2). Nonetheless, it is the only institutional instrument that is in place to generate a unity of purpose across the GTA for those areas or issues involving the spatial scale that corresponds to the full global city-region economy (Gertler 1999: 16). And the GTSB is beginning to respond to this challenge.

By way of illustration, it is instructive to focus in more detail on the GTA physical infrastructure challenge. Berridge (1999) addresses this in terms of the following "paradox" or trade-off:

> Toronto can help keep Canada economically dynamic only through greater integration with the U.S. economy. To do so, however, it must go head to head with some very substantial cities south of the border that are in the midst of a renaissance spurred on by massive investment.... To maintain our ranking... in the face of well-capitalized U.S. urban competition will require both a strategy and a scale of public and private financial investment not now evident.

These U.S. cities have benefited from very substantial *federal* infrastructure spending. This is a nonstarter, politically, in Canada since the federal government must go *through the provinces* with respect to municipal initiatives. Ottawa is mounting a modest infrastructure program, but it requires provincial matching and will presumably be subject to provincial priorities. Thus, "the fundamental strategic goal for the Toronto area must be to become financially self-sufficient, not only from an operating perspective, but generating a significant portion of capital requirements for new investment" (Berridge 1999). As noted in the next section, Toronto has limited financial capacity to meet its operating budget, let alone embark on infrastructure spending.

But the solution to the infrastructure challenge goes well beyond the financial issue. Again, Berridge (1999) merits quotation:

> Toronto also desperately needs the management capacity for urban regeneration that is characteristic of every other world city. We have no development corporations for public–private projects comparable to the agencies typically responsible for transforming waterfront and industrial lands in U.S. and British cities.

And further:

> Toronto cannot remain a competitive global city without the active involvement of the business, financial, and voluntary sectors. All successful cities have broadened the constituency commitment to productive management of their urban future beyond the

narrow framework of home-owner based local politics. Without such business intelligence and community resources, no effective business plan can be realized. How we achieve this may be Toronto's biggest challenge.

If the GTSB were to get its act together in terms of the above challenges, then it is Ontario (and Queen's Park), not the GTA, that will be on the defensive. The government of Ontario has clearly recognized (as elaborated earlier) that the province's success as a powerful North American region-state will depend on the viability of the GTA as a global city-region. This leaves Queen's Park with two polar options (and combinations thereof): on the one hand to accommodate the GTA's needs either by providing the necessary capital funds or by allowing the GTA enhanced fiscal flexibility to undertake these initiatives on its own (more on this later) or, on the other, to witness a concerted effort on the part of the GTA and other Canadian city-regions to pressure the Canadian federal government to play a U.S.-type role in providing infrastructure funds for Canadian cities. Assuming that the latter option will not sit well with Ontario, this directs focus to the fiscal position of the GTA.

The Fiscal Flexibility Dimension

Toronto and the GTA are, as a result of the recent Ontario reallocation of provincial-municipal powers and finances, arguably the most fiscally restrained of Canadian cities. Fully 20 percent of GTA operating expenses are allocated to social and family services, over which the GTA has limited control.[5] On the revenue side, property taxes and associated levies, which account for half of the budget, are now increasingly subject to provincial rate-setting. A further 20 percent of revenues come in the form of conditional grants from the province to be spent in line with provincial priorities. The remaining revenues consist of user fees (16 percent) plus a variety of other revenue sources. Beyond this, municipalities cannot borrow to meet operating deficits. This leaves the GTA in a vulnerable position in the best of times and will likely generate a fiscal crisis in the face of a future recession.

In general, the GTA can pursue three main approaches to enhancing its fiscal flexibility. One is to "upload" selected expenditure categories to the provincial level. An obvious candidate here is "social housing" which should in any event appropriately be a provincial, if not national, responsibility. Indeed, if the earlier analysis is correct, namely that region-states will focus more on wealth creation than on income-distribution concerns, then there probably is a rationale for a greater federal presence on the distributional front. In any event, to the extent that any such uploading leads to a compensating decrease in provincial conditional grants, this will do little to ameliorate the financial straightjacket, although it will help cushion the financial implications of an economic downturn.

A second approach relates to the general area of cost-containment and, in particular, a more extensive approach to user fees. In terms of the latter, Toronto could follow the increasing trend to extend user fees to other services such as garbage collection. Along similar lines, Berridge (1999) notes:

> [Toronto and the GTA] have to decide what activities the city-region should *not* finance off the tax base, scrutinizing all the operating municipal services businesses—electricity, water and waste water, garbage, transit—and creating new organizations largely able to meet their own needs. Toronto is one of the few world cities that still operates these services as mainline businesses. The ability to use the very substantial asset values and cash flows of these municipal businesses is perhaps the only financial option to provide the city region with what is unlikely to be obtainable from other sources: its own pool of re-investment capital. Such an urban infrastructure fund would have remarkable leverage potential, both from public-sector pension funds and from other private-sector institutions.

But this has never been the Canadian way. We pride ourselves in our universal, no-user-fee, medicare system and are extremely loathe to rely on user fees elsewhere in the policy arena, lest they become the thin edge of the wedge in terms of spreading to the health system. Indeed, this national characteristic is part of the reason why Canada's aggregate government debt load (federal and provincial) is now 100 percent of our GDP. This is yet another reflection of the fact that we Canadians are having a difficult time making the transition from the former resource-dominated and behind-tariff-walls paradigm to the new realities of the emerging global order. Nonetheless, Berridge's comments are, arguably, the way of the future.

The third and most obvious avenue for achieving fiscal flexibility is to gain access to new revenue sources. Because of municipal amalgamation, and the creation of much larger municipal entities, this is a much more feasible alternative than heretofore was the case. One area under some discussion (and suggested by the Golden Report) is for the GTA to share in the provincial motor fuels tax, along the lines of current practice in the Greater Vancouver area: "the ability . . . to receive a share of the fuel tax (and possibly license fees and other transportation-related charges) to fund road or transit improvements would increase Toronto's financial self-sufficiency and its ability to pay for transit and transportation needs in the region" (Slack 1999: 8). Beyond this option, Slack notes that city-regions such as Stockholm and Frankfurt have access to a share of income taxation. Allocating a portion of the provincial sales tax to the city level is yet another potential option. It may not be surprising that none of these options are even on the provincial government's radar screen. What is surprising is that they do not feature prominently, except for the fuel tax, in terms of the priorities of Toronto and the GTA. In my view, the underlying issue here is political, not economic. Toronto and the GTA are still locked into the constitutional mind set that they are creatures of the province. However, with the creation of the megacity and with the potential for the GTSB to evolve into a GTA-wide instrument for integrating physical and human capital infrastructure, the political dynamics of Ontario will alter significantly. In admittedly speculative fashion, I now address this potential for greater self-determination for Toronto and the GTA.

Political Evolution

With its over 4.5 million residents, the GTA has a larger population than all but two Canadian provinces—Ontario (or the rest of Ontario) and Quebec. If and when the GTA embraces a "unity of purpose" and conceives of itself as an integrated global city, it may well become a political arrangement that will be able to rival Queen's Park in selected policy areas. And if the GTA were ever to become a single political entity, it would not take long before it harbored aspirations of becoming a city-province along the lines of the German city-laender—Hamburg, Bremen, and Berlin. Presumably the existing province would veto any such aspirations, but the fallback position would certainly be a degree of GTA self-determination that Queen's Park could no longer ignore. But even without political amalgamation, the Toronto megacity will possess a cadre of civil servants that will have sufficient information, analytic, and implementation capacity to generate alternative approaches for policy and program development to those emanating from Queen's Park. Of and by itself, this will change the political dynamics between the GTA and the province.

Relatedly, Toronto itself has the possibility for significantly altering the politics of Ontario. The new city's fifty-seven councilors represent, in my view, an unstable equilibrium. Presumably the rationale for such a large body had to do with either or both of the following: to allow for "neighborhood" representation in order to make the new megacity more acceptable to the six constituent municipalities, or to ensure that the sheer number of members would, from Queen's Park's view, effectively constitute a "divide and conquer" strategy and prevent Toronto from speaking with a unified collective voice. However, the unwieldy nature of the status quo will likely become apparent to Torontonians, once the initial adjustment to the reality of the megacity is complete. If the numbers of councilors are not reduced in order to facilitate more effective governance, the likelihood is that this will be an open invitation for the introduction of party politics at the Toronto level which, in turn, *will* influence the provincial political environment.[6]

There is, of course, a close relationship between economic/financial and political self-determination. The more that Toronto (and particularly the GTA), embraces the conception of itself as a global city-region that has to make its way in the context of competing North American global city-regions, the more likely that Queen's Park will be pressured to accommodate this political thrust with a greater degree of fiscal self-determination.

In any event, the purpose of this speculation is not to attempt to predict the future of the GTA. Rather, it is to suggest that recent Ontario initiatives in reconfiguring provincial-municipal powers are best viewed as a temporary equilibrium, with the seeds for further evolution ready to germinate.

Canada Matters Too

To this point, the analysis has focused on Toronto as a global city-region through the lens of Ontario's emergence as a North American region-state. Where is Canada in all this? The correct answer is that it is omnipresent. It was the Canada–U.S. Auto Pact that put Ontario and the GTA on the North American manufacturing map. It was Canada that boldly spearheaded in the Canada–U.S. Free Trade Agreement and, later, NAFTA. And it was Canadian macro policy in the mid-1990s that tamed the deficit, reduced inflation to near zero, generated thirty- or forty-year lows in interest rates that, in tandem with the fall in the dollar, engineered the most competitive Canadian and Ontario economies in the postwar period. Without these initiatives, there would be no Ontario region-state and Toronto's star as a global city-region would be shining a lot less brightly.

Nonetheless, globalization and the information revolution present Canadian governance with additional challenges. As already noted, one of these is to provide pan-Canadian leadership and policy in terms of ensuring not only that our human capital infrastructure is consistent with the reality that knowledge is at the cutting edge of competitiveness but, as well, to ensure wherever possible that the best and the brightest among us can find in Canada a productive and innovative environment to ply their skills. One of the major concerns here is that Canadian income taxes are not only too high but are triggered at very low thresholds of income. For example, apart from the fact that marginal tax rates are much higher in Canada (at the "average production wage," marginal rates in Canada and the United States are 45.9 percent and 29.9 percent respectively (Courchene 1999*a*)), the top marginal rate kicks in at roughly C$64,000 in Canada, whereas the top marginal rate in the United States takes effect at an income level of C$400,000. And it is the Americans that appear to be the more determined to implement a substantial further reduction in income tax rates. To a large extent, the significant rate reductions in Ontario's (and Alberta's) component of the shared income tax are designed to attempt to ameliorate the overall Canada–U.S. marginal-tax-rate differential. If Ottawa does not act, the provinces will continue along this path. Hence, it is now imperative that the federal government bring its tax rates more in line with U.S. rates. If this places its social agenda in the balance, then the appropriate response is to increase the tax rate on the export–import neutral GST (VAT).

This reference to social programs relates to another Canadian concern—namely that North American integration is undermining Canadian support for its generous social contract. To a degree, this is indeed the case—all nation-states are reevaluating the magnitude of, and incentives within, their social envelopes. But there is a related issue that, arguably, is as important when it comes to Canadians' views of social policy and government generally: increasingly, citizens perceive that the value of government programs falls short of the tax cost of these programs. And in this they are surely correct, since the huge debt overhang means that over one-quarter of every federal tax dollar goes to debt servicing. Generating a lower debt-to-GDP ratio would thus serve several goals, e.g. it would make Canada more competitive (by allowing for tax reductions or for programs that would enhance Canada's knowledge capital) and it would restore citizens' faith in government spending since more of each tax dollar could be devoted to program spending. In the process, this would surely enhance the future of Toronto as a global city.

There is, however, another challenge facing Ottawa, namely to find creative instruments that would allow Canadian industry more flexibility in adjusting to its new NAFTA opportunities. As Gertler (1999: 14) perceptively notes:

> it is foolish or misguided to presume that, just because city-regions have become the key locus for innovation and learning, they must now be expected to provide the full wherewithal to support these activities themselves. If one looks at the world's great clusters of economic activity, the influence of senior (especially federal) governments is almost universally very strong. While this is most obvious in great capital cities like London and Paris, it is equally true in Silicon Valley, which has risen, fallen, and risen again at least in part on the basis of national defence policy and military procurement in the United States, and whose high-tech firms show more than passing interest in *federal anti-trust and competition policy*. [Emphasis added.]

The most important exemplar of the need for rethinking competition policy in terms of Toronto and the GTA is the banking sector. In the new global era, countries are lucky if they have a few "national assets" to help propel them forward competitively. The Canadian banking sector is clearly one such Canadian asset. We must not allow this sector to languish into second-class status in North America. Yet, we must also recognize that the existing east–west banking infrastructure represents both national social capital and economic capital for other Canadian regions. Hence, we need a solid dose of innovative statecraft to generate creative instruments that will allow the banks to pursue their inevitable north–south future and at the same time ensure that all Canadians continue to have access to effective, efficient and accessible financial services. Toronto as a global city-region needs banks with a greater international capacity and reach. Arguably, so does the rest of Canada. Here, the ball is in Ottawa's court.

CONCLUSION

The geoeconomies of the FTA, NAFTA, and, more generally, the emerging global order are having a profound and permanent impact on the economic and political underpinnings of Canadian society. While east–west trade is far more open and efficient than the cross-border trade, the sheer size of the NAFTA economy and the associated "open borders" dictates that the volume of north–south trade is beginning to dominate the economic fortunes of our east–west economies. Consistent with the downward transfer of powers associated with the globalization thrust of the new paradigm, the various Canadian regions and provinces are, to varying degrees, donning the mantle of North American region-states. Nowhere is this more apparent than for Ontario. The thesis of this chapter is that the emergence of Ontario as a North American region-state is providing the governance architecture and the needed restructuring and incentives for Toronto to make its likewise inevitable transition from Canada's economic, financial, and cultural capital to a global city-region in the North American context and beyond. This is a politically troublesome transition for Canadians, since the undeniable economic strengths and potential of Toronto and the GTA have been derived either from national policy (e.g. the Auto Pact) or from their role as the provider of national goods and services to all Canadians. To now redeploy this power and influence in a north–south pursuit of economic advantage and prosperity may well be (and in areas like banking, is) viewed as a reneging of sorts on a long-standing, implicit east–west "societal contract."

But Toronto has no meaningful alternative. Fortunately, the future of Toronto has been well-served by the recent and impressive series of reports and research papers, all of which focus on creative ways in which Toronto and the GTA can not only better govern themselves but, in the process, more effectively make their way competitively within the open-borders framework of North America. Unfortunately, from the vantage point of many, Ontario did not embrace the full policy and structural thrust of these reports. Yet it has gone a considerable way towards this end. To be sure, this does not imply that the province's initiatives, particularly in the area of provincial-municipal restructuring and the political structure of the GTA, are appropriate, let alone the final evolutionary word. What can be said is that the important and significant steps Ontario is taking toward becoming a North American region-state are serving to provide a framework that will facilitate, if not propel, Toronto toward its inevitable future as a powerful global city-region. These include Ontario embracing an economic mission statement that assigns high priority to human capital, to innovation, and, more generally, to privileging Ontario as an attractive location in North America, and steps to implement institutional and structural changes in Toronto and GTA governance. Indeed, in its mission statement Ontario recognizes that its future as an effective North American region-state depends on Toronto's success as a global city region.

The intriguing irony is that Ontario may have overplayed its hand here. Internal and external pressures on Toronto and the GTA will be such that the GTA will indeed evolve towards Gertler's vision of a "unity of purpose" and that the GTSB will become an effective body for developing infrastructure and other GTA-wide initiatives to capitalize on the opportunities presented by the NAFTA geoeconomy. Unwittingly, perhaps, Ontario may well have laid the framework for the creation not only of a powerful global city-region but for an increasingly influential political countervailing power to Queen's Park as well. The consolidation of Toronto as a global city-region will begin to alter Ontario's view of itself and its role in the federation, and, indeed, alter the federation itself.

NOTES

1. With its 11.1 million people, Ontario accounts for 37 percent of Canada's population and 40 percent of Canadian GDP. With its rougly 4.5 million people, the Greater Toronto Area (defined below) accounts for just over 40 percent of Ontario's population but

generates 50 percent of Ontario's GDP. Thus, the GTA accounts for nearly 20 percent of Canada's GDP.

2. Note that these exports, both interprovincial and international, are defined in terms of total value, not value-added.
3. One might note here that the provinces collect, on average, just under 40 percent of all personal income tax revenues, so that a 30 percent reduction in Ontario's tax rate is a significant decrease in overall income taxes.
4. On the cultural side, this statement applies only to "English Canada."
5. The data in this paragraph are adapted from Slack (1999).
6. As this paper is being revised (December 1999), Ontario is "forcing" a reduction of the number of Toronto councilors. As an associated comment, it may be instructive to note that party politics currently plays no role in municipal elections in Canada.

REFERENCES

Beach, C. M., and Slotsve, G. A. (1996). *Are We Becoming Two Societies? Income Polarization and the Myth of the Declining Middle Class in Canada.* Toronto: C. D. Howe Institute.

Berridge, J. (1999). "There's No Need to Sit and Wait for a Handout." *Globe and Mail*, 7 June.

Bird, R., and Chen, D. (1998). "Federal Finance and Fiscal Federalism: The Two Worlds of Canadian Public Finance." *Canadian Public Administration*, 51–74.

Castells, M. (1996). *The Rise of the Network Society*. Cambridge: Blackwells.

Courchene, T. J. (1999*a*). "Provincial Perspectives on the Role and Operation of the Tax Collection Agreements." *Canadian Tax Journal* (forthcoming).

—— (1999*b*). "From Heartland to North American Region-State." Acceptance remarks for the 1999 Donner Prize, *Policy Options*, 20 (4/July–August).

——, and Telmer, C. R. (1998). *From Heartland to North American Region-State: The Social, Fiscal, and Federal Evolution of Ontario.* Toronto: Faculty of Management, University of Toronto.

Gertler, M. (1999). "Self-Determination for Toronto: What Are the Economic Conditions, and Do They Exist?" Paper presented to the Evolution of Toronto Forum (23 June).

Golden Report. (1996). See Task Force on the Future of the Greater Toronto Area (1996).

Graham, K. A., and Phillips, S. D. (1998). "Who Does What in Ontario: The Process of Provincial-Municipal Disentanglement." *Canadian Public Administration*, 41 (2): 175–209.

Lecoq, B. (1991). "Organisation industrielle, organisation territoriale: une approche intégrée fondée sur le concept de réseau." *Revue d'Économie Régionale et Urbaine*, 34: 321–42.

Mendelson, M. (1999). "The Emancipation of Cities." Paper presented to the Evolution of Toronto Forum (23 June).

Ohmae, K. (1993). "The Rise of the Region-State." *Foreign Affairs*, 72: 78–87.

Ontario Jobs and Investment Board. (1999). *A Road Map to Prosperity: An Economic Plan for Jobs in the 21st Century.* Toronto.

Scott, A. J., Agnew, J., Soja, E. W., and Storper, M. (2000). "Global City Regions." Chapter 1, this volume.

Slack, E. (1999). "The Road to Financial Self-Sufficiency for Toronto: What Are the Impediments and How Can They Be Overcome." Paper presented to the Evolution of Toronto Forum (23 June).

Storper, M. (1995). "The Resurgence of Regional Economics Ten Years Later." *European Urban and Regional Studies*, 2 (3): 191–221.

Task Force on the Future of the Greater Toronto Area. (1996). *Greater Toronto.* Toronto: Queen's Printer for Ontario. This report is referred to as the Golden Report, after its chair, Anne Golden.

United Nations. (1990). *Regional Economic Integration and Transnational Corporations in the 1990s: Europe 1992, North America and Developing Countries.* United Nations Center on Transnational Corporations, series A, no. 15. New York.

PART V

GLOBAL CITY-REGIONS IN AFRICA, ASIA, AND LATIN AMERICA: POLITICAL AND ECONOMIC CHALLENGES

In the less economically developed, as in the more economically developed, parts of the world, city-regions are critical engines of economic growth. This positive attribute of city-regions, however, comes with high social costs, most especially in developing countries where, as both Stren and Douglass argue, large-scale urbanization is endemically associated with massive problems of poverty, inequality, crime, congestion, environmental degradation, and so on.

The tasks of managing this explosive combination of desirable and undesirable urban outcomes frequently far exceed the political and administrative capacities of municipal governments in the developing world. These tasks are made all the more onerous by the additional stresses and strains that are sparked off in these city-regions as globalization works its effects, a point that is dramatically exemplified by the devastating impacts of the recent financial crisis on many aspects of urban life in East and Southeast Asia (Douglass and Kim). In light of these remarks, Campbell's account of political changes at the local level in Latin America over the 1990s strikes a welcome note of optimism. A revival of urban leadership, improving levels of professionalism in municipal administrations, and rising democratization of local public decision-making are all becoming increasingly apparent in a number of large cities throughout Latin America, and are beginning to produce extremely positive results. In addition to the cases cited by Campbell, the so-called ABC municipalities in the southeast quadrant of the São Paulo metropolitan region in Brazil represent a remarkable example of these trends. Here, a deepening process of social mobilization has been occurring since the early 1990s, leading to the search for a new regional political dispensation with greatly expanded popular participation and active efforts to construct a new collaborative knowledge-intensive regional economy.

In some parts of Africa, Asia, and Latin America, however, intensifying levels of competition between large city-regions is leading to wasteful development races. This condition is strongly exemplified by the recurrent contests that occur in many Latin American countries, with municipalities competing against one another in the effort to attract foreign direct investments. In their most exacerbated expression, these contests assume the guise of interregional fiscal wars in which rival municipalities aggressively bid to make the most generous concessions to foreign corporations searching for locations for new plants, a process that often leads in the end to sharply reduced social benefits for all. In circumstances like these, either some higher-level political authority or some institutionalized form of interregional cooperation is required in order to bring the costs of rivalry under control, as well as to unleash greater developmental potentials. Both Kim and Douglass write in very positive terms about the benefits that can be expected to flow by bringing together the major cities of northeast China, the Russian Far East, the west coast of Japan, and the two Koreas into a collaborative network, thus pushing the Northeast Asian area as a whole to a new and higher stage of development. It can be argued, indeed, that as lines of political cleavage in the area begin to soften, Northeast Asia might eventually come to display a similar economic dynamism to that which characterizes Southeast Asia today.

In certain other parts of the globe, especially in the poorest countries comprising the Fourth World, the outlook is much less sanguine. As Stren suggests, there appears to be little prospect for spontaneous positive development in many of the urban areas of these countries. Significant and sustained support from the wider national and international communities is thus likely to be important in order to stimulate the takeoff of these areas into a virtuous circle of growth. Should it be possible to initiate such growth, there is some chance that the cities of the world's poorest countries—despite their manifold social problems—may eventually come to function as motors of durable overall development. Some measure of confidence in this judgment may perhaps be derived from the observation that cities located in parts of the world that were once thought of as development-resistant Third-World peripheries (such as Mexico, Taiwan, or Thailand) have been in the vanguard of significant economic advances in recent years.

11

Local Governance and Social Diversity in the Developing World: New Challenges for Globalizing City-Regions

RICHARD STREN

COMPETITIVE CITIES IN THE NORTH AND SOUTH: IS THERE A DIFFERENCE?

Cities, as many experts have been telling us, are increasingly involved in a globalizing international system, in which they (and their constituent firms and populations) must successfully compete in order to survive. As a British writer puts it:

> The acceleration of the globalisation of economic activity and the growing internationalisation of investment flows have accentuated competitive pressure on businesses and led many cities to seek competitive advantage in the urban hierarchy. . . . Cities are now part of an increasingly competitive world and place marketing has become an important part of economic development strategies. This emphasis on inter-area competition and place marketing has become clearly articulated and transparent in initiatives such as City Challenge, the SRB [Single Regeneration Budget], Local and Sector Challenge, City Pride and the National Lottery. (Oatley 1998: 5.)

There is a legitimate debate over whether cities as such (rather than firms and enterprises, for example) can be competitive (Krugman 1996, 1997) and even whether the notion of "competitiveness" has substantial and verifiable meaning (Begg 1999). In this discussion, the dean of the "competitiveness" school, Michael Porter, has made his position clear: cities and regions have an important role to play in assuring the competitiveness of their local firms and enterprises:

> The importance of geographic concentration [in enhancing competitive advantage] raises interesting questions about whether the nation is a relevant unit of analysis. The conditions that underlie competitive advantage are indeed often localized *within* a nation, though at different locations for different industries. . . . While classical factors of production are more and more accessible because of globalization, competitive advantage in advanced industries is increasingly determined by differential knowledge, skills, and rates of innovation which are embodied in skilled people and organizational routines. The process of creating skills and the important influences on the rate of improvement and innovation are intensely local. Paradoxically, then, more open global competition makes the home base more, not less, important. (Porter 1998: 157–8.)

Porter's well-known position has no doubt contributed to the widely held belief among local politicians and urban managers throughout the world that their cities must be competitive if they are to succeed. This view was reinforced by the work of Rosabeth Moss Kanter, whose influential work on so-called world-class American cities suggests a range of possible strategies that cities can follow if they wish effectively to connect with the global economy.[1] It was further strengthened by the spread of the idea of "best practices" at the Habitat II Conference in Istanbul in 1996. The notion that there were certain "best practices" that—if clearly documented and disseminated—could assist municipalities everywhere to improve their urban management was not new. But it was given a much higher profile at the Habitat II Conference when twelve initiatives received "Awards for Excellence" in a public ceremony. The twelve were chosen by a technical advisory committee, and then an independent international jury, out of a total of 700 original submissions from around the world. These submissions were the basis of the creation of a major database, currently available from Habitat-UNCHS. In 1998, the Municipality of Dubai presented an Award to ten initiatives, offering a $30,000 prize, a trophy, and a commemorative certificate to each of the winners (UNCHS website).

Recently, the World Bank cosponsored a meeting for businesses and municipal officials, entitled "The World Competitive Cities Congress." The meeting was attended by mayors and senior officials of both northern and southern cities. In a paper written for the meeting, William Barnes and James Brooks (of the National League of Cities) took the competitive premise for granted:

> As a local leader, you're concerned about your local economy. . . . The highly competitive global economy that has emerged in the closing years of the 20th century places new demands on local economies and local leaders. . . . No matter what your city's location is or its size, the global economy is all around you—on your main street, in your districts and in your schools. Your local economy is a part of it, just like every other local economy around the world. Your job as a local leader is to accept this fact, to help others accept it and to ensure that your local economy lives up to worldwide standards. You want your local economy to be . . . "world class."
>
> World-class means being competitive—meeting the highest standards set anywhere for goods and services and for residents' quality of life. (Barnes and Brooks 1999: 32.)

At the same meeting where the Barnes and Brooks paper was presented, senior officials of five major cities in the developed world, and eight major cities in the developing/transitional world presented their ideas on local efforts to address the competitiveness challenge. In a paper on Rio de Janeiro's experience in financial reform during the period 1993–96, for example, the current secretary of finance discussed the steps undertaken by the city's newly elected administration to make the accounting and budget management system more transparent and professional. Partly as a result, she said, the city became "the first Latin American city to issue securities abroad . . . thus ratifying investors' confidence in the soundness of the municipal finances" (Braule Pinto 1999: 66). In a companion piece, the current mayor, Luiz Paulo Fernandez Conde, argued that "[t]oday, we can no longer ignore the evidence that it is up to the cities to determine the greater or less degree of countries' competitiveness," summarizing the evidence as showing that "there exists, and will continue to exist, growing competition among cities, regions and countries, in which there will be winners and losers." Detailing a number of areas in which major initiatives were undertaken during his term of office (in tourism, the hosting of international meetings, infrastructural projects, nuclear energy, and software development), he approvingly referred to a 1998 survey in *Fortune* magazine, in which the city was highlighted "as the best city for investment in Brazil, and the fourth best in Latin America" (Fernandez Conde 1999: 92, 94). (Perhaps inadvertently, the authors made little or no reference to the city's other side: high local crime and murder rates, a high and increasing level of poverty and homelessness, deteriorating local services, and widespread unemployment.)

Another, albeit more balanced, presentation on Cape Town, South Africa (written by the mayor and chief finance officer of the city) also stressed the needs of the city to compete. While the writers rightly acknowledged that a major goal of the city is to achieve better racial integration as well as to reduce widespread poverty, they nevertheless highlighted a number of large infrastructural projects in the planning stage (including a major conference center), the effort to gain the Olympics for Cape Town in 2004, and the fact that the city "has hosted a stream of key international dignitaries in recent times." They concluded that Cape Town "is well set to compete successfully in the new millenium" (Mfeketo and van Ryneveld 1999).

At international meetings of mayors and urban specialists, the point is constantly brought home that cities need to develop "strategic plans," a "vision," or a unique approach to their economic challenges, if they are going to be among the world's winners rather than losers. In his introduction to a book entitled *Competitive Cities: Succeeding in the Global Economy* (Duffy 1995), the former mayor of Seattle says, "[s]uccessful cities of the future, both large and small, and regardless of where they are on the world map, must use all their resources if they hope to compete and prosper in a new world economy" (Royer 1999: x). Since the late 1980s, many cities have been undertaking "strategic planning" in order to achieve these objectives.[2] The basic elements of municipal strategic planning include such sequential steps as:

1. analyzing past, present, and potential future trends than can impact on a city;
2. adopting a goal-setting exercise that articulates what the city is and what it wants to be;
3. establishing a range of targets and operating principles to guide decision-making and use of resources;
4. involving the community and other stakeholders to respond and provide input;
5. producing a strategic plan document including an implementation and evaluation phase.

As the adepts of strategic planning are quick to point out, the process involves technical expertise (particularly in the early stages) but is essentially a political exercise, one of the most essential ingredients of which involves participation by major stakeholders in the elaboration of a "vision" for the city.

The notion of developing a "vision" in order to succeed in an international competitive environment has been supported by some important donor agencies. In late 1998, the World Bank (with collaboration of UNCHS and UNEP, and support from the Japanese government) established a "Cities Alliance," which had as one of its two main goals to formulate effective "city development strategies" (CDS) for a representative sample of developing country cities. By August 1999, thirty-two CDS exercises had been planned, of which twenty-two were fully active, covering all major regions of the developing world. The Bank defined the city development strategy as "an analytical approach which takes a city and its surrounding region as the unit of analysis. . . . A CDS will examine at least four aspects of cities: livability, competitiveness, good governance and management, and bankability. A CDS engages all city stakeholders in understanding the opportunities and constraints faced by their cities. The process aims to develop a realistic long term vision for the city, helping to define and prioritize actions needed to achieve these goals." Interviews with Bank officials in August of 1999 indicated that there were many more cities that had applied for CDS support than could be included under the current program (World Bank 1999).

In the midst of all these analyses and initiatives, do we need to distinguish between cities that are located in relatively more affluent regions from those in the poorer parts of the developing world? The competitiveness literature, insofar as it focuses on cities, city-regions, and subnational governments, tends to assume that factors that enhance the potential success of a city (such as Michael Porter's determinants of national competitive advantage, which include factor conditions; firm strategy, structure, and rivalry; demand conditions; and related and supporting industries) are generic, whether we have in mind a city with relatively ample resources, or a city with very limited resources. This assumption of generic approaches for North and South is becoming more common in the 1990s, partly because the world is internationalizing and disparate locations tend to have more in common (notwithstanding the fact that they also have many differences); but also because development ideas are increasingly being applied on a worldwide basis. At least for these reasons, such a generic assumption would at least be plausible. But to the extent that cities need to develop strategies—and strategic plans and visions—to respond to economic challenges, they need to take into account their basic resources, social structures, and governance institutions. It is at this point that we need to review some of the emerging realities in the larger cities of the South. In the section that follows, I will attempt to establish the point that southern cities—in spite of energetic attempts to incorporate them into the competitive global economy—need to take account of their special circumstances. These special circumstances—which include very rapid growth, extensive development that both defies conventional planning and harbors a high degree of social and physical fragmentation, high levels of poverty, and (often) increasing violence and insecurity—require a more nuanced approach to strategic planning than has commonly been evident in the published literature on northern cities.

URBANIZATION IN DEVELOPING COUNTRIES

While we must interpret comparative demographic statistics with caution, the most recent estimates of the United Nations Population Division (United Nations 1997) indicate a world that is relentlessly urbanizing, albeit more rapidly in the more rural southern regions (Latin America, Africa, Asia), than in Europe, North America, and Japan. The *rate of urbanization*, defined as the average annual rate of change of the proportion urban (equivalent to the difference between the urban and the global rate of growth for a country's—or region's—whole population) is a useful indicator of this change. Thus, while the rate of urbanization in the more developed regions has been hovering around 0.3 percent per annum from 1980 to 1995, "and should remain relatively unchanged for the near future," the rate of increase in the urban areas of the South has been estimated at 1.5 percent from 1980 to 1995, after which time it is expected to decline to approximately 1 percent in thirty years (United Nations 1997: 4). At the very least, therefore, these figures show the rate of urban growth—at the most aggregated level—in developing countries to be at least *three* (and up to *five*) times the rate of urban growth in the more developed countries of the world. In more conventional figures, the overall urban growth level (based on compound net population increases) in developed countries was about 0.8 percent per annum in 1990–95, while the figure was 3.5 percent per annum during the same period in developing countries—again, about 4–5 times higher in the South than in the North. As cities in the South continue to grow many times more rapidly than cities in the North, more and more of the world's urban population is found in southern, rather than northern, cities.

The distribution of this growing urban population is uneven. By 1995, about one third of the people in the less developed regions of the South lived in cities, while about three out of every four lived in cities in the North. This gap is gradually narrowing as the South urbanizes, although it is changing unevenly. Latin America (especially South America) and the Caribbean constitute the most urbanized region of the South, while Africa and parts of Asia (particularly the southcentral, southeast, and eastern parts of the region) lag considerably behind. In general, the least urbanized parts of the developing world are also urbanizing at the fastest annual rate. This statement applies *within* as well as *between* regions and continents.

The size of cities is another dynamic element in this narrative. As Mattei Dogan and John Kasarda put it a decade ago, "[t]he world is becoming more and more a world of giant cities, and these cities are increasingly located in less-developed countries" (Dogan and Kasarda 1988: 12). Rather than "giant cities," these days

Table 11.1. *The 14 largest urban agglomerations, ranked by population size, 1995 (in millions)*

1. Tokyo, Japan	27.0
2. Mexico City, Mexico	16.6
3. São Paulo, Brazil	16.5
4. New York, United States	16.3
5. Bombay, India	15.1
6. Shanghai, China	13.6
7. Los Angeles, United States	12.4
8. Calcutta, India	11.9
9. Buenos Aires, Argentina	11.8
10. Seoul, Republic of Korea	11.6
11. Beijing, China	11.3
12. Osaka, Japan	10.6
13. Lagos, Nigeria	10.3
14. Rio de Janeiro, Brazil	10.2

Source: United Nations 1997: 20.

we tend to speak of "megacities"—commonly defined as cities (or city-regions) with a total population of 10 million or more. The growing importance of these cities is remarkable. Thus, in 1950, only one city—New York—had a population of 10 million or more. By 1975, there were five: New York, Tokyo, Shanghai, Mexico City, and São Paulo. In 1995, ten of the fourteen megacities were located in the less developed regions; and by 2015 predictions are that twenty-two of the twenty-six megacities will be located in the less developed regions (United Nations 1997: 19). Table 11.1 lists the populations of the fourteen megacities as of 1995. Tokyo is by far the largest, at 27 million, with New York, Mexico City, and São Paulo clustering together near the 16 million mark. As Table 11.2 shows, the growth rates of the southern megacities have generally been much higher than the growth rates of the northern megacities (during the period 1975–95), and they will continue to be higher in almost all cases through to the year 2015, even though the growth rate of most megacities is expected to slow down over the next two decades.

The extent to which a city, or a city-region, is involved in the global economy is affected by many factors—its trading patterns, the origins and overseas connections of its people, its political status (capital cities are more involved than provincial cities), and its location (coastal cities, other things being equal, tend to have more international ties). Population size, however, relates to many of these factors: the largest cities are more likely to be capital cities, or at least major regional centers in most developing countries; the largest cities tend also to have more diverse populations, more complex trading economies, specialized financial institutions, large airports and/or seaports, and more high-level institutions such as universities, large industrial or research complexes, and cultural centers. Saskia Sassen's "global" cities are among the world's largest: Tokyo, Paris, and

Table 11.2. *Average annual rate of change in population, 1975–95 and 1995–2015, for urban agglomerations ranked as megacities in 2015 (percentage)*

Urban agglomeration and country	1975–95	1995–2015
A. Less developed regions		
Beijing, China	1.40	1.60
Bombay, India	3.96	2.74
Buenos Aires, Argentina	1.27	0.80
Cairo, Egypt	2.33	1.99
Calcutta, India	2.06	1.86
Delhi, India	4.05	2.64
Dhaka, Bangladesh	7.45	4.12
Hangzhou, China	6.72	4.99
Hyderabad, India	4.83	3.25
Istanbul, Turkey	3.94	3.22
Jakarta, Indonesia	2.91	2.40
Karachi, Pakistan	4.47	3.44
Lagos, Nigeria	5.68	4.37
Lahore, Pakistan	3.68	3.48
Metro Manila, Philippines	3.10	2.28
Mexico City, Mexico	1.94	0.73
Rio de Janeiro, Brazil	1.30	0.76
São Paulo, Brazil	2.49	1.03
Seoul, Republic of Korea	2.67	0.56
Shanghai, China	0.86	1.40
Teheran, Iran	2.35	2.05
Tianjin, China	2.12	1.81
B. More developed regions		
Los Angeles, United States	1.65	0.68
New York, United States	0.14	0.37
Osaka, Japan	0.37	0.00
Tokyo, Japan	1.55	0.34

Source: United Nations 1997: 23.

New York (Sassen 1991). And John Friedmann's thirty "world" cities are also among the largest—even in the 1980s, all were over a million in population, and most were at least several million in size. In Friedmann's three highest ranked categories of world cities (those with "global financial articulations," those with "multinational articulations," and those with "important national articulations") nine out of fifteen (again according to 1980s population figures) exceeded 5 million in size (Friedmann 1995: 24). While size is probably a necessary, if not a sufficient, condition for large-scale engagement in the international system, the growth of very large cities in the southern hemisphere is an important element in the increasing involvement of their regions and nations in the globalizing economy.

SOCIAL AND PHYSICAL FRAGMENTATION IN SOUTHERN CITIES

Coincident with the very rapid demographic growth that many cities in the South have been experiencing over the last several decades, their social and geographic morphology has been evolving in some unanticipated directions. In a detailed study of urbanization in Southeast Asia, T. G. McGee and Ira Robinson note the intermingling of rural and urban functions in very heterogeneous and far-flung city-regions.

> A distinguishing feature of recent urbanization in the ASEAN countries is the extension of their mega-cities beyond the city and metropolitan boundaries. This process has particularly affected the largest cities but it is also now occurring in the largest secondary ones, such as Chiang Mai in Thailand, Bandung in Indonesia, and Cebu City in the Philippines. Metropolitan regional growth tends to sprawl along major expressways and railroad lines radiating out from the urban cores, and leapfrogs in all directions, putting down new towns, industrial estates, housing projects, and even golf courses in areas hitherto agricultural and rural. In such areas, regions of dense population and mixed land uses are created, in which traditional agriculture is found side by side with modern factories, commercial activities, and suburban development. T. G. McGee has termed these *desakota* zones, drawing on the Bahasa Indonesia words for town and village.
>
> Extended metropolitan development tends to produce an amorphous and amoebic-like spatial form, with no set boundaries or geographic extent and long regional peripheries, their radii sometimes stretching 75 to 100 km from the urban core. The entire territory . . . is emerging as a single, economically integrated "mega-urban region", or "extended metropolitan region." . . . No single authority is responsible for overall planning or management. (McGee and Robinson 1995: ix–x.)

Elsewhere in the same book, McGee notes the social heterogeneity of these urbanizing regions. "Villages with households that still rely upon agriculture for some of their income exist side by side with golf courses, industrial estates, and squatter encampments. The outer regions of the zones exhibit a remarkable mixture of lifestyles and income-earning opportunities" (McGee 1995: 16).

If the expansion of very large cities in Southeast Asia has led to a pattern of extreme heterogeneity in land use and community lifestyles, the pattern in some other parts of the developing world has been one of physical extension from the central core, along with social fragmentation and polarization. A recent study of Buenos Aires by an Argentinian planner notes how land use in the city has taken the form of a series of concentric rings spreading outwards from the historic center where government offices and major commercial and financial services are located. Densities are highest in the center, decreasing towards the various municipalities in the periphery. Population growth has been fastest toward the outside, with the center (the Federal Capital) growing only 1.3 percent in total between the censuses of 1980 and 1991. (In 1991, the Federal Capital district recorded a population of 2,960,976, while the whole region had a population of 10,887,355.) By contrast, districts in the first, second, and third "ring" areas grew

15.83 percent during that period. While this growth was taking place, the city was experiencing serious economic problems, reflected in a decline in formal employment. This has resulted, argues Luis Ainstein, in "acute" social segregation in the city. High quality infrastructure and personal services are concentrated in the northern and western parts of the Federal Capital district, where most of the affluent live. "In the rest of the area, there has been an unprecedented decline in the physical fabric, including the growth of large areas of slums. Low-income settlements have developed in all parts of the periphery, but particularly in the south and west" (Ainstein 1996: 149).

This social and physical fragmentation—more visible in the "giant" cities in the South, but nevertheless present in many other cities—has been remarked by many observers. In a classic article on urban planning in developing countries, Marcello Balbo observes that the city of the Third World "is a city of fragments",

> where urbanisation takes place in leaps and bounds, creating a continuously discontinuous pattern. In the fragmented city, physical environment, services, income, cultural values and institutional systems can vary markedly from neighbourhood to neighbourhood, often from street to street. . . .
>
> Even in Latin America, where most cities date from the sixteenth century, a process of "tribalisation" seems to be under way: the city is splitting into different separated parts, with the apparent formation of many "microstates". Wealthy neighbourhoods provided with all kinds of services, such as exclusive schools, golf courses, tennis courts and private police patrolling the area around the clock intertwine with illegal settlements where water is available only at public fountains, no sanitation system exists, electricity is pirated by a privileged few, the roads become mud streams whenever it rains, and where house-sharing is the norm. Each fragment appears to live and function autonomously, sticking firmly to what it has been able to grab in the daily fight for survival. (Balbo 1993: 24–5.)

The continued growth of cities in Africa has followed the pattern established in other regions, but at a much lower level as a consequence of the overall marginalization of the continent in terms of trade, investment, and infrastructural development (Halfani 1996). Except for South Africa, which has been relatively buoyant, aggressively investing over the rest of the continent, most other countries have been experiencing low or negative investment, high and increasing unemployment, and (in many cases) political and civil unrest over the last decade. While African cities have been growing both spatially and demographically (although their growth increasingly derives from natural increase rather than migration), the two most prominent features they exhibit are increasing informality in major areas of economic activity, and a declining capacity to provide services and infrastructure to their populations. Agriculture (including both cultivation and animal husbandry) is practiced extensively in many cities, with the result that the economic and cultural differences between city and rural areas have become blurred (Stren and Halfani forthcoming). Municipal revenues are puny by international standards. As one Tanzanian town director explained his dilemma: "Even if I collect all the fees, rates, and levies in my district for two years, and suspend all other expenditures, I will not be able to buy one septic tank" (Halfani 1996: 89). Even a relatively wealthy (by African standards) city such as Abidjan has succumbed to "crisis" and "recession." "Once a formidable integrative machine," says Alain Dubresson, "the 'pearl of the lagoons' has today become a city of excluded people, with 15.7 percent of its total economically active population and 22.4 percent of its Ivoirian population unemployed" (Dubresson 1996: 264). Inequalities between wealthy and poorer districts in the distribution of services and capital investment in Abidjan are palpable. In the early 1990s, for example, the three wealthiest of the ten communes of the City of Abidjan spent, per resident, an average of 49 times the amount spent by the three poorest communes on recurrent expenditures, and six times the amount in capital expenditures (Dubresson 1996: 285).

The social and spatial fragmentation of many Third World cities is further exacerbated by the current wave of concern with the issues of security and violence.[3] Thus, Teresa Caldeira (1996) discusses the development of social and spatial segregation in São Paulo from the early twentieth century to the present. During this period, São Paulo went from being a "concentrated city" (from the early part of the century to the 1930s), through a city with "a rich centre and a poor periphery" (from the 1940s to the 1980s), to its present form in the 1990s, which she describes as "proximity and high walls." Her study of a rapidly growing wealthy suburban neighborhood (Morumbi) shows that fear of violence and crime is a pervasive subject in everyday conversation. However, talk of crime is common throughout all social groups in the city, as "people from all social classes fortify their homes, change their habits, and end up transforming the city and its public areas" (1996: 63). The result is a new urban landscape made up essentially of "fortified fragments" from which the poor and marginalized are excluded:

> As the spaces for the rich face inwards, the outside space is left for those who cannot afford to go in. In fact, the public is treated as leftover both by the design of the enclaves and by the citizens who create the new private order. The modern public space of the streets is increasingly the area abandoned to the homeless and the street children . . . fragmentation enforces separation and expresses not simple differences but irreconcilable inequalities. (Caldeira 1996: 64–5.)

Newspaper advertisements for closed condominiums published between 1985 and 1995 illustrate this trend; these advertisements (aimed at the rich) both reflect and promote an image of security, isolation, racial and class homogeneity, and high levels of services and facilities (Caldeira 1999: 120). In another analytical approach to fragmentation in São Paulo, Raquel Rolnik has collected data on a large sample of areas of "territorial exclusion" (where communities are deprived of legal rights to land that they occupy, to social and physical infrastructure, and to good housing). Data on land ownership, infrastructure, and housing was then matched to statistics on violence and crime. In general, Rolnik found that the areas with the worst infrastructure have the highest crime rates, and those with the best facilities have the lowest crime rates (Rolnik 1999). Physical and social fragmentation appear strongly related.

Urban crime rates in Latin America are a continuing source of alarm. Not only have homicide and violent crime rates (however they are calculated) been going up in many countries, but some countries—such as Colombia, Brazil, and Mexico—have among the highest rates in the world (Ayres 1998: 3). Homicide rates, as are well known, are particularly high for young males but have reached alarming proportions among women and children. A paper prepared for the World Bank concluded that "the 'net accumulation of human capital' in Latin America and the Caribbean had been cut in half because of the increase in crime and violence over the past 15 years" (ibid.). A study on Colombia prepared for the Interamerican Development Bank (IDB) in 1996 concluded that the cost of crime and violence to the country amounts to about one-third of its per capita income (cited in Ayres 1998: 8). The IDB has called violent crime "the principal barrier to regional economic development," and estimated that its annual cost is 14 percent of regional GNP (*Newsweek* 20 April 1998: 12). Except in Chile, Uruguay, and Bolivia, personal safety is the "top public concern throughout Latin America" (ibid.).

In response to the deteriorating crime and homicide situation in Rio de Janeiro—and in particular the problem of street violence against marginalized people and youth—a major social movement known as Viva Rio began in late 1993. An analysis of this movement by Hilda Maria Gaspar Pereira (1996) points out some of the connections between urban form and violence. For example, the structure of the drug trade (involving control over various *favelas* by different criminal groups) is one of exaggerated spatial fragmentation. Alba Zaluar, a sociologist who has studied this problem for years, argues that the drug trade is a form of war, but

> [i]t is a peculiar war in which all sides finish behind bars: law-abiding bourgeois behind the bars of their condominiums and houses, surrounded by vigilantes and bodyguards; peaceful workers at the hands of bodyguards, soldiers and the terror of the drug gangs in shanty towns, or at the hands of extermination groups in Rio's poor periphery; poor bandits in penitentiaries or in the vicious circle of the eternal debts with their enemies, the gangs, the criminal organisation. (Zaluar in Pereira 1996: 6.)

As for the movement itself, its members decided at the outset that violence was closely related to social inequality (a major concern in Brazilian cities). As a result, many of Viva Rio's major activities involve strengthening social ties at the community level through projects of community policing, reuniting street children with their families, establishing a community center for poor youth, and training of the unemployed as well as providing health services at the local level (Pereira 1996).

Just as Brazil is the largest and most populous country in Latin America, South Africa is among the largest in Africa, and at the same time, the wealthiest country on its own continent. One of the most urbanized countries in Africa, South

Africa is home both to very large cities and a very fragmented and even polarized social structure. Based on the 1991 census, the greater Johannesburg area contains some 6.8 million, followed by Cape Town metropolitan area and Durban with its surrounding areas, both at 3.2 million, and the large cities of the Eastern Cape Province (East London and Port Elizabeth) at 2.6 million. Although the legislative framework of apartheid no longer exists in a democratic South Africa, the extreme distribution of wealth and political power that was institutionalized by apartheid has not disappeared from either the urban or rural areas of the country. Formerly "white" areas of the major cities are still typically well maintained and well serviced, with housing interspersed with public and private amenities like parks and shops. The other side of this picture is that of lower-income residential areas (mostly formerly "black" areas), notably the so-called former townships and informal settlements. These neighborhoods are usually located far from major centers of employment, in the periphery of the major towns and cities, and are marked by poverty and squalor. They are simultaneously overcrowded and underserviced, lacking both formal retail facilities and community and recreational services, particularly open space. Violence and crime are widespread in these areas. Partly for political reasons (for example, a long-standing struggle between the ANC and the Inkatha Freedom Party) but for many other complex reasons, violence has become a central fact of life in South African cities. Overall, South Africa has one of the highest rates of homicide in the world, with a murder rate in 1994 of 53.5/100,000 (Gilbert 1996: 876)—this is exceeded only by Colombia at a rate of 89.5/100,000 in the early 1990s (Ayres 1998: 3). Although political violence may be receding in importance since the 1994 election, criminal violence has spread outward from its earlier confines in the black townships and shantytowns.

Whatever the escalating situation in the wealthier areas of South African cities, exposure to violence of all kinds is, and has been, endemic in the poorest areas. As observers have pointed out (Hindson, Byerley, and Morris 1994; Hindson 1996; Adam and Moodley 1997), the rise in political violence after the mid-1980s and the high level of violent crime that has plagued South African cities are related to structural cleavages and extreme inequality in the society in general, and to the physical separation of groups from each other—a pattern that is not receding quickly with the end of apartheid. Describing Durban in the mid-1990s, Michael Sutcliffe (1996) talks in turn of the city of survival, the city of hope, the city of entitlement, the city of superfluity, and the city of death. The city of death "includes at least 10 percent of the residents of Durban, people who are the most marginalized, living in absolutely terrible conditions of squalor, poverty and violence in migrant worker hostels . . . and . . . informal settlements (such as Bambayi and Mshayazafe—which means literally to 'hit him with a stick until he dies')" (1996: 68). The extreme inequality that this violence at least partially reflects is indicated in the fact that South Africa—along with Brazil—is among the most unequal societies in the world, as measured by Gini coefficients (World Bank 1998: Table 2.8).

STRATEGIC PLANNING UNDER "SPECIAL CIRCUMSTANCES": THE POLITICS OF GOVERNANCE

The strategic planning approach to improving the economic prospects of city-regions, as originally developed in northern cities (in particular the United States), incorporates two main elements: a *technical* component (collecting information on the performance and prospects of various economic sectors, developing a "niche" approach to economic and social development that maximizes the particular strengths of the particular city or region, and promoting this approach, or "vision," to other levels of government as well as investors and the international community); and a *political* component (which includes the emergence of an effective local leader or leadership coalition, the involvement of major social and economic groups in the development of the planning strategy, and the ability to collaborate with higher levels of government in obtaining support for the strategy). Not all cities can successfully negotiate these threshold conditions, even in the North where the pace of urban expansion is modest; human resources are relatively plentiful; planners have good data to work with; municipal revenues are, for the most part, adequate; and there is a reasonable prospect (at least in a good number of countries and city-regions) of bringing major stakeholders into the decision-making process. In the South, however, conditions are much more challenging: urban expansion may be very rapid (at least in terms of aggregate population increase), there is a severe lack of good information, municipal revenues are extremely limited, professional and technical support is both scarce and inexperienced, and the social and physical fragmentation of many urban areas constitutes almost a structural barrier to a successful political exercise. Assuming they are competing in the same arena with their northern compatriots, southern cities are severely handicapped in their efforts to establish the necessary conditions for investment and economic growth.

A very important element in this emerging scenario is the nature and quality of governance. In the 1990s, the term "governance" has been employed in a number of ways by different authors and agencies. My understanding of "governance" is that it denotes a wider field of action than the term "government," in that it comprises both the formal institutions of the state, and the cultural and social context within which the state operates. This wider field is what Patricia McCarney, Mohamed Halfani, and Alfredo Rodriguez (1995: 95) have in mind when they propose a definition of governance: "Governance, as distinct from government, refers to the *relationship* between civil society and the state, between rulers and the ruled, the government and the governed." Going well beyond the idea of a relationship, many agencies and writers concern themselves with the *quality* of "good governance." This latter concept may be formalized and even measured, based on such indicators as accountability, transparency, the regularity of electoral choice of political leadership, and the existence of supportive legal and constitutional structures to protect citizens from arbitrary actions.[4] To some, governance is linked to strategic planning. Thus, Om Prakash Mathur suggests that "governance has acquired a new meaning wherein it is seen as a process of setting priorities and sets of actions not only by the government but by other stakeholders as well—the non-governmental sectors, business, industry and, in fact, the civil society as a whole" (Mathur 1999: 235). Certainly, as Mathur implies, the process of "setting priorities and sets of actions" should be enhanced by involving a wide range of local stakeholders; but the degree to which this can effectively be done will depend on how well civil society and other groups are engaged with municipal institutions, and how much power and effective authority these institutions command. These issues ultimately relate to the degree of local democracy and openness in the political system.

Many southern cities have achieved some success in "streamlining" their administrative systems, in reorganizing the provision of services, and in bringing their populations into the decision-making process. Such examples as Ahmedabad (Mathur 1999), which reorganized its tax collection procedures in order to achieve a positive credit rating that would enable it to issue municipal bonds; or Porto Alegre (Abers 1998), which instituted an extremely effective system of participatory budgeting, with the result that its revenue collections were substantially increased, are well known. And we also have a number of other examples of cities (such as Rio de Janeiro, mentioned above; Curitiba; and Coimbatore [in southern India]) that have achieved at least partial success in attempting to improve selected aspects of their municipal management. But many more cities have been severely hampered in their efforts to undertake reform. Let me give two examples: Salvador, Brazil, and Mombasa, Kenya. While these cases are certainly not "best practices," they are not "worst practices" either, in that certain innovations and planning efforts were successful either for a short time or in some (rather than other) sectors. I would call them "cautionary examples."

Salvador, Brazil

Salvador, with a population of 2,211,539 in 1996, is the capital and the most important city of the state of Bahia in the northeast region of Brazil, one of the poorest regions of the country. Salvador was one of the first settlements of the Portuguese, and the capital of Brazil during most of the colonial period. As such, says Renato Boschi, "it was the cradle for an unequal social structure grounded on slavery and in which the black population would eventually play a prominent role in terms of shaping today's distinctive culture and local traditions" (Boschi 1997: 2). During the period from 1980 to 1991, Salvador experienced the highest rate of population growth of all state capitals in the country. At the same time, it had among the highest rates of urban poverty in the country, and the lowest level of average income among all state capitals. An analysis of three major areas of policy during the period 1993–96—the development of a Master Plan *(Plano Diretor)*, the elaboration of a participatory budget, and the organization of a "Mother City" program designed to assure social assistance to poor children and adolescents—shows that the city's political leadership experienced only modest success. In spite of its initial commitment to the task of "making the city more human and more equal," and its determination to overcome the poverty and misery in which the majority of the city's population lives by appealing to the business community to invest in tourism, the government of Mayor Lidice de Mata fell short in many areas. Among its interesting initiatives was a strategic planning exercise for all sectors of the mayoralty, which involved the upgrading of infrastructure in poor peripheral neighborhoods in collaboration with local communities. Boschi attributes the failure of this left-of-center administration to a relative absence of strong local associational linkages ("social capital") on which the government could build; and the determined resistance of a state government whose governor, the nationally powerful conservative politician Antonio Carlos Magalhaes (or ACM as he is known in Brazil) refused to grant resources to the municipality, and waged a fierce campaign in the media (many of which were owned by himself) to discredit the mayor and her administration. The fragility of the electoral alliance holding the municipal administration together, along with the lack of explicit support at the federal government level after 1995, only added to these difficulties.

Mombasa, Kenya

Mombasa, the second largest city in Kenya, had an approximate population in the late 1990s of 1.2 million. The current capital of the Coast Province, Mombasa was the first capital of Kenya, having grown over many centuries as a major node in the East African trading system. As the major Kenyan city in the coastal region, Mombasa boasts a large port facility, and is the center of a major beachfront tourist industry, which extends to the north and south of the town. In spite of its importance as a port and the attractiveness of its hotels and other tourist facilities, the economy of Mombasa and its surrounding region has been in decline for several decades. This decline was explosively accelerated in the run-up to the December 1997 elections, when a major outbreak of interethnic violence threatened to cut even further into the trickle of business investment coming into the town. During the violence (which lasted over several weeks in August) nearly eighty people were killed, up to two hundred were maimed, and nearly one hundred thousand were displaced and forced to relocate their houses. While many tourist establishments subsequently went bankrupt, those who suffered most of the physical harm were so-called up-country Africans, living in and around Mombasa. For many decades, antagonism between the coastal African groups (who tended to have lower education and to obtain less remunerative employment) and the up-country groups has been a central element of Mombasa politics. At this point in Mombasa's history, the up-country groups were expected to vote for opposition parties. In effect, the dislocation of many of these people probably increased the chances of the governing party (KANU—the Kenya African National Union) to win the Coast Province elections.

Partly as a response to this severe deterioration in the town's business environment, KANU nominated a young businessman to the municipal council following the 1997 elections. Najib Balala, who had previously been the chairman of the Mombasa Tour Operators' Association, was subsequently elected as mayor by the other councilors in early 1998. In the short time he was in office, Balala attempted a number of major reforms in the operations of the municipal council—reforms that were to gain him immense popular support among the population of the city. In an account of his experience as mayor, Balala stresses the ineffectiveness of the municipality when he first took office in early 1998. Among the many problems he discusses are the controls over expenditures and over municipal staff exercised by the Minister in Nairobi; poor municipal infrastructure and services; and lack of adequate revenue. His approach to these problems was radical and participatory. Thus, upon taking office, he immediately called a full meeting of the senior council staff with the mayor and councilors. "We have no record of any such thing having taken place . . . since Independence. The novelty of this approach immediately helped to boost morale" (Balala 1999: 5). Soon thereafter, he invited the whole town to meet the councilors and staff. "Over a thousand people of all social classes attended. The ground was packed to capacity. . . . The citizens had a field day. Nobody was spared. I restrained the councillors and Council staff from replying. . . . The session left citizens feeling like their problems were being heard and we in turn were further educated about the deficiencies of our services" (Balala 1999: 6).

From this base, Balala launched a program to beautify the town's open spaces, attempted to bring the city's major religious groups (Christians, Muslims, and Hindus) together for major holidays, improved services (particularly garbage collection) and infrastructure, and began to crack down on the hundreds of "ghost workers" inhabiting the council's payroll. He also moved to stop the granting of land in road reserves and parks to councilors and local businessmen. From all accounts, tax collections began to increase, people began to paint and refurbish their houses and buildings, and a sense of pride returned to the town. Unfortunately, the mayor was too successful and popular. Powerful local politicians and developers, in alliance with senior politicians in the capital, appeared determined to contain Balala's reforms (*Daily Nation*, 13 February 1999). When it became known that he would not be reelected for a second term, and following a number of threats on his life, Najib Balala resigned from the municipal council entirely in early 1999. His short political career was over.

In spite of their differences, these two cases illustrate a number of common features. First, both were coastal cities with a long history, and a substantial population living below the poverty line. Neither has enjoyed—during recent years—a buoyant economy. For both cities, tourism has been one of the leading sectors. Second, although both cities passed through a brief period during which political reforms and urban management innovations were undertaken, neither was able to withstand the opposition of higher-level political forces. Partly as a result, their reforms were stalemated. Thus, while local political leaders carved out a political space within which participatory initiatives were featured and even promoted, these initiatives threatened the position of more powerful political and economic interests, leading to their neutralization. In other words, developing a good local strategy was not enough: the larger system needed to give support, or at least remain neutral in the face of changes at the municipal level. Given the complex of forces invested in the existing system in so many countries, these conditions are likely to be relatively rare.

Global economic influences have clearly had an impact on both Salvador and Mombasa, although these influences have more often had negative rather than positive consequences. Different political leaders and coalitions in each city attempted to improve the economic performance at the municipal level, and to support an increased level of investment by the private sector. These leaders and coalitions achieved success in some sectors, or over a short period of time, but long-term, sustained growth proved elusive. This small comparison suggests, as Michael Leaf and Ayse Pamuk have convincingly argued, in the context of pervasive globalization, that local differences are extremely important (1997) and that local politics is perhaps the most powerful organizing framework we can find to understand the potentialities for successful or unsuccessful strategic planning. Unlike the situation in the North, where we can take for granted many aspects of the "good governance" paradigm, the political aspect of strategic planning may be problematic. But politics involves the resolution of conflicts and differences, and as long as many southern cities harbor very diverse and even fragmented social groups and actors, the political system (which includes both local politicians and the higher levels of political organization that may either support or constrain their actions) will be a multifaceted and ambiguous context with which urban planners will have to contend.

CONCLUSIONS

Models of strategic planning, originally developed in northern cities, are being applied in southern cities with considerable energy but with mixed success. Although many of the reasons for the application of these models are similar on both sides of the development divide, the conditions under which strategic planning can be successful may differ in complex ways. To explore these differences, we have looked at some of the key factors in the urbanization of the developing world: rapid urban growth, extensive development of city-regions, social diversity and physical fragmentation, and (in many areas) extremely low and unpredictable sources of revenue for municipal development. This review suggests that conditions for successful strategic planning exercises in the South are (in general) more challenging than they are in the North, particularly in cities where economic and human resources are limited, and the engagement of major social groups with the political leadership is problematic.

Given these inherent difficulties, what should southern cities (and their leaders) do in the event they still wish to compete? In the South, successful strategic planning appears to be more dependent on governance relationships (or on the existence of the preconditions for "good governance") than is the case in the North where a wider institutional framework is normally in play to assure transparency, accountability, regular electoral choice, and the effective rule of law. Southern mayors will have to be very inventive to overcome their lack of resources. One solution—attempted by a number of cities—has been to call upon civil society (and in particular the local NGO community) for support in educating the local population about the stakes and issues involved in strategic planning. This may well involve, on the one hand, a better understanding on the part of the people as to how local services are financed and managed; and on the other hand, more transparency and accountability on the part of local governments, which need to obtain popular support for new strategic directions. Whatever the approach selected, the local political context becomes crucial, as each city attempts to find its own voice both to respond to competitive demand, and to incorporate its disparate and often fragmented citizens in a more coherent project. But however this project is constructed, it cannot ignore the central reality of the intergovernmental structure and the support that poor cities must obtain from other levels of the political system.

NOTES

1. According to Kanter, "Communities must open their connections to the world. Success for locals in the global economy will derive from their ability to become more cosmopolitan, to forge linkages to the rest of the world. And local communities must exert leadership to develop these links, with or without the help of national governments. In the global economy of the future, national opportunities will be led by world class metropolitan centers within nations" (1995: 353).
2. Strategic planning originated in the 1960s in the private sector. It began to be applied to the public sector, and to local planning in the United States, in the late 1980s. A symposium on strategic planning published in the *Journal of the American Planning Association* in the Winter 1987 issue stated that this was, at the time, "a hot topic—the subject of an increasing number of professional conference sessions and journal articles" (Bryson and Einsweiler 1987: 6). In another article in the same issue of the *Journal*, Jerome Kaufman and Harvey Jacobs argued that, while strategic planning had many points in common with (then) conventional long-range, or master, planning, it tended to be more broadly participative and more action-oriented than the earlier approach (Kaufman and Jacobs 1987).
3. Parts of this section on violence and fragmentation are adapted from Stren 1998: 11–15.
4. Dinesh Mehta has noted three current lists of "good governance" characteristics: a Habitat II list (including accountability, transparency, participation, the rule of law, and predictability); a UNDP list (participation, rule of law, transparency, responsiveness, consensus orientation, equity, effectiveness and efficiency, accountability, and strategic vision); and a list compiled by the Konrad Adenauer Stiftung for the "Better Cities Network of East and South-East Asian Cities" (accountability, responsiveness,

management innovation, public-private partnership, local government-citizen interaction, decentralized management, networking, human resource management). In each of the lists, explanatory text describes how the criteria might be applied. See Mehta 1999.

REFERENCES

Abers, R. (1998). "Learning Democratic Practice: Distributing Government Resources through Popular Participation in Porto Alegre, Brazil," in M. Douglass and J. Friedmann (eds.), *Cities for Citizens: Planning and the Rise of Civil Society in a Global Age*. Chichester: John Wiley, 39–65.

Adam, H., and Moodley, K. (1997). "'Tribalism' and Political Violence in South Africa," in J. Gugler (ed.), *Cities in the Developing World: Issues, Theory, and Policy*. New York: Oxford University Press, 314–26.

Ainstein, L. (1996). "Buenos Aires: A Case of Deepening Social Polarization," in A. Gilbert (ed.), *The Mega-City in Latin America*. Tokyo: United Nations University Press, 133–54.

Ayres, R. (1998). *Crime and Violence as Development Issues in Latin America and the Caribbean*. Washington: World Bank Latin American and Caribbean Studies.

Balala, N. (1999). "Challenges of Local Governance: One African Mayor's Experience." Unpublished paper, Centre for Urban and Community Studies, University of Toronto.

Balbo, M. (1993). "Urban Planning and the Fragmented City of Developing Countries." *Third World Planning Review*, 15 (February): 23–35.

Barnes, W., and Brooks, J. (1999). "World-Class Local Economies," in World Bank, *Business Briefing: World Urban Economic Development*. London: World Markets Research Centre, 32–6.

Begg, I. (1999). "Cities and Competitiveness." *Urban Studies*, 36 (May): 795–809.

Boschi, R. R. (1997). "Democratic Governance and Participation: Tales of Two Cities." Paper presented at GURI Conference on Governance in Action: Urban Initiatives in a Global Setting, Washington, DC.

Braule Pinto, S. G. (1999). "Financial Management of the City of Rio de Janeiro—a Change of Mindset," in World Bank, *Business Briefing: World Urban Economic Development*. London: World Markets Research Centre, 66–9.

Bryson, J. M., and Einsweiler, R. C. (1987). "Strategic Planning: Introduction." *Journal of the American Planning Association*, 53 (Winter): 6–8.

Caldeira, T. P. R. (1996). "Building Up Walls: The New Pattern of Spatial Segregation in São Paulo." *International Social Science Journal*, 147 (March): 55–66.

—— (1999). "Fortified Enclaves: The New Urban Segregation," in J. Holston (ed.), *Cities and Citizenship*. Durham and London: Duke University Press, 114–38.

Daily Nation (Nairobi). (1999). 13 February.

Dogan, M., and Kasarda, J. D. (1988). "Introduction: How Giant Cities Will Multiply and Grow," in M. Dogan and J. D. Kasarda (eds.), *The Metropolis Era. Vol. 1. A World of Giant Cities*. Newbury Park, CA: Sage, 12–29.

Dubai International Award web page: http://www.sustainabledevelopment.org/blp/awards/1998winners/

Dubresson, A. (1996). "Abidjan: From the Public Making of a Modern City to Urban Management of a Metropolis," in C. Rakodi (ed.), *The Urban Challenge in Africa: Growth and Management of Its Large Cities*. Tokyo: United Nations University Press, 252–91.

Duffy, H. (1995). Competitive Cities: Succeeding in the Global Economy. London: Chapman and Hall.

Fernandez Conde, L. P. (1999). "Rio de Janeiro—Towards Competitiveness," in World Bank, *Business Briefing: World Urban Economic Development.* London: World Markets Research Centre, 921–94.

Friedmann, J. (1995). "Where We Stand: A Decade of World City Research," in P. L. Knox and P. J. Taylor (eds.), *World Cities in a World-System.* Cambridge: Cambridge University Press, 21–47.

Gilbert, L. (1996). "Urban Violence and Health—South Africa 1995." *Social Science and Medicine,* 43 (5): 873–86.

Halfani, M. (1996). "Marginality and Dynamism: Prospects for the Sub-Saharan African City," in M. A. Cohen, B. A. Ruble, J. S. Tulchin, and A. M. Garland (eds.), *Preparing for the Global Future: Global Pressures and Local Forces.* Washington, DC: Woodrow Wilson Center Press, 83–107.

Hindson, D. (1996). "The Apartheid City: Construction, Decline, and Reconstruction," in E. le Bris (ed.), *Villes du Sud: Sur la route d'Istanbul.* Paris: ORSTOM, 75–106.

——, Byerley, M., and Morris, M. (1994). "From Violence to Reconstruction: The Making, Disintegration, and Remaking of an Apartheid City." *Antipode,* 26 (4): 323–50.

Kanter, R. M. (1995). World Class: Thriving Locally in the Global Economy. New York: Simon and Schuster.

Kaufman, J. L., and Jacobs, H. M. (1987). "A Public Planning Perspective on Strategic Planning." *Journal of the American Planning Association,* 53 (1): 23–33.

Krugman, P. (1996). "Making Sense of the Competitiveness Debate." *Oxford Review of Economic Policy,* 12: 17–25.

—— (1997). *Pop Internationalism.* Cambridge, Mass.: MIT Press.

Leaf, M., and Pamuk, A. (1997). "Habitat II and the Globalization of Ideas." *Journal of Planning Education and Research,* 17 (1): 69–76.

Mathur, O. P. (1999). "Fiscal Innovations and Urban Governance," in O. P. Mathur (ed.), *India: The Challenge of Urban Governance.* New Delhi: National Institute of Public Finance and Policy, 231–74.

McCarney, P., Halfani, M., and Rodriguez, A. (1995). "Towards an Understanding of Governance: The Emergence of an Idea and Its Implications for Urban Research in Developing Countries," in R. Stren and J. Bell (eds.), *Urban Research in the Developing World, vol. 4. Perspectives on the City.* Toronto: Centre for Urban and Community Studies, University of Toronto, 91–141.

McGee, T. G. (1995). "Metrofitting the Emerging Mega-Urban Regions of ASEAN: An Overview," in T. G. McGee and I. M. Robinson (eds.), *The Mega-Urban Regions of Southeast Asia.* Vancouver: University of British Columbia Press, 5–26.

——, and Robinson, I. M. (1995). "Preface," in T. G. McGee and I. M. Robinson (eds.), *The Mega-Urban Regions of Southeast Asia.* Vancouver: University of British Columbia Press.

Mehta, D. (1999). "Urban Governance: Lessons from Best Practices in Asia." New Delhi: unpublished paper.

Mfeketo, N., and van Ryneveld, P. (1999). "Cape Town: An Emerging City," in World Bank, *Business Briefing: World Urban Economic Development.* London: World Markets Research Centre, 135–6.

Newsweek. (1998). "Latin America: Living in Fear." 20 April: 10–14.

Oatley, N. (ed.). (1998). *Cities, Economic Competition, and Urban Policy.* London: Paul Chapman Publishing.

Pereira, H. M. G. (1996). *The Viva Rio Movement: The Struggle for Peace.* London: University of London, Institute of Latin American Studies Research Papers.

Porter, M. (1998). *The Competitive Advantage of Nations.* Revised edition (originally published 1990). New York: Free Press.

Rolnik, R. (1999). "Territorial Exclusion and Violence: The Case of São Paulo, Brazil." Washington, DC: Woodrow Wilson International Center for Scholars. Occasional Paper no. 26, Comparative Urban Studies.

Royer, C. (1995). "Foreword" to H. Duffy, *Competitive Cities: Succeeding in the Global Economy.* London: Chapman and Hall, ix–x.

Sassen, S. (1991). *The Global City: New York, London, Tokyo.* Princeton: Princeton University Press.

Stren, R. (1998). *Urban Research in the Developing World: From Governance to Security.* Occasional Paper no. 16, Comparative Urban Studies Project, Woodrow Wilson International Center for Scholars. Washington, D.C.: Woodrow Wilson Center.

——, and Halfani, M. (Forthcoming). "The Cities of Sub-Saharan Africa: From Dependency to Marginality," in R. Paddison (ed.), *Sage Handbook of Urban Studies.* London: Sage Publications.

Sutcliffe, M. (1996). "The Fragmented City: Durban, South Africa." *International Social Science Journal*, 147 (March): 67–72.

United Nations. (1997). *World Urbanization Prospects: The 1996 Revision.* New York: United Nations. Draft version.

World Bank. (1998). *World Development Indicators.* Washington, DC: World Bank.

—— (1999). "The Cities Alliance: A Global Partnership Designed to Achieve the Promise of Well-Managed Cities." Washington, DC: World Bank, unpublished document.

12

Innovation and Risk-taking: Urban Governance in Latin America

TIM CAMPBELL

Decentralization in Latin America has dramatically transformed the public sector, producing a quiet revolution of popular participation in public choices at the local level. The process of decentralization has had its share of frustrations, dangers, and false starts in the Latin American region. Fuzzy or overlapping divisions of labor, associated threats of fiscal instability, and sustained finance for urban infrastructure still remain to be resolved in many countries. But decentralization has also produced a new generation of leaders, particularly at the local level. Several opinion polls have shown that local, elected officials were more trusted by voters and more responsive than ever to their constituents. They were also energetic, proactive, and vocal. New leaders exhibited a drive to deliver, and this made them eager consumers of new ideas and techniques. They have invented or adopted many ways to mobilize local participation, strengthen organizational capacities, and even raise local taxes, despite increasing flows of shared revenues from central governments.

A wave of innovations appeared in many local governments shortly after decentralization in the early 1990s, and many novel approaches introduced at that time had positive impacts in many of the areas of interest in global city-regions, such as economic competitiveness, governance, and participation. This chapter draws from an in-depth study, conducted by the author and colleague Harald Fuhr (Campbell and Fuhr forthcoming), which examined seventeen innovations at the local level in Latin America. The study probed into the mechanisms by which innovation and reform were advanced in each case and how risks to local leaders were overcome. The study found that the drive to innovate is an engine much more powerful than national fiats at achieving and sustaining the next stages of reform in Latin America. These experiences offer useful lessons into the reform process and a glimpse into the dynamics of change, dynamics that must be engaged in order to handle the many challenges of global city-regions in the decades to come.

CONTEXT AND PROBLEM: SUSTAINING INNOVATION AFTER THE QUIET REVOLUTION

Coping with the Quiet Revolution

The decentralization of governance began in much of Latin America well before the 1980s, but progress was intermittent and marked by dramatic financial rearrangements and stunning political reforms (Campbell forthcoming). Nearly all governments took actions in three areas of reform: fiscal relations, democratization, and local governance.

Political and Fiscal Reform

Many governments were in a rush to share power, and they promulgated decentralization without fully thinking through how national objectives in areas such as health, education, and welfare, could be reconciled with decentralized powers of decision-making and spending being given to subnational governments. Thus, for the first few years of decentralization, transferred moneys in large quantities were, to caricature the situation, "finances chasing functions" (although in some cases local governments were saddled with new responsibilities without transferred revenue). Most local governments were left with a good deal of spending discretion, and this ambiguity, plus continued local spending by national governments, left excess funds at the local level, at least during the initial years of decentralization. Local governments from Guatemala to Argentina have been spending 10 to 40 percent of total public spending, amounting to significant fractions of GDP. (See Table 12.1.)

But though some state governments sank into debt—São Paulo and Cordoba are two outstanding examples—by and large municipal governments avoided precipitous spending and did not create destabilizing pressures as many observers feared. Much work in intergovernmental fiscal affairs aims to restore the balance between finance and spending. Some of the most progressive local governments show how this can be done, and this chapter covers the examples of Manizales and Valledupar in Colombia, and Mendoza Province in Argentina.

Table 12.1. *Local spending as a percentage of total public spending (selected countries)*

Country	1980	1992
Argentina	36.4	48.1
Colombia	27.2	33.0
Chile (1970)	4.7	12.7

Source: Lopez Murphy (1994).

Democratization

Another trend which is still sweeping the region and bolstering the fiscal nature of reform in Latin America is the democratic transition. Since the mid-1980s, countries are not only selecting national leaders democratically, but are also choosing virtually every executive and legislative officer in the more than 13,000 units of state (i.e. intermediate) and local governments. All but a few islands have completed this transition. Moreover, electoral reforms—for instance, switching to uninominal elections and requiring candidates to publish intended spending programs during electoral campaigns—have been promulgated in a dozen countries and are under active consideration in many others. Electoral choice—together with widespread popular participation in decision-making, planning, spending, and implementation of projects—amounts to a quiet revolution of local governance.

A New Model of Governance

Ironically, spending power and transferred revenues fueled democratization at the local level and created new energies. Many in the new generation of leaders, fresh with mandates and ideas of reform, began to rejuvenate municipal institutions and to create a new model of governance. The new governance model is characterized by (1) a new leadership style; (2) more professional staffing in executive branches; (3) tax and revenue increases; and (4) much stronger participation in public choice making.

- Perhaps the most startling change is that more qualified persons are seeking local public office. Surveys of office holders elected in the first five years of the 1990s in Central America, Paraguay, and Colombia revealed that the ratio of professionals to nonprofessionals jumped from around 11 percent in the early 1980s to more than 46 percent in the 1990s.
- More qualified office holders brought in more professional staff. A sample of sixteen municipalities in Colombia for which detailed data were gathered in the early 1990s showed that over the previous ten years, the ratio of total staff to professionals dropped from 12:1 to 4:1. Mayors reported that these changes were aimed at increasing capacity to deliver better services.
- Contrary to many predictions, many local governments were able to increase levies on their populations, because, to paraphrase many local executives, "when taxpayers see they are getting new services, they are willing to pay" (see Table 12.2). The rate of property tax increases doubled over the past decade across the entire spectrum of Colombia's more than 1,000 municipalities. The average increase in the late 1980s was 7.5 percent; the average increase in the early 1990s was 15 percent. The Colombian increases were partly due to requirements for revenue sharing, and partly, in specific cities, because mayors sought to tie levies, like gasoline surcharges and betterment taxes, to specific improvements in service. Some mayors simplified cadastres (La Paz), or introduced self-assessments (Bogota), or both (Quito). Still others (Puerto Alegre, Tijuana) simply raised property tax collections.

Table 12.2. *Recent local revenue increases (selected countries)*

City	Year	Increase (%)
Porto Alegre	1991–95	22
Tijuana	1989–94	58
Manizales	1988–94	165
La Paz	1990–95	218
Valledupar	1988–94	246
Villanueva (HO)	1991–93	373

- Mayors have also stepped up participatory consultations, using a large variety of communications and consultative techniques to sound out preferences of their constituents. In many cities, we observed that once this participatory process was unleashed, a new frontier of expectations was created, making it difficult to ignore the voice and preferences of voter-taxpayers in succeeding rounds of programs and elections.

Sustaining Innovation and Reform

These and many other changes—for instance the incorporation of civil society and the private sector into local public life—have transformed the nature and style of local government. More importantly, a wave of reforms created new opportunities for self-sustained growth. The development community has been focused on sustaining fiscal balance and redressing the mismatch between local functions and financial resources. Efforts to operationalize this concern—in public sector modernization and state reform loans—often fail to address municipal levels and ignore the growing cultural and business matrix in cities and regions. Several countries exhibited robust new horizontal linkages forged by business interests and actors in civic affairs. These alliances underpin local and regional economic activity in industrialized countries. Still another feature of the new era of governance is that local governments are claiming a more prominent place in national and local growth.

Taken together these changes (newly emerging regional interests, innovators, and proactive local governments) constitute an opportunity for the development community to leverage assistance capacity by taking advantage of and building on the new dynamic already underway in Latin America. A key step in moving toward self-sustaining change is to understand the process of innovation.

THE DYNAMICS OF CHANGE

Purpose and Scope of the Study

Following the momentous changes in decentralization reforms in Latin America in the 1990s, a large number of startling changes were noted in governance, management, and public and private sector participation at the local level. These became apparent in routine field missions and conferences of local government officials (see for example Peterson 1995 and Campbell *et al.* 1996, reporting on two Inter-American Conferences of Mayors). Consequently, the author and colleague Harald Fuhr, now at the University of Potsdam, launched a survey of innovations in order to take stock and explore the causes and mechanisms of change. The present article, and a more complete series of case studies, are drawn from a compilation of cases and analysis now in manuscript form (Campbell and Fuhr 1999). Five areas of local government were examined:

- *Administrative performance*—increase in professional capacity, initiation of administrative reorganization and strengthening, expansion of training programs, etc.
- *Fiscal management*—establishment of efficient and transparent intergovernmental transfer systems and creative mechanisms to mobilize and manage local financial resources.
- *Public service provision*—improvement in delivery efficiency, institution of more effective coordination among levels of government and new options for service delivery, such as outsourcing, privatization, etc.
- *Enhancing private sector development*—implementation of arrangements that foster local private investment, activation of private sector participation in policy and services at the local level and improvement in public responsiveness to private sector needs.
- *Participation in local and regional decision-making*—expansion of options for local voice, participatory planning, and consultative mechanisms, among others.

Methods: Selecting Cities Indicative of the New Generation of Change Makers

Criteria and Selection

Cities reflecting change in the five areas of innovation noted above were selected mostly on the basis of reputation. A first cut of more than thirty cases was compiled, with nominations based on anecdotal evidence gathered in the course of professional work, on published studies and unpublished reports, and on interaction among professionals in conferences and seminars. An effort was made also to include cases that are relatively new, as well as older innovations that have spawned secondary changes at the local level and beyond. In this respect, the study seeks to take account of conditions before decentralization. Also, not all of the innovations were completely successful, but all moved toward an improved standard of practice, and all but one have survived multiple political administrations. In addition, geographical and sectoral criteria were applied to achieve a broad cross section of experiences within Latin America.

Table 12.3. *Cases by area of impact*

Case	Administrative	Fiscal	Service	Private	Participation
Cali Waste	*		***	**	
Cali Private			**	***	*
Conchali	*		**		***
Curitiba Planning	***		**		
Curitiba Transport	*		***	**	
El Salvador			***	*	**
Manizales Admin.	***		*		
Manizales Fiscal		***			
Manizales Waste			**	***	
Mendoza Budget	**	***			
Mendoza Infrast.	*	**	***	*	***
P. Alegre Budget	*	**			***
Tijuana Manos	*	*	**		***
Tijuana PAU	*	***	**	*	**
Valledupar Fiscal	*	***			
Valledupar Paving	*	*	***	*	*
Valledupar Police	*		**		***

Key to impacts: *** = primary, ** = secondary, * = tertiary

Source: Campbell, Fuhr, and Eid 1995.

Preparation of City Cases

From the first-cut list, the study team selected twenty city cases and, together with consultants and country collaborators in Brazil and Colombia, produced seventeen case studies emphasizing the context and origins of the innovation.[1] Table 12.3 summarizes each of the cases studied and indicates the primary, secondary, and tertiary areas affected by the innovation.

Five cases are briefly summarized below (Table 12.4). They are representative of all the cases prepared in the course of the study. Many of the cases spill over across categorical boundaries. "Participation," for instance, is found everywhere. Sometimes cases impact several major areas. Tijuana, for example, is about participation, fiscal reform, and infrastructure services. And it would be undesirable and counterproductive to attempt an exclusive separation of these aspects.

Sample Cases: Old and New, Simple and Complex

Before delving into the cases, it is helpful to see them in four broad, somewhat overlapping, categories—"simple" and "complex" and "first" and "mature" generations. The term "simple" refers to an innovation of a tool, technique, or process familiar and central to the everyday flow of municipal business, such as training of municipal officials, budgeting, city planning, management and finance, and the like. In reality, simple projects are simple only in one sense of the word.

Table 12.4. *Selected cases—age, context, and scope*

City/Country	Innovation	Scope	Complexity	Generation year launched
Cali, Colombia	private role in public life	planning, finance, and management of public business by private sector	simple	multiple 1920s
Curitiba, Brazil	transportation	integrated urban transport system building on sequence of innovations	complex	multiple 1960s
Manizales, Colombia	municipal training institute	integrated training program with city job categories and career advancement	simple	first 1990
Mendoza, Argentina	social censure to guarantee credit	infrastructure finance in low-income households	complex	first 1991
Tijuana, Mexico	public choice on infrastructure program and costs	investment program and costs to taxpayers were subjected to public referendum	complex	first 1991

The distinguishing feature of simple cases is that they do not involve extensive contact with large segments of the public. More than half the cases selected in this study fall into this "simple" category. The balance, of "complex" cases, involve extensive participation of the public, neighborhood groups, volunteer organizations, and voters at large. For instance, some experiences have convened thousands of meetings to determine city spending priorities or to work out neighborhood indebtedness arrangements. These cases are more elaborate and more complicated, and in our scheme, "complex." Simple and complex cases can be either a first innovation in the city or fall into a series of several or more. Manizales, for instance, set up a training institute, reformed its finances, started new health care, and launched innovative waste service, all primarily within one political administration. Curitiba on the other hand launched a long series of innovations branching out from land use to transport to solid waste and management of commercial vendors, among many other innovations, all over a period of thirty years.

Complex and mature cases build sequentially on past innovations, and this broadens the scope of inquiry somewhat to include the conditions for sustained change, often under the assumption that a propitious environment has been enriched, and management of the innovation process becomes a new level of endeavor. In all cases, we focus on the "breakthrough" of the initial innovation. These aspects of complexity and age, together with more detail about the scope of innovations, are also presented in Table 12.4.

Cali, Colombia: Private Sector Roles in Public Administration and Management

The Cali case represents a style of administration and management based on tight-knit interaction between public and private sectors at the local (municipal) and intermediate levels of government (*departmentos* in Colombia) and with multinational corporations. Cali and the Valley of Cauca were chosen specifically for the study because for more than fifty years, large family enterprises and multinational corporations worked closely with local administrations in a variety of joint ventures. Both public and private sectors were characterized by openness to innovations, were engaged in administrative initiatives, and maintained strong links with each other and with the church, the regional university, and local and international NGOs and corporations. More than half of the corporations that founded the *Fundación para el Desarrollo Integral del Valle* (FDI), the main development organization for consensus building in the region, were multinationals.[2]

Public–private cooperation in Cali took many forms, including rotations of businessmen and managers in public posts, open consultations, advisory boards, revenue generation, and direct provision of public services by private foundations, as in the case of public parks (Rojas 1996*b*). Private enterprise also shared costs of training personnel and carrying out market and consumer research. Generally speaking, these interactions were instigated by the private sector as a way to streamline government and make necessary public functions more efficient and less subject to bureaucracy, clientelism, and administrative corruption. Both public and private interests stood to gain from improved quality of public management. This cooperative attitude was extended into parks, planning, services and housing for the poor, and other areas (Rojas 1996*a*).

Cooperative arrangements in Cali had an impact beyond proficiency in services or infrastructure. Perceptible repercussion can be seen in: (1) a stronger orientation of public servants towards the client; (2) changes in the form and quality of management in all its dimensions—planning, finance, coordination and controls, and efficiency; and (3) the establishment of precedents and indirect competition with traditional administrative structures. The novel forms of interaction stood as precursors to state-society relations needed in a decentralized system of government.

The Cali style of interaction also had its drawbacks. Close ties of public and private sectors were not always conducive to efficiency in resource allocation, nor in production, as both public and private interests can sometimes be dominated by rent-seeking. Also, not all bureaucratic rigidities were eliminated, nor were personalistic and clientelist behaviors weeded out of the middle levels of the public sector. Another problem was that the Cali style also set up a kind of shadow government, parallel to the mayor's and governor's professional staffs, and this created confusion and raised costs of both. The style also encountered inevitable tensions between the administrative procedures of the state on the one hand, and on the other, the modern business practices of strategic planning, flexibility, risk management, and the like. But entrepreneurs succeeded in imparting a private sector drive, and both sides achieved a cooperative mentality and a larger vision. These achievements established significant gains in the composition and orientation of administrative personnel, buttressed by a network of corporate associations and managerial expertise in the region.

Many contextual circumstances—such as its historical development, civic pride and sense of place, strong regional identity—may have been decisive in explaining the Cali innovations, and these factors therefore may limit the applicability of the public–private styles invented there. But many big city-regions, and even smaller ones on the periphery of regional centers such as Cali, can benefit from the self-interests of private enterprise, rich with human and financial resources usually found in large national and international firms, regional universities, research centers, and nonprofit foundations.

Curitiba, Brazil: Integrated Transport System

Curitiba has been successfully innovating in the transport sector over the past twenty-five years (Leitman, Santoro, and Campbell 1996). Successful public transit in Curitiba is a good example of "public authorities thinking private and private enterprise thinking public." Curitiba explicitly favored public transportation over the private automobile by developing or adapting technologies appropriate to the transit problems, ridership needs, street and city layout, and availability of capital in the city. Furthermore, Curitiba pursued strategic principles, guided by a master plan and bolstered by good data on land and transit needs and land use enforcement tools. The key innovations in the transportation system were the following:

- integrating conscientiously land use planning, road design, and public transport;
- operating the transportation system jointly with the private sector;
- establishing an integrated system with revenue sharing of fares;
- building in flexibility to expand the system (special buses, boarding stations, advanced ticket sales);
- devising measures to keep costs low and assure high quality service to the poor and sparsely populated areas of the city.

These innovations were rooted in a visionary, flexible master plan that challenged the strong momentum built up by the growing use of the private automobile in the 1960s and 1970s. The plan and early innovations—a pedestrian mall serving as a downtown terminus—were maturing and being accepted while technical capacity was gaining strength in the city planning agency. The bold departures in Curitiba were mainly home-grown and nurtured by consistent political support across many municipal administrations and by the positive effects of federal and metropolitan relations with Curitiba.

Curitiba's transport innovations evolved in several directions at the same time. The principal axes of the road system were preserved as rights of way, and these were inherited from early land-use plans. The city was fortunate to have consistent guidance of local leaders who were convinced of the advantages of the plan and were able to draw upon technical data and analysis by the city's planning agency, IPPUC. An integrated public transportation system evolved into a kind of surface metro. All of these elements were implemented with innovative and workable enforcement measures. Basic data on land use and ridership were indispensable to sustained success in Curitiba.

These innovations have resulted in tangible economic and environmental benefits for the city. Although Curitiba has more than 500,000 private cars, three-quarters of all commuters take the bus. Affordable fares mean that the average low-income family spends only about 10 percent of its income on transport, which is relatively low for Brazil. The efficient system improves productivity by speeding the movement of people, goods, and services. Nearly 75 percent of passenger trips in Curitiba are carried by buses at one thousandth the cost of an underground metro system. Environmentally, the city has achieved a 25 percent reduction in fuel consumption with related reductions in automotive emissions. The transportation system is directly responsible for the city having one of the lowest rates of ambient air pollution in Brazil.

Curitiba's innovations in urban transport had to overcome a range of obstacles: the predominant thinking about how cities should respond to rapid growth; threats to long-term transportation planning that are posed by short-term political decisions; and lack of financing. In overcoming these obstacles, lessons have spread throughout Brazilian cities and beyond. Many cities have adopted articulated buses, dedicated lanes, boarding stations, and other features of Curitiba's system. Furthermore, the spread has been spontaneous, and not really a product of a deliberate dissemination strategy. More deliberate strategies could be easily justified on environmental grounds alone, and central government and donors might have achieved much greater impact in the global city-regions of Brazil and beyond.

Mendoza, Argentina: Social Contract for Infrastructure in Poor Neighborhoods

The Mendoza Provincial Program on Basic Infrastructure (hereafter referred to as MENPROSIF) is a program to supply basic sanitation and other services to low-income households at the neighborhood level in the Province of Mendoza, Argentina (Campbell 1996). In the five years between its inception and the date it was studied in 1996, MENPROSIF implemented 274 small-scale projects (averaging under $100,000 each) which benefited more than 50,000 households in more than half the municipalities in the Province. MENPROSIF was innovative in its reliance on social censure—pressure of friends and neighbors on participants—to secure loans given to low-income residents, rather than requiring a pledge of material or monetary collateral they rarely have. This system enabled the poor to afford 70–80 percent of total project costs and minimized state subsidy for works improvements of broad social interest. The program also lowered costs of works and achieved extremely high rates of repayment and project completion.

Many other features of the MENPROSIF were innovative. For instance, the MENPROSIF worked out collaborative partnership arrangements among public agencies, private contractors, NGOs, and neighborhood organizations, each playing a role in planning, designing, bidding, contracting, and building neighborhood improvements. High levels of community organization among beneficiary groups were also a key ingredient in achieving extensive participation in selection and implementation of works. Each neighborhood organized beneficiaries to take part in identifying needs, selecting solutions, taking individual responsibility for short-term (two year) credits, choosing contractors, and overseeing implementation of works.

Although the role of the Province remains indispensable in MENPROSIF's success, the program moved key responsibilities away from the state. The Province's Ministry of Environment played a strong fostering and brokerage role in getting local groups to agree on neighborhood preferences and verifying willingness to pay. These were expressed in frequent, open, participatory meetings at the neighborhood level. Securing consensus on projects and payments obviated such key public sector tasks as cost and benefits evaluation of projects. The next stages of evolution would include a reduced role of the state; explicit, targeted subsidies for the poorest citizens; and longer term, more market-based, credit.

The rich successes exhibited in this program also depended strongly on unusual contextual factors such as the reform-minded spirit in Argentina in the early 1990s, the threat of cholera, and the special leadership qualities of the governor. But MENPROSIF also showed that the innovations of incorporating social censure can be replicated in many global city-regions where motivation is strong and emphasis is given to social organization among low-income beneficiaries.

Manizales, Colombia: Municipal Training Institute

The Manizales experience demonstrated the effectiveness of intervention by an outside agent—technical assistance and finance by international NGOs—to set up a tailor-made training facility for the city's municipal employees (Maldonado 1996). The establishment of the Instituto de Capacitación de Manizales (ICAM) helped reinforce the process of decentralization by improving and sustaining the city's capacity to deliver public services transferred to the municipal level. ICAM's training budget grew from $70,000 in 1994 to around $614,000 in 1996, and affected more than 6,500 local civil servants since its first year of operation in 1994. Since then, the effectiveness of the ICAM has been diluted by a drop in student enrollment and disarticulation of matriculation from salary and job promotion.

Although the ICAM drew on similar experiences in Ecuador and Venezuela, several factors were key to its adaptation in Manizales. Most notable among these were:

1. new incentives for mayors to implement innovative policies created by the resumption of elections and reinforced by new measures of accountability;
2. various policies that served to enlarge the fiscal base of municipalities, both by increasing the sources of local revenue and by augmenting central government transfers;
3. the transfer of additional responsibility for service delivery to municipal governments in areas such as water and sanitation, health, education, agriculture, and transportation;
4. legal requirements aimed at enhancing human resource management in municipalities by linking quality service at the local level to upward mobility in the national civil service and by requiring that municipalities earmark a minimum percentage of investment expenditures to training activities.

ICAM's budget was allocated under this legal provision.

Certain features of ICAM's structure and function stand out and have been central to its success. The ICAM project was approved by the Manizales Municipal Council as a special training "fund" with a small but highly qualified staff, and a minimal administrative apparatus. ICAM's work was contracted out to specialists in various components of the municipal training plan, which was produced by ICAM staff in close coordination with the division of human resources, and the mayor's office. Organizationally, this status allowed ICAM flexibility and autonomy in the design and implementation of its programs. ICAM's programs ranged from seminars, to address problems of accounting and rigidities in procurement, to awareness sessions aimed at reorienting work attitudes (service orientation, importance of the client) of municipal employees.

The ICAM idea was diffused vertically as well as horizontally. Among the effects of its vertical diffusion was a national government plan to institute permanent systems of technology transfer between municipalities, drawing on the training and technical assistance information collected by ICAM. Following the example of Manizales, sixteen other training institutes were established in Colombia by the end of 1996.

Consistent institutional strengthening of the kind that was implemented with ICAM is needed in most large cities in the world, and this model shows some of the incentives—decentralized local government, specific legal provisions—that worked to foster ICAM in Manizales.

Tijuana: Political Contract for Public Financing of Infrastructure

The case of Tijuana consisted of an amalgam of a half-dozen innovations, introduced in sets of two and three in sequence (Campbell and Katz 1996). Each innovation in Tijuana shared a direct or indirect connection with the others, and these, in turn, built upon, and then helped to advance, a qualitative change in the character of governance within the municipality. The innovations included:

- property tax reform;
- restraint in public spending;
- cadastre modernization;
- a citywide referendum on public works (PAU);
- small-scale public works program for the poor (*Manos a la Obra* (Katz and Campbell 1996));
- long-term strategic planning with the private sector.

The central innovation in terms of scope, novelty, risk, and impact was the Plan de Activación Urbana (PAU), a package of civil works designed to rehabilitate the city following disastrous floods in 1993. The PAU was novel in its design process, its extensive consultation with the public, its linkage of costs to financing by an improvement levy on affected property owners, and its use of a citywide public referendum and opinion poll to verify demand and public willingness to pay for the $170 million program.

The PAU was striking for its participation, communication, and involvement of the public in decision-making, particularly in the decision to borrow for capital investment. More than any case we have seen, the public investments in the PAU were linked, through consultation and voting, to expressed preferences and willingness to pay by beneficiaries or voter-taxpayers. PAU and other innovations in Tijuana confirmed findings of cases analyzed elsewhere about the indispensable roles of leadership, continuity, simplicity, and participation.

In addition, the analysis of Tijuana takes a step further into the dynamics of innovations. The multiple innovations in Tijuana, one laying the groundwork for the next, allow us to begin formulating hypotheses about sustained change. Each of the innovations in a city built and extended the climate of expectations and eventually produced an emerging quality in the style of governance and particularly the relationship between the executive and the electorate. In the case of Tijuana, we refer to this qualitative change as a transformation in the character of government.

But whether by single or multiple innovations, the Tijuana experience allowed new insights into the policy options and conditions of civil society that financial and technical assistance organizations must understand to foster and promote reform in decentralized city-regions. Above all, the new style of governance is marked by the terms of a new political contract forged in Tijuana. In it, the links between public works and the voter-taxpayer were made more explicit and subjected to public debate. This relationships goes to the heart of governance.

FINDINGS AND CONCLUSIONS: CARE AND MAINTENANCE FOR ENGINES OF CHANGE

All five cases profiled here have idiosyncratic features of one kind or another, but they do share features, at least a family resemblance, in three specific phases of Hopkins's cycle of innovations—origins, launch, and dissemination (1995). Table 12.5 summarizes this information for the five cases described in the preceding section. Except where noted, the generalizations made here hold for all cases documented in this study and they offer many insights into policy and practice that might be employed to advance the interests of global city-regions.

Origins and Context

Who Innovates and How Do They Learn?

As observed in related literature (e.g. Hopkins 1995; Leeuw, Rist, and Sonnichsen 1994) a champion or visionary is found in virtually every experience of innovations, and these cases are no exception. A champion—a mayor, entrepreneur, or leader—was able to "read" what is possible at a given historical moment, to understand what the public wants, and to visualize a new way of doing things. Above all, the champion is able to convert this vision into reality. Leadership is another aspect of the visionary champion. It is hard to imagine the successful beginnings, let alone positive outcomes, of the innovations we documented without the driving force of leadership. Leaders play a role of provocateur challenging citizenry to *see* how a venture might be formulated. Leaders are on the lookout for good ideas, and find or invent ways to offset or hedge the risks of failure. More than a few of the initiatives were actually adaptations from experiences observed elsewhere, for instance the referendum and improvement levy introduced in Tijuana was inspired by local government referenda in the United States.

Another inspirational factor, visible in more than half the cases, was an environment of reform or crisis—fiscal, natural, or political. Leaders and champions

Table 12.5. *Features of urban innovations in Latin America and the Caribbean: summary table*

Feature	Mendoza	Curitiba	Tijuana	Cali	Manizales
Context of Origins	political renewal; cholera	congestion, oil crisis	floods, opposition government	historical identity	decentralization, restored democracy
Conceptual Model	previous program *(ahorros previous—prior savings)*	buses as metros	betterment levy	company town	French institute
Who Acted	governor	mayors	mayor	mayors, private sector	mayors
Outside Help	no	help in later phases			outsiders recruited
Preconditions	prior experience; political leadership	urban plan, wide streets; commitment to sustain land use	cadastre records, spending reform	history of commitment; decentralization of authority	electoral and municipal reforms created need for professionalization
Launch	small, contained pilot	single axis, large redesigned buses	full-blown program	revolving management in parks and planning	founding of institute
Evolution	limited expansion of basic concept	extensive elaboration of basic concept	revised to smaller programs, different forms of participation	gradual elaboration and extensive application	elaboration and integration with career plan and pay
Next Steps	longer term credits; market finance; bigger projects	?	borrow and implement	tighter linkages with regional and national development schemes	integrate with hiring criteria and career; application to other public authorities
Dissemination	limited impact on other provinces; municipal governments alert	moderate; many Brazilian and LAC cities have adopted "pieces"	via municipal associations	ideas spreading to other cities in Colombia	contributed to reform in other cities
Replication	good potential	good potential; but not fully realized (need for land use controls and dedicated lanes)	good potential (for referendum and communications)	possible for selected applications	good potential

were acting in an environment of larger imperatives, such as Argentine political reform felt in Mendoza in the early 1990s, or the wave of renewal in Manizales, or the floods in Tijuana. Even the fuel crisis of the 1980s helped give the Curitiba transport system extra momentum.

How do Mayors and Other Local Leaders Learn?

The answer we discovered is that mayors learn from each other more than any other single source. They may get ideas from afar, in print or as a result of interacting with technical experts, but independent, foreign, or external sources, though important as a means sometimes to legitimate a new venture, usually follow a prior consultation or series of consultations with other elected leaders. This pattern is seen elsewhere in the literature, for example Clark (1995) and Leeuw, Rist, and Sonnichsen (1994). Furthermore, our seminars revealed that leaders learn best in oral terms, mostly from each other, and much less often in written form. This was true in the cases of El Salvador's Programa de Educación con Participación de la Comunidad (EDUCO), Porto Alegre's participatory budgeting, and Mendoza's neighborhood infrastructure. Mayors are doers, not academics, and they can go far with visually demonstrable examples. Some experiences also show that mayors are especially effective as retransmitters of ideas.

Sustained Commitment

An extension of the importance of leadership, particularly in local governments, is that a leader must be able to articulate convincingly commitment and be able to sustain public trust. This is particularly difficult in Latin America where short mayoral administrations are the rule. Often continuity in trust is achieved by means of periodic "doses" of direct contact with neighborhoods participating in the project. Mayor Lerner of Curitiba sustained a consistent vision during three nonconsecutive terms as mayor spanning more than twenty years. The longest track record, in Cali, dates to the 1920s. Tijuana accomplished a great deal in only six years.

Contexts and Models with Basic Tools

Each innovation has some sort of mental model—a precedent, a nearby example, or visually concrete scheme as a starting point. But high quality current information about the city was also important for innovators to see the connection between an inspirational idea and the local circumstances of a city. Land use and cadastre information were decisive in both Curitiba and Tijuana. This clue suggests a new justification for fostering the basic building blocks of city management. Without basic data, creative management of cities is more difficult.

Scale and Launch: Keeping it Simple, Gradual Elaboration

The origin of complex, multigenerational experiences, such as the novel innovations reported among these cases, was a simple idea, built on a simple model, visible and in operation somewhere nearby. Training institutes in Ecuador and Venezuela helped launch the ICAM in Manizales, for example. No experience is more illustrative of the power of simplicity than in Curitiba, where a fundamental concept—controlling the automobile and making buses have some of the speed and passenger volume of metro systems—was extended in a dozen different directions over a fifteen-year period. From today's perspective, these innovations in Curitiba appear grandly complex and impossibly complicated to replicate. But it began with a single conceptual change, based on the premise that the city could control the automobile, and to do that it needed to control land use. Dozens of cities already know this is true, but cannot yet find a way to get started.

Where this pattern of "small and simple first" was broken—and Tijuana is the best example because of the breadth of scope proposed with the PAU—the innovation ran into trouble. The trouble, and eventual defeat of the PAU, arose not so much because the idea was bad, or poorly carried out, although errors in tactics and design might have been part of the problem. The bigger problem was that, as with all large undertakings, they create more institutional friction and are more vulnerable to outside forces, in this case the monetary and fiscal crises that swept Mexico.

Small Scale

Small scale of operations is critical, especially for neighborhood works. The small, 200 to 300 family, block-by-block scale of the Mendoza infrastructure program, seen also in Conchali and the Tijuana *Manos a la Obra*, for example, facilitated sustained personal contact of program officials and leaders, and hence made legitimacy easier to achieve. A small scale also fosters a sense of partnership between neighborhood residents and program officers. Increasing the face-to-face contact among neighbors engaged in a project tends to heighten mutual responsibility, and this in turn, is key to managing the risks for community members who undertake credit obligations. Finally, small projects get built faster.

Start in a Safe Harbor

The cases also suggest that launching in a safe harbor—that is, protecting new ventures from political and social reactions—helps foster success. The incubator in Mendoza was an office in a provincial ministry; in Manizales, a small-scale training program; and in Valledupar and Conchali local infrastructure programs were started in a few neighborhoods. Others, like El Salvador's EDUCO, expanded very quickly building on a basic program piloted in a few rural districts, but overseen and protected by a unit in the Ministry of Education.

Social Relations and Communications to the Public

Social Organizations as Building Blocks

A corollary to the idea of simplicity in innovative startups is that basic social building blocks at the local level are needed to advance common purposes. Mendoza and Manizales—like their cohorts Valledupar, El Salvador, Conchali, and Porto Alegre—depended heavily on organizational strengthening of grassroots, often single-purpose, organizations that were gradually mobilized to move beyond their original objectives. Grassroots interests are the moving forces of participatory innovations. In many cases their very presence becomes the organizing principle around which community efforts are mobilized. The community organizations in Mendoza typically involved 100 to 300 families living in contiguous city blocks, but ranged from as small as five to as many as four thousand families. Similar ranges were found in Conchali, Tijuana, and Porto Alegre.

The architects of the innovations were acutely aware of the importance of the organized community, and project implementers exhibited skill and experience in communicating with and promoting organizations and managing community relations. But though donor experience corroborates the importance of participation, very little attention has been paid to shaping the message or mobilizing the modes of communication to the public.

Communications and Public Education

The champions' use of various devices for public communication to define ideas, provide an identity, reduce uncertainties raised by the opposition, and persuade or convince the public and other political leaders that the innovations were a good idea is a common factor of successful cases. Private firms marketing products understand the value of advertisement and consumer awareness. Public agencies are generally inexperienced, except in electoral campaigns. The successful cases in this study are conspicuous by the quality of publicity generated to win over the public. Potential innovators, development institutions and governmental institutions alike, need to pay much more attention to the media and the message in transmitting ideas to the public about good practice. Too often public officials are not cognizant of the quality of their message and are unaware of ways to improve communications to the public. Many local leaders, like donors, are rarely willing to pay what seem to be high costs of strengthening this critical communications linkage in the process of making public choices.

POLICY DIRECTIONS FOR DONORS: MOVING FROM INNOVATION TO REFORM

Policy and Strategic Focus

Perhaps the most important conclusion from this study is that the arena in public sector reform has shifted to the local level, and the momentum and mechanisms of these changes can be applied to the critical problems of economic development, management, and governance in city-regions in the coming decades. Although this study documents only a few cases, many additional experiments have been launched by cities and intermediate levels of government in Latin America and many other parts of the world. This energy represents an engine of reform, and

move from first attempts of single innovations to a sustained sequence of changes by focusing on strategic incentives and tactical tools that foster innovation to solve problems of the global city-regions.

NOTES

1. Unless specifically referenced, detail about specific cases can be found in relation to specific cities (Campbell and Fuhr forthcoming).
2. The author observes from recent visits to Cali that the strong civic and social ties noted in this case appear to have been eroded recently under the intense pressure of economic crisis coupled with armed assaults and threats from the organized drug trade, left wing guerilla groups, and right wing paramilitary forces.

REFERENCES

Campbell, T. (1996). "Mendoza Provincial Program for Basic Social Infrastructure (MENPROSIF), Case Study," in *Regional Study on Best Practices and Policy Lessons in Decentralization.* Washington, DC: Latin America and the Caribbean Technical Department, World Bank.

—— (Forthcoming). *The Quiet Revolution: The Rise of Political Participation and Local Government in Latin America and the Caribbean.* Washington, DC: Urban Partnership, TWU (Transportation, Water, and Urban Development Department), World Bank.

——, and Fuhr, H. (eds.). (Forthcoming). *Leadership and Innovation in Latin American Cities.* Washington, DC: World Bank Institute, World Bank.

——, and Katz, T. (1996). "The Politics of Participation in Tijuana, Mexico—Inventing a New Style of Governance," in *Regional Study on Decentralization: Best Practices and Policy Lessons in Latin America.* Washington, DC: Latin America and the Caribbean Technical Department, World Bank.

——, Bidus, M. H., Cárdenas, J. H., Fisher, J., and Rosenbaum, A. (1996). *An Emerging Policy Agenda for Local Government.* Final report of the Second Inter-American Conference of Mayors. Sponsored jointly by the World Bank, OAS, IDB, USAID, and IAF, Miami, 17–19 April 1996. Washington, DC: Latin America and the Caribbean Technical Department, World Bank.

Clark, T. N. (ed.). (1995). *Urban Innovation—Creative Strategies for Turbulent Times.* Thousand Oaks, CA: Sage Publications.

Hopkins, E. (1995). "The Life Cycle of Urban Innovations." Vol. I, Urban Management Program Working Paper Series. Washington, DC: World Bank.

Jacobs, J. (1968). *Life and Death of Great American Cities.* New York: Doubleday.

Katz, T., and Campbell, T. (1996). "Manos a la obra" (Hands to work), in *Regional Study on Decentralization: Best Practice and Policy Lessons in Latin America.* Washington, DC: Latin America and the Caribbean Technical Department, World Bank.

Leeuw, F., Rist, R., and Sonnichsen, R. (eds.). (1994). *Can Governments Learn? Comparative Perspectives on Evaluation and Organizational Learning.* New Brunswick, NJ: Transaction Publishers.

Leitman, J., Santoro, R., and Campbell, T. (1996). "Transport System in Curitiba: A Successful Challenge to Conventional Wisdom," in *Case Study of Decentralization in Latin America: Policy Lessons and Best Practices.* Washington, DC: World Bank.

Maldonado, A. (1996). "Creación del Instituto de Capacitación Municipal de Manizales" (The creation of the Manizales Municipal Training Institute). *Regional Study on Decentralization: Best Practice and Policy Lessons in LAC.* LACTD Regional Study. Washington, DC: Latin America and the Caribbean Technical Department, World Bank.

Marris, P. (1974). *Loss and Change.* New York: Pantheon.

Peterson, G. (1995). *First Inter-American Conference of Mayors.* Washington, DC: Latin America and the Caribbean Technical Department, World Bank.

Rojas, F. (1996*a*). "Administrative Decentralization and Management: Private Park Provision in Cali," in *Regional Study on Decentralization: Best Practice and Policy Lessons in Latin America.* Washington, DC: Latin America and the Caribbean Technical Department, World Bank.

—— (1996*b*). "Innovaciones en el manejo de la ciudad de Cali y el Departamento del Valle de Cauca (Colombia)" (Innovations in the city management of Cali and Valle de Cauca Department [Colombia]), in *Regional Study on Decentralization: Best Practice and Policy Lessons in Latin America.* Washington, DC: Latin America and the Caribbean Technical Department, World Bank.

World Bank (1996). *The World Bank Participation Sourcebook: Environmentally Sustainable Development.* Washington, DC: World Bank.

13

Intercity Competition and the Question of Economic Resilience: Globalization and Crisis in Asia

MICHAEL DOUGLASS

THE PACIFIC ASIA URBAN TRANSITION

Policymakers in Asia will have to plan for megacities of a size and complexity never before seen in history. Ronald Skeldon (1998: 3)

Globalization—here concerned with the integration of circuits of finance, commerce, and production on a world scale—is recent, incomplete, and undergoing dynamic transformations in organizational structures and local impacts. Although industrial production began to globalize in the 1970s, very few countries in the world actually achieved "newly industrialized economy" status. The most well-known economic miracles in the developing world emerged in east and southeast Asia (Pacific Asia). Erstwhile successes in Latin America faltered in the late 1970s with only sporadic recovery since. Other would-be success stories in the Third World generally failed to get beyond the textile, garment, and shoe fabrication stage of industrialization (Athukorala 1989). By the early 1990s, the record showed that with only a few Pacific Asia countries becoming the principal sources of higher value-added manufacturing outside of the OECD, economic disparities among nations were continuing to widen (Pritchett 1996, Rao 1998).[1]

The rise of Pacific Asia in the world economy is both a source of and ultimately dependent upon accelerated rates of urbanization, which have been among the highest in the world. From now to 2025 the expected annual growth rate of the urban population in Pacific Asia will be roughly four times that of the highest-income countries, resulting in a doubling of the number of city dwellers, while in several countries rural populations will begin to decline for the first time in history (UN 1994, 1997; Douglass 1999). During the next quarter of a century Pacific Asia is expected to add more than 700 million people to its cities, accounting for about 30 percent of the world's urban population increases as well as 30 percent of the total world urban population in 2025, with China accounting for most of the increases. Cities in Southeast Asia, where the global factory has arrived later than in east Asia, are predicted to grow five times faster than OECD cities. These cities have been experiencing increases of several hundred thousand new residents every year, a large share of whom are locating in peri-urban areas beyond urban boundaries and thus have no municipal government to oversee urban management and planning issues.

The global unevenness of capitalist development is mirrored by highly uneven spatial patterns of growth within the economies that have been successful in creating accelerated export-oriented industrialization platforms. These have largely been driven by transnational enterprises and investment. In Pacific Asia this has fundamentally restructured the economic as well as social and political space in an astonishingly short period of less than three decades. Among the most prominent elements of the spatial restructuring accompanying globalization are (Douglass 1998, 1999):

- spatial polarization in a few metropolitan centers;
- formation of very large megaurban regions around these centers that are growing in excess of 10 million and as much as 80 million or more in population;
- government promotion of candidate world cities at the top of an emerging hierarchy of urban nodes in the Pacific Asia region;
- emergence of a pan-Pacific Asia development corridor from northeast to southeast Asia;
- slow rates of urbanization and economic growth in inland regions, including densely settled agricultural heartland regions away from metropolitan centers.

The concerted global and national energy focused on megaurban regions and corridors has been a fundamental underlying dimension of the recent economic crisis as both a source and arena of impacts. As a source, the polarization of economic growth fostered stellar urban land price increases that fueled the circulation of global finance capital through Asian banks and into land development schemes. With major urban regions doubling in population every two decades or so, land price rises far outpaced per capita income growth to create seemingly endless opportunities to turn speculative land investments into high returns through ambitious development schemes.

The rationale put forth for many of these schemes was the imperative of intercity competition for world-city status, a concept that emerged as a critical look at the urban condition in a select number of global centers but which quickly turned into a banner for national development in Asia (Friedmann 1986, Knox and Taylor 1995). "Waterfront fever," "Manhattan skylines," "cyber" cities, superexpress rail lines, world-hub airports, huge industrial estates and technoparks, large-scale international convention sites, elite business districts, and massive new town developments were but a few of the many types of megaprojects launched by global finance capital channeled through manipulated domestic finance systems and the pursuit of world-city status.

In most countries global urban pursuits resulted in a de facto absence of policy for most of the national territory. By the mid-1980s any pretense of trying to divert the growth of major urban centers to regions away from key metropolitan cores was effectively dropped from national development plans. Attitudes toward the "big city" switched from cautionary concern to outright advocacy of concentrating investment in them as a way to accelerate national economic growth. Even though rural revitalization continued to receive token mention, rural regions—which had been reduced to green revolution grain crop zones and contract farms for international agribusiness—and their rural towns continued to experience chronic population losses and aging farm populations accompanied by a parallel decline of local urban functions and transportation services.

Japan represents an extreme case in which rural areas have already been decimated by decades of polarization along the Pacific Belt. Approximately 80 percent of the national population lives in the urban belt stretching from Tokyo to Osaka. In a majority of rural areas, the farm population is over age sixty-five, schools are closing for lack of students, and transportation services have been reduced to a minimum. Despite earlier prognoses that a "U"-turn to rural areas or a "J"-turn to rural towns would occur, there is no evidence that this is happening. The idea of thriving rural economies with vibrant communities for all generations of people seems to have passed into history.

Dramatically slowing population growth rates now becoming prevalent throughout the Pacific Asia region are amplifying the aging of rural populations already produced through rural–metropolitan migration. In the case of Korea, by 1990 areas with absolute population decline were accounting for 40 percent (up from 17 percent in 1980) of the national population and 61 percent (up from 32 percent in 1980) of the national territory (Kim 1996/97: 243). One of the most critical aspects of Korea's rural depopulation is that it has been more rapid since 1980 rather than during the nation's decade of accelerated industrialization in the 1970s. Thus, paradoxically, rural depopulation began reaching its highest levels even when industrial regions such as the southeast coast around Pusan were experiencing serious economic downturn as Korean corporations began moving low-wage assembly operations from these regions to locations in southeast Asia and other parts of the world. This has further stimulated growth of the greater Seoul metropolitan region, which now accounts for almost one half of the national population, as global management and service functions gravitate to it.

In these growing metropolitan regions, the impacts of economic growth and population concentrations have produced great stress on all aspects of urban life and habitat. Environmental degradation, monumental traffic congestion, housing shortages, the growth of slums are among the daunting conditions summarized as threats to sustainable development and the attributes of unlivable cities (UNESCAP 1993). Megaprojects launched for "internationalization" have also led to the forced resettlement of tens of thousands of small enterprises and urban households from their communities in the city and periurban households from their villages and agricultural land (Douglass 1998). Yet, as the crisis revealed, the huge amounts of investment required by these projects also turned out to be far beyond local capacities to absorb and turn into profitable ventures, leading to economic collapse throughout the region in the late 1990s.

THE CRISES AND THEIR URBAN IMPACTS

The Crises

The economic turmoil that swept through the open economies of east and southeast Asia from 1997 has been generally portrayed as one solely created in the nexus of the globalization of finance capital coupled with "crony-capitalism." It is, however, a much more complex set of crises that collectively threaten both the economic future of societies and the livability of their cities:

Environmental Crisis

Resulting from excessive concentration on economic growth over environmental management, this is now resulting in significant losses to urban productivity and personal health as well as the unwanted growth of what can only be called dysfunctional urban habitats that require working people to make exceptionally arduous commuting arrangements that, in some cases, are undermining family life and intergenerational continuity.[2]

From almost every perspective—air pollution, water quality, toxic wastes in water and land—a majority of cities are less livable today than a decade or two ago (Douglass and Ooi 1999). Severe water shortages and seasonal flooding have become more pronounced, and Pacific Asia has cities with the highest levels of air pollution in the world. Waterways do not support life; land is heavily polluted with toxic wastes; human waste seeps into drinking water supplies; acid rain is affecting plants and human health. For many urban residents, and especially the urban poor, the urban environment is life-threatening. Issues surrounding the idea of livable cities have become the rallying points for the emergence of environmental movements in Asia, and have thus become among the most politically salient topics of the day (Lee 1995; Ho 1997; Hsiao 1995; Hsiao and Liu 2000; Douglass, Ard-Am, and Kim 2000). The socially uneven burden of environmental degradation has raised the parallel issue of environmental justice.[3]

Health costs extend beyond personal well-being to include time lost from work. The average cost of all known pollution in Pacific Asia's metropolitan regions is estimated to be close to 10 percent of urban GDP, with these regions now accounting for as much as half of the national GDP in most countries. The health and productivity costs of air pollution are estimated to amount to billions of dollars a year in the large Asian cities. With pollution levels increasing 10–20 percent per year in some energy, industry, and transport subsectors, the costs to productivity are expected to rise not only in the form of health costs and mortality, but also in rising resource costs due to deterioration of environmental quality (Brandon 1994).[4]

The World Bank (1996) concludes that urban regions that cannot successfully sustain their environments may begin to be abandoned in favor of other "new" regions where environmental deterioration is not as pronounced. In this context, it should be noted that with China just beginning its period of accelerated industrialization, as much as 80 percent of the industrial structure expected for Pacific Asia is not yet in place.

Lack of Economic Resilience

In export-led industrialization this has been creating a "shallow capitalist" development. Even before the crisis, higher income Pacific Asia economies had entered a period of marked decline of industrial regions located outside of metropolitan regions. Southeast Asia's export engines were also faltering as local capacities for innovation remained weak and China began out-competing them for lower-end assembly operations.[5] Limited localized interindustry linkages, low levels of local research and development needed to create innovative "learning regions," and high dependence on external investment created economies with low capacity to generate new industries or alternative sectors for economic growth. In addition, the nesting of national economic eggs in a few urban baskets neglected potentials for economic growth over the national territory.

Governance Crisis

The growing difficulty in governing has resulted from several factors, including continuing high levels of corrupt corporate-state relationships and absence of serious measures to increase capacities of municipal governments to manage urban growth. Lack of transparency and weak institutional arrangements for citizen involvement are part of this crisis that has become more acute with the awakening of civil society throughout the Pacific Asia region. Weak local governments limit both urban management capacities and democratization processes.

Human Welfare Crisis

A sharp decline in the quality of life has resulted from overt dependence on economic growth to deliver households from poverty and sustain minimum levels of welfare. Little attention has been paid to the need to create alternative forms of entitlements to basic goods and services outside of wage-based economic exchange. In this context, with surplus rural labor supplies disappearing and natural population growth turning negative in Japan and reaching toward zero in many other countries in the region, ratios of nonworking to working populations will steadily increase, and with this increase will come heavier burdens on wage workers to support the elderly. Midline projections show that Japan will only have four-fifths of its current population of 126 million by the year 2050 and as little as 40 percent in 2100 (*Jinko Mondai Shingikai* 1997: 4). By the early 1990s the number of people over age 65 had already surpassed the number under age 15 (*Nikkei Weekly*, 27 January 1997: 6). Although Japan is the first to experience negative population growth rates, they are expected to begin in South Korea, Singapore, and Taiwan before midcentury.

Foreign workers also represent a growing segment of unprotected urban populations who not uncommonly live in substandard accommodations and have no health or other welfare benefits. Some estimates show that 10–15 million Asians are involved in global migration of all types (Tran 1998), with low-wage migrant workers in Pacific Asia totaling 2.6 million (Silverman 1996). In 1994 alone about one-half million people were reported to have moved from lower to higher income economies in Asia, with Japan, Korea, Taiwan, Singapore, and Hong Kong each receiving 30,000–150,000.

Financial Crisis

The roots of the financial crisis lie in policies to attract short-term rather than long-term capital through liberalization of banking, encouraging foreign borrowing and high debt–equity ratios. With currencies linked to the U.S. dollar to reduce risks and local interest rates high, investors were virtually guaranteed high returns and easy, quick withdrawal from host banks. This strategy allowed land developers and other local enterprises to rely heavily on bank credit. By international standards, firms in the region become extraordinarily highly leveraged in the 1990s. In Korea and Thailand, the average debt–equity ratios in 1996 were above 200 percent, and were only slightly lower in other Pacific Asia economies (Sachs 1999). This left little immunity to external shocks.

Previously, tight controls on external sources of bank finance had insulated weak local banking systems from external vulnerability to short-term foreign debt. This changed during the 1990s with the opening and deregulation of domestic banking without parallel improvements in supervision and regulatory oversight. Increases in foreign borrowing in the 1990s were dramatic and pushed financing through inadequately prepared local lending systems into projects with little chance of making economic returns, thus creating a financial house of cards over the urban landscape. By mid-1997 borrowers in the five most highly leveraged countries—Indonesia, South Korea, Malaysia, the Philippines, and Thailand—had an estimated $274 billion in outstanding international bank loans, with two-thirds of this amount in short-term deposits with a maturity of less than one year.

Impacts

When the international banks started to sniff trouble in 1996, with overvalued currencies, weakening exports, and overcapacity, these banks began to reduce their lending. After the devaluation of the Thai baht in mid-1997, they started to flee. When the IMF panicked—ostentatiously declaring that Asia needed drastic financial surgery such as immediate and widespread bank closures, astronomical interest rates, and drastic fiscal cuts—the investors panicked right alongside (Sachs 1999: 1). The Asian finance debacle became a catalyst setting off chain effects through the other crises already underway. In comparison, the finance crisis in the United States in the 1980s had a rather limited impact on the U.S. population—principally on those who had their money in savings and loan banks. The Asian finance crisis had an immediate and profound impact throughout the region:

Systemic Business Failures

Company bankruptcies were linked to the collapse of finance institutions and the withdrawal of global finance, reducing national economic growth to negative rates.

Mass Unemployment

Unemployment of wage workers in Bangkok rose by one-quarter to one-half million people (out of a total work force of 4 million). In South Korea the unemployment figures reached 1.8 million, or 8.7 percent of the labor force by early 1999 (Kim, W. B. 1999*b*), and the number of households falling apart over financial problems and inability to pay debts tripled in 1998; an estimated 30 percent of house loans were nonperforming (Song 1999).

Declining access to basic needs as a result of lost income and rising import costs occurred throughout the region. In Indonesia, employees in some sectors experienced real wage cuts greater than 50 percent. Even in Singapore, which was only indirectly affected by the crisis, wages were down by as much as one-third in some sectors. A more pervasive pattern than open unemployment has been underemployment in terms of less than 40 hours worked per week and/or less than a living wage, which is resulting from firms adopting job-sharing and reduced hours rather than outright firing of employees.

"New" Urban Poverty

This has taken the form of a pauperization of large segments of society—not just migrants from rural areas trapped in some kind of stylized "informal sector," but rather white- and blue-collar workers in the global factory and office. Increases in outright destitution, and dissolution of marriages and families, are widely reported. Street people have also greatly increased in number in cities in Korea (Cha 1999), and homeless camps have suddenly appeared in major cities such as Tokyo, Nagoya, and Osaka in Japan. Suicide rates among self-employed men and middle-aged people, who were hit hardest by the prolonged recession in Japan, reached record levels in 1997 and 1998.[6] With restructuring and international bailouts generally favoring the rich over the poor, inequalities have also been heightened.

Other members of the new poor are the elderly, who are increasing in their share of national populations in almost all countries. Little has been done by governments to create the health and other supports, such as housing and assured food sources, needed by this growing, vulnerable segment of society.

Foreign workers, millions of whom faced mass deportation from the crisis-ridden countries that had previously recruited them, have become another major category of the new urban poverty (Douglass 1999).[7] With the crisis, foreign workers were the first to be targeted for immediate deportation, with little, if any, severance pay or benefits actually given. More often than not, they face an even more severe crisis and prospects of long-term unemployment in their home countries, and large numbers have stayed in host countries as illegal entrants. Antiforeign-worker sentiments, mixed with racism, emerged throughout the region. Wanted when labor shortages were critical, they were suddenly seen as undesirable aliens with little effective protection under the law. Korea initiated a program to expel almost 100,000 foreign workers. Japan stepped up drives to arrest and deport illegal migrants.[8] In Taiwan the government required firms to reduce the share of foreign workers among their employees, and a crackdown was initiated to locate some 20,000 "runaway foreign workers" who had left their places of employment without official permission. The Taiwan government also proposed an amendment to the Labor Standards Act to exclude foreign workers from the protection of the minimum wage policy. In Hong Kong the target was Filipina maids, who number almost 140,000 and who were subjected to as much as a 35 percent reduction in their minimum wage.

Striking parallels arise between the crisis and Sen's (1990) concept of entitlement failures associated with famine. With the crisis leaving millions of people unable to obtain basic commodities that are widely available on world markets, the situation can be likened to a "slump" famine, in which the purchasing power in a particular location is so deflated that entire populations are impoverished by losses of jobs and savings combined with rising costs of imports due to falling currency exchange rates.[9] Almost no government or industry safety nets exist for the newly unemployed in most of the affected countries. The traditional systems that supported the poor in the past—the ability to retreat to subsistence production and call upon close family links and home communities for support—have been seriously weakened with the advent of a modern urban economy. In Indonesia, where official levels of poverty jumped from 12 to 50 percent on Java, school enrollment of children has also fallen, which is just one indicator of the intergenerational spillover effects of the crisis.

"Moth-eaten" Urban Landscapes

These have been described as vistas of vacant lots, half-finished construction projects, and empty high-rise buildings (Amaha 1998). The collapse of what Korten (1998) terms casino-pyramid schemes of finance capital channeled into dubious land development projects has left bizarre urban landscapes mottled with the failures of fast-track capitalism. Called *mushikui* (moth-eaten) by local residents in Tokyo, some 1,000 communities in cities across Japan are blighted with plots of empty or half-developed land scattered among their neighborhoods. In Bangkok vacancy rates in the central business district stood at 40 percent in May 1999, which was an increase of 10 percent over the end of 1998 (*Week in Review*, 9–15 May 1999). In the same city, developers abandoned 364 unfinished buildings in response to credit problems and lack of demand. Some have become magnets for crime, and all are deteriorating to the point that they must first be demolished before rebuilding (*Week in Review*, 30 May–5 June 1999). In most cities, the now defunct projects were launched by demolition and, in many instances, forced relocation of preexisting communities and businesses (Douglass 1998).

Declining Public Expenditures

These reductions are evident in welfare, environmental management, and urban management in general. Although in some ways the environment abruptly improved due to the precipitous decline of industrial production, the decreased ability of government to enforce environmental regulations and monitor performance has had the opposite effect (World Bank 1998).

Changing Competitive Positions

Comparative strengths have been shifting among economies and cities, especially candidate world cities, as a variety of impacts take on their own localized forms and trajectories (Douglass 1999). There are indications, for example, that the relative position of Tokyo as an international finance center may have eroded with the collapse of several of its largest financial institutions. Seoul is having similar experiences with the decline of some of Korea's largest corporations that are headquartered there, undermining its rise as a potential world regional center in northeast Asia.

Hong Kong's relatively milder impacts from the finance crisis masks more profound crises stemming from its loss of comparative advantage in both small-scale manufacturing and higher level services such as banking to adjacent regions in China. This is compounded by its high levels of pollution and their health impacts.[10] Sensing a potential decline in Hong Kong's position seems to underlie the spate of proposals to create competing island sanctuaries for global capital in other countries. In addition to Cheju Island in Korea (*Korea Herald* 1999), Thailand has proposed that the tourist island of Phuket be turned into an international Silicon Island free from government taxes and regulation (*Nation 1999*). In the late 1980s a "Cosmopolis Plan" was launched by the Japanese government and Mitsubishi to fill in completely Tokyo Bay with an artificial island that would also be a deregulated international zone (Douglass 1993).

All of these impacts suggest that just as the crises are manifold and widespread, the search for solutions must be equally so. The greatest risk would be that of seemingly quick economic recovery that fails to attend to the more entrenched problems of environmental degradation, slow pace of political reform, continuing shallow economic structures, and vulnerability of populations to global economic shocks.

RECOVERY: THE LIMITS OF INTERCITY COMPETITION FOR GLOBAL INVESTMENT AND STATUS

> The landscape of global business is changing rapidly. Major factors behind the accelerating tempo of foreign direct investment are the soaring levels of cross-border mergers and acquisitions (M&As), increasing numbers of privatizations, and strong efforts by countries to attract foreign investment. (UNCTAD 1998*d*)

> The goal of infrastructure investment is to provide the bases for prosperous and comfortable lives. In the 21st century, the needs for a beautiful natural environment, a

comfortable and safe life, and individual cultural circumstance will increase, and infrastructures to match these needs will be more important. However, during the past decade, although large public works have been carried out continuously to help out an end to the economic recession that followed the bubble economy, local economies remain impoverished, and infrastructures in urban areas are getting obsolete. In fact, inefficient public works are carried out only to stimulate the economy temporarily. Today, from a global perspective, it is doubted that Japan is an attractive country in Asia for investors. The Economic Strategy Council of Japan (ESCJ), "Strategies for Reviving the Japanese Economy; Report to Prime Minister Obuchi," 26 February 1999.

"Local competition for business expansions and new plants has grown fierce."
Upjohn study of state and local investment incentives offered in the United States in the 1990s (Bartik 1995).

Several of the Pacific Asia economies in crisis, including Japan, began to show signs of possible recovery by mid-1999. Optimism began to run high that the worst was over and that past growth rates could be reestablished to lift the Pacific Asia "geese" led by Japan to ever higher levels of per capita income. Without discounting the possibility of a long-term economic recovery, there are at least four major reasons why a return to the past formula of national and urban development is problematic.

1. First, as the foregoing discussion indicates, the IMF package of reforms, namely, transparent banking, floating exchange rates, and the entire range of neoliberal policies to open economies further to globalization and foreign investment, will not address—and might even exacerbate—the other crises of shallow economic development, low economic resilience, environmental deterioration and its economic impacts, governance, or social justice issues. If, as expected, past patterns of development are reasserted, these crises will continue unless they are simultaneously and directly addressed. It is not clear, however, that foreign-investment-driven national development can be achieved while also adopting policies to improve the environment, create social safety nets, or any number of programs to make cities more livable and supportive of human welfare.

2. The second reason is that economic recovery will probably not reach levels of past growth. Should they achieve averages of OECD countries, expectations of economic growth rates of under 5 percent per year would be reasonable. Under such a scenario, and judging from the OECD experience, economic growth could no longer be expected to maintain high levels of employment, particularly if some countries, such as China, attract the lion's share of foreign investment previously going to other Pacific Asian economies.[11] In such circumstances, chronic unemployment and income inequalities are likely to persist and require other forms of entitlements to attenuate.

3. Third, even proglobalization institutions such as the World Bank (1999) and the IMF (1999) are predicting that the globalization of finance capital is creating heightened propensities for the type of finance crises that have already visited Mexico, Pacific Asia, Brazil, and, most recently, Russia. The World Bank

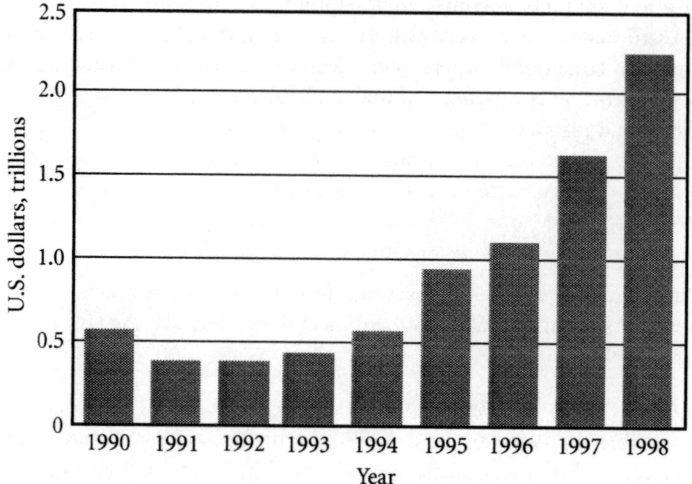

Figure 13.1. *Total value of announced worldwide mergers and acquisitions, 1990–98*

Source: Bloomberg Financial Markets: Securities Data company as reported in the *New York Times*, 8 December 1998

(1999: 1) warns that "financial crises are on the rise in developing countries" and declares that the expected slowdown in global economic growth will "hurt people the most in countries that . . . depend on private capital flows to finance large current account deficits." With reform in banking and government still partial and proceeding slowly in Pacific Asia, there is no guarantee that episodes of economic collapse and sudden loss of exchange entitlements for local populations will not occur again. Because such crises invariably lead to a shrinking of the public purse, the impacts can also be expected to be redoubled in terms of declining attention to other outstanding environmental, social, and economic problems.

4. Fourth, with regard to the appearance of new candidates for foreign investment, prospects for less rapid rates of economic growth stem from the trends showing a substantial heightening of international competition among cities, which is resulting in increasing subsidies to investors with less surety of long-term benefits. This is occurring as a result of increasing concentrations of control over investment into the hands of fewer and larger global enterprises, giving them extraordinary leverage power over local conditions for investment. With the increasing global reach of finance capital, the world is now witnessing an unprecedented level and pace of megamergers and acquisitions (M&A) among large-scale corporations. As shown in Figure 13.1, between 1994 and 1998 annual amounts expended on M&A activity worldwide increased almost five-fold to reach nearly $2.5 trillion. As finance capital spins its own circuits of expansion, much of this activity is being driven by rising stock prices rewarding mergers and acquisitions even when new production or increased productivity is not the result.

Increasingly, a very large share of M&As are cross-border as corporations expanding from one national base penetrate, merge, or form strategic alliances with those in other countries and regions. For the world as a whole, cross-border mergers and acquisitions amounted to US$359 billion in 1997, with the number of megatransactions involving the world's largest transnational corporations (TNCs) on the rise (UNCTAD 1998*e*, 1998*f*). Cross-border M&A activity in 1998 and early 1999 greatly surpassed even the 1997 levels, propelling a doubling in world foreign direct investment (FDI) from 1990 to reach $440 billion in 1998. This is having a snowball effect of compelling more and more corporations to participate in mergers and acquisitions as a means of maintaining market shares and positioning among rivals.[12]

TNCs are achieving their goals of strategic positioning not with M&As alone, but also through a growing numbers of cross-border interfirm agreements and alliances, many of which focus on technology that is particularly important for enhancing competitiveness. More than 8,000 interfirm agreements in technology-intensive activities were concluded from 1980 to 1998, with the annual volume increasing over time.[13] Korean and Japanese firms, for example, are investing in California's Silicon Valley with an interest in gaining access to cutting-edge technology. Even the Tokyo Metropolitan Government is setting up an office in Silicon Valley to introduce small Japanese companies to U.S. investors (*Asia Pulse* 1999*b*).[14]

The outcomes are increasing shares of local economic activities in the hands of global monopolies. As one of many examples, major world automakers are predicted to decline from the current number of fifteen to as few as five over the coming decade (UNCTAD 1998*e*). The world's one hundred largest TNCs alone now account for more than US$2 trillion in foreign sales and 6 million foreign employees. According to UNCTAD (1998*a*), two-thirds of world trade is now taking place within corporate networks. With many large corporations now entering into alliances with each other effectively to divide world markets into oligopolistic regional spheres, associating international trade with unfettered free trade among nations is increasingly anachronistic.

Pacific Asia has become both a source and target of cross-border mergers and acquisitions. Japanese firms and banks, principal sources of global finance a decade ago but mired with heavy debts, are now selling off assets in the United States, Europe, and elsewhere at prices well below those they originally paid (*Asia Pulse* 1999*a*). As part of the economic crisis and subsequent sell-off of assets by defunct banks, Japan and South Korea have also begun to witness wholesale asset buyouts of domestic enterprises by U.S. and European firms. In Japan, for example, Ford Motor Corporation has purchased one-third ownership of Mazda (*Nikkei Weekly*, 26 July 1999). "Thanks to sweeping liberalization measures and the availability of cheap assets," in 1998 cross-border M&As in Pacific Asia increased by 28 percent in value over the previous year, swelling the M&A share of FDI to 16 percent, compared to 3 percent before the economic crisis in 1996.[15] South Korea received its largest-ever volume of FDI inflows in 1998, mostly in the form of $6 billion of its corporate assets sold in cross-border acquisitions

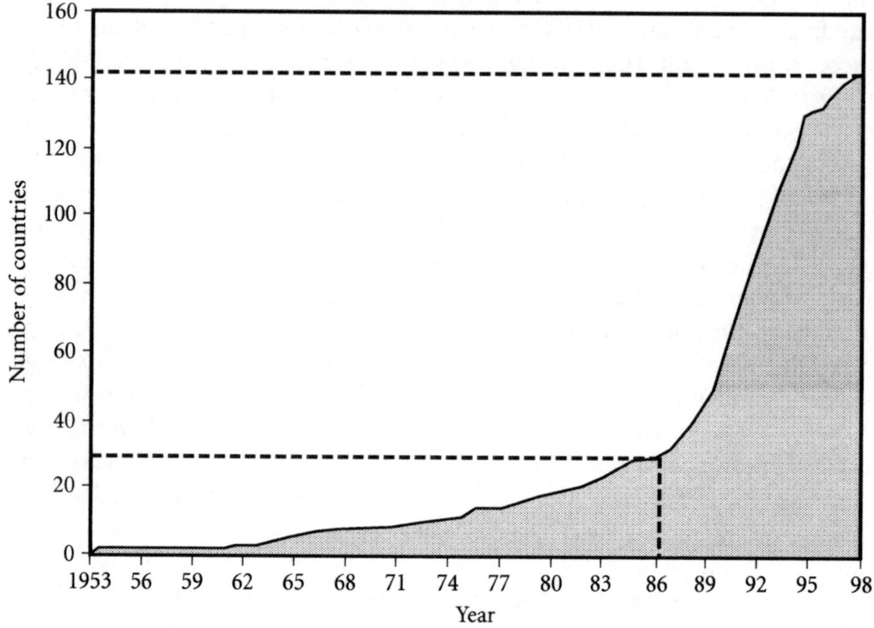

Figure 13.2. *Cumulative number of countries and territories with special FDI regimes, 1953–98*

Source: UNCTAD 1999

(UNCTAD 1999). This was four times the average annual inflow of FDI during the economic surge of the early 1990s.

All of the growth in FDI and M&A activity is occurring despite slower world economic growth and in the same time frame as the appearance of economic crises in world regions, the most recent of which has been the Pacific Asia meltdown (UNCTAD 1998*f*). In 1998 world output grew by only 1.9 percent in real terms (*Christian Science Monitor*, 21 July 1999).[16] As noted, concentrations of control in global corporate networks are also generating substantially increased competition among countries and cities for investment. As shown in Figure 13.2, the number of countries adopting favorable FDI regimes jumped from 40 in 1986, the year in which the yen began to skyrocket against other currencies to create a global rush for Japanese investment, to more than 140 by 1998. Table 13.1 provides more details on the types of policy changes toward foreign investment that were made in 1997, a year in which 76 countries introduced changes. Approximately 90 percent of the changes were made to make conditions more favorable to investors, and among these about one-third involved increasing tax incentives and subsidies.

These dramatic trends are occurring around the world and help to explain how a subsidy of $11,000 per job created that was given by Tennessee to win a Toyota assembly plant in 1980 grew to $168,000 per job provided by Alabama

Table 13.1. *National regulatory changes by type of distribution, 1997*

Number of countries introducing changes	76
Number of changes	151
More favorable for FDI	135
More liberal entry conditions and procedures[a]	3
More liberal operations[b] conditions and frameworks[a]	61
More incentives	41
More promotion (other than incentives)[c]	8
More sectoral liberalization	17
More guarantees and protection	5
Less favorable to FDI	16
Less incentives	7
More control	9

Notes:

[a] Includes changes applying across the board.

[b] Includes performance requirements as well as other operational measures.

[c] Includes free-zone regulations.

Source: UNCTAD 1999 (based on national sources).

to win a Mercedes plant in 1993. Despite these inflating give-aways, a U.S. study by the Upjohn Institute (Bartik 1995) found that the effects of such incentives on business locations are actually modest, with many decisions unchanged by higher offers of subsidies or tax relief. Further, the costs to governments have exceeded revenues generated by the new activity in the local area.[17]

In addition to concentrating ownership, cross-border M&As also reflect the strategies of TNCs to divest lower end production activities and strengthen control over worldwide systems of production, distribution, and finance through acquisitions in higher level network control functions.[18] Low-wage, labor-intensive, and low value-added manufacturing and assembly activities are increasingly arranged through subcontracting or licensing. As the Oregon-based Nike Corporation has demonstrated by setting up subcontractors in Korea and soon using these Korean firms to move and manage production to Indonesia and Vietnam, subcontracting can readily be shifted among locations according to conditions of local hospitality to investors and relative costs of labor. Reflecting these trends, longitudinal data on FDI show that employment has been declining per dollar of foreign direct investment worldwide, while at the same time it has been increasing among subcontractors (UN 1994). The total number of jobs directly associated with the top 500 TNCs at end of the 1980s was lower than in 1980, and it is likely to have further declined since.[19]

In witnessing mergers and buyouts of once domestically owned enterprises, cities and their governments are further compelled to provide the infrastructure and other investments in the built environment to host industries and create the communications and transportation networks facilitating globalization. In 1997, for example, a major jump occurred in the number of export processing zones and free trade zones, adding a substantial number to the 800 government-sponsored zones already in place around the world (UNCTAD 1998*c*).[20] China alone has 124 such zones, and is adding several more (*Asia Pulse* 1999*c*). By the end of 1998, its 32 state-class development zones had approved the establishment of 13,454 foreign-funded enterprises with a total contractual foreign capital reaching US$51 billion.

In engaging in this intercity competition for global investment, the Korean government announced in 1998 its intentions to establish four customs-free zones at key ports (Inchon, Kwangyang Bay, and Pusan) and airports (Kimpo in Seoul), the first in that country, which are intended to become trade and distribution hubs for northeast Asia (Cha 1998). All of the exemptions typical of such zones will apply.

Similar initiatives are being pursued in countries throughout the region, with the result that a strong proinvestment public policy is now a given factor in attracting FDI throughout the world. As noted above, over the past fifteen years, the overwhelming majority of governments have introduced measures to liberalize substantially their foreign investment regulations and have in this way opened the door for TNCs to an increasing degree. This has meant that the "old" incentives for attracting FDI—tax holidays and other subsidies directly to investors, trade liberalization, government control of labor organizations—are so widely available that, while still minimum requirements, they are insufficient by themselves to gain the more sought after levels of economic activity above the assembly line.

Governments are thus directing much of their attention and resources to creating new assets and imaginative schemes to give them an edge over other cities and to move upward in a perceived global hierarchy of cities. This has kept paramount the sense among governments that public investments to respond to global competition have overriding priority. While successful in some locales at particular moments, in others, such as Osaka, local governments have been driven to near-bankruptcy by their unsuccessful investments of public money in huge megaprojects and spectacular global events aimed at winning global economic prominence.[21]

In sum, spatial changes taking place in economies in crisis reveal important considerations about globalization. As core regions experience the most pronounced impacts, their economic troubles coupled with low levels of economic performance in other subnational cities and regions reveal a general lack of national economic resilience. Even though many economies are now apparently showing signs that they are improving, the future is still uncertain as effects of the crisis and new crises reverberate through other quarters of the world. Achieving economic resilience through local capacity building to resolve crises as they appear, rather than simply intensifying competition to attract global capital, needs to be given greater policy attention. As city-regions become the home of greater shares of the world's population, making them more livable as human habitats requires equal priority. Rather than treating urban economic resilience and livability as competing objectives, strategies to incorporate them as complementarities for the longer term sustainability of city-regions must be devised.

BUILDING CAPACITIES IN AND AMONG CITIES: FROM INTERCITY COMPETITION TO COOPERATION

One reason for the nationwide economic slump is sagging local economies. Their economic futures may not become rosy unless they succeed in producing area-based industries and culture, one after another, everywhere, by recovering a self-supporting mechanism that avoids the current dependency on the central government. For this, "local sovereignty" should be firmly established (ESCJ 1999).[22]

Three dimensions of capacity building—localization, collaborative governance, and intercity networks—are fundamental to the task of making cities more livable and economically resilient.

Localization of Capacity-building

The above quote from the recent report on the path toward economic recovery commissioned by the Prime Minister of Japan captures the paradox that while globalization proceeds into new, more encompassing modes, responsibilities for creating more resilient economies are seen to be increasingly localized. As cities are more directly integrated into the world economy and their economies are less mediated through national political processes, they are compelled to act as arenas for policymaking about global economic interaction. Municipal governments are now being charged with devising their own strategies for globalization and to engage in overt campaigns to attract world investment. In addition, most of the IMF reforms being undertaken in response to the crisis are exposing local economies to even greater direct influences of globalization. Countries that had tightly controlled foreign direct investment are now dismantling barriers to buyouts and cross-border mergers by global enterprises. Property markets have also been opened for the first time to foreign investment and land ownership.

While such liberalization might have positive effects in some aspects of particular sectors, its broader impacts on the resilience of local urban and regional economies, not to mention the quality of local living, cannot be gauged from spaceless sector models of economic efficiency that cannot capture either the interplay of economic with political, social, and environmental dynamics or the distributional effects of economic growth. There is a pressing need to improve local government and social capacities to develop more strategic approaches to urban development in its fullest sense. Economic restructuring, movements for political reform, and urban development are all intertwined but are also animated in strikingly different ways among cities and regions. Efforts to secure the longer term sustainability of cities and nations will thus rest greatly on building local capacities.

Enlarging this capacity will in turn call for a sharper focus on cities not simply as economic agglomerations, but also as arenas for the formation of political communities that can meaningfully address other outstanding issues. Often unperceived at the center, such concerns as managing the environment and citizen welfare are the daily concerns of local governments. Yet most are ill-prepared to take them on as urban policy; planning in Asia continues to be directed principally by central governments. Municipal governments remain notoriously weak, with insufficient revenues to cover basic infrastructure and management needs, and with inadequate staff to meet the challenges of contemporary urban economic, social, and environmental concerns.

For their part, central governments tend to focus attention and money on a few large metropolitan regions, leaving even less for other cities and rural regions. If cities are to find and nurture their own strengths through either local or global linkages, and if this is to be accomplished in a manner that allows opportunities to be seized more widely among cities and regions, there is a manifest need to strengthen local governments at all levels over national space.

Localization of capacity-building has traditionally been discussed under the banner of decentralization. To varying degrees, most governments in the region have adopted policies at least selectively to decentralize decision-making powers and management capacities to local urban and regional scales. In some cases, such as in Korea and Taiwan, progress in this direction has been impressive. In most other societies, decentralization in practice remains a form of deconcentration of administrative tasks still tightly controlled by central bureaus rather than devolved and effective local decision-making power.

A more authentic process of decentralization to build local government capacities would entail several key actions. First, local governments need to be given much greater decision-making and management authority over an array of areas, including selecting economic activities for public support, managing the environment, and creating their own policies toward the welfare of local residents, including foreign workers (Tegtmeyer Pak 2000).

Greater decision-making power is of little real meaning without parallel enhancements of autonomous sources of revenue. In most instances, municipal governments have very limited authority and capacity to engage in such routines as collecting property taxes or recouping expenditures through locally initiated cost-recovery programs. Local revenues typically account for less than one-third of actual expenditures, with the remainder being allocated and controlled from the center.[23] Local governments are also generally without the authority to raise funds for large-scale public projects through borrowing or selling bonds.

Local governments also need substantially to raise the quality of personnel in both technical skills, such as environmental monitoring, and organizational skills, such as working proactively with businesses in creating "learning regions" in which knowledge and its economic applications are locally generated in dynamic, continuous cycles of innovation (Edgington 1998). Equally important skills are needed in working with citizens toward establishing routines of collaborative governance.

Collaborative Governance

Localization of public decision-making is a principal channel for bringing civil society and other local economic interests into a more inclusive political process. Command and control styles of planning associated with the "developmental state" of the 1960s and 1970s are yielding to more democratic and inclusive forms of governance. Institutional arrangements within public bureaucracies have, however, lagged behind popular demands for openness and transparency. They have tended to remain difficult to access and rigidly hierarchical in structure.

The weakness of local public decision-making and its still bureaucratic forms of working with the public continue to limit the possibilities for more collaborative governance among government, civil society, and private enterprise. Without more collaborative forms of governance—the processes by which public decisions are made and put into practice (Friedmann 1999)—relations become reactive and adversarial. Without government facilitation, communities face great difficulties in engaging businesses in public discussions on their environmental and quality of life concerns. Confronted with antigovernment protests, governments tend to try to withdraw from interface with the public or, worse, feel compelled to resort to old-style police and military control of citizen ire.

The stresses of globalization will also continue to magnify reactive, sometimes violent, confrontations in cities and communities throughout the region. The countless projects launched in the name of internationalization that are radically destroying and reconstructing urban space in Pacific Asia are also targets of local protest and antigovernment movements. Even where civil society remains thoroughly repressed, the possibilities for large-scale citizen mobilization—over such issues as entitlements and rights to the city, including land and housing, and incidents of environmental degradation by polluting factories—occur and cannot be continuously suppressed.

In viewing the deep social as well as physical changes attending urbanization and globalization in Pacific Asia, contests over the shaping of cities, access to their amenities, and, ultimately, their livability have already become the substance of much of urban politics. How to transform this social energy into a positive source of collaborative planning is of fundamental importance to the future of Pacific Asia cities. Where advances have been made in this direction, results have been impressive. Assessments of environmental movements in the region show, for example, that democratization and social mobilization have resulted in positive improvements (Douglass, Ard-Am, and Kim 2000). In Korea following political reforms from the late 1980s, NGOs active in environmental management issues multiplied, reaching a reported 175 groups nationwide in 1993 (Kim 1994). In 1995 the consolidation of various environmental groups led to the foundation of the Korea Environmental Movement Federation, which claimed 20,000 members and twenty-one local chapters (KNCFH 1996). Along with local elections held for the first time in the same year, two environmental candidates won mayoral elections. Environmental movements were also able to persuade the national government to reorganize environmental planning bureaus and adopt an environmental impact assessment system.

Intercity Networks

With urbanization no longer simply a "national" phenomenon, a Pacific Asia urban network has begun to emerge as part of globalizing flows of information, services, goods, people, and decision-making power (Kim, W. B. 1999*a*). Although the current pattern of relations among cities in this network is one of heightening competition for segments of the global economy, the ease and frequency of interaction make it possible for cities to use a variety of media and venues for exchanging ideas and information about contemporary policy issues and their possible solutions. Concerted attention to fostering more cooperative intercity networks has potentially high payoffs in terms of raising awareness of common problems, availability of technologies, and opportunities for collaborative innovations across urban and national boundaries. They can also be promoted as a means of leveling the playing field in vying for global investment. By establishing agreements or guidelines among cities on conditions for investment and identifying the types of incentives that are more likely to have positive local impacts, the bidding-down process in which local governments lower claims on and regulation of investors while increasing subsidies to attract them can possibly be attenuated.

Building more cooperative intercity relations faces enormous obstacles. Most cities continue to view themselves as being in a zero-sum game of economic competition with other cities. In the absence of a national-level player such as a central government to prevent "cheating," it will be difficult to establish practical intercity agreements to set standards for foreign and domestic enterprises—for example, basic environmental regulations. National governments would certainly need to be part of the process at the international level as well.

Nonetheless, there are opportunities to use more positive elements of urban performance to challenge other cities to reach higher levels of livability as a way of attracting and keeping investment. Performance-focused approaches to development programs and projects rest on local-level setting of performance measurements and supporting information systems rather than on centrally standardized programs that are frequently inappropriate in local contexts, fail to tap local knowledge, and do not take advantage of local resources (Metzembaum 1998).

Cities can facilitate improvements in other cities through sharing of performance achievements, which can be used to stimulate improvements among all cities. Such achievements can be further spotlighted by such practices as giving national and international awards to "best cities" in, for example, reducing air pollution. Networking could also involve creating or envisioning urban futures and developing strategies to realize them.

Intercity networks are already being formed among countries in many regions of the world. Given the general weakness of local governments, most only play an information exchange or goodwill role. There are, however, many leagues of city organizations within countries, including some in Pacific Asia.[24] There is also a growing interest and support for strengthening intercity government relations, as evidenced by the convocation of the World Assembly of Cities and Local Authorities at the Habitat II Conference in 1996, and the growing activity of the International Union of Local Authorities. Such national and international intercity organizations are bound to grow in number as cities increase their awareness of common problems and find greater ease in exchanging information through advances in global communications systems. Whether they can begin to develop a policy voice in the international arena remains to be seen. It is clear, however, that the time has come for cities to try to find more room for cooperative engagement as an antidote to the extremely competitive pressures they now face.

CONCLUSIONS

Building local capacities, formulating policy through citizen-government-business dialogue and collaboration, and finding common ground for cooperation among cities are suggested as important elements of any strategy for strengthening economic resilience and making cities more livable, including supporting the basic welfare of all urban residents. The intention is not to isolate cities from globalization, but rather to create greater room for manouver for cities to secure improvements in all of these vital dimensions of their existence and development.

The challenge for cities is how to overcome immediate global pressures that foster trade-offs between economic growth and other goals of development. The proposition put forth here is that this challenge can be met and that possibilities exist for making progress in both economic resilience and livability. Endowing cities with a positive image of livability is increasingly seen as being a key element in capturing investment. Similarly, cities that can assist households in maintaining access to basic goods and services in times of economic turbulence are arguably more likely to avoid the problems of homelessness, crime, and other forms of social dysfunction that ultimately work against economic vitality. From this perspective, the challenge is not one of finding opportunities for improving the potential of city-regions, but rather one of generating local level synergies to be able creatively to seize and use them.

NOTES

1. Pritchett (1996) estimates that between 1970 and 1985 the ratio of incomes in the richest and poorest countries increased sixfold, and the average income gap between the richest and poorest countries grew almost ninefold (from $1,500 to over $12,000).
2. An urban Japanese father is found to spend an average of about seven minutes per day with his children.
3. Three general objectives have been associated with environmental justice and the movements it has spawned: healthy communities for all citizens, rights of redress and access to legal institutions, and citizen participation with government and business in decision-making on environmental matters.
4. Improvements are being made in several countries, but gaps remain large. In Japan, for example, the National Environmental Agency announced in 1998 that air pollution from dioxin emissions had been cut by almost half compared to the previous year, but this level is still 6 to 9 times those of other OECD countries. In most other countries, gains in improved engine efficiencies to lower pollutants are being negated by the still rapid growth in vehicle ownership, which is typically occurring at rates in excess of 10 percent per year.
5. In the first quarter of 1996, the increase in exports slowed from 28 to 8 percent in Thailand, 20 to 6 percent in Hong Kong, from 23 to 17 percent in Malaysia, 32 to 21 percent in Korea, 23 to 9 percent in Taiwan, and 20 to 10 percent in Indonesia (Lewis 1996).
6. In Japan in 1998 the life expectancy of men actually decreased for the first time since World War II due to increases in suicides among older men losing their jobs. Increasing numbers of middle-aged people were also abandoning their homes due to debts and related economic misfortunes (*Hawaii Hochi* 1999).
7. The demand for supplies of cheap foreign labor is already established in Pacific Asia's higher income economies. In 1992 the Korean Federation of Small Business stated that the country needed an additional 360,000 workers, or the equivalent of 7.5 percent of the nation's labor force, to fill shortfalls in low-wage labor availability. Among the 200,000–300,000 foreign workers in Taiwan are 40,000 Thais, Filipinos, Malaysians, and Indonesians working in retirement homes, an activity that is so dependent on cheap foreign labor that in 1999 the government officially allowed small establishments openly to recruit workers from abroad for this work (*China News* 1999). In Japan, electric machinery, plastics and certain chemical processing industries, construction, and auto parts making are well known for their reliance on foreign workers to keep wages down and carry out jobs that Japanese workers will no longer take even in the recession (Douglass and Roberts 2000).
8. In Japan the government has linked the period of residence permits to employment contracts. This has allowed employers unilaterally to terminate contracts with foreign workers by using the justification that their visas would soon expire. With the usual practice of deducting about US$5,000 from the wages of foreign contract workers for the expenses of bringing them from Latin America to Japan, sudden termination has proved to be disastrous as they end up with no money for either themselves or their families in their home countries (Terasawa 2000).
9. Sen (1990) defines entitlements as the endowments and means of exchange to achieve expanded human capabilities, which he uses to define the idea of develop-

ment. As he details, even in times of plenty people were found to be starving in huge numbers due to entitlement failures, i.e. the lack of economic power to obtain what was, in fact, plentiful.

10. Hong Kong's 1999 "winning" of the only Disneyland theme park in Asia outside of Japan, for which it is paying 90 percent of the costs while Disney Corporation receives 43 percent of the equity and all receipts from Disney brand merchandise sales, is portrayed as a major event in revitalizing its drifting economy, but is not expected to generate a positive rate of return for another twenty or thirty years. Hong Kong's subsidies to Disney are estimated to be equivalent to $100,000 per job created (*Honolulu Advertiser* 1999).
11. Of the all-time-high $97 billion in direct foreign investment in developing countries in 1994, about two-thirds was absorbed in East Asia, with China receiving 40 percent of the total (UNCTAD 1995). Of the worldwide foreign investment going to developing countries in 1995, most went to just four countries: China, Indonesia, Malaysia, and Thailand (UNCTAD 1996).
12. Mitsubishi, for example, has created a large fund to buy up Japanese companies that are going bankrupt. Financing for the buyouts is to be set up by Ripplewood Holdings, a U.S.-based firm with 10 percent Mitsubishi ownership, that is being used to raise US$1 billion from Japanese, U.S., and European institutional investors. Mitsubishi states that it intends to buy about ten businesses over the next decade, priced at about 30–40 billion yen each (*Asia Pulse* 1999*b*). In Korea, in addition to Samsung's slated takeover of Daewoo, Hyundai Electronics is absorbing LG Semiconductor, and Kia Motors is merging with Hyundai (Mo 1999). The latter merger is expected to lead to a reduction of shop floor employment by 20 percent and management by 30 percent (Kim, Y.-s. 1999).
13. Their number has increased from an annual average of fewer than 300 in the early 1980s to more than 600 in the mid-1990s.
14. Daewoo, a giant South Korean *chaebol* with $15 billion in foreign assets and about 40,000 employees in foreign countries (1996), topped the list of transnational enterprises from the South with the largest value of foreign assets, while South Korea has experienced negative GDP growth rates (UNCTAD 1998*b*). Samsung's buyout of Daewoo announced in the heat of the Asia economic crisis in 1998 represents a substantial concentration of corporate power.
15. UNCTAD 1998*a*. This same source observes that rarely before has there been so much activity undertaken by national governments and international organizations in the realm of investment negotiations. The number of bilateral framework agreements has been expanding, reaching more than 1,500 by the end of 1997. About 1,800 double taxation agreements covering 178 countries were in effect at the end of the same year.
16. The United Nations predicts that for the foreseeable future in the majority of countries growth will fall far short of what is necessary to effect a substantial improvement in living standards and a reduction in the number of people in poverty. Of the 95 developing countries for which they have reliable data, only 13, including China, will grow enough in 1999 to experience a rise in living standards and a decline in poverty. Approximately 1.2 billion people living in 40 countries suffered declining living standards (*Christian Science Monitor*, 21 July 1999).
17. The study advises governments to use incentives in a more targeted way to attract firms that have high employment payoffs at higher wages. It also suggests that governments

adopt mechanisms such as "clawback" provisions that require corporations to repay subsidies if promised employment does not last for a specific period.

18. In 1998 a total of fifty-eight transactions were individually valued at over US$1 billion each. TNCs from OECD countries accounted for 90 percent of them. Trade liberalization (including the financial services agreement reached in 1998 under the World Trade Organization) and deregulation and privatization in some key areas (for example, telecommunications) have further stimulated the M&A activity (UNCTAD 1999).
19. Jobs created directly by FDI are still substantial. In the early 1990s TNCs were estimated to employ directly 10 percent of world's and 20 percent of the OECD's nonagricultural labor force (UNCTAD 1998*a*).
20. In these zones, firms are typically exempt from customs duties, value-added taxes, and various other indirect taxes. The process of entry and exit of goods at these points is also usually abolished, with activities such as storage, manufacturing, and production guaranteed to be allowed. Foreign businesses are also typically exempt of all corporate income taxes; land rental charges will be exempt as well.
21. Osaka Prefecture launched a number of megaprojects in the late 1980s, including the waterfront Izumisano Cosmopolis, Rinku Town, the new Kansai International Airport, and what has turned out to be several unsuccessful bids for the 2008 summer Olympics. All of these have either been failures, have been substantially scaled back, or have performed far below the levels projected by their promoters. By early 1996, of 29 such projects, 22 had losses of more than ¥386 billion. By 1998 the prefecture had a ¥230 billion deficit from its contributions to them (Johnston 1997).
22. The Economic Council goes on to state that Japan's current economic problems are not simply the result of cyclical recession but rather the legacy of an over-rigid administrative and industrial system that has discouraged individual initiative and innovation. It also notes that major intellectual activities have been concentrated in Tokyo, while other regions have been pressed to adopt the same standards as the capital city in order to create a unified market. Japan's educational system has also been oriented toward standardization rather than individual creativity. Government and corporations have created an ethic of corporate loyalties above family and community. Accomplishing reforms in these areas is declared to require a complete change in the Japanese mentality toward greater individual freedom, gender equality, and ethnic diversity.
23. Comparative studies show that an average of about 90 percent of public revenues is collected and spent by national governments in developing countries; for high-income countries, the level averages about 65 percent (Oates 1993).
24. In 1994 a Korea Local Authorities Foundation for International Relations was established under the Ministry of Home Affairs. Its purpose is to cooperate with local authorities abroad to improve the "international competitiveness of local authorities." In July 1999 it hosted an international conference on strengthening international relationships between local governments in Korea, China, and Japan (KLAFIR 1999).

REFERENCES

Amaha, E. (1998). "Land of Despair." *Far Eastern Economic Review*, 14 September (Internet version).

Asia Pulse (1999*a*). "South Korea Attracts Japanese Firms to Media Valley Project." 28 June (Yahoo, Internet).

—— (1999*b*). "Mitsubishi to Invest in U.S. Fund to Buy Japanese Firms." 28 June.

—— (1999*c*). "China Development Zones to Attract More Foreign Capital." 28 June.

Athukorala, P. (1989). "Export Performance of 'New Exporting Countries': How Valid the Optimism?" *Development and Change*, 20 (1): 89–120.

Bartik, T. (1995). "Economic Development Incentive Wars." *Upjohn Institute Employment Research*, Spring: 1–4.

Brandon, C. (1994). "Reversing Pollution Trends in Asia." *Finance & Development*, 31 (2/June): 21–23.

Cha, B.-h. (1998). "Four Customs-Free Zones to Be Set Up." *Chosun Ilbo*, 22 December.

Cha, H.-b. (1999). "Street People Relocated to Temporary Houses." *Chosun Ilbo*, 5 January.

China News (1999). "Workers Needed for Elderly." 11 February.

Corporate Watch. (1998). "Financial Crisis: Our Responses—Final Statement from Conference Organised by Hong Kong Based Regional NGOs." 15–18 June. http://www.corpwatch.org.

Douglass, M. (1993). "The 'New' Tokyo Story: Restructuring Space and the Struggle for Place in a World City," in K. Fujita and R. C. Hill (eds.), *Japanese Cities in the Global Economy: Global Restructuring and Urban-Industrial Change.* Philadelphia: Temple University Press, 83–119.

—— (1998). "World City Formation on the Asia Pacific Rim: Poverty, 'Everyday' Forms of Civil Society, and Environmental Management," in M. Douglass and J. Friedmann (eds.), *Cities for Citizens: Planning and the Rise of Civil Society in a Global Age.* London: John Wiley, 107–37.

—— (1999). "Unbundling National Identity—Global Migration and the Advent of Multicultural Societies in East Asia." *Asian Perspectives*, 23 (3): 79–128.

——, and Ooi, G. L. (1999). "Industrializing Cities and the Environment in Pacific Asia: Toward a Policy Framework and Agenda for Action." Working paper. Washington, DC: U.S.–Asia Environmental Partnership.

——, and Roberts, G. (2000). "Japan in a Global Age of Migration," in M. Douglass and G. Roberts (eds.), *Coming to Japan—Foreign Workers and Households in a Multicultural Age.* London: Routledge.

——, Ard-Am, O., and Kim, I. K. (2000). "Urban Poverty and the Environment—Social Capital and State-Community Synergy in Seoul and Bangkok," in P. Evans (ed.), *Livable Cities? The Politics of Urban Livelihood and Sustainability.* Berkeley: University of California Press (forthcoming).

Edgington, D. W. (1998). " 'Learning Regions': Lesson for Developed and Developing Countries." Paper presented at UNCRD Global Forum on New Directions in Regional Planning, 1–4 December, Nagoya, Japan.

ESCJ (Economic Strategy Council of Japan). (1999). "Strategies for Reviving the Japanese Economy: Report to Prime Minister Obuchi." Tokyo.

Friedmann, J. (1986). "The World City Hypothesis." *Development and Change*, 17: 69–83.

—— (1996). *World City Futures: The Role of Urban and Regional Policies in the Asia-Pacific Region.* Hong Kong: Chinese University of Hong Kong, Hong Kong Institute of Asia-Pacific Studies.

—— (1999). "The Common Good: Assessing the Performance of Cities," in J. Friedmann (ed.), *Urban and Regional Governance in the Asia Pacific Region.* Vancouver: University of British Columbia, Institute of Asian Research, 1–16.

Hawaii Hochi (1999). "Suicide Rate Up 35% to Record." 3 July: 1.

Ho, K. C. (1997). "From Port City to City-State: Forces Shaping Singapore's Built Environment," in W. B. Kim, M. Douglass, S. C. Choe, and K. C. Ho (eds.), *Culture and the City in East Asia.* Oxford: Oxford University Press, 212–33.

Honolulu Advertiser (1999). "Disney Treads Carefully in Asia." 3 November.

Hsiao, H.-H. M. (1995). "Assessing Taiwan's Environmental Movement." First Workshop on Asia's Environmental Movements in Comparative Perspective," Honolulu, 29 November–1 December.

——, and Liu, H.-J. (2000). "Degradation, Livelihood, and Sustainability in Taipei: Emerging Issues and Public Action," in P. Evans (ed.), *Livable Cities? The Politics of Urban Livelihood and Sustainability.* Berkeley: University of California Press (forthcoming).

IMF (International Monetary Fund) (1999). *World Economic Outlook.* Washington, DC.

Jinko Mondai Shingikai (1997). "Shoshika ni Kansuru Kihonteki Kangaekata ni tsuite" (Basic viewpoint on the problem of the trend toward fewer children). Tokyo: Koseisho, 4: 7.

Johnston, E. (1997). "Prefecture's Mega-Projects Seen Bankrupting Osaka." *Hawaii Hochi*, 15 April: 1.

Kim, D.-C. (1996/97). "Economic Growth, Migration, and Rural Depopulation in the Republic of Korea: Comparison with Japan's Experience." *Regional Development Studies*, 3: 239–59.

Kim, I. K. (1994). "The Environmental Problems in Urban Communities and the Protection of the Environment in Korea." *Korea Journal of Population and Development*, 23 (1): 63–76.

Kim, W. B. (1999*a*). "Urban Dynamics in Northeast Asia and the Future of Korean Cities." Sixteenth Pacific Regional Science Conference, 12–16 July, Seoul.

—— (1999*b*). "Desperately Seeking Foreign Direct Investment: About-Face of Korean Cities." Paper presented at the Third Intercity Network Workshop on Urban Impacts and Responses to the Economic Crisis in the Asia-Pacific Region, Osaka, 1–4 September.

Kim, Y.-s. (1999). "Hyundai Plans More Layoffs at Kia." *Chosun Ilbo*, 18 January.

KLAFIR (Korea Local Authorities Foundation for International Relations). (1999). Seoul: http://www.klafir.or.kr/eng/sub1/main.htm.

KNCFH (Korean NGOs and CBOs Forum for Habitat II). (1996). *Voices of the Korean NGOs and CBOs to Habitat II.* Istanbul, 30 May.

Knox, P., and Taylor, P. J. (eds.). (1995). *World Cities in a World-System.* Cambridge: Cambridge University Press.

Korea Herald (1999). "Korea Eyes Hong Kong-Style Free-Trade City on Cheju Island." 21 June.

Korten, D. (1998). "The Financial Casino and Corporate Rule." Corporate Watch Feature, 15–18 June. http://www.corpwatch.org.

Lee, S.-H. (1995). "Environmental Movements in South Korea." First Workshop on Asia's Environmental Movements in Comparative Perspective." Honolulu, 29 November–1 December.

Lewis, P. (1996). "Export Growth Slows for Asia's Tiger Economies." *New York Times*, 3 August.

Metzembaum, S. (1998). *Making Measurement Matter: The Challenge and Promise of Building a Performance-Focused Environmental Protection System.* Washington, DC.: Brookings Institution.

Mo, T.-j. (1999). "Big Cost for 'Big Deal' Delay," *Chosun Ilbo*, 26 January.

Nation (1999). "Phuket, Thailand." 18 January.

Nikkei Weekly (1997). "Latest Population Forecast Should Be 'Call to Action.'" 27 January: 6.

Oates, W. (1993). "Fiscal Decentralization and Economic Development." *National Tax Journal*, 46 (2): 237–43.

Pritchett, L. (1996). "Divergence, Big Time." Washington, DC.: World Bank. http://www.worldbank.org/growth/abs1522.htm.

Rao, J. M. (1998). "Development in the Time of Globalization." New York: UNDP, Working Paper 2, September.

Sachs, J. (1999). "Missing Pieces." *Far Eastern Economic Review*, 25 February.

Sen, A. K. (1990). "Food, Economics, and Entitlements," in J. Staatz and C. Eicher (eds.), *Agricultural Development in the Third World.* Baltimore: Johns Hopkins University Press, 189–205.

Silverman, G. (1996). "Vital and Vulnerable: Migrant Workers Reach Unprecedented Numbers in Asia." *Far Eastern Economic Review*, 159 (21): 60–64.

Skeldon, R. (1998). "Urbanization and Migration in the ESCAP Region." *Asia-Pacific Population Journal*, 13 (1): 3–24.

Song, H.-y. (1999). "Bankrupt Households." *Chosun Ilbo*, 13 January.

Tegtmeyer Pak, K. (2000). "Foreigners Are Local Citizens, Too: Local Governments Respond to International Migration in Japan," in M. Douglass and G. S. Roberts (eds.), *Japan and Global Migration: Foreign Workers and the Advent of a Multicultural Society.* London: Routledge.

Terasawa, K. (2000). "Labor Law, Civil Law, Immigration Law, and the Reality of Migrants and Their Children," in M. Douglass and G. S. Roberts (eds.), *Japan and Global Migration: Foreign Workers and the Advent of a Multicultural Society.* London: Routledge.

Tran, P. (1998). "Migrant Workers in Asia: The Call by the Synod for Asia to Assist Migrants." *Migration World Magazine*, 26 (5): 32–5.

UN (United Nations). (1994). *World Urbanization Prospects: 1994 Revision.* New York.

—— (1997). *World Urbanization Prospects: 1996 Revision.* New York.

UNCTAD (United Nations Conference on Trade and Development) (1995). *World Investment Report.* Geneva.

—— (1996). "Global Foreign Direct Investment Flows Reach $325 Billion in 1995: An All-Time High." UNCTAD fact sheet. Geneva.

—— (1998*a*). *Trade and Development Report 1998.* New York: http://www.un.org/publications.

—— (1998*b*). "General Electric Heads List of World's Top 100 Transnational Firms—Daewoo Leads List of Largest TNCs from Developing Countries." New York: UNCTAD Press Release TAD/INF/2778, http://www.un.org/publications.

—— (1998*c*). *World Investment Report 1998: Trends and Determinants.* New York.

—— (1998*d*). "Important Shifts Are Emerging in the Key Factors Influencing Foreign Business Investments." New York: UNCTAD Press Release TAD/INF/2777, November, http://www.un.org/publications.

—— (1998*e*). "Cross-Border Mergers and Acquisitions Dominate Foreign Direct Investment Flows." New York: UNCTAD Press Release TAD/INF/2776, http://www.un.org/publications.

—— (1998*f*). "New Records Being Set in Global Foreign Direct Investment Despite Financial Crises—Some Gain Possible for 1998." New York: UNCTAD Press Release, TAD/INF/2775, http://www.un.org/publications.

—— (1999). "Foreign Direct Investment into Developing Asia Has Weathered the Storm." New York: UNCTAD Press Release, TAD/INF/2803, http://www.un.org/publications.

UNESCAP (1993). *State of Urbanization in Asia and the Pacific.* Bangkok.

Week in Review (1999). Internet e-mail supplement of the *Bangkok Post.*

World Bank (1996). *1996 Regional Perspectives: East Asia and Pacific.* Washington, DC: World Bank. Also available from the Bank's website at http://www.worldbank.org/html/extpb/annrep96/wbar08a.htm.

—— (1998). *The Social Impact of the Asian Economic Crisis on Cities.* Washington, DC: World Bank. Also available from the Bank's website at http://www.worldbank.org/poverty/eacrisis/library/varma.htm.

—— (1999). *Global Development Finance 1999.* Washington, DC: World Bank.

14

Repositioning of City-Regions: Korea after the Crisis

WON BAE KIM

As the Asian economic crisis unfolded, the regional geography of East Asia changed. The role of large city-regions in the regional and national economy has been emphasized again, especially with respect to the recovery of the ailing economies of East Asia. As economic competitiveness takes policy priority after the crisis, interstate and intercity competition is being intensified in the economic sphere. In order to secure a share of export markets and mobile capital, city-regions and nation-states are competing fiercely with one another. They are also jockeying for superior position in the international urban hierarchies along the Asia Pacific corridors.

Across city-regions, the economic crisis has brought a renewed emphasis on global competitiveness, redirecting public resources for building infrastructure and urban space for global industries. A strong proinvestment public policy is now sweeping throughout East Asia to attract foreign direct investment. Regulations concerning foreign investment have either been removed or relaxed substantially in the crisis-afflicted countries. On the other hand, the spatial dimension of the crisis seems to receive inadequate attention. The crisis has brought uneven economic impacts across city-regions within the region. For example, the decline of production, the sudden loss of jobs, wage cuts, and asset depreciation were uneven across city-regions. Moreover, the effects of policy responses to the crisis at the national level varied between city-regions.

Despite the rhetoric for regional economic cooperation in East Asia, regional polarization seems to have been intensified after the crisis. At the international front, region building in East Asia is slow to make tangible progress except for ASEAN countries. Such ideas as an Asian Monetary Fund, Free Trade Area, and East Asian Economic Group have been circulated but have yet to materialize. Intercity networking is often regarded as a tool for the promotion of individual cities' own-interests instead of sharing benefits with other cities in the network. Even if an agreement is formed to create an intercity network, many issues, including the governance of transborder regions, need to be resolved by local government and nongovernmental organizations.

The purpose of this chapter is to examine impacts and responses to the recent economic crisis, with a particular focus on the spatial dimension of such impacts and responses. The first part will introduce major spatial impacts of the crisis, and the second part policy responses such as deregulation in housing and land markets, and relaxation of restrictions on foreign direct investment. The third part will discuss long-term, macrospatial strategies to secure Korea's position in East Asia. While these strategies and policy responses may help the Korean economy regain its competitiveness, they raise several issues concerning social well being, regional equality, and regional governance both at domestic and international levels. The last part of the paper will address some of these issues for the purpose of identifying alternative forms of regional governance in large city-regions of East Asia.

SPATIAL IMPACTS OF THE CRISIS

The 1997 Asian economic crisis, whatever its root causes, had a devastating impact on the economies of five countries—Indonesia, Thailand, South Korea, Malaysia, and the Philippines. Its impact, however, was not so severe on China, Taiwan, and Singapore. As the crisis unfolded, its force shifted from the financial economy to the real economy—currency devaluation, fall in real estate prices, and increases in unemployment. The crisis brought uneven spatial impacts as well. Large cities were hit hard and directly. They are also where an intensive reform and restructuring has been taking place. Since large cities produce a major proportion of national income and wealth, the economic recovery of national economies depends on how these cities perform in coming years. As the impacts of the crisis are different between cities and countries in East Asia, the relative international position of these cities and countries is changing as well.

Devalorization of Urban Space

It is well known that rapid economic growth in the East Asian economies created bubbles in the real estate market. One could argue that the real estate bubble in major cities of East Asia was one of the reasons for the crisis (Quigley 1999).[1] In any case, the financial crisis in 1997 burst the bubble and real estate prices in major cities across East Asia have plummeted. In Jakarta, commercial property values fell by two-thirds between mid-1997 and the end of 1998. Bangkok's office vacancies rose from 20 percent in mid-1997 to 30 percent at the end of 1998. Property values in Bangkok fell by 44 percent during the same period. Singapore was dragged in by its neighbors' fall (*The Economist* 1999*a*). Seoul and other Korean cities experienced a sharp fall in property values since 1997.

Obviously, the commercial properties in large cities recorded the biggest loss in prices. Properties used as collateral were put on sale to reduce bad bank loans. Firms had to sell properties to pay back debt. Closure of a few banks and slimming-down of large corporations decreased the demand for office space. Thus, many office buildings in the business districts of Seoul and other large cities became vacant and rents for office space came down. Residential and industrial properties experienced price declines as the demand for them shrank. As a result, the value of urban space in large Korean cities declined in 1998. Together with the currency depreciation, the devalorization of urban space in East Asian cities provided incentives for foreign investors who were interested in low-cost business and production sites.

Uneven Economic Decline and Recovery between Regions

As the financial crunch began to affect the production sector, many small-sized firms went bankrupt and others reduced the scale of their operations. Firm closures were heavily concentrated in the cities, especially those that specialized in production of labor-intensive, price-sensitive segments of export markets. For example, the decline of industrial production was more pronounced in Korea's industrial cities such as Inchon and Ulsan (Bank of Korea 1999, Cho 1999). Less industrialized regions with a narrow economic base were also hard hit by the crisis. As the economic recovery began in the latter part of 1998, it took a different pattern. The capital region, which consists of Seoul, Inchon, and Kyonggi, recorded a faster recovery of industrial production, while other regions lagged behind. It reflected the advantage of the capital region in terms of access to information and resources, in particular, to new capital both from abroad and within. The second largest city, Pusan, was exceptionally slow to recover from the crisis. The reasons may be twofold: the industrial structure of Pusan, which is characterized by small-scale, labor-intensive firms, and the collapse of the region's bank.

Such uneven impacts are revealed in the size of unemployment. The rise of unemployment in Korea was phenomenal. The number of officially unemployed increased from 470,000 in the third quarter of 1997 to 1,785,000 in February 1999, recording an unemployment rate of 8.7 percent, which is unprecedented in the recent history of Korea (National Statistical Office 1999*a*). Such an enormous increase in the number of unemployed was observed in the other crisis-afflicted economies as well. Common to the crisis-afflicted economies was the concentration of unemployment in large cities. For example, the number of unemployed in the seven largest cities in Korea accounted for more than 50 percent of the total unemployed as of June 1999. The unemployment rates varied even among these seven. Pusan experienced a persistently high unemployment rate, even after unemployment rates for other cities and the country as a whole began to decline from the peak of February 1999. Compounded with regionalism in Korean politics, the deep recession of Pusan's regional economy raised an issue for policymakers at the national level.

The massive unemployment that resulted from the 1997 crisis increased the number of households below the poverty line. According to one estimate, the share of households below the poverty line more than doubled between 1997 and 1998 (Bark 1999). It is not difficult to see the concentration of those poor households in large cities because of a close relationship between unemployment and poverty. Another related feature wrought by the crisis was the emergence of homeless people in major cities. It is estimated that there were about 6,000 homeless persons as of December 1998. Of these, more than 90 percent were concentrated in large cities and 60 percent in Seoul alone (Ha 1998).

Income disparity within cities has been increasing after the crisis. The average household income of the lowest 20 percent of urban workers decreased by 3.3 percent between the first quarter of 1998 and the first quarter of 1999, whereas that of the upper 20 percent increased by 9.2 percent during the same period (National Statistical Office 1999*a*). This means that the costs of the crisis and the benefits of economic recovery are unequally shared by different income classes. It also reflects the tendency of labor-market segmentation in cities during the course of economic recovery. As the number of manufacturing jobs in the urban economy decreases, more jobs are created either in high-wage professional, technical, and administrative positions or low-wage simple manual positions.

Changing Relative Position of Cities in International Urban Hierarchies

As the role of large city-regions increases through a global network of cities, the geoeconomic power of city-regions determines the relative position of a country in the global economy. Particularly in East Asia, the fortune of the national economy depends greatly on a few city-regions in a country. For example, more than 40 percent of Korea's GDP is produced by the six largest cities. The prime city-region of Seoul (called as "Capital Region") alone produces more than 40 percent of GDP (National Statistical Office 1999*b*).

The primacy of Bangkok is known to be more pronounced than that of Seoul in Korea. Even in an economy as advanced and large as Japan, the role of three large city-regions, namely Tokyo, Osaka, and Nagoya, is critical.

As a variety of impacts of the Asian economic crisis appeared in those large city-regions, their relative position in the international urban hierarchies changed. For example, the relative position of Seoul may have eroded with the decline of some of the country's largest corporations that are headquartered there. The world city Tokyo may have lost its competitive edge with the collapse of several of its largest financial institutions (Douglass 1999). Hong Kong's competitive position declined somewhat because of actions that were taken to protect its currency and stock market for the stability of mainland China (*The Economist* 1999*b*). The geoeconomic power of Singapore was somewhat weakened because of its links with its once-booming neighbors that have been suffering most severely from the crisis. On the whole, as the region's economic balance tilted toward Greater China—mainland China, Hong Kong, and Taiwan—major city-regions such as the Pearl River delta, the Greater Shanghai region, and the Taipei metropolitan area may have improved their relative position in the East Asian urban hierarchy (Kim 1999). Jakarta, Bangkok, and Kuala Lumpur, once contenders to become major regional business centers in Southeast Asia, seem to have lost an opportunity, at least in the short run.

The changing position of city-regions is partly reflected in the global competitiveness ranking of countries (IMD 1999). Asia's competitiveness suffered in 1998. Taiwan and China contained the damage, while others slipped downward. Korea's competitiveness rank fell from 35th in 1998 to 38th in 1999, below the standing of several other crisis-affected Asian economies: Thailand (34), Malaysia (27), and the Philippines (32).

On the other hand, the combined effects of currency depreciation, property value decline, and wage cuts have somewhat improved the cost competitiveness of cities in the crisis-afflicted economies (JETRO 1998*a* and 1998*b*). For example, between December 1997 and June 1998, wage costs in Beijing became more or less equal to those in Bangkok and twice as expensive as those in Jakarta. In other words, China's attractiveness as a low-cost production site was weakened by decreased investment costs in Southeast Asian countries. Korean cities became less costly places for foreign investors, compared with the period before the economic crisis. This may enhance the chance to receive more foreign investment seeking low-cost production sites but would not help much in the long run to regain the economic power of Korean cities and other cities in the crisis-hit economies.

POLICY RESPONSES

The crisis called for immediate government responses. As for short-term crisis management, the government took austerity measures recommended by the IMF, including high interest rates, a tight monetary policy, and current deficit reduction. The government's next steps were to restructure the inefficient banking sector, the financial markets, debt-ridden big corporations, and the inflexible labor market. In addition, various short-term policy measures were taken to relieve unemployment, to arrest the decline of property values, and to boost the construction sector. Some long-term responses were also set in motion with respect to infrastructure building and foreign direct investment.

Preventing Asset Deflation

Alarmed with the rapid decrease in housing and land prices in large cities in 1998, the Korean government has taken various measures to stop the further decline of real estate prices.[2] About 4 trillion won (US$3 billion) was released in 1999 in the form of special loans for housing purchase or rent. Temporary exemption of real estate income transfer tax was granted for the resale of new housing (*Hankukkyongje* 1998). More important, the government policy reducing interest rates (which had gone up to more than 20 percent in the first quarter of 1998) was a principal factor in arresting the fall of real estate prices. Diverse measures to deregulate real estate were another contributing factor for the recovery of the market in 1999.

The decline and recovery of the real estate market reveals an interesting spatial pattern. While both housing and land prices fell by large margins in large cities, the speed of recovery in land price has been slow. On the other hand, housing prices in large cities (especially in Seoul) were picking up faster than in smaller cities in the first half of 1999 (Korea Land Corporation 1999, Housing and Commercial Bank 1999). There is, however, a concern with the overheating of the housing market in the capital region. If the price increase is simply led by speculative housing investment, this will not assist the economic recovery of the capital region.

Relieving Unemployment

The government adopted several programs to deal with the unprecedented high level of unemployment. With inadequate social safety nets, unemployment became a major issue for the government in 1998. About 4 trillion won (US$3 billion) was spent for unemployment-related programs in 1998 and 7.2 trillion won (US$6 billion) was budgeted for 1999 (Bark 1999). These programs included measures to create and retain jobs, and to provide direct relief to unemployed persons. These programs, however, seemed to pay inadequate attention to the regional dimension of the unemployment problems. Public works programs and unemployment compensation were primarily based on head counts. Region-specific factors were not taken into consideration. A region with a large number of unemployed people, therefore, received more funds. Government programs, if intended to assist regional economic recovery rather than simply relieving pain from unemployment, should consider regional labor market conditions, regional industrial and occupational structures, and other relevant factors.

Infrastructure Building

Apart from the short-term crisis management programs, the government placed an emphasis on infrastructure building as a long-term policy response to the crisis. There were two major reasons: first, to create jobs through infrastructure construction and thus absorb unemployed workers, and, second, to raise the country's competitiveness through the provision of modern and efficient infrastructure. According to the medium-term fiscal plan, the Korean government came up with an infrastructure budget of around $10 billion for 1999, which meant a more than 10 percent increase from the previous year. Infrastructure budgets will increase by more than 10 percent annually until 2006 (Lee 1999).

Major projects to be completed in a few years' time are the high-speed rail link between Seoul and Pusan, the new international airport at Inchon, and new construction and expansion of ports in Pusan, Kwangyang, and Inchon. Port and airport construction are expected to elevate Korea's position in the regional transportation system of East Asia. The Inchon international and Pusan airports are envisioned as hub airports in Northeast Asia. The location of international functions is encouraged in and near these facilities. In July 1999, the government announced a plan to establish custom-free zones in the new international airport, the new port in Pusan, and Kwangyang port. The primary purpose of these custom-free zones is to promote logistics and related industries by attracting world-class logistics companies by means of tax exemptions (*Hankukilbo* 1999).

Deregulation and Liberalization of Foreign Direct Investment

Even before the crisis, the Korean economy suffered from high costs and low efficiency. After the crisis, the government placed a special emphasis on reforming the high-cost and low-efficiency economy. High land prices, wages, capital costs, and circulation costs were known to be the reasons for the high-cost economy. Bureaucratic red tape and cumbersome procedures were the major factor causing low efficiency and the reason for it being difficult to do business in Korea. Therefore, the government began to carry out economywide deregulation and liberalization programs in conjunction with the governmental restructuring since 1998.

As widely heralded by supranational agencies such as the World Bank and the International Monetary Fund (IMF), open markets are emphasized as a condition for a bailout from the financial crisis. According to the OECD (1998), more open economies enjoy higher rates of private investment, which is a major determinant of economic growth and job creation. Foreign direct investment (FDI), in particular, is said to bring higher wages and to be a major source of technology transfer and managerial skills in host countries. Crisis-afflicted countries including Korea came to recognize once again that, unlike speculative investment for short-term gains, foreign direct investment is essential for economic recovery. All of them sought to improve their investment environment by either relaxing or abolishing restrictions on FDI (JETRO 1999).

Before the crisis, Korea was one of the least open economies with respect to FDI. The ratio of cumulative FDI to the 1996 GDP was only 2.6 percent, which is far below that of competing Asian economies (24.7 percent in China, 72.4 percent in Singapore, and 48 percent in Malaysia) (MOIR 1999). This low ratio can be attributed to restrictive FDI policies including a ceiling on foreign equity ownership per issue and a maximum of 10 percent foreign ownership of outstanding shares in case of hostile mergers and acquisitions (M&A). These restrictions were abolished in early 1998. One hundred percent foreign equity ownership is permitted and M&A rules were liberalized. Another important change was the opening of property markets to foreigners in June 1998. This was a radical departure from the past, when nationalistic sentiment against foreign ownership of land prevailed.

In November 1998, the Foreign Investment Promotion Act was put into effect. According to the act, one-stop service and investment incentives are provided to foreign investors. Another notable feature was that Free Investment Zones can be established anywhere, if a few conditions are met (MOFE 1998).

With this policy shift, the investment environment of Korea improved. FDI inflow increased in 1998 but this increase was largely led by M&A rather than greenfield investment. M&A were obviously attracted to the bargain prices of ailing Korean firms. As the restructuring of Korean firms has been actively carried out, the pace of foreign direct investment through cross-border M&A picked up markedly in 1998. Compared to US$698 million or 10 percent of total FDI in 1997, foreign acquisitions of outstanding Korean stocks increased to US$1,241 million or 14 percent in 1998. If the acquisition of assets were included in the number, the amount of M&A would be more than 50 percent of total FDI inflow in 1998. These M&A activities were most active in the manufacturing sector, where firms were pressured to restructure.

During January to July 1999, however, foreign acquisition of outstanding Korean stocks decreased to 14.4 percent, compared to 23.3 percent in the same period of 1998. Also decreased was FDI by asset acquisition (from 42.4 percent in January–July 1998 to 7.9 percent in January–July 1999). The decreased importance of M&A and asset acquisition appears to be related to the pace of firm restructuring and the acquisition costs. As the Korean economy recovered, the speed and scale of firm restructuring slowed down. Thus, the share of FDI inflow in the manufacturing sector declined, while that in the service sector increased. The total amount of FDI inflow, however, grew continuously during the first half of 1999, indicating an improved investment environment in Korea.

Growing FDI inflow was reflected in the land market as well. Since land acquisition was allowed in June 1998, there has been increasing purchase of land by foreign entities. Land acquired by foreign companies and joint ventures amounted to more than 80 percent of total land acquisition. The major purpose was to buy factory and commercial sites (MOCT 1999).

On the whole, the liberalization of foreign direct investment and the land market has brought the intended results. Korea has surpassed other crisis-afflicted countries in terms of total amount of FDI inflow. A refinement of FDI policy is, however, called for to increase the benefits of FDI to national economic development. It has been pointed out that FDI should be selectively promoted in certain strategic sectors so as to enhance Korea's industrial competitiveness (MOIR 1999). This applies to city-regions as well. Instead of hosting FDI blindly, a city or region should selectively invite foreign enterprises matching local characteristics, i.e. local resources and industrial strength, so as to enhance local assets.

Another aspect is the regional distribution of FDI. It is known that FDI tends to reinforce spatial polarization. Although it may be too early to assess the regional effect of FDI, available statistics suggest that it tends to concentrate in the prime city-region of Seoul. Foreign investors' preference for the capital region is clearly manifested in the amount of FDI inflow (Table 14.1). This provides supporting evidence for advocates of markets who strongly believe that only the capital region can lead the economic recovery of the country. Outside of the capital region, there is no evidence of any preference for large cities. The data suggest that local efforts may be a factor in hosting FDI. Cities and provinces that actively promoted their locational advantages under the initiative and leadership of mayors and governors recorded better results.

Table 14.1. *Regional distribution of foreign direct investment*

Region	Jan.–Oct. 1997		Jan.–Oct. 1998		Cumulative as of Oct. 1998	
	Establishments (number)	Amount (million US$)	Establishments (number)	Amount (million US$)	Establishments (number)	Amount (million US$)
Capital Region	381	1,770	430	3,080	3,399	11,988
Seoul	305	1,297	337	2,290	2,502	8,365
Inchon	12	66	26	165	211	851
Kyonggi	64	407	67	625	686	2,772
Rest of country	87	4,026	88	2,073	1,129	12,057
Unknown	55	47	96	378	436	788
Total	523	5,843	614	5,531	4,964	24,833

Notes: The regional distribution is based on head office location not on actual location of factories.

Source: Ministry of Finance and Economy, Investment Promotion Bureau 1999.

MACROSPATIAL VISIONS OF KOREA IN A CHANGING REGIONAL GEOGRAPHY

In the aftermath of the economic crisis, the need to enhance the global competitiveness of the major city-regions in Korea became apparent. It is widely acknowledged that restructuring inefficient economic institutions—in particular, financial institutions and upgrading the industrial structure of city-regions—is essential for enhancing Korea's competitiveness. As for Korean cities, the main strategy has been to move forward to a knowledge- or information-intensive structure. Constructing a knowledge-based economy is understood to be the only way to survive in an increasingly competitive global environment in coming decades.

On the other hand, there is growing recognition that the survival of the Korean economy will depend on how it forms external linkages with other economies in Asia and the world. In this regard, it is important to identify and strengthen the comparative advantage of Korea vis-à-vis other countries, especially in relation to the two neighboring economies of Japan and China. It is widely known that Korea will be in the jaws of a nutcracker in the coming decades, squeezed between cost-competitive China and technology-competitive Japan (Booz-Allen & Hamilton 1997). It is also advised that head-on competition with these two economic giants would not be wise for Korea. Instead, it should find its own niches.

One avenue for Korea's geostrategic move can be to utilize its geoeconomic and geopolitical position in Northeast Asia (Kim 1998*a*, 1999). By taking advantage of its middle position between China and Japan economically, politically, and geographically, Korea could avoid the nutcracker predicament. To achieve this, it is necessary to transform the Korean economy from a low-cost production base to a regional platform or center for advanced manufacturing and logistics functions. Although there is no consensus yet for the long-term vision of Korea, there are three main visions of Korea in the future. The first is a regional business center for Northeast Asia. The second foresees a regional platform for a few manufacturing industries in which Korea has comparative advantage. The third is Korea as a regional logistics and information center. It is of course possible to have some combination of all three ideas.

As for the first idea, there exist doubts whether Korea (for example, the Seoul megacity-region) can compete with the existing business and financial centers of Tokyo, Hong Kong, and Singapore. In terms of current distribution of transnational business and financial functions, Seoul is not comparable to other major cities in East Asia (Kim 1999, Rimmer 1999). Seoul, however, can play a role in northeastern China as Hong Kong has done in southern China since China's reform in 1978. But as of now, China's economic growth is mainly concentrated in the south. It will take time for north China to develop. Furthermore, Seoul does not yet have the capability—such as manpower and institutions that are familiar with Chinese institutions and the Chinese language—that Hong Kong does.

With respect to the second idea of Korea as a regional manufacturing platform, this is not a bright prospect either. Korea's major exports industries—steel, automotive products, semiconductors, and consumer electronics—are facing competitive challenges from both ends—cost and knowledge (Booz-Allen & Hamilton 1997). Korea cannot compete with China and Southeast Asian countries in cost terms, whereas it is inferior to Japan, the United States, and European countries in knowledge competence. If Korea can overcome knowledge gaps[3] through educational reform internally and active networking with global corporations, it may have a chance to survive as a knowledge-based competitor in some manufacturing industries, i.e. not as a low-cost manufacturing center but as a regional manufacturing platform integrated with low-cost production bases in Northeast and Southeast Asia.

The third vision of Korea as a regional logistics and information hub in Northeast Asia is based on Korea's advantage in geoeconomic and geopolitical aspects. Geographically, Korea is located between China and Japan. Because of this geographical position, the Korean peninsula has historically played a role as a bridge between the continental cultures and economies and the marine-centered cultures and economies. But the division of the Korean peninsula and the ideological confrontation between capitalist and socialist camps has impaired this cultural and technological conduit function. Restoring this bridge role with enhanced logistics and information functions is argued to be the best feasible option for Korea (Kim 1998*a*, 1999). To realize this vision, however, the Korean peninsula must be reunited or at least functionally integrated. Given the uncertainties surrounding the Korean peninsula, the idea of a logistics and information hub remains a long-term vision.

Economically and politically, Korea is certainly not a major power like China and Japan. It is a middle power country in Northeast Asia (even a unified Korea would not be comparable to China or Japan). This fact, in turn, provides Korea with greater latitude in international relations than China and Japan. As Scalapino (1998) pointed out, Korea can make a significant contribution to regional cooperation in Northeast Asia if it plays a role of mediator. In economic terms, Korea can also play a role of intermediary between Japan's advanced and yet expensive technology and China's lagging technology in the civilian sectors.

In conclusion, it is possible for Korea to pursue the vision of a high value-added regional manufacturing platform combined with regional logistics and information hub functions. What this national vision implies for city-regions is, first of all, to strengthen networking with other city-regions in East Asia and the world. Second, it points toward enhancing the knowledge base of the local economy with cross-cultural skills, especially in the services sector such as accounting, law, advertising and marketing, financing, information services, transportation and logistics, management consultancy, and art and cultural services. Third, the vision implies a need to develop the transportation and information infrastructures in line with Korea's bridge role in Northeast Asia.

URBAN AND REGIONAL ISSUES

As economic competitiveness becomes a key focus for the economies affected by the crisis, earlier concerns with balanced development and social welfare seem to have been either pushed aside or postponed. Short-term responses to the crisis were mainly focused on economic recovery. Markets instead of government or planning were declared to be the guiding mechanism for the Korean economy. But these so-called market-conforming policies seem to aggravate social and spatial polarization. Although liberalization policies including foreign direct investment are adopted to enhance competitiveness, there is no guarantee that they necessarily strengthen long-term competitiveness of the Korean economy. On the other hand, long-term strategies of making Korea a regional manufacturing platform and logistics center need to be refined further in order to achieve intended results since they involve intercity relations across the national border. Three main issues are discussed here for repositioning Korean cities in the twenty-first century.

Economic Competitiveness and Sustainable Local Development

Competitiveness is usually defined at the level of the firm or industry. For example, the semiconductor industry in Korea is known to be competitive worldwide. When competitiveness is discussed at the city and country level, it incorporates many more factors than just product competitiveness. The competitiveness of a city depends on a whole series of factors, including its process of governance, the social and economic infrastructure, the quality of its human capital, the quality of its natural environment, its business environment, and the capacity of local institutions (Friedmann 1998, Kim 1997).

Even though industrial competitiveness, which often arises from the cluster of competent firms in related industries, provides an important source of the city's and the country's competitive advantage (Porter 1990), it should not be equated with the competitiveness of a city or a region. Firm or industry competitiveness may not last forever since a firm or industry has a life cycle (Norton 1992). If new ideas and innovations are not created within a firm or industry, its competitiveness may eventually disappear. The key factor in affecting the rise and fall of industry clusters and eventually of local economies lies in local adaptability or local economic resilience (Douglass 1999). Local adaptability involves collective responses to external changes, in particular, to high global turbulence. It requires local leadership to create common goals and a shared vision among managers, workers, citizens, and politicians within the city. Ultimately, local culture including norms and values provide a source of institutional creativity (Kim 1997).

As Friedmann (2000) proposes, competitiveness should not be interpreted as simply as the production of more outputs and trade surpluses. Hosting foreign direct investment may boost local production but may drain the region's precious assets rather than add to them if it is not tied up with local competitive advantage. The example of Pusan illustrates the unfortunate cycle of asset degradation. Here a succession of declining industries (plywood, apparel, and shoes) in the regional economy pushed out local talent and weakened industrial capacity. Moreover, the steady deterioration of the city's waterfront occurred as commercial interests were left to govern land development in the local area. Hence, identifying local competitive advantage is the first task for cities and regions in a globalized environment. Finding strategies to enhance economic competitiveness without asset degradation is the next step for sustainable local development.

Balanced and Resilient Regional Development

Balanced regional development has been the national goal for the past three decades. As the survival of the national economy is at stake, balanced regional development appears to be a difficult goal to maintain. Riding the wave of deregulation and liberalization, promarket forces are gaining weight in urban and regional economies. For example, the Korean Chamber of Commerce and Industry together with liberal economists advocate the deregulation of what they consider unnecessary government intervention in the urban land market, especially in the capital region. They believe that the capital region is the only region in Korea that is able to compete with other major city-regions in the world. Impairing its competitiveness through excessive regulations and restrictions is said to be detrimental to the stable growth of the Korean economy (Korean Chamber of Commerce and Industry 1997, Lee 1998).

It is proposed that more advanced service functions, high-technology industries, universities and research institutions, and other international functions are needed in the capital region to enhance its competitiveness (Lee 1998). Large office buildings that can accommodate multinational corporations' regional headquarters should be allowed to be built without penalty. Restrictions on factory construction within the capital region are no longer needed, because these restrictions drive firms out of the country to seek low-cost production sites. Moreover, as revealed in the locational preference of foreign-invested firms, the capital region is a preferred place of foreign direct investment. If they are discouraged by regulations, foreign investors will go to other Asian countries, which offer better and more incentives (Park 1999).

Local governments within the capital region endorse the above line of argument. The provincial government of Kyonggi proposed to amend the regulations governing the capital region. In contrast, however, the leaders of provinces just outside the capital region—Chungchong, Cholla, and Kangwon—strongly protested the idea of relaxing restrictions. They are concerned with the prospect that deregulation would bring another round of concentration of investment in the capital region, while leaving nothing much for the relatively poor, less industrialized provinces. Considering the limited effects of the containment policy, the government faces a dilemma of balancing regional development and national economic growth. This seeming trade-off relationship between regionally balanced development and national economic growth, however, may be resolved if we take a longer-term perspective.

Since the national economy is composed of regions, the diversity in regional industrial structures and cultures provides vitality in the national economy (Norton 1992). Therefore, it is necessary to promote region-specific development strategies instead of a uniform regional policy across the nation.[4] A more locally oriented, endogenous approach is required to enhance local capacities to manage the regional economy (Douglass 1999). An endogenous approach, however, should not mean regional development independent of other regions within and outside the country. City and provincial governments should try to avoid excessive interregional rivalry by seeking interregional cooperation. In this regard, the central government can certainly help city and provincial governments in two respects: first, in resolving potential conflicts between regions by taking a mediator's role and second, in raising the local capacity by offering more fiscal and planning power and skills to city and provincial governments.

Transborder Intercity Cooperation

After the crisis, intercity competition to attract mobile global capital has intensified. Cities in East Asia are bidding against each other by offering higher subsidies or greater tax relief to host transnational firms. Moreover, many cities are competing to move upward in a perceived global hierarchy of cities (Douglass 1998). Governments are thus directing much of their attention and resources to building new assets such as international airports, ports, high-technology parks, and information networks. As discussed earlier, Korea is planning to become a trade and distribution hub for Northeast Asia. But competition to become the regional hub in air and maritime transport is stiff in East Asia. For example, Narita airport in Tokyo, a new Kansai international airport in Osaka, Chek Lap Kok in Hong Kong, and Shanghai's new airport are contending for a superhub position. Korea's aim to become a regional hub for marine transportation will not be easy to achieve either because of competition from Kobe, Kaohsiung, and Shanghai.

Creating new assets alone is not enough to move up the global hierarchy of cities. Re-positioning a city-region in a global network of city-regions requires intercity cooperation strategies. Theoretically, intercity cooperation is premised upon a transaction costs argument and partly upon economies of scale and scope. A region can benefit much more by cooperating with other regions since it cannot be competent in all functions—trade, production, research and development, finance, and management. The principal rationale derives from the theory of the firm, in which multiple firms form an alliance for the purpose of sharing different core assets owned by each firm (Chandler 1990). This logic of cooperation can be applied to regions and nations (Dunning 1998). Through intercity cooperation, redundant investments in the same industry and infrastructure can be saved. Furthermore, intercity cooperation can have a high payoff in terms of sharing best practices of urban management and creating opportunities for a collaborative approach to common problems.

Fortunately, Korea is in a strategic location to promote intercity cooperation. Across the Yellow Sea, Korea can establish intercity networks with China's growing coastal regions. It is also possible to form intercity networks along the rim of East Sea (Japan Sea) with Japan, Russia, and with China's northeastern provinces. The Yellow Sea subregion, which encompasses the Bohai Gulf Zone —one of the three most promising economic zones of China—and the Seoul megacity-region, has great potential for transborder intercity cooperation. Indeed, there has been some intercity network formation in the subregion through sister-city or sister-province relationships, trade, and investment. Currently, the cities along the Yellow Sea rim are linked by air and sea connections. Although the 1997 crisis has dampened somewhat Korean investment in Shandong and other provinces in the subregion, cross-investment is likely to increase across the Yellow Sea in coming years (Kim 1998*b*).

With a combined population of more than 100 million, the subregion provides opportunities for intercity cooperation in the areas of industry, environment, and transportation among others. Intercity and interstate cooperation are essential to combat increasing regionwide air pollution, acid rain problems, and ocean pollution, and to promote sustainable fishery development in the Yellow Sea; and to tackle industrial pollution and municipal waste problems in heavily industrialized cities along the Yellow Sea rim. In particular, Korean firms can extend their network of production into the cities of the Yellow Sea subregion. The new international airport, which will open in 2001, and the ports of Pusan and Kwangyang, depend on transfer cargo and passengers departing from and arriving at the ports in the northern part of China (Kim 1998*b*).

In the East Sea subregion, cities and provinces have more or less a common problem of underdevelopment. The western provinces of Japan are lagging behind the provinces located along the Pacific belt. The Russian Far East, once subsidized by the central government of the USSR for security purposes, is suffering from its remoteness from Moscow and underdevelopment. Korea's East Coast has the problem of underdevelopment as well. Thus, intercity cooperation in the East Sea subregion has a special meaning for Northeast Asia, namely the development of a lagging region. The region has also a common purpose of fighting against nuclear dumping in the East Sea and of utilizing natural resources and tourist opportunities with which the subregion is endowed.

CONCLUDING COMMENTS

I have examined major spatial impacts of the economic crisis in Korea and Northeast Asia. Some of the policy responses for both short-term crisis management and long-term development were discussed with a specific focus on cities and regions. With the crisis and the globalization trend in general, however, three urban and regional issues are emerging. They are economic competitiveness and sustainable development, balanced and resilient regional development, and transborder intercity cooperation. The first two issues are not new, but the economic crisis and the neoliberal strategies taken by the Korean government in turn accentuate them. The third issue has arisen in the current round of globalization and is closely related with a new round of intercity competition triggered by the Asian economic crisis.

Given that large city-regions are the major engines of the national and global economy, managing city-regions effectively and efficiently is widely acknowledged to be critical for the future of cities and nations. With the progress of globalization and local autonomy in many Asian countries, including Korea, the monopoly of the state in territorial management is no longer possible and hence the state-centered structure of governance is being challenged. Alternative forms of governance are yet to develop. Given the history of a highly centralized political system in Korea and other Asian countries, a radical departure from the centralized model of governance of the past may not be feasible in the near future. Instead, a compromise model, which combines some elements of both a hierarchical and a horizontal approach would be realistic. As for large city-regions like the Seoul megacity-region, an association of local governments coordinated by the central government is feasible. This lies between the inter-municipality governance model and the supramunicipality governance model. As a matter of fact, there are signs that such a mixed form of governance is in formation in Korea.[5] As scholars concerned with Asian urban issues have proposed (Douglass, Jones, and Kim 1998), collaborative forms of governance are the keys for managing large city-regions in Korea and other Asian countries. A collaborative model of governance, which is based on principles of citizen participation, self-governance, and intergovernmental cooperation, will increase the chance of solving problems of social and spatial polarization, interregional rivalry and competition, and environmental degradation.

With respect to transborder intercity cooperation, the above line of reasoning can be equally well applied. Regional development should not be focused exclusively on the interests of a single region. Through intercity cooperation, more benefits can be obtained. Each city-region has to consider ways and means of creating joint competitive advantages through collaboration and alliances. Korean cities in this regard are better situated than other Asian cities. How to utilize this window of opportunity depends on local capacities of city-regions. This may, in turn, call for a redesign of local governance so as to develop more effective agencies to handle international linkages. The central state can help local governments in strengthening local capacities to deal with international problems arising from transborder interactions. This enhanced domestic and international coordination will certainly reduce unnecessary competition and facilitate cooperation between cities and regions across the border. Locally driven exchanges and cooperation, if facilitated by national governments, will contribute to building regional identity and community, the lack of which is apparent in Northeast Asia.

NOTES

1. According to Quigley (1999), a financial crisis can happen under the following conditions in the real estate market: when firms have incentives to increase leverage and to borrow against the book value of assets for business expansion, when foreign entities find it difficult to enter the market (for example, Korea until June 1998), when property appraisals tend to be inflated for reciprocal benefits between banks and firms, and when developers seek loans to fuel the general expansion of the economy. The crisis can occur without any macroeconomic or balance of payments problems.
2. Another purpose was to save the construction industry, which was hardest hit by the crisis, and thereby to help absorb unemployed labor.
3. Korea needs to fill in the knowledge gaps, especially in product development, design, marketing, financing, and human resource management.
4. The central government in the third quarter of 1999 announced a new policy to promote the development of regions other than the capital region (*Chosunilbo* 24 August 1999). This policy includes more incentives to firms moving out of the capital region. The difference from the past policy is granting urban development rights to the firms, which are relocating their headquarters. There is doubt whether these strengthened incentives may contribute much to building resilient and diversified regional economies.
5. The mayors of cities in the Seoul region and the governor have become sitting members of the capital regional management review committee. They are also engaging in negotiation processes of specific sectoral issues such as water supply and transportation, with the participation of the central government agencies as a mediator and coordinator.

REFERENCES

Bank of Korea (1999). "Major Economic Indicators." http:/www.bok.or.kr/kb/princip-l/pei9.html.

Bark, S. I. (1999). "The Social Impact of Mass Unemployment in Korea." Paper presented at the Conference on Mass Unemployment and Policy Responses, 13 March, Seoul, Korea (in Korean).

Booz-Allen & Hamilton (1997). *Revitalizing the Korean Economy Toward the 21st Century*. Seoul, Korea.

Chandler, A. D., Jr. (1990). *Scale and Scope: The Dynamics of Industrial Capitalism*. Cambridge, Mass.: Harvard University Press.

Cho, M. R. (1999). "The Urbanization of the IMF Crisis in Korea." Paper presented at the Sixteenth Pacific Regional Science Conference, 12–16 July, Seoul, Korea.

Douglass, M. (1998). "Urban and Regional Policy after the Era of Naïve Globalism." Paper presented at the Global Forum on Regional Development Policy, 1–4 December, Nagoya, Japan.

—— (1999). "Problems and Policies in the Urban Regions of Northeast Asia." Paper presented at the Sixteenth Pacific Regional Science Conference, 12–16 July, Seoul, Korea.

—— Jones, G., and Kim, W. B. (1998). "Collaborative Governance for Mega-Urban Regions in Pacific Asia." Paper presented at the Expert Workshop on the Governance of Mega-Urban Regions in Pacific Asia, Bellagio, Italy.

Dunning, J. H. (1998). "Globalization, Technological Change, and the Spatial Organization of Economic Activity," in A. D. Chandler, Jr., P. Hagstrom, and O. Solvell (eds.), *The Dynamic Firm: The Role of Technology, Organization, and Regions.* Oxford: Oxford University Press, 289–314.

The Economist (1999*a*). "Asian Property: Sad Storeys." 13 March: 94, 97.

—— (1999*b*). "Asia's Hubs: Last Man Standing." 3 April: 59–60.

Friedmann, J. (1998). "Rethinking Urban Competition and Sustainability in East Asia." *International Journal of Urban Sciences*, 2: 1–11.

—— (2000). "Intercity Networks in a Globalizing Era." Chapter 8, this volume.

Ha, S. K. (1998). "The Status of Homeless in the IMF Era and Policy Responses." *Korean Social Policy Review*, 5: 194–220 (in Korean).

Hankukilbo 30 July 1999.

Hankukkyongje 14 December 1998.

Housing and Commercial Bank (1999). "Housing Price Index." http://www.hcb.co.kr/bankkor/html/inform/price/9907_a01.html.

IMD (International Institute for Management Development) (1999). "The World Competitiveness Scoreboard." http:/www.imd.ch/wcy/factors/overall.html.

JETRO (Japan External Trade Promotion Organization) Censor (1998*a*) *The Fifth Comparison of Investment Costs in Major Cities and Regions in Asia.* Tokyo: Japan.

—— (1998*b*). *The Sixth Comparison of Investment Costs in Major Cities and Regions in Asia.* Tokyo: Japan.

—— (1999). *Trends in Global Foreign Direct Investment.* http://www.jetro.go.jp/whitepaper/invest99/inv1–1.html.

Kim, W. B. (1997). *Strategies for Enhancing Local Competitiveness of Large Cities.* Anyang, Korea: Korea Research Institute for Human Settlements (in Korean).

—— (1998*a*). "Restructuring Design for the Korean Peninsula in a New Regional Economic Order of Northeast Asia," in W. B. Kim (ed.), *Restructuring the Korean Peninsula for the 21st Century.* Korea Research Institute for Human Settlements and the East-West Center. Anyang: Korea, 43–84.

—— (1998*b*). *Prospects for Sino-Korean Economic Cooperation and Collaborative Development of the Coastal Areas of Shandong and West Korea.* Anyang, Korea: KRIHS (Korea Research Institute for Human Settlements) (in Korean).

—— (1999). "National Competitiveness and Governance of the Capital Region of Seoul," in J. Friedmann (ed.), *Urban and Regional Governance in the Asia-Pacific.* Vancouver: University of British Columbia Press, 33–50.

Korean Chamber of Commerce and Industry (1997). "Policy News." *Industrial Location Newsletter.* Seoul: Korea. October (in Korean).

Korea Land Corporation (1999). "Land Price Index." http://www.koland.co.kr/ldp_index/stat/1999/quarter1_1999_1.html.

Lee, B. S. (1998). "Land Use Regulations and Efficiency of Seoul's Economy." *International Journal of Urban Sciences*, 2: 48–72.

Lee, C. H. (1999). "Infrastructure Investment Plan after the Financial Crisis." *Planning and Policy*, 3: 6–21 (in Korean).

MOCT (Ministry of Construction and Transportation) (1999). "News Release." http://www.moct.go.kr/mctu/.

MOFE (Ministry of Finance and Economy) (1998). http://www.mofe.gov.kr.

MOIR (Ministry of Industry and Resources) (1999). "Foreign Direct Investment: Trend and Policy Issues." http://epic.kdi.re.kr/cgi-bin/fulltext.cgi?name=D9901076.

National Statistical Office (1999*a*). "Major Economic Indicators." http://www.nso.go.kr/majorecono/5.html.

—— (1999*b*). "1997 Gross Regional Domestic Product." http://www.nso.go.kr/report/data/sagr9700.htm.

Norton, R. D. (1992). "Agglomerations and Competitiveness: from Marshall to Chinitz." *Urban Studies*, 29: 155–70.

OECD (1998). "Open Market Matter: The Benefits of Trade and Investment Liberalization." *OECD Policy Brief*, 6.

Park, H. (1999). "Maeil Kyongje." 13 August.

Porter, M. (1990). *The Competitive Advantage of Nations.* New York: The Free Press.

Quigley, J. (1999). "Real Estate and the Asian Crisis." Paper presented at the Sixteenth Pacific Regional Science Conference, 12–16 July, Seoul, Korea.

Rimmer, P. (1999). "Flows of Goods, People, and Information between Cities in Northeast Asia." Paper presented at the Sixteenth Pacific Regional Science Conference, 12–16 July, Seoul, Korea.

Scalapino, R. (1998). "The Role of a Unified Korea in Northeast Asia," in W. B. Kim (ed.), *Restructuring the Korean Peninsula for the 21st Century.* Anyang: Korea: Korea Research Institute for Human Settlements and the East-West Center, 9–24.

PART VI

SOCIAL INEQUALITIES AND IMMIGRANT NICHES IN GLOBAL CITY-REGIONS

Some of the most strenuous debates in the social sciences in recent years have revolved around the combined effects of urbanization and globalization on patterns of social stratification.

Many theorists have claimed that large-scale metropolitan development in modern capitalism is endemically associated with a tendency for urban society to fragment into two disjoint layers, one of them represented by a top tier of high-wage professionals, managers, technicians, and so on, the other represented by a bottom tier composed of unskilled low-wage workers, with the middle ground between them steadily being vacated as traditional skilled and semiskilled blue-collar jobs disappear due to processes of technological and organizational change in modern production systems. This claim is often accompanied by a leitmotif to the effect that globalization in the specific guise of massive immigration from less developed to more developed parts of the world is virtually everywhere causing the ranks of the lower social tier to swell profusely in large city-regions. In addition, some analysts have proposed that the same process, in combination with intensifying international economic competition, is actually leading to decreasing wages and living standards of the working poor in urban areas.

There can be little question that several aspects of this story are quite accurate. Certainly, contemporary post-Fordist urban society displays greater levels of income inequality than did Fordist urban society, and the lower echelons of urban labor markets in most if not all of the world's great city-regions are increasingly occupied by immigrants from much poorer countries. However, there continues to be wide disagreement about the specific forms that social segmentation and labor-market inequalities take in large city-regions, as well as about the trajectories of these variables over time. The two chapters that make up this part of the book help significantly to clarify elements of this debate.

Fainstein analyzes income inequalities in five of the world's most important city-regions (New York, London, Tokyo, Paris, and the Randstad). She shows that inequalities are indeed increasing in these centers, but that this is largely due to rising incomes at the top rather than to falling incomes at the bottom. There is very little evidence, according to Fainstein, that the middle stratum is disappearing. Significant differences among the five city-regions can be detected in regard to levels of income inequality over the 1980s and 1990s, but these appear mainly to be due to differences in welfare regimes (rather than, say, differences in their susceptibility to global competition), with New York showing the greatest range of inequality and the Randstad the least.

Waldinger's critical review of the immigrant niche hypothesis neatly complements Fainstein's analysis of income inequalities. Waldinger, along with many other analysts, observes that particular immigrant groups often occupy distinctive occupational and sectoral niches in any given urban economy. This phenomenon is also associated with rising levels of immigrant entrepreneurialism in the same niches. Waldinger goes on to argue that the concentration of particular immigrant groups within these niches occurs not so much because of preferential hiring of coethnics on the part of immigrant entrepreneurs, but because of the existence of indurated networks through which flows of information about job openings pass by word-of-mouth within ethnic communities. The more recent the arrival of any given immigrant cohort in the host society, the more concentrated its occupation of any given employment niche tends to be. By contrast, cohorts that arrived earlier (or their descendants) tend to occupy jobs that are relatively more scattered through the economy at large. Specific immigrant niches in large city-regions are usually quite durable over time, though they are occasionally subject to sharp succession as particular migration streams dry up and as others begin to fill the void.

Notwithstanding the continuing debate about the nature and causes of social disparities in global city-regions, their existence remains a stubborn fact of daily life. Above all, the economies of virtually all major city-regions are marked, on the one hand, by high-wage industries in white-collar and advanced-technology sectors, and, on the other hand, by dense networks of sweatshops and low-wage service activities, and this situation inevitably breeds wide income inequalities. These inequalities are all the more visible and politically problematical in view of the disproportionate concentration of racial and ethnic minorities in the lower echelons of urban labor markets. Even if some individuals display significant social mobility and rapidly ascend the income ladder, these enduring contrasts in the internal structure of global city-regions are a constant source of social friction, sometimes to the point of civil disorder, particularly in periods when unemployment levels are on the rise.

15

Inequality in Global City-Regions

SUSAN S. FAINSTEIN

Within the developed countries, business and governmental leaders of large cities typically aspire to reach global-city status. Yet no convincing evidence shows that the inhabitants of global cities and their surrounding regions fare better than the residents of lesser places. Indeed "the global-city hypothesis" argues that these metropolises are especially prone to extremes of inequality (Friedmann 1986). Despite being, in aggregate, the wealthiest areas of their respective nations, global city-regions tend to have large, dense groups of very poor people, often living in close juxtaposition with concentrations of the extraordinarily wealthy. According to Sassen (1991), the particular industrial and occupational structure of global cities produces a bifurcated earnings structure that in turn creates the outcome of the "disappearing middle." This paper shows that global city-regions in wealthy countries do display high levels of income inequality (although not necessarily of class polarization) but that the explanation given by global-city theorists in terms of earnings is not wholly satisfactory. It further indicates that the five wealthy global city-regions of New York, London, Tokyo, Paris, and the Randstad (Netherlands) vary in terms of the extent of inequality. It concludes by examining the reasons for inequality in such regions and the effects of public policy on it.

THE SKEWED EARNINGS CURVE ARGUMENT

Crudely put, global-city theory makes the following argument: Global flows of capital produce similar economic structures in those few cities where the industries that control these flows have their home. Such control rests preeminently with financial institutions, business-services firms, and corporate headquarters (Friedmann 1986; Sassen 1991, 1994, 1998); thus, the mark of a global city is its disproportionate share of finance and business services and corporate headquarters. In Sassen's terms, global cities constitute "strategic sites" in which leading-edge global functions are performed. Moreover, the most significant linkages between these cities' leading industries and other economic enterprises are international rather than national. Because the sectors of the economy performing global roles dominate the economic base of the affected cities, the cities display similar labor markets. In turn, these produce similar occupational and earnings hierarchies resulting in similar social outcomes. In Sassen's view, the economic structure of the global city leads to social polarization, as the leading sectors, on the one hand, employ a group of extraordinarily high-earning individuals and, on the other, create a demand for low-paid, low-skilled service workers. Global-city theory implies that such cities will have similar social characteristics, despite differing culture, history, governmental institutions, or public policy. This outcome is not just the product of a globalized world in which all cities increasingly look alike, but rather of ineluctable economic forces that impose a particular economic and social structure on these nodal sites.[1]

THE EMPIRICAL EVIDENCE

Analysis of the social structures of the global city-regions of New York, London, Tokyo, Paris, and the Randstad supports an argument of increasing inequality, but it is much more ambiguous on the issues of the declining middle and of growth at the bottom.[2] Global-city theory, as noted above, predicts that the income distribution in global cities will become increasingly polarized—i.e. not only will the relative shares of total income attained by different strata of the population shift, but the numbers of people at the top and bottom will increase relative to the modal point in the income distribution curve. Testing this hypothesis, however, is a complicated proposition. First, there is the question of what to measure: earnings, income (of individuals, families, or households), occupation. Global-city theory is based on an argument concerning earnings—that the types of industries which cluster in global cities disproportionately hire high- and low-wage workers. But much of the evidence that has been used to support it consists of household income data rather than earnings data. Second, measures of income distribution only take into account income that is realized in any particular year as a result of earnings, transfers, dividends, and interest. Thus, unrealized capital gains are not included, even though in the last twenty years a small group of people has become enormously richer as a consequence of soaring growth in equity markets. The fact that these gains have not been cashed out does not prevent them from being used as collateral for loans or differentiate them from earnings that have been used to buy equities.

What is clear is that incomes within the five city-regions are becoming more unequal as the upper strata receive an increasingly large share of earnings.[3] In all five regions most of the cause of growing inequality is very large increases in both individual earnings and household incomes at the top (if unrealized capital gains were included, the skew would be even greater). To put this another way, only a small proportion of households is profiting very much from the growth in aggregate income that has occurred in these regions over the last twenty years. The argument of the disappearing middle does not seem to hold up except in the sense that the shares of all income quintiles are declining relative to the top. In New York, Tokyo, and the Randstad, where there has been a steady outmigration of middle-class families to the suburbs, this statement applies more to the metropolitan region as a whole than to the central cities.[4]

Table 15.1. *Income distribution, New York City and the Randstad*[a]

	1979	1981	1997	
	New York[b] %	Randstad %	New York[b] %	Randstad %
Share of bottom 20%	4.9	7.0	2.3	6.2
Share of middle 60%	50.5	55.6	41.6	54.6
Share of top 20%	44.6	37.4	56.1	39.2

Notes:

[a] Figures for New York are families with children; for the Randstad, households

[b] Data are combined for three-year periods, 1977–79 and 1995–97.

Sources: Fiscal Policy Institute 1999 and data supplied by the Netherlands Central Bureau of Statistics, Division of Social-Economic Statistics.

Although inequality increased in all five global city-regions, the extent of the increase, and especially the situation of those at the bottom, varies. The contrast is most marked between New York City and the Randstad. As Table 15.1 shows, in both cases the relative share of the bottom diminished during the last two decades, while the proportion of income captured by the top quintile grew. In New York, however, the bottom quintile lost more than half its share, and the top 20 percent gained 25 percent; the comparable figures for the Randstad were about a 10 percent loss for the bottom and approximately 5 percent gain for the top. Moreover, the 1997 share of the Randstad's bottom quintile is 2.7 times that of New York City's.

A brief individual look at each city-region permits a better picture of their social structure.

THE CITY-REGIONS

New York

Characterizations of the income structure of New York depend on which years one chooses to analyze. During the 1980s the trend of declining median income that had characterized the previous decade in the city was reversed. According to Mollenkopf (1997), real median household income grew more than 28 percent compared to a national rate of 6.5 percent. The total real income of the bottom decile fell, but all other deciles gained, with the gains increasing as one went up the income scale. The principal reason for income gains was the upward movement of earnings in different economic sectors: health, education, and social service employment produced improved incomes in the middle ranks, while finance and business service earnings pushed up the top. Only the bottom decile had no increase in labor force participation. Most importantly the bottom suffered from a decline in the real value of retirement benefits and welfare payments. Thus, loss of income at the bottom resulted from social exclusion and the retrenchment of the welfare state, not globalization and downgraded jobs.

A more recent study of the New York region (New York City Council 1997: 47–48) shows general improvement during the 1980s but reversal in the 1990s. In the period 1977 through 1989, poor households increased in number due to overall population growth, but they decreased as a proportion of total households. At the same time upper income households increased numerically as well as in the relative share of total income they received. The size of the middle class, defined in relation to a middle-class standard of living, also increased. Between 1989 and 1996, however, a period of sharp recession and slow recovery, almost all gains went to the upper income group, resulting in an aggravation of regional inequality and a hollowing out of the middle, especially in the city (New York City Council 1997: 13–14). Manhattan, nevertheless, retained a dominant position within the region—income losses in New York City were almost entirely in the four outer boroughs of Queens, the Bronx, Brooklyn, and Staten Island (Hughes and Seneca 1993: 21). The result was that, in 1977, 41 percent of the city's population was classified as middle or upper class (based on standard of living); 48 percent were at this level in 1989; and in 1996 the figures had sunk back to the total of 1977 (but with a larger proportion classified as upper class).[5] The explanation for this finding was the failure of the city to regain all the jobs it had lost during the recession. Since 1996, however, the regional labor market has improved substantially as both employment and wages have increased; improvement was especially sharp during 1998 (*Crain's New York Business*, 5–11 July 1999: 12). By 1999 all lost jobs had been regained, and unlike in the earlier period the city shared equally with its suburban areas in job growth (Port Authority 1999: 2). It is therefore likely that the situation of those at the bottom has improved in the last year, although income data are not yet available to allow a firm conclusion.

London

The massive increase in income inequality that occurred in London during the period 1979–93 resulted almost wholly from increases in earnings at the top rather than loss at the bottom of the income distribution. Within London the share of the top income decile increased from 26 percent to 33 percent, as compared to Great Britain as a whole, where the shift was from 25 percent to 31 percent. Hamnett (1997) argues that even while the very top was increasing its share, there was an upward socioeconomic shift whereby the number and proportion of professional, managerial, and technical workers have been increasing, while the number and proportion of manual workers have been falling dramatically. Even within the service sector there has been a decline in clerical and blue-collar occupations, contravening the argument that globalization increases the demand for unskilled service workers. Hamnett finds that between 1979 and 1993 the number of people with a high standard of living (i.e. earning an amount that would have put them in the top 25 percent of earners in 1979, adjusted for inflation) had increased by fifteen times. Moreover, this growth was substantially greater for London than for Britain as a whole. Hamnett finds more evidence for polarization when examining household income rather than earnings, as a consequence of including the unemployed and of looking at households rather than individuals.[6] He therefore concludes, as did Mollenkopf for New York, that the cause of increased poverty at the bottom is exclusion from the labor force not globalization.

Tokyo

Central Tokyo displays strong evidence of polarization, although the Tokyo region does not show the same trend. Within central Tokyo there has been growth in both the top and bottom occupations within fast-growing industries; at the same time middle-level clerical and manufacturing jobs are disappearing. Thus, according to Sonobe and Machimura (1997), social polarization is more significant than professionalization in describing socioeconomic changes in the last decade. Nevertheless, overall income distribution remains less skewed in central Tokyo than in the core areas of the New York, London, or Paris regions.

Sonobe and Machimura relate trends in earnings and income distributions to the effect of the 1986–91 bubble economy. During that period income inequality grew both inside Tokyo and between Tokyo and the rest of the nation; after the bubble burst, the reverse occurred as a result of losses at the top. Occupational polarization, however, has continued in the aftermath of the period of excessive speculation. Foreign workers who immigrated during the expansionary time remain in menial jobs within the service sector, and homelessness has emerged.

Paris

Paris has also seen occupational restructuring but in ways somewhat different from that experienced in New York, Tokyo, and London. As elsewhere there has been a decline in the stable working class as a result of economic restructuring but not directly as a consequence of globalization. Earnings have increased for all but the lowest decile of households, with the strongest growth at the top; again, as in the other cities, the household income distribution, which includes the unemployed, is more unequal than the earnings distribution. Although some industries associated with globalization have increased their size, as in Tokyo upper-level occupations have not expanded. Thus, Preteceille (1997) does not find in Paris the professionalization of the workforce that Hamnett discovered in London. Preteceille finds that the most important reason for income growth at the top results from the return on assets. Nevertheless, the range of salary inequality has also increased; the lowest level has received a decreasing share but stable wages, while the top has made disproportionate gains. Unexpectedly, within the context of both globalization and regulation theory, the size of the public sector has increased. There has been a limited but noticeable enlargement of intermediate groups and increased stability of their share. Opposite to the other four regions, salary inequality has increased more quickly outside the core area of the Ile-de-France than within it.

The Randstad

The Randstad, a conurbation of nearly seven million people that includes the cities of Amsterdam, Rotterdam, the Hague, and Utrecht and their surrounding suburbs, is smaller than the other global city-regions discussed here, lacks a primate city, and is not a major site for headquarters of multinational firms. It is less dependent on finance than the others, although like them it has a large and rapidly growing business services sector. Its significance as a global center depends on its key role as a transit point; the port of Rotterdam and Amsterdam's Schiphol Airport are the biggest transshipping points in continental Europe, and they have spawned a huge, trade-dependent commercial sector.[7] The Randstad is included in this analysis because it points to the importance of policy mediation in affecting social outcomes, thereby making problematic the determinism of global-city theory. It contrasts with the other four regions by being more planned, more environmentally sensitive, and more egalitarian (Table 15.1). Moreover, in the words of *The Economist* (1995: 43), it "combine[s] Germanic efficiency with creative individualism." The Randstad is thus of particular interest because it points to the extent to which national governmental policy can counter global economic imperatives.[8]

Like the other global city-regions, the Randstad endured severe loss of manufacturing jobs and above-average growth in producers services during the 1970s and 1980s (Atzema and Smidt 1992). Changes in the workforce paralleled the London pattern, with a trend toward increasing professionalization during the 1980s. Within both service and manufacturing industries, the categories of technical and executive personnel grew rapidly, while unskilled work diminished. Atzema and Smidt argue that economic restructuring proceeded more smoothly in the Randstad than in U.S. and British cities, without causing such enormous losses of jobs and income as occurred in those places; nevertheless, a 14 percent average level of unemployment within the big Dutch cities during the 1980s pointed to considerable economic hardship.

The central Dutch state provides a high level of support for the poor of the Netherlands, who are primarily clustered in the Randstad's four cities. According to Kloosterman and Lambooy (1992: 127), "the Netherlands has developed a unique model: a high degree of centralization of tax collection and social contributions combined with a high degree of decentralization of expenditure on welfare." High direct subsidy to individuals combines with large governmental supply side subventions to support the provision of housing, transport, medical services, and education. Consequently the cost of living for those on low incomes is substantially less than is the case in other countries, a fact that is not revealed by income distribution data. Moreover, the overall Dutch unemployment rate, which exceeded 10 percent at the time Atzema and Smidt performed their analysis, dropped to 5 percent in 1998 (*Statistics Netherlands* 1999). We can therefore expect that the duality of the Randstad's urban centers, resulting mainly from unemployment rather than low wages, has substantially diminished.

COMMON PATTERNS, DISSIMILARITIES, AND CAUSAL FACTORS

The five regions are most alike in containing a very wealthy segment of their nations' population and supporting the economic and cultural institutions that sustain this group. Their economic bases are similar but by no means identical, and the similarities are only partly a consequence of globalization. New York and London have the strongest resemblance to each other of the five in economic structure, but they differ in social composition, with New York having a population with much larger racial and ethnic minorities and London having seen a greater professionalization of its labor force. At the end of the decade, Tokyo and Paris seemed to be diverging from the trajectory of the other three regions, largely as a result of changes in the economic position of their respective nation-states, which are themselves the consequence of both global and internal factors. Japan continued to be in recession, and France has had only a limited recovery from the recession of the early 1990s—Japan had rising unemployment and sluggish growth, while France had failed to diminish high unemployment despite positive economic growth. In contrast, the United States, the United Kingdom, and the Netherlands were all sustaining both robust rates of economic growth and diminishing unemployment. All five regions had seen increasing income inequality, but polarization was not the most accurate description of this phenomenon in that, as a term, it failed to capture the improving position of the largest proportion of the middle mass.

Global-city theory associates the widening gap between the (shrinking) middle and the (growing) bottom of the income distribution with the demand by upper-income people for the services of casual, very poorly paid workers and the resurgence of sweatshop manufacturing using immigrant labor. The studies referred to here, however, do not support this argument but rather show that exclusion from the labor force is the principal cause of poverty, rather than a large increase in the number of working poor. Moreover, the severity of poverty is largely a consequence of public policy. As is reflected in Table 15.1, the least support for the indigent is in New York and the most in the Randstad. The growth in income of high-end households, as well as arising from individual earnings and equity market gains, reflects the presence of women in the upper reaches of the workforce, making possible the existence of families or housemates with two high-earning individuals. Couples where one partner is an investment banker and another a corporate lawyer bring in a total income double that which once supported a well-to-do family dependent on a male breadwinner.

If labor force exclusion is the principal impetus causing downward pressure on incomes, and returns from financial markets a main cause of growth in wealth, then we can expect income distribution to respond to cyclical economic changes. This makes comparisons of the regions quite difficult if their business cycles are not synchronous. During the 1980s boom it appeared as if there was a single business cycle that operated in all these regions simultaneously, but in the 1990s their courses have diverged. The studies that focused on global cities during the 1980s boom found increasing inequality in all of them and concluded that trends in income distribution were common to all global cities. More refined analysis, however, shows a number of cross-cutting forces that make generalizations about social outcomes extremely complicated.

First, the particular sectoral composition of the region affects its response to economic forces. During the 1970s and 1980s, workers in American and European cities suffered severely from loss of jobs in manufacturing while Japanese workers did not. In the 1990s, the New York, London, and Randstad regions, which had already lost a substantial proportion of their manufacturing jobs, were fairly immune to downturns in the production of manufactured goods. In contrast, Tokyo and, to a lesser extent, Paris, which had until recently remained major manufacturing centers, continued to be particularly susceptible. Second, geographic location matters. The New York region is currently benefiting from its location within the expanding American market, while the Tokyo region is suffering from being within the Asian Pacific zone, still emerging from the sharp recession of the last several years. Third, governmental policy considerably affects the situation of people in the bottom deciles of the income curve.

GLOBALIZATION AND GOVERNMENTAL POLICY

Global-city theory considers governmental policy as a response to global economic pressures. In this light, the increasing deregulation of financial markets and privatization of industry that occurred in the five regions can be viewed as the consequence of global forces. And, in turn, that deregulation and marketization have stimulated the growth of the financial services and international-trade-related sectors that are the leading edge of the economies of the global cities. Deregulation of labor markets can similarly be viewed as a response to international pressure (and also to ideology spread through international channels). The effects of these moves toward freer markets on income distribution and job security can therefore be attributed to globalization. But we also see that the extent of national state withdrawal from intervention in the economy varies among the five regions with differing consequences for industrial structure, labor markets, and income and earnings distributions. Furthermore, there is a question of the direction of causality. Does (national) governmental policy create the conditions for the development of global cities? Or do global forces cause governments to act as they do? And, is the growth initially stimulated by deregulation primarily speculative and part of a longer term destabilization that will ultimately result in increased economic volatility and insecurity? The great dependence of global city-regions on international financial flows makes them particularly susceptible to fluctuations in the increasingly volatile global financial system.[9]

The policies that matter the most for the economic situation of global-city residents are made by their national governments and have to do with securities regulation, interest rate levels, and labor-market restrictions. The greater income equality of Tokyo and the Randstad and the better situation of groups at the bottom in Paris than in New York or London indicate that ideology and governmental policy mediate tendencies toward the worsening of poverty. Nevertheless, policymakers within the five regions have deliberately embarked on courses that have been given the name "global-cities strategy." By this is meant subsidies and loosened land-use regulation to encourage office development and intensive place marketing to international business, especially financial and producers services firms.

Is there a usefulness in adopting such a program? Tokyo has lately retreated from its global-cities strategy and its government is now emphasizing quality of life. Policymakers in the other regions, however, continue to emphasize global-city functions. London and Paris have mounted a number of projects aimed at increasing their cultural prominence and improving infrastructure for the conduct of business. New York during the 1980s was strongly committed to development projects that enhanced the role of finance and business services in the city's economy, while in the 1990s the main emphasis has switched to tourism and entertainment. In the Randstad considerable rhetoric has emphasized the global-city ideal, and massive infrastructure investment has aimed at improving the area's importance in international shipping and communication.[10]

Emphasis on global-city status means a reinforcement of the tendencies toward dependence on international finance rather than an attempt to counterbalance them. To the extent that being a global city results in increased instability and income inequality, a global-cities strategy may worsen conditions for those worst off, although, as is discussed below, globalization is a less important factor than some others for this sector of the population. As the Paris and Randstad cases show, however, a global-city strategy can be combined with a redistributional one. Moreover, even in New York and London, where inequality has increased substantially, global-city strategy contributed to rising incomes for most of the population, thereby benefiting far more people than just the very highest earners, even though the latter group gained the most.

The four-region comparison of New York, London, Tokyo, and Paris found that the first two of these regions saw a considerably greater increase in inequality and worsening of the situation of those at the bottom than in the latter two. Adding the Randstad to the analysis reveals even greater variation. Despite the small size of the Dutch state, it demonstrates the possibility of overcoming global ideological pressures in favor of the dismantling of the welfare state. During the nineties the Dutch have managed simultaneously to stimulate economic growth, reduce unemployment, protect sectors of the economy from full-scale marketization, and maintain the standard of living of those at the bottom through welfare state policies (Terhorst and van der Ven 1998, Fainstein 1997).

IMMIGRATION, RACE, AND ETHNICITY

In all five regions there is a correlation between low income and membership in marginal ethnic or racial groups. One aspect of the global character of these regions is that, to a considerably greater extent than other parts of their nations,[11] they have been a destination for immigrants. Nevertheless, there is not a simple relationship between the existence of large foreign-born populations and inequality. The five regions differ considerably in their level of racial/ethnic difference, the amount of immigration they have sustained, the length of time that foreign-born residents have resided within them, and the ability of immigrant groups to improve their economic situation. New York has received by far the largest number of immigrants both absolutely and proportionally of the five regions, and it continues to be a major recipient. On the whole, foreign-born residents who have lived in the region have done quite well (Waldinger 1996). In New York race is highly correlated with income, yet within the black population West Indian immigrants fare better than African Americans. In London and the Randstad ethnicity is strongly associated with low income, with East Indians in London and Turks and Moroccans in the Randstad being relatively poorly educated and having a high unemployment rate (although immigrants from the former Dutch colonies of Indonesia and Surinam, with greater facility in Dutch and higher educational levels, have fared better). In Paris changes in income distribution are not attributable to immigration. The rate of immigration has remained more or less stable, with the total foreign-born population increasing by 11 percent from 1982 to 1990, a rate that has changed little in the past several decades (Preteceille 1997). On the whole, immigrants to France have not retained their ethnic identity as strongly as their American counterparts, although this is perhaps changing. There has, however, been an increase in the level of ethnic spatial segregation. Although the Tokyo metropolitan area had a rise in immigration during the 1980s, its level of immigration has always been quite low in comparison to the other four regions. Its current economic troubles have discouraged increases in immigration, and foreigners living in Japan have been the group most severely affected by rising unemployment.

LINKAGES BETWEEN GLOBAL CITY-REGION STATUS AND INEQUALITY

There do appear to be some significant links between global-city status and inequality. First, as described above, global city-regions encompass particularly high-earning individuals resulting in an upward skew in the income distribution curve. The second correlation is a spatial one: the high cost of living in the core areas of these global-city-regions either forces low-income people into unaffordable housing at the center or pushes them, along with industries not associated with the global economy, to the periphery. (The Randstad is largely an exception, as generous rent subsidies and a large stock of social housing have mainly stabilized central city housing occupancy, despite some gentrification.) To the extent that they contribute to a spatial mismatch that reinforces labor-market exclusion, global-city characteristics may then be an indirect cause of income inequality. Third, those global cities whose fortunes are particularly tied to financial markets are supersensitive to swings in those markets, with the consequence of serious instability in the livelihoods of their residents. Although globalization is not the direct cause of polarization in Tokyo, its connection to the speculative frenzy of the 1980s and subsequent bursting of the bubble makes it an indirect determinant. The well-to-do, of course, are also vulnerable to loss of jobs and income, but their superior asset position and educational credentials insulate them from the extreme insecurity that affects the bottom strata; consequently their long-term prospects of emerging from the downswing relatively intact are much higher.

The nation-state continues to matter. Peter Taylor (1995), expressing a view popular among global-city theorists, asserts that "cities are replacing states in the construction of social identities. Hence, alongside the erosion of national economy we can glimpse the erosion of nation-state." The evidence from the study of global city-regions is highly ambiguous on this point. Although international forces clearly do shape the economic possibilities open to any region, national policy mediates the impact of those forces in ways that strongly affect the life chances of urban residents. And, from this perspective, the nation is far more potent that the city-region. National governments may not be able to affect the global economy, but they can shield their citizens from the most pernicious effects of that economy. Without such an effort occurring at the national level, local governments are largely helpless. As the Randstad illustrates, a combination of national initiative and local commitment can provide the basis for a region that both enjoys economic growth and sustains the well-being of the poorer section of the population.

NOTES

1. As it has been developed, global-city theory describes the core city rather than the region. Whether its hypotheses concerning income inequality apply also to the region is not altogether clear. To the extent possible with available data, this chapter looks at the issue of inequality regionally.
2. Between 1991 and 1997, I was part of a group of scholars from the United States, the United Kingdom, France, and Japan who participated in a series of conferences entitled "Nodes in the Global System of Cities." The purpose of the conferences was to investigate the relationship between economic structure and social outcomes that prevailed in four global cities—New York, London, Paris, and Tokyo. The discussion here of those four regions is mainly based on papers written for these conferences: Warf and Grimes (1997), Beckouche (1997), Mollenkopf (1997), Sonobe and Machimura (1997), Preteceille (1997), Hamnett (1997), Gordon (1997), and Kamo

and Sasaki (1997). They are intended for inclusion in a volume to be edited by John H. Mollenkopf.

3. This conclusion is based on data and analyses set forth in the papers listed in note 2. The data for the various cities is not precisely comparable because income data is not collected in the censuses of all the countries and because, even where available for the country, recent data for the core city and region is not available. Thus, I am depending on the inferences made by the authors of the papers from available statistics, as summarized in the sections on the specific areas, below. A recent analysis of a special census for New York City and a special analysis provided by the Netherlands Central Bureau of Statistics for the Randstad do allow comparison of these two areas (see Table 15.1).
4. Studies of the New York region show that income in the suburbs for both middle- and upper-income groups grew substantially more than in the city (Hughes and Seneca 1993; New York City Council 1997). Sonobe and Machimura found that the Tokyo region as a whole did not show income polarization but the central city did. Similarly in the Randstad the poor grew as a proportion of central city populations, due to selective in- and out-migration, but not as a proportion of the overall region (Kruythoff, Jobse, and Musterd 1992).
5. In 1977, 33.3 percent were middle class and 8.0 percent upper class; in 1996, the figures were 29.2 percent and 12.2 percent respectively. The number classified as lower class had increased from 45.7 percent to 48.6 percent. (New York City Council 1997: 14).
6. Looking at households rather than individuals captures the marked difference in incomes between multiple earner households and households with either a single earner or a nonearner.
7. See Atzema, Kruyt, and van Weesep 1992. The Randstad contributes approximately half of production, value-added, investment, and employment to the Dutch economy (Atzema and Smidt 1992, Smidt 1992). Dieleman and Faludi (1998) assert the Randstad, Rhine-Ruhr, and Flemish diamond can be considered as a single polynucleated macrourban region, characterized by high population density, a large number of core areas, rapid urbanization of the corridors linking them, and a high degree of interaction.
8. At its 1983 peak Dutch unemployment rose to 18 percent of the workforce. The term the "Dutch Disease" was coined to refer to a national economy with high unemployment that is able to sustain itself through a trade surplus caused by the export of raw materials (in the Dutch case natural gas). In 1982 the government negotiated an agreement with organized labor by which wage demands were suppressed, public expenditures cut, and eligibility requirements for state benefits tightened. In later years the agreement was extended to allow more flexibility in labor markets. At the same time, most welfare state benefits, including massive housing subsidies, were maintained (Terhorst and van der Ven 1998). Recently the Dutch housing support system has been modified to encourage more owner occupancy and to shift public subsidy away from support of new construction; rent subsidies, however, have been continued and strengthened (Priemus 1998). Terhorst and van der Ven (1998: 469) comment that whereas other European countries have witnessed the decline of corporatism, the Netherlands has seen "a revitalized cooperation between capital, labor, and the state."
9. This is especially the case for New York. A recent study of the dependence of New York City on Wall Street found that, while it represents only 5 percent of the city's

employment, it accounted for 56 percent of the increase in aggregate real earnings in New York City between 1992 and 1997 (Office of the State Deputy Comptroller (OSDC 1998: 2). It was estimated that between 1995 and 1997, when Wall Street firms themselves added about 9,800 jobs, the full economic impact of Wall Street (direct, indirect, and induced effects) may have accounted for more than 55,000 new jobs, representing well over half of all job growth in New York City over this two year period (OSDC 1998: 14–15). Although the region as a whole is more diverse in its economic base, Manhattan dominates the economic fortunes of the region, having not only the greatest number of jobs but also the region's highest paying jobs (Port Authority 1999: 13). According to the Port Authority (1999: 12) the average wage in the securities industry was a breathtaking $175,316 in 1997.

10. At the same time efforts to create an office center comparable to La Défense in Paris or Docklands in London have foundered. Modern office space is scattered throughout the Randstat but no area has sufficient preeminence to make it extremely attractive to the headquarters of multinationals.
11. The New York region is a slight exception to this generalization in that the Los Angeles–San Diego region has received more immigrants. Nevertheless, New York vastly exceeds all other regions of the United States in its proportion of foreign-born residents.

REFERENCES

Atzema, O., and Smidt, M. de (1992). "Selection and Duality in the Employment Structure of the Randstad." *Tijdschrift voor Economische en Sociale Geografie*, 83 (4): 289–304.

——, Kruyt, B., and Weesep, J. van. (1992). "The Randstad Today and Tomorrow." *Tijdschrift voor Economische en Sociale Geografie*, 83 (4): 243–9.

Beckouche, P. (1997). "Globalization and Economic Change in Paris." Paper presented at the Workshop on Global Cities, CUNY Graduate Center. New York.

Dieleman, F. M., and Faludi, A. (1998). "Randstad, Rhine-Ruhr, and Flemish Diamond as One Polynucleated Macro-region?" *Tijdschrift voor Economische en Sociale Geografie*, 89 (3): 320–7.

The Economist. (1995). "Holland: A New City State." 19 August: 43.

Fainstein, S. S. (1997). "The Egalitarian City: The Restructuring of Amsterdam." *International Planning Studies*, 2 (3): 295–314.

Fiscal Policy Institute. (1999). *The State of Working New York: The Illusion of Prosperity: New York in the New Economy.* New York: Fiscal Policy Institute, September.

Friedmann, J. (1986). "The World City Hypothesis." *Development and Change*, 17: 69–83.

Gordon, I. (1997). "The Role of Internationalization in Economic Change in London over the Past Twenty-five Years." Paper presented at the Workshop on Global Cities, CUNY Graduate Center. New York.

Hamnett, C. (1997). "Social Change and Polarization in London." Paper presented at the Workshop on Global Cities, CUNY Graduate Center. New York.

Hughes, J. W., and Seneca, J. J. (1993). "The Tidal Wave of Income Suburbanization: New Jersey, New York, and Philadelphia Metropolitan Dynamics." *Rutgers Regional Report.* New Brunswick, NJ: Edgar J. Bloustein School of Planning and Public Policy, Rutgers—the State University of New Jersey, Issue Paper no. 8, October.

Kamo, T., and Sasaki, M. (1997). "Tokyo: The Asian Global City at the Crossroads." Paper presented at the Workshop on Global Cities, CUNY Graduate Center. New York.

Kloosterman, R. C., and Lambooy, J. G. (1992). "The Randstad—A Welfare Region?" in F. M. Dieleman and S. Musterd (eds.), *The Randstad: A Research and Policy Laboratory*. Dordrecht: Kluwer, 123–39.

Kruythoff, H., Jobse, R., and Musterd, S. (1992). "Migration and the Socio-Economic Structure of the Four Big Randstad Cities and the Daily Urban Systems." *Tijdschrift voor Economische en Sociale Geografie*, 83 (3): 180–95.

Mollenkopf, J. (1997). "Changing Patterns of Inequality in New York City." Paper presented at the Workshop on Global Cities, CUNY Graduate Center. New York.

New York City Council. (1997). *Hollow in the Middle: The Rise and Fall of New York City's Middle Class*. New York: City Council.

Office of the State Deputy Comptroller (OSDC) for the City of New York. (1998). *New York City's Economic and Fiscal Dependence on Wall Street*. Report 5–99, 13 August. New York: OSDC.

Port Authority of New York and New Jersey (1999). *Regional Economy: Review and Outlook for the New York–New Jersey Metropolitan Region*. August. New York: Port Authority.

Preteceille, E. (1997). "Social Restructuring of the Global City: The Paris Case." Paper presented at the Workshop on Global Cities, CUNY Graduate Center. New York.

Priemus, H. (1998). "Improving or Endangering Housing Policies? Recent Changes in the Dutch Housing Allowance Scheme." *International Journal of Urban and Regional Research*, 22 (2): 319–30.

Sassen, S. (1991). *The Global City*. Princeton: Princeton University Press.

—— (1994). *Cities in a World Economy*. Thousand Oaks: Pine Forge.

—— (1998). *Globalization and Its Discontents*. New York: New Press.

Smidt, M. de (1992). "A World City Paradox—Firms and the Urban Fabric," in F. M. Dieleman and S. Musterd (eds.), *The Randstad: A Research and Policy Laboratory*. Dordrecht: Kluwer, 97–122.

Sonobe, M., and Machimura, T. (1997). "Globalization Effect or Bubble Effect? Social Polarization in Tokyo." Paper presented at the Workshop on Global Cities, CUNY Graduate Center. New York.

Statistics Netherlands. 1999. "Macroeconomic Overview of the Netherlands 1998." http://www.cbs.nl/en/products/recent/economy/991118.htm.

Taylor, P. J. (1995). "World Cities and Territorial States: The Rise and Fall of their Mutuality," in P. L. Knox and P. J. Taylor (eds.), *World Cities in a World System*. Cambridge: Cambridge University Press, 48–62.

Terhorst, P., and van der Ven, J. (1998). "Urban Policies and the 'Polder Model': Two Sides of the Same Coin." *Tijdschrift voor Economische en Sociale Geografie*, 89 (4): 467–73.

Waldinger, R. (1996). *Still the Promised City?* Cambridge: Harvard University Press.

Warf, B., and Grimes, J. (1997). "New York City's Economy at the Fin de Siècle." Paper presented at the Workshop on Global Cities, CUNY Graduate Center. New York.

16

The Immigrant Niche in Global City-Regions: Concept, Patterns, Controversy

ROGER WALDINGER

As America enters the twenty-first century, it is now clear that the twentieth was the century of immigration. True, the doors closed in the mid-1920s—and for many, especially during the dark days of World War II, they remained fatally shut until it was too late. But even during the heyday of immigration restriction, the back door remained open, which means that the Mexican presence also then grew. However, the advent of a temporary migrant farm labor program in 1943—known as the Bracero program—augured the shape of things to come: immigration began growing in the late 1940s, and the path has been ever upwards, indeed at an ever sharper slope. At the end of the century, the numbers of newcomers added up to the flow seen at the century's dawn.

So immigration is again transforming the United States. It does so in a particular way, since the newcomers head for urban America. Today's newcomers are far more likely than their native-born counterparts to live in the nation's largest urban regions, making immigration, now as in the past, a quintessentially urban phenomenon.

Thus, the immigrant masses are once again huddling; they are also congregating, as they did before, in just a handful of places. Nonetheless, the new map of immigrant America looks very different from the old. New York still ranks as a premier immigrant place; likewise, Chicago retains a significant attraction for the foreign-born. But immigration's center of gravity has decisively shifted south and westward. San Francisco, earlier an immigrant town, remains a magnet for the foreign-born, its importance magnified by the region's vastly greater population. However, the capital of today's immigrant America is unquestionably Los Angeles, a still-growing mass, sprawling over five southern California counties. And at the other end of the country, Miami, though a much smaller metropolis than the rest, reigns as the nation's densest immigrant concentration, the very first to receive the new immigrant tide, and still an entry-point of extraordinary magnitude.

At the top of the agenda stands the question of how the newcomers to these American global city-regions change after they have arrived. The conventional wisdom, both academic and popular, says that immigrants *should* change by entering the American mainstream. The concept of assimilation stands as a shorthand for this point of view.

In its canonical form, the theory of assimilation began with the assumption that the immigrants would arrive as "ethnics," an identity reinforced by their tendency to re-create their own social worlds. Cultural change would come first, as Americanization made the second generation quite different from their forebears in tastes, everyday habits, and preferences. But Americanization could proceed even as the ethnic social structure of interpersonal relations largely stood still: as long as immigrants and their descendants remained embedded in ethnic neighborhoods, networks, and niches, integration into the fabric of American society would have to wait. Once ethnic boundaries were crossed by moving to occupations or neighborhoods of greater ethnic diversity, increasing exposure to outsiders would inevitably pull ethnic communities apart: with the move from ethnic ghetto to suburb, interethnic friendships, networks, and eventually marriages would all follow in due course. Thus, the advent of structural assimilation, to borrow the influential term coined by Milton Gordon, signaled entry into the "mainstream," and the beginning of the end for any distinctiveness associated with the immigrant generation (Gordon 1964).

All this is now entirely familiar to the students of American ethnicity. But perhaps too much so, since the canonical view had little, if anything, to say about the driving force behind changing contact probabilities—namely, movement out of the socioeconomic cellar. All that one can do is to infer the likeliest answer: that economic progress took the form of dispersion from the occupational or industrial clusters that the immigrants initially established. After all, from the assimilationist standpoint, concentration is a source of disadvantage, to be explained by lack of skills and education. With acculturation and growing levels of schooling and American experience, the immigrants and their children would naturally move upward by filtering outward from the ethnic niche.

Today's scholars, however, tend not to agree. The emphasis, instead, is on the connections that bind the newcomers together and the resources generated by the contacts that crisscross the immigrant communities. These ties constitute a source of "social capital," providing social structures that facilitate action, in this case the search for jobs and the acquisition of skills and other resources needed to move up the economic ladder. Networks tying veterans to newcomers allow for rapid transmission of information about openings in workplaces or opportunities for new business startups. Networks also provide better information within workplaces, reducing the risks associated with initial hiring, and similarly connecting coethnic entrepreneurs, who take membership in the community as an index of trust (Bailey and Waldinger 1991). Once in place, the networks are self-reproducing, since each incumbent recruits friends or relatives from his or her own group, and entrepreneurs gravitate to the cluster of business opportunities that their associates in the community have already identified. Relationships among coethnics are likely to be many-sided, rather than specialized, inducing community effects to go beyond their informational value, and engendering both codes of conduct, and the mechanisms for sanctioning those who violate norms (Portes and Sensenbrenner 1993). In other words, concentration is the way to go, with the search for advancement taking a *collective*, not an individual, form, as network-dense communities provide the informational base and support mechanisms for a pattern of parallel movement up the economic ladder (see Waldinger 1996*b*).

So goes the now conventional wisdom among many of today's immigration specialists. These views are most likely to resonate with sociologists and anthropologists, but they are hardly confined to these particular disciplinary tribes alone. The economist Glenn Loury was one of the first to invoke "social capital" as a factor facilitating movement up from the bottom, arguing most recently that "each individual is socially situated, and one's location within the network of social affiliations substantially affects one's access to various resources" (Loury 1998: 125). George Borjas, a neoclassical economist, has essentially endorsed the same point of view, showing that access to resources shared by the group as a whole can redound to the individual's benefit (Borjas 1994). And similar perspectives can be found among political scientists and other authorities of the same type.

Of course, not everyone has signed on to the program. There remain numerous defenders of the old-time religion, who continue to argue that dispersion remains the best, and more importantly, the most common way by which immigrants and their descendants move up the economic ladder (Alba and Nee 1997). And even the exponents of the new point of view are divided on almost as many points as those on which they agree. There is uncertainty as to how best to characterize the clusters that immigrants have established—are they ethnic economies, ethnic enclaves, ethnic niches, or perhaps even some other neologism that better captures the phenomenon? Just what name to use matters, because each concept denotes a somewhat different phenomenon, each varying in nature and extent. Whether one opts for the most restricted or most expansive appellation, questions of size and persistence loom large, since there is always the possibility that attention is grabbed by an exceptional phenomenon, not the everyday, more prosaic, mean. And even if concentration is pervasive at any one point in time, it may simply result from the large immigrant inflows received in recent years, and thus be a phenomenon of passing importance.

This chapter is designed to provide an entry into the scholarship in this emerging area, focusing on the five global city-regions of Los Angeles, New York, Chicago, San Francisco, and Miami on which the bulk of the U.S. foreign-born population has converged. I start out with a summary of the relevant U.S. literature on ethnic niches, moving on to an overview of the economic concentrations that contemporary immigrants have established in America's largest urban regions, and ending with a discussion of how immigrant niches take root, develop, and change over time. As I shall show, clustering is indeed pervasive, a characteristic found in every place, and typical of every major immigrant type, whether high skilled or low, refugee or economic migrant. Moreover, niches represent an enduring phenomenon: as we will see toward the end of the chapter, once established, patterns of concentration exercise an enduring attraction for immigrants, even as they deepen roots in the United States.

ETHNIC ENCLAVES, ECONOMIES, OR NICHES: THE PLAY OF DEBATE

That immigrants tend to gravitate toward a narrow set of economic activities and then stay there is not new. The historical literature on American immigration is replete with observations on the predilections of immigrants for trades and occupations of various kinds. Scholars studying chain migration naturally noticed that newcomers moving from the same hometown not only became neighbors in the new world, but often worked alongside one another. As is the case today, clustering was always more pronounced among some groups than among others. Jewish immigrants from Poland were a particularly noticed and noticeable example, establishing not only *landsmannschaften*—hometown associations—but also a *landsmannschaft economy*, a striking concept coined by Moses Rischin, but one that somehow never got much intellectual circulation (Rischin 1962).

So immigration scholars were always sensitive to the specializations with which the newcomers so frequently began. But ideological and academic preoccupation with assimilation led attention to wander elsewhere: the social science analysis of immigrant adaptation developed analytic tools and concepts to study such phenomena as intermarriage or residential change, but not the ethnic structuring of the occupational order. For the most part, the state of thinking was pretty much captured by Stanley Lieberson, in his influential 1980 book *A Piece of the Pie*, who used the term "special niches" to note that "most racial and ethnic groups tend to develop concentrations in certain jobs," reflecting cultural characteristics, special skills, or opportunities available at the time of arrival, but pretty much left the matter there (Lieberson 1980: 379).

The Ethnic Enclave

What led social scientists to think differently was renewed interest in, and appreciation of, that much maligned social category, the petty bourgeoisie. Small business had always been an immigrant and ethnic specialty, but too insignificant to get more than the passing academic nod, until Ivan Light wrote his seminal *Ethnic Enterprise in America*. Light's central point, that ethnic solidarity propelled business growth among Japanese, Chinese, and West Indian immigrants, can now be seen as a formulation of embeddedness *avant la lettre*; but widely as the book was read, its historical focus blunted its broader impact on the ways in which social scientists thought about immigrant progress (Light 1972).

Instead, the catalytic intellectual development resulted from the publication of Franklin Wilson and Alejandro Portes's article on the Cuban "Immigrant Enclave" in Miami, twenty years ago (Wilson and Portes 1980). Reporting on the initial wave of a longitudinal survey of newly arrived Cuban refugees and their labor-market experiences in Miami from 1973 to 1976, Wilson and Portes found that a sizable proportion of the newcomers went to work for coethnics. They also discovered that those who worked for immigrant bosses were doing better than refugees employed in white-owned, secondary sector firms—which in turn prompted a piece of scholarly revisionism that became known as the "ethnic enclave hypothesis." What earlier observers had seen as a sweatshop, Wilson and Portes recast as an apprenticeship: low wages for a couple of terms of labor in the ethnic economy—dubbed the "enclave"—in return for which one learns the tools of the trade in order to set up on one's own and thus move ahead.

The scholarly news about Miami's Cuban ethnic economy and its impact provoked immense interest, for reasons having to do with policy and theory. After all, the central question in immigration research concerns the prospects for immigrants and their children. The research on the Cubans suggested that at least some would move ahead successfully; and more startlingly, they would do so on their own, turning disadvantage to good account. But if Cubans, and possibly other, entrepreneurially active, groups, could use business as a stepping stone, how was one to account for this state of affairs? An earlier wave of research had shown that other visibly identifiable minorities were trapped in the "secondary labor market," unable to move into the "primary labor market," where employment was more stable, job arrangements allowed for upward mobility, and workers were rewarded for investments in skill and training (D. Gordon 1972, Piore 1979). Indeed, Portes's own research showed that this same pattern persisted among recent Mexican immigrants (Portes and Bach 1985). The puzzle was all the more compelling because the industries that comprised the Cuban ethnic economy also made up the "secondary sector." The same structural factors that impeded skill acquisition, attachment (to a particular firm, industry, or labor market), and upward mobility in the secondary sector also characterized the ethnic enclave. Yet, work in the enclave appeared to possess some of the features associated with the primary sector.

The ethnic enclave hypothesis quickly led to an ethnic enclave debate. It soon became apparent that the phenomenon to which Portes drew attention was not so easily identified in the other capitals of immigrant America. In the unusual immigrant metropolis of Miami—where the largest group of newcomers were also middle-class refugees—Cubans appeared to provide ample employment to others of their own kind. Though by definition, employment of coethnics served as a distinguishing feature of the enclave, scholars eventually noted that this characteristic was relatively uncommon: immigrant entrepreneurship could be found aplenty; instances where immigrant owners *and* workers were over-represented in the very same activity were a good deal more rare (Logan, Alba, and McNulty 1994).

The concept of the ethnic *enclave* also proved limiting. *Enclave* denotes segregation within a particular territorial configuration. And Portes's original elaboration made the enclave into a case of a still more special kind, depicting the enclave as not only geographically distinct, but as a self-supporting economy generating a variety of inputs and outputs itself. The notion of self-sufficiency was a nonstarter from the very beginning: if the largest cities are far from being self-supporting, how could small ethnic enclaves do any better? Moreover, our knowledge of immigrant economies shows that they are not spread throughout the economy, but rather highly specialized in a few industries or business lines where ethnic firms can enjoy competitive advantages. Likewise, the emphasis on spatial concentration proved a red herring: though many immigrant neighborhoods serve as the fount of business activity, immigrant entrepreneurs spring up throughout the urban landscape—whether there are lots of coethnic customers to be found or not. Clearly, space may be a variable affecting the immigrant entrepreneurial outcomes, but there seems little reason to treat it as a defining characteristic.[1]

But the greatest problems had to do with the central finding itself: that immigrant workers laboring for a coethnic boss did better than those employed in *comparable jobs*, but engaged by an Anglo employer. The immediate issue was how to explain this apparent anomaly; the initial literature did not help matters by offering a number of different accounts. Ethnic solidarity was one of the possibilities invoked: "Immigrant entrepreneurs," wrote Portes and Bach in *Latin Journey*, "rely upon the economic potential of ethnic solidarity":

> ethnicity modifies the character of the class relationship—capital and labor—within the enclave. Ethnic ties suffuse an otherwise "bare" relationship with a sense of collective purpose in contrast to the outside. But the utilization of ethnic solidarity in lieu of enforced discipline in the workplace also entails reciprocal obligations. If employers can profit from the willing self-exploitation of fellow immigrants, they are also obliged to reserve for them those supervisory positions that open in their firms, to train them in trade skills, and to support their eventual move into self-employment. It is the fact that enclave firms are compelled to rely on ethnic solidarity and that the latter "cuts both ways," which creates opportunities for mobility unavailable in the outside. (Portes and Bach 1985: 345.)

This story was plausible, but *Latin Journey* did not adequately tie down the case. In the end, one is forced to conclude that Portes and Bach *assumed* solidarity, a presupposition that they never had any necessity to entertain. A more parsimonious view would simply have suggested that the development of ethnic networks would generate the infrastructure and resources for ethnic small businesses *before* a sense of group awareness or solidarity need develop. In the end, Portes himself moved on to a view of this sort, arguing that "bounded solidarity" and "enforceable trust"—*emergent* community characteristics related to the development of ethnic networks—provided the necessary ingredients for both mobilizing resources and limiting obligations, thereby making exchanges within the ethnic enclave reciprocal, and *not* exploitative (Portes and Sensenbrenner 1993, Portes and Stepick 1993).

Conceptual niceties aside, the nub of the problem involved replication. Victor Nee and Jimy Sanders fired the opening salvo: looking at the Chinese in San Francisco and the Cubans in south Florida, they found that self-employment was good for the immigrant bosses, but much less satisfactory for the immigrants most likely to work in their shops (Sanders and Nee 1987). Min Zhou and John Logan then added nuance, showing that male Chinese immigrants in New York did indeed benefit from working in industries of Chinese concentration, but that their female counterparts had no such luck (Zhou and Logan 1989, and see M. Zhou 1992). Greta Gilbertson, who examined the experience of Colombians and Dominicans in New York, came up with results that essentially supported Nee and Sanders's critique (Gilbertson and Gurak 1993; Gilbertson 1995). Portes, needless to say, fired back, but with conclusions a good deal more modest than those that he had originally advanced—namely, that workers in the enclave *do no worse* than those at work elsewhere (Portes and Jensen 1989).[2] Debate on the matter continues, but in the meantime the theoretical action has moved elsewhere.

The Ethnic Niche

As we have noted above, the particular economic configuration identified as an "enclave" is a relatively rare element in the immigrant employment scene. Miami may have an enclave, as conventionally defined, of sizable dimensions; so too, do the Chinatowns of San Francisco and New York, but one then quickly begins to run out of cases. Moreover, some of the immigrant groups with the highest self-employment levels seem to be particularly unlikely to exhibit the pattern associated with Miami's Cubans. The Koreans, for example, are renowned for their entrepreneurial success, with self-employment rates well above the levels attained by the Cubans. But Korean owners largely make do with a non-Korean workforce, in part because small-business ownership has simply swept up so many Korean immigrants that there are too few coethnics for Korean bosses to hire (Kim 1981, Min 1996). And the Korean story is hardly unique, as Ivan Light and his collaborators have shown in their work on the Iranians in Los Angeles. Admittedly, this last group is not typical, as they are refugees with the good fortune of arriving with ample capital, and entrepreneurial experience to boot. But even so the example is entirely relevant: Iranians have scored tremendous business success and have done so without a coethnic labor force (Light *et al.* 1994). Similar stories can be told for Israelis, Arabs, Russians, Greeks, Indians, and a variety of other immigrants who have made their mark in small business (Der-Martirosian 1996, forthcoming; Gold and Phillips, 1996). In effect, the old middleman minority pattern, exemplified in earlier immigration history by American Jews, remains alive, well, and a good deal more common than the ethnic enclave of immigrant bosses and their coethnic workers.

Moreover, the underlying sociological processes—involving the mobilization of information, capital, and support through ethnic social networks—characterize both the middleman minority phenomenon and the ethnic enclave as well. While there may well be differences between immigrant-owned firms that recruit outsiders and those that rely on insiders, these seem to be differences of degree, not kind, with plenty of within-group variation along the coethnic employment axis, as well as movement over time. Just as one would consider immigrant businesses that sell to a coethnic clientele and those that sell on the general market as variants of a common type, so too does it seem appropriate to think of the ethnic enclave and the middleman minority situation exemplified by Koreans or Iranians as special cases of the "ethnic economy" writ large—as convincingly argued by Ivan Light (Light and Karageorgis 1994).

Self-employment is a particularly prominent, and these days, much discussed, instance of immigrant economic specialization; but it is hardly the major feature. As an *ethnic* phenomenon, employment concentration shows up elsewhere —most notably, in the well-known propensity by some ethnics to find jobs in the public sector, a tradition pioneered by the Irish and taken up by others, most notably African Americans. As I have shown elsewhere, the public sector story has some distinctive elements, but the crucial ingredients involved in the establishment of an employment concentration seem much the same, whether the locus is private or government sectors, or for that matter, wage and salary work as contrasted to entrepreneurship (see Waldinger 1996*b*: chapter 7).

Most importantly, immigrants tend to cluster in activities where others of their own kind have already become established. Initial placements, just as Lieberson noted in *A Piece of a Pie*, may be affected by any range of factors—prior experience, cultural preferences, or historical accident. But once the initial settlers have established a beachhead, subsequent arrivals tend to follow behind, preferring an environment in which at least some faces are familiar and finding that personal contacts prove the most efficient way of finding a job. More germane, the predilections of immigrants match the preferences of employers, who rely on their workers for recommendations. Managers appreciate network recruitment for its ability to attract applicants quickly and at little cost; they value it even more for its efficiency. Hiring through connections upgrades the quality of information, reducing the risks entailed in acquiring new personnel; since sponsors usually have a stake in their job, they can also be relied on to keep their referrals in line. The process works a little differently in business, where early success sends later arrivals an implicit signal about the types of companies to start, and the business lines to seek out or avoid. An expanding business sector then provides both a mechanism for the effective transmission of skill and a catalyst for the entrepreneurial drive: the opportunity to acquire managerial skills through a stint of employment in immigrant firms both compensates for low pay and motivates workers to learn a variety of jobs (see Waldinger 1996*b*: chapters 1 and 9, and Waldinger 1994).

The sociological literature prepares us to expect that niches are the refuge for immigrants lacking in skill, education, or language ability; others, more equipped to enter the mainstream of the U.S. labor market, should disperse out of the ethnic concentration in short order. The matter is of no small moment, since contemporary immigration to the United States is characterized by socioeconomic diversity: unlike the past, when the newcomers were concentrated at the bottom of the socioeconomic ladder, today's arrivals span the entire occupational spectrum, with a sizable portion in the middle or above. But the literature, otherwise so emphatic about the importance of ethnic clustering—whether thought of as ethnic enclave or ethnic niche—assumes that these highly educated immigrants are quickly assuming the occupational or industrial distribution of other workers with like skills. Portes, for example, has long argued that professional immigrants "are primarily hired according to ability rather than ethnicity," enjoying "mobility chances comparable to those of native workers," and "work conditions and remuneration not . . . different from those of domestic labor at similar levels" (Portes 1981). Ironically, the reasoning follows from the arguments of Victor Nee and his collaborators, otherwise highly critical of Portes's point of view: firms "may be predominantly Anglo in character" but "have formal rules and procedures" and "legally . . . cannot discriminate by race or ethnicity and may be pressured to hire and promote minorities and women" (Nee, Sanders, and Sernau 1994: 852). And thus, there is considerable consensus as to how these high skilled immigrants make it in America: as Portes and Rumbaut put it in their influential synthesis, *Immigrant America*, professionals "tend to enter at the bottom of their respective occupational ladders and to progress from there according to individual merit," overcoming initial difficulties with "remarkable success" (1990).

And yet the conventional wisdom has probably had more influence than it truly deserves. Clearly, immigrant professionals are not quite so convinced, as evidenced by the ongoing and increasingly prominent controversy over the "glass ceiling." And the controversy itself sends an important signal about the phenomenon in question: one would hardly expect complaints about promotional obstacles, were there no sizable immigrant concentrations at upper reaches of the occupational spectrum. It is precisely the establishment of notable clusters—in engineering, computer specialties, and other like fields—that draws attention to potential problems experienced in moving ahead (U.S. Federal Glass Ceiling Commission 1995; Tang 1993, 1994). As we shall show, high skilled immigrants are in fact highly likely to develop ethnic niches, though, as one would expect, those niches take a very distinctive form.

ETHNIC NICHES IN THE IMMIGRANT METROPOLIS

Regardless of whether the linkages involve connections among high- or low-skilled workers, the repeated action of immigrant social networks yields the ethnic niche: a set of economic activities in which immigrants are heavily concentrated. Convention now defines an ethnic niche as an occupation or industry in which the percentage of workers that are group members is at least one-and-a-half times greater than the group's percentage of all employment.

Though most scholars seem willing to concur with this highly generalized definition, just how to put it into practice has been a matter of some uncertainty. Almost all will agree that a niche denotes a "job" or, at best, a set of clearly related jobs, as specified by Suzanne Model in her pioneering article on "The Ethnic

Niche and the Structure of Opportunity." But Model then left considerable ambiguity as to what she meant by a "job," writing that a job could denote "an occupation, an industry, even a set of related industries" (1993). One could argue that niches are best thought of in occupational terms, in which case the emphasis rests on the *similarity* of jobs, as they extend horizontally across a number of industries, themselves very possibly unrelated. To the extent that niches are the product of networks developing in a particular institutional context, one would prefer to underscore *relatedness* among a set of somewhat different, but usually interacting, occupations. For that reason, I have previously argued for the industrial view: whatever the portal of entry, niches grow as immigrants move into the related jobs *within an industry* to which initial starting-points provide access, information, and opportunities to pick up the relevant skills.[3] In the sections that follow, I examine both occupational *and* industrial niches, in each case defining a niche as a category in which immigrants of a particular group are over-represented by 50 percent or more.[4]

What can we say about the extent, nature, and persistence of these niches? As the literature has repeatedly shown, the category of "immigrant" hides almost as much as it reveals. Not only are today's immigrants socioeconomically diverse; they also vary according to the circumstances of their arrival, some coming as economic migrants, others as refugees. Portes and Rumbaut's now well-known schema—differentiating among entrepreneurial, professional, labor migrant, and refugee types—nicely captures these crucial lines of variation, and we have used this framework to select the groups in question (Portes and Rumbaut 1990). Asian Indians, Filipinos, and, to some extent, Chinese, exemplify professional migration; Koreans serve as the exemplar of the entrepreneurial type; Vietnamese and Cubans fit into the refugee category; Mexicans and Dominicans belong to the genus of labor migrant. Needless to say, this linkage of particular national flows with specific migration types involves considerable simplification: even if some type of skew characterizes every flow, each one also exhibits at least some degree of heterogeneity. But for the purposes of this chapter, the skew is precisely what we seek to capture; at the very least, the type captures the modal category for the group.

Moreover, there seems to be only modest within-group variation among the key categories, with the Chinese most likely to fall across types—recently arrived Chinese in Los Angeles, for example, mainly fit into the professional/entrepreneurial category, whereas their counterparts in New York and San Francisco are far more proletarian in origin (Waldinger and Tseng 1992; Y. Zhou 1998; M. Zhou and Kim 1999). Only the West Indians seem to provide an awkward fit with the available categories: while clearly not refugees, and certainly not entrepreneurs, their migration histories and occupational position are such that they straddle the professional/labor migrant divide. Though including this group slightly muddies our comparisons, the gain outweighs the costs, if only because of the group's numerical importance and intrinsic interest (Kasinitz 1992, Waldinger 1996*b*: chapter 4).

The relationship between immigration type and settlement pattern precludes the type of interurban consistency that I would have preferred. In general, the networked nature of immigration makes for local concentration, impeding geographic diffusion. The more dependent on networks for information and support—a characteristic usually linked to lower levels of marketable skills—the more likely are the immigrants to converge on a limited number of places. Take Mexicans, for example, whose presence in California has a long and distinguished pedigree, and who have only recently added a sizable concentration in New York. Likewise, West Indians and Dominicans are highly concentrated, having yet to penetrate far beyond the East Coast in any numbers, while the Vietnamese have developed a very noticeable Southern California concentration, but none other of significant magnitude. By contrast, the higher-skilled groups—Koreans, Chinese, Filipinos, and Asian Indians—scatter more widely, showing up in sufficient number in four out of the five global city-regions of interest.

Another part of the story involves a sort of regional specialization: geography, history, and accident ensure that the immigrant regions themselves receive certain flows and not others. Though Miami is a heralded immigrant region, it is also a deviant one because it hosts a very small Asian population. Thus, none of the groups that I have selected span all five immigrant urban regions. Koreans, Chinese, Filipinos, Asian Indians, and Mexicans are found in four regions, having yet to establish a large base in Miami; Cubans cluster in three (Miami, a veritable sun, surrounded by the distinctly lesser moons of New York and Los Angeles); West Indians, Dominicans, and Vietnamese have built up settlements in two (Miami and New York in the former two cases, and Los Angeles and San Francisco in the latter).

However, economic clustering seems to be a pervasive phenomenon, wherever the immigrants settle, as can be seen in Table 16.1. As the conventional wisdom would suggest, the labor migrant groups have moved heavily into a limited number of occupations and industries. Thus, Mexican immigrants working in Los Angeles are particularly likely to be employed in niches, as has been shown elsewhere (Waldinger 1996*a*, Ortiz 1996). But the Mexicans who head to San Francisco or Chicago or any of the other urban regions in question appear no different in this respect: in each place, ethnic niches account for a very sizable share of Mexican employment. And the same generalization applies to the other group that clearly qualifies for the labor migrant designation—the Dominicans. The Koreans, a relatively well-educated group, but one renowned for their entrepreneurial activity, are also heavily concentrated in niches in each of the global city-regions to which they have gravitated.

But neither the Mexicans nor the Koreans are out of line with the other groups in question. My selection of groups and cities, each divided into occupational and industrial niches, yields a matrix of 54 cells—in which ethnic niches account for more than 50 percent of a group's employment in more than half of the cases. To be sure, Mexicans are the only group with concentrations above the 50 percent mark in every place, whether assessed from the occupational or

Table 16.1. *Percent employed in niches*

	Chicago		Los Angeles		Miami		New York		San Francisco	
	Occcupational	Industrial	Occcupational	Industrial	Occcupational	Industrial	Occcupational	Industrial	Occcupational	Industrial
Dominicans					41	50	54	59		
West Indians					31	31	43	40		
Mexicans	58	68	55	55			68	74	62	64
Chinese	60	64	50	49			49	51	39	41
Filipino	55	57	47	50			49	53	41	50
Korean	50	57	47	45			59	54	53	53
Asian Indians	57	57	49	53			50	43	54	54
Cubans					15	19	35	33		
Vietnamese			48	50					57	57

Note: Niches are industries or occupations in which members of a group are over-represented by 50 percent, relative to their share of total employment in the economy of a global city-region. The table displays the percent of *all employed* persons in any group at work in an industry or occupation classified as a niche. Data apply to employed persons, ages 25–64 only.

Source: 1990 Census of Population, Public Use Microdata Sample.

industrial standpoint. Still, the others follow shortly behind. Consider, for example, the Filipinos, the purest instance of the "professional migrant" type, as members of this group are particularly unlikely to work on their own, indeed far more so than the native-born population against whom the immigrants are typically compared. Notwithstanding the usual insistence that professional migrants filter into a broad cross-section of occupations at the level for which their education qualifies them, the Filipinos look much like their less-skilled counterparts in their tendency to cluster in niches. At least half of Filipino employment falls into industrial niches in each of the four regions where Filipinos are found in sizable numbers; only in San Francisco do Filipinos display a notably lower tendency to cluster in a narrow tier of industrial niches, though even here the level of concentration is far from trivial. Overall, we see little deviation from this pattern among the remaining groups, and considerable parallelism from place to place, with the high-skilled groups quite like the low-skilled groups in the propensity to gravitate to a clearly defined tier of jobs.

Only one group—Cubans in Miami—clearly departs from the general pattern. This was an unexpected exception, given the widely accepted depiction of the Cuban ethnic enclave, whose importance no one has yet disputed. Though a full explanation for the discrepancy between the conventional wisdom and my findings goes beyond the scope of this chapter, consideration of group and city size and characteristics may provide the clue to the puzzle. While Miami may be a notable immigrant concentration, as a metropolis it is far smaller than the other urban regions in question. Cubans are Miami's very largest immigrant group, which may make it more difficult for them than for the far less numerous Dominicans or West Indians to secure a distinctive position within the region's economy. The Cubans also comprise a population of at least average qualifications. Thus, unlike Los Angeles's Mexicans, whose numbers lead to dominance in many occupations and industries, but whose limited schooling impedes movement out of the low-skilled sector, the Cubans have more options; the Cubans' *relatively* large numbers, within the Miami context, also reduce the potential that a small set of industries or occupations could absorb much of the group, yielding the diffusion implied by the low levels of concentration recorded.

NICHES: PERVASIVE *AND* PERSISTENT? OR SIMPLY TRANSITIONAL?

Thus, the ethnic niche stands out as a characteristic of almost every major immigrant group, a phenomenon to be found in each of America's major immigrant places. With only one major exception, immigrant groups pile up in occupations or industries where they achieve high levels of concentration. Clustering occurs regardless of immigrant type—holding among labor migrants *and* professionals, among refugees *as well as* entrepreneurial groups.

The nature of the niches established by the groups that I have surveyed suggests that the concept of an "ethnic division of labor" provides an apt description for

But the declines of the 1970 to 1980 period left all the groups at high levels of concentration. Cubans in New York and Los Angeles registered the lowest levels of clustering; even this low ebb saw just over 40 percent of Cubans employed in occupational niches in each place. In both places Cubans were also unique in yet another respect: namely, their numbers had increased only slightly over the decade, reflecting the extraordinary magnetism exercised by Miami. Consequently, the relatively low concentration levels of Cubans are probably most suggestive of the pressures towards continued clustering, even under those circumstances most conducive to diffusion. In any case, the new groups, many of them highly educated, as in the case of the Filipinos or the Indians, began with a high proportion of the group nested in a narrow tier of occupations.

In general, the 1980 to 1990 data yield a picture consistent with a tendency toward dispersion, but only to a very modest degree. Concentration fell off most drastically among the Cubans in Los Angeles, with the proportion employed in niches down almost 25 percent, as compared to 1980; but this remains a highly unusual case, as numbers remained unchanged during this period of rising immigration. Of greater relevance is the experience of the Chinese and Vietnamese in Los Angeles, and the West Indians, Cubans, and Koreans in New York, where concentration levels slipped modestly, though the decline was in the one-sixth to one-fifth range. Other groups, such as the Filipinos or Indians of both regions, or the Dominicans and Chinese in New York, saw much lower levels of diffusion toward occupations of lower ethnic density. In Los Angeles, the Mexicans actually increased the tendency to cluster in niches. Regardless of the rate of attenuation—reversed in the Mexican case—all groups retained levels of concentration close to, or above, the 50 percent level, as noted above.

Immigrant Cohorts

Thus, the immigrant niche is a phenomenon with staying power, at least in the short run. But its apparent persistence might be an artifact of a spurious correlation: if immigrant numbers are growing rapidly, as they are, and the newest immigrants converge on the industries of highest ethnic density, as they do, we may fail to observe the underlying tendency that involves long-term immigrants heading toward jobs where their compatriots are less likely to work.

Examining the behavior of veteran immigrants offers one way to assess this possibility. Figure 16.2 displays concentration rates, as of 1970, for those immigrants who moved to the United States between 1960 and 1969, and then shows how those patterns changed over the course of the next two decades. Once again, we observe a marked decline from the peaks registered in 1970, though in this case, samples are still small, providing some ground for caution. While attenuation persisted from 1980 to 1990, it took place at a greatly reduced rate; only the Cubans, a group whose numbers actually declined during this period, appear to deviate from the broader pattern. In general, a large portion of the cohort of the 1960s—though not quite a majority—remained in occupations of high ethnic density, at least twenty years after arrival in the United States.

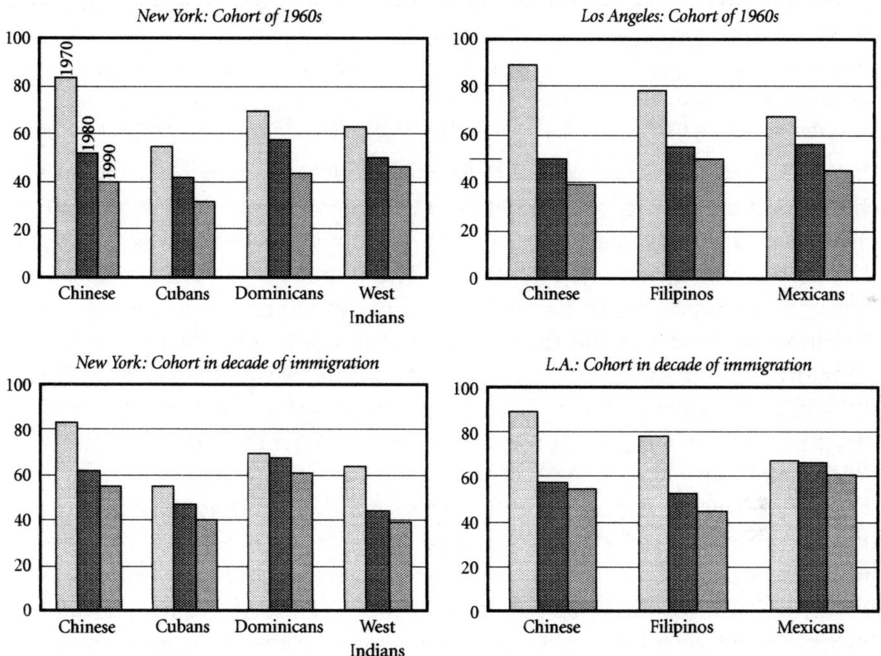

Figure 16.2. *Percent of labor force working in occupational niches*

But one could look at the question from a different angle: if it is newness that leads immigrants to cluster, with the first wave most dependent on help from the limited number of veterans, and the group is still small enough to find accommodation in a handful of occupations, then later cohorts might be less likely to start out by clustering. Stated baldly, this proposition garners support, as suggested by the data graphed in the bottom two panels Figure 16.2. Insofar as small sample size does not distort the experience of the cohort of the 1960s, no other group of newcomers seems to have begun with comparable levels of clustering. But the situation of the arrivals of the 1980s looks barely different from the pattern established a decade earlier by their predecessors of the 1970s. In four of the seven groups, the cohort of the 1980s began with concentration levels above the 50 percent mark. And in the case of the two labor migrant groups in question—the Dominicans in New York and the Mexicans in Los Angeles—the degree of clustering in niches barely changes from one cohort to another. To be sure, data such as these hardly settle the matter: more time is needed if we are fully to assess persistence; and it would be useful if we could compare persistence in the niche against some other benchmark. Nonetheless, concentration does appear to be a trait that lasts over an extended period of time, shaping the experience of both new and old cohorts. If we recall that the concentrations are truly distinctive, separating the groups from one another, then the tendency to maintain employment in occupations of high ethnic density highlights a fundamental aspect of ethnic social structure.

SOCIAL REPRODUCTION OR SOCIAL DISCONTINUITY?

But if one can make the case for the ethnic niche as a social phenomenon worthy of attention, its origins remain fully to be explained. Like most other researchers who have treated the topic, the account that I offered earlier in this chapter provides a network explanation: The immigrant niche is made by the repeated interaction of the networks that link immigrant newcomers to more established compatriots and the recruitment networks that firms use to obtain labor. In turn, networks sort categorically distinctive groups of immigrants into different positions within the economy. Since newcomers converge on those places where their compatriots are already established, immigrant concentrations quickly build up.

The problem is that this view suffers from a built-in contradiction: it explains why tomorrow's workforce looks a good deal like today's; it does not tell us how today's labor force was put in place. The relationship between today and tomorrow is not difficult to understand: the established immigrant workers learn about job openings before anyone else; once in the know, they run to tell their friends and relatives. They also reassure the boss that their referrals are just the right candidates to fill the vacancies, a reassurance all the more meaningful when the boss thinks that birds of a feather flock together, and likes the birds he currently has.

But today is *not* like yesterday: at some point, today's immigrant veterans were outsiders, knocking on doors, with few if any contacts inside. Moreover, a network explanation puts the immigrants in the position of possessing the resources—information, support, assistance in training—needed to help out kith and kin. But as we know, the process of migration is also one whereby established groups create outsiders, the latter's "otherness" largely defined by the functions which they fill, a status that aggravates any stigma attached to foreign origins. Often as not, the immigrants' (socially constructed) characteristics are such as to define them as *ineligible* for the very authority positions access to which are largely assumed by a network explanation.

So how do the tables turn? To some extent, conditions at the bottom of the labor market are such that workers engage in extensive churning; in other words, a high turnover rate constantly creates vacancies. Furthermore, immigrants may be more apt to apply for these jobs than anyone else, since the conditions and stigma associated with the economy's "bad jobs" motivates natives to search out other options whenever possible. So even if excluded, the immigrants can rapidly build up concentrations; as they do so, the number with the ability to help a friend or family member get and keep a job quickly increases. Given bosses' "natural" preference to recruit from inside, the immigrant presence automatically grows.

This explanation may apply at the very bottom of the labor market. But as I have shown above, immigrant networks get implanted at higher levels of the labor market, funneling into jobs where conditions and compensation are not unattractive. Often, immigrants move into positions previously dominated by some prior, established, group, which until then had displayed an effective track record of foreclosing entry to others.

As I argued in *Still the Promised City?*, changes in the shape of the labor queue create the conditions under which immigrant networks can connect with positions at various reaches of the job structure. Changes in the *shape* of the labor queue—that is, the relative sizes of groups—create the potential for *ethnic succession*. The critical development occurs when the relative size of the established group declines—usually as the result of economic growth which pulls it up the labor queue, or as a consequence of a change in the group's *ranking* of available jobs. Erosion in a job's relative pay, prestige, or security may trigger its abandonment by members of the established group; in the United States, with its history of serial migrant recruitment, job rankings also shift as generations change, as the children and grandchildren of immigrants "assimilate" the preferences shared by natives.

Thus, in New York, succession processes of this sort provided the backdrop for the new immigrant story that progressively unfolded after 1965. At the population level, the disproportionately declining Euro-American presence had a ladder effect, creating empty spaces for newcomers up and down—though mainly down—the economic totem pole. With the exception of construction and a few other skilled trades, New York's Euro-American proletariat disappeared after 1970. Consequently, immigrants could move in and replace departed Euro-American workers, without conflict or opposition from incumbents. Ethnic succession even generated opportunities in declining industries, where the rate of outflow among European-origin ethnics often outpaced the rate of job erosion. New York's small-business sector was home to the same game of musical chairs: newcomers repeatedly moved in as Euro-American ethnics abandoned petty retailing, garment contracting, and other less remunerative business lines. Since changes in the standing of occupations *relative* to a group's opportunities or preferences are the key to shifts in or out of a niche, succession processes occurred at relatively high levels of the occupational structure—as was the case among municipal engineers or accountants, who were once uniformly Jewish, Italian, or Irish, but are now increasingly dominated by Asian, Middle Eastern, and Russian professionals from abroad.

THE MICROPOLITICS OF THE IMMIGRANT NICHE

Network-based explanations of the implantation of immigrants into the economy, and then the gradual transmutation of ethnic clusters into niches, provide an account of *social reproduction*. But the first task at hand is to account for an instance of *social discontinuity*, that is the buildup of an immigrant concentration in a context where there had been little, if any, immigrant presence before. As I have suggested above, *ethnic succession*, if conceptualized as a process driven by contingent, not inevitable, changes in the availability of established groups, can explain why immigrant outsiders suddenly get inserted into structures from which they have previously been excluded.

But once inside, the formerly excluded can turn their situation to good account. Hiring is a risk, as is investing in human capital, and the search for risk reduction leads to network recruitment, which both improves the quality and the quantity of information that both workers and employers need. The social closure potential of immigrant networks accounts for much its effectiveness: it is precisely the latent power inherent in a dense, overlapping set of immigrant connections that provides veterans with the ability to ensure that the referrals whom they sponsor will behave as promised. Likewise, in business, the web of contacts within a community serves a somewhat similar function, the history of prior exchanges with members of an ethnic network providing a baseline against which future behavior can be assessed. Since relations among coethnics are likely to be many sided, rather than specialized, community effects go beyond their informational value, engendering both codes of conduct and the mechanisms for sanctioning those who violate norms.

Thus, the formation of an immigrant niche almost inevitably yields exclusion. To some extent, exclusion results from the simple operation of network recruitment: reliance on incumbents and their contacts also makes those lacking similar contacts ineligible. But exclusion also results from more deliberate efforts at social closure: the same connections that bring ethnic communities into the workplace also provide the motivation and opportunities for excluding those workers who are not members of the same ethnic club. After all, work is a fundamentally social activity, where the basic skills are learned through interaction with others on the job: if the numerically dominant group will not accept you, it is hard to get by and complete the tasks to which one is assigned, which means that trouble is sure to be lurking around the corner.

Moreover, the symmetry between workers' and employers' interests only goes so far. To begin with, incumbents are naturally positioned to exercise influence over the hiring process, whether management likes it or not. Possessing lateral contacts that managers do not possess, coethnic workers are often more likely than management to know when a vacancy will arise—and have a networked associate in place to fill the job before anyone has ever had a chance to post it. Though hiring through networks involves incumbents as enforcers of implicit contracts regarding effort and reward, it also tends to bind management, constraining its freedom to ignore the spontaneous referrals provided by the key workers. Since workers have to get along to get the job done, management ignores these hiring preferences at its peril. Under conditions of job scarcity, moreover, workers seek to maximize employment opportunities for their kin and associates, a goal unlikely to always coincide with management's objectives. Consequently, the ties that bind the workforce comprise a resource that workers can use to expand the scope of network hiring, against management's preferences.

Thus, the immigrant niche tends to expand through two types of closure strategies, one involving *exclusion*, the other, *usurpation*. Exclusionary closure occurs when ethnically distinctive insiders attempt to monopolize job opportunities for members of their core network and restrict outsiders. By contrast, usurpationary closure occurs when workers expand the scope of network hiring, restricting management's ability to access the labor market, and enforce their own-group preferences as against those of the employer.

CONCLUSION

In a sense, this chapter tells the oldest of stories, confirming that today's immigrants are following the timeworn paths of immigrants' past: linked by connections to established residents, and moving with the help and guidance provided by veterans, newcomers gravitate to the jobs where their compatriots have started. Because migration is driven by networks, it also involves a process of social reproduction, in which the current crop of workers begets a new bunch that looks very much like themselves.

But there is also something new under the sun: the ethnic niches of today are not quite the same as the ethnic niches of yore. Yes, they are often to be found at the bottom rungs of the occupational ladder, where workers with no other resource but social support necessarily rely for help on others of their own kind. But the distinctively new breed of immigrants—the newcomers who arrive with high levels of education—turn out to be no less likely to converge on niches than their less-skilled counterparts. Whether high or low skilled, the nature of the migration tends to feed the newcomers into clusters of similar type. Though the economies of America's major immigrant urban regions offer striking contrasts, immigrants of any one group secure niches of much the same type, regardless of place.

At once pervasive and persistent, the ethnic niche shows that ethnicity is not simply an imported cultural characteristic, but rather a principle of social organization, deeply shaping the role that immigrants play in the dynamic economies of turn-of-the-twenty-first-century America. The product of the largely unconscious actions of employers and workers, natives and immigrants, the niche also activates a set of boundary creating and maintaining mechanisms, providing groups with the motivation and the opportunity for excluding all those who are not members of the same ethnic club.

NOTES

1. For further elaboration along these lines, see Waldinger 1993. For a further discussion of the impact of spatial factors on ethnic economies, see Waldinger, McEvoy, and Aldrich 1990 and Kaplan 1998. Of course, the paragraph above constructs the

problem in relatively narrow terms, implying that the issue at hand involves the relationship between the spatial configurations of ethnic entrepreneurs and a set of economic outcomes (such as wages or business foundings), and nothing else. But, as Portes and Rumbaut (1990) argued in *Immigrant America*, to considerable success, the ethnic enclave, as *form of immigrant community*, can affect the process of immigrant incorporation in any number of ways. That effect is largely due to the enclave's status as an encompassing entity, crosscut by a web of complex relations among coethnics of various sorts, where the density and multiplexity of ties produces considerable social control. The question is how those social control effects vary according to the spatial configuration of a community: are they dependent on recurrent face-to-face contacts, or do they persist under conditions of greater decentralization? To my (very possibly imperfect) knowledge, this question has not been systematically addressed.

2. As suggested earlier, my summary may be framing the debate in excessively narrow terms. To some extent, the discussion may simply have taken a different turn, no longer concerned with the narrow economic effects of the enclave, but rather with its broader, and possibly longer-term social consequences. If it is the case that participation in an ethnic enclave exposes members to broader social resources not available to those group members with lower levels of community attachment, then the economic consequences of employment in an enclave firm—whether positive, negative, or simply benign, as compared to the generally unattractive alternatives—may be of lesser significance. For an argument along these lines, see Zhou and Bankston 1997. In my view, again possibly mistaken, the case is not settled.
3. See Waldinger, 1996*b*, Chapters 3 and 4 and the footnote on p. 340.
4. The occupations and industries on which this chapter focuses involve the detailed, three-digit, categories identified in the Census of Population. Though sometimes overlapping, occupations and industries are distinctive categories. For example, most carpenters tend to work in the construction industry; but those who work for the University of California would be categorized as employees in the "higher education" industry.

REFERENCES

Alba, R., and Nee, V. (1997). "Rethinking Assimilation Theory for a New Era of Immigration." *International Migration Review*, 21 (4): 826–74.

Bailey, T., and Waldinger, R. (1991). "Primary, Secondary, and Enclave Labor Markets: A Training Systems Approach." *American Sociological Review*, 56 (4): 432–45.

Borjas, G. (1994). "Long-run Convergence of Ethnic Skill Differentials: The Children and Grandchildren of the Great Migration." *Industrial and Labor Relations Review*, 47 (4): 553–73.

Der-Martirosian, C. (1996). "Economic Embeddedness and Social Capital of Immigrants: Iranians in Los Angeles." Unpublished Ph.D. dissertation, University of California, Los Angeles.

—— (Forthcoming). "Immigrant Self-Employment and Social Capital." *Ethnic and Racial Studies*.

Gilbertson, G. (1995). "Women's Labor and Enclave Employment: The Case of Dominican and Colombian Women in New York City." *International Migration Review*, 29 (3): 657–70.

——, and Gurak, D. (1993). "Broadening the Ethnic Enclave Debate." *Sociological Forum*, 8 (3): 205–19.

Gold, S., and Phillips, B. (1996). "Israelis in the United States," in *American Jewish Yearbook 1996*. New York: American Jewish Committtee, 51–101.

Gordon, D. (1972). *Theories of Poverty and Unemployment: Orthodox, Radical, and Dual Labor Market Perspectives.* Lexington, MA: Heath.

Gordon, M. (1964). *Assimilation in American Life.* New York: Oxford University Press.

Kaplan, D. (1998). "The Spatial Structure of Urban Ethnic Economies." *Urban Geography*, 19 (6): 489–501.

Kasinitz, P. (1992). *Caribbean New Yorkers.* Ithaca: Cornell University Press.

Kim, I. (1981). *The New Urban Immigrants.* Princeton: Princeton University Press.

Lieberson, S. (1980). *A Piece of the Pie.* Berkeley: University of California Press.

Light, I. (1972). *Ethnic Enterprise in America.* Berkeley: University of California Press.

——, and Karageorgis, S. (1994). "The Ethnic Economy," in N. Smelser and R. Swedberg (eds.), *The Handbook of Economic Sociology.* Princeton: Princeton University Press and New York: Russell Sage Foundation, 647–72.

——, Sabagh, G., Bozorgmehr, M., and Der-Martirosian, C. (1994). "Beyond the Ethnic Enclave Economy." *Social Problems*, 41: 65–80.

Logan, J. R., Alba, R., and McNulty, T. R. (1994). "Ethnic Economies in Metropolitan Regions: Miami and Beyond." *Social Forces*, 72 (3): 691–724.

Loury, G. (1998). "Discrimination in the Post-Civil Rights Era: Beyond Market Interactions." *Journal of Economic Perspectives*, 12: 2117–126.

Min, P. G. (1996). *Caught in the Middle: Korean Communities in New York and Los Angeles.* Berkeley: University of California Press.

Model, S. (1993). "The Ethnic Niche and the Structure of Opportunity: Immigrants and Minorities in New York City," in M. Katz (ed.), *The Historical Origins of the Underclass.* New York: Princeton University Press, 161–94.

Nee, V., Sanders, J., and Sernau, S. (1994). "Job Transitions in an Immigrant Metropolis: Ethnic Boundaries and the Mixed Economy." *American Sociological Review*, 59 (6): 849–72.

Ortiz, V. (1996). "The Mexican-Origin Population: Permanent Working-Class or Emerging Middle-Class," in R. Waldinger and M. Bozorgmehr (eds.), *Ethnic Los Angeles.* New York: Russell Sage, Chapter 9.

Piore, M. (1979). *Birds of Passage.* Cambridge: Cambridge University Press.

Portes, A. (1981). "Modes of Immigrant Incorporation," in M. M. Kritz, C. B. Keely, and S. M. Tomas (eds.), *Global Trends in Migration: Theory and Research on International Population Movements.* Staten Island: Center for Migration Studies, 262–83.

——, and Bach, R. (1985). *Latin Journey.* Berkeley: University of California Press.

——, and Jensen, L. (1989). "The Enclave and the Entrants: Patterns of Ethnic Enterprise in Miami before and after Mariel." *American Sociological Review*, 54 (6): 929–49.

——, and Rumbaut, R. G. (1990). *Immigrant America: A Portrait.* Berkeley: University of California Press.

——, and Sensenbrenner, J. (1993). "Embeddedness and Immigration: Notes on the Social Determination of Economic Action." *American Journal of Sociology*, 98: 1320–50.

——, and Stepick, A. (1993). *City on the Edge.* Berkeley: University of California Press.

Rischin, M. (1962). *The Promised City.* Cambridge: Harvard University Press.

Sanders, J., and Nee, V. (1987). "Limits of Ethnic Solidarity in the Ethnic Enclave Economy." *American Sociological Review*, 52: 745–67.

Tang, J. (1993). "The Career Attainment of Caucasian and Asian Engineers." *Sociological Quarterly*, 34 (3): 467–96.

—— (1994). "Caucasians and Asians in Engineering: A Study in Occupational Mobility and Departure." *Research in the Sociology of Organizations*, 11: 217–56.

U.S. Federal Glass Ceiling Commission. (1995). *Good for Business: Making Full Use of the Nation's Human Capital.* Fact-Finding Report. Washington, DC.

Waldinger, R. (1993). "The Ethnic Enclave Debate Revisited." *International Journal of Urban and Regional Research*, 17 (3): 428–36.

—— (1994). "The Making of an Immigrant Niche." *International Migration Review*, 28 (1): 3–30.

—— (1996*a*). "Ethnicity and Opportunity in the Plural City," in R. Waldinger and M. Bozorgmehr (eds.), *Ethnic Los Angeles.* New York: Russell Sage, Chapter 15.

—— (1996*b*). *Still the Promised City? African-Americans and New Immigrants in Post-industrial New York.* Cambridge: Harvard University Press.

——, and Tseng, Y. (1992). "Divergent Diasporas: The Chinese Communities of New York and Los Angeles Compared." *Revue Européene des Migrations Internationales*, 8 (3): 91–116.

——, McEvoy, D., and Aldrich, H. (1990). "Spatial Dimensions of Opportunity Structures," in R. Waldinger, H. Aldrich, and R. Ward (eds.), *Ethnic Entrepreneurs: Immigrant Business in Industrial Societies.* Newbury Park, CA: Sage, 106–30.

Wilson, K., and Portes, A. (1980). "Immigrant Enclaves: An Analysis of the Labor Market Experiences of Cubans in Miami." *American Journal of Sociology*, 88 (July): 295–319.

Zhou, M. (1992). *Chinatown: The Socioeconomic Potential of an Immigrant Enclave.* Philadelphia: Temple University Press.

——, and Bankston, C. (1997). *Growing Up American.* New York: Russell Sage.

——, and Kim, R. (1999). "A Tale of Two Metropolises: Immigrant Chinese Communities in New York and Los Angeles." Paper presented at the conference on New York and Los Angeles in the New Millenium, University of California, Los Angeles, May 1999.

——, and Logan, J. (1989). "Returns on Human Capital in Ethnic Enclaves: New York City's Chinatown." *American Sociological Review*, 54: 809–20.

Zhou, Y. (1998) "How Do Places Matter? A Comparative Study of Chinese Ethnic Economies in Los Angeles and New York City." *Urban Geography*, 19 (6): 531–53.

PART VII

QUESTIONS OF CITIZENSHIP

With the historical emergence of the modern state, citizenship came almost exclusively to be defined in terms of *national* political rights and obligations transcending all internal social differences. In its full normative sense, the idea of citizenship signified—as it still does in much current political theory—the universal equality of all individuals formally incorporated by birthright or by legal contract into the fold of the state.

In democratic and protodemocratic societies throughout the nineteenth and twentieth centuries, this idea—in spite of its abstraction—has typically struck deeply responsive chords. It is an idea, however, that now appears to be entering a moment of crisis. In the first place, globalization is in certain respects eroding confidence in the nation-state as the final and absolute source of identity and political allegiance. In the second place, a discourse of democracy and human rights is rapidly diffusing to all corners of the world, leading many intranational social groups to assert political demands based on particularities of their culture, ethnicity, ways of life, and so on. As Holston argues, demands such as these undermine the already precarious theory of universal citizenship, and since they are an expression of real needs as opposed to universal norms, they are often most clearly articulated and acted upon in local contexts. One major instance of local context in this connection is the global city-region, which in and of itself is a basic kind of sociogeographic community as well as being a sort of composite of multiple smaller communities. We might say that global city-regions are on the way to becoming critical test-beds for and repositories of alternative visions and practices of citizenship and democracy in the twenty-first century. Once that has been said, however, we must be wary of assimilating this turn of events into something approximating a revival of Greek or Medieval European city-states. The actual and potential role of global city-regions as laboratories of new political practices is itself an expression of a multiple rescaling of political life in an era of intensifying globalization. In this process, we are at one and the same time caught up in overlapping webs of relationships in which the local is but one element alongside a number of other (e.g. national and supranational) ranges of political action and allegiance. Equally, optimism about the prospects for enhanced democracy and citizenship in global city-regions needs to be tempered by an acknowledgment of possible countercurrents as national governments jettison many of the social responsibilities that they formerly shouldered, leaving local governments to deal with the ensuing problems as best they can.

Classical theories of citizenship and democracy are deeply rooted in Western historical experience. For this reason, questions of democracy and citizenship in non-Western societies, when viewed through the lenses offered by these theories, are often subject to distorted evaluations. One of the most egregious expressions of this tendency, as Isin writes, can be found in late nineteenth century European "orientalist" thought, which asserted that in the absence of processes of city growth and social change like those associated with the Western European urban tradition, Islamic societies were unable to construct equivalent legal and political freedoms. Isin challenges this notion and then uses this platform to launch a detailed discussion of citizenship and democracy in contemporary Istanbul. Here, in the most economically developed and globalized city in Turkey, issues of citizenship and democracy are unambiguously on the political agenda, but they are, in addition, filtered through a deeply Islamic sense of identity. Isin goes on to argue that this filtering should be seen not as a deformation but as an extension of the central meaning of these issues.

Concomitantly, while a common rhetoric of individual rights, democratic participation, and the rule of law is spreading across the globe at the present time, social manifestations of this rhetoric vary widely from place to place and across all levels of geographical scale. Perhaps nowhere is this variety of response more evident than in the practical political experiments currently proceeding on all sides in the world's main city-regions.

17

Urban Citizenship and Globalization

JAMES HOLSTON

What it means to be a rights-bearing member of a territorial nation-state has changed significantly over the last quarter of the twentieth century. After several centuries of triumph over other forms of membership in the political community, the very notion of national citizenship appears unsettled. In a few of the world's 191 sovereign states, processes of disintegration have advanced to the point that the nation-state is no longer the locus of primary affiliation. In some cases, more local and sometimes shifting memberships replace it; in others, more diasporic and deterritorialized affiliations seem paramount. In most nations, however, national citizenship is still the primary envelope of affiliation and loyalty. Yet, in the last several decades, global processes of change of unprecedented force have so affected the meaning and substance of many national citizenships that the resulting social morphologies seem unfamiliar even to their members.

In many instances, nations have become patchworks of culturally heterogeneous urban spaces. Some of these city-regions are a veritable babble of polyglot, marginalized, and nonnational migrant populations. In most cases, heterogeneity is not so extreme because processes of assimilation to a national language and culture remain strong. Nevertheless, most cities experience a remaking of political mobilization through local civic affiliation that is significant. As the inequalities and injustices with which so many people live are great, such changes may well be for the better if they force a reformulation of the principles of membership and the distribution of resources. In the context of this kind of world transformation, it becomes imperative to understand in what ways and by what forces citizenship has changed as a fundamental status of membership in modern society. How does contemporary globalization affect citizenship and the prospects of both local and national democratic participation? Which global forces, in what contexts, by which processes, and with what consequences?

I propose that of the major forces of contemporary globalization, the one of particular importance for citizenship is the globalization of democracy. Since the mid-1970s, the rights-discourses of democracy have circulated throughout the world with remarkable force. They have turned democracy into both a global value and a global process of transformation that no single bloc of nations or cultural tradition can claim exclusively. Moreover, this globalization has severed democracy from its tight historical association with national citizenship and thereby with discrete, unified, neatly bordered nation-states. In the most diverse societies, the rights-discourses of global democracy have mobilized new forms and forces of citizenship to engage many of the consequences of other processes of globalization. I argue that the discourses of democratic rights are particularly engaging because they address the social and economic inequalities that so many people suffer and that the globalization of capital and labor in recent decades has intensified. I am not suggesting, let me emphasize, that democracy is either necessary or preparatory for global capitalism. Rather, the globalization of democracy is a force in its own right, sometimes benefiting and sometimes restraining capital markets. The fact is that people use democratic rights to fight not only authoritarian rule but also ruthless capitalism.

I further suggest that cities—and metropolitan regions especially—are the crucial sites for the impact of global democracy and the strategic arenas for the development of new citizenships. Cities make the consequences of global capitalism and migration a lived experience for masses of people, manifest in urban spatial forms, social (dis)organization, property relations, living conditions, service and resource distributions, job opportunities, and economic crises. As people struggle over the conditions of urban life, they mobilize around right-claims that address the inequities of these conditions. In the process, they become active citizens, developing new sources of rights and new agendas of citizenship. In this way, the lived experience of cities becomes both the context and the substance of emergent forms of citizenship. I will refer to these forms as urban citizenship (1) when the city is the primary political community, (2) when urban residence is the criterion of membership and the basis of political mobilization, and (3) when right-claims addressing urban experience and related civic performances are the substance of citizenship. Thus, I propose that one of the significant consequences of the globalization of democracy for city-regions is the generation of new urban citizenships. In these terms, urban citizenship does not necessarily supplant or negate national citizenship. But it has two important consequences. It leads to a reformulation of national citizenship and it is available to nonnationals. By the latter, I mean that resident nonnationals can become urban citizens, exercising substantive but not formal (i.e. national) citizenship.

There are many urban conditions that become the substantive concerns of new citizenships. I will focus on one condition that seems to me a fundamental and predictable catalyst, namely, illegal residence, a category that encompasses diverse forms of illegality and that characterizes the urban experience of masses of people in metropolitan regions throughout the world. Some of these residential illegalities are consequences of recent globalization and some are consequences of earlier processes of urbanization that recent changes exacerbate. Typically, the urban poor—many of whom are disenfranchised—are drawn to the rights-discourses of democracy as a means to redress the many disabilities that their illegal residence produces. They use the newly legitimate language of rights to advance an agenda of "rights to the city," claiming rights to resources not in the name of national citizenship—not, in other words, because they are Brazilians or Mexicans—but because they are city residents. Thus, illegal residence in the city becomes the basis both for new citizenship mobilizations and for a conception of citizenship based on urban residence. Furthermore, when city governments respond to illegal residence, their policies often lead, paradoxically, to new legal regimes that legitimate this urban citizenship. As a result, the city's poor succeed in expanding citizenship to new social bases. In this situation, urban policymakers and city residents together generate new forms of citizenship and reform legal codes around agendas for a more social democracy. As I suggest below, nationalistic and xenopbohic reactions such as the criminalization of the poor and the dismantling of state social services may undercut this new urban citizenship. However, they do not abolish it.

In evaluating the effects of recent globalization on citizenship, it is important to recognize that the rights-discourses of democracy are themselves heterogeneous and are variably absorbed and utilized. Such variation produces significantly different results in the context of illegal city residence. In what follows, I first discuss the globalization of democracy and its discourses of rights, and then use two examples to demonstrate its impact on citizenship, the importance of cities and illegal residence, and the differing results. The first case is the metropolitan region of São Paulo, Brazil, and the second is the city of Oceanside, located within the suprametropolitan region of San Diego and Los Angeles in Southern California. If São Paulo is more typical of city-regions structured by national populations of rich and poor in emerging democracies, Oceanside represents the development of more polyglot and nonnational cities within established democracies.

THE GLOBALIZATION OF DEMOCRACY

The recent expansion of democracy has taken root in remarkably varied ground. I will use data for electoral democracy to illustrate its globalization. In just twenty-five years, since the mid-1970s, the number of electoral democracies has more than doubled. During this period, approximately seventy-four countries changed from nondemocratic to democratic political systems. In 1972, there were 52 electoral democracies, constituting thirty-three percent of the world's 160 sovereign nation-states. By 1996, the number had risen to 118 democracies out of 191 states, or sixty-two percent of the total, for a net gain of 66 democratic states. Among the larger countries, those with a population of one million or more people, the number of political democracies nearly tripled during the same period. Significantly, the number of nondemocratic states has declined by a third since the early 1970s, after rising steadily from the beginning of the century. If it took almost two hundred years of modern world history to generate about fifty democratic states by 1970, it has taken only ten years of political change since the mid-1980s to yield the same number of new democracies. The wave of democratic change that began in the mid-1970s—the third or fourth wave since the Age of Revolution—is by far the strongest. As Tables 17.1 and 17.2 indicate, never before has the world experienced such democratization as in the late twentieth century.[1]

Table 17.1. *Democratization in the twentieth century*

Year	Total states	Electoral democracies	Nondemocratic states	% electoral democracies of total states
1922	64	29	35	45.3
1942	61	12	49	19.7
1962	111	36	75	32.4
1973	122	30	92	24.6
1990	129	58	71	45.0
1996	150	87	63	58.0

Note: Huntington's estimates omit countries with a population of less than one million. I use "Electoral Democracies" where Huntington has "Democratic States" to emphasize the defining role of elections in the political conception of democracy he employs. For comparative purposes, I also omit countries with a population of less than one million for year 1996.

Sources: Years 1922–90 are from Huntington 1991: 26 (Table 1.1); Year 1996 is derived from Freedom House 1997.

Table 17.2. *Third-wave democratization, 1972–96*

Year	Total states	Electoral democracies	Nondemocratic states	% electoral democracies of total states
1972	160	52	108	32.5
1977	164	56	108	34.2
1982	167	60	107	35.9
1986	167	67	100	40.1
1992	186	99	87	53.2
1996	191	118	73	61.8

Note: Includes all sovereign states in each year.

Source: Derived from the annual surveys of political rights and civil liberties in Freedom House 1978, 1983, 1987, 1993, 1997.

This movement for political democracy has swept over every region of the globe. The sheer number of national transformations reveals a world politically remade. In the early 1970s, one-party regimes and military dictatorships of various sorts held power over most of Latin America, Africa, Asia, and Eastern Europe. In 1975, only three countries in all of Latin South and Central America had democratically elected national leaders, namely Colombia, Costa Rica, and Venezuela. At the same time, the Soviet empire held much of Eastern and Central Europe and Central Asia in undemocratic union. Of the thirty-six countries that gained independence in Africa between 1956 and 1970, thirty-three became authoritarian at birth or shortly thereafter. The exceptions were Botswana and short-lived electoral democracies in Ghana and Nigeria. If African decolonization produced most of the world's new states in the 1960s, it also yielded the most sustained wave of authoritarian new governments in history (see Bratton and Walle 1997). In the Asia-Pacific region, only a handful of countries had democratic regimes in 1975, including Australia, Fiji, Japan, New Zealand, Papua New Guinea, and Sri Lanka. Others, such as India, Pakistan, the Philippines, and South Korea had suffered democratic reversals in the 1960s and 1970s.

By 1996, however, democracy had dramatically transformed the political development of all these regions. Among the 35 states that compose the Americas, 31 are today electoral democracies (89 percent). In South and Central America, of 20 nations, only Peru and possibly Mexico cannot be called at least formally democratic. Of the 53 countries in contemporary Africa, the number of electoral democracies has increased to 18 (34 percent). In the Asia-Pacific region, 24 of its 38 nation-states are now politically democratic (63 percent). With the collapse of the Soviet Union, 19 countries have become democratic out of 27 in the region it used to control (70 percent). Only in the Middle East has democracy been stagnant in terms of national rule, where 2 out of 14 states (Israel and Turkey) are democratic (14 percent)—though it is important to observe that *local* democratic projects and debates about democracy abound throughout the region.

Indisputably, with this new wave of democratization, democracy has become a global value, adopted by the most diverse societies and cultures. This transcultural scope raises a host of questions as to how to assess democracy's quality and its relation to citizenship in such diverse situations. I doubt that the political theories of democracy anchored in Western history and culture remain adequate for understanding its global reach and its non-Western experience. Elsewhere, I have suggested an alternative approach (see Holston, forthcoming). Here, I want to emphasize a number of related points about citizenship. Although I have just relied on a survey of electoral democracy to establish its globalization, it is crucial for researchers and policymakers alike to understand the limited importance of elections in evaluating emerging democracies. A deeper study of these cases than surveys permit shows beyond doubt that political democracy is not enough to secure the civil rights of citizenship or to produce a democratic rule of law. Without both, the realization of democratic citizenship remains disabled. To get a better understanding of the quality of democracy, it is necessary to study not only elections but also the realization of the substance of citizenship in a much fuller sense. That means evaluating its full array of socioeconomic, civil, and cultural rights in addition to political rights. It means studying its cultural and social conditions in addition to its formal institutionalization. Certainly, this kind of anthropological analysis is more difficult and untidy than electoral minimalism. But it is vastly more accurate of the actual conditions that legitimate or discredit democracy, citizenship, and law.

From this more complex perspective, it is clear that in both emerging and established democracies the distribution of democratic citizenship is typically uneven among citizens in a given political space. That is, it is normal for democracy to expand in some areas of citizenship while contracting in others and for those who are formally citizens to experience it differently. In this sense, democratization is normally what I call disjunctive: It comprises processes in the institutionalization, performance, and meaning of citizenship that are always uneven, unbalanced, and heterogeneous. Two types of democratic disjunction are especially prevalent and suggest why cities are such salient sites for the constitution of different citizens. First, my research indicates that approximately 65 percent of third-wave democracies experience a similar disjunction: Although their political institutions democratize with considerable success in the sense of promoting reasonably free and fair elections, respected political rights, and functioning elected institutions, and although they promulgate constitutions and legal codes based on the rule of law and democratic principles, their citizens suffer systematic violations of civil rights. With the civil component of citizenship seriously impaired, the citizens of these electoral democracies usually experience violence, injustice, and legal disability more than they realize the stated norms of their constitutions (see Holston, forthcoming).

Thus, these democracies are both electoral and uncivil (as I call them) at the same time. As a result, uncivil electoral democracies share certain significant features of citizenship: Their institutions of law and justice undergo delegitimation; violent crime and police abuse escalate; the poor and the ethnically other are criminalized, dehumanized, and attacked; civility and civil protection in public space decline; people abandon the public to retreat behind private security; and illegal measures of control receive massive popular support. Across the nation, the civil components of citizenship are unevenly and irregularly distributed among citizens. In emerging democracies, the impairment of the civil component of citizenship often affects the majority of citizens, especially the poor. In established democracies, this disjunction more usually affects racial or cultural minorities. Other types of democratic disjunctions also occur and often at the same time. For example, in the United States the civil rights of innercity minorities are regularly violated, legally resident nonnationals—a significant segment of many American cities—have no political rights (though they did before World War I), and social rights for all Americans are scant.[2]

The second prevalent democratic disjunction concerns the relation between the formal status of citizenship and the substantive rights people exercise. Although in theory membership entails full access to rights and access depends on membership, in practice the two are often independent of each other. Thus, formal membership is increasingly neither a necessary nor sufficient condition for substantive citizenship. For the urban poor, for example, formal membership in the state is not sufficient to prevent exclusion in fact or law from the rights of citizenship and effective participation in its organization. This disjunction also affects what I would call life-style minorities, groups particularly important in cities. Often their preferences for "the good life" as they define it—for example, in terms of religious practice or sexual orientation—are not embodied in the national consensus of rights. Even though these groups are comprised of national citizens and form residential communities that overwhelmingly approve their preferences, they can neither exercise nor protect the identities most important to them with security. It is now evident that the disjunction of formal membership without much substantive citizenship characterizes the quality of democracy in many of the societies around the world that have experienced democratic transitions in the last twenty-five years.

That formal citizenship is less necessary for access to substantive rights is also apparent, especially in established democracies that have large populations of legally resident noncitizens such as the United States. Although formal membership may be required for some rights, like voting, it is not for most. Hence, legally resident noncitizens (and sometimes illegally resident ones) often have virtually identical social and civil rights as citizens. Furthermore, those rights that are exclusively reserved for citizens are often perceived as onerous, like military service and jury duty. As a result, immigrant noncitizens may not be interested in acquiring national citizenship, particularly if naturalization compromises their rights of return or of property and inheritance in their homelands. Thus, though they are not citizens, these residents have access to citizenship rights similar to those of national citizens of comparable socioeconomic experience, except that they have no political representation. This condition is typical, for example, of the large number of long-term legally resident Mexicans in the United States, most of whom live in cities. As I will show in the case of Oceanside, their lack of political representation is a major problem for American democracy.

It may also be said that many citizens perceive the near parity of social and civil rights with noncitizens as unfair and demoralizing. They may even perceive it as devaluing the institutions of national citizenship in both a moral and an economic sense. Such is the case in the United States and is the motivation behind ballet initiatives in several states to ensure that illegally resident noncitizens do not receive the social benefits of citizens—the most famous being California's Proposition 187 of 1994 which made "illegal aliens ineligible for public social services, public health care services (unless emergency under federal law), and attendance at public schools [and required that] state/local agencies report suspected illegal aliens." Such perceptions of the demoralization of national citizenship are also the source of recent federal acts in 1996 and 1997 that the Republican-dominated Congress passed to restrict welfare rights to even legally resident noncitizens. Perhaps paradoxically, perhaps intentionally, one consequence of this legislation is that more resident noncitizens applied for and received national citizenship in 1998 than ever in the history of American naturalization.

These two types of disjunction—uneven citizenships and discrepancies between form and substance—are today characteristic of global democracy. They make it impossible to define contemporary citizenship in terms of uniform national membership. This is not to gainsay nationalism as a global force today or to deny that many cases of democratization involve national self-determination through elections. It is rather to observe, first, that democracy's project of national identity through citizenship is different from the homogenization of ethnicity and polity on which nationalism depends (see Gellner 1983); and, second, that although this project may include democratic elections, it entails a more complex notion of membership. Indeed, the disjunctions I have described make it difficult to attribute to contemporary democratic citizenship the unifying social ground that T. H. Marshall's classic study supposed would be its national foundation, namely, "a direct sense of community membership based on loyalty to a civilization which is a common possession" (1977: 94, originally 1950). This normative ideal of a nation of commensurable citizens who share a culture of citizenship rights, practices, and meanings *in spite of all other differences* may have been fundamental to the modern origins of democracy. Ironically, however, this project seems less plausible today with democracy's global expansion.

If neither the drive for commensurable national identity nor the sense of common culture fuels this expansion, what does? What makes democracy resonate deeply with the aspirations of so many different peoples and societies? Part of the answer is surely that democracy has become overwhelmingly identified with rights and not with other components that might conceivably make up its understanding, such as civic duty, direct participation in the business of rule, institutionalized accountablity, or procedural justice. It is the rights version of democracy that has such universal appeal. Over the last several decades, the language of democratic rights has become a universally legitimate mode of contestation. Casting claims in these terms seems to legitimate them. Moreover, this universality derives from the United Nation's Universal Declaration of Human Rights of 1948 and not from the hegemony of any specific national (e.g. American) version. As I will show with the case of São Paulo, the discourses of rights that are especially motivating refer to the new collective and personal spaces of the modern metropolis—especially the experiences of daily life and residence rather than of work. As this urban residential experience is largely new, the rights-discourses that address it give the urban poor an unprecedented sense of power and creativity to forge new kinds of citizenships outside the old normative, institutionalized, and often outdated and repressive definitions of the state. Thus, the rights-discourses of global democracy are grounded in both personal and collective urban experience.

That said, let me also stress that democracy's rights-discourses are variable and fluid. They acquire different meanings in different contexts to the extent that I do not think it useful to attempt a general and systematic definition. In Brazil, the language of rights that mobilizes most people concerns socioeconomic (but not civil) rights; in Argentina, rights to memory and to justice; in the United States, rights to difference. Perhaps it is possible to conjecture that democracy mobilizes such diverse peoples globally because, at least in part, its aura of rights draws them to the animating idea that as human beings they have an inalienable "right to rights," as Hannah Arendt put it. Perhaps, less mystically, the answer is also that as people become modern urban workers, they feel that they have a right to rights because they are productive and contributing members of the public sphere of the city.

RIGHTS TO THE CITY: SÃO PAULO, [illegible]

Beginning in the 1940s, the vast urban periphery of the c[illegible] veloped as a region of mainly residential neighborhoods [illegible] In many ways, its development is paradigmatic of the growth o[illegible] pheries around most of the major cities in the developing world[illegible] these cities into metropolitan regions, the urbanization of the hint[illegible] enormous social, political, and economic consequences. I will use [illegible]o's periphery to illustrate the impact of global democracy on a city-regio[illegible] spatially and socially structured by nationally oriented processes of industrialization. To evaluate this impact, I need first to outline this structure and to establish the model of citizenship for the urban poor prior to the onset of global democracy.

The structuring of São Paulo's periphery as an urban space occurred during the postwar period of nationalist industrial development that peaked in the early 1970s under military dictatorship. The periphery began to take urban shape in the 1940s as the place for the settlement of masses of new migrants drawn to the city's flourishing industries. It emerged as the "solution" to the housing crisis of the 1940s: As São Paulo received waves of new migrants, its market in new housing shifted from rent to ownership, excluding most of them. The state encouraged this shift through a number of policies, the most important of which were rent control and master urban plans. The Renters Law, 1942–64, discouraged investment in new rental units by freezing rents well below inflation for two decades. At the same time, the state implemented a series of urban plans—such as the haussmanian Plan of the Avenues in 1938—to remodel the center of the city and to open the periphery through road construction. Linked to these policies of urban management was the creation of federally funded banks that were supposed to enable qualified workers to become home owners but whose funds were mostly usurped by the middle classes. As a result, investors lost interest in cheap rental units in centrally located tenements and row houses that had been the initial types of housing for the urban lower classes. Instead investors turned their attention to the largely undeveloped hinterland. City government also made this area attractive to investors by continuing to consider it under the legal category "suburban" until the 1960s and by ignoring the tangle of property relations that characterized it. Thus, zoning laws did not require urban infrastructure or centralized title searches. As a result of this shift in interest, new kinds of speculators arose in bus transportation, construction materials, and tract housing to open the periphery for low-income residence.

Tethered to city jobs, São Paulo's workers were pushed out of the central city and into the empty hinterland to fend for themselves. Occasionally, they found cheap tract houses to buy through installments paid to a private developer. Mostly, however, they had to find a plot of accessible land on which to build their own homes. This latter process is called autoconstruction (*autoconstrução*) and refers to the transformation, usually over decades, of an initial shack of wood or concrete block into a finished, furnished, and decorated masonry home—a dream house that is for most autoconstrutors their greatest lifetime project. As each wave of migrants went further out into the hinterland, where the only infrastructure they found was the dirt road speculators put in to sell the land, these house builders became modern pioneers of city-building.

The force of their expansion of São Paulo's periphery has been astonishing. In 1940, this hinterland was essentially unpopulated. In 1991, according to the last national census, 32 percent of the entire city, more than three million people, resided in the poorest areas of the periphery, in the eastern, southern, and northern districts. One of the largest of these districts, São Miguel Paulista, has annual population growth rates that are typical: for 1940–50, 7.7 percent; 1950–60, 15.2 percent, 1960–70, 13.6 percent; 1970–80, 6.6 percent (Caldeira 1984: 38). The change from rent to ownership is just as impressive. According to national census data in 1940, renters occupied 68 percent of the total residences in the municipality of São Paulo. By 1980, this proportion had dropped to 40 percent and the number of owner-occupied residences had increased from 25 to 51 percent (Bonduki 1983: 146). Among low-income households, home ownership is practically the norm: in 1987, almost 60 percent of them throughout the municipality lived in their own homes (Metrô 1990: 30). In São Miguel Paulista, as in the other poorest districts of the periphery, the number is even higher: 69 percent were home owners and only 23 percent renters in the 1991 census.

By the end of the 1970s, the industrialization of metropolitan São Paulo had produced a rich urbanized center, some urbanized areas of concentrated industrial development (such as the so-called ABCD region of the municipalities of Santo André, São Bernardo, São Caetano, and Diadema), and a dispersed, largely unurbanized residential periphery of enormous extent for the poor. In her study of this periphery at the time, Teresa Caldeira (1984) presents the following contrasts: With only 7 percent of the households, the center was almost completely served by electrical and sewage lines and its roads paved. Nearly 75 percent of its households had telephones and less than 20 percent made under five minimum salaries a month.[3] By contrast, with 22 percent of the city's households, the periphery was "the bush" as residents called it. Almost 75 percent of its roads were dirt, which became mud in the rainy season. The vast majority of residents worked far from home, spending about 3.5 hours a day commuting on overcrowded buses and trains. Although 79 percent of the periphery's households had potable water and 97 percent electricity by 1980, only 19 percent were served by sewage lines and less than 5 percent had telephones. Nearly 65 percent of its households made less than five minimum salaries a month. The infant mortality rate was a staggering 81 deaths in the first year for every 1,000 live births. A longer list of contrasts would only show the same thing: a city-region systematically segregated through a combination of market forces and government policies.

The periphery is also overwhelmingly illegal. One study by São Paulo's department of urban planning estimates that in 1990 approximately 65 percent of the city's entire population resided in violation of housing or property laws

(Rolnik, Kowarik, and Somekh 1990: 95)! In many parts of the periphery that figure is even higher.[4] Migrants initiate their settlement in the periphery either by purchasing a house or, much more likely, a house lot on which to build. A relatively small number of people seize their lots without any payment.[5] All of these options almost invariably result in some form of illegal residence. People who squat on seized land have no legal rights to it, though the law tends to recognize their ownership of what they build. Those who purchase lots or houses thereby have some legal claims to own them. However, they usually find that the developer's illegal methods of selling—ranging from outright fraud to the failure to provide the basic urban services required by law—jeopardize legal recognition of the deed.

I want to spend a moment discussing the "illegalization" of residence in the periphery to demonstrate how it is structured (if not promoted) more by urban land law and policy than by illegal activity on the part of the urban poor, though the contrary is often assumed. Without understanding that structuring of illegality, it is not possible to understand why issues of residence galvanized people's interest in democratic rights. As defined in zoning codes, people buy house lots in four types of subdivisions: the legal, irregular, clandestine, and fraudulent. The fully legal is rare. The last three usually exist side-by-side in the same neighborhood, combining the illegalities of several types. The most serious problem is that irregular and clandestine subdivisions are also usually developed on the basis of larger or smaller frauds by developers who claim to have legitimate title to the land. Moreover, especially when the land is relatively unbuilt, developers often sell subdivisions to other developers (swindler to swindler) who redivide the land on paper and sell the lots again to other home builders. Sometimes, the same developer redivides and sells the land over and over. Each new subdivision brings threats of eviction to those who have already built, as developers superimpose layers of lots, frauds, and victims.

When people buy a lot in an illegal subdivision, they cannot register their deed of title in the appropriate public registry until they correct the infraction. Without registration, there is no ownership. However, it may take residents years to discover that there is a problem for two reasons. First, they can only apply for a registered title by proving that they have completed all payments on their "promissory contract" of purchase, usually stipulated in terms of ten years of installments. This bureaucratic regulation sustains many a swindler. Second, swindlers typically provide reams of bona-fide records—such as sales receipts, tax documents, lot surveys, and protocols for preliminary deed registration—of transactions based on frauds not yet discovered. These bona fide records are the basis for leading people to believe that they will eventually be able to register their deed. However, the documents are mostly useless for purposes of registration. When residents finally discover that their purchased lot and/or residence is illegal, they learn that they cannot obtain title, that their claims of ownership are endlessly entangled in bureaucratic procedure, that their lifetime investment is imperiled, and that they are threatened with eviction.[6]

I have analyzed elsewhere the historical and legal specificities of this overwhelming condition of residential illegality (see Holston 1991). Here, I want to suggest some of its sources in the institutions of Brazilian law and urban policy. The developers' stratagems themselves suggest that such sources are paramount. Drawing inspiration from the intricate formalism of the Brazilian legal codes and bureaucracies—one that requires notarized copies and signatures with appropriate stamps and seals for even the most banal transaction—these stratagems model their deceptions on the very laws they violate. That is, they use bureaucratic complication as a means to deceive. The endless formalisms and procedural complexities of Brazilian law provide swindlers many opportunities to give their operations the appearance of legality. They can weave together so many apparently legal documents that even lawyers and judges are fooled, let alone humbler folk who are apt to be more intimidated by official-looking papers. Given that registries are decentralized and that some kinds will register as "original" any document without having to attest to its content, documents that are legally registered in one may be based on false or irregular documents from another. The result is that it is usually exceedingly difficult to determine who owns what beneath the layers of legal complication.

Hence, if disputes are litigated, they are frequently impossible to settle in court. Rather, they circulate forever through the bureaucratic system, awaiting more conclusive but nonexistent evidence on the merits of competing claims. As long as the disputes are left unresolved, the judicial system itself enhances the sense of impunity and thereby encourages further illegalities. Eventually, often twenty to fifty years later, land disputes get solved through extrajudicial maneuvers, such as amnesties and accords, in which executive or legislative institutions of government intervene to declare the judicial system checkmated and to legalize claims. By that time, the illegalities are indelibly established. Thus, such governmental interventions legalize usurpations of land and thereby insinuate illegal and extralegal practices into law. This process of legalizing the illegal is, in fact, an ancient practice, having been perfected by colonial elites as a dependable means to increase their patrimony at the expense of the Portuguese crown (Holston 1991).

The analysis of land tenure in the periphery demonstrates the fundamental, if paradoxical, role of illegal residence in this kind of city-regional development. Both developers and migrants seem to understand that the very illegality of land in the periphery makes it accessible to those who could not afford the prices of legal residence. Land policy, bureaucratic complexity, and judicial irresolution make it possible for developers to get away with illegally opening the periphery to new settlement for a very long time. In many cases, extrajudicial and political solutions eventually legalize the precarious land claims. Illegal land occupation is, therefore, a good bet in Brazil; that is, a reliable way for speculators to make money and for the urban working poor to win legal access to land and housing that would otherwise be beyond their means. Thus, a fundamental relationship between illegality and legitimation characterizes the periphery's development: usurpation initiates settlement and reliably precipitates the legalization of land claims. This relation indicates, moreover, that distinctions between the legal and the illegal, which often seem conceptually "hard," are rather strategically unstable as it is one of the important social functions of land law to facilitate the transformation of one into the other. I am not defending this system. Its social and institutional costs are exorbitant. Rather, I am emphasizing its importance in structuring the periphery through illegal residence. The point is not that "the law doesn't work" or that "there is no law" as one often hears in Brazil, but rather that it works differently from the way one might expect. By facilitating complication to the point of judicial impasse and by establishing a reliable path to eventual extrajudicial legalization, law stimulates regional development through illegal occupation.

The urban periphery thus structured through illegal residence developed most intensely from the early 1950s to the early 1980s. During this entire period, the model of citizenship in force was that established during the 1930s and 1940s by the government of president and dictator Getúlio Vargas. As Santos (1979) and others have shown, Vargas structured a restrictive citizenship at the core of which was a set of state-sponsored social rights focused on labor. Access to these rights depended on the possession of a registered labor contract in a state-regulated occupation and not only on the status of national citizenship. However, only a fraction of workers were thus registered and entitled to rights. For these workers, Brazilian citizenship was entirely defined within the political and legal boundaries of the state and amounted to privileges of particular labor categories rather than common rights of membership in the nation. Citizenship did not refer to the new urban conditions of workers' residence in the periphery. It emphasized social rights relating to labor but lacked political rights and many kinds of civil ones during the dictatorships of 1937–45 and 1964–85. For the rest of the population, rich and poor, citizenship was more or less an empty category: political rights were often curtailed by authoritarian regimes, social rights were restricted, and civil rights—either as legal norms or cultural values—were hardly woven into its fabric.

Into this regional structure of developed center and unurbanized residential periphery, military rule and restricted citizenship, democracy began to appear in the mid-to-late 1970s—as it did in many countries—as a force for change. Initially, it was the notion of rights more than the banner of democracy per se that inspired three broad movements: an interclass coalition of forces opposed to the military and demanding renewed political rights and direct elections; a trade-union movement demanding new labor rights such as the rights to strike and to organize freely; and the so-called new social movements of the urban poor demanding rights to the city. The latter in particular mobilized people around the redistributive right-claims of citizenship—the conviction that people have a right, because they are rightful citizens (i.e. not criminals or bums), to a just distribution of resources. Not concerned with traditional issues of labor rights and political parties, these grassroots movements were new because they were located in the neighborhoods of the urban periphery and focused on the residential conditions there of the urban poor. They focused their demands on the new collective and personal spaces of daily life in the modern metropolis, especially on the inadequacies and disabilities of their residential conditions. They demanded urbanization of their neighborhoods, forcing the state to respond to their needs for infrastructure and housing.[7] They claimed, and won, access to local health services, schools, and child care. With these claims, they brought the concerns of women and children into the traditionally male sphere of citizenship. Above all, they were concerned with the lives of the urban poor who had been excluded from citizenship. For the first time in Brazilian history, these people won rights by exercising social power from the bottom up.[8]

The new urban movements also expanded the scope and notion of social rights because many of the urban problems they posed as issues of citizenship were not covered in current legal codes and constitutional definitions, most of which predated the periphery. For example, though they lobbied for the legalization of their land and houses, they also argued that property should not be amassed without a social utility. They claimed that property had to fulfill a "social function" or risk expropriation and redistribution. Such a claim relativizes the traditionally absolute right to property enshrined in the Civil Code and subjects it to a social evaluation. Thus, the urban social movements were unprecedented because they argued for new kinds of rights outside of the normative and institutional definitions of the state. These arguments culminated in the promulgation of a new federal constitution in 1988 that framed many of them as constitutional principles. During the Constitutional Assembly of 1986–88, grassroots forces gathered more than 12 million signatures in support of Popular Amendments, successfully pressuring the state to relinquish its juridical monopoly and include their concerns in the new constitution. During the next two years, state and municipal constitutional assemblies occurred throughout Brazil with similar results.[9] Thus, the grassroots social movements of the urban periphery created a new substance of citizenship by bringing the urban experience of the poor under the calculus of rights.

The expansion of rights to new sources (the experience of the city) and to new types of citizens (the urban poor) has also changed the conception of rights. In the positivist or "civil law" tradition that characterizes Brazil's legal system, the state is the only source that can establish the norms to which individuals must conform their behavior. These norms constitute the "objective law" over which the state exercises a monopoly of authority. In turn, individuals derive legal power from the norms. This power constitutes the "subjective rights" that individuals hold against the world. In this conception, rights are a kind of property that some possess and others do not. Influenced by the Liberation Theology of the Catholic Church in this regard, the urban social movements pose the idea of rights not as possessions but more as claims on society for the resources necessary to meet the basic needs and interests of members. In this sense, rights are rethought as claims for the minimums necessary to lead a dignified life. This change in the conception of rights applies mostly to the sphere of social rights rather than civil rights, as the latter remain undeveloped as a component of the new urban citizenship. Nevertheless, in terms of rights to the city, rights are more thought of as deriving from social relatedness than from "objective norms." By that, I mean that although the state may formalize them, society establishes what the necessary minimums are and what they mean. An example of this rethinking is that of the social function of property I just discussed. In the Anglo-American tradition of common law, this idea of law-in-society is almost a taken-for-granted. But in the civil law tradition, it is a radical alternative for new sources of citizenship rights.

The idea that rights derive from social needs and relations rather than from abstract norms, and that new social experience is therefore a source of new rights, resonates with and amplifies a new sense of personal agency among urban workers. In the experience of being autoconstructors and city pioneers, of working in the modern city and becoming modern, residents of the periphery gain deeply felt capacities to contribute morally and politically to the public sphere. Even though poor, even if illegal, they have rights and dignity because they are modern urban workers, consumers, and taxpayers. These are people whom elites have traditionally viewed as marginals, excluded by class and race from their cosmopolitan modernity. Hence, the change over the course of one generation is significant. It also suggests the more radical proposition in Brazil that people's rights to the necessary minimums of life do not depend on their relative market worth or inherited social capital but rather on their absolute rights as citizens to a measure of economic well being and dignity. Potentially, this idea is radically redistributive of society's wealth because it attacks entrenched and elite-based explanations for relative worth and inequality.

In sum, with the globalization of democracy and its language of rights, the experience of residential illegality in the urban periphery of São Paulo generated a new legal regime of urban citizenship, with new types of citizens and new sources of rights. This regime defines the city-region as the primary community of citizenship for many of the poor for whom urban experience and especially illegal residence provides the basis of mobilization and substantive demands. Urban land law and policy promoted (and still does) the illegalization of the poor. But the rights-discourses of citizenship motivated people to redress the disabilities and injustices of illegal residence by making these very conditions the substance of their demands for a more just distribution of society's resources. For these people, urban experience sets the agenda through which they think themselves into politics and into the exercise of democratic rights.

The urbanized and politicized city-region that emerges under this impact of global democracy is thus quite different from the one structured under nationalist industrialization. As in many other metropolises around the world, the urban poor of São Paulo established a space of opposition—the periphery—within the city-region. This space confronts an old culture of citizenship with a new imagination of democratic values. Its insurgent citizenship opposes the modernist and developmentalist political projects of absorbing citizenship into a plan of nation-building monopolized by the state. Such state projects homogenize the multitude of social and cultural identities of modern society to produce formally commensurable national subjects often, as in Brazil, without much substantive citizenship. Urban citizenship does the opposite. It has no formal standing in the sense that it is not recognized in the constitution along with national and state memberships. Rather, it is a de facto regime of new rights and identities. Having no formal status per se, urban citizenship is all substance and symbol. Rather than homogenize and dematerialize difference to arrive at a formal (national) identity, urban citizenship takes as its substance the heterogeneity and materiality of urban experience.

The citizenship of city-regions does not replace national citizenship. It does not obliterate the importance of the nation-state in continuing to sustain a type of citizenship. That end is nowhere in sight. However, in most emerging democracies, like Brazil, the new urban citizenship produces a reformulation of national citizenship because the new urban citizens are also, for the most part, national citizens. But they were citizens who had been effectively excluded from exercising their citizenship. Their new rights to the city changed this de facto disqualification because their new sense of empowerment as urban citizens made them demand a renewed national citizenship as well. Thus, a transformed national citizenship emerged after military rule in Brazil. In the last direct presidential election in 1960 before the military coup of 1964, there were 15 million registered voters, approximately 21.4 percent of the population. The rest of the adults were disqualified, mostly by literacy requirements. In the first direct presidential election after military rule, in 1989—after nearly two decades of urban social movements, abolishing literacy requirements, and lowering the voting age to sixteen—there were 82 million registered voters, approximately 58.0 percent of the population. For the elites, a new and uncertain Brazil of mass national citizens had emerged on the basis of the substantive citizenship of its metropolitan regions.

URBAN CITIZENSHIP AMONG NONNATIONALS: OCEANSIDE, CALIFORNIA

The emergence of the urban periphery as a space of insurgent citizenship in São Paulo is typical of the impact of global democracy on many city-regions in the developing world. Its impact on Oceanside is quite different but equally emblematic. Oceanside is a small incorporated city at the northern Pacific edge of the county of San Diego. Its sluggish economy revolves around agriculture, the U.S. Marine base at Camp Pendleton, and tourism. With about 150,000 inhabitants, it is not itself a metropolitan region. Rather, Oceanside is one of the many urban incorporations within the suprametropolitan region of Southern California that stretches from Tijuana, Mexico, north through the cities of San Diego and Los Angeles. As in São Paulo, illegal residence in Oceanside catalyzes the rights-discourses of global democracy and the emergence of an urban citizenship. But Oceanside is an urban space marked by a very different kind of heterogeneity. Whereas São Paulo is structured by a national population that is overwhelmingly Brazilian and Portuguese-speaking regardless of other differences, Oceanside has significant numbers of resident noncitizens, mainly poor labor migrants and refugees from Central America, who primarily speak Spanish and who are often undocumented. It is a city divided culturally, socially, and politically between English and Spanish, Anglo and Latino, national and nonnational, citizen and noncitizen, legal and illegal, richer and poorer.

As such, Oceanside confronts a problem faced by many cities within established democratic nations that have both governments committed to democracy and significant resident populations of poor, linguistically heterogeneous, noncitizens: Either rule these noncitizens undemocratically or establish civic participation and democratic practice among them even though they are, by official national definition, politically disenfranchised and unrepresented, democratically unorganized, formally excluded, and often illegal residents. By less official but pervasive reckonings, these residents are also culturally "other." I will use an example from the innercity neighborhood of Crown Heights in Oceanside to analyze this dilemma and the impact of globalized democracy on it.[10]

Correlated with access to American national citizenship, these divisions of politics and culture visibly structure Oceanside's urban space into a poor center, inhabited predominantly by Latinos, and richer suburbs, inhabited predominantly by Anglos. With a population of about 4,000 people, Crown Heights is located in this center. Its foundations date from the mid-nineteenth century. Until the early 1970s, its residents were middle-class, primarily English-speaking, Anglos who owned and lived in single-family homes. Today, the residents of Crown Heights are 93 percent Latino and primarily speak Spanish. They have low incomes (43 percent of the households earn less than $15,000 a year) and generally little formal education (34 percent have six years or less). Often living in small apartments with several families at once, 93 percent of the residents rent. According to data from the City Planning Department, 70 percent of the households live in renter-occupied buildings that have a utility service turnover rate of 60 percent. The department interprets this rate to mean that Crown Heights has a significant population of transient renters who arrive illegally from the border and await transportation further into California. There are high levels of un-, under-, and unstable employment in the neighborhood. Typically, men find work as agricultural laborers and women either stay at home with the children (about 75 percent of the households have children under eighteen) or work as domestics in suburban homes. Crown Heights has only one active grassroots organization, sponsoring neighborhood cleanups on Saturday mornings, that is more or less independent of public sector or religious affiliation. There are a number of governmental and nongovernmental organizations administering various projects of social benefit in the neighborhood, such as the YMCA Pryde Program at the Americanization School, Partners for Healthy Neighborhoods, and the Teen Pregnancy Prevention Project. Drug use and gang violence are serious problems.

The adult residents of Crown Heights overwhelmingly do not have U.S. citizenship. They are predominantly recent immigrants from Mexico, though some have come from El Salvador and Guatemala. Most do not speak English or understand it well. Some are fluent only in an indigenous language and not Spanish. Their arrival in Crown Heights began in the early 1970s and increased dramatically during the next two decades as a result of changes in U.S. immigration laws in 1965 that altered the preference system from one that selected immigrants on the basis of national origin (favoring Europeans) to one that gave priority to people with family members already in the United States; the wars in Central America of the 1970s and 1980s that created a steady stream of refugees; and the economic boom in California in the 1990s that drew immigrants across the border. Many of those who came in consequence of the last two factors are undocumented and therefore illegal residents. It is, however, difficult to determine precisely the numbers among them of citizens and noncitizenss and legal and illegal residents because local census takers and service providers rigorously do not ask questions about citizenship or the legality of residence. As far as I can determine, they do so primarily to avoid having to report illegal residents for deportation or to deny them public services as mandated by Proposition 187. Rather, with regard to these issues, local government and service providers appear to have adopted an unofficial policy of "don't ask, don't tell." Therefore, regardless of status, residents of Crown Heights generally receive a number of welfare benefits similar to poor American citizens. However, unlike the latter, most have no political representation of any kind in either local or national government.[11] Moreover, they have little recourse to defend their civil rights if they are violated. Long suspicious of anything official, they avoid the law.

In 1998, the City Planning Department asked me for an "anthropological evaluation" of a series of problems relating to illegal food services in Crown Heights. The Planning Department felt that it needed an anthropologist to understand the "foreign culture" of the neighborhood. Due to residential zoning, Crown Heights has no local commerce of any kind—not even food stores or pharmacies—to serve the population. Although extreme in Crown Heights, the lack of accessible and reasonably priced commerce is a typical characteristic of poor innercity neighborhoods in the United States. Grocery stores at the margins of the neighborhood sell high priced and poor quality foodstuff and domestic supplies. Lower-priced and higher-quality chain supermarkets are not within walking distance, and most do not stock items that residents consider culturally appropriate to their kind of cooking. For a number of reasons, residents in Crown Heights like to shop daily: they generally do not have the money or freezer space for large purchases; women do the shopping and they usually do not have cars to transport such purchases; women like to bring their children shopping and make it a social event and consequently enjoy the urban public markets typical of their home countries; residents prefer fresh foods, especially meat that is butchered daily, and do not like the "old food" of the Anglo supermarkets.

For all these reasons, in the absence of local stores, two sorts of illegal operations arose in Crown Heights. One was in-home stores that sell fresh and prepared foods. Some also sell and administer medicines obtained in Mexico. In addition, mobile food venders appeared, selling groceries from trucks and vans parked on the street. Most have licenses for this commerce. But, for a number of reasons, they operate illegally in the neighborhood and create serious safety and trash problems. In response, the police began to close the in-home stores and ticket the venders who, in turn, stopped going to the neighborhood. The residents protested that the police were driving away their only sources of groceries. Realizing that the problem has significant social consequences for the neighborhood, the police turned to the Planning Department for a more comprehensive solution.

In addition to considering issues of code, zoning, enforcement, and safety, the Planning Department thought of the problem in cultural terms, presenting me with the following issues: What kind of neighborhood installation would not only solve the problem of food supply but also that of transience, in the sense that it would "enhance community attachment and stability" in the absence of home ownership? How could the planning of this facility involve residents and thus benefit from a "bottom-up" participation—or at least benefit from ethnographic information about the needs, habits, and desires of residents? Should the Department "try to encourage a Latino cultural pattern of business to take hold in a new home"—that is, food shopping as a public urban event in an open-air market—"or try to Americanize food shopping by encouraging the development of a suburban-type [i.e. private and interior] supermarket?" Thus, in Crown Heights, the experience of various kinds of residential illegalities—themselves a consequence of recent changes in the global economy—has mobilized not so much residents, as in São Paulo, but city government to seek greater civic participation, democratic practice, and redistribution of resources for the marginalized.

In framing their initiative in these ways, the city's policymakers show the influence of a particular rights-discourse of the recent global wave of democracy, namely, that of cultural rights and their politics of difference. Among several planners I interviewed, this influence is conscious and deliberate though not theorized as such. Whereas in São Paulo (and Brazil generally) an interest in social rights characterizes the impact of democracy, in Oceanside (and in the United States generally) it is cultural rights. Even though the United States is an established democracy, it is not a static one. It too has experienced a significant debate about citizenship and rights that derives directly from democracy's recent global expansions and realignments. In the United States, this debate is known mainly by the terms multiculturalism, cultural rights, and the politics of difference. Whether or not they use these terms or are conscious of this debate, the policymakers of Oceanside demonstrate that they are influenced by it and engaged in the rethinking of citizenship it entails.

The question of cultural rights involves recent developments in what I discuss elsewhere as the moral dimension of citizenship (see Holston, forthcoming).

This dimension concerns the meaning of citizenship and focuses on the concept of equality. Classically, the moral sense of citizenship opposes the inequalities of legalized status hierarchies—traditionally based on differences of race, property, gender, age, religion, ancestry, culture, and so forth—with the universal equality of citizens. That is, the concept of modern citizenship entails an equalization of rights regardless of other differences. It demands that all citizens have the same rights on the basis of the uniform and identical status of citizen rather than special rights on the basis of personal differences. However, in the last few decades, the notion of equality has increasingly come to mean, as well, that each person equally is distinctive and unique. This sense of individual worth resonates deeply in American culture. Yet, it also contradicts American notions of uniform treatment: Especially with regard to global human rights, the recent debates about democracy base the idea of distinctive individual worth on the absolute right of people to a measure of well-being necessary to cultivate their distinction, rather than on their market value to do so. This other sense of equality demands a differentiation of rights, not an equalization, based on the sustenance of distinctive differences, such as those of culture, language, and gender. It demands, in other words, a difference-specific rather than difference-neutral or difference-blind citizenship. In the United States, this disjunction in the meaning of citizenship between equalization and differentiation of rights has been debated under the banner of the politics of difference. The debate asks whether difference-specific rights may constitute a more just basis for the participation of some people in the polity, especially for those who have been traditionally excluded on the basis of identity differences that remain important to them, such as ethnicity.

The city officials of Oceanside are applying a version of this sort of consideration of difference to the Latino residents of Crown Heights. They are willing to commit city resources to the propositions that these residents ought to have a different urban space (an open-air market) from other (Anglo) residents, a different zoning (mixed residential and commercial), a government subvention that protects their special benefits from market forces, and treatment different from that given to others engaged in illegal activity. Policymakers justify this politics of difference by arguing that the Latino residents have a "right" to sustain their Latin culture, that Oceanside benefits from a diversity of cultures, and that by supporting this right to cultural difference planners hope not only "to improve neighborhood conditions" but also "to foster [the residents'] own self-help initiatives" (i.e. encourage their civic participation), as a memorandum on the issue put it. The planners cannot be considering that this "right" to sustain cultural difference is, in this case, a right of national or state citizenship as the residents of Crown Heights are mostly noncitizens. Rather, they must base their consideration of right either on the idea of global human rights or on the idea of urban citizenship—or on both. I am not suggesting that, at this point, city officials articulate the issues using either platform exactly as I have expressed them. But I am proposing that these ideas are present in their deliberations and ground their attempts to formulate new policies to address the unevenness of democracy in their city and include the formally excluded. Ironically, they direct these attempts at noncitizens rather or more than at the poor American citizens in Oceanside who are also marginalized from local democratic participation but not formally excluded.

In sum, recent changes in the global economy have generated heterogeneous urban spaces such as Oceanside with significant polyglot, marginalized, and noncitizen populations. In the case I have examined, the experience of residential illegality motivates city government to address the dilemmas of democratic exclusion with innovative policies. These policies are grounded in notions of cultural rights and a politics of difference. In this process, residential illegality is like a chemical catalyst that starts a reaction but is not changed by the consequences: Illegality precipitates processes in realigning democratic participation that do not necessarily resolve the underlying conditions of illegal residence. Nevertheless, when city governments respond to illegal residence, their policies may generate new legal regimes and what I have called an urban citizenship. As in the case of São Paulo, the latter is a de facto system comprised of new rights and identities. It has no formal standing in the regime of national membership. It does not convert immigrant noncitizens into American citizens, members of a nation and at least one of its states. Rather, given the current definitions of American membership, urban citizenship for the residents of Crown Heights is substantive only. That substance comprises difference-specific considerations—some conceived as cultural rights—and processes of participation concerning the very heterogeneity and material conditions of urban experience. For the city's excluded, that substance constitutes a change of fortune indeed and amounts to a new agenda of urban democracy.

Oceanside is emblematic of many city-regions, especially in established democracies, that are extensively divided by the cultural and social heterogeneity of national citizen and noncitizen. It is emblematic of the dilemma of undemocratic rule that results. The emergence of urban citizenship as a policy initiative presents the possibility of engaging these problems in a significant way because it converts resident nonnationals into urban citizens who exercise a substantive democratic membership in the city. Urban citizenship of the Oceanside type is not, as that in São Paulo, an insurgence against the state. To the contrary, it is much more government-initiated and directed, as policymakers apply new concepts of rights and citizenship. Moreover, it does not reformulate national citizenship the way São Paulo's does because its urban citizens remain nonnationals. It may, however, realign national citizenship in other ways by driving wedges between a national space and its urban centers. The new urban citizenship of Crown Heights may very well sustain a multicultural society and economy at odds with mainstream visions of American identity. Thus, the new urban citizens of Crown Heights are probably not commensurable, in the sense I discussed earlier of national identity, with many American citizens who live in much less heterogeneous places. Cities have often maintained a different relationship than their hinterlands to national processes of integration and to global processes of change. Moreover, this relationship often differs from the policies that their nation-states endorse. Yet, the localization of global forces of capital, labor, and democracy in city-regions may generate an urban citizenship at fundamental odds with principles of national membership. In the United States, Britain, and France, such antagonisms are already evident. They have prompted national governments to curtail the economic and social resources they provide to local government and thus to leave cities more on their own to manage the ensuing problems.

At this point, it is difficult to see how such deeper divergences between nations and cities will develop. But it is possible to observe that in many city-regions, as in both São Paulo and Oceanside, the urban experience of the poor, the excluded, and the illegal may become, through its engagement with global democracy, the basis of a new kind of urban citizenship. In this process, both urban residents and their city governments confront the dilemma of undemocratic rule with new agendas for a more civic and social democracy.

NOTES

1. International watchdog organizations use standard criteria of electoral procedure and political freedom to arrive at the number of electoral democracies in the world. As I have written elsewhere (see Holston and Caldeira 1998), I am strongly critical of the electoral approach in evaluating democracy. I use its data to grasp both the importance of elections and their limitations in the evaluation. In this essay, I use the research that Freedom House has compiled since 1972 in annual world surveys of political rights and civil liberties. Thus, in my analysis, the attribution "democracy" is not a matter of a country's self-nomination. For example, although the governments of the Democratic Republic of Congo and Egypt declare themselves democratic, international organizations disagree and do not count them among the world's 118 electoral democracies. With regard to the number of waves of democratization since the late eighteenth century, Samuel Huntington (1991) argues for three waves (and, thus far, two reversals) while Philippe Schmitter (1993) proposes four. At this point, the phrase, "the third wave," has caught on. Of the seventy-four third-wave democracies, eight had been formally democratic in 1972, became authoritarian, and then re-democratized by 1996 for a net gain of sixty-six electoral democracies over the twenty-four year period.
2. In the literature and legislation on citizenship, social rights refer to socioeconomic minimums that guarantee a basic standard of living. In comparison with most Europeans, for example, it is clear that Americans of all social classes have few of these rights to a minimum standard of living that do not depend on the market value of individual claimants. Some conceptions of citizenship, however, include the principle of a minimum standard that depends not on market worth but rather on the absolute right of citizens to a measure of dignity. Such social rights usually refer to conditions of health, education, housing, and work.
3. Defined by law and periodically readjusted, one minimum salary is the amount supposedly necessary to cover basic staples for a household.
4. Caldeira (2000: chapter 6) has devised a useful way to indicate the extent of illegal residence in São Paulo.

5. Although not a measure of the number of lots seized, the number of people living in squatter settlements (*favelas*) gives a rough idea of their extent. In 1980, 4.4 percent of São Paulo's population lived in favelas and in 1993, 19.1 percent.
6. In 1979, Caldeira (1984: 70) found that among those purchasing lots in a neighborhood of São Miguel Paulista, 57 percent had completed payments based on contracts initiated on average ten years earlier, but only 16 percent declared that they had definitive title. Researching the same neighborhood several years later, I discovered that even such declarations cannot be accepted at face value because residents often refuse to admit that their property, purchased with such sacrifice, might not be secure. If pressed, they show documents that the seller provides, some of which may indeed be legitimate but of little use for registration. If they do not have the registered title, which most do not, nothing is proved.
7. For example, by 1991, 74 percent of the poorest periphery had sanitation services, up from 19 percent ten years earlier.
8. Manuel Castells (1983) was one of the first to demonstrate, in his book *The City and the Grassroots*, both the importance of social movements of protest in the development of cities and the significance of urban issues in the formation of social movements. Although he continued to call them "marginals" and "lumpenproletariat," he challenged the traditional Marxist dismissal of the nonindustrial urban poor by showing that these people could mobilize collective movements that transform the material and social conditions of the city.
9. One of the most significant sources of this process is popular participation in urban reform and municipal administration. Growing out of the National Movement of Struggle for Urban Reform founded in 1986 to influence the federal Constitutional Assembly, this participation has rallied around rights to the city and around the concept of urban self-management (*auto-gestão*). In many major cities, including São Paulo, Rio de Janeiro, and Recife, the movement for urban reform succeeded in building these rights into innovative municipal codes, charters, and master plans. See Silva (1990) for a discussion of some of these innovations. Even where these plans have not passed city council, as in São Paulo, they have nevertheless animated local administrations in unprecedented ways. Perhaps the most well known is the city-wide popular participation in making the annual budget of Porto Alegre (see Abers 1998 and Ottman 1995).
10. It is important to note that resident nonnationals in the United States have not always been politically disenfranchised. According to legal scholar Jamin Raskin (1993), aliens voted in local, state, and even national elections in twenty-two states and federal territories before World War I. They also held local public offices, such as coroner and alderman. Raskin writes that "from the moment the Declaration of Independence was signed (including by several aliens), alien enfranchisement seemed to many states, such as Vermont and Virginia, the logical thing to do. In a regime built on federalism, state citizenship was deemed central and nation-state citizenship peripheral. The key suffrage qualifications in the states centered on property ownership, race and gender, not national citizenship" (1993: 451). Moreover, the Supreme Court has repeatedly indicated that alien suffrage is constitutional and therefore up to localities to institute. Nevertheless, antiimmigrant forces have campaigned against it from the early decades of the twentieth century—perhaps, as Raskin suggests, because U.S. immigration became significantly less Northern European. By the mid-1920s, these forces had succeeded in eliminating alien suffrage from the American political landscape.

11. The City Council of Oceanside is elected through citywide elections. Thus, council members do not represent specific neighborhoods or areas of the city.

REFERENCES

Abers, R. (1998). "Learning Democratic Practice: Distributing Government Resources through Popular Participation in Porto Alegre, Brazil," in M. Douglass and J. Friedmann (eds.), *Citizenship in Cities.* Chichester: John Wiley & Sons, 39–65.

Bonduki, N. G. (1983). "Habitação popular: contribuição para o estudo da evolução urbana de São Paulo," in L. Valladares (ed.), *Habitação em Questão.* Rio de Janeiro: Zahar Editores, 135–68.

Bratton, M., and Walle, N. (1997). *Democratic Experiments in Africa: Regime Transitions in Comparative Perspective.* New York: Cambridge University Press.

Caldeira, T. P. R. (1984). *A Política dos Outros: O Cotidiano dos Moradores da Periferia e o que Pensam do Poder e dos Poderosos.* São Paulo: Brasiliense.

—— (2000). *City of Walls: Crime, Segregation, and Citizenship in São Paulo.* Berkeley: University of California Press.

Castells, M. (1983). *The City and the Grassroots.* Berkeley: University of California Press.

Freedom House. (1978–97). *Freedom in the World: The Annual Survey of Political Rights and Civil Liberties.* New Brunswick: Transaction Publishers.

Gellner, E. (1983). *Nations and Nationalism.* Ithaca: Cornell University Press.

Holston, J. (1991). "The Misrule of Law: Land and Usurpation in Brazil." *Comparative Studies in Society and History,* 33 (4): 695–725.

—— (Forthcoming). *Unsettling Citizenship: Disjunctions of Democracy and Modernity.*

——, and Caldeira, T. P. R. (1998). "Democracy, Law, and Violence: Disjunctions of Brazilian Citizenship," in F. Agüero and J. Stark (eds.), *Fault Lines of Democracy in Post-Transition Latin America.* Miami: University of Miami North-South Center Press, 263–96.

Huntington, S. P. (1991). *The Third Wave: Democratization in the Late Twentieth Century.* Norman: University of Oklahoma Press.

Marshall, T. H. (1977 [1950]). "Citizenship and Social Class," in his book *Class, Citizenship, and Social Development: Essays by T. H. Marshall.* Chicago: University of Chicago Press, 71–134.

Metrô (Companhia do Metropolitano de São Paulo). (1990). *Pesquisa OD/87 (Pesquisa Origem e Destino 1987): Região Metropolitana de São Paulo, Síntese das Informações.* São Paulo: Metrô.

Ottmann, G. (1995). "Movimentos sociais urbanos e democracia no Brasil: uma abordagem cognitiva." *Novos Estudos,* 41: 186–207.

Raskin, J. B. (1993). "Time to Give Aliens the Vote (Again)." *The Nation,* 256 (13): 433, 451–2.

Rolnik, R., Kowarik, L., and Somekh, N. (eds.). (1990). *São Paulo: Crise e Mudança.* São Paulo: Brasiliense.

Santos, W. (1979). *Cidadania e Justiça.* Rio de Janeiro: Campus.

Schmitter, P. C. (1993). "The International Context for Contemporary Democratization." *Stanford Journal of International Affairs,* 2: 1–34.

Silva, A. A. (1990). "A luta pelos direitos urbanos: novas representações de cidade e cidadania." *Espaço e Debates,* 30: 29–41.

18

Istanbul's Conflicting Paths to Citizenship: Islamization and Globalization

ENGIN F. ISIN

POSTMODERNIZATION, GLOBALIZATION, AND THE GLOBAL CITY-REGIONS: AN APPROACH TO ISTANBUL

Any discussion of citizenship inevitably involves related issues of modernization and postmodernization and economic, cultural, and political globalization (Isin and Wood 1999). If we define postmodernization as both a process of fragmentation through which various group identities have been formed and discourses through which "difference" has become a dominant ideology, its effect on citizenship has been twofold. On the one hand, various groups that have been marginalized and excluded from *modern* citizenship have been able to seek recognition (Fraser 1997; Young 1990). Groups based upon ethnic, "racial," ecological, and sexual concerns have articulated claims for citizenship to include group-differentiated rights. Women have fought to expand their citizenship rights to include social rights such as access to childcare, pay equity, and rights to safe cities; ethnic and racialized minorities have sought recognition and representation; aboriginal peoples have sought representation and self-government rights; gays and lesbians have struggled to claim rights that are already extended to heterosexual couples, such as spousal benefits and common-law arrangements; immigrants have struggled for naturalization and political rights; and various ability groups have demanded recognition of their needs to become fully functional citizens of their polities. This challenged one of the most venerable premises of modernization—universalization—by exposing its limits. On the other hand, these various claims have strained the boundaries of citizenship and pitted group against group in the search for identity and recognition. As a result, while ostensibly making claims to citizenship, some members of these groups have become trapped or encased within specific identities, unable to move beyond the straitjacket that they have unintentionally created. This called into question another venerable premise of modernization that would have us

I am grateful to Allen Scott, Warren Magnusson, Evelyn Ruppert, and Bryan S. Turner who read earlier drafts and provided critical comments. I am also indebted to the participants in the Global City-Regions conference and of a seminar at the Faculty of Social and Political Sciences, University of Cambridge, who have provided critical response to earlier drafts of this chapter.

believe in the disappearance of such allegiances. Either way, postmodernization of politics has, therefore, stressed the capacity of the modern nation-state and citizenship to accommodate and recognize these diverse and conflicting demands.

If we define globalization as both a process by which the increasing interconnectedness of places becomes the defining moment and as a discourse through which "globalism" becomes a dominant ideology, its effect on citizenship has also been twofold. On the one hand, with the rise of global flows of capital, images, ideas, labor, crime, music, and regimes of governance, the sources of authority of citizenship rights and obligations have expanded from the nation-state to other international organizations, corporations, and agencies such as the World Bank, IMF, IBM, Internet, Greenpeace, Amnesty International, Microsoft, and Coca-Cola. On the other hand, the dominance of such global agents was accompanied by the decline of the ability of the nation-states to set sovereign policies. In a very complex relay of events, nation-states retrenched from certain citizenship rights and instead imposed new obligations on their citizens, which intensified tensions within states where taken-for-granted citizenship rights began to disappear (e.g. unemployment insurance, welfare, or right to legal counsel) and new obligations (e.g. workfare) were implemented. Similarly, increased international migration has raised the question of rights and responsibilities of aliens, immigrants, and refugees.

While some believe that globalization means the rise of the world as one single place, others dispute whether globalization has become as widespread as claimed and point to increased postmodernization of culture and politics where diversity, fragmentation, and difference dominate. But few would disagree that both postmodernization and globalization are occurring simultaneously and are engendering new patterns of global differentiation in which some states, societies, and social groups are becoming increasingly enmeshed with each other while others are becoming increasingly marginalized. A new configuration of power relations is crystalizing as the old geographic divisions rapidly give way to new spaces such that the familiar triad of core-periphery, north–south, and First World–Third World no longer represents these new spaces. Globalization has recast modern patterns of inclusion and exclusion between nation-states by forging new hierarchies, which cut across and penetrate all regions of the world (Held *et al.* 1999: 8). North and south, First World and Third World, are no longer "out there" but nestled together within global city-regions. It is doubtful whether we can any longer divide the world into discrete, contiguous, and contained zones as a representation of reality. Instead, the sociopolitical geography of the world seems to be crystalizing as overlapping networks of various flows of intensity in which global city-regions are the primary nodes. These complex overlapping networks connect the fate of one global city-region to the fate of another in distant parts of the world.

As such, postmodernization and globalization are not simply a continuation of modern capitalism on a global scale, but political, economic, and cultural transformations of modern capitalism into new regimes of accumulation and modes of regulation (Hoogvelt 1997). That cities and regions, or more precisely, global city-regions, are the fundamental spaces of this emerging political economy further erodes the credibility of modernization theories that would have us believe in national trajectories that will follow the disappearance of religion, tradition, and particularism. Instead, in global city-regions we are witnessing a general trend toward the proliferation of identities and projects and an overall incredulity toward grand narratives. If global city-regions give us not only the geographic metaphors with which we think about the social world, they are also the concrete sites in which to investigate the complex relays of postmodernization and globalization (Isin 2000). This chapter outlines some observations on Istanbul, which vividly illustrates that globalization and postmodernization engender spaces for new identities and projects, which modernization either contained or prohibited, and generate new citizenship rights and obligations.

A "global city" for more than fifteen centuries, first as an imperial city in both Byzantine and Ottoman Empires and later as a major port city in the Turkish Republic, Istanbul raises these citizenship issues in rather complex and profound ways. Istanbul began its life as an occidental city and was transformed into an oriental city. It therefore articulates both elements. During both the Byzantine and Ottoman Empires, Istanbul was undoubtedly a cosmopolitan city, home to diverse ethnic, religious, and language groups. After the birth of the Turkish Republic, Istanbul occupied an ambiguous position as a symbol of imperial power while Ankara became the symbol of republican order. Between the 1920s and 1980s, Istanbul was of secondary importance to the project of nation building and the formation of a national, Western, secular, Turkish identity. Since the 1980s, however, with economic globalization (liberalization and the transition from import substitution to export-led production in Turkey), Istanbul became the nation's center of globalized consumption, production, and exchange.

With these complex transformations, Istanbul defies traditional sociological and political categories with which we consider citizenship. The usual and foundational distinctions between oriental and occidental or between civil, political, and social forms of citizenship are thrown into disarray. The aim of this chapter, however, is not to argue that Istanbul is an exception that proves the rule. Rather, it argues that the postmodernization and globalization of Istanbul with its articulation into global flows challenges our conceptions of citizenship in an acute and a very significant way. Take, for example, the issue whether concepts generated by Western social scientists for Western societies can be fruitfully used to explore Istanbul, which is ostensibly an Eastern society. While this issue forces us to reconsider orientalism in the social sciences, as we shall see, the distinction is not an easy one to maintain. The chapter, therefore, opens with a brief discussion of the orientalist theories that located uniqueness of the Orient in terms of citizenship, and their most recent reincarnation. While this distinction has been rejected on many grounds, recently it has also become the founding principle of new forms of orientalism. The following section considers whether orientalism can even grasp the nineteenth century Istanbul with its hybrid forms of urban citizenship and municipal government. After a description of Kemalism and the project of the modern Turkish nation-state with its roots in the nineteenth century reform movements of the Ottoman Empire, the chapter illustrates the conflicts and contradictions in the foundations of the project, particularly its hypermodern implementation of secularism and sovereignty. While these faults remained relatively benign throughout the twentieth century, still, it required three military interventions to contain their consequences. With the more recent military-led and IMF-OECD-World Bank-sponsored liberalization, these faults have become more visible and have created conditions for the questioning of sovereignty by a major Kurdish movement and of secularism by further Islamization of politics. Istanbul is at the political, if not geographic, center of these transformations in which conflicting paths of citizenship offered both by Islamization and globalization become acutely visible, which is the focus of this chapter.

ORIENTALISM, CITIZENSHIP, AND THE CITY

The interpretation that citizenship is essentially an occidental institution and that it distinguishes the West from oriental civilizations can be traced to orientalist discourse in the late nineteenth century. As studies by Edward Said (1978, 1993) and Bryan Turner (1974, 1978, 1994) and the subsequent postcolonial studies have illustrated, orientalism as both a discipline and an outlook dominated nineteenth century European and American attitudes toward the societies outside them, especially those based on Islam, Buddhism, Confucianism, and Hinduism. When compared with other world-religions and civilizations, however, Islam has had the unique if dubious distinction of having always been regarded by the West as a cultural "other," an adversary. While rivalry over exclusive claim to a one and indivisible transcendent God, the share of their respective Holy Land, and their geographic proximity partially explain this relationship, the Western civilization has become dependent upon this other to articulate its own identity. As Hoogvelt (1997) argued, as much as "orientalism" may be a product of Western culture, which Said illustrated, it is also a product of its search for itself. For Hoogvelt it is this dependency that perhaps explains the West's special fear of Islam. Be that as it may, in the intertwining histories of the West and Islam, the nineteenth century stands apart with the emergence of orientalism as a special discipline and outlook that inexorably fixes on the difference of Islam as the anchor that defines the nature of the West. While buttressing the confidence of Europe in its own cultural superiority, orientalism cast Islam in the role of contemptible victim, in need of correction. The discipline linked itself up with broader interpretations that explained the trajectories of Islam on the basis of race, language, and religion.

If orientalism were merely a historical matter, it would remain a rather innocuous and benign curiosity. But both in the beginning and at the end of the twentieth century orientalism penetrated into social-scientific theories of modernization and democratization. Max Weber became the main protagonist using orientalism to explain the difference between the Orient and the Occident.

For Said, "Weber's studies . . . blew him (perhaps unwittingly) into the very territory originally charted and claimed by Orientalists. There he found encouragement amongst all those nineteenth century thinkers who believed that there was a sort of ontological difference between Eastern and Western economic (as well as religious) 'mentalities' " (Said 1978: 259). For Turner, "At the centre of Weber's view of Islamic society is a contrast between the rational and systematic character of Occidental society, particularly in the fields of law, science, and industry and the arbitrary, unstable political and economic conditions of Oriental civilizations, particularly the Islamic" (Turner 1974: 14). Weber made this distinction between the occidental and the oriental civilizations at various levels, not necessarily consistent with each other. But whatever the level, Weber was concerned with explaining the rise of capitalism in the West and its "lack" in the East. Islam and patrimonialism were two running themes of his considerations of the difference between the two.

While orientalism has been discussed at some length in the literature, what is less emphasized is that for Weber citizenship was *the* institution that came to explain the difference between the Orient and the Occident. For Weber while Christianity played a fundamental part in the development of the associational character of occidental city, Islam impeded the development of such a character with its emphasis on clan and kinship (Turner 1974: 97). While in oriental cities one finds a collection of distinct and separate clan and tribal groups, which do not join common action, Christianity helped break tribalism in Europe. "The internal development of a rich and autonomous guild and associational life within the city was closely connected with the legal and political freedom of the city from interference from patrimonial or feudal officials. Not only were cities legal persons, they were also independent political agents" (Turner 1974: 97). They fought wars, concluded treaties, and made alliances. Their autonomy was fundamentally connected with their military independence. It was in the city that urban piety, legal autonomy, occupational associations, and political involvement developed; hence, the autonomous city had very important connections with the rise of European capitalism. In Islam, Weber argued, "it was the combination of a warrior religiosity with patrimonialism which limited the growth of autonomous cities and which in consequence precluded the growth of urban piety within the lower middle classes" (Turner 1974: 98).

For Weber, therefore, the oriental city-states "lacked" a concept and status of citizenship. While some rights did exist in oriental cities, citizenship as a status or concept was "absent." That Weber wanted with this difference to explain why capitalism and its distinctive rationality emerged in the occident need not concern us here (Turner 1996: 257–86). But how Weber explained this "absence" is of consequence for considering citizenship in "oriental" societies. For Weber did not stop at the level of religious difference but claimed that citizenship was "absent" in the Orient because of the persistence and omnipotence of theocratic rule. That oriental cities were centralized and hierarchical would not allow for the rise of citizenship. The necessity of irrigation and water regulation in Mesopotamia, Egypt,

India, and China, which required financing and coordinating large projects and disciplining masses of laborers, forced the development of a governing class responsible for these activities (Weber 1909). These large-scale undertakings enabled the kings to control the military and administration. The soldiers were simply the officers of the royal army and the subjects were dominated by the monopoly of this force. In other words, the rule of the king and the royal bureaucracy was, though not total, omnipotent. Under such conditions, although certain rights were secured by the subjects, neither an association of subjects as citizens nor a special status for them was possible (Weber 1921: 1261). For Weber citizenship embodied and expressed this unique aspect of the occidental city.

Orientalism has, therefore, connected cities and citizenship in a theoretical framework in which the absence of associational solidarities became an explanatory factor for "lacking" capitalism and hence "progress." It formed the foundation of modernization theories later in the century that associated "underdevelopment" with religion and authoritarianism and "development" with secularism and democracy. Throughout the twentieth century, modernization theories anticipated that the underdeveloped states, with secularization, rationalization, and democratization, were on the linear path to industrialization and urbanization and hence modernization. While both alternative theories and the actual trajectories taken by non-Western states in the second half of the twentieth century have discredited these theories, they still form the bedrock of how we think about the world of states. Moreover, while postmodernization and globalization may have made orientalist theories of modernization and secularization redundant, a new wave of neo-orientalist discourse emerged at the end of the twentieth century. The new orientalism explains the absence of democratic regimes in Muslim states, for example, with an *essential* incompatibility between Islam and democracy. Islam is said to nurture group solidarities that are incompatible with universal ideas of democracy and citizenship. For Sadowski (1997) an irony with neo-orientalist discourse is that while orientalism focused on the "absence" of associations that explained underdevelopment, neo-orientalism is focusing on the cultural essences such as the persistence of solidarities to illustrate why societies based on these can never become democratic or civilized (Sadowski 1997: 41). Another irony is, of course, democratic theorists such as Iris Marion Young have become influential precisely because they argue that behind the claims to universality, modern democratic citizenship fostered group privileges (Young 1989). To understand these complex processes, it is not, therefore, enough to critique orientalism and neo-orientalism as theories. We need genealogies that empirically explore their effects in historically and geographically specific circumstances that link up with contemporary trajectories.

ORIENTALISM AND THE OTTOMAN ISTANBUL

Leaving aside the objections that the occidental cities did not dissolve clan and tribal ties purely and totally in the way Weber envisaged and the historicism of orientalism (Isin 2001), does the Ottoman administration conform to the distinction between the occidental and oriental cities? It is worthwhile to explore briefly this question. While it is true that the Ottoman cities never explicitly articulated a conception of citizenship expressed in the autonomy of cities, there are other historical reasons for this than Ottoman centralism or the inability to dissolve clan and kinship ties. First, the Ottoman cities evolved right from the beginning in the context of a highly developed and extensive imperial government and administration and thus were not under pressure to constitute themselves as politically and legally autonomous corporations (Kafadar 1995; Karpat 1974; Köprülü 1992). The inhabitants of Istanbul were already Ottoman subjects and were entitled, in law and in custom, to certain property and associational rights (Gerber 1994; Quataert and Inalcik 1994). Second, Ottoman cities did develop various merchant and craft guilds, religious and political associations, and articulated a complex combination of attributes that resulted in a unique status for the urban dweller (Faroqhi 1984). That this status was not expressed in the occidental language of citizenship should not lead us to believe in its absence as an institution.

Beyond these reasons, however, there is a third reason, which is perhaps even more damaging to the orientalist thought about urban citizenship. Ottoman cities and their administration did not evolve in isolation from the contacts imperial elite and rulers developed over the years with occidental states and their systems of law and administration. As early as the sixteenth and seventeenth centuries, Ottoman officials were already developing a positive view of the absolutist states and their urban administration, with which they could easily find affinities and parallels (Christensen 1990). Moreover, the administration of cities in absolutist Europe of the sixteenth and seventeenth centuries was nowhere close to Weber's ideal type and it is remarkable that Weber chose to remain entirely silent about the "absence" of citizenship in the absolutist state of early modern Europe (Friedrichs 1995).

By the eighteenth and nineteenth centuries, the decline and disintegration of the Ottoman Empire was obvious to Ottoman intelligentsia and there were various reform movements to restructure the Ottoman state and its institutions (Göçek 1996; Kasaba 1988; Quataert 1983). Not surprisingly, municipal reform increasingly occupied an important place in these efforts and several models were experimented with, especially in Istanbul (Çadirci 1991). As Rosenthal (1980) has illustrated, a municipal council introduced in Galata District in the nineteenth century, while it eventually failed, constituted a major experiment to implement Western-style municipal government in the Ottoman Empire. The traditional administration of Istanbul, which persisted until the mid-nineteenth century, was based not on the rights and duties of citizenship understood in the modern sense, but on a social system of disconnected, self-contained, and largely autonomous groups. It was through membership of groups such as guilds or religious communities that the status of town dweller was defined and taxes were paid, obligations of membership were imposed, and rights exercised

(Rosenthal 1980: 33). The role of the central government was largely limited to the work of judges (*kadis*), the patrols of the police, and the demands of the tax collector. Even in the comparatively rare instances when the government impinged on the life of the residents of Istanbul, it usually did so through an intermediary such as the guild chiefs or the head of a millet. How Istanbul was administered was remarkably similar to the maelstrom of corporations that dominated especially the medieval north European city, which also had to contend with powerful states (Nicholas 1997*a*; 1997*b*).

While Ottoman administration did not immediately follow major municipal reforms in England, America, and France in the 1830s and 1840s that established cities as self-governing polities (Isin 1992), by the 1850s there was a reform experiment in Istanbul. Galata was a district dominated by the Christian subjects of the Ottoman Empire. In 1859, with the hopes of creating a common Ottoman citizenship, the Ottoman government ceded significant autonomy and financial resources to the district and constituted it as a municipal corporation with a council and municipal machinery. As Rosenthal (1980: 193–5) argues, while the experiment failed to create a model of common Ottoman citizenship (the municipality was abolished by 1872), its direct influence on subsequent Ottoman municipal history was far-reaching. Moreover, the district illustrates not only the willingness of Ottoman intelligentsia to experiment with *modern* occidental institutions of citizenship but also how difficult it was to impose a modern occidental national citizenship on Ottoman subjects who were Christians, Muslims, Turks, European proteges, and foreigners. Nonetheless, by the opening decades of the twentieth century neither municipal nor imperial reforms were able to avoid the decline and disintegration of the Ottoman Empire.

These elements—advanced imperial administration, advanced commerce, and guild structures, and early encounters and hybridization with Western municipal institutions—severely limit the orientalist interpretation as a framework either to understand the fundamental differences between the Occident and the Orient or to explain why capitalism did not emerge in the latter. Orientalism becomes even more limited when it layers certain expectations on the consequences of modernization that followed the disintegration of the Ottoman Empire and the birth of the modern Turkish Republic.

ISTANBUL FROM OTTOMAN COSMOPOLITANISM TO KEMALIST REPUBLICANISM

That the modern Turkish republic was born of the ashes of the mighty Ottoman Empire that had dominated Europe, Asia, and Africa for centuries is well known. What is less known is that a movement, the Young Turks, laid its foundations well before the republic was declared according to Kemalist principles (Kemal being himself a Young Turk) in 1923. In the 1890s the Ottoman Empire was defined by the European states as the "Eastern Question"—the complex series of strategic conundrums surrounding the fate of the entire Ottoman Empire—

and new states were emerging in the Balkans such as Serbia, Bulgaria, and Albania from the remains of the Empire. The movement of Young Turks, mainly led by émigré army officers educated in European cities, mostly Paris, against the ramshackle imperial system, was laying the foundations of a secular, modern nation-state, modeled after European nation-states (Keyder 1987: 49–70). Many of the leaders of the movement were from Macedonia, one of the most economically prosperous and European segments of the Empire. They were also mostly educated and trained in the European-influenced schools and traditions and were divided between European liberalism and nationalism as a recipe for the post-Ottoman constitutional order (Hanioğlu 1995; Kayali 1997; Ramsaur 1957).

While the Young Turks were unable to halt the disintegration of the Empire and rescue the "sick man of Europe," despite a revolution in 1908, their legacy played a significant role in the future of the country. The most obvious was, of course, a future leader and founder of the republic, Mustafa Kemal who became the military and political leader of a movement that culminated in the birth of the Turkish Republic in 1923. The new nation envisaged itself as secular, modern, and Western with an industrial future against the background of the Islamic, imperial, and quasifeudal past. The contradictions and dilemmas that tear Turkey apart today can be in part traced to the closing days of the nineteenth century and the opening decades of the twentieth century. A new nationalism and republicanism were being forged to which Mustafa Kemal eventually gave his name and stamp as their heir. (The depiction of Mustafa Kemal as the Mother Turk who invented modern Turkey with his genius was a myth generated after the formation of the republic as part of its national identity.)

Atatürk and Kemalism—a set of ideas or ideals with which he is associated—has a powerful presence in the Turkish psyche. When *Time* magazine editors made an international call for the man of the century, they were surprised how many Turks inundated their inboxes with a confident and irreverent reply that there was no doubt in their minds as to who the man of this century was. Yet, while the portraits, busts, and sculptures of Atatürk dominate the Turkish landscape, Kemalism was a contested and fractured movement and it remains that way today. Its dominant position in the media, government, and military ideology and the popular imagination belie the fact that there are conflicting and contesting interpretations of Kemalism in modern Turkey. These contradictory and ambivalent elements are also embedded in the person who was the ostensible founder of the movement. Mustafa Kemal was born and raised in a cosmopolitan European city, Salonika, and his parents had more European lineage and sensibilities than many Turks would care to admit. The streets of Salonika were full of Ladino-speaking Jews, Slav speakers from the northern Balkans, Greeks, Bulgarians, Serbs, Romanians, Albanians, Vlachs, Armenians, and Gypsies. As well, being a trading center, it brought in numerous different people and professions. While Atatürk is regarded as the ultimate Turk who came from the East and swept away the invading British, Greek, Italian, and French forces to found the modern Turkish Republic, his origins were not in Turkey, let alone eastern

Turkey, but Europe. He may even have had some Albanian or Slav blood among his ancestors. Finally, his piercing blue eyes and blonde hair constitute perfect symbols of Western modernization rather than an Ottoman past. But his legacy and the reforms he instigated are open to interpretation and have been differently appropriated by various dominant groups in the country throughout the latter part of the twentieth century.

The republican reforms for modernization—secularization and modernization of the state, abolishing the Arabic script and the introduction of the Latin alphabet, literacy campaigns, the end of the reign of religious leaders, and the introduction of Western dress codes—are seen as the effective end of the Ottoman rule in Turkey. Following the manifesto of the single party that ruled Turkey under the leadership of Atatürk until the 1950s, the six elements of Kemalism—republicanism, secularism, nationalism, populism, statism, and revolutionism—did not include democracy (Ahmad 1993; Zürcher 1993). Secularism and nationalism had been among the distinctive characteristics of the Young Turk movement. But during the 1930s both were carried to their extremes, secularism being interpreted not only as a separation of state and religion, but as the removal of religion from public life and the establishment of complete state control over remaining religious institutions. An extreme form of nationalism, with the attendant creation of historical myths, was used as the prime instrument in the building of a Turkish national identity, and as such was intended to take the place of religion in many respects. Republican citizenship meant a commitment to a constitutional order against the return of the Ottoman monarchical rule. It did not mean a democratic republicanism with free and multiparty elections, freedom of speech and expression, and freedom of association. On the contrary, Kemalist Turkey was ruled in the 1930s and 1940s with an iron hand, resembling authoritarian states, especially that of Fascist Italy in the 1930s, rather than a democratic state. Populism meant national solidarity and placing the interests of the nation before those of any group or class. According to Kemalism there were no social classes in Turkey in the sense European nations had them. Revolutionism meant the continuance of reforms to rid the nation of its Ottoman past until no traces of it were left. Finally, statism was a very significant aspect of Kemalism, which regarded the state not only as a guardian of but also an active player in the economic field. It is of vital importance to understand that Kemalism positioned itself against both capitalism and socialism. It was its defining aspect to embark upon a program of nationalization (acquisition of railway companies, agricultural sectors, and creation of state monopolies) and liberalization (allowing selective foreign investment) simultaneously.

What is important from the point of view of Istanbul is that it occupied an ambiguous position in the new republican order. In the ethos of the nationalist discourse, Istanbul became the symbolic vestige of the corrupt Ottoman cosmopolitanism. The new valorization of the Anatolian peasant as the core of the new state was coupled with the identification of commerce with profiteering. Ankara thus became not only the symbol of political power in the new republic but also a symbol of the new national economy and the site of the emergence of a secular, bureaucratic elite. Until the 1960s, Istanbul continually lost prominence to Ankara and experienced only moderate population and economic growth by postwar Turkish standards (Keyder and Öncü 1994: 392–3). Ankara became the symbol of a balanced approach to economic growth, allowing limited foreign direct investment, encouraging import-substitution, nationalization of major services in transportation and communications, and developing a program of national production symbolized in national monopolies. While citizenship did not feature explicitly, nor was the regime prepared to experiment with, democratic rights, underlying Kemalism was a strong sense of national identity and belonging, and guarantees that came with that belonging. Kemalism was then a delicate, if not effective, balance of competing forces that threatened to tear apart the young republic, with its contradictory roots in Islam and expansionism expressed in Turan and its precarious situation in the world economy and polity (Karpat 1973; Weiker 1981).

It was this balance that was threatened with the onset of the Cold War and the rising interest of the United States in Turkey after the Second World War. Turkey increasingly found itself drawn to the orbit of American capitalism, and foreign policy, the state, and the army were increasingly articulated as the guardians of a new kind of Kemalism (Keyder 1987). Beginning with the Truman Doctrine and the Marshall Plan, the World Bank and IMF (backed by the United States) began increasingly influencing Turkish economic policy. Throughout the remainder of the 1940s and 1950s, the statism of Kemalism was already slowly being replaced with economic liberalization and political oppression. Every movement that questioned this secularist alignment was brutally and violently suppressed, with major military coups and interventions in 1960 and 1971. While the 1960 coup and the resultant new constitution introduced some civil and political rights, they did not live long and were suspended by martial law in 1970. These interventions showed how far the interpretation of Kemalism had shifted from its original principles. While Kemalism extolled the virtues of sovereignty and independence, these military interventions increasingly brought Turkey into the orbit of Western capitalism and made Turkey the cornerstone of American expansionism against the Soviet Union. Yet, the paradoxical consequence of being brought into the orbit of American capitalism and accepting the policies of the World Bank and IMF also meant the gradual weakening of the state, without a corresponding strengthening of a civil society. While the 1960 and 1971 interventions remained rather limited, neoliberalism was instituted by a total revolution by the military in 1980.

GLOBALIZATION, IDENTITIES, AND PROJECTS: ISLAMIZATION OF POLITICS

To assert that the republican modernization project failed in Turkey is too simplistic. For it seems that the trajectory of globalization that Turkey followed since 1980 paralleled the trajectories followed by other states as diverse as Chile, Argentina, Brazil, Pakistan, Egypt, Indonesia, Malaysia, and Taiwan (Hoogvelt 1997). There has been a general trend from import-substitution developmental projects to neoliberal deregulation, privatization, and market-led reforms. That these neoliberal policies have resulted in different consequences for each state is beyond doubt, but to explain the turn toward neoliberalism with the ostensible failure of modernization without taking into account broader economic, cultural, and political globalization is inadequate. Accordingly, that the 1980 military coup in Turkey coincides with the major takeoff moment of globalization is perhaps less a symbol of the failure of modernization than a signal of a structural readjustment. It is a telling fact that while the coup gave the military leaders a grip on power to begin a political cleansing, their attention turned astonishingly rapidly toward economic liberalization and modernization. Throughout the remainder of the 1980s, while the military loosened its grip on political power and allowed "democratic" elections, the elected governments continued the program of rapid economic liberalization (Ahmad 1993: 181–212; Zürcher 1993: 292–6).

Throughout the 1980s, the linchpins of Kemalism, the strong state and import substitution, were replaced with a weak state involvement in the economy and export-led growth, driven by foreign direct investment, the opening up of markets, and the dismantling of regulations and public sector producers. By the end of the 1980s, the coup succeeded in its aims. Having effectively dismantled and suppressed civil and political rights, the regime implemented an entirely different set of economic policies than Kemalism. While all this was done under the banner of protecting the legacy of Atatürk, the military-induced neoliberalism in Turkey was a fragile interpretation of Kemalism that, while emphasizing his European aspirations, ignored his insistence on statism. Within a few years the Kemalist legacy of strong state institutions and monopolies was nearly dismantled, trade protections lifted, many regulations abandoned, and the Turkish money and commodity markets opened to foreign investors and products. While the results were devastating for some, especially in the large public sector, they also created a new, secular, middle class, a parvenu class, whose fortunes and mentalities were more integrated with American and European sensibilities and lifestyles than any other social group Turkey had ever experienced. The Turkish economic liberalization program and its consequences are well documented (Nas and Odekon 1988, 1992; Togan and Balasubramanyam 1996). Istanbul played a special role in this program, which requires further discussion.

That Istanbul has experienced these transformations in globalization more than any other city in Turkey is not surprising. But that Istanbul became virtually synonymous with globalization in Turkey as the vanguard of all those transformations reveals that the city played a qualitatively different role from a typical postwar economic engine. For Keyder and Öncü (1994) Istanbul was *the* center of the ambitious liberalization program embarked upon by postmilitary governments after 1983. It is in this interpretation that Istanbul begins to reveal new regimes of regulation for these governments that created new financial sources, allowed the opening of a stock exchange market, created a new metropolitan government, and transformed the city into a competitive global city-region. They also embarked upon policies to mitigate the negative effects of liberalization in Istanbul, especially on the public sector employees and their dependants. They adopted a populist approach toward squatter settlements, which made up between 60 and 75 percent of the overall residential settlement in Istanbul. Their dwellers were allowed legally to convert their low-density houses to multistory apartment buildings, which created opportunities for attaining instant wealth by selling these properties to "developers." Within a decade a rapid shift from low-density squatter settlements to relatively high-density shantytowns with substandard housing radically transformed Istanbul. While public sector workers endured a decline in real wages, and those in the marginal sector suffered both from decreasing employment opportunities and lower wages, deregulation of the residential property market provided opportunities to more or less the same population via their new ownership of houses in shantytowns. For Keyder and Öncü (1994) this was the essence of the urban populism of neoliberalism.

Furthermore, the significant increase in foreign direct investment and the arrival of, first, the headquarters of major multinational corporations, then, major producer-service firms in accounting, advertising, marketing, fashion, design, and entertainment, and finally the dramatic rise of the hospitality industry, transformed Istanbul. New wealth engendered new social groups. While the public sector professions such as teachers, writers, bureaucrats, trade unionists, suffered an identity crisis and loss of public confidence, the new private sector professions in engineering, journalism, marketing, and advertising experienced a dramatic growth of confidence (Göle 1993). The spatial organization of the city changed dramatically as well. While its traditional polarization between the rich and the poor increased, it was obvious that the new rich were those connected with the internationalized and liberalized economy. The regeneration and renovation of the historic core of the city for both the tourist industry and the new chic quarters of the wealthy continued as poverty was increasingly suburbanized further and further out from the city.

Of relevance for us is the fact that while new groups in the city developed a new sense of ownership of the city, both symbolically and materially, they also engendered new forms of alienation and marginalization, especially of recent migrants from Anatolia. Their sense of belonging and entitlement were very different from those of the new, Western, elite that began shaping Istanbul in its own image. For many social groups westernization and modernization—hence globalization though the vocabulary is hardly vernacular—increasingly and obviously meant marginalization, impoverishment, and outright abandonment. Islamization of politics as a credible world view among them and its articulation of an alternative development path bypassing westernization must be seen against that background. But it must also be seen against a broader background of political and economic change that allowed Islam to make its case to the Turkish electorate.

To speak of Islamization of politics is more accurate than an Islamist revival or resurgence since the 1970s in Turkey. For Islam has always been present as a political force in the republican order (Göle 1996). Nonetheless, that it has become increasingly prominent in electoral politics and won major electoral victories in the 1990s has usually been explained by immiseration of lower and middle classes from neoliberal policies and the inability of the modernization project to deliver political and economic stability (Margulies and Yildizoğlu 1997). While undoubtedly useful, these explanations, however, reveal vestiges of orientalism and forms of new orientalism. They assume that if political and economic stability were on offer to the lower and middle classes, Islam would lose its attraction. The complex ways in which Islamist politics appeal to various groups and how postmodernization and globalization relay these complex identifications belie such explanations. Many Western observers, for example, especially those who would like to see Turkey admitted into the European Union, consider the rise of Islamist politics in Turkey as a temporary setback to the secular and nationalist project of Kemalism. But, the roots of Islam in Turkey are far deeper than capitalism, westernism, or even secularism (Akpinar 1993). With the unexpected decline of the socialist and communist ideals in Europe, Asia, Africa, and Latin America, Islam emerged as a real and credible alternative for many Turks to the Kemalism of the army and the secular elite. There are three other reasons that account for Islamization of politics as an instance of postmodernization and globalization of Istanbul rather than an ostensible revival of Islamic jihad against a McWorld (Barber 1995).

The first reason concerns the Eastern European revolutions in 1989, which could not have come at a worse time for the secular Turkish elite. Turkey had applied to become a member of the European Union in 1987. Just when it was preparing for its final admission—a long and protracted story that goes back to the 1950s—the emphasis of both Europe and America had already shifted rather rapidly to the new zones liberated from communism and their transition to capitalism. In the frenzy of the billions of dollars that American and European capitalism invested in the formerly communist states, Turkey had become overnight the "forgotten man of Europe." The reasons for the protracted battle to be European are too complex to enter into here. Official reasons such as human rights violations are less important than the strategic regional interests of the United States, which would like to keep Turkey outside the European Union, and of Europe, which would like to keep Turkey as its isolated other (Keyder 1993). Be that as it may, the protracted battle to be European in the wake of a weakening state unable to provide social security gradually destabilized the fragile balance between secularism and nationalism and opened the way to the Islamization of politics (Ayata 1993; Davison 1998; Toprak 1981). To put it another way, neoliberalism, dressed up as Kemalism, was not sufficiently convincing to many groups to provide them with an adequate sense of identity (Keyder 1995). Islamist politics provided an alternative to Western-style consumerism, as a source of identity, belonging, and identification.

The second reason concerns the tragic Gulf War in 1991–92. This not only left Turkey with a trade deficit of billions of dollars in fulfilling its NATO "obligation," but also placed stress on the political fault line between the West and the Muslim states. As soon as the prospect of war with Iraq over the invasion of Kuwait loomed, the United Nations imposed economic sanctions on Iraq. This meant the important pipeline exporting Iraqi oil running through Turkey had to be closed, at an estimated cost of $250 million a year. Iraq was also an important market for Turkish agricultural exports. Although the alliance led by the United States explicitly promised to meet the cost of these measures, it never did so, and many Turkish companies went bankrupt and the Turkish economy was hit very badly. This was a turning point in the emergence of Islam as a political force in politics in that it illustrated vividly who the masters of Turkey were in international relations. Aligning with the West against another Muslim country and its people and culture made it clear, if anyone had any doubts, that in the New World Order, Turkey was subjected to the rules set by Western, especially American, policies.

A third reason for Islamization of politics in Turkey was the impact of the military coup on associations, unions, and organizations that followed a leftist politics, especially in large cities such as Istanbul and Ankara. For in installing Western hypercapitalism by force and dismantling civil and political liberties such as free speech, expression, and association so absolutely that an independent and associational life became stultified and stale, the cultural imagination was left open to Islam. Islam has become credible among the critical middle classes precisely because, especially in its moderate versions, it provides an alternative to Western subjugation and modernization, and a link to tradition and history. The left, which was so effectively dismantled by the military, had previously been able to provide an alternative vision, borrowing elements both from Kemalism and secularism and even from Islam.

Still, despite the merits of explanations that highlight immiseration of lower and middle classes from neoliberalism and the inability of the modernization project to deliver political and economic stability, shifting identities of the Turkish people due to the 1989 revolutions and the Gulf War and the disappearance of the left tend to underestimate the organizational skills of Islamist politics as an urban movement. That Islamization of politics may be an instance of post-modernization and globalization of Istanbul and may be offering a new path to citizenship should be considered seriously.

ISLAMIC CITIZENSHIP

While these accounts contextualize the rise of Islamist politics in Turkey, still, without understanding its organization, ideologies, and sources of identity, it is impossible to understand let alone come to terms with it. Islamization of politics in Turkey can be understood as the emergence of an *urban* social movement that is compatible with notions of democracy and citizenship rather than displaying immutable and essential fundamentalisms that relegate it to marginal and fringe politics. To be sure, Islamization of politics takes various forms, from fundamentalist to moderate and progressive currents, but this is not any different from any urban or social movement that characterizes post-modernization of politics in the West. Similarly, deepening democracy and strengthening progressive aspects of these movements requires taking their claims seriously and recognizing their legitimacy. This is impossible to do if one adheres to a perspective that sees an immutable incompatibility between Islam and democracy, either because of the absence of associational solidarities (orientalism) or their strong presence (new orientalism). From such a perspective, Islamic citizenship is impossible precisely because Islam is considered incompatible with democracy (Esposito and Voll 1996; Krämer 1997; Nielsen 1992; Sadowski 1997).

As more studies conclude that Islamization appeals to various groups not because it offers a jihad mentality but because it offers practical and reasonable choices in people's everyday lives it becomes more difficult to sustain an interpretation that casts the Islamic revival as a movement against modernity and democracy. Practical Islamic politics are concerned with issues such as poverty, the environment, transportation, people's conduct of their public selves, consumption, and neighborhood protection. When in 1994 the Islamist Welfare Party (RP) won 19 percent of the popular vote and captured twenty-six of the seventy-two metropolitan municipalities in the country, including Istanbul and Ankara, the entire secular establishment was deeply concerned. When this was followed by a national election victory in 1995 in which the RP became the largest party and eventually formed the government, Western commentators and observers joined the panic. The political geography of the 1995 general election provided some evidence for this concern. Over the great mass of central and eastern Anatolia, Refah was the largest party, with Islamist victories stretching to the heart of Istanbul, not only in the poor working-class and underclass suburbs but also in fashionable districts. Islamists organize very effectively through municipal institutions, as witnessed by their persistent victories in local elections, and have become a major part of Turkish political life. The irony of maintaining democracy via undemocratic measures was not lost on Islamist intellectuals when, in 1997, the army through the National Security Council delivered an ultimatum to the Islamist government to resign because of its failure to uphold secularism. While the party was closed down in 1998, it was reincarnated in time for the 1999 general elections in which it succeeded remarkably well by gaining 15 percent of the popular vote as the third largest party in parliament.

Behind these electoral successes is a grassroots organization that uses a network of mosques and Islamic brotherhoods and operates at the neighborhood level. While mounting legitimate and serious criticism of globalization and the Western path to citizenship, the Islamic organization operates at the level of people's everyday experiences and provides alternative sources of identity and identification to consumerism, westernization, and capitalism (Göle 1997; Gülalp

1997). Simultaneously, rather than refusing globalization as such, it presents an alternative path to globalization by looking eastward and envisaging Turkey as part of a global Islam.

CONCLUSION

Islamization of politics in Istanbul and its articulation of an Islamic citizenship are neither ephemeral nor necessarily a fundamentalist phenomena. The project of westernization and modernization already rested on fragile grounds and with the globalization and postmodernization of Istanbul these grounds became even more fragile and made possible the articulation of various identities and projects that compete with dominant nationalist narratives. While the secular elite is divided between those who look to the West to articulate a vision of modern citizenship based upon the state and those who look to civil society and market institutions, other social groups, among them Islamists, are articulating alternative forms of identity and citizenship that look eastward (Toprak 1996). The fact that Turkey now finds it difficult to secure acceptance by the West helps the Islamist leaders and intellectuals to articulate a vision of Turkish citizenship without incorporating these contradictions from the West (Ayata 1993; Heyd 1968; Tapper 1991; Toprak 1993).

Some Islamic intellectuals have articulated the choices available to the Turkish Republic as the "city of virtue" that Islam represents against an "empire of consumerism" that the West represents (Mehmet 1990; Toprak 1993). To them the virtuous path of Islam is far superior to a path towards narcissistic consumption, elevating it into a form of fundamentalism, which is all too visible on the streets of Istanbul. To interpret the Islamization of politics in Istanbul and the paths to citizenship it provides it is clear that the orientalist and neo-orientalist dualities between occidental and the oriental forms of citizenship will be inadequate. The ostensibly occidental institutions of citizenship already existed in Istanbul before modernity and the modernization of its constitution and citizenship left a complex legacy of citizenship that cannot be captured by orientalist concepts. Accordingly, understanding visions of citizenship offered by Islamic thought must be taken seriously to come to terms with a globalizing Istanbul.

REFERENCES

Ahmad, F. (1993). *The Making of Modern Turkey.* London: Routledge.

Akpınar, T. (1993). *Türk Tarihinde Islâmiyet.* Istanbul: İletişim Yayınları.

Ayata, S. (1993). "The Rise of Islamic Fundamentalism and Its Institutional Framework," in A. Eralp, M. Tünay, and B. A. Yesilada (eds.), *The Political and Socioeconomic Transformation of Turkey.* Westport, CO: Praeger, 51–68.

Barber, B. (1995). *Jihad vs. McWorld.* New York: Times Books.

Çadırcı, M. (1991). *Tanzimat Döneminde Anadolu Kentleri'nin Sosyal ve Ekonomik Yapıları.* Ankara: Türk Tarih Kurumu Basımevi.

Christensen, S. T. (ed.). (1990). *Violence and the Absolutist State: Studies in European and Ottoman History*. Copenhagen: Akademisk Forlag.

Davison, A. (1998). *Secularism and Revivalism in Turkey: A Hermeneutic Reconsideration*. New Haven: Yale University Press.

Esposito, J. L., and Voll, J. O. (1996). *Islam and Democracy*. Oxford: Oxford University Press.

Faroqhi, S. (1984). *Towns and Townsmen of Ottoman Anatolia: Trade, Crafts, and Food Production in an Urban Setting, 1520–1650*. Cambridge: Cambridge University Press.

Fraser, N. (1997). *Justice Interruptus: Critical Reflections on the "Postsocialist" Condition*. New York: Routledge.

Friedrichs, C. R. (1995). *The Early Modern City, 1450–1750*. London: Longman.

Gerber, H. (1994). *State, Society, and Law in Islam: Ottoman Law in Comparative Perspective*. Albany: State University of New York Press.

Göçek, F. M. (1996). *Rise of the Bourgeoisie, Demise of Empire: Ottoman Westernization and Social Change*. New York: Oxford University Press.

Göle, N. (1993). "Engineers: 'Technocratic Democracy,'" in M. Heper, A. Öncü, and H. Kramer (eds.), *Turkey and the West: Changing Political and Cultural Identities*. London: I. B. Tauris, 199–218.

—— (1996). "Authoritarian Secularism and Islamist Politics: The Case of Turkey," in A. R. Norton (ed.), *Civil Society in the Middle East*, vol. 50. Leiden: E. J. Brill, 17–43.

—— (1997). "The Quest for the Islamic Self within the Context of Modernity," in S. Bozdogan and R. Kasaba (eds.), *Rethinking Modernity and National Identity in Turkey*. Seattle: University of Washington Press, 81–94.

Gülalp, H. (1997). "Modernization Policies and Islamist Politics," in S. Bozdogan and R. Kasaba (eds.), *Rethinking Modernity and National Identity in Turkey*. Seattle: University of Washington Press, 52–63.

Hanioğlu, M. S. (1995). *The Young Turks in Opposition*. New York: Oxford University Press.

Held, D., McGrew, A., Goldblatt, D., and Perraton, J. (1999). *Global Transformations: Politics, Economics, and Culture*. Cambridge: Polity.

Heyd, U. (1968). *Revival of Islam in Modern Turkey*. Jerusalem: Magnes Press, Hebrew University.

Hoogvelt, A. (1997). *Globalisation and the Postcolonial World: The New Political Economy of Development*. Houndmills, Basingstoke, Hampshire: Macmillan.

Isin, E. F. (1992). *Cities without Citizens: Modernity of the City as a Corporation*. Montreal: Black Rose Books.

—— (ed.). (2000). *Democracy, Citizenship, and the Global City*. London: Routledge.

—— (2001). *Being Political: Citizenship as Alterity from Polis to Cosmopolis*. Minneapolis: University of Minnesota Press.

——, and Wood, P. K. (1999). *Citizenship and Identity*. London: Sage.

Kafadar, C. (1995). *Between Two Worlds: The Construction of the Ottoman State*. Berkeley: University of California Press.

Karpat, K. H. (1973). *An Inquiry into the Social Foundations of Nationalism in the Ottoman State: From Social Estates to Classes, From Millets to Nations*. Princeton, NJ: Center of International Studies, Princeton University.

—— (1974). *The Ottoman State and Its Place in World History*. Leiden: Brill.

Kasaba, R. (1988). *The Ottoman Empire and the World-Economy: The Nineteenth Century*. Albany: State University of New York Press.

Kayalı, H. (1997). *Arabs and Young Turks: Ottomanism, Arabism, and Islamism in the Ottoman Empire, 1908–1918.* Berkeley: University of California Press.

Keyder, Ç. (1987). *State and Class in Turkey: A Study in Capitalist Development.* London: Verso.

—— (1993). "The Dilemma of Cultural Identity on the Margins of Europe." *Review,* 16 (1): 19–33.

—— (1995). "Afterword: The Current Condition of the Popular Classes," in D. Quataert and E. J. Zürcher (eds.), *Workers and the Working Class in the Ottoman Empire and the Turkish Republic, 1839–1950.* London: I. B. Tauris, 147–58.

——, and Öncü, A. (1994). "Globalization of a Third-World Metropolis: Istanbul in the 1980s." *Review,* 17 (3): 383–421.

Köprülü, M. F. (1992). *The Origins of the Ottoman Empire* (Gary Leiser, trans.). Albany: State University of New York Press.

Krämer, G. (1997). "Islamist Notions of Democracy," in J. Beinin and J. Stork (eds.), *Political Islam.* Berkeley and Los Angeles: University of California Press, 71–82.

Margulies, R., and Yıldızoğlu, E. (1997). "The Resurgence of Islam and the Welfare Party in Turkey," in J. Beinin and J. Stork (eds.), *Political Islam.* Berkeley and Los Angeles: University of California Press, 144–53.

Mehmet, O. (1990). *Islamic Identity and Development: Studies of the Islamic Periphery.* London: Routledge.

Nas, T. F., and Odekon, M. (1988). *Liberalization and the Turkish Economy.* New York: Greenwood Press.

—— (eds.) (1992). *Economics and Politics of Turkish Liberalization.* Bethlehem: Lehigh University Press.

Nicholas, D. (1997*a*). *The Growth of the Medieval City: From Late Antiquity to the Early Fourteenth Century.* London: Longman.

—— (1997*b*). *The Later Medieval City, 1300–1500.* London: Longman.

Nielsen, J. S. (1992). *Religion and Citizenship in Europe and the Arab World.* London: Grey Seal.

Quataert, D. (1983). *Social Disintegration and Popular Resistance in the Ottoman Empire, 1881–1908: Reactions to European Economic Penetration.* New York: New York University Press.

——, and Inalcik, H. (eds.) (1994). *An Economic and Social History of the Ottoman Empire, 1300–1914.* Cambridge: Cambridge University Press.

Ramsaur, E. E. (1957). *The Young Turks: Prelude to the Revolution of 1908.* Princeton: Princeton University Press.

Rosenthal, S. T. (1980). *The Politics of Dependency: Urban Reform in Istanbul.* Westport, CT: Greenwood Press.

Sadowski, Y. (1997). "The New Orientalism and the Democracy Debate," in J. Beinin and J. Stork (eds.), *Political Islam.* Berkeley and Los Angeles: University of California Press, 33–50.

Said, E. S. (1978). *Orientalism.* New York: Random House.

—— (1993). *Culture and Imperialism.* New York: Vintage Books.

Tapper, R. (ed.) (1991). *Islam in Modern Turkey: Religion, Politics. and Literature in a Secular State.* London: I. B. Tauris.

Togan, S., and Balasubramanyam, V. N. (eds.) (1996). *The Economy of Turkey since Liberalization.* New York: St Martin's Press.

Toprak, B. (1981). *Islam and Political Development in Turkey.* Leiden: Brill.

—— (1993). "Islamist Intellectuals: Revolt against Industry and Technology," in M. Heper, A. Öncü, and H. Kramer (eds.), *Turkey and the West: Changing Political and Cultural Identities.* London: I. B. Tauris, 237–57.

—— (1996). "Civil Society in Turkey," in A. R. Norton (ed.), *Civil Society in the Middle East,* vol. 50. Leiden: E. J. Brill, 87–118.

Turner, B. S. (1974). *Weber and Islam: A Critical Study.* London: Routledge & Kegan Paul.

—— (1978). *Marx and the End of Orientalism.* London: George Allen & Unwin.

—— (1994). *Orientalism, Postmodernism, and Globalism.* London: Routledge.

—— (1996). *For Weber: Essays on the Sociology of Fate,* 2nd edn. London: Sage.

Weber, M. (1909 [1976]). *The Agrarian Sociology of Ancient Civilizations* (R. I. Frank, trans.). London: New Left Books.

—— (1921 [1978]). *Economy and Society: An Outline of Interpretive Sociology* (G. Roth and C. Wittich, trans.). Berkeley: University of California Press.

Weiker, W. F. (1981). *The Modernization of Turkey: From Atatürk to the Present Day.* New York: Holmes & Meier.

Young, I. M. (1989). "Polity and Group Difference: A Critique of the Ideal of Universal Citizenship." *Ethics,* 99 (January): 250–74.

—— (1990). *Justice and the Politics of Difference.* Princeton, NJ: Princeton University Press.

Zürcher, E. J. (1993). *Turkey: A Modern History.* New York: St Martin's Press.

PART VIII

THE NEW COLLECTIVE ORDER OF GLOBAL CITY-REGIONS

The new regionalism, as Keating reminds us, is as much a political construction as it is an expression of shifting patterns of economic production and location. As such, the puzzles posed by the new regionalism are also very much focused on the internal collective order of global city-regions, i.e. on their status as communities with overarching needs and purposes, whether these be in the domain of cultural identity, social welfare, or competitiveness and growth. By the same token, the internal collective order of global city-regions is subject to varied and confusing political crosscurrents. Although a dominant neoliberalism has succeeded in many parts of the world in putting issues of competitiveness and the extension of markets at the top of the policy agenda, other kinds of political demands remain strongly evident in dense urban communities, and, given their enduring structural roots, they are not likely to remain in the background indefinitely. As a corollary, some sort of social market arrangement in global city-regions would seem to offer a viable compromise between political demands for various kinds of sociocultural programs on the one hand and high levels of economic performance on the other.

In Chapters 20 and 21, Henton and Schmitz deal with the collective order of global city-regions in two sharply contrasting empirical situations, the one involving Silicon Valley, the other the shoe-manufacturing complex of the Sinos Valley in Brazil. Henton and Schmitz demonstrate the benefits of—but also the difficulties of building—the institutional bases of robust regional clusters of firms and workers. The discussion in these two chapters is consistent with views that are more and more commonly to be found in the literature on regional development to the effect that definite governance mechanisms and collaborative associations are essential if regional economies are to function at their most competitive and innovative levels of performance. Even so, local business communities and their associated labor markets are subject to many centrifugal forces, and, as Schmitz indicates, these can often undercut the hard work of building the institutional structures that would otherwise enable them to function more effectively.

19

Governing Cities and Regions: Territorial Restructuring in a Global Age

MICHAEL KEATING

THE RISE OF THE REGION

One of the most striking features of the late twentieth century world is the rise of cities and regions as important spaces and as actors in national and global politics. This is all the more remarkable in that it defies the wisdom of generations of modernization theorists who argued that there was an inexorable trend to integration within consolidated nation-states. Equally it calls into question some of the theories of globalization. Both modernists and postmodernists have argued that globalization and European integration will mark the "end of territory" (Badie 1995), superseding both the nation-state and the territorial units within it. In a world of instant communication, free trade, frictionless capital flows, and global culture, this would seem a logical outcome. Yet once again the integrationists have been confounded. Instead of a homogeneous world order, we are faced with a resurgence of regionalist movements, minority nationalisms, and the renaissance of cities as global actors. Observers have ceased to regard this conjunction of globalization and regionalization as a paradox and to appreciate that both are related to each other as the nation-state faces twin pressures from above and below. Political, economic, and social space is restructuring, at various territorial levels and new types of regulation are emerging. What is still lacking is a clear appreciation of how these effects work. Functionalist and reductionist accounts have postulated an automatic connection between economic and technological change and political transformation. My argument is that there is no automatic link between economic and political change, that politics itself still matters, and that the new territorial politics is extremely diverse. The tasks of government, to facilitate economic growth, to foster social solidarity, and to respect cultural pluralism,[1] are the same, but the context is different and the challenge more difficult.

As the state system consolidated from the seventeenth to the nineteenth centuries, it came largely to dominate and structure older patterns of territorial action based on cities and regions with their control of resources and trade routes (Tilly and Blockmans 1994). By the late nineteenth century, European stat
were engaged in complex policies of territorial management, seeking to imp

cultural unity while juggling tariff policies to secure the loyalty of key territories and using intermediaries to broker relationships between center and periphery (Keating 1988, 1998). After the Second World War, states extended their intervention to a panoply of urban and regional policies intended to secure balanced development within national economies with each region assured its role in the national division of labor according to principles of comparative advantage. They widely practiced diversionary policies, steering investments from booming to declining or underdeveloped regions, using infrastructure investment, grants, and tax breaks, and physical planning controls. In centralized states with a large technical bureaucracy, this was extended to sophisticated forms of integrated spatial planning, organizing investment, infrastructure, and urban development around growth poles. In various forms, similar approaches were adopted elsewhere, although American state and federal governments were less inclined to regulate and plan their spatial economies and tended to leave matters more to competition among states and cities themselves. Since the 1980s, this model of planned and state-regulated spatial development has come into question as a consequence of the changing role of the state, economic and technological change, and a greater protagonism on the part of cities and regions themselves. The American model of competitive development seems to have spread more widely, along with the American model of capitalism. Some observers see this as an inevitable and welcome consequence of modernization. Yet we can legitimately ask whether it is also the product of ideology, a close relative of the neoliberal mind set that has become almost hegemonic in the modern world.

There has been an intense debate in recent years about the decline of the state, whether it is in retreat, being "hollowed out," or merely reshaping so as better to maintain its power and authority. Certainly, the share of public spending in GDP has not fallen sharply in developed countries, although it has stabilized in some countries from the 1980s (UK, USA, Canada) while continuing to increase elsewhere. Nor has there been a dramatic withdrawal of the state from welfare provision across the OECD, although there has been a sharp decline in federal responsibility in the USA and, to a lesser extent, Canada. Change has been most marked in the area of economic policy, where Keynesian economic management has formally been abandoned (although still practiced surreptitiously by conservative governments in the USA and United Kingdom in the 1980s and 1990s). Interventionist state policies have given way to deregulation and privatization. There are many explanations for this but they can conveniently be divided into two, those that put the emphasis on ideological and political change, and those that attribute it to technological change and globalization. It is clear that market values have come to dominate, not only in economic policy in the strict sense, but over large swaths of public policy generally, and that these are increasingly uncontested. "Globalization" has become a difficult and contested term and, rather than enter into this debate, I shall use it as shorthand for referring to a bundle of effects including freer international trade, capital mobility, and the rise of the transnational corporation.

Whether driven by ideological change or by global trends, the restructuring of the state has had marked effects on the management of the spatial economy. By the 1970s centralized regional policy was under strain and in the 1980s and 1990s has given way to a more competitive approach in which regions are obliged to seek their own place in the European and global division of labor. In a world where investors, denied the opportunity to invest in their preferred region, can relocate out of the country altogether, governments can no longer steer investment into priority regions. Privatization and deregulation deprive them of key instruments of control. Continental free trade regimes like NAFTA and the European Union reinforce this effect, limiting subsidies and encouraging national governments to favor their most competitive sectors and locations. With the partial disengagement of states, regions themselves have become more active. Political restructuring has also changed the incentive structure for local politicians. Competition among regions for investment has given regional political leaders a *leitmotiv*, producing a neomercantilist form of politics in which regions are presented as pitched into a zero-sum game for advantage. In a world of weakened ideologies, class attachments, and parties, territorial advantage becomes a tempting theme for politicians to use to broaden their electoral bases.

There is certainly an intellectual basis for this shift in emphasis, but it is less clear and more complex than it is sometimes presented and does not always point to clear answers or policy prescriptions. New academic theories about local and regional development focus on the importance of place and the global-local interface. Traditional approaches in regional development policy largely confined themselves to thinking about location, that is distance from markets, labor, or raw materials. The new approaches see *place* (Agnew 1987) as a complex of social relationships, norms, institutions, and understandings, drawing on the literature on economic sociology (Swedberg 1993) and on the *social construction of the market* (Bagnasco and Trigilia 1993) to show that economic development is about more than assembling factors of production in a physical space. Place itself becomes a factor of production as does *social capital* (Coleman 1988; Putnam 1993). This refers to the patterns of social relationships and trust that permit a balance of cooperation and competition, allowing the production of public goods and long-term collective investment (Sabel 1993) and overcoming the division between individual short-term rationality and long-term collective interest that is one of the abiding problems of market capitalism. Traditional approaches to regional development allowed for the existence of traded dependencies, in which complementary industries can reduce their costs by locating together; growth pole policies of the 1960s and 1970s sought to foster these to encourage self-sustaining development. Recent approaches extend this to *untraded interdependencies* (Courchene 1995; Storper 1997; Morgan 1995) arising from the proximity of innovators, manufacturers, and suppliers within a region or locality and the dense pattern of informal exchanges that this encourages. These allow for the production of regional public goods, for a longer term approach to development and for nonimmediate forms of reciprocity or trust. The *associational economy*

(Cooke and Morgan 1998) is presented as a form of enterprise different from individualistic capitalism, blending cooperation and competition in complex ways. Another key idea is that of the *learning region* (Morgan 1995) in which innovation is self-sustaining and success, by fostering trust and cooperation, lays the ground for future success. Many observers have also noted a change in production technologies and systems of innovation such that the old idea of comparative advantage under which every region had a place in the national and international division of labor, and which underlay traditional regional policy, has given way to absolute or *competitive advantage* (Scott 1998).

In response to these economic, technological, political, and intellectual changes, regional development policy has been refocused. It now tends to be more *decentralized*, to the regional or local level where the capacity for horizontal integration and knowledge of problems is greatest (Cappellin 1995*a*,*b*; Begg, Lansbury, and Mayes 1995). There is a strong emphasis on *institution building*, especially on regional-level institutions to build networks of cooperation and partnership, and foster strategic planning (Wannop 1995). Institutionalist approaches (Amin 1999), which bear a striking similarity to the "new institutionalism" in political science (Peters 1999), point to learned behavior, routines, and norms, together with the capacity to change. Institutions are defined broadly to include both government and associational patterns, with the emphasis on the latter.

National governments have tended to be more selective in their interventions and an urban focus has in many cases replaced the broader regional focus of earlier years. Policy places less emphasis now on physical infrastructure and more on *human resources* development. Training policies have widely been decentralized to complement other instruments of intervention, and education has often been tied into economic policy in a more direct way than before. *Research, development, and technology transfer* are stressed through science parks and university-business linkages. Networks and linkages among firms and between them, universities, research centers, and governments, are encouraged, to foster the untraded interdependencies typical of successful regions. There is less emphasis on synoptic planning or large-scale intervention and more on "steering" and selective intervention to remedy market failures. While governments tend to beware of trying to pick winners, they do think about the region's niche in the global economy and how to foster clusters of industries that can exploit this best and sustain each other. Industry itself is defined more widely, to include traded services as well as manufacturing. Small firms and *endogenous development* are especially targeted, although the promotion of inward investment is still important.

These developments have spawned a rich literature but have also given rise to some simplistic explanations and extrapolations and a new set of critiques (Lovering 1999). One problem is a tendency to functional reductionism and economic determinism, in which the competitive region is seen as both inevitable and as marking the end of the nation-state and of politics as we know it. Typical of this type of reasoning is Ohmae (1995) who jumps directly from the rise of regional economies to the rise of global city-regions, to the end of the nation-state, or the "borderless world." In fact, neither the nation-state nor national borders came into being for economic/functional reasons and there is no reason to suppose they will disappear even if they do become functionally redundant. There is also a tendency to project the model of the global city-region everywhere around the world, interpreting just about any manifestation of territorial specificity as a response to global restructuring. This constructed model is then propagated and sold back to urban and regional leaders as a model to emulate, so creating further material for the original observers. So scholars, rather than being detached analysts of political and economic restructuring, become themselves agents for the elaboration and diffusion of the model. One is then forced to ask how far this model is an interpretation of the world and how far it is a mere construction.

Another ideological construction is elaborated around the model of the competitive region. If it is indeed the case that comparative advantage, in which all regions can find their place in the national division of labor, has given way to competitive advantage, in which regions are pitched into competition in global markets, then development is a zero-sum game. This is implied in the very meaning of the word "competition." We are also led to believe that any region can make itself competitive, since raw materials or location are no longer determinant. Yet even if *any* region can be competitive, it follows from the premises given by the model that not *all* regions can be competitive. It may be that comparative advantage has given way to competitive advantage in some sectors; whether it has done so in all areas of economic activity is much more doubtful. Yet the insistence that competitive advantage is the imperative driving development has important political implications. It means that, if a region does not succeed, then in effect that is its own fault. There is nothing wrong with the market system itself, with the global order, or with state policies, since some regions do well in spite of these. This provides a rationale for disregarding issues of spatial equity, for cutting back on redistributive programs, and for wealthy regions to disengage themselves from concern for poorer ones, a process already visible across Europe, North America, and other parts of the world. As the region or city is reconceptualized as an actor in the global order, there is a reification of what is really a complex and plural system and a further closure of political options. Globalization is then brought in to serve what the French call the *pensée unique*, another form of the old "one best way" philosophy in which political debate about the future of social and economic life is largely precluded.

In the remainder of this chapter, I am going to argue that regionalism is in fact a highly diverse phenomenon (Keating 1998). The effects of economic change are powerfully mediated by culture, by institutions, and by politics. It is true that regions are being built and rebuilt as systems of social regulation and as actors in national and global spaces, but this is a complex and multifaceted process. Economic determinism, whether of the Marxist or neoliberal type, does not explain a great deal.

THE POLITICS OF DEVELOPMENT

One of the paradoxes of the "new paradigm" of regional development is that, by emphasizing the importance of place, it makes it impossible to construct a single model for all cases (Storper 1997). Even the meaning of region or city-region is contested, both intellectually and politically. The goals of policy can be multiple and the policy process, the policy mix, and the means of implementation will all be specific to particular places.

Regions may be defined in purely topographical terms but usually they are taken to have a broader economic, social, and political meaning. Economic functionalism provides one way of defining the region, either as a homogeneous production space or as an interlinked set of production systems. Cultural criteria may give another definition. A political region may be defined as a "political space" (Keating 1998) whose inhabitants have a sense of territorial identity and in which issues are appraised by reference to their impact on the region. Administrative regions are defined by states for the delivery of policy and services. These varied meanings of the region do not always coincide and, where they do, it is usually as a result of a process of region-building and political leadership. Wales, for example, is far from being a functional economic region but it may be that political leaders and state policies are building one around a common history, cultural elements, and new institutions, guided by a vision derived by intellectuals from the theories of new regionalism (see Lovering 1999). There is a perennial conflict between planners and social policymakers who want to define regions and cities broadly, so as to include the whole functional system and its interdependencies, or to share wealth more evenly, and the interests of wealthy neighborhoods and towns who want to keep what they have. In the United States, the wealthy areas tend to be in the suburbs and the poorer areas in the inner city, while in much of Europe it is the other way around; but the basic issue is the same. There are also conflicts between politicians established at the larger regional level and those whose power base lies in the city or city-region. In Catalonia, there have been regular conflicts between the autonomous government of the Generalitat and the town hall of Barcelona. French regions have tended to lose out in the competition with large cities and even the old *départements*. The vacuum caused by the collapse of the central party system in Italy has been partly filled by city mayors, now directly elected, with the regions still looking for their place.

The new development paradigm has obvious political attractions. It recognizes the constraints of the global economy and the need to insert the region into the international division of labor. It ties in with trends to decentralization and regionalism and has affinity with communitarian ideas and the "small is beautiful" philosophy. The political right like it because it is against big government and large-scale intervention and social engineering. The left can buy into it because it is critical of unbridled capitalism of the "Anglo-Saxon" variety and stresses the importance of social relations and community. There are affinities with the "new public management" which seeks to replace hierarchy and control with new forms of compliance, often without facing up to the realities of conflict, power, and interests, but taking refuge in superficially appealing analogies such as "steering not rowing."[2] It is, in other words, an ideal philosophy for "third way" politicians and thinkers uncomfortable with the hard choices of real politics. Yet there are both analytical and normative difficulties with the idea.

Much of the thinking behind the model stemmed from studies of industrial districts in central Italy (Ritaine 1989) and, later, southern Germany. These findings have then been extrapolated elsewhere. Critics, however, have suggested that many of these studies are wishful thinking or a generalization from selected features of specific cases (Hadjmichaelis and Papamicos 1991; Ritaine 1989; Amin and Thrift 1994; Hudson 1999). They note that the dense networks of small firms in these districts may rely on low wages, family exploitation, and tax evasion; and that some of these districts have subsequently experienced economic difficulties. The extrapolation of the model is also criticized. The transition from Fordism to flexible specialization can be overstated. Many regions have never been truly Fordist while others still are. Small firms might be important generators of jobs and innovation but they are very often dependent on the presence of large firms or government. The growth of business services, for example, is often the result of large firms outsourcing these services rather than a form of endogenous development. Indeed, insofar as the model is based on the need to tailor policies to the needs of specific locations and the recognition that there is no "one best way" to success, one might ask whether there is a model at all (Storper 1997). Imitation of success stories in other regions is likely to be counterproductive, because the circumstances are different and because the other region has got there first, occupying that niche in the international division of production.

The new approaches to regionalism too often either sweep aside questions of distribution and welfare (Ohmae 1995), insist that this choice is no longer available in a global economy, or suggest that the new paradigm may be both more efficient and socially just (Cooke and Morgan 1998). This last claim may be true insofar as the welfare state helps avoid some of the social cost of deprivation, security may enhance social cooperation, and investment in people may have both economic and social benefits. One could say the same about environmental policies. Indeed it seems likely that investors will be more attracted to cities and regions without the burden of social stress and environmental degradation. Yet this is not self-evidently true everywhere or at all times. These are long-term policies requiring long-term investment, while the incentives that politicians face are for short-term results. Some regions may be in a better market position or endowed with high levels of technology and skills and so be able to pursue a high cost strategy of trading up into higher value-added production. Others have concluded that their competitive advantage lies in low wages, deregulated labor markets without trade unions, or low social overheads. Even where the welfare state has survived, as it generally has in western Europe, it is being reshaped to the needs of economic competitiveness rather than social integration. This explains measures like "workfare" or the shifting of priorities in education towards economic competitiveness. One could make the same argument about environmental quality. Some regions have a good environment and are able to use this to attract high quality development. Others are burdened with obsolete industrial infrastructure, pollution, or contaminated land and cannot compete without outside help in tackling these problems.

So the tension between growth and redistribution, which is the staple of American urban political economy, is still there. Globalization and free trade have exacerbated this tension and, together with decentralization, have introduced it into other countries. Globalization, technological change, and the crisis of the state have added to the tension, generating new forms of social movements and identity politics at multiple levels (Castells 1997). These include environmentalism, gender issues, and neighborhood movements, as well as new types of criminality and social pathology. Indeed it seems that city-regions are becoming internally more pluralist, with a wider range of social demands made on them, just at the time when the external global environment and the needs of competition are restricting their policy options (Kantor 1995; Keating 1991). This is the essence of politics and makes it ever more difficult to reduce city-regions to a form of functional determinism.

Another important political issue is interterritorial justice. A degree of inequality is inherent in the very idea of the competitive regions (Dunford 1994) and as this model gains intellectual acceptance it may be used to justify inequality. Wealthy regions are showing increased resistance to paying for fiscal transfers to their poorer compatriots on the ground that this hampers their ability to compete in global markets. The rise of Italy's Northern League is due in large part to an unwillingness to pay for subsidies to the Mezzogiorno. These were tolerated in the past, when the money mostly came back in the form of orders for northern goods, and redistribution was seen as a price to pay to keep the Italian state together. In an integrating Europe, neither rationale is as convincing. Southerners can buy their goods on European and world markets, and Europe provides an alternative political and economic frame for the north. Similar tensions are undermining the Canadian federation. In Germany, a group of wealthy Länder has gone to the constitutional court to complain about the system of horizontal equalization. Catalonia and the Basque Country are complaining vociferously about their disproportionate contribution to the common expenses of Spain and increasingly looking to Europe. Flemish interests are seeking to transfer the Belgian social security system to the linguistic communities, so reducing their payment to Wallonia. In the United Kingdom, Scottish devolution has sparked a renewed debate on territorial allocations and one of the few items on which candidates for mayor of London seem to agree is the need to cut back transfers to the Scots. The fact is that nation-states are still responsible for massive resource transfers (Davezies 1997). Public expenditure and employment are often the key factors in regional development, despite the tendency of the new approaches to focus on the private sector (Lovering 1999).

These questions show that regional politics is still alive and well in the era of the global city-region. Structures of government, access to power and resources, and social relationships are still important. Too often, however, we lack the analytical tools to appreciate and assess these changes. There has been a great deal of talk recently about "governance" as a new form of social regulation distinct from "government." There are many definitions of this term—Rhodes (1996) gives six—but the central idea appears to be a system of policymaking and regulation going beyond the state, to take in the private sector, civil society, and, in some versions, multiple territorial levels of action. I have never really understood why we need this neologism[3] since government was always about more than the formal structures of the state.[4] The vaguely pluralistic basis of the idea seems to represent a loss rather than a gain in analytical capacity. Perhaps more worrying is its normative bias. Combined with some interpretations of the new development paradigm and the "new public management" it feeds into forms of "Third Way" politics in which the great issues of politics and social conflict simply disappear. They are replaced by markets, by management nostrums, or a concentration on the minutiae of politics at the expense of the big picture.

BUILDING A DEVELOPMENT MODEL

We can analyze the new forms of competitive development and their impact on politics through the concept of a "development coalition," a place-based interclass coalition dedicated to economic development in a specific location. This places the emphasis on competitive development, but recognizes that policy will be the outcome of political competition within the region and of the composition of the dominant coalition. Of course, external factors are of vital importance. Not all regions have the same locational advantages or resource endowments and development politics will thus be influenced greatly by the difficulty of the task (Stone 1989). The competitive situation is also critical in determining the room for maneuver of political and other leaders.

Five other factors are critical in the construction of a development coalition: culture, institutions, leadership, social composition, and external relations.

Culture

Culture is an expansive term, with many meanings. There is a distinction between the "high culture" of literature and the performing arts, and the everyday culture of social norms and practices. Although there are links between the two, our main interest is in the latter. The new development paradigm places great emphasis on social relationships, shared understandings, and norms of cooperation and reciprocity and, while some authors shy away from using the term "culture," this is a type of cultural explanation. There does appear to be something here, but there are serious problems in identifying and measuring the importance of culture and behavioral norms. One approach is based on case studies of success or failure and exploration on the ground of the nature of the local societies. These almost invariably yield one or two "stories." There is the success story, in which people tell the researchers that the society is cohesive, cooperative, and efficient, and has a strong sense of identity and social responsibility. Then there is the failure story, in which one is told that the people are too "individualist," that there is no capacity for sustained action, and that there is a lack of entrepreneurial spirit. These stories are usually so similar as to appear rehearsed and one has the impression that respondents are merely rationalizing success or failure. This becomes even more apparent when old failures suddenly become successes and the same factors that explained failure are now adduced to explain success—Ireland being an obvious example. So "collectivist attitudes" become "cooperation"; the blockage of "special interests" becomes "social concertation"; "individualism" becomes "self-reliance"; and "traditionalism" becomes "sensitivity to history and culture."

The second approach is based on surveys, seeking to explain economic performance by mass attitudes. Apart from the difficulty of making a connection between mass attitudes and economic action, this comes up against methodological problems. The survey is an individualized instrument in which people are asked out of context what they feel about various things. It is often a poor guide to how they act in social situations. Surveys often yield no more than stereotypes paralleling the stories mentioned above rather than getting into the dynamics of social behaviors. For example, a Spanish survey showed respondents in Catalonia believing that Catalans were dynamic and businesslike, but not attributing the same qualities to themselves as individuals, another example of a learned story (Sangrador García 1996).

Cultural reductionism, then, does not get us very far. We need to look at the way in which culture is created, transmitted, and used. We also need to explore apparent contradictions and conflicts and the way in which culture can bridge these. We find often that successful territorial political movements and development coalitions are those that can play two contradictory themes at once. A localist theme, rooted in tradition and particularism, helps consolidate local solidarity and collective action, yet threatens parochialism, xenophobia, and the crushing of local pluralism. A cosmopolitan theme, on the other hand, reaches out to the international market and seeks to integrate the region into wider circuits, but on the other hand threatens to erode social solidarity, attachment, and culture, subordinating communities to the impersonal market. In some places, these two coexist in more or less uneasy partnership, producing a "rooted cosmopolitanism," which allows regions to operate in the global economy without losing their own distinct characters (Friedmann 1991). Another way of capturing the formula is the "strength of weak ties" (Granovetter 1973), that is, ties that bind communities but are not exclusive and allow multiple channels of communication, so fostering innovation and change. Much of the work on the importance of community and of associations in regional development has failed to make this kind of distinction between functional and dysfunctional kinds of solidarity and ties.

Little is known as yet about the way in which these local norms are constituted historically and sustained over time. In France, the *annales* school, and the quantitative analyses of Todd (1990), Le Bras (1995), and others have contributed greatly to the understanding of territorial identity and its transmission, but there is a lack of similar work elsewhere. Putnam's work on Italy (Putnam, Leonardi, and Nanetti 1985; Putnam 1993) emphasizes the importance of historical patterns and inheritance and argues for a form of path-dependency. Comparative study, however, shows us that cultures and identities are continually created and recreated (Rohe 1990). The critical factor here becomes the instrumentalization of identity by region-builders and leaders of the development coalition. Regions with a "usable past" will find this reinterpreted and pressed into service to forge a vision of the future. In Catalonia, which has traditions of both conflict and social cooperation, the latter are being valorized, while Catalonia's history as a medieval stateless trading nation provides an image for its role in an integrating Europe and globalizing world. Welsh traditions of cooperation and mutualism can be stressed over the more recent history of class conflict. Galicia, on the other hand, is burdened by negative stereotypes and the political will and mobilization are not present to create more positive images. These images and motifs serve as myths, that is stories that may be true, false, or (usually) partially true but whose mobilizing capacity is largely independent of their truth. One could even see Ohmae's global city-regions as such a myth and its adoption by regional elites as part of the process of the invention of regions.

Institutions

Institutional analysis has enjoyed a new vogue in recent years in the guise of the "new institutionalism" (March and Olsen 1984) or "institutional economics" (North 1990). These new approaches go beyond formal organizations to show how behavior is shaped by institutions of all types. They provide a corrective to pure rational choice explanations of behavior by showing how choices are constrained by the operating environment. They also add to cultural explanations by showing how norms and routines can be inculcated through practice and how routine can build trust. In fact, so close have cultural and institutional analysis become that it is sometimes difficult to tell where one ends and the other begins. Institutions are also important as arenas in which choices can be debated and preferences formed and reshaped in interaction with others.

Four aspects of the institutional structure of regions are important for our theme. First is the degree of territorial fragmentation or consolidation. There is a long debate between supporters of fragmentation and consolidation. Supporters of fragmentation, who once emphasized the value of community, identity, and tradition, have now been joined by exponents of the "public choice" approach. These argue that fragmented local government gives citizens a choice of different locations with differing bundles of services, promotes efficiency through competition, and limits the power of bureaucracy by dividing it. Supporters of consolidation used to urge the benefits of economies of scale in service provision. Nowadays they put more emphasis on the need for coherent metropolitan planning, building metropolitanwide competitiveness, and the need to avoid beggar-my-neighbor competition for development, in which business sets local governments against each other to offer the most attractive incentives at the taxpayers' cost. Consolidation was in fashion across Europe and North America in the 1960s and 1970s. In the 1980s it was halted and even reversed, as large-scale planning lost popularity and the promised economies of scale often seemed elusive. It was also politically very difficult to get agreement on forms of metropolitan government strong enough to make their plans stick, and the usual compromise was a two-tier structure with the main powers at the lower level. In the 1990s, there has been a revived interest in metropolitan government but of a more modest type, with the task of coordinating infrastructure and planning and attracting economic development. France has introduced new types of interurban consortia. A council for Greater London, abolished in 1986, is being restored on a more modest scale, with a directly elected mayor. Italian cities have been encouraged to try metropolitan structures. The Dutch are restoring something like the old Rijndmond authority. The cities of metropolitan Toronto have been consolidated, although only a weak services board has been allowed for the wider Greater Toronto area.

The second issue is that of functional fragmentation. In the 1960s and 1970s the emphasis was on integrated planning and corporate management, with governments seeking a synoptic view of social and economic problems and trying to link their interventions across multiple policy spheres. In the 1990s, the tendency is to privatization, ad hoc agencies, and contracting to business and the nonprofit sector. This is impelled largely by the desire to save money but it is rationalized by reference to public choice theories and the new public management. Efficiency is supposedly ensured by making agencies compete for contracts or in the provision of services. This may happen, although the evidence is inconclusive and studies are almost always tainted by the ideological bias of the researcher or the interest of the body commissioning the work. Perhaps more significant is the growth in power of producer interests and the tendency for policy to fragment further into separate segments, discouraging links and new thinking. In a situation where the public sector is highly fragmented and disorganized, private interests, by being only slightly organized, have a major advantage. Matters are not helped by misleading analogies, such as the idea that government can now retreat to a role in "steering," leaving others to do the "rowing." A tendency of particular interest to our theme is the trend to separating economic development issues from social or distributive ones, by entrusting them to separate agencies dominated by business interests. This type of functional regionalism can produce outcomes very different from those produced by elected regional governments with broad representation.

Related to this is a third issue, that of public–private relationships. The relationship between public and private power, always a key issue in U.S. cities, has become a concern now in other parts of the world. The very emphasis on economic development as an imperative for cities and regions enhances the power of the private sector, since they are the ones with the mobile resources to invest. This is increased by the trend to using private instruments and organizations for public purposes, and the growth of public–private partnerships. Partnerships, which are regarded with almost universal approbation as heralding an end to the old types of politics, may be an effective way of mobilizing resources for development and tying capital into cities and regions. They also present a series of dangers, which are less often appreciated. They alter the balance of power in favor of private interests, by bringing them into the policy process, and often by the way in which the terms of the partnership work. Since private business operates on the basis of commercial secrecy while governments are obliged to publish full accounts, the private partner usually knows more about the public one than vice versa. The need for commercial confidentiality often leads to a lack of transparency and accountability, to the point that details of contracts are often kept secret.

There are concerns about costs, which are not always as favorable to the public sector as might seem at first sight. Large public infrastructures built with private capital almost invariably come with an implicit government guarantee since the public authorities, having undertaken the project, will not allow it to fail. So the public bailout, whether directly or by providing complementary spending, is common. Partnerships involving private developers supplying the upfront capital and leasing facilities back to government have also been criticized for providing poor value for taxpayers. With the credit of the taxpayer behind them, governments can nearly always borrow money more cheaply than private developers and do not need to add a profit margin. Britain's Private Finance Initiative, relabeled but essentially unchanged under the new Labour government, is regarded almost unanimously by specialists in public finance as a bad deal for the taxpayer, since it transfers to future generations the costs of providing capital facilities in the present. Public–private partnerships can also lead to a policy bias, in which public resources go into those activities of most interest and profit to the private sectors. These are often property and land deals, or construction of facilities for the new consumption economy. High-income leisure facilities ("playgrounds for the rich"), congress halls, and sports stadia are typical examples.

The final institutional issue is intergovernmental relations. There has been a tendency in recent years for senior governments to decentralize functions and responsibilities to local and regional units. This has a positive side, enabling cities and regions to devise local solutions to the problems posed by global competition. Its permits experimentation and policies geared to the characteristics of place, in line with modern thinking. On the other hand, it exposes cities and regions more directly to the discipline of the market and may reinforce the bias to development politics against social integration. Cities and regions cannot be independent, they can only manage various forms of interdependency, and there may be a trade-off to be made between dependence on the state and dependence on private capital.[5] A widespread fear is that decentralization and downloading will produce a "race to the bottom" as regions and cities cut back social provision to enhance their competitive edge. This is too simple. Many cities and regions do not need to compete hard for development, while some cannot attract it whatever they do. As we have noted, an attractive environment and social stability may be development assets. Local responses to external pressures will always be mediated by local political pressures and conditions. So there are a variety of responses. Some cities and regions are forced to cut back on social provisions. Others are able to invest in social and environmental infrastructure. Others again adopt a more selective approach to social assistance, redefining the "deserving poor" in a way to maximize political gain and minimize political cost.

Leadership

An important element in development coalitions is leadership. This can provide the discursive element in constructing the "imagined" city or region, a symbolic realm in which identities can be formed. This in turn helps create a political space, a frame of reference in relation to which issues can be debated and appraised. The creation of this public political space is an element notably lacking in public choice approaches, which tend to assume that people's preferences are ready-formed and that politics is merely a matter of arbitrating between them. Political leadership can also serve to create a broader, city or regionwide, rationality, allowing issues to be appraised for their impact on the whole area or in the long term, rather than just on their immediate and local impact. Leadership may be individualized, in a charismatic personality, or it may be collective, lodged in a political party. Parties have been weakening in city and regional politics, and this may result in a diminished ability to integrate policy concerns and interests.

Social Composition

The strategy of the development coalition and the content of policy will be affected by the representation of social interests, notably those of capital and labor. International and European market integration itself redistributes power from labor to capital since capital is more mobile than labor and can play off regions against each other. Within regions, the presence of organized class interests varies. Some regions, such as many parts of Germany, have retained their indigenous bourgeoisies, with a continued social investment in the place. In the United Kingdom, by contrast, regional bourgeoisies of the old industrial regions often sold out, moved to London, or moved socially into the leisured upper classes through the purchase of land, from the early part of the twentieth century, and especially after World War I. British capital has also been more internationalized than that of other European countries. In both France and Britain, the centralization of the financial systems on the capital which in the nineteenth century contrasted with the dispersal of industrial ownership and production at the periphery, tended in the twentieth century to concentrate industrial ownership at the center too.

This is not to say that indigenous control is essential for economic development; that argument has long been abandoned. The point that I am making is about the qualitative aspect of development. Where local business elites have a stake in the place, as in some U.S. cities, this may foster a commitment to regenerate the city rather than merely seek out the conditions for investment, and can facilitate a social dialogue about priorities and social and environmental issues.

Business leaders are always wedded rhetorically to the idea of the free market and neoliberal nostrums, but in practice usually support regional development efforts, as long as these are delivered by depoliticized agencies with a strong business input. They appreciate the functional rationale for organizing government at the regional level to deliver training policies, infrastructure, and land use planning, but this is in tension with their suspicion of regional government as a basis for nonbusiness or antibusiness forces, producing an ambivalent attitude to territorial politics (Lange 1998).

Labor has become more territorialized as class struggles have shifted to the defense of threatened plants and sectors. Sometimes, it has been able to mobilize wider social movements of territorial defense committed to broader goals and regional development strategies but these have been rather precarious, as the French cases show. Labour and the social democratic parties have become increasingly supportive of decentralization and regionalism, as their faith in the centralized state has diminished and they have been drawn into territorial-based conflicts. Yet at the same time, unions insist on the maintenance of national labor-market regulation so that they too are ambivalent on the question of regionalism.

The new regionalism has produced many examples of capital-labor cooperation in pursuit of a common territorial interest. Labor, however, has been at a disadvantage. It is less mobile than capital and less able to exploit the opportunities of globalization. Also, where policy and the constitution of the dominant coalition is driven by the needs of competitive development, business is able to pose as a representative of a general, as well as a particular, interest. In France, where union membership is particularly low, they hardly feature at all. In the UK, they were marginalized by the Conservative government, not only in national policymaking but also in the construction of the new instruments for local and regional development, including the Urban Development Corporations and Training and Enterprise Councils (in Scotland, Local Enterprise Companies). In Germany, trade unions feature more strongly in the Social Democratic stronghold of North Rhine-Westphalia than in Baden-Württemberg. In Spain, control of autonomous communities by either the socialists or the Christian democrats of the Catalan CiU or Basque PNV produces a willingness to recognize trade unions as social partners, although, given the low level of unionization in Spain, as very junior ones. In France, Italy, and Spain, the division of the trade union movement on political lines also weakens its influence and allows regional leaders to choose their favored union partners. In North American city-regions, organized labor rarely features these days as an important partner in the development coalition. Unorganized labor has even less of a place.

The External Dimension

The context for the new regionalism is supplied not only by the nation-state, but by global and continental markets and new transnational institutions. Regions have consequently developed international strategies, forms of "paradiplomacy" (Aldecoa and Keating 1999) aimed at securing their position. The most important things they seek are inward investment, markets, technology, and alliances with other regions in development promotion or political action. A great deal has been made of the emergence of transnational or cross-border regions bound together by functional ties and common interests. Yet this activity, too, is highly constrained by politics and once again functionalist explanations do not always fit. In the first place, before a region can engage in external activities it must constitute itself as an actor and, as we have seen, not all regions are in a position to do this. It requires institutions, leadership, and an ability to carry a definition of the interests of the region. Those who are able to define the region's external interest have a big advantage in internal politics and so this becomes highly contested. Second, the state framework is still very important and state elites, both political and bureaucratic, tend to be jealous of their monopoly of external action and can place all manner of obstacles in the way of regions. Third, regions are, according to the prevailing theory, engaged in a neomercantilist competition for absolute advantage. In these circumstances, it is not clear why they should want to cooperate with each other. Border regions, in particular, are likely to be competing for the same markets and investment opportunities. So, although there may be economies of scale to be achieved, for example by investing in one large airport rather than two, there is no political advantage to be achieved by politicians on either side in letting the other side have it. Common interests will only be realized if they are institutionalized by providing a framework in which costs and benefits will be shared and additional resources brought in.

The evidence that we have shows that interregional cooperation and cross-border regionalism will happen where there are clearly identifiable common interests, political leaders able and willing to articulate these and use external action as a political resource at home, and an external support system such as that offered by the regional programs of the European Union. This explains the explosion of paradiplomacy and cross-border regionalism in Europe and their almost complete absence, apart from rhetoric and sloganizing, in North America (Keating 1996).[6]

CONCLUSION

There have been two approaches in the study of regionalism, an internally focused one which looks at the mobilization of actors on the ground and the social, political, and historical basis of regional identity and demands; and an externally focused one which concentrates on the reshaping of the global economy and the place of regions within this. A proper appreciation of the phenomenon needs to take both into account. On the internal dimension, city-regions are becoming more heterogeneous, multicultural, and pluralist. New demands are being placed on the political agenda, from strategies of economic development, through environmental concerns, to issues of social justice and identity politics. Yet the policy options available to city-regions as political systems are constrained by the external competitive environment. Here lies the dilemma of contemporary urban and regional politics. It is through politics that these tensions and conflicts will be resolved but this must be a democratic and inclusive politics, not one subordinated to a narrow policy agenda of boosterism and growth. The principal mechanism is government. Markets alone cannot substitute for government. Nor can vague notions of self-regulation or "governance," however soothing, help us resolve the conflicts of interest and values present in the urban context. Instead, the interests of business and development become synonymous with the general interest of the region. It is not surprising, then, that the issue of government keeps on reappearing on the policy agenda. Designing new institutions and promoting democratic participation is thus an urgent priority.

NOTES

1. Of course, there are other tasks of government, notably to ensure security, but I list only the ones relevant to my theme.
2. Like so many fashionable cliches, this is based on a false understanding of the analogue. In a rowing boat, most of the steering is provided by the oarsmen.
3. It is not strictly a neologism, since the word is an old one, but its current usage is new.
4. In more than thirty years studying political science in universities, I have never found the mythical "textbook" that says otherwise.
5. In rare cases, such as the traditional French system, local governments can have the best of both worlds. They can use state resources to reduce their reliance on the market, but effectively control the allocation of those resources through their position in national politics. The desire to end this state of affairs was one of the motives behind the state's decentralization program of the 1980s.
6. There are many examples of cross-border initiatives in North America, but our researches show that so far they have not amounted to much in practice.

REFERENCES

Agnew, J. (1987). *Place and Politics: The Geographical Mediation of State and Society.* London: Allen and Unwin.

Aldecoa, F., and Keating, M. (eds.). (1999). *Paradiplomacy in Action: The External Activities of Subnational Governments.* London: Frank Cass.

Amin, A. (1999). "An Institutionalist Perspective on Regional Economic Development." *International Journal of Urban and Regional Research*, 23: 365–78.

——, and Thrift, N. (1994). "Living in the Global," in A. Amin and N. Thrift (eds.), *Globalization, Institutions, and Regional Development in Europe.* Oxford: Oxford University Press, 1–22.

Bachtler, J. (1993). "Regional Policy in the 1990s: The European Perspective," in R. T. Harrison and M. Hart (eds.), *Spatial Policy in a Divided Nation*. London: Jessica Kingsley, 254–69.

Badie, B. (1995). *La fin des territoires: Essai sur le désordre international et sur l'utilité sociale du respect*. Paris: Fayard.

Bagnasco, A., and Trigilia, C. (1993). *La construction social du marché*. Cachan: Editions ENS Cachan.

Begg, I., Lansbury, M., and Mayes, D. G. (1995). "The Case for Decentralized Industrial Policy," in P. Cheshire and I. Gordon (eds.), *Territorial Competition in an Integrating Europe*. Aldershot: Avebury, 179–205.

Cappellin, R. (1995*a*). "Una politica regionale nazionale 'orientata al mercato' tra i nuovi modelli organizzativi e federalismo," in G. Gorla and O. V. Colonna (eds.), *Regioni e Sviluppo: Modelli, politiche e riforme*. Milan: Franco Angeli, 331–51.

—— (1995*b*). "Regional Development, Federalism and Interregional Cooperation," in H. Eskelinen and F. Snickers (eds.), *Competitive European Peripheries*. Berlin: Springer, 41–58.

Castells, M. (1997). *The Information Age: Economy, Society, and Culture*, vol. 2, *The Power of Identity*. Oxford: Blackwell.

Coleman, J. (1988). "Social Capital in the Creation of Human Capital." *American Journal of Sociology*, 94 (supplement): S95-S120.

Cooke, P., and Morgan, K. (1998). *The Associational Economy: Firms, Regions, and Innovation*. Oxford: Oxford University Press.

Courchene, T. (1995). "Celebrating Flexibility: An Interpretative Essay on the Evolution of Canadian Federalism." C. D. Howe Institute, 1994 Benefactors Lecture. Montreal.

Davezies, L. (1997). *Interregional Transfers from Central Government Budgets in European Countries: A Fragmented Cohesion Process?* Paper published singly from the April 1997 Conference on Territorial Politics in Europe: A Zero-Sum Game? Florence: Robert Schuman Centre, European University Institute.

Dunford, M. (1994). "Winners and Losers: The New Map of Economic Inequality in the European Union. *European Urban and Regional Studies*, 1: 95–114.

Friedmann, J. (1991). "The Industrial Transition: A Comprehensive Approach to Regional Development", in E. Bergman, G. Maier, and F. Tödtling (eds.), *Regions Reconsidered: Economic Networks, Innovation, and Local Development in Industrialized Countries*. London: Mansell, 124–48.

Granovetter, M. (1973). "The Strength of Weak Ties." *American Journal of Sociology*, 78: 360–80.

Hadjimichaelis, C., and Papamicos, N. (1991). "'Local' Development in Southern Europe: Myths and Realities," in E. Bergman, G. Maier, and F. Tödtling (eds.), *Regions Reconsidered: Economic Networks, Innovation, and Local Development in Industrialized Countries*. London: Mansell, 241–69.

Hudson, R. (1999). "The Learning Economy, the Learning Firm, and the Learning Region: A Sympathetic Critique of the Limits to Learning." *European Urban and Regional Studies*, 61: 59–72.

Kantor, P. (1995). *The Dependent City Revisited: The Political Economy of Urban Development and Social Policy*. Boulder: Westview.

Keating, M. (1988). *State and Regional Nationalism: Territorial Politics and the European State*. London: Harvester Wheatsheaf.

—— (1991). *Comparative Urban Politics: Power and the City in the United States, Canada, Britain, and France.* Aldershot: Edward Elgar.

—— (1996). "Les provinces canadiennes dans la concurrence inter-régionale nord-américaine," in R. Balme (ed.), *Les politiques du néo-régionalisme.* Paris: Economica, 283–301.

—— (1998). *The New Regionalism in Western Europe: Territorial Restructuring and Political Change.* Aldershot: Edward Elgar.

Lange, N. (1998). *Zwischen Regionalismus und europäischer Integration. Wirtschaftsinteressen im Spannungsfeld.* Baden-Baden: Nomos.

Le Bras, H. (1995). *Les Trois France.* Paris: Odile Jacob.

Lovering, J. (1999). "Theory Led by Policy: The Inadequacies of the 'New Regionalism.'" *International Journal of Urban and Regional Research,* 23: 379–90.

March, J. G., and Olsen, J. P. (1984). "The New Institutionalism: Organizational Factors in Political Life." *American Political Science Review,* 78: 734–48.

Morgan, K. (1995). *The Learning Region: Institutions, Innovation, and Regional Renewal.* Papers in Planning Research, no. 157. Cardiff: Department of City and Regional Planning, University of Wales College of Cardiff.

North, D. C. (1990). *Institutions, Institutional Change, and Economic Performance.* Cambridge: Cambridge University Press.

Ohmae, K. (1995). *The End of the Nation-State: The Rise of Regional Economies.* New York: Free Press.

Peters, B. G. (1999). *Institutional Theory in Political Science: The "New Institutionalism."* London: Pinter.

Putnam, R. (1993). *Making Democracy Work: Civic Traditions in Modern Italy.* Princeton: Princeton University Press.

——, Leonardi, R., and Nanetti, R. (1985). *La pianta e le radici. Il radicamento dell'istituto regionale nel sistema politico italiano.* Bologna: Il Mulino.

Rhodes, R. A. W. (1996). "The New Governance: Governing without Government." *Political Studies,* 44: 652–67.

Ritaine, E. (1989). "La modernité localisée: Leçons italiennes sur le développement régional." *Revue française de science politique,* 39: 154–77.

Rohe, K. (1990). "Political Alignments and Realignments in the Ruhr, 1867–1987: Continuity and Change of Political Traditions in an Industrial Region," in Karl Rohe (ed.), *Elections, Parties, and Political Traditions: Social Foundations of German Parties and Party Systems, 1867–1987.* New York: Berg, 107–44.

Sabel, C. F. (1993). "Studied Trust: Building New Forms of Cooperation in a Volatile Economy," in R. Swedberg (ed.), *Explorations in Economic Sociology.* New York: Russel Sage Foundation, 104–44.

Sangrador García, José L. (1996). "Identidades, actitudes y estereotipos en la España de las Autonomías." *Opiniones y Actitudes, 10.* Madrid: Centro de Investigaciones Sociológicas.

Scott, A. J. (1998). *Regions and the World Economy: The Coming Shape of Global Production, Competition, and Political Order.* Oxford: Oxford University Press.

Stone, C. (1989). *Regime Politics: Governing Atlanta, 1946–1986.* Lawrence: University of Kansas Press.

Storper, M. (1997). *The Regional World: Territorial Development in a Global Economy.* New York and London: Guilford.

Swedberg, R. (1993). "Preface," in R. Swedberg (ed.), *Explorations in Economic Sociology*. New York: Russel Sage Foundation, xiii–xxiv.

Tilly, C., and Blockmans, W. P. (eds.). (1994). *Cities and the Rise of States in Europe, AD 1,000 to 1,800*. Boulder: Westview.

Todd, E. (1990). *L'invention de l'Europe*. Paris: Seuil.

Wannop, U. (1995). *The Regional Imperative: Regional Planning and Governance in Britain, Europe, and the United States*. London: Jessica Kingsley.

20

Lessons from Silicon Valley: Governance in a Global City-Region

DOUGLAS HENTON

Who governs in the global city-region? What governance institutions are most appropriate for the new economy? This chapter addresses these questions by examining lessons from Silicon Valley, a global city-region that has become the world's leading new economy. This innovative region has helped to pioneer the information age and may now be ready to demonstrate new governance institutions for the new economy.

As the economy has changed, so has the governance of Silicon Valley. A commitment to laissez-faire in the early days of the Valley gave way to business-led models of governance in the 1970s as the region began to address quality of life issues. Global competition and the end of the Cold War in the late 1980s led to new models of business-government-community collaboration. The Internet has promoted networking as a form of regional governance. Joint Venture: Silicon Valley Network has become a model of network governance for the new economy. Lessons from Silicon Valley should be useful to other regions searching for new governance institutions more appropriate to the new century.

GOVERNANCE CHALLENGES FOR THE TWENTY-FIRST CENTURY

Governance is how people come together to address common problems. Governance is more than government. At the city-region level, it involves citizens, businesses, nonprofit organizations, and educators as well as government working in various ways to set directions, solve problems, and take action in a region.

Regional governance in the United States requires solving problems across multiple jurisdictions—cities, townships, and counties. The evolution of regional governance has gone through three distinct phases. The first phase in the 1950s and 1960s involved attempts at *government consolidation*—creating unitary governments from several jurisdictions. Examples included Indianapolis and Miami-Dade County, Florida. A second phase in the 1970s and 1980s involved creating *regional councils of government*, which attempt to coordinate separate local governments around specific functions such as transportation. The third phase in the 1980s and 1990s has involved *regional public–private cooperation* in a variety of partnerships and alliances among business, government, and community groups. This third phase is often called the *new regionalism* to distinguish it from prior efforts focused primarily on efforts to create regional government.

City-regions face a number of governance challenges as they enter the twenty-first century:

- *Scale:* As city-regions grow they continue to expand beyond traditional political jurisdictions. Many city-regions now encompass many cities, towns, and counties. How to deal with this political fragmentation in the face of growing economic regions is a challenge to most city-regions.
- *Speed:* The new economy is based on speed. Governance institutions are having trouble keeping up with the pace of change. Few institutions have learned how to operate on "Internet time," but they are being asked to respond more quickly to economic changes.
- *Effectiveness:* In the end, what matters is how well do regional institutions respond to the changing needs of the region. Fragmentation of responsibility and the increasing pace of change have made it difficult for institutions to meet those needs. Worse, a lack of effective regional governance leads to conflict and competition among jurisdictions and between the public and private sectors, which leads to gridlock.
- *Participation:* How much civic engagement is possible in regional governance today? The scale and speed challenges combine with a lack of trust due to ineffective institutions to discourage participation in regional governance. On the other hand, without civic engagement, regional governance will not be responsive to citizen needs. According to Robert Dahl, a leading thinker on democracy, "Scale, complexity and greater quantities of information impose ever-stronger demands on citizens' capacities. As a result, one of the imperative needs of democracy is to improve citizens' capacities to engage intelligently in political life" (1998: 187).
- *Accountability:* How are public and private leaders working in a variety of public–private partnerships and hybrid institutions held accountable to citizens for outcomes? If there is a growth of new regional organizations that are not directly elected by the people, how is the leadership in these organizations selected and replaced?

ALTERNATIVE INSTITUTIONS

There are a variety of different institutions that can be used to address the governance challenges of city-regions as we move into the twenty-first century. Just as regional economies have been changing, so too must our institutions for regional governance. As Dahl says, "Perhaps our institutions created in democratic countries during the nineteenth and twentieth centuries are no longer adequate. If this is so, then democracies will need to create new institutions to supplement the old" (1998: 80).

Oliver Williamson and other institutional economists have outlined alternative types of institutions that are appropriate for different situations. Williamson believes that institutions seek ways to reduce transaction costs either within an organization or in relationship with other organizations (Williamson 1975). His work and that of others lead to three alternatives:

1. *Hierarchies.* In stable environments, hierarchical forms of organization make sense because they can internalize transaction costs through vertical integration.
2. *Markets.* In environments of uncertainty, market forms of organization make sense because transaction costs can be reduced through external contracts.
3. *Networks.* In environments where speed is critical, networks make sense because they reduce transaction costs by combining flexibility of markets with the trust relationships of hierarchy.

Between vertical hierarchy (or bureaucracy) and horizontal markets (or laissez-faire) are networks. According to Francis Fukuyama, author of *Trust* and *The Great Disruption*, a "network is a group of individual agents who share informal norms beyond those necessary for ordinary market transactions" (Fukuyama 1999: 199). In other words, networks are markets with memory.

Another way to look at alternatives is provided by Elinor Ostrom in *Governing the Commons.* Ostrom addresses the challenge of common resource problems illustrated by the "tragedy of the commons" where rational decision-making by individuals pursuing their own self-interest results in a loss of the common resource for all (Ostrom 1990). She poses three possible solutions to this challenge:

1. *Regulation*, based on the belief that only an external government authority can mandate the outcome that is in the best interest of all.
2. *Privatization*, based on the belief that the best way to avoid the tragedy of the commons is to create a system of private property rights.
3. *Voluntary agreements*, based on the belief that individuals can make binding contracts that commit them to mutually beneficial cooperative strategies that they themselves can work out.

Ostrom maintains that the key to establishing voluntary agreements is sharing information and recognizing incentives to collaborate. If the parties involved do not know what their individual choices are ultimately doing to the commons and are unable or unwilling to adjust their behavior, then external regulation may be required. If information is available, however, individuals may see it in their long-term interest to adjust their behavior by forming voluntary cooperative agreements with each other.

These alternatives suggest that there are a variety of ways to organize governance institutions in city-regions depending on the environment and situation. Traditionally, governance institutions have been organized as public bureaucracies with regulatory powers. An alternative approach that has been emerging in regions in the United States in the 1990s involves a variety of collaborative models with public, private, and community organizations working with networks based on voluntary agreements.

SILICON VALLEY AS A LABORATORY FOR NEW APPROACHES TO GOVERNANCE

If Silicon Valley were choosing a name today, it would probably choose the "Innovation Region." This ever-changing place has moved well beyond silicon to become a prototype network economy that creates wealth by linking new ideas with people, capital, and enterprises across a wide range of industry clusters. How does the Valley continue to keep pace with changing technology, and what is its next step?

Since World War II, the Valley has shifted from defense, to semiconductors, to computers, and the Internet in a series of Schumpterian waves of technology. Today, Silicon Valley is going through another transition as it pushes the frontier of innovation toward a knowledge economy. Throughout these innovation cycles, a powerful set of innovation networks have formed based on tight relationships among entrepreneurs, venture capitalists, university researchers, marketing professionals, accountants, lawyers, and other support.

Francis Fukuyama describes the importance of networks to innovation in Silicon Valley:

> [T]he whole of Silicon Valley can be seen as a single large network organization that can tap expertise and specialized skills unavailable to even the largest vertically integrated Japanese electronics firms and their *keiretsu* partners. . . . [T]he impersonal sharing of data over electronic networks is not enough to create the mutual trust and respect evident in places like Silicon Valley. (Fukuyama 1999: 210.)

An important parallel social innovation has helped connect the Valley's resources and make the transition to a new economy. Joint Venture: Silicon Valley Network was created in 1992 in response to the economic slowdown resulting from the end of the Cold War and competitive pressures on both the semiconductor and computer industries. Joint Venture has joined business, government, and community leaders in an unprecedented regional network that promotes innovative solutions to the region's economic and community issues. These include preparing the workforce for the new economy and creating innovative strategies for quality growth.

As technology products and services become commodities over time, the Valley has continued to search for higher value activities, moving from components to systems to software to the Internet. Along the way, the productivity of the Valley's firms continues to increase as it innovates to the next level. The foundation for this innovation process is the rich innovation networks that connect and reconnect the Valley's human, technology, and capital assets in new ways. The role of Joint Venture in helping the Valley make the transition into the new economy will be highlighted as a social innovation as important as the Valley's economic innovation. In fact, the networked economy needs a more connected community to prosper, and Joint Venture has helped to create a more connected community through its collaborative initiatives. (See Joint Venture 1995.)

EVOLUTION OF THE SILICON VALLEY ECONOMY

There have been at least five major technology waves that have shaped Silicon Valley since World War II. Each wave has built innovation networks of talent, suppliers, and financial service providers that have helped make the next technology wave possible.

1. *Defense.* World War II and especially the Korean War had a dramatic impact on the Valley by increasing demand for electronics products from Valley firms such as Hewlett Packard and Varian Associates. Defense spending helped to build the technology infrastructure of firms and support institutions in the 1950s. During the Cold War and space race it was not just the level of spending, but how the Defense Department procured technology that mattered. Often the defense agencies specified their requirements and let the firms innovate to find solutions. In addition, the Defense Department required second-source arrangements, in which producers ensured that alternative suppliers of their products existed, spreading technology capabilities within the region.

2. *Integrated circuits.* The invention of the integrated circuit in 1959 led to the explosive growth of the semiconductor industry in the 1960s and 1970s. Starting with Shockley Semiconductor—which begat Fairchild and its many offspring including Intel, Advanced Micro Devices, and National Semiconductor—more than thirty semiconductor firms were started in the Valley during the 1960s. Only five of the forty-five independent semiconductor firms started in the United States between 1959 and 1976 were located outside Silicon Valley. This is the period when Silicon Valley got its name, from Don Hoefler, a reporter for *Electronic News.* This technology wave got an additional push with the invention of the microprocessor at Intel in 1971, which established the foundation for the next wave led by the personal computer.

3. *Personal computers.* The technology foundation established by the defense and integrated circuit waves created a rich environment for launching this next wave. Silicon Valley had attracted a critical mass of technology firms, support industries, venture capital, and talent that helped ignite the PC revolution. Young talent meeting at the Homebrew Computer Club eventually gave birth to more than twenty computer companies, including Apple. The explosive growth during this technology wave led to an increase in the total number of Valley firms from 830 in 1975 to 3,000 in 1990 with an increase of employment from 100,000 to 267,000. The initial focus on personal computers quickly led to the development of more sophisticated workstations led by firms such as Sun Microsystems. During this wave, the seeds were sown for the next innovation, built around software.

4. *Software.* Since the mid-1980s, the fast growth in employment in Silicon Valley has been in software not hardware. As competition in the computer industry intensified during the decade, Silicon Valley computer firms greatly increased their productivity by shifting to higher value-added products and outsourcing routine production either to contract manufacturers in the region or outside of the region. Software companies such as Oracle, Adobe, and Electronic Arts became the fast growing firms in the Valley. Inside most leading technology firms such as Hewlett-Packard, Sun, and Silicon Graphics, the intensive work was in software design.

5. *Internet.* After a period of slow economic growth in the early 1990s during the defense cutbacks following the end of the Cold War and growing global competition in both the semiconductor and computer hardware industries, the question arose about what would be Silicon Valley's next act. Could the Valley reinvent itself once again? The answer became clear with the commercial development of the Internet in 1993 and the creation of the World Wide Web. Building on its prior technology strengths, the region became a leader in the Internet revolution. The result was the explosive growth of Internet-related firms. At the forefront were Netscape, Cisco, and 3Com. Between 1992 and 1998, software jobs in the Valley grew by more than 150 percent, and jobs in computer networking doubled. Computer firms such as Sun and Hewlett-Packard and semiconductor firms such as Intel and AMD grew along with their Internet markets.

CHANGING GOVERNANCE IN SILICON VALLEY

As the Silicon Valley economy was going through transition, so were its governance institutions in a rough parallel to the economic changes. Silicon Valley has shifted from essentially a laissez-faire limited government, market-driven region, first into a more business-driven model, and then into new models of collaboration and networks. Each stage was impelled by the realities of both the changing economy and the community. Table 20.1 illustrates this parallel transition process.

Table 20.1. *Economic eras and their form of regional governance*

Economic era	Regional governance
Semiconductors 1959–75	Laissez-faire Semiconductor Industry Association
Personal computers 1975–85	Business led Santa Clara Manufacturing Group
Software 1985–95	Collaboration Joint Venture: Silicon Valley Network
Internet 1995–	Networking Silicon Valley Civic Action Network

1. *Laissez-faire.* The prevailing attitude in the Valley during the boom years of the 1960s and 1970s was essentially laissez-faire. "Keep government out of the way." Local governments were relatively weak and exerted little influence over the early technology firms. Governance in Silicon Valley was organized around industry associations such as the Semiconductor Industry Association, SEMI (Semiconductor Equipment and Materials International), and the Western Electronics Association (later renamed the American Electronics Association), which formed to promote the interests of the industry primarily at the national level.
2. *Business-led.* The environment changed in the mid-1970s as the economic boom began to put pressure on the region's housing and transportation. David Packard, founder of Hewlett-Packard, helped create the Santa Clara Manufacturing Group, composed of the largest employers. The business-led manufacturing group began to promote quality-of-life issues and negotiate with local government on public policy issues that impacted technology firms.
3. *Collaboration.* The economic slowdown at the end of the 1980s and early 1990s caused by the end of the Cold War and foreign competition led to the creation of Joint Venture: Silicon Valley. Unlike the previous eras, Joint Venture was a public–private partnership that involved both business leaders and elected officials. It promotes a collaborative approach to addressing key regional issues such as education.
4. *Networking.* With the Internet boom has come major pressure on the quality of life of the region, including rising housing costs, traffic congestion, and environmental concerns. Joint Venture commissioned a group of business, community, and government leaders to chart a vision for 2010. From this effort has come the Silicon Valley Civic Network, which will promote civic engagement around the goals of the Silicon Valley 2010 effort.

This trajectory suggests that new regional governance approaches have been evolving as the economy has been moving. In both cases, the transformations are driven by the need for more innovative ways to solve problems in both the economy and society. The later stages of the governance approaches—networking—have been shaped by the nature of the Internet economy.

EXAMPLES OF HOW SILICON VALLEY GOVERNANCE WORKS

The history of Joint Venture and its evolution into a Silicon Valley Civic Action Network illustrates the new governance models that are now evolving in the region. This history clearly demonstrates how new hybrid models of collaboration have emerged, employing networks and voluntary agreements rather than either markets or hierarchies. Joint Venture represented a "step function" in Silicon Valley governance. Before Joint Venture, business and government were separate and often in conflict. There were over twenty-seven local jurisdictions in the region and little cooperation. Silicon Valley had become so big and complex it had trouble dealing with regional challenge. No city by itself had the resources or authority to meet the big challenges.

Technology business leaders and local government leaders agreed that a new regional governance model was needed. They knew that laissez-faire or business-led models would not work anymore. They also knew that a regional government would not be feasible or desirable. They chose a network model grounded on broad-based participation by business, government, and community leaders. The board of Joint Venture was divided into one-quarter each of business, government, education, and community leaders. It involved all twenty-seven cities in Silicon Valley in a public sector roundtable of mayors and on an economic development team of development officials. The mayor of San Jose and the chairman and CEO of Hewlett-Packard chaired Joint Venture. Its funding came three-quarters from private and foundation sources and one-quarter from local government. Joint Venture was organized as a nonprofit.

In its first five years, Joint Venture had a number of accomplishments for its collaborative model:

- Smart Valley helped connect schools, local governments, and libraries to the Internet.
- Challenge 2000 provided $30 million in "venture capital" to help reform local schools.
- Twenty-seven cities joined together to reform the permit process, create a uniform building code, and promote smart permitting over the Internet.
- The Healthy Community project promoted a major program for early childhood health.

These and other initiatives were developed using a collaborative process led by civic entrepreneurs. Civic entrepreneurs are leaders from businesses or the community who apply the same entrepreneurial energy to address community problems that business entrepreneurs do to create their businesses. Silicon Valley 2010 (SV2010) was a major initiative by Joint Venture to address the broad community issues arising from the rapid growth of the economy. Involving more than two thousand people, SV2010 developed a series of nineteen goals divided into four areas to move the region forward:

1. *Innovative economy* that increases productivity and broadens prosperity for all;
2. *Livable environment* that protects nature, preserves open space, and promotes livable communities;
3. *Inclusive society* that connects people to opportunity; and
4. *Regional stewardship* that develops shared solutions through civic engagement.

The Silicon Valley 2010 project is based on new ways of thinking about the region that involve shifting from quantitative growth (more jobs, more consumption) to qualitative growth (better jobs, better use of resource), from sprawl to land reuse, and from fragmented social networks to connected social networks. Silicon

Valley 2010 creates a framework for growing together by broadening prosperity, promoting livable communities, and transcending traditional political boundaries.

To promote these goals, Joint Venture has created Silicon Valley-Civic Action Network (SV-CAN)—a broad-based coalition of business, government, community, and environmental leaders. SV-CAN is the latest evolution of the network governance model. It will seek to build a grassroots movement around the SV2010 vision through civic engagement and broad-based civic dialogue.

Silicon Valley is moving toward a model of regional stewardship. The idea is to identify and support leaders who want to work on the long-term future of the region in a more integrated way. SV2010 has made clear it is not possible to have an innovative economy without a livable environment that attracts and retains talent or an inclusive society where everyone shares in the region's prosperity. SV-CAN is about creating a network of regional stewards.

HOW SILICON VALLEY INNOVATIONS RELATE TO TWENTY-FIRST CENTURY GOVERNANCE CHALLENGES

How well do the evolving governance mechanisms in the Silicon Valley relate to the governance challenges faced by global city-regions?

- *Scale.* Joint Venture has addressed the problems of fragmentation of local governments by creating a regional network of relationships based on voluntary agreements. It provides regular information on a regional scale (*The Index of Silicon Valley*) and has developed a regional vision (SV2010). It has not become a regional government but it promotes regional cooperation on key issues such as permit streamlining and economic development.
- *Speed.* Joint Venture has helped local institutions including local government and schools get more connected to the Internet and has helped to bring local government permitting up to speed. Time is critical in the new economy, and many public and community institutions in the Valley are now more responsive.
- *Effectiveness.* Joint Venture has promoted collaboration among business and government in a variety of areas including education and regulation that have increased the effectiveness of governance institutions. Less conflict and competition has led to better performance.

There are a number of areas where issues remain and more work clearly needs to be made:

- *Participation.* Joint Venture has been primarily a network of leaders. It has involved citizens in specific projects, but it has not been a grassroots organization. It has been criticized by some community groups as not representative of the total community. SV-CAN will attempt to reach out to a broad group of citizens through a variety of civic engagement tools over the next few years.
- *Accountability.* The hybrid nature of public–private organizations such as Joint Venture raises issues about accountability to the public. While elected officials

are included on the boards and working groups, private and community leaders are selected by Joint Venture. How to maintain accountability over time remains an issue.

LESSONS LEARNED

An innovative region like Silicon Valley will have to invent continually new governance institutions. As the economy makes transitions, it will create new demands on the community, requiring new approaches. Silicon Valley has evolved from a laissez-faire approach through business-led models to collaboration and networks just as the economy has evolved toward networking. Joint Venture employs a collaborative model based on networks and voluntary agreements rather than hierarchy or markets. It has changed over the years and is now experimenting with new approaches such as SV-CAN.

Silicon Valley's experience is an example, not a universal blueprint. Every global city-region has a different environment. Still, there is much to learn from the Valley in how a region struggles to reshape its institutions to participate effectively in a rapidly changing world.

REFERENCES

Dahl, R. (1998). *On Democracy.* New Haven: Yale University.

Fukuyama, F. (1995). *Trust: The Social Virtues and the Creation of Prosperity.* New York: Free Press.

——. (1999). *The Great Disruption: Human Nature and the Reconstitution of Social Order.* New York: The Free Press.

Joint Venture Silicon Valley Network. (1995). *The Joint Venture Way: Lesson for Regional Rejuvenation.* San Jose, CA: Joint Venture Silicon Valley Network.

Ostrom, E. (1990). *Governing the Commons.* Cambridge: Cambridge University Press.

Williamson, O. (1975). *Markets and Hierachies.* New York: Free Press.

21

Local Governance and Conflict Management: Reflections on a Brazilian Cluster

HUBERT SCHMITZ

What does it take to respond successfully to the challenges posed by globalization? What kind of local governance is required to enhance competitiveness and earning opportunities? These are central questions for proactive regions.

These are also questions that Rodrik (1999) addresses in a recent book concerned with *Making Openness Work*. He concludes that societies with weak institutions of conflict management find it more difficult to cope with the turbulence caused by globalization. This is precisely what I found to be the key problem in a Brazilian industrial cluster that was attempting to fend off intensifying global competition. The lack of conflict management contributed to the collapse of a promising clusterwide upgrading strategy.

This chapter shows the challenges the cluster was up against, where it succeeded, and where it failed. The progress that was made was achieved through interfirm cooperation. And the failure came with conflict among enterprise groups and associations. Due to the centrifugal forces of globalization, conflicts among such private actors are inevitable. Without mediation by public agencies, such conflicts pull local economies apart and upgrading strategies fail. This is one of the main messages of this chapter.

CLUSTERS IN DEVELOPING COUNTRIES

A paradoxical feature of the recent globalization debate is the increasing importance given to geographical proximity. Terms such as economies of clustering, synergy, systemic competitiveness, collective efficiency, or local innovation system express the main concerns in this debate. Research on industrial clusters and local sources of competitive advantage has grown enormously in recent years. Scott (1996) predicted that this concern would accelerate further as the globalization of product markets intensifies. In the literature on advanced countries, the convergence on the locality straddles four lines of work:

1. *New mainstream economics*. Since the mid-1980s economists have found a way of modeling increasing returns that has led to a new body of growth theory.

Paul Krugman (1991, 1995; Krugman and Venables 1995), particularly in his work on trade and geography, has put the increasing returns from economic clustering on the mainstream agenda. These concerns have been reinforced by econometric evidence that innovative activity tends to cluster due to knowledge spillovers (Audretsch and Feldman 1996).

2. *Business economics.* Michael Porter also emphasizes the importance of clustering (Porter 1990, 1998; Porter and Wayland 1995). He argues that competitive advantage in the global economy derives from a constellation of local factors that sustain the dynamism of leading firms. He has stressed the importance of proximity, not just of suppliers but also of rivals and customers for dynamic business development.[1]
3. *Regional science.* The interest of economic geographers and regional scientists in clustering is reflected in the recent industrial district literature, which focused initially on Italy and then on many other countries in Europe and elsewhere (Becattini 1990; Brusco 1990; Markusen 1996; Pyke and Sengenberger 1992). It has also contributed to a new emphasis on the region as a nexus of untraded interdependencies—for example in the work of Michael Storper (1995) or francophone writings on the milieu innovateur (Maillat 1996).
4. *Innovation literature.* In the literature concerned with technological development there has long been a focus on the individual firm and a strong distinction between innovation and diffusion. Over the last ten years this has given way to a greater concern with learning-by-interaction (between producer and user) and first national, then increasingly regional, systems of innovation (Braczyk, Cooke, and Heidenreich 1996; Cooke and Morgan 1998; Edquist 1997; Freeman 1995; Heidenreich 1997; Lundvall 1993).

For the purpose of this chapter, one difference between these lines of work deserves particular emphasis: in the former two, gains from clustering arise spontaneously, whereas the latter two stress the need for local governance. In other words, public agencies and private self-help organizations are thought to be important for steering or coordinating local responses to external challenges. The need for such governance is also emphasized in recent research on industrial clusters and local innovation systems in developing countries (Cassiolato and Lastres 1999; Meyer-Stamer 1999; Schmitz 1995, 2000). Since this chapter refers mainly to this group of countries, this section provides a brief summary of the relevant literature.

Just as in the advanced country literature, so also in the studies of developing countries, there has been an increasing recognition of the local sources of competitiveness. This is most clearly expressed in the fast-growing research on industrial clusters (Humphrey and Schmitz 1996; Nadvi and Schmitz 1999; Pedersen, Sverisson, and van Dijk 1994; van Dijk and Rabellotti 1997). Summarizing the conclusions of this work is difficult because the growth and upgrading experiences have been diverse. At one end of the spectrum, there are artisanal clusters that have shown little dynamism and seem unable to expand or innovate (e.g. McCormick 1998). At the other end are clusters that have been able to deepen their interfirm division of labor, raise their competitiveness, and break into international markets (e.g. Meyer-Stamer *et al.* 1996; Nadvi 1999; Tewari 1999). Along this spectrum, there are many intermediate cases (e.g. Knorringa 1996; Rabellotti 1997).

In spite of this diversity, a range of clear findings has emerged from these studies. The main conclusions are as follows:[2]

- Industrial clusters are common in a wide range of developing countries and sectors.
- Clustering has helped small enterprises to overcome well-known growth constraints and compete in distant markets, nationally and abroad.
- However, collective efficiency only emerges where trust sustains interfirm relations and where traders connect clusters to sizable markets.
- Joint action of local firms enhances their ability to cope with the new quality and speed requirements imposed by global competition.
- Within clusters, greater cooperation is positively correlated with improved performance.
- Increases in vertical cooperation have been more substantial than increases in horizontal cooperation.
- Global competitive pressures have led to increasing differentiation within clusters.
- Future research on upgrading needs a shift in emphasis from internal to external linkages and from production systems to knowledge systems.

The main policy lessons from this body of work are:

- Successful clusters cannot be created from scratch; there needs to be a critical mass of enterprises and skills (however rudimentary) that outside assistance can "hook into."
- External support for clusters works best where industrial policy is decentralized and builds on public–private partnership.
- The lessons from fostering clusters and networks are summed up in "the triple C": to be effective, interventions need to be customer-oriented, collective, and cumulative.
- Strategic responses to global competitive pressures cannot just rely on private joint action but require public agencies as catalysts or mediators.

The next section moves from the general to the specific and shows how the overall findings presented above apply to one of Latin America's most significant industrial clusters: the footwear exporting Sinos Valley in Brazil.

LOCAL COOPERATION AND GLOBAL COMPETITION IN THE SINOS VALLEY

Brazil is a major exporter of women's leather shoes to North America and Western Europe. Most producers are clustered in the Sinos Valley in Brazil's southernmost state of Rio Grande do Sul. This cluster includes some 400 shoe manufacturers and 1,000 suppliers and subcontractors, giving employment to 160,000 people. Historically, the Sinos Valley has been an embodiment of cooperative competition: fierce rivalry among local producers accompanied by cooperation to deal with common problems.

A major problem hit the cluster in the early 1990s: other producer countries with even lower wages were infiltrating their main export markets. Simultaneously, buyers in these markets began to insist on better quality and faster delivery. The first challenge for the Brazilian cluster was therefore to raise quality, speed, and flexibility. The second challenge was to open up new markets and marketing channels.

This section summarizes how local producers responded to the challenges. It draws on research that was driven by the following hypothesis: responding to major crisis requires more and better cooperation between the clustering firms. In other words, the (incidental) economies of agglomeration are important to growth but are not sufficient to ride out major changes in product or factor markets: that requires joint action. This section examines whether—in line with this hypothesis—enterprises stepped up cooperation and what role public agencies played in this process.

The information comes from a number of sources and was collected using a combination of methods: a survey of sixty-five enterprises; in-depth interviews with selected manufacturers and their suppliers; interviews with the officials of business associations and public agencies; participant observation at meetings of industrialists; screening of the local press; and the usual secondary sources. This section distils some of the results of this work recorded in detail in Schmitz (1998).

Local Cooperation

The concern with interfirm cooperation in this paper does not imply that individual excellence does not matter. Far from it. Performance within clusters varies and the excellence of one firm tends to have incidental positive effects on others. Proximity ensures that such external effects do not "evaporate." The proposition is that relying merely on such spontaneous effects is not sufficient to cope with crisis, hence the concern with joint action.

One of the main results of the survey was the positive and significant relationship between cooperation and performance. Enterprises that increased cooperation tended to perform better than those which did not. The scatter diagram (Figure 21.1) gives visual evidence of the positive relationship between improvements in performance and increases in cooperation.

The survey, combined with other fieldwork methods, showed, however, that changes in cooperation over the period 1992/93–1997/98 varied with the *type* of cooperation considered. Four types can be captured in a simple matrix which, on one axis, distinguishes between bilateral and multilateral, and, on the other, between horizontal and vertical cooperation. The findings are summarized in Figure 21.2.

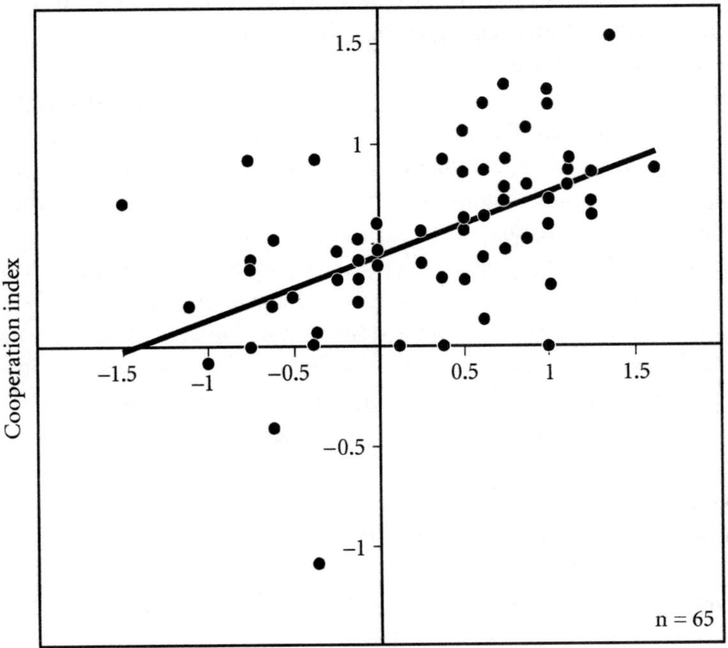

Figure 21.1. *Scatter diagram of changes in cooperation and in performance, Sinos Valley, Brazil*

Source: Author's survey

What stands out is the strong increase in bilateral vertical cooperation, notably between shoemakers on the one hand and their input suppliers and subcontractors on the other. The reasons for stepping up this form of cooperation are straightforward. Certain demands of the new global competition can only be met if the whole chain responds; better product quality and greater speed cannot be attained by enterprises individually. The recognition of interdependence —even if it is at times asymmetrical—has led to more cooperative behavior. The survey data are very clear in this respect. Detailed case studies of shoe

	BILATERAL	MULTILATERAL
HORIZONTAL	No change	Varies with association
VERTICAL	Substantial increase	First increase, then decline

Figure 21.2. *Changes in interfirm cooperation in the Sinos Valley, Brazil, 1992/93–1997/98*

manufacturers and related firms confirmed the increase but also provided important qualifications. For example, in subcontracting relationships, close cooperation was selective in that it was limited to core subcontractors.

As shown in Figure 21.2, bilateral horizontal cooperation between the manufacturers changed little. Beyond exchange of information and lending each other equipment, little such cooperation occurred. There certainly was no major increase in response to the new challenges noted earlier. As regards horizontal multilateral cooperation, the results are difficult to summarize because there are six business associations in the Sinos Valley, which reacted differently. For example, the Association of Synthetic Component Manufacturers (ASSINTECAL) was a strong force for innovation, whereas the Association of Shoe Manufacturers (ABICALÇADOS) was more ambiguous in its response. Despite such differences, the associations were able to launch a joint initiative, the Shoes from Brazil Program, a not-so-common example of vertical multilateral cooperation.

The mere existence of this program commands attention because it encompassed associations representing the entire local value chain, because it was based on the explicit recognition of interdependence, and because raising competitiveness was its mission. This included a number of upgrading proposals, which ranged from the targeting of new markets, to raising the image of "Made in Brazil," eradicating child labor, joint participation in fairs, and creating a local design capacity. While a lot of the groundwork was carried out by local consultants and association officials, the entrepreneurs themselves were involved in the analysis and formulation of proposals. The program was an example of the private sector taking an initiative in local governance. Based on a combination of in-depth interviews and participant observation, the rise and fall of this program was traced. Its eventual decline was due to conflict generated by the centrifugal forces of globalization. Before discussing these forces, the significance of succeeding or failing in local cooperation needs to be brought out.

As stated above, bilateral vertical cooperation increased and multilateral cooperation across the entire local value chain collapsed. These findings are of wider concern because they have direct implications for the ability of the cluster to compete globally and create jobs and income locally.

The increasing cooperation in bilateral vertical relationships (between shoe manufacturers and suppliers) was essential for achieving increases in quality, speed, and flexibility. The survey findings (Figure 21.3) show very clearly this improvement in performance. This advance is confirmed by another study based on information from European and U.S. buyers; they suggest that—on the above parameters—their Brazilian suppliers are close to the Italian competitors (Schmitz and Knorringa 1999). In this sense, stepping up cooperation has helped the Sinos Valley to live up to the global competitive pressure.

The problem is that these improvements in production have merely enabled the cluster to stand still. Exports in 1997 were at the level of 1990—with some fluctuations in between. More problematic still, profits declined. The survey (see Figure 21.3) shows this very clearly, particularly for exporting firms. Detailed interviews suggest that this is not just the usual tendency of entrepreneurs

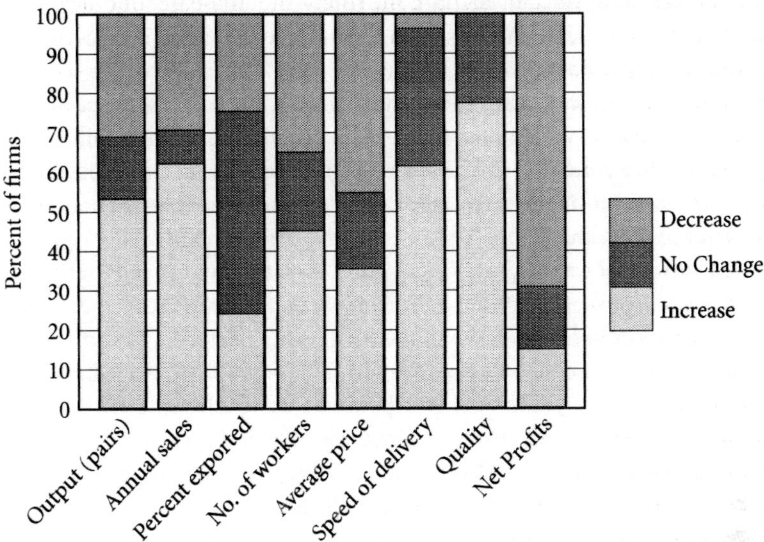

Figure 21.3. *Changes in performance in the Sinos Valley, Brazil, 1992/93–1997/98*
Source: Author's survey

understating their profits and that profits fell by more than half. As a result there is a downward pressure on wages.

Thus this case study confirms recent writings on globalization (e.g. Kaplinsky 1998), warning that a focus on manufacturing alone may not lead to sustainable income growth and that a shift to other stages of the value chain—such as design or marketing—may be a more rewarding target. Upgrading outside production has, however, been very limited in the Sinos Valley. While the cluster is a world-class producer, it has not been able to establish a positive and recognizable image in the European and U.S. market, it has not exhibited in a substantial and regular way at the world's key trade fairs, it has very few of its own brands in its main export markets, and very little capacity for innovative design. Progressing in these nonproduction areas was one of the main objectives of the Shoes from Brazil Program. Its failure means that the chances of the Sinos Valley to reposition itself in the international market are a more distant prospect. The next section provides a brief anatomy of this collective failure.

The Centrifugal Forces of Globalization

Understanding the failure of the Shoes from Brazil Program is of potential interest to all those concerned with local governance for industrial upgrading. While ambitious, the program had good chances of being carried out for two reasons: first, the Sinos Valley has a long history of cooperation; while this process was punctured during an earlier phase of fast and easy growth, the Valley entered the 1990s with a formidable number of collective actors: six subsectoral associations, two professional associations, four technology and training centers, and a trade fair organization. Second, the footwear and related industries entirely dominate the Valley, giving discussions about its future a focus difficult to attain in regions with a wide spread of sectors.[3]

Given that, at least by Latin American standards, the preconditions in the Sinos Valley were favorable, why did its clusterwide upgrading strategy fail? The search for an answer needs to consider the forces of globalization and their capacity to erode local cooperation. Before elaborating on specifics and its general lessons, it is worth recalling that globalization can also strengthen local cooperation.

These centripetal forces were highlighted in the previous section: upgrading within the sphere of production, that is, increasing quality and speed, required closer cooperation between firms in the local value chain. As already noted, this was achieved and helped the cluster to maintain its position as a production center. It was not, however, sufficient to reposition the cluster internationally, move into design and marketing, and develop a positive and recognizable image. The latter would have required individual and collective investments that were not made due to the centrifugal forces of globalization.

There were several such forces at work—clearly visible in this Brazilian case but by no means unique to it. First, a key feature of the current globalization phase is that political authorities, especially local and regional governments, compete with each other to attract enterprises from other regions or countries. Tax concessions, cheap labor, and subsidized infrastructure are the key weapons in this competition. While fiscal wars are not a new phenomenon, they became particularly ferocious in Brazil in the course of the 1990s. States and municipalities of the Northeast of Brazil were targeting especially labor-intensive export industries in competition with Asian industry. The footwear enterprises from the Sinos Valley were among the key targets. Even though only some of the large enterprises set up subsidiary plants in the Northeast, the debate on whether to join "Operation Northeast" upstaged the ambitious upgrading plans for the Sinos Valley. As a result, much entrepreneurial energy remained focused on production and failed to shift to design, marketing, and image building—all aims set out in the Shoes from Brazil Program.

Second, exporting local firms are not just part of local networks but also belong to global networks and in some circumstances global and local networks are in conflict with each other. This point is worth elaborating not just because it is critical to understand the governance question in the Sinos Valley but because it is rarely recognized in the literature on local production or innovation systems. The latter emphasizes, quite rightly, that enterprises are embedded in local networks, and that these networks are critical to the ability to compete. However, this literature tends to assume that this competition takes place in anonymous markets and fails to recognize that competing in distant markets, especially export markets, often requires joining networks controlled by lead firms that focus on trading and/or retailing. Gereffi (1999) calls them buyer-driven global commodity chains. The Sinos Valley manufacturers exporting to the United States and Europe feed into such buyer-driven networks. And the allegiance to these buyers proved

—in some critical instances—to be stronger than the allegiance to local networks. The issue came to a head because key parts of the Shoes from Brazil Program was in conflict with the foreign buyers' interests.

When local manufacturers seek to develop their own design and marketing capabilities they encroach on the core competence of their buyers. This explains why some of the leading export manufacturers did not support the Shoes from Brazil Program. The details are set out elsewhere (Schmitz 1998). The critical point to be registered here is the potential conflict between local cluster governance and global chain governance. Global forces prevailed in the Sinos Valley but, as will be argued in the next section, public agencies could have helped to bring about a different outcome.

The Absent Mediator

In the course of the research—notably through confidential interviews and participant observation at meetings of the entrepreneurs—it became clear that some of the largest and most influential enterprises were not interested in the Shoes from Brazil Program becoming effective. They put their alliance with a powerful foreign buyer above local cooperation. Producing for this buyer served them well for many years, but it kept their strategies firmly limited to upgrading in the sphere of production whereas the Shoes from Brazil Program envisaged upgrading beyond production and moving into design and marketing.

Presumably such conflicts of interest are not unique to the Sinos Valley. The question is whether their resolution follows a global or local rationale. The research suggests that the collapse of the joint upgrading program was not a necessary or predictable outcome. There were moments in the evolution of the program that could have triggered an upward rather than a downward spiral in local cooperation. Informed political mediation was required for the alliance of private sector institutions to work. But government agencies did not recognize their opportunity of industrial policy by mediation.

One of the conflicts that required public mediation concerned the export of semiprocessed leather (wet blue). In the course of 1996, leather exports were increasing fast, infuriating tanneries specialized in final processing, and also shoe manufacturers. Their concerns were that (1) local raw material prices rose; (2) the best leather was exported, especially in the specification needed for high-quality shoes; and (3) most of this leather went to the countries which were Brazil's main competitors in the international footwear market—especially Italy and Hong Kong (for reexport to other Asian countries). The proposal that they put forward was that a 7 percent export tax be levied on semiprocessed leather. The reasoning came from a differential in EU tariffs of zero import tariff on wet blue and 7 percent import tariff on finished leather. This regulation clearly benefited the Italian (and other European) tanners so the proposal that the Brazilian government should counterbalance the differential seemed modest and reasonable. Yet the issue remained unresolved, harming the Shoes from Brazil Program far beyond the immediate issue at stake.

What distorted the local alliance was the (not always overt) position of the largest shoe exporters. For reasons set out above, they were not interested in the success of the joint program and gave priority to their alliance with their global buyer. Moreover, in addition to manufacturing shoes, they produced and speculated in wet blue, and were therefore against restrictions on exports—some of which went to the Asian shoe suppliers of the global buyer. The global network unhinged the local alliance, but well-positioned participants of the process stressed that—with public mediation—the outcome might have been different.

Another conflict concerned the *frequency and timing of trade fairs* for footwear machinery and components. While the final decision in such matters lay with FENAC, the local trade fair organization, there was a tradition and well-defined mechanism of consulting the various sections of the local business community. Frictions always existed, for example, between the footwear manufacturers and the machinery producers, but these were usually overcome through negotiation and compromise. Conflicts deepened, however, because FENAC itself (and not only the exhibiting firms) was increasingly forced to compete nationally and globally. It sought to hold the number-one Latin American trade fair in footwear, leather, components, and machinery, attracting exhibitors and customers from all over the world. Competition itself and the need to establish itself in the overcrowded international trade fair calendar had implications for frequency and timing decisions of FENAC. The external influence on local decisions became even stronger when FENAC entered an alliance with an Italian trade fair organization. Whatever the long-term benefits of this alliance, it resulted in FENAC deciding timings for its own trade fairs that suited its international partner more than the local machinery and component industry. A negotiated settlement was only reached after several years of fierce conflict (including boycotts) from which all sides emerged weakened.

These are two examples of conflicts in which public mediation was required and openly requested. The positions of the various protagonists have been set out in detail elsewhere (Schmitz 1998). My main message here is that there was no capacity within government to assess different claims and assess their validity and likely impact. Nor was there much interest in building up such a capacity. Neither at the federal, nor at state, level did a serious attempt exist to conduct industrial policy. Neoliberalism might have been on its way out in Washington (World Bank 1997) but it continued to dominate in Brazil, a country which in earlier decades used to practice an active industrial policy. The actors involved in the Shoes from Brazil Program were not hoping for a return to the old-style top-down industrial policy. On the contrary, they had taken the initiative, they had done the institutional groundwork, they had explicitly recognized their interdependence in the value chain, they had created a forum for discussing their differences. But there were cases where they could not overcome these differences. What they were hoping for was intelligent mediation by a public actor. This did not materialize.

Instead, government adopted the position that, since the private sector could not agree, it would take no action—which was conveniently in line with the dominant neoliberal sentiment that "the free market with its potentially perverse effects—is better for the private sector than a situation of state intervention" (*Exclusivo*, 3–9 June 1996). It is impossible to know whether private multilateral cooperation would have succeeded with public mediation. It is, however, clear that with public mediation there would have been a much greater chance of resolving conflicts in the private sector.

Policy Lesson

There is a potentially important policy conclusion for the debate on who should provide business development services. One of the main tenets of the current debate is that such services can be provided by the private sector itself—either through specialized enterprises or collective organizations such as business associations, consortia, or the like. The Shoes from Brazil Program both underlines this view and also shows its limits. The private sector did all the preparatory work for what could be called a program of local sectoral governance but it could not—on its own—resolve the emerging conflicts. What is striking is that even in Brazil, where inefficiency and corruption have discredited the state, it is still seen as the most legitimate mediator. But in addition to legitimacy, mediation requires knowledge of two types: knowledge of the industrial sector in question and expertise in techniques of conflict resolution. In summary, conflict mediation is an important role even, or especially, for the lean state which relies on the self-help of the private sector.[4]

This policy conclusion is also important for the recent debates on regional or local innovation and employment policy. Both have stressed the importance of institutions, especially the relevance of collective institutions. The Sinos Valley has this kind of "institutional thickness" in its professional associations, business associations, and technology centers. Clearly this is not sufficient because fragmentation occurs and conflicts arise. Even in an institutionally well-endowed region, government is needed to mediate conflicts and help foster an upgrading consensus.

Such a conclusion is inevitably controversial, given the dangers of incompetence and corruption in the public agencies. The development literature of the last decade has given a great deal of attention to the failures of public agencies. The conclusion to be drawn from this debate is not, however, to minimize public intervention but the need for a shift towards different kinds of intervention. My contention is that conflict resolution is one of those interventions that deserves more attention in future.

FUTURE RESEARCH ON GLOBALIZATION AND CONFLICT MANAGEMENT

The role of conflict management for coping with the centrifugal forces of globalization certainly requires closer attention from researchers. The overall hypothesis, to drive such a new line of work, can be taken from Rodrik's (1999) study cited earlier: societies with strong institutions of conflict management are better at handling external turbulence and experience higher growth than those with weak institutions of conflict management. Such a proposition, stressing the crucial role of mediation and arbitration, can also be found in Sabel's (1992) work on European industrial districts: "whenever the parties to these conflicts regulate their disputes through arbitration boards or councils . . . the districts flourish; when not, then not" (228). Perhaps the best way for further research to proceed is to focus on turning points in the development of clusters, communities, or regions. Investigating why—at these turning points—some manage to respond strategically to globalization and others do not, is crucial; and examining the processes through the lens of how conflicts are managed should provide some particularly policy-relevant findings. The remainder of this section elaborates on this agenda for new research on globalization and conflict management.

Concerns with understanding conflicts and their resolution are hardly new. What is new is the proposition that avoiding or managing such conflicts is essential for reaping economic and social gains from globalization. Moreover, it is proposed that the focus on conflict management is of *increasing* importance to understand and influence the developmental impact of globalization. The latter proposition is triggered by the observation that globalization in the course of the 1990s has been associated with increasing inequality and with increasing volatility. These trends are apparent at the international, national, and subnational (regional and local) level (IDS 1999; Fainstein, Chapter 15 in this volume). Finding solutions to the resulting conflicts is essential if the powerful global forces are to be harnessed to local advancement.

The focus proposed here has the advantage of being able to draw on recent practical experience with conflict mediation. U.S. organizations such as the Conflict Management Group or the Consensus Building Institute have been successful in finding negotiated solutions to entrenched conflict in a number of fields such as environmental, industrial, or community disputes. Professionals in conflict mediation (a field which is increasing rapidly but still at the stage of a cottage industry) are moving towards the formulation of best practice in conflict assessment and consensus building (Susskind, McKearnon, and Thomas-Larmer 1999). Most of this work has, however, concentrated on developed countries. It would now seem useful to examine its relevance for developing countries. This would provide the proposed research with an almost immediate practical edge in the analysis and mediation of institutionalized conflicts.

New research would, however, also need to go beyond studying such conflict mediation. The very idea of mediation assumes that conflicts are expressed and that the stakeholders are, if not "sitting round the negotiating table," voicing their concerns through organized representation. The problem is that in many conflicts the weaker sides are not organized and are not at the table. Or negotiation does not take place because the stronger side prefers to remain absent. The weak side cannot negotiate because it is not organized and the strong side does not want to negotiate because it is (or feels it is) in a position to impose its view. In such situations, the conflict is not articulated but latent. Many conflict situations in developing countries are of this type. Such situations are difficult to resolve but the importance of strengthening the organizational capacity of the underrepresented sections of society has been recognized. This is clearest in the support of the international donor community for NGOs in developing countries. The effectiveness of this outside support for NGOs has, however, been challenged (Howell 2000) and needs to be assessed.

The emphasis on interests being articulated and organized is thus not new. It is central to recent concerns with strengthening civil society in developing countries. It also extends to debates on poverty alleviation and social policy that have embraced the need to empower the poor (e.g. Wolfensohn, Chapter 3 in this volume). What is proposed here is examining the connection between strong organization and the ability to respond to opportunity and crisis generated by globalization. This connection has been explored very little.[5] The cluster analyzed in this chapter had many of the sought-after institutions of civil society, at least on the entrepreneurial side. However, this institutional thickness on its own was not sufficient. Conflict mediation was required to turn it into effective local governance.

In conclusion, the above agenda for new research on globalization and conflict management in developing countries is driven by three propositions:

- the road to development is increasingly conflictual due to the centrifugal forces of globalization;
- the organization of stakeholders is essential for conflicts to be expressed and outcomes to be negotiated;
- new "techniques" of conflict mediation make it more likely that constructive solutions can be found.

NOTES

1. The term "cluster" is also central to Porter's (1990) analysis, where it is sometimes used, as in this chapter, to refer to a sectoral and geographical concentration of firms; for example, the ceramic tile cluster of Sassuolo, Italy. In other parts of Porter's work, however, "cluster" is much broader, referring to a group of industries with strong vertical ties and located within one country, but not always geographically close.
2. Many of the papers from which these conclusions are drawn can be downloaded or are summarized on: www.ids.ac.uk/ids/global/coleff.html.
3. For example, Rabellotti (1999) found in Mexico that responses to external pressure in Leon (which relies on the footwear industry) were more strategic than in Guadalajara (which hosts a footwear and several other industries).
4. It could be argued that also the mediation of conflicts can be left to the private sector. In the United States, for example, there are private firms specializing in conflict management (most such organizations are not-for-profit). However, expertise in

conflict assessment and mediation is probably not sufficient. Especially in conflicts between sections of the private sector, the involvement of the local or state government can exert the required pressure on the parties to find a solution which favors local collective efficiency. Of course, governments can hire the services of mediation specialists to facilitate the process. See also the final section of this chapter, on "Future research on globalization and conflict management."

5. One of the few exceptions is a review of labor market institutions in Asia and Latin America which concludes that countries with well-organized social groups, especially labor unions, have been more successful in riding out economic crises (Banuri and Amadeo 1991). This chapter has not been concerned with labor unions but the discussion in this section applies equally to conflicts between employers and workers.

REFERENCES

Audretsch, D. B., and Feldman, M. P. (1996). "R & D Spillovers and the Geography of Innovation and Production." *American Economic Review*, 86 (3): 630–40.

Banuri, T., and Amadeo, E. (1991). "Worlds within the Third World: Labour Market Institutions in Asia and Latin America," in T. Ban (ed.), *Economic Liberalization—No Panacea: The Experiences of Latin America and Asia.* Oxford: Clarendon Press, 171–206.

Becattini, G. (1990). "The Marshallian Industrial District as a Socioeconomic Notion," in F. Pyke, G. Becattini, and W. Sengenberger (eds.), *Industrial Districts and Interfirm Cooperation in Italy.* Geneva: International Institute for Labour Studies, ILO: 37–51.

Braczyk, H.-J., Cooke, P., and Heidenreich, M. (eds.). (1996). *Regional Innovation Systems: The Role of Governances in a Globalized World.* London: University College of London Press.

Brusco, S. (1990). "The Idea of the Industrial District: Its Genesis," in F. Pyke, G. Becattini, and W. Sengenberger (eds.), *Industrial Districts and Interfirm Cooperation in Italy.* Geneva: International Institute for Labour Studies, ILO: 10–19.

Cassiolato, J. E., and Lastres, H. M. M. (1999). *Globalização e Inovaçã Localizada: Experiências de Sistemas Locais no Mercosul.* Brasília: IEL/IBICT.

Cooke, P., and Morgan, K. (1998). *The Associational Economy: Firms, Regions, and Innovation.* Oxford: Oxford University Press.

Edquist, C. (1997). *Systems of Innovation: Technologies, Institutions, and Organizations.* London and Washington: Pinter.

Freeman, C. (1995). "The National System of Innovation in Historical Perspective." *Cambridge Journal of Economics*, 19 (1): 5–24.

Gereffi, G. (1999). "International Trade and Industrial Upgrading in the Apparel Commodity Chain." *Journal of International Economics*, 48 (1): 37–70.

Heidenreich, M. (1997). "Wirtschaftsregionen im weltweiten Innovationswettbewerb." *Kölner Zeitschrift für Soziologie und Sozialpsychologie*, 49 (3): 500–27.

Howell, J. (2000). "Manufacturing Civil Society from the Outside—Challenges for Donors." *European Journal of Development Research*, 12(1): 3–22.

Humphrey, J., and Schmitz, H. (1996). "The Triple C Approach to Local Industrial Policy." *World Development*, 24 (12): 1859–77.

IDS (1999). *Background Notes for Workshop on the Spreading of Gains from Globalisation.* Mimeo. Brighton: Institute of Development Studies, University of Sussex.

Kaplinsky, R. (1998). *Globalisation, Industrialisation, and Sustainable Growth: The Pursuit of the* nth *Rent.* Discussion Paper, 365. Brighton: Institute of Development Studies, University of Sussex.

Knorringa, P. (1996). *Economics of Collaboration: Indian Shoemakers between Market and Hierarchy.* New Delhi and London: Sage.

Krugman, P. (1991). *Geography and Trade.* Cambridge, MA: MIT Press.

—— (1995). *Development, Geography, and Economic Theory.* Cambridge, MA: MIT Press.

——, and Venables, J. (1995). *The Seamless World: A Spatial Model of International Specialization.* Discussion Paper 1230. London: Center for Economic Policy Research.

Lundvall, B.-A. (1993). "Explaining Interfirm Cooperation and Innovation: Limits of the Transaction-Cost Approach," in G. Grahber (ed.), *The Embedded Firm: On the Socio-economics of Industrial Networks.* London: Routledge, 52–64.

Maillat, D. (1996). *From the Industrial District to the Analyses of Territorialized Productive Organisations.* Working Paper 9606b. Institut de Recherches Economiques et Regionales, Université de Neuchâtel.

Markusen, A. (1996). "Sticky Places in Slippery Space: A Typology of Industrial Districts." *Economic Geography,* 293–313.

McCormick, D. (1998). *Enterprise Clusters in Africa: On the Way to Industrialisation?* IDS Discussion Paper 366. Brighton: Institute of Development Studies, University of Sussex.

Meyer-Stamer, J. (1999). "What Can We Learn from the Ceramics and Textiles/ Clothing Clusters of Santa Catarina, Brazil?" Paper presented at Conference of the Inter-American Development Bank on Business Development Services, Rio de Janeiro, 3–5 March.

——, Adam, B., Bantle, S., Lauer, A., and Mohaupt, D. (1996). *Industrielle Netzwerke und Wettbewerbsfähigkeit: Das Beispiel Santa Catarina.* Berlin: Deutsches Institut für Entwicklungspolitik.

Nadvi, K. (1999). "The Cutting Edge: Collective Efficiency and International Competitiveness in Pakistan." *Oxford Development Studies,* 27 (1): 81–107.

——, and Schmitz, H. (eds.) (1999). *Industrial Clusters in Developing Countries.* Special Issue of *World Development,* 27 (9).

Pedersen, P. O., Sverisson, A., and van Dijk, M. P. (eds.). (1994). *Flexible Specialization: The Dynamics of Small-scale Industry in the South.* London: Intermediate Technology.

Porter, M. E. (1990). *The Competitive Advantage of Nations.* London: Macmillan.

—— (1998). "Clusters and the New Economics of Competition." *Harvard Business Review* (November–December): 77–90.

——, and Wayland, R. E. (1995). "Global Competition and the Localization of Competitive Advantage." *Advances in Strategic Management,* 11A: 63–105.

Pyke, F., and Sengenberger, W. (eds.). (1992). *Industrial Districts and Local Economic Regeneration.* Geneva: International Institute for Labour Studies, ILO.

Rabellotti, R. (1997). *External Economies and Cooperation in Industrial Districts: A Comparison of Italy and Mexico.* London: Macmillan.

—— (1999). "Recovery of a Mexican Cluster: Devaluation Bonanza or Collective Efficiency?" *World Development,* 27 (9): 1571–86.

Rodrik, D. (1999). *The New Global Economy and the Developing Countries: Making Openness Work.* Baltimore and Washington: Johns Hopkins University Press for the Overseas Development Council.

Sabel, C. (1992). "Studied Trust: Building New Forms of Cooperation in a Volatile Economy," in F. Pyke and W. Sengenberger (eds.), *Industrial Districts and Local Economic Regeneration.* Geneva: ILO, International Institute for Labour Studies, 215–50.

Schmitz, H. (1995). "Collective Efficiency: Growth Path for Small-scale Industry." *Journal of Development Studies*, 31 (4): 529–66.

—— (1998). *Responding to Global Competitive Pressure: Local Cooperation and Upgrading in the Sinos Valley, Brazil.* IDS Working Paper 82. Brighton: Institute of Development Studies, University of Sussex.

—— (2000). "Does Local Cooperation Matter? Evidence from Industrial Clusters in South Asia and Latin America". *Oxford Development Studies*, 28(3): 323–36.

——, and Knorringa, P. (1999). *Learning from Global Buyers.* IDS Working Paper 100. Brighton: Institute of Development Studies, University of Sussex.

Scott, A. J. (1996). "Regional Motors of the Global Economy." *Futures*, 28 (5): 391–411.

Storper, M. (1995). "The Resurgence of Regional Economies, Ten Years Later." *European Urban and Regional Studies*, 2 (3): 191–221.

Susskind, L., McKearnon, S., and Thomas-Larmer, J. (eds.) (1999). *The Consensus Building Handbook.* Thousand Oaks, London, New Delhi: Sage.

Tewari, M. (1999). Successful Adjustment in Indian Industry: The Case of Ludhiana's Woolen Knitwear Cluster." *World Development*, 27 (9): 1651–72.

van Dijk, M. P., and Rabellotti, R. (1997). *Enterprise Clusters and Networks in Developing Countries.* EADI book series. London: Frank Cass.

World Bank. (1997). *World Development Report: The State in a Changing World.* London: Oxford University Press for the World Bank.

PART IX

CODA: ENVIRONMENTAL ISSUES

In this final part of the book, Panayotou provides a review and critique of environmental policies and practices in global city-regions, with special emphasis on developing countries.

Global city-regions in all parts of the world are susceptible to serious environmental degradation in the form of blight and pollution. The problem is compounded both by the density of emission points and by the serious market failures that often make it problematical or inefficient for private agents to provide appropriate levels of corrective action. In developing countries, environmental degradation in large cities is all the more severe due to high levels of population growth and poverty. Panayotou documents the enormous social and economic costs associated with these predicaments. He is critical of the performance of governmental agencies in dealing with them, and suggests that current policy paradigms based on the principle of centralized regulation are actually poorly designed and tend to be inefficient in practice, especially in the case of developing countries where administrative capacities are frequently quite limited. His solution is not to abandon public policy altogether in the domain of environmental control, but to advocate a new sort of partnership between the public and private sectors, in which the particular strengths of each are allowed fuller play. For Panayotou, this means opening up certain kinds of environmental servicing activities to private firms while decentralizing regulatory oversight as far as possible to individual communities and civil organizations. As he writes in his chapter, "there is a need for enabling legislation and new rules of the game that would allow greater flexibility of response and wider involvement of the private sector in the provision of environmental services while protecting the public interest and accommodating distributional concerns."

If Panayotou's discussion of environmental sustainability tilts perceptibly toward the market side of this formulation, his analysis nevertheless points more generally to a still quite open question. In brief, how can the public interest best be served in a world of global city-regions where regulatory authority tends to be increasingly diffuse and contested, but where particular kinds of systemic social and physical infrastructures and coordinating services are indispensable for continued growth and development? The answers to this question that we construct in practice—some of which are sketched out in embryonic form in the present volume—will unquestionably have profound effects on the shape and functional characteristics of global city-regions as they develop over the twenty-first century.

22

Environmental Sustainability and Services in Developing Global City-Regions

THEODORE PANAYOTOU

Global city-regions have enormous advantages in terms of economies of scale and agglomeration and ability to attract investment and to create jobs and wealth. At the same time, megacities, and even cities of moderate size, require continuous investment in expansion and maintenance of a broad range of infrastructure and public services if they are to work efficiently and to continue to attract investment and provide a satisfactory quality of life to their expanding and increasingly demanding populations. Even in developed countries, providing adequate infrastructure and public services to meet the growing demand and to ensure improving—or at least not deteriorating—environmental quality has always been a challenge.

The rapid rate of urbanization experienced by developing countries creates even greater challenges for cities in developing countries, which have fewer financial, human, and institutional resources to respond to the growth. The demand for infrastructure and public services quickly outpaces the supply, creating an ever-widening gap between the two. The result is urban slums and shantytowns that lack even the most basic of services: clean water, sanitation, paved roads, and electricity. Compoundng the failure of urban infrastructure and public services to meet the increasing demands, traffic congestion, deteriorating water and air quality, and uncollected solid waste add to the array of problems facing developing-country megacities.

State-owned utilities and other state enterprises providing these services often find themselves lacking the necessary financial resources, unable to maintain or increase coverage and access, despite—or perhaps because of—governments' efforts to provide subsidized services affordable to the poor. Since most of the poor have no access to these services, the wealthier urban inhabitants tend to be the main beneficiaries of subsidized water, power, and other services. Both subsidies and underpricing result in excessive and wasteful use by those who have access and in failure to cover even the operating costs of existing services. As a result, infrastructure is not properly maintained and the quality of service deteriorates further, causing users to be even less willing to pay for these services and to seek more reliable alternatives. This, in turn, further deprives public providers of the badly needed revenues in a vicious circle of ratcheting down to lower and lower quality of service that has come to be known euphemistically as a low-level equilibrium trap.

The consequence of this trap is deteriorating environmental quality in cities, with dire consequences for the health and productivity of millions of people who are exposed to harmful pollutants. Damage to property and traffic congestion further diminishes the net wealth and welfare generated by megacities. Yet, as long as the average level of services and job opportunities in cities is better than that in rural areas, rural urban migration continues unabated, putting further pressure on a system that is already unable to cope, totally overwhelming city governments and other public service providers. It is this inability to cope with the expanding demands of growing urban population, along with the absence of negative feedbacks to reverse the process, that is the greatest threat to urban environmental sustainability.

How does globalization (and concurrently, liberalization and privatization) change the sustainability picture in global city-regions? Globalization has the potential to make things better by making available the necessary financial resources, technology, and management to escape the low-level equilibrium trap. On the other hand, globalization may make things worse if it simply increases the demands on the already heavily burdened infrastructure and services and adds to pollution and congestion while continuing to make the megacities more attractive to rural migrants because of increased employment prospects. Indeed, this is what is happening to most of the developing world's megacities, but there are also positive examples of innovative approaches to tapping globalization and putting it to the service of environmental improvement and sustainability. While developed-country cities as a group have been more successful in marshaling outside resources to alleviate infrastructural bottlenecks and to improve environmental quality, they are not always a good example for developing countries to follow. Indeed, in some cases, they may be an example to avoid.

The purpose of this chapter is (1) to analyze the environmental challenges of global city-regions, especially in developing countries, where they are more severe; (2) to examine the implications of globalization for these challenges; and (3) to explore public policy options, private sector involvement, and innovative, flexible instruments for addressing these challenges. I focus particularly on the Asian region, because it has been the most active participant in the globalization process. Examples from Latin American countries, such as Argentina and Chile, which have also been active participants not only at the national level but also at the global-city level, are also discussed. Based on this analysis, the chapter proposes a new paradigm for environmental management of global city-regions, driven by the private sector and civil society, with government playing a regulatory and facilitating role.

ECONOMIC GROWTH AND URBANIZATION

Megacities are the creation of the powerful process of urbanization, which is in part derived from economic growth and in part from government policies. As

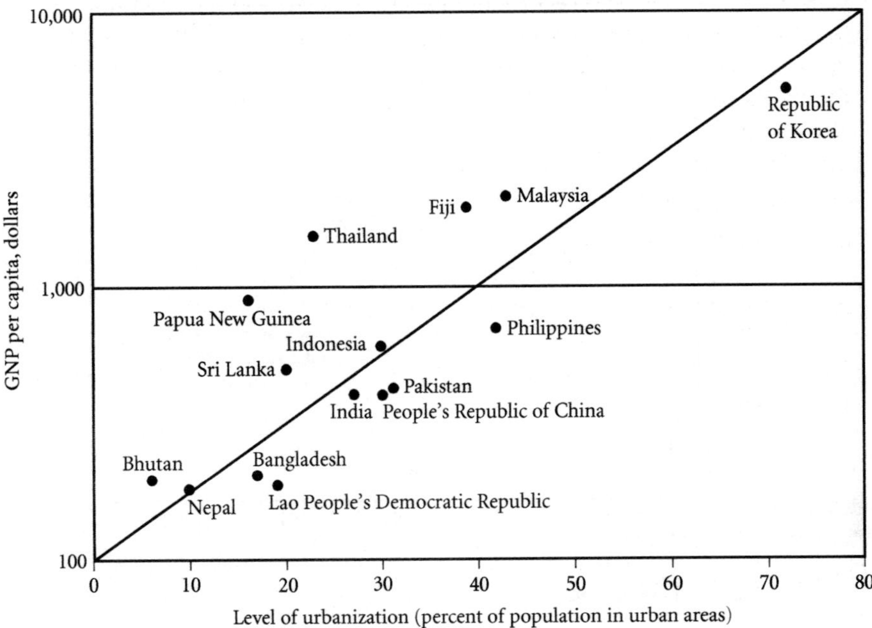

Figure 22.1. *Level of urbanization and GNP per capita of selected Asian countries*
Source: Asian Development Bank 1995

per capita income grows, structural change from agriculture to industry also occurs. In fact, the two processes are simultaneous and mutually reinforcing. What drives both economic growth and urban migration is the movement of resources from low-return activities and environments (agriculture, rural) to high-return activities and environments (industry, urban). The strong relationship between urbanization and GNP per capita for selected Asian countries is seen in Figure 22.1. Economic boom, accompanied by rapid urbanization and slow growth in the supply of infrastructure and public services (including environmental protection), has caused a precipitous decline in environmental quality, as seen in Figure 22.2 for the case of the Bangkok global city-region of eight million people: urban congestion, notorious traffic jams, anaerobic water bodies, clogging air pollution, and ubiquitous uncollected solid waste mark Bangkok's golden economic decade, 1985–95.

URBANIZATION AND ENVIRONMENTAL QUALITY: THE CASE OF ASIA

While the level of urbanization in Asia is considerably lower than that of Latin America, it has been growing faster. As a result, Asian cities are becoming dirtier, noisier, and ever more congested. Particulate levels are twice the world average and five times the levels in other developing regions. Ambient levels of

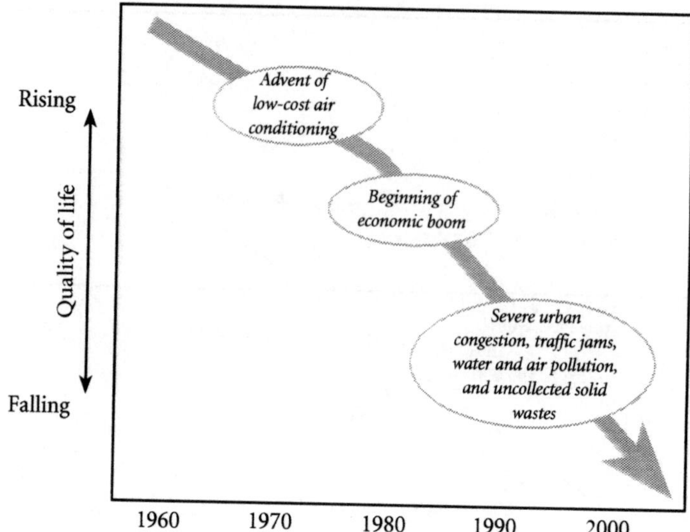

Figure 22.2. *Change in quality of life in Bangkok metropolitan region*
Source: Kiravanich and In-na 1996

sulfur dioxide (a precursor of acid rain and a major regional pollutant that damages crops and materials) are 50 percent higher in Asia than in Latin America (GEMS 1996), corresponding to Asia's higher rates of economic growth during the 1980s and early part of the 1990s. Figures 22.3 and 22.4 compare selected Asian cities to selected North American cities, while Figures 22.5 and 22.6 show the sources of particulate and SO_2 emissions in one Asian global-city airshed. Although Asian emissions of CO_2 (a global pollutant suspected to contribute to global warming) are less than half of the world average in per capita terms, they are growing at four times the world average. Fecal coliform count and suspended solids in Asian rivers are three to four times the world average, while surface waters in urban centers are replete with pathogens, organic material, and heavy metals, exceeding national and WHO standards. Thirteen of the world's fifteen most polluted cities are in Asia.

How well protected are Asians from this increasingly unhealthy environment around them? Despite the rapid, steady growth in income and wealth, a third of the population in developing Asia has no access to safe drinking water, and one half has no access to sanitation services; only in Africa is the situation worse. For those with access to a public water supply, service is intermittent and poor, averaging between four and fourteen hours per day, while system leakages exceed 40 percent. At least one-third of a billion tons—and growing at rates of 3–7 percent a year—of solid waste remain uncollected, becoming the breeding ground for disease vectors. Millions of tons of untreated hazardous waste are disposed of in dumpsites and landfills, threatening both groundwater and the food chain.

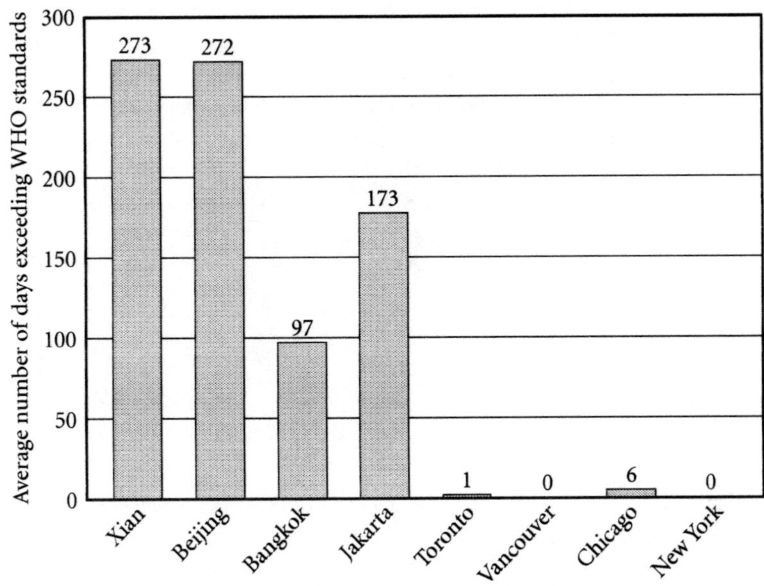

Figure 22.3. *Cities exceeding World Health Organization standards for suspended particulate matter of 230 micrograms per cubic meter*

Source: Lohani and Whitington 1996

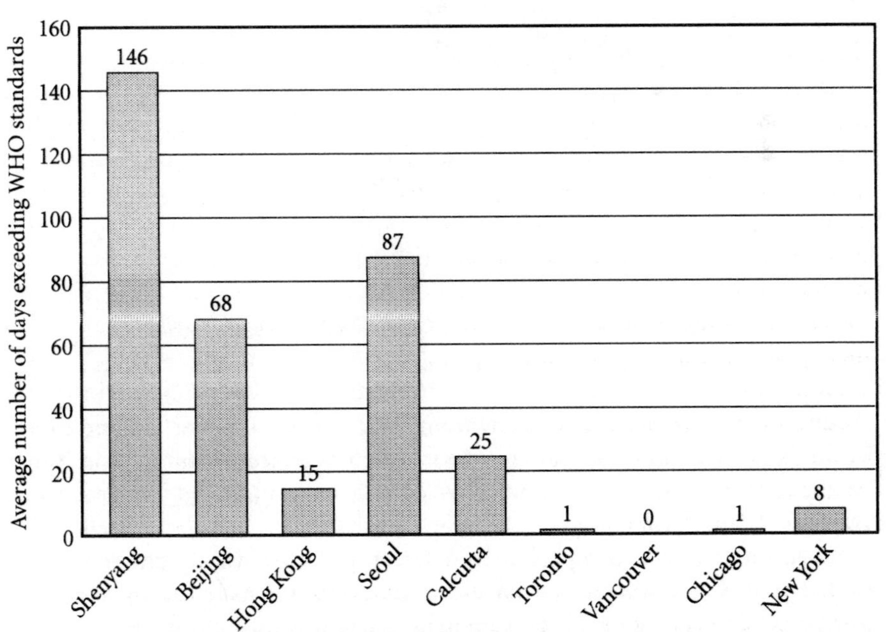

Figure 22.4. *Cities exceeding World Health Organization standards for sulfur dioxide of 150 micrograms per cubic meter*

Source: Lohani and Whitington 1996

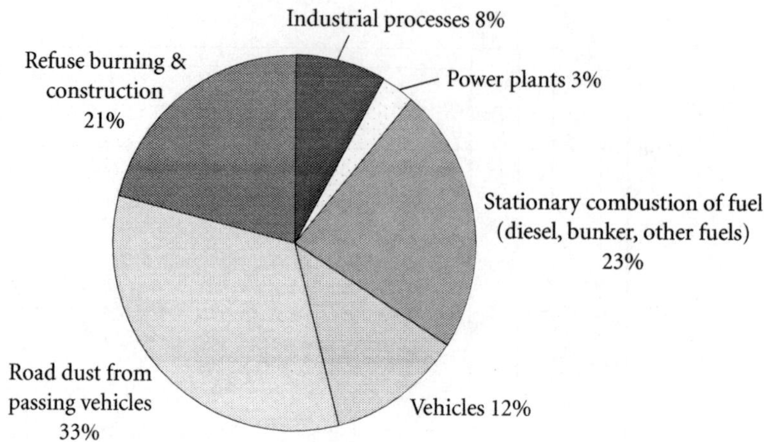

Figure 22.5. *Emission sources in Manila airshed: suspended particulate matter*
Source: Lohani and Whitington 1996

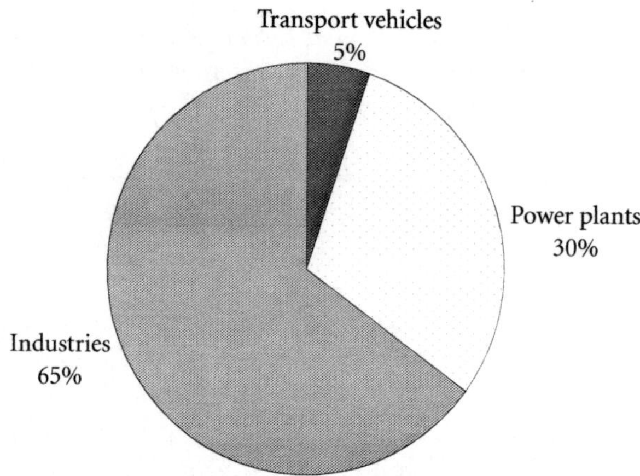

Figure 22.6. *Emission sources in Manila airshed: sulfur dioxide*
Source: Lohani and Whitington 1996

What is the economic cost of environmental damage in Asia? Is there effective demand (willingness to pay) for environmental improvement in Asia? What are the expected benefits from different levels of environmental improvements, and how do they compare with the likely costs?

While there are no comprehensive estimates of the costs of environmental degradation in Asia, existing partial estimates indicate costs in the range of 2–10 percent of GDP, depending on the comprehensiveness of the estimate. For example, the Chinese Academy of Social Sciences has estimated environmental damages in China in 1990 to be US$31 billion, or 8.5 percent of GDP, while Smil (1996) puts the figure between 5.5 percent and 9.8 percent of GNP. Far less comprehensive

Table 22.1. *Social costs of different fuels in selected cities (US$ millions unless otherwise noted)*

City	Damages	Coal	Fuel oil	Diesel	Gasoline	Total
Bangkok	Health costs	—	170	392	71	633
	Nonhealth costs	—	25	39	4	78
	Total costs	—	195	431	85	712
	Total local costs per ton of fuel (US$)	—	33	718	102	—
Manila	Health costs	—	143	316	33	492
	Nonhealth costs	—	16	36	11	63
	Total costs	—	159	352	44	555
	Total local costs per ton of fuel (US$)	—	31	392	62	—
Shanghai	Health costs	892	39	57	9	996
	Nonhealth costs	46	3	6	2	57
	Total costs	938	42	63	11	1055
	Total local costs per ton of fuel (US$)	33	10	138	13	—
All three cities	Cost of contribution to global climate change as $20 per ton of carbon (US$/ton of fuel)	15	18	18	18	—
World market price, 1995 (US$/ton)		44	118–135	148	158	

Source: Lvovsky *et al.* 1994.

estimates for Indonesia, Pakistan, and the Philippines range between 2 percent and 3.3 percent. The Indonesian estimate of 2.0 percent includes only health effects of particulates and lead levels above WHO standards in Jakarta alone: premature mortality accounts for 80 percent of the $844 million damages from particulates, and IQ loss in children for 90 percent of the $1,320 million damages from lead emissions (Ostro 1994; DeShazo 1996). Table 22.1 shows estimates of social costs of different fuels in selected Asian cities. A reasonable average figure for annual damages and production losses for the typical Asian country would be around 5 percent of GDP. There are also significant additional welfare losses arising from damages to health, amenity, and existence value not captured by GDP losses.

ECONOMIC GROWTH AND ENVIRONMENT

Environmental quality follows an inverted U-shaped curve during the course of economic development. It first deteriorates, during the industrialization process, and then tends to improve during the postindustrial stage, as the center of gravity of the economy moves from industry to services (Panayotou 1993, 1997). However, the environmental price of economic growth is in part policy-determined.

It is generally higher when policies subsidize extractive industries, such as capital-intensive industries, and inputs such as energy and water; when property rights are undefined or insecure and externalities pervasive and unmanaged; and when institutions are weak and enforcement is lax. Since all these policy, market, and institutional failures have been present throughout the developing world during the past several decades, it is very likely that megacities paid an unnecessarily high environmental price for their economic growth. While economic growth generated the structural changes, demand shifts, and financial resources for significant environmental improvement—especially in large cities such as Bangkok and Manila that produce about 50 percent of national GDP—the institutions and policies were not in place to ensure a supply response.

THE INEFFECTIVENESS OF CURRENT POLICIES

There is a general perception among developing-country policymakers that people are not willing to pay for environmental improvements, even for such basic services as access to safe drinking water. There is accumulating evidence from surveys and from revealed behavior (e.g. water purchases from water vendors and transport of water from distant sources) that the great majority of households, including the poor, are willing to pay the full costs of improved municipal water supply and indoor sanitation, though not for outdoor sanitation. Defensive expenditures also indicate considerable willingness to pay for improvements in air quality. For instance, in the absence of access to reliable and safe public water supply, hundreds of millions of Asians are buying water from vendors at three to eight times the price of metered tap water (World Bank 1992). Surveys have found that people in developing countries are as concerned about environmental degradation as people in the developed world and are willing to pay higher prices or to trade growth for environmental protection.

Thus, while willingness to pay may be constrained by market and institutional failures, as in the case of outdoor sanitation, the lack of effective demand is not a binding constraint on environmental improvement. There is significant unmet effective demand because of unresponsive supply (see Figure 22.7). The public sector has been unresponsive because of under-appreciated benefits and perceived high cost, as well as because of institutional weakness and a lack of funds. Excessive centralization of environmental management, lack of public participation, and institutional paternalism prevented individual and collective preferences from influencing public decisions concerning the supply of environmental services. Supply costs are inflated by the choice of costly—and largely ineffective—instruments, such as end-of-the-pipe command-and-control regulations, mandated best-available technologies, and centralized public capital investments, rather than least-cost alternatives such as price reforms, pollution charges, and decentralized provision. For example, the end-of-the-pipe investment program for controlling SO_2 and particulates in China and India is costing 3–10 times as much as the least-cost alternatives, because it focuses on power

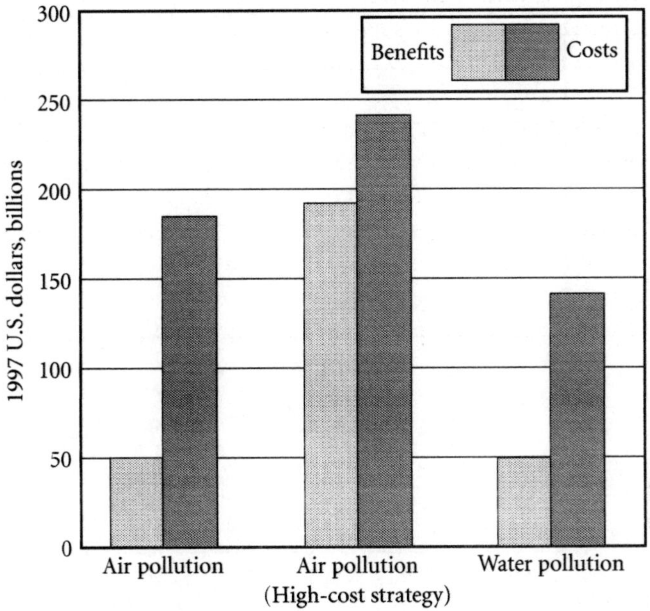

Figure 22.7. *China: costs and benefits of pollution controls*

Source: Lohani and Whitington 1996

sector investments and ignores lower-cost alternatives outside the power sector, such as reduction of emissions from coal burning households and industrial boilers. The supply costs of environmental improvements are compounded by the failure to take advantage of the wide variability in control costs among sources and pollutants and to allow the flexibility of response needed to achieve least-cost solutions (see Figure 22.8).

Environmental infrastructure, such as water supply, sanitation systems, solid waste collection, and wastewater treatment, is severely underfinanced because of inadequate cost recovery (itself the result of not charging users the full cost of supply), and a reluctance to involve the private sector in order to lower cost and to leverage private capital. The private sector itself is unresponsive to the growing demand for improved environmental services because it is either legally prohibited (natural monopolies) or unable to recover costs due to free-riding (public goods).

Sustainable improvements can only be achieved through changes of behavior, which in turn require changes of the incentive structure facing individual economic agents as consumers and producers. As long as property rights remain ill-defined and insecure, as long as polluting inputs and extractive industries are being subsidized, as long as polluters free-ride on the environment and users of public services free-ride on the treasury, and as long as the dynamics of the private sector and the spirit of civil society are bureaucratically constrained from making their full contributions, current trends cannot be reversed, and the gap

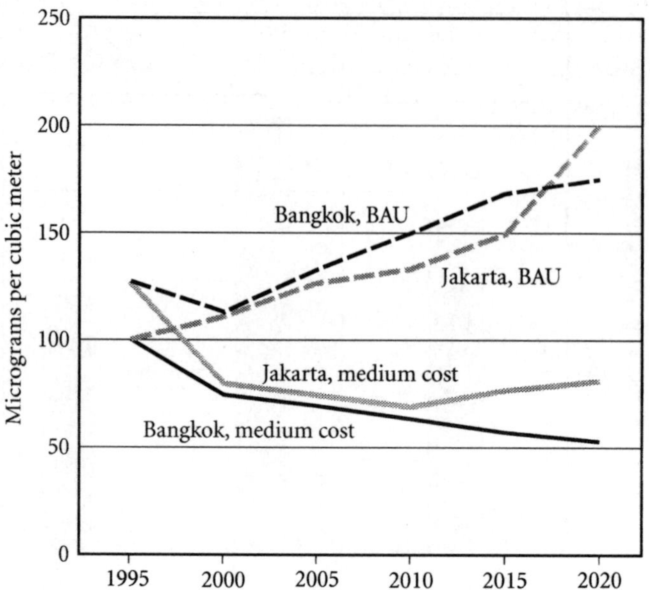

Figure 22.8. *Air quality in Bangkok and Jakarta under alternative scenarios*

Source: Lohani and Whitington 1996

between economic and environmental performance will continue to grow. Only a policy paradigm shift can put the developing world on the fast track to environmental recovery that parallels its fast track of economic growth. The new policy paradigm involves less government bureaucracy, an enhanced role for the private sector and civil society, and the aggressive pursuit of untapped win-win policy reforms and high-return investment opportunities that would result in both environmental and economic gains: (1) phasing out environmentally harmful subsidies, (2) using economic instruments to save on costs, and (3) making environmental investments with high returns. This new policy paradigm does not ignore the role of redistributive interventions by the state, which may actually increase in importance as the state's role in economic activity and environmental management is diminished in favor of the private sector and the civil society, but seeks to pursue social justice by the most efficient and targeted means.

PROBLEMS WITH PUBLICLY OPERATED INFRASTRUCTURE

A major rationale and catalyst for increased private sector participation in infrastructure and public sector provision has been posed by the poor performance and mismanagement characterizing most publicly owned and operated utilities. Well-managed public systems are the exception rather than the rule. A combination of technical, financial, institutional, and environmental problems of public service monopolies have resulted in unreliable service, unsatisfied consumers, poor cost recovery and financially insolvent systems, unnecessary environmental damage, and unacceptable health hazards. The following problems have been identified based on an assessment of public water supply and sanitation systems (Idelovitch and Ringskog 1995) but apply at varying levels to other public services, such as power, telephone, and transport.

1. *Low-quality service and inadequate coverage* (50–75 percent for water, 30–50 percent for sanitation); inability to cope with expanding population. The intermittent, low-pressure water supply is mirrored in the power sector by frequent brownouts and a variable electric current.
2. *Inefficient operational practices and poor maintenance*, resulting in large water losses, unaccounted-for water, and power losses as high as 40–50 percent (compared to 10–20 percent for well-managed systems).
3. *Excessive and wasteful use.* For example, water consumption may reach 500–600 liters per capita, which is twice the norm in metered and well-managed water supply systems; this is largely the result of water pricing, nonmarginal cost pricing, and lack of metering. In the energy sector, underpricing leads to energy intensities (energy use per unit of GDP) that are two to three times the norm for full-cost priced energy.
4. *Poor cost recovery and financial problems*, which arise from underpricing, limited consumption metering, irregular meter reading, and billing not based on actual consumption. Water and electricity tariffs typically do not reflect the incremental costs of future supplies, resulting in inadequate funds for expansion. Poor maintenance consequent on poor cost recovery causes a vicious circle of falling revenues and deteriorating service.
5. *High labor costs and low labor productivity*, because of excess staff, generous benefits, and low skills. For example, public water companies often employ five to ten employees per 1,000 water connections compared with only two to three employees per 1,000 connections for efficient water companies.
6. *Poor management and inability to attract management talent* and qualified technical staff, due to noncompetitive wages, political appointments, high turnover, lack of disciplined labor force, and lack of incentives to attract qualified managerial and technical staff.
7. *Large and growing state subsidies*, which benefit mainly the middle class and the wealthy who are large consumers of water and power while the poor are either not connected or too small users to benefit much from untargeted subsidies.
8. *Lack of clear regulatory responsibility*, and conflict of interest between the regulator and operator functions of the public utility. Underperformance or undercompliance is often dealt with by lowering standards rather than by improving operations.

In sum, public service monopolies are usually among the largest sources of environmental problems, for reasons that range from soft budget constraints and inefficiency to low tariffs and bureaucratic shielding. Water and electricity tariffs rarely include environmental costs. For example, water rates do not cover the cost of collecting and treating wastewater. Moreover, the general lag of sewage connections behind water supply connections results in sewage being deposited in septic tanks that contaminate shallow aquifers, often a major source of urban water supply.

The poor performance and mismanagement characterizing most publicly owned and operated utilities created the impetus for considering private sector participation. A second and equally important catalyst has been the increasing needs of urban infrastructure (power, water supply and sanitation, roads, ports, telecommunications, etc.) and the inability of the public sector to mobilize these resources. A declining ODA, unsustainable levels of budget deficits and external debts, and the need to maintain fiscal discipline to control inflation and spur economic growth have convinced governments to seek private sector resources.

THE PROMISE AND CHALLENGE OF PRIVATE SECTOR PARTICIPATION

The promise of the private sector lies in (1) improved management and higher efficiency and (2) increased access to private capital for maintenance and expansion. The two are related since greater efficiency results in cost savings and greater availability of funds for investment; improved management results in easier access to private capital; and investment of private capital constitutes an added incentive for operational efficiency.

While the potential benefits from private sector participation are clear, the obstacles are often formidable. Infrastructure investments tend to be capital intensive and lumpy, have long gestation and even longer payback periods. For example, in water and sanitation, the ratio of investment in fixed assets to annual tariff revenues is ten to one. This means that private financing is contingent upon the existence of long-term capital markets and guarantees and rewards offered for high risks. The private sector risks are many and varied: demand for the services provided may turn out to be lower than expected; tariffs may be too low and not be permitted to adjust to reflect costs; the condition of infrastructure may turn out to be worse than represented, while delays of construction prove to be longer and costs higher than anticipated. Other risks include the financial risk of currency devaluation, legal risks in dispute resolution, and the political risk of asset appropriation. As a result of one or more of these hazards, the private contractor may be unable to recover costs and earn a reasonable profit. Indeed, how these risks are quantified and mitigated turns out to be the key to private sector participation in infrastructure projects. The principle is that whoever controls a particular risk best should assume it and be compensated for it.

The public sector that invites private sector participation in areas that have been traditionally reserved for the state also faces risks: procured services may be substandard or costs may turn out to be higher than those charged by the public utility. There are also political risks, arising from public opposition to privatization, especially by labor unions. Water supply, sanitation, and power (as well as other utilities) are natural monopolies; it is uneconomical to duplicate the water and sewage pipes or the power lines in city streets, and, therefore, competition is difficult to achieve. Moreover, regulation is necessary to protect against monopolistic practices. Regulation is also necessary to control externalities related to public health and the environment. When the social benefits exceed private benefits, investments must be promoted above what is privately profitable.

The obstacles to private sector participation may appear formidable. Lack of adequate legislation for private sector involvement and nonenforcement of property rights and contracts are common obstacles, as are bureaucratic inertia and lack of confidence in the private sector among policymakers. Other constraints include unfavorable public opinion, fear of foreign operations, and reluctance to deal with labor problems. The constraints may also be on the supply side, with the private sector showing too little interest to ensure competitive bidding. Despite these obstacles a number of poor and middle-income countries succeeded in attracting private sector participation in urban environmental management through a variety of innovative instruments (see Table 22.2).

Table 22.2. *Private sector activities and institutional arrangements in financing water and sanitation services*

Country	Activity—institutional arrangement
Bangladesh	Solid waste disposal—contractual basis per piece of work
	Operation of community latrine—lease
	Community maintenance—advance prequalification and quotation (similar to retainership)
India	Garbage collection and disposal—contractual
	Maintenance of parks and gardens—contractual
	Operation of water supply and sewerage pumping stations—contractual
	Informal markets for water supply, solid waste collection, recycling—contractual
	Water distribution—private vending of water
Indonesia	Water source/water supply system development—BOT
	Water distribution—private vending of bottled
Malaysia	National Sewerage System
	Water supply—BOT
	Garbage disposal—contractual
Pakistan	Water and Power Development Authority—sale of equity
Thailand	Water supply—BOT
Philippines	Water distribution—private vending of water
	Garbage disposal—contractual

Source: Pernia and Alabastro 1996.

PHASING OUT DISTORTIONARY SUBSIDIES

The World Bank (1994) estimated that the cost recovery of urban water supply systems in developing countries averaged 35 percent, imposing a fiscal burden of $13 billion a year. Developing country governments, like those of OECD, intervene heavily in their energy markets through direct and indirect producer and consumer subsidies. OECD energy subsidies are estimated to be in the range of $60–75 billion (OECD forthcoming). Larsen and Shah (1994) have estimated non-OECD energy subsidies to be in the range of $270–330 billion in 1991, equivalent to 5–7 percent of GDP. China and India's combined energy subsidies were put by the same source at $36 billion, also in 1991. There are no estimates for the whole region but a figure of $50 billion would be conservative. Petroleum prices in China in 1991 were 76 percent of world prices, in India 44 percent, while electricity prices were 37 percent and 54 percent respectively. In Indonesia, petroleum prices were as low as 37 percent of the world price. Coal—Asia's dirtiest fuel—responsible for millions of deaths and billions of dollars of damages a year, received an 18 percent subsidy in China and a 38 percent subsidy in India. Ingram and Fay (1994) estimated that avoidable power losses in the transmission, distribution, and generation stages amounted to $30 billion in developing countries or 0.6 percent of GDP.

Subsidy removal promises large environmental benefits including reductions of NO_x, SO_2, and CO_2, and in the case of transport fuels, reduction of congestion and particulates. In addition, $3 billion can be saved from eliminating illegal connections and $2.5 billion from increased efficiency of use resulting from full-cost pricing. Full-cost pricing could save as much as 30 percent of residential water consumption and over 60 percent of industrial consumption[1] while repairs to the distribution systems and elimination of illegal connections can save another 25 percent of water supply (World Bank 1994). In total, 50 percent of current water supply in developing countries can be saved and used to supply the uncovered population by using better pricing and demand management and only modest investments in repair and expanded distribution systems. With few exceptions, no major investment in new sources of supply would be needed.

In Beijing, for example, 70 million cubic meters of water per year or 15 percent of current domestic consumption could be saved through improved efficiency in public utilities, leakage repair, and recycling of cooling water used in air conditioning at the cost of $0.02–0.04 per cubic meter. Another 300 million cubic meters per year or 33 percent of current industrial consumption can be saved by increasing recycling of cooling water in manufacturing and in power plants, at the cost of $0.02–0.05 per cubic meter (World Bank 1992). For comparison, the cost of the next lowest cost water development project is $0.11 per cubic meter or more than three times the average cost of water savings through efficiency improvements. The savings equal $28 million per year and do not exhaust the opportunities for water conservation and increased coverage through demand management. At a price of $0.08 per cubic meter, installation of water-efficient toilets in households and wastewater recycling in industry become profitable,

Table 22.3. *Environmental, economic, and social effects of energy subsidy removal in developing countries*

Environmental	
CO_2 reduction	–7% (–18%)[a]
SO_2 reduction	–65%
No_x reduction	–40%
Economic	
Welfare (US$ billions, 1991)	35
Real income (% per annum)	1.6
Social	
Maximum welfare loss	–1% to –3%
Health benefits	positive

Note:

[a] 7% reduction in global CO_2 emissions in 2010; 18% reduction in 2050.

Sources: IEA 1994; Larsen and Shah 1994; Burniaux, Martin, and Oliveira-Martines 1992; Hope and Singh 1995; and Earth Council 1996.

saving additional quantities of water, still at two-thirds of the cost of water from new water development projects. Table 22.3 reports estimates of a 65 percent reduction in SO_2, a 40 percent reduction in NO_x, and a 7–18 percent reduction in global CO_2 emissions from removing subsidies in countries such as China and India. Removal of subsidies also removes the incentive to produce energy-intensive products and encourages the production of more energy-efficient consumer goods, resulting in further reductions in energy use and air emissions.

The economic benefits from energy subsidy removal are also substantial. Larsen and Shah (1994) estimate that eliminating consumer subsidies of energy in non-OECD countries would raise welfare by $35 billion. Burniaux, Martin, and Oliveira-Martins (1992) estimate that discounted real income would increase by 1.6 percent in non-OECD countries, real world income by 0.7 percent annually while the terms of trade would improve by 0.5 percent per year. The major exceptions are China, which is expected to experience an average real income loss of 0.7 percent per year, and the oil exporters. Hope and Singh (1995) present evidence from developing countries that raising energy prices by removing subsidies does not harm competitiveness; GDP growth rates were the same or higher than before the reform. Furthermore, the removal of energy subsidies has public revenue effects (higher public savings, lower deficits) that are supportive of economic growth. While there was a small welfare loss for urban poor using commercial fuels, the overall conclusion is that energy subsidy removal has not harmed the poor.

COST SAVINGS FROM THE USE OF ECONOMIC INSTRUMENTS

The very same environmental protection achieved today in Asia through the existing rigid command-and-control regulations can be achieved at a fraction of the current cost, possibly a third or lower, through a more flexible incentive-based system that combines economic and regulatory instruments. Indeed such an environmental policy reform is likely to be both economically less costly and environmentally more effective as countries that make even a partial move (Malaysia, Singapore, Korea, Indonesia, Thailand, and Chile) discover.

The cost savings in moving from command-and-control to economic instruments or to a mixed system can be demonstrated by comparing the costs of the existing combination of discharge permits and fines on over-standard emissions to a full emissions charge system. Based on a sample of 260 enterprises in Beijing and Tianjin, China, with multiple water pollution sources, for which abatement varied from 0 to 100 percent with a median abatement level of 70 to 80 percent, Dasgupta *et al.* (1996) derived a marginal cost curve and determined the emission charge that would achieve the current abatement rate for each pollutant. Abatement costs were reduced from $47 million to $13 million, a saving of $34 million from this set of enterprises alone, or a 70 percent reduction from the command-and-control cost level.

The large cost savings from a shift from command-and-control regulations to least-cost instruments is well-documented in the United States, where most studies show ratios of CAC-cost to least-cost ranging from 2 to 22 (Teitenberg 1990). It is particularly notable that the savings are greatest in the case of particulates, the developing world's most serious and widespread air pollution problem. Even if only two-thirds of the current cost of environmental protection could be saved from a more efficient regulatory system, the effect would be equivalent to that of tripling environmental expenditures under the existing system.

The economic benefits of a more flexible and effective regulatory regime go beyond cost savings to the enhancement of competitiveness. A World Economic Forum survey of business executives in fifty countries revealed a strong correlation between the flexibility of environmental regulations and international competitiveness. Countries that rank high in terms of competitiveness, such as Singapore, Hong Kong, New Zealand, Chile, and Norway, also rank high in terms of the flexibility of environmental regulations, while countries such as Russia, Venezuela, and Hungary that rank low in terms of competitiveness also rank low in terms of the flexibility of environmental regulations, at least as perceived by investors and business executives (Panayotou and Vincent 1997). There are, of course, several mediating variables, such as openness to trade, taxation, and condition of infrastructure.

ENVIRONMENTAL INVESTMENTS WITH HIGH ECONOMIC RETURNS

The environmental neglect, in the cities of the emerging world, during the takeoff process of economic growth left unexploited countless public investment opportunities that at modest cost can yield large economic and environmental benefits. The scope and magnitude of these opportunities is exemplified by the following examples:

- *Water supply*. In Phuket, Thailand, increased access to water and improvement of service would yield returns in the range of 14 to 300 percent. The higher returns are due to the fact that water shortage affects Phuket's lucrative tourist industry. In Gujnamwala, Pakistan, increased access to safe water would yield a 20 percent rate of return.
- *Energy efficiency improvements*. In electricity generation in Asia this would result in savings of $9 to $13 billion, while similar improvements in residential and commercial energy use (including electricity consumption) would result in net savings of $26 to $39 billion, not including productivity gains from health improvement and reduced agricultural damages resulting from reduced emissions (ADB 1992, Saunders and Gandhi 1994).
- *Pollution control*. Investment of $20 million to reduce BOD discharges from the top 100 polluters in the Metro Manila Area would result in labor productivity gains and reduced fishery losses valued at $250 million. Investment of $35 million in fuel reformulation to reduce lead in gasoline and sulfur in diesel would result in productivity gains from avoided illness and reduced damages to forestry and agriculture valued at $85 to $160 million (Table 22.4).

Table 22.4. *Annual benefits and costs of reduced pollution in the metro Manila area and vicinity (early 1990s)*

Water pollution control		
Intervention	• Reduction of industrial BOD discharges from top 100 polluters (40 tons of BOD reduction/day)	
Benefits	• Metro Manila area productivity gain from reduced incidence of water pollution-related illness	US$100 million/yr.
	• Reduced risk on fishery resources in the vicinity of Metro Manila area	US$150 million/yr.
Total benefits		US$250 million/yr.
Costs	Amortized capital and operating costs (US$400 per ton of BOD)	US$20 million/yr.
Net benefits		US$230 million/yr
Air pollution control		
Interventions	• Fuel reformulation to reduce lead in gasoline and sulfur in diesel; emission control devices; installation of flue gas desulfurization	
Benefits	• Metro Manila area productivity gain from reduced incidence of air pollution-related illness	US$20 million/yr.
	• Reduced risk on agricultural and forestry resources in the vicinity of Metro Manila area	US$65–140 million/yr.
Total benefits		US$85–160 million/yr.
Costs	Fuel reformulation program to reduce lead in gasoline and sulfur in diesel	US$35 million/yr.
Net benefits		US$50–125 million/yr

Source: World Bank 1993.

THE CASE OF URBAN TRANSPORT, CONGESTION, AND AIR EMISSIONS

One of the greatest challenges facing developing global city-regions is how best to respond to the rapidly increasing number of vehicles and increasing traffic congestion, reflecting a growing demand for transport services by expanding urban populations enjoying rising income levels. While developing global city-regions such as Bangkok, Jakarta, Cairo, and Mexico City are at different stages of development and face different problems from cities in developed countries (see Table 22.5, comparing Jakarta and Detroit), the response has often been not unlike that of North American cities. The central feature of the North American approach has been to help the city decentralize and disperse by (1) keeping transport fuel prices low and (2) investing heavily in an extensive road infrastructure network (often subsidized). This demand-response, rather than demand-management approach gives high priority to the automobile in the city-region's overall transport system; this, in turn, means high priority for new roads and parking spaces. The construction of new roads linking the suburbs with the city center creates pressure for new suburban infrastructure at the fringe of the suburbs, as the extra speed afforded by new roads makes it possible to live further out and to travel greater distances. Subsidized roads, suburban infrastructure, and low transport fuel prices create low-density suburbs that cannot be profitably served by public transport, and this, in turn, raises fuel use per person (see Figure 22.9), and creates pressures to keep fuel prices low and to raise further the priority of car-related infrastructure as the private automobile becomes no longer a choice but a necessity for the sprawling suburbs.

North American and Australian cities, after fifty years of automobile-based growth, have spread as far as 40–50 kilometers from the city center, stretching the limits of comfortable car commuting. The average private automobile travel per person, per year, was 12,507 km for American cities and 10,680 km for Canadian cities. This contrasts with 5,600 km for European cities and 1,800 km for Asian cities (see Table 22.6). Low fuel prices and subsidized road infrastructure have been among the driving forces of suburban sprawl in North American and Australian cities. The consequences have been many and profound: land use, infrastructure, urban development, energy pricing, voting behavior, and even attitudes toward efforts to control global warming have been shaped by the now culturally ingrained long-distance commuting and automobile dependence. Not only driving costs, but also land value, housing mortgages, and even lifestyles are perceived to be threatened by any proposal to introduce carbon taxes or any other policies that might result in increased gasoline prices. This is why policies aiming to control the environmental impact of transport have focused on producing cleaner and more efficient vehicles, rather than fully internalizing the environmental costs of private driving or shifting transport policies towards public transit systems. Such systems are not viable at the low population densities

Table 22.5. *Comparison of transport- and energy-related problems between developing and developed global cities: Jakarta vs. Detroit*

Jakarta	Detroit
Land use	
Expanding outward—since 1955, the metropolitan region has increased more than threefold. As is the case with most megacities, Jakarta's urban fringe is growing much faster than the city itself in some areas at nearly 18 percent per year. The expansion is different from the suburbanization of U.S. cities. Although some neighborhoods are richer enclaves, most of the expansion is due to population pressures.	Urban sprawl leads to energy inefficiency. In U.S. cities (such as Detroit), it is not only housing that has gone to the suburbs, but also jobs and services. Whole new "edge cities" have evolved, further exacerbating the chasm between inner city and suburb.
Transportation	
The number of cars is increasing rapidly. As wealth grows, people turn to cars as status symbols. The city has been unable to respond with an adequate number of roads. Traffic congestion has increased dramatically in recent years.	Lack of public transportation limits job opportunities for inner-city residents, who cannot go to the edge cities where the jobs are. Despite an extensive network of freeways, Detroit still suffers rush hour traffic jams.
Energy use	
Residents use much less energy per capita than people living in the United States.	U.S. cities use much more energy than other cities around the world, in part because of the greater number of cars. Carbon dioxide emissions in U.S. cities—from the burning of fossil fuels such as gasoline—are 2 times higher than in European cities and 5 to 10 times higher than in developing-country cities.
Air quality	
As with many other megacities, Jakarta faces a serious and growing problem of air pollution. Ambient levels of particulate matter exceed health standards at least 173 days per year. Vehicle emissions constitute the most important source of harmful pollutants. Lead levels in the environment regularly exceed health standards by a factor of 3 or 4.	Air quality has improved dramatically since the passage of the Clean Air Act in 1970. However, in 1992, the city still had 154 days when air pollution levels were high enough to cause discomfort to asthma or allergy sufferers or to be annoying or aesthetically displeasing. The city also experienced 11 days of unhealthful air pollution levels.

Source: Excerpted from World Resources Institute 1998.

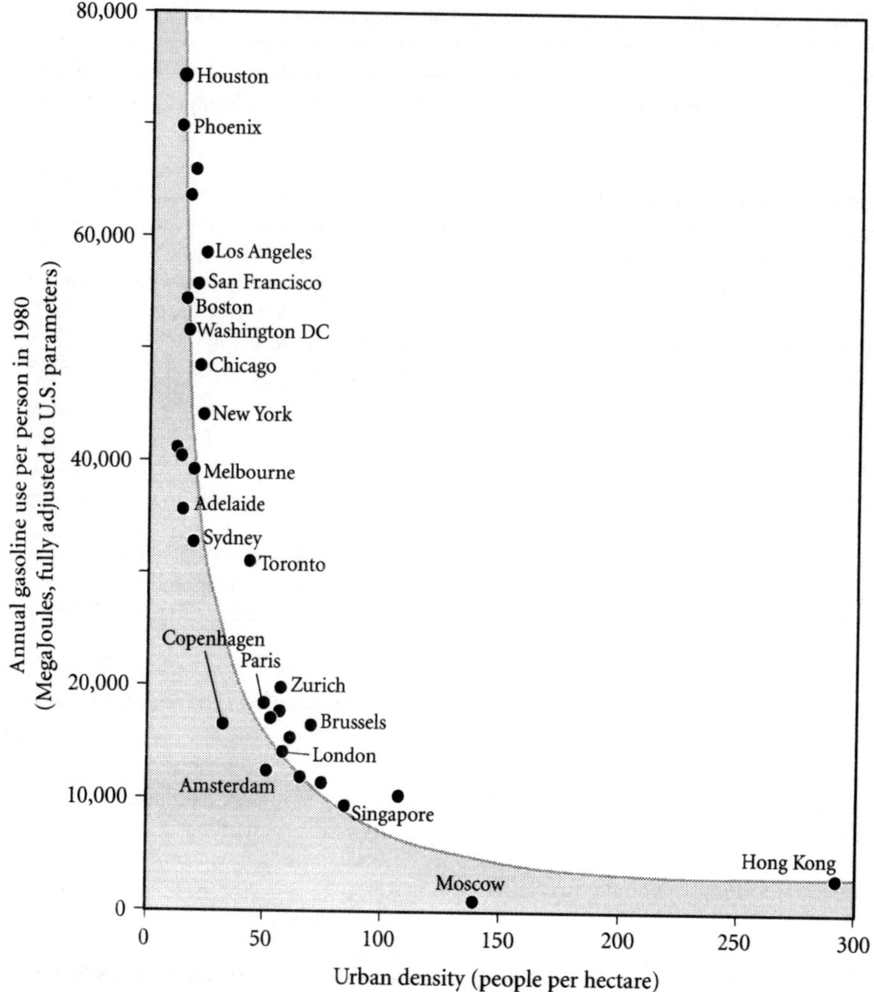

Figure 22.9. *Gasoline consumption and urban densities in major world cities, 1980*
Source: Pahelke 1991

of American cities: 45 persons per hectare compared to 91 for European cities and 464 for Asian cities (Table 22.6).

Automobile-dependent cities are generally characterized by low economic efficiency in at least two respects. First, the social costs of automobile-based transport are 30–40 percent higher than those of transit-based systems and are usually not fully paid by the users. Second, the overall infrastructure costs are also higher as new suburban infrastructure is constantly being developed while older city infrastructure is underutilized. Automobile-dependent cities are also characterized by high environmental and social impact. Environmental impact includes: (1) air pollution, especially substances such as nitrogen oxide, particulates,

Table 22.6. *Urban density and gasoline consumption in major cities, 1980*

City	Gasoline consumption per person	Overall population density	Inner-city population density	Overall job density	Inner-city job density	Private automobile travel
American cities[a]	58,541	14	45	7	30	12,507
San Francisco	55,365	16	59	8	48	13,200
Chicago	48,246	18	54	8	26	11,122
Australian cities[a]	29,849	14	24	6	27	10,680
Melbourne	29,104	16	29	6	40	10,128
Sydney	27,986	18	39	8	39	9,450
Metro Toronto	34,813	40	57	20	38	9,850
European cities[a]	13,280	54	91	31	79	5,595
Frankfurt	16,093	54	63	43	74	6,810
Stockholm	15,574	51	58	34	62	6,570
Paris	14,091	48	106	22	60	4,199
Asian cities[a]	5,493	160	464	71	296	1,799

Notes: Gasoline consumption per person is given in megajoules; overall population density in people per hectare; inner-city population density in people per hectare; overall job density in jobs per hectare; inner-city job density in jobs per hectare; and private automobile travel in per person per kilometer.

[a] The figures given for American, Australian, European, and Asian cities in the table are average for the cities in those regions studied by Newman and Kenworthy (1989). The data reflect results from ten American, five Australian, and twelve European cities. The Asian data are for the three "Westernized" Asian cities of Tokyo, Singapore, and Hong Kong.

Interpretation: The extent to which people choose to use private passenger cars is a direct function of urban density. Cities that are more compact are significantly less dependent on automobiles. Residents of U.S. cities drive their cars, on average, two to three times as far as do residents of European cities. Toronto is about midway between a typical American and a typical European city in this regard.

Sources: Hough 1995: 167. This material originated from Paehlke 1991. Compiled from material originally presented in Newman and Kenworthy 1989.

hydrocarbons, carbon monoxide, sulfur dioxide, ground-level ozone, carbon dioxide, and, in many developing countries, lead emissions; (2) noise, visual pollution, and traffic congestion, which exacerbate pollution problems; (3) loss of countryside to urban sprawl, green spaces to roads, and rainwater infiltration to paved areas. Social impact includes higher accident rates (compared to transit-based systems) and loss of community and urban vitality.

Given the path dependence and the lock-in effects of demand-responsive energy and transport policies (e.g. low fuel prices and subsidized road infrastructure) and the high cost of retrofitting transport and urban infrastructure, there should be a heavier emphasis on prevention (rather than remedy) through demand management. This is particularly important for developing global city-regions where transport infrastructure and urban development are in their formative stage and still have many options open to them. For example, cities in China and India, which still have low levels of vehicle ownership but are experiencing exponential rates of motorization, can avoid the spectacular failures of Bangkok, Jakarta, and Manila by reordering their transport policy priorities from open-ended supply of transportation infrastructure to more sustainable systems of demand-management and public transit development.

An urban transport policy that is proactive and demand-oriented, rather than simply demand-responsive and reactive encompasses land-use changes that reduce the demand for travel, development of efficient public transport systems, elimination of hidden subsidies for roads and fuels, and introduction of economic and regulatory instruments to control vehicle emissions. The latter include:

1. instruments to control the type and age of vehicles, such as differentiation of taxes and registration fees to discourage large, inefficient, and older vehicles;
2. instruments to control vehicle use such as fuel taxes, differential parking fees, and restricted area permits;
3. instruments that control vehicle emissions such as mandatory inspections and emission charges; and
4. instruments that reduce congestion such as road tolls and congestion fees.

Such policies aim to internalize fully the economic, environmental, and social cost of private driving and to restore a level playing field between private commuting and public transport. The private sector has a key role to play in the development and management of efficient public transit systems, toll roads, vehicle inspection stations, and brownfield development. The benefits of such integrated demand management policies go beyond reduction of pollution and congestion to creating a more livable urban environment and to enhancing competitiveness and sustainability of the global city-region.

TOWARDS A NEW POLICY PARADIGM

It is generally recognized that environmental degradation in developing-country megacities has reached unprecedented levels, and it is likely to get worse. It is appreciated that it carries a heavy price in productivity losses, health costs, and human suffering. It is also recognized that it is easier to deal with these problems in a growing rather than a stagnant economy. The need for new legislation and new institutions is widely acknowledged, as is the general weakness of enforcement throughout the region. A consensus is emerging that punitive regulation would be less effective than a collaborative effort that encourages industries and communities to set standards and guidelines for their members and to monitor themselves with only spot checks by the regulators. It is increasingly recognized that nongovernmental organizations and the civil society have an important role to play in environmental management. It is also beginning to be recognized that consideration of benefits and costs in environmental policies and projects is just as important as it is in economic policies and projects.

The emerging new policy paradigm is one of smaller central government and stronger local and city-region governments capable of good governance and effective management (see Table 22.7) by virtue of this reduced and more focused mandate. It involves a far greater role for the private sector and civil

Table 22.7. *Allocation of expenditures and taxes in selected global cities in the Asian and South Pacific region*

	Expenditures	Taxes
For local and metropolitan governments	Street cleaning	Property taxes
	Water distribution	Pollution fees
	Urban transport	Registration fees
	Power distribution	Motor vehicle taxes
	Garbage collection	Excise taxes
	Ports	Sales tax
	Water production and storage	Business taxes
	Airports	Natural resources tax
	Telephone	Corporate Income tax
	Rural roads	Value-added tax
	Primary education	Personal income tax
	Secondary education	
	Power production and transmission	
	Railroads	
	Sanitation	
	Highways	
	Higher education and research	
	Justice	
For the central government	Defense	Custom duties

Source: Prud'homme 1996.

society in the provision of environmental infrastructure, public services, environmental investments, and even monitoring and enforcement of environmental regulations, areas in which governments and bureaucracies dominated in the past. But this policy shift cannot take place in an institutional and legal vacuum. There is a need for enabling legislation and new rules of the game that would allow greater flexibility of response and wider involvement of the private sector in the provision of environmental services while protecting the public interest and accommodating distributional concerns.

At the same time, it is equally critical to strengthen the capacity of governments to set priorities, to establish and clarify property rights, to undertake reforms and redeploy resources, to introduce flexible yet consistently enforced regulations and economic instruments, to outsource services competitively, and to design and carry out targeted interventions to achieve distributional objectives at least cost. The new policy paradigm envisages only limited and targeted increases in public environmental expenditure, a major overhaul and redeployment of existing resources to increase their efficiency and effectiveness, and considerable mobilization of domestic and external private capital sources to finance the needed environmental improvements. (See Table 22.8)

Table 22.8. *Investment and control actions relating to environmental sectors*

Needs for infrastructure and/or controls	Affected environmental sectors									
	A Air quality	B Water quality	C Land quality	D Public health	E Traffic	F Environmental quality	G Recreation	H Socioeconomic	I Economics	
									Long-term	Short-term
Infrastructure										
Water supply		3	1	3		3	1	3	3	3
Waste management										
Sewage[a]		3	1	3		3		3	2	1
Solid wastes	1	3	3	3		3		1	2	1
Drainage/flood control		2	3	2		2		3	3	3
Transportation										
Roads/highways	3	1	1	3	3	1	1	3	3	3
Mass transit	3	1		3	3	1	1	3	3	3
Harbors		3	1	2		1		1	3	3
Inland waterways		2		1	2	1	1	3	3	3
Urban slums housing	1	3	3	3	1	3	1	3	3	3

Water supply/sanitation										
Thermal power	3	1		2				3	3	3
Green areas			3			3	3	3		
Natural resources						3				
Controls										
Air pollution control[b]	3	1		3		3		1	3	1
Environmental impact assessment	3	3	3	3	3	3	3	3	1	1
Permit system for wastes	3	3	3		1	2		1	3	1
Megacity development planning	3	3	3	3	3	3	3	3	1	1
Environmental standard	3	3	1	3	3	3	3	3	3	3

Notes: F = overall community environmental quality; H = all socioeconomic values excepting public health; 3 = major influence; 2 = moderate; 1 = significant but minor.

[a] Includes people and industries.

[b] Includes vehicles and industries.

Source: Clarke 1996.

In order to achieve both environmental improvement and continued economic growth, global city-regions will do best to adopt the best available policy (BAP) rather than the best available technology (BAT). The best available policy is one that (1) minimizes the costs of environmental protection by judicial choice of instruments and (2) gradually internalizes it to the generators of environmental damage and/or the beneficiaries of environmental improvement. The new policy paradigm leverages limited and targeted public environmental expenditures by tapping the private sector and market competition to supply environmental infrastructure that is least cost, self-financed, and well maintained (see Box 22.1 on the Buenos Aires Consortium for Water Supply and Sanitation). Under this scenario, environmental expenditures can be kept under 2 percent of GDP with less than half provided by the public sector. Since public environmental expenditures in the developing world are just under 1 percent, this scenario will not involve substantial increase in public expenditure on the environment but a significant redeployment of existing resources toward a more targeted and strategic portfolio (see Table 22.9 for investment and control actions relating to the environmental sustainability of global city-regions).

Box 22.1. *The Buenos Aires concession for water supply and sanitation*

The Greater Buenos Aires water supply and sanitation system, operated by a public company (Obras Sanitarias de la Nación, OSN) was plagued through the years by problems common to public water utilities throughout the developing world. Coverage was only 70 percent for water supply and 58 percent for sanitation. The service was of poor quality and unreliable, while only 5 percent of the wastewater received any treatment before dumping into natural water bodies. Infrastructure was poorly maintained and unaccounted-for water was as high as 45 percent of the water produced. Water meters were installed at only 20 percent of the connections; meter reading and billing were highly irregular; and water consumption reached 400–500 liters per capita a day—twice the norm for metered and well-managed systems. The public utility was grossly overstaffed with 8,000 employees, or 8–9 employees per connection compared with 2–3 by efficiently operating systems. At the same time, population growth and urbanization were expanding the demand for additional coverage. The costs of rehabilitating the deteriorating system and expanding to reach 100 percent coverage were estimated at several billion dollars over the next twenty to thirty years, which was clearly beyond the capacity of both the utility and the state to mobilize.

In 1993, the government of Argentina privatized water and sewage services for Greater Buenos Aires as part of a massive privatization program that began in 1990, with World Bank support, and included virtually all public services and federally owned enterprises such as electricity, telephone, railways, airlines, roads, and ports. The private sector participation option chosen for water and sanitation was a thirty-year full concession that allowed the assets to remain under public ownership while the operation, maintenance, rehabilitation, expansion, and wastewater treatment were transferred to a private concessionaire. After a successful process of preparation

Table 22.9. *Impact of Greater Buenos Aires water concession*

Indicator of performance	Change from May 1993 to December 1995
Increase in production capacity (%)	26
Water pipes rehabilitated (kms)	550
Sewers drained (kms)	4,800
Decline in clogged drains (%)	97
Meters upgraded and installed	128,500
Staff reduction (%)	47
Residents with new water connections	642,000
Residents with new sewer connections	342,000

Source: Crampes and Estache 1996.

and bidding, the concession was awarded to Aguas Argentinas, a consortium of foreign and local firms led by Lyonnaise de Feax-Dumez, that offered a 27 percent discount to the prevailing public water tariffs. Thus, competition was effective in reducing costs. It also mobilized $4 billion over the life of the contract to meet the performance targets of the concession, which included 100 percent coverage in water supply and 90 percent coverage in sanitation by year thirty, a reduction in the unaccounted-for water from 45 to 25 percent, and an increase in sewage treatment from 4 to 93 percent. Over the first five years alone, the concessionaire will invest $1.2 billion, or $240 million a year—twelve times more than the annual investment made by the public utility in the previous decade. To regulate and control the concession and protect the consumers against monopolistic practices, the government established a regulatory agency, Ente Tripartito de Obras y Servicios Sanitarios (ETOSS) with participation of the federal, provincial, and local government with a budget of $8 million to be financed through a user surcharge of 2.7 percent of the water and sewage bill collected by the concessionaire. The regulatory agency also enforces water and effluent quality standards based on international norms introduced prior to the bidding.

During the first three years of operation, accelerated rehabilitation of the system led to a reduction of water losses from 45 to 25 percent and coverage increased by 10 percent with no increase in production. The population receiving sewage services increased by 8 percent. Prices were reduced initially by 27 percent but increased by 13.5 percent in 1994 to further accelerate rehabilitation as provided in contract clause; still, water prices are 17 percent lower than those charged by the public utility. The staff was reduced by 47 percent through severance payments by the government and a voluntary retirement program by the concessionaire. Labor productivity rose and new recruitment is now underway as the concessionaire is responding to increasing demand for water and sanitation services. Table 22.9 summarizes these improvements.

While the overall experience has been clearly positive and the model is now being adopted by other Argentine provinces and other countries in Latin America, there have also been teething problems with regard to negotiations with the labor unions and regulation. Indirect labor costs remain high as the concessionaire continues to provide fringe benefits traditionally available to civil servants. The regulatory agency staffed with former utility employees finds it difficult to give up the state's day-to-day management role and focus on its regulatory and contract enforcement role.

The successful privatization of the supply and sewage services in Buenos Aires contains many important lessons for private sector participation in water and sanitation throughout the developing world. First, privatization must receive the endorsement of major stakeholders, enjoy political commitment at the highest level, and be part of a comprehensive program of economic reforms. Second, political, technical, legal, commercial, and financial risks must be assessed and alleviated through appropriate mechanisms. Third, all available options for private sector participation should be considered and the one best suited to the country's political and cultural conditions and the sector's features must be selected; the assets need not be privatized to improve efficiency and attract private capital. Fourth, the regulatory framework and regulatory institution must be established, and the technical and financial feasibility of the concession studied prior to bidding. The regulatory entity must be strong enough to regulate an experienced international concessionaire. Fifth, while adequate preparation and time should be allowed to ensure universal bidding, eligibility should be confined to qualified bidders through a prequalification process. Sixth, sensitive staff reduction issues can be effectively dealt with through attractive retirement packages jointly financed by the government and the concessionaire. A final lesson is that the contract should be realistic and specific to minimize conflicts yet be flexible enough to allow for adjustments for unforeseen or substantially altered circumstances.

Sources: Idelovitch and Ringskog 1995 and Crampes and Estache 1996.

CONCLUSION

Globalization combined with population growth and urbanization brings unparalleled challenges and opportunities for developing global city-regions, in terms of both wealth creation and environmental sustainability. The quality of the governance of these megacities, and of the countries of which they are part, will determine whether they will grow into sustainable entities, fully integrated into the global economy while preserving their individuality, or will become an unmanaged sprawl of built-up areas imposing externalities on each other and underpinning their long-term sustainability and competitiveness. To a considerable extent, this will depend on how much responsibility, authority, and accountability as well as resources is devolved from central governments to local governments, the private sector, and civil society. A new policy paradigm is emerging that emphasizes prevention over remedy, incentives over regulations, and private over public provision of city services. Demand management, full-cost pricing, competitive bidding, targeted assistance to low-income groups, and independent regulatory oversight replace subsidized state monopoly provision. In the new paradigm, public policy aims to reintegrate land use, infrastructure, and transport and energy policies (defined by technological and socioeconomic changes) in order to avert suburban sprawl, urban slums, and city-center decay; to ease traffic congestion; and to maintain the environmental quality, livability, and sense of community in the rapidly expanding cities of the developing world. The experience of a good number of innovative cities in recent years offers grounds for optimism.

NOTE

1. Assuming a residential water price elasticity of −0.45 and an industrial of 0.9, Bathia, Cestti, and Winpenny (1995) report residential elasticities of −0.3 to −0.6 and industrial of −0.4 to 1.4. These are very conservative estimates.

REFERENCES

ADB (Asian Development Bank). (1992). *Energy Indicators of Developing Member Countries of ADB*. Manila: ADB.

—— (1995). *Key Indicators of Developing Asian and Pacific Countries*. Hong Kong: Oxford University Press.

Bathia, R., Cestti, R., and Winpenny, J. (1995). *Water Conservation and Reallocation: Best Practice Cases in Improving Economic Efficiency and Environmental Quality*. Water and Sanitation Program Publications. Washington, DC: World Bank.

Burniaux, J.-M., Martin, J. P., and Oliveria-Martins, J. (1992). "The Effects of Existing Distortions in Energy Markets on the Costs of Policies to Reduce CO2 Emissions." *OECD Economic Studies*, 19 (Winter): 141–65.

Clarke, G. T. R. (1996). "Megacity Management: Trends and Issues," in J. Stubbs and G. T. R. Clarke (eds.), *Megacity Management in the Asian and Pacific Region: Policy Issues and Innovative Approaches. Vol. 1: Recommendations of the Working Groups, Theme Papers, and Case Studies*. Manila: Asian Development Bank, 53–9.

Crampes, C., and Estache, A. (1996). "Regulating Concessions: Lessons from the Buenos Aires Concession," in *Public Policy for the Private Sector*. Viewpoint Note no. 114. Washington, DC: World Bank (September).

Dasgupta, S., Huq, M., Wheeler, D., and Zhang, C. (1996). *Water Pollution Abatement by Chinese Industry: Cost Estimates and Policy Implications*. Washington, DC: World Bank.

DeShazo, J. R. (1996). "The Level of and Demand for Environmental Quality in Asia." Background paper for *Emerging Asia: Changes and Challenges*. Manila: ADB.

Earth Council. (1996). *Economic Incentives for Sustainable Development*. The Hague: Institute for Research on Public Expenditure.

GEMS (Global Environmental Monitoring System). (1996). "Airs Executive International Programme." World Health Organization, http://www.epagov/airs/aeint.

Hope, E., and Singh, B. (1995). *Energy Price Increases in Developing Countries*. Policy Research Paper 1442, Washington, DC: World Bank.

Hough, M. (1995). *Cities and Natural Process*. London: Routledge.

Idelovitch, E., and Ringskog, K. (1995). "Private Sector Participation in Water Supply and Sanitation in Latin America: Executive Summary." World Bank. URL: www.worldbank.org/html/lat/english/summary/ewsu/ps_water.htm

IEA (1994). "Energy and Environmental Technology to Respond to Global Climate Concerns." Scoping study, IEA/OECD. France.

Ingram, G., and Fay, M. (1994). "Valuing Infrastructure Stocks and Gains from Improved Performance." Background paper for *World Development Report 1994*, 130. Washington, DC: World Bank.

Kiravanich, P., and In-na, Y. (1996). "Case Study of Pollution Management in the Bangkok Metropolitan Region," in J. Stubbs and G. T. R. Clarke (eds.), *Megacity Management in the Asian and Pacific Region: Policy Issues and Innovative Approaches. Vol. 1: Recommendations of the Working Groups, Theme Papers, and Case Studies.* Manila: Asian Development Bank, 99–110.

Larsen, B., and Shah, A. (1994). "Global Climate Change, Economic Policy Instruments, and Developing Countries." Paper prepared for the Fiftieth Congress of the International Institute of Public Finance, 22–25 August. Cambridge, MA: Harvard University.

Lohani, B. N., and Whitington, T. P. (1996). "Environmental Management in the Megacities of Asia," in J. Stubbs and G. T. R. Clarke (eds.), *Megacity Management in the Asian and Pacific Region: Policy Issues and Innovative Approaches. Vol. 1: Recommendations of the Working Groups, Theme Papers, and Case Studies.* Manila: Asian Development Bank, 131–74.

Lvovsky, K., Maddison, D., Margulis, S., and von Amsberg, J. (1994). *Air Pollution and the Social Costs of Fuels.* Environment Department Working Paper. Washington, DC: World Bank.

Newman, P., and Kenworthy, J. (1989). *Cities and Automobile Dependence: An International Sourcebook.* Hampshire: Gower Publishing.

Ostro, B. (1994). *Estimating the Health Effect of Air Pollution: A Method with an Application to Jakarta.* Policy Research Paper WPS 1301. Washington, DC: World Bank.

Pahelke, R. (1991). "The Environmental Effects of Intensification." Prepared for Municipal Planning Policy Branch, Ministry of Municipal Affairs. Based on Canadian Urban Institute (1990), *Housing Intensification: Policies, Constraints, and Challenges.* Toronto: Canadian Urban Institute, p. 13.

Panayotou, T. (1993). "Empirical Tests and Policy Analysis of Environmental Degradation at Different Stages of Economic Development," in *Technology, Environment, and Employment.* Geneva: International Labour Office.

—— (1997). "Demystifying the Environmental Kuznets Curve: Turning a Black Box into a Policy Tool." *Environment and Development Economics*, 2: 465–84.

——, and Vincent, J. R. (1997). "Consumption: Challenge to Sustainable Development . . . or Distraction?" *Science*, 276 (4): 53–5.

Pernia, E., and Alabastro, S. (1996). *Aspects of Urban Sanitation in the Context of Rapid Urbanization in Developing Asia.* Economics and Development Resource Center, Asian Development Bank. Manila.

Prud'homme, R. (1996). "Management of Megacities: The Institutional Dimensions," in J. Stubbs and G. T. R. Clarke (eds.), *Megacity Management in the Asian and Pacific Region: Policy Issues and Innovative Approaches. Vol. 1: Recommendations of the Working Groups, Theme Papers, and Case Studies.* Manila: Asian Development Bank, 97–129.

Saunders, R. J., and Gandhi, S. (1994). *Global Energy Paths: Energy Policy Prescriptions for Sustaining the Environment.* Washington, DC: World Bank.

Smil, V. (1996). *Environmental Problems in China: Estimates of Economic Costs.* Special Report no. 5. Honolulu: East-West Center.

Teitenberg, T. H. (1990). "Economic Instruments for Environmental Regulation." *Oxford Review of Economic Policy*, 6: 17–33.

World Bank. (1992). *Water Resources Management.* Policy Paper. Washington, DC: World Bank.

—— (1993). *Watershed Development Sector Study: Towards Improved Management of Environmental Impacts.* Washington, DC: World Bank, East Asia and Pacific Region, Industry and Energy Division.

—— (1994). *World Development Report 1994: Infrastructure for Development.* New York and Oxford: Oxford University Press.

World Resources Institute. (1998). "Problems and Priorities in Jakarta and Detroit: A World of Differences," in *Teacher's Guide to World Resources: Exploring Sustainable Communities.* Washington, DC: World Resources Institute. www.wri.org/sdis.

Notes on Contributors

John Agnew is Professor and chair of the Department of Geography at UCLA. He taught previously at Syracuse University. He has been a visiting professor at the University of Chicago, University College London, and the University of Cambridge. Some of his publications are *Place and Politics* (London, 1987), *The Geography of the World Economy* (London, 1998), *Rome* (New York, 1995), and *Geopolitics: Re-Visioning World Politics* (London, 1998).

Lucien Bouchard has been Premier of Quebec and Chairman of the Parti Québécois since 1996. He was appointed Canadian Ambassador to France before launching his political career as Secretary of State of Canada and Minister of the Environment. From 1991 to 1995, Mr Bouchard was the leader of the Bloc Québécois, forming, after 1993, the Official Opposition in the House of Commons of Canada. He earned a bachelor's degree in social science as well as a degree in law at Laval University. Lucien Bouchard has published a number of specialized articles in legal and labor relations journals in addition to an essay on political change in Quebec and an autobiography.

Roberto Camagni is Professor of Economics and of Urban Economics, Politecnico di Milano, Italy, since 1994. He was previously Professor of Regional Economics at the University of Padua and Professor of Economics at Bocconi University, Milan. Professor Camagni was also Visiting Professor at Université de Toulouse in 1996, at Paris at the Sorbonne, and at the University of California, Santa Cruz, in 1995. During the Prodi Government (1997–98), he was Head of the Department for Urban Affairs at the Presidency of the Council of Ministers, Rome. He also served as Vice President of the Group of Urban Affairs, TDS, at OECD, Paris. Since 1987, Professor Camagni has been President of the GREMI, an international association for the study of innovative environments or "milieux," located in Paris, Sorbonne University. He was President of AISRE, the Italian Section of the Regional Science Association, from 1989 to 1992. He has worked extensively on technological diffusion models, regional and urban development, city networks, and urban sustainability.

Tim Campbell is an Adviser in Urban Development at the World Bank, and manages the Urban Partnership, established by the Bank in 1997 to create new products for the Bank to meet the world's challenges in urban development in the decades to come. The partnership works actively to develop new partners from outside the Bank and to strengthen linkages across the disciplines within the World Bank Group. Before taking this position, he was a member of an advisory group responsible for quality enhancement in urban development and decentralization in Latin America and the Caribbean. His expertise is in areas of policy, planning, and intergovernmental arrangements, particularly in countries in the process of decentralizing spending and decision-making powers to sub-national governments. Dr Campbell is the author of numerous publications on subjects related to urban development, with emphasis in the last few years on decentralization. Recent work includes *Innovations and Risk Taking: The Engine of Reform in Local Government*, World Bank Discussion Paper 357 (1997) and *Decentralization in Latin America: National Strategies and Local Response in Planning, Spending, and Management* (1991). He holds a master's in City and Regional Planning from the University of California, Berkeley (1970), and a Ph.D. in Urban Studies and Planning from MIT (1980).

Thomas J. Courchene is the Jarislowsky-Deutsch Professor of Economic and Financial Policy at Queen's University (Kingston, Ontario, Canada) and Senior Scholar at the Institute for Research on Public Policy (Montreal). Dr Courchene is the author of some two hundred and fifty articles and books on a wide range of Canadian policy issues. His 1994 book *Social Canada in the Millennium* was awarded the Douglas D. Purvis prize for the best Canadian economic policy contribution in 1994 and his 1998 book (with Colin Telmer) *From Heartland to North American Region State: The Social, Fiscal, and Federal Evolution of Ontario* won the inaugural annual Donner Prize for the best Canadian public policy treatise. Dr Courchene was chair of the Ontario Economic Council from 1982 to 1985, is a past-president (1991–92) of the Canadian Economics Association, is a Fellow of the Royal Society of Canada, and earlier this year was invested as an Officer in the Order of Canada.

Michael Douglass is Professor and former chair of the Department of Urban and Regional Planning, University of Hawaii. He received his Ph.D. in Urban Planning from UCLA. He has lived and worked for many years in Asia, including Japan, Korea, Indonesia, and Thailand. He has been a consultant to the United Nations, World Bank, USAID, and World Resources Institute, as well as to national and local governments in Asia. He has been a Visiting Scholar (2000) and Shorenstein Distinguished Lecturer (1998) at Stanford University; Rockefeller Foundation Scholar at Bellagio (1998); Perloff Chair in Urban Planning at UCLA (1996); and visiting scholar at Tokyo University (1985). His latest books are: *Japan and Global Migration: Foreign Workers and the Advent of a Multicultural Society* (Routledge, 2000); *Cities for Citizens: Planning and the Rise of Civil Society in a Global Age* (John Wiley, 1998), and *Culture and the City in East Asia* (Oxford, 1997).

Susan S. Fainstein is Professor of Urban Planning and Policy Development at the State University of New Jersey at Rutgers. Her teaching and research have focused on comparative urban public policy, planning theory, and urban redevelopment. Among her books are *The City Builders: Property, Politics, and*

Planning in London and New York (Blackwell, 1994). She is coeditor of *Divided Cities: New York and London in the Contemporary World* (Blackwell, 1992) and of two readers on planning theory and urban theory that were published by Blackwell in 1996. With Dennis Judd she is coeditor of *The Tourist City*, published in 1999 by Yale University Press.

John Friedmann is Professor Emeritus in the School of Public Policy and Social Research, University of California, Los Angeles. Author of many books and more than one hundred and fifty articles, he is convenor of a network of scholars studying policy aspects of urbanization in East Asia. His most recent book is a coedited collection with Michael Douglass, *Cities for Citizens: Planning and the Rise of Civil Society* (Wiley, 1998). Friedmann now lives in Melbourne, Australia.

Sir Peter Hall is Professor of Planning at the Bartlett School of Architecture and Planning, University College, London. From 1991 to 1994 he was Special Adviser on Strategic Planning to the Secretary of State for the Environment, with special reference to issues of London and South East regional planning including the East Thames Corridor and the Channel Tunnel Rail Link. He has taught at the London School of Economics, and at the University of California at Berkeley (1980–92). He is author or editor of nearly thirty books on urban and regional planning and related topics, including *Cities in Civilization*, which was published December 1998. He was a founder member of the Regional Studies Association and first editor of its *Journal of Regional Studies* (1967–78). He is a trustee and former chairman of the Town and Country Planning Association. His extensive consultancy experience includes advising the London and Continental Railway Company on the high-speed rail link from London to the Channel Tunnel (1994–95); and direction of the Bartlett/UCL study of Four World Cities for GOL (1995–96). He is currently a member of a team researching economic competitiveness and social cohesion in London.

Douglas Henton, President of Collaborative Economics, has more than twenty years of experience in economic development at the national, regional, state, and local levels. He managed the startup of the Joint Venture: Silicon Valley Network and serves as consultant to the California Economic Strategy Panel. With colleagues John Melville and Kim Walesh, he authored *Grassroots Leaders for a New Economy: How Civic Entrepreneurs Are Building Prosperous Communities* (Jossey-Bass, 1997). Prior to founding Collaborative Economics in 1993, he was assistant director of SRI International's Center for Economic Competitiveness, where he led regional projects in the United States, Hong Kong, Japan, and China. He holds a bachelor's degree in political science and economics from Yale University and a master of public policy degree from the University of California, Berkeley.

James Holston is Associate Professor of Anthropology at the University of California, San Diego. His current research focuses on citizenship and democratic change in the Americas, especially Brazil, and related transformations in the social and spatial organization of cities. He is also conducting research on the emergence of urban citizenship among recent immigrants in Southern California and has organized a civic initiative there focused on public space, markets, and micro-enterprises. His publications include *The Modernist City* (University of Chicago Press) and *Cities and Citizenship* (Duke University Press), as well as essays on citizenship and law, democracy and violence, architecture, planning, and new religions. He is finishing a book on dilemmas of citizenship in new democracies.

Engin F. Isin is Associate Professor in the Division of Social Science at York University, Ontario, and Visiting Fellow, Faculty of Social and Political Sciences, University of Cambridge. He teaches courses on comparative urbanization, the culture of cities, and the culture of citizenship. His research focuses on the origins and transformations of the city as a locus of citizenship. He has completed a four-year (1993–97) grant from the Social Sciences and Humanities Research Council of Canada (SSHRC) to investigate the role of the city in Canadian federalism, and a two-year (1997–99) grant from the Center for Settlement and Immigration (CERIS) to investigate the status of immigrants in the Toronto metropolis. He is the author of *Cities without Citizens: Modernity of the City as a Corporation* (Montreal, 1992), and numerous essays on the city, politics, and citizenship. He is the North American chair of the international journal, *Citizenship Studies*. His most recent book, written with Patricia Wood, entitled *Citizenship and Identity*, was published by Sage (London, 1999). Two books forthcoming are *Being Political: Citizenship and Alterity from Polis to Cosmopolis* (University of Minnesota Press, 2000) and an edited collection, *Democracy, Citizenship, and the City: Rights to the Global City* (Routledge, 2000).

Michael Keating is a political scientist and holds chairs in Scottish Politics at the University of Aberdeen and in Regions at the European University Institute in Florence. Between 1988 and 1999 he was Professor of Political Science at the University of Western Ontario and before that was at the University of Strathclyde in Glasgow. He has held visiting posts in the United States, France, Spain, Italy, and Norway. He has published widely on urban and regional politics in Europe and North America. His most recent book is *The New Regionalism in Western Europe: Territorial Restructuring and Political Change* (Edward Elgar, 1999). His textbook *The Politics of Modern Europe* appeared in its second edition in 1999.

Won Bae Kim is currently Senior Fellow at the Korea Research Institute for Human Settlements. He has been working extensively on urban and regional issues in East Asia for the past fifteen years. He holds a Ph.D. from the University of Wisconsin. He is lead editor of *Culture and the City in East Asia* (Oxford

University Press, 1997) and coeditor of *Asian NIEs and the Global Economy: Industrial Restructuring and Corporate Strategy in the 1990s* (Johns Hopkins University Press, 1995). His recent research projects include Industrial Cooperation and Regional Development in Northeast Asia (1996), Restructuring the Korean Peninsula for the Twenty-first Century (1998), and Intercity Networking Strategy in the Yellow Sea Subregion (1999).

Kenichi Ohmae, management consultant, visionary, and best-selling author, has been described as "Mr Strategy." A former director of McKinsey & Company and now Managing Director of Ohmae & Associates and Chancellor's Professor of Public Policy at UCLA, he has served companies in a wide spectrum of industries. Cited by the *Financial Times* as "Japan's only management guru," his counsel is much in demand from U.S., Asian, and European multinational corporations and governments. Dr Ohmae graduated from Waseda University (B.S.), Tokyo Institute of Technology (M.S.), and Massachusetts Institute of Technology (Ph.D.).

Theodore Panayotou is a Fellow of the Harvard Institute for International Development and Director of the Institute's International Environment Program as well as Director of the Environment Program of the Center for International Development at Harvard University. He lectures on environmental and resource economics at the Department of Economics and the Kennedy School of Government and serves as an environmental adviser to many governments and international organizations. Among his recent publications are *Green Markets* (ICS Press, 1993), *Not by Timber Alone: Economics and Ecology for Sustaining Tropical Forests* (with Peter Ashton, Island Press, 1992), and *Instruments of Change: Motivating and Financing Sustainable Development* (Earthscan, 1998).

Michael E. Porter is the C. Roland Christensen Professor of Business Administration at the Harvard Business School and a leading authority on competitive strategy and international competitiveness. Professor Porter is the author of fifteen books and more than seventy-five articles. His books on strategy include: *Competitive Strategy: Techniques for Analyzing Industries and Competitors* (53rd printing), *The Competitive Advantage: Creating and Sustaining Superior Performance* (32nd printing), and *On Competition* (1998). His 1990 book, *The Competitive Advantage of Nations*, developed a new theory of how nations, states, and regions compete, and has guided economic policy throughout the world. Professor Porter has led competitiveness programs in nations and states such as New Zealand, Portugal, the Basque Country, and Connecticut; guides regional projects in Central America and the Middle East; and is cochairman, with Harvard colleague Jeffrey Sachs, of the Global Competitiveness Report. In 1994, Professor Porter founded The Initiative for a Competitive Inner City, a nonprofit private sector initiative formed to catalyze business development in distressed inner cities across the United States. The holder of eight honorary doctorates, Professor Porter has won numerous awards for his books, articles, public service, and influence on several fields.

Saskia Sassen is Professor of Sociology, University of Chicago, and Centennial Visiting Professor, London School of Economics. Her most recent book is *Globalization and Its Discontents* (New York: New Press, 1999). Her books have been translated into ten languages. Two of her books are being reissued in updated editions in 2000, *The Global City* (Princeton University Press) and *Cities in a World Economy* (Pine Forge/Sage). Her edited book *Cities and Their Cross-border Networks* sponsored by the United Nations University will also appear in 2000. She is currently completing a research project on "Governance and Accountability in a Global Economy." She is a member of the Council on Foreign Relations and a Fellow of the American Bar Foundation.

Hubert Schmitz is a Professorial Fellow of the Institute of Development Studies (IDS) at the University of Sussex, United Kingdom. He has more than twenty years' experience in research on industrialization and employment. He was coordinator of the IDS Collective Efficiency Project, which studied clustering and networking in Pakistan, India, Kenya, Mexico, and Brazil. This work focused on two policy questions: how to achieve economic development on the basis of small local industry, and how local clusters cope with global competition. For a summary of findings and publications see: http://www.ids.ac.uk/ids/global/coleff.html. He is now coordinator of a new project concerned with the interaction of local and global governance and the implications for industrial upgrading.

Allen J. Scott was born in England and educated at Oxford University. He is currently professor jointly appointed to the Departments of Policy Studies and Geography at the University of California, Los Angeles, and the director of the Center for Globalization and Policy Research in the university's School of Public Policy and Social Research. He was a recipient of a Guggenheim fellowship in 1986–87, and was awarded Honors by the Association of American Geographers in 1987. He was elected as corresponding fellow of the British Academy in 1999. In the winter of 1998–99 he occupied the André Siegfried Chair in the Institut d'Etudes Politiques, Paris. His most recent books are *Regions and the World Economy* (Oxford University Press, 1998), and *The Cultural Economy of Cities* (Sage 2000).

Edward W. Soja is Professor of Urban Planning, School of Public Policy and Social Research, University of California, Los Angeles, where he teaches courses in regional planning, urban political economy, and planning theory. After starting his academic career as a specialist on Africa, he has focused his research and writing over the past twenty years on urban restructuring in Los Angeles and more broadly on theories of space and critical studies of cities and regions. His major publications include *Postmodern Geographies, Thirdspace*, and the recently published *Postmetropolis*. He is also coeditor, with Allen Scott, of *The City: Los Angeles and Urban Theory at the End of the Twentieth Century*. His policy interests are primarily involved with questions of regional development, planning, and governance, and the effects of ethnic and cultural diversity in Los Angeles.

Michael Storper is engaged in research dealing with theories and processes of regional development: where economic activity goes and why, and why city and regional economies grow and decline. Dr Storper's most recent major work is a book comparing economic organization in French, U.S., and Italian regions, another book on the cognitive and institutional foundations of regional development, and an edited book on industrial policies among latecomers to industrialization. Fluent in French and Portuguese, he has lectured throughout Europe, in Canada, and Brazil. His current work includes a project on globalization and inequality, another on the new economic geography of Europe, a related project on the relationship between globalization of production and the globalization of consumerism, and another on development strategies for the Northeast Region of Brazil. He currently holds a permanent joint appointment with the University of California, Los Angeles, and the University of Paris/Marne-la-Vallée in France, and has consulted widely with the European Union, the OECD, and many national and regional governments.

Richard Stren is Professor of Political Science at the University of Toronto, and Director of the Center for Urban and Community Studies. He received his B.A. in economics from the University of Toronto, and his Ph.D. in political science from the University of California at Berkeley. Over the past thirty years he has carried out extensive research in African cities, although he has also worked in Latin America in recent years. His major thematic interests are urban policy and the environment, urban management, and comparative urban politics. He has published more than fifty articles in journals and a number of books on these themes. His major book-length publications include *Housing the Urban Poor in Africa*, *African Cities in Crisis* (edited with Rodney White), and a four-volume edited collection, *Urban Research in the Developing World*, the result of the Global Urban Research Initiative, a major international collaborative research project of which he was the coordinator. With Mario Polèse, he has edited *Socially Sustainable Cities*, which will be published in early 2000 by the University of Toronto Press.

Roger Waldinger is Professor and chair, Department of Sociology, UCLA. He holds a B.A. from Brown University and Ph.D. from Harvard University. Waldinger is the author of four books, most recently, *Still the Promised City? African-Americans and New Immigrants in Post Industrial New York* (Cambridge: Harvard University Press, 1986; 1996 Best Book in Urban Politics, American Political Science Association; 1998 Robert E. Park Award, American Sociological Association); and *Ethnic Los Angeles* (New York: Russell Sage Foundation, 1996; 1997

Thomas and Znaniecki Prize, American Sociological Association). He is completing two new books, *How the Other Half Works: Immigration and the Social Organization of Labor* (with Michael Lichter) and *Strangers at the Gates*, a collection of essays on new immigrants in urban America.

James D. Wolfensohn is the ninth President of the World Bank Group since its establishment in 1946. He took office with the Bank in June 1995. On 27 September 1999, Mr Wolfensohn was unanimously reappointed by the Bank's Board of Executive Directors to a second five-year term as President beginning 1 June 2000. Since becoming President, he has visited more than one hundred of the Bank's one hundred and eighty-one member countries and sought a dialogue not only with the Bank's government clients but also with civil society, the private sector, religious groups, regional development banks, and other bilateral and multilateral donors. Mr Wolfensohn was born in Australia in December 1933 and is a naturalized U.S. citizen. He holds B.A. and LL.B. degrees from the University of Sydney and an M.B.A. from the Harvard Graduate School of Business. Prior to becoming President of the World Bank Group, Mr Wolfensohn had established his career as an international investment banker with a parallel involvement in development issues, the global environment, and the arts.

Index

QM LIBRARY
(MILE END)